A Butler Brothers Catalog Collection

Original Catalog Reprints

from the Glass and Pottery Sections

of "Our Drummer" Wholesale Catalogs

Volume 1: 1896 - 1906

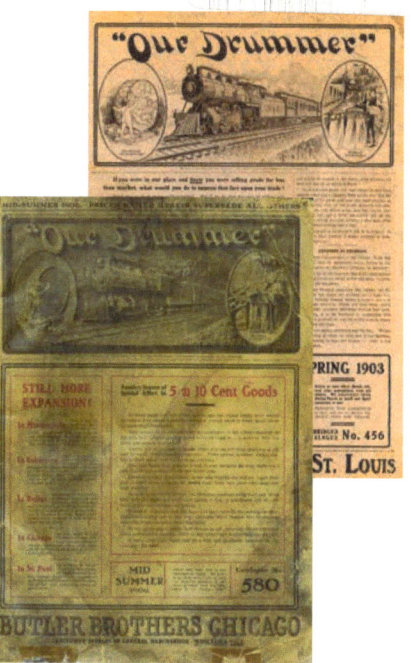

Compiled by Craig S. Schenning

An Old Line Publishing Reference Book

If you have purchased this book without a cover you should be aware that this book may have been stolen property and was reported as "unsold and destroyed" to the publisher. In such case neither the author nor the publisher has received any compensation for this book.

Copyright © 2009 by Old Line Publishing, LLC

All rights reserved. No part of this book may be reproduced or transmitted in any form or by any means; graphic, electronic or mechanical, including photocopying, recording, or by any information storage and retrieval system, without expressed permission from the publisher. The scanning, uploading and distribution of this book or any part thereof via the internet or via any other means without the expressed permission of the publisher is illegal and punishable by law.

Printed in The United States of America

Compiled and designed by Craig S. Schenning

ISBN-13: 978-0-9841065-3-0
ISBN-10: 0-9841065-3-7

Looking for a publisher?
At Old Line Publishing we are always looking for authors and original manuscripts. We hope that you will contact us and share your thoughts, ideas, stories, and/or already written material with us so that we can help you turn your idea into a timeless treasure and share it with the world.

Old Line Publishing, LLC

P.O. Box 624

Hampstead, MD 21074

Toll-Free Phone: 1-877-866-8820

Website: www.oldlinepublishingllc.com

Be sure to look for these future volumes in our
Catalog Collection Series from Old Line Publishing.

Volume 2: 1907 - 1914

Our Drummer, #596, Winter 1907
Our Drummer, #878, Spring 1911
Our Drummer, #1142, Fall 1913
Our Drummer, #1202, May 1914

Volume 3: 1917 - 1923

Our Drummer, #1502, June 1917
Our Drummer, #1752, Spring 1920
Our Drummer, #1888, Summer 1921
Our Drummer, #2102, September 1923

Volume 4: 1924 - 1928

Our Drummer, #2148, February 1924
Our Drummer, #2409, November 1926
Our Drummer, #2477, August 1927
Our Drummer, #2597, November 1928

Volume 5: 1929 - 1932

Our Drummer, #2648, July 1929
Our Drummer, #2716, May 1930
Our Drummer, #2801, May 1931
Our Drummer, #2897, July 1932

Volume 6: 1933 - 1936

Our Drummer, #3020, April 1933
Our Drummer, #4112, Summer 1934
Our Drummer, #4259, July/August 1935
Our Drummer, #4410, November/December 1936

Volume 7: 1937 - 1941

Our Drummer, #4445, Spring 1937
Our Drummer, #4545, Spring 1938
Our Drummer, #4752, Spring 1940
Our Drummer, #4787, Spring 1941

Table of Contents - Index

Our Drummer, #150, November 1896

Front Cover	7
Inside Front Cover	8
Yellow & Rockingham Ware	9
Peerless White Granite Ware	10
Decorated American Tea & Dinner Sets	12
Decorated Toilet Sets	13
Glassware	14
Tumblers	17
Lamps	19
Decorated Lamps	20
Inside Back Cover	23
Back Cover	24

Our Drummer, #194, Spring and Summer 1898

Front Cover	25
Inside Front Cover	26
Open Stock Glassware	27
Glassware	29
Lamps	31
Yellow & Rockingham Ware	33
Decorated Lamps	34
Inside Back Cover	37
Back Cover	38

Our Drummer, #456, Spring 1903

Front Cover	39
Inside Front Cover	40
Glassware	41
Competition Glassware	55
Tumblers	60
Open Stock Glassware	61

Table of Contents - Index (continued)

Boxed Tumblers	62
Salts and Peppers	65
Gold Decorated Glassware	67
Glass Specialties	68
Lamps	70
Decorated Table Lamps	73
Suns-Rays Lamps	76
Peerless White Granite Ware	77
Green Print Decorated Ware	79
Decorated Semi-Porcelain Ware	80
White and Gold Decorated Semi-Porcelain Ware	81
Decorated Chamber or Toilet Sets	82
American Decorated Tea and Dinnerware Sets	84
Crockery	87
Yellow & Rockingham Ware	88
Assorted Glassware	89
Inside Back Cover	91
Back Cover	92

Our Drummer, #580, Spring 1906

Front Cover	93
Inside Front Cover	94
American Cut Glass	95
Glassware	97
Table Sets	108
Specials in Glassware and Crockery	109
White Granite Ware	111
Water or Lemonade Sets	113
Glass Vases	115
Tumblers	116
Punch Sets	117
Boxed Tumblers	118
Salts and peppers	121
Syrups	122

Table of Contents - Index (continued)

Lamps	123
Decorated Lamps	128
White Granite Ware	131
Semi-Porcelain Ware	132
Decorated Semi-Porcelain Ware	133
English Semi-Porcelain Ware	134
Yellow & Rockingham Ware	140
American Tea and Dinner Sets	141
Decorated American Toilet Sets	144
Planters and Jardinières	146
Inside Back Cover	147
Back Cover	148

Catalogs On CD

Old Line Publishing is now offering an extensive line of eCatalogs. We have digitally reproduced every page of these trade catalogs in high resolution and in full color. We have then placed these images on compact disc for you to use. The quality of these images is so good that you can print them right on your home printer if you like, or you can simply view them on your computer.

There are nearly fifty catalogs available to choose from. Each compact disc catalog comes with a printed label and case for safe storage and easy identification.

All shipping and handling fees are included in the price of the catalog. All orders are shipped within 24-48 hours from when your order is received. These eCatalogs are designed to be used with Adobe Acrobat Reader 5.0 or greater. To order simply go to www.oldlinepublishingllc.com.

BUTLER BROTHERS,
NEW YORK AND CHICAGO.

SANTA CLAUS EDITION

HOLIDAY NUMBER,
NOVEMBER, 1896.

"Our Drummer"
1896

The title of this Catalogue, "Our Drummer," was registered at Washington, 1886, as a Trade-mark—Butler Brothers, New York and Chicago.

THE FALL TRADE OF 1896.

Notwithstanding the excitement of one of the most stirring political campaigns in this country's history, the issue of our holiday catalogue finds us in the midst of one of the most successful seasons we ever experienced, and this in the face of the general cry of business depression heard on every hand. How do we account for it? There are two answers to that question: one is that we without doubt handle a larger line than does any other concern of those goods which the majority of people are able to purchase, and the other is that whenever a dull season threatens we do exactly what we have always advised our customers to do—*push all the harder.* Our enormous sales therefore have not been made without a great effort; we frankly admit that.

In taking a careful diagnosis of our own business condition by which we arrive at the above facts, we are also equally confident that a large number of retailers, the most conservative ones, have undoubtedly held back their purchases until after the presidential election is decided. For us this means that on top of the enormous trade we have already had November promises to be simply a "crusher." In every year the months of October and November are particularly trying to our entire working force, but November, 1896, promises to eclipse all previous records.

By the time this catalogue is issued the people of the United States will practically know who is to be the next president and will as a rule settle down again to hard work. Merchants who have refrained from buying their fall stocks until after November third will come forward with orders and all will want to be waited on first. While we ask for your orders therefore we also request you to bear these facts in mind and be patient.

We have a larger and finer variety of Fall and Holiday Goods than ever before and believe we have enough for everybody, because each year we place larger orders, and notwithstanding the rumpus of the presidential election, we have full faith that the Fall trade of 1896 will be all that could be desired to those who push for it. Get your orders in early and we will give them as prompt despatch as it is possible for any house to do.

DON'T SEND ADDITIONS TO ORDERS

Do not send a "please add to my order" tagging along 24 or 48 hours after your main order has been sent. No one unacquainted with the system necessary for a large house like ours can appreciate the difficulty of finding an order after it has once started on its way through the house. It is not that we are unaccommodating in this matter but often it is practically an impossibility to make such additions.

TIME IS MONEY.

We cannot too strongly urge on customers who have not already purchased a line of Toys and Holiday Goods, to do so now. Do not wait for a convenient opportunity to look through our offerings but *take the time at once,* make up your mind what you want and order without further delay.

For several years past we have endeavored to offer such inducements to buyers of Holiday Goods as would cause them to place their orders in September and October. Possibly the political canvass has prevented many from accepting our liberal terms this season, though a large number have come forward and shown their confidence in a good trade for November and December.

In the best of seasons however there are many who for various reasons put off the purchasing of their holiday stock until practically the last moment. By the last moment we mean the last two weeks in November and the first week in December. This is a bad practice in any year and will be particularly so this season, because so many will do the same thing, and we cannot too strongly urge that orders be placed the earliest day possible.

Do not think for a moment that you are the only man who is going to wait. Hundreds are saying to themselves "O well, I have this or that thing to attend to now and the holiday season is still two months off." That is true so far as retailing is concerned, but the time when you will be *compelled* to get your stocks in is scarcely a month away, and there are so many hundreds of people who put off buying in this manner that we find great difficulty in satisfying them when the rush comes.

At the time this catalogue is issued our stock is practically complete, very few items being out, but before long several items will be completely exhausted every day, and imported goods particularly it is impossible to replenish.

CATALOGUE No. 150.

Prices take effect October 30, 1896.
We sell to merchants only.
Terms—2 per cent 10 days. Net 40 days. See page 1 for Special Terms on Holiday Goods.

HOLIDAY EDITION.

We are compelled to place our orders not only on foreign goods but on most American manufactures many months in advance of the time they will be required by the retailer and this is getting to be more and more the case with successful retailers, who likewise look ahead and prepare for their own season before it is actually upon them. Don't delay your orders for Holiday Goods. Send them in now.

POLITICS AND TRADE.

The political campaign being over the thoughtful industry of the American people will assert itself. Whatever disappointment the result may bring to some the bustle of business will soon take the place of the stump speaker and fife and drum. Competition for dollars will supplant the rivalry for votes.

None of us, not even the most partisan, believes the result of a presidential contest can more than temporarily retard the wheels of progress. The map of this glorious United States will not be removed from the world's atlas, our farms will be as productive, the brains and muscle of commerce as ready and as capable as before.

Within a very few weeks we predict that all business will resume its normal condition and people be as intent on making money as they have been within the past few weeks on saving the country.

Whatever the result of the election the country will be saved and we undoubtedly voice the sentiment of a very large proportion of Americans, aside from the professional politician, when we express the wish so often heard that these presidential disturbances, if they may be so designated without disrespect, could be six or eight years apart instead of four.

TO BUYERS OF HOLIDAY GOODS.

Judging this holiday season by those of former years, we shall doubtless run out of certain items in Christmas goods before the season is closed. Therefore, merchants who order such goods will be disappointed, unless they give us a list of "second choice," items or instruct us to put in the nearest thing we have in case we are out of anything ordered.

We know from experience that three out of four buyers *prefer* us to do this rather than to omit such "outs" entirely, since owing to the lateness of the season there is often not time to re-order other goods and they would therefore miss altogether the sale of a portion of their Christmas goods. We prefer however that customers instruct us *definitely* on this point.

Bear in mind the holiday goods which run out first are *not* the most desirable. The simple fact that the supply of same is exhausted so early shows that our buyers did not consider them quite good enough to order in the usual generous quantities.

In ordering Holiday Goods please send a list of "second choice" items, or else tell us to send the nearest thing we have when anything is "out." In that event we will of course use our best judgment and give something to suit about the same want and sell at about the same price.

BUTLER BROTHERS, 495 AND 497 BROADWAY, NEW YORK.   Also 230 to 236 Adams Street, CHICAGO.

Whatever Is Found in the Pages of "OUR DRUMMER" ORIGINAL WITH BUTLER BROTHERS.

NO ORDERS LESS THAN $5.00.

Orders for less than $5.00 will not be filled. This is for your economy as well as ours. Transportation charges on such bills eat up your profits, and our expense for filling is as great as on large orders.

QUALITY FIRST, THEN PRICE.

It is only when it comes to the matter of comparing quality that we regret our inability to SHOW SAMPLES OF THE GOODS. A lean and stingy looking doll will look just as well on paper when described as a "7-Inch China Limb Doll" as a plump-bodied well made one, but the latter may be better worth 42 cents than the former is 36 cents. We may offer a 12-inch trumpet at 42 cents and some neighbor list a 13-inch one in his catalogue at 39 cents. On paper we are badly beaten, whereas the superior quality of our trumpet may make ours very much the better value.

After all is said and done, you must, whether buying from a flesh-and-blood salesman or a paper one, depend to a large degree upon the character and integrity of the house. The salesman may show you a sample better made and better finished than the goods will run, and not one buyer out of a hundred could remember the goods well enough to be sure of the difference. The catalogue may deliberately misrepresent, and yet make the description in too general terms to found a complaint.

Wise buyers will keep these things in mind in making up their holiday goods orders. When they are acquainted with us we have no fear of the results. We simply wish to say that we seek no business to obtain which we are required to misrepresent.

PRICE REDUCTIONS.

A large number of price reductions will be found throughout this catalogue. The market for several months has been a declining one in many lines of trade, consequently we have obtained concessions on nearly every important purchase. As our old customers well know we reduce prices whenever we get a chance and the frequent issue of our various Bulletins enables us to place the latest and lowest quotations before our customers very soon after it has been possible to make them. All the reductions shown on recent Bulletins are embodied in this catalogue.

THE HOLIDAY TRADE OF 1896.

There will practically be just as many holiday gifts made this year as though the business of 1896 had not been dwarfed by an exciting presidential contest and the general cry of hard times heard on every hand. The only difference will be that people will invest nickels instead of dimes and seek to make a dollar buy two presents instead of one. There may be fewer grand pianos, fewer diamonds and fewer pretty but useless nick-nacks sold this year than last but of the popular toys to retail at from a penny to a dollar—of albums, dolls, low-cost books and practical household chinaware—there will be *more goods sold than ever before.*

Has your fall trade been disappointing? Have your patrons been "feeling poor" or discouraged for fear the country was "going to the dogs" and in consequence contracted their purchases to the absolute necessities? If so the holiday trade offers you a chance to average up the season. By wisely reading the signs of the times, by freely preparing for the holiday trade, by prudently avoiding the goods which your judgment tells you are unsafe to touch, you may insure for yourself a season of good times.

WHAT ARE HOLIDAY GOODS?

There was a time when the term Holiday Goods offered a scare to every conservative merchant. He instinctively had in mind a certain class of merchandise which could not be put to practical use and shivered to think of the nicknacks which would possibly be dead stock the next week after Christmas.

Such conditions do not now exist, and it is the shrewd conservative merchant who now puts in a liberal supply of merchandise which will sell rapidly just before Christmas, and the proportion of goods generally sold under this classification that will not prove good property twelve months in the year is insignificant.

A certain degree of usefulness is now combined with the gift character of nearly everything sold for the holiday trade. This assertion will be easily proven by your making a 30-minute inspection of the goods shown on the pink pages of this book.

Do not therefore be frightened when we talk Holiday Goods to you. They are the ones which for the next six weeks will attract customers to your store and unless you handle a fair variety of them the public is likely to be attracted elsewhere for their staples.

KEEP THE STAPLES MOVING TOO.

It is of course wise at this season to give special attention to toys and fancy goods and other peculiarly holiday merchandise, but don't neglect your staple lines altogether. People want pots and pans, glassware and gloves, wire goods and watches, pocket books and pipes, cutlery and crockery, just as much in December as in January, and you can't afford to let this all-the-year-'round trade get away from you.

THE "BARGAIN TREE"—*Specially Adapted for Holiday Goods.*

The most effective automatic salesman ever invented—Holds as many goods as a 20-foot counter—Takes a floor space less than 4 feet square—Always in bloom and always the center of a crowd—An ornament to any store—Makes people talk about you—Sells more goods than any two salesmen.

The "BARGAIN TREE" is the invention of one of our bright salesmen who set out to solve the problem how to make space for the merchant who thinks he "hasn't room for a bargain counter." The result is a grand success. Not only does it enable you to display 150 articles in a space less than 4 feet square, but it presents a unique and splendidly attractive appearance which helps to make your store the bargain hub of your town.

STANDS ABOUT EIGHT FEET HIGH from base to top of ball at summit. Diameter at widest part about 48 inches. Trunk formed of japanned iron with ornamental base and fancy cast fixture at top, surmounted with ball enameled in bright color. Five tiers of round-shape holders RICHLY ENAMELED—deep blue outside, red inside—ranging in size from 14 inches in bottom tier to 7½ inches at top; each of the five tiers contains seven holders. Above these is the sixth holder divided into ten compartments, the right size and shape for pencils, tooth brushes, combs, etc. Rising above this in turn is a fancy cast fixture having around its edges various devices for holding items such as shown in illustration. The ball top also has a number of hooks for hanging small articles such as spoons, thermometers, etc.

Suppose we allow three different items for each of the 35 circular holders, total 105; one item each for the 10 compartments at top; 20 for the cast fixtures above and 15 for the ball. This makes a grand total of 150 DIFFERENT ITEMS.

THE "BARGAIN TREE" IS REVOLVING (that is, each tier of holders can be easily revolved around the standard), so that your customer can stand still and pass every item on the tree in procession before him. The lowest tier of holders is far enough from the floor to be out of the way of dust and dirt and the top tier is on a level with the eyes of any person of ordinary height. Each holder is on an arm by itself and can be removed independently, the arm locking into hub by a simple device. Not a single screw is required to put the "Bargain Tree" together, except those fastening holders to arms.

THE USES to which the "Bargain Tree" can be put are endless. It can be used for goods of any character but is peculiarly adapted for displaying house furnishing goods in tinware, hardware, glassware, woodenware, etc. It is also admirably adapted for the display of holiday goods. The "Bargain Tree" will be shipped knocked down, properly packed, with full instructions for putting together. The following price of course does not include goods shown in cut.

PRICE, $15.00 COMPLETE.

A "BARGAIN TREE" FREE.

We have such thorough faith in the "Bargain Tree" as a means of selling goods for the retailer, that we make the following liberal offer:

Order a "Bargain Tree" now and same will be shipped at once, to be paid for on our regular terms. Then in case you buy from us, within the six months following, $200 more than you bought between the same dates one year ago, we will send you our check for $15.

It should be understood that the "Bargain Tree" must be **bought now** and paid for on regular terms. At the end of six months from date "Bargain Tree" is billed we will compare your purchases for that period with your purchases for the corresponding six months of the preceding year and in case same have increased $200 or more will send you check for the full cost of "Bargain Tree"—$15. If the gain is less than $200 no credit will of course be due you. No more than one tree given to any customer under any circumstances.

We can afford to make this offer for two reasons: Because we believe every merchant who puts a "Bargain Tree" in his store will sell so many more goods that his purchases from us will increase *very much more* than $200; and because, in reaching out to extend his purchases he will naturally dip into lines he has not bought from us before, and we thus count on a permanent gain in sales.

A SUGGESTION. During the short time the "BARGAIN TREE" has been in use a number of customers have bought **two**, using one for 5-cent and one for 10-cent goods. We also call the attention of buyers to the fact that price tickets and ticket holders suitable for use with the "BARGAIN TREE" will be found listed in this catalogue—see index for pages.

The "BARGAIN TREE" Proves Again That "GOODS WELL DISPLAYED ARE HALF SOLD."

We Urgently Invite Those of Our Customers Who Have Never Sold Crockery to GIVE IT A TRIAL.

"PEERLESS" WHITE GRANITE WARE
SHIPPED DIRECT FROM POTTERY.

EVERY PIECE ABSOLUTELY WARRANTED NOT TO CRAZE.

NEW PATTERN OF MATCHLESS FINISH AND UNEQUALED STRENGTH.

60, 5 and 5 PER CENT FROM W. G. LIST.—The net prices given below are figured at exactly 60, 5 and 5 per cent from the standard White Granite List, adopted July 1st, 1895.

Economy in packing requires that at least one barrel be filled. Therefore if you should happen to require some one or two items to "sort up" you will please add a few staples so that the shipment will amount to at least $10.00.

NOTE.—Packages will be charged according to the never-broken rule among crockery manufacturers. **No charge for cartage.**

SHIPPED DIRECT FROM OUR CENTRAL WAREHOUSE.

In order to make possible the prices here named we have made arrangements to fill all orders for "Peerless" ware **direct from our warehouse** near **Bellaire, Ohio**, from which point we have obtained advantageous freight rates.

N. B.—All these goods are "run of the kiln" firsts, absolutely guaranteed not to craze.

OUR STANDING CHALLENGE.—Our "Peerless" ware is positively worth **10 to 20 per cent more** than some well known lines. Send for a package and if the ware is not *equal to any other* hold it *subject to our order*.

For two years we have kept the above challenge standing at the head of this department in our catalogue. During that time not one single complaint has been made nor one shipment returned. Next time any traveling man tries to tell you that *"Butler Brothers' W. G. ware is seconds"* please remember the above.

CROCKERY BUYERS. Any merchant who has been in the habit of buying his crockery at a certain discount (W. G. or A.) from the regular list and prefers to so continue can buy these best goods from us at best terms to be obtained from any pottery. N. B.—Any merchant preferring to buy from the long list will please mention it when ordering.

C. O. D. SHIPMENTS.—Customers dealing with us on a C. O. D. basis, when ordering Crockery to be shipped from factory in the same order with goods to be shipped from our house, should send a separate deposit for each shipment.

LIST OF OUR "PEERLESS" WHITE GRANITE WARE—From Which to Sort Up Package Lots to Suit Your Wants.

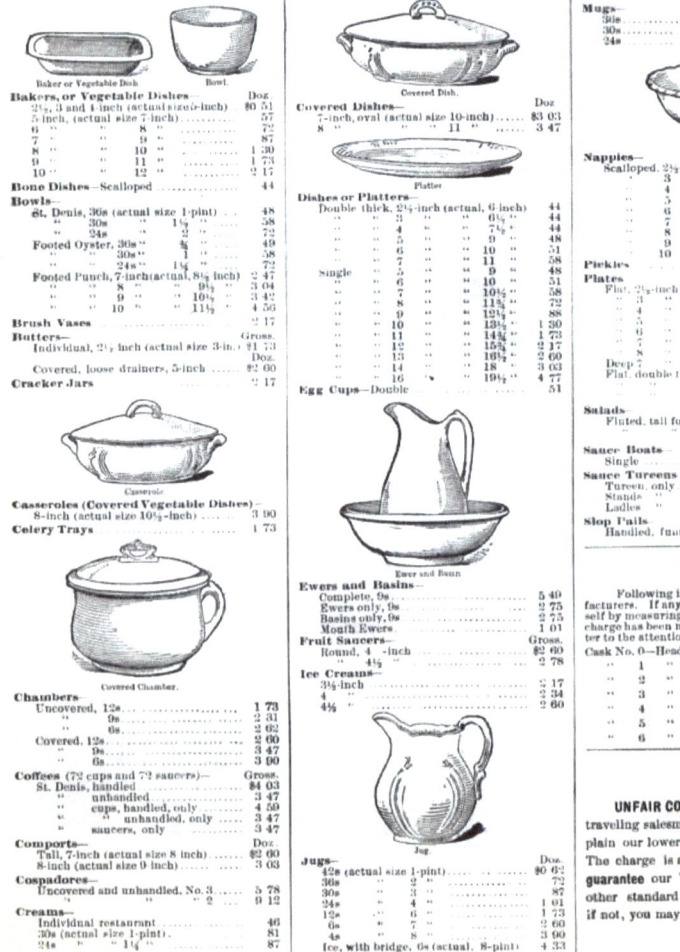

Our "Peerless" Ware Is Not Merely Equal to Any Other—It Is Positively THE BEST.

Order One Lot of Our "Peerless" White Granite Ware and Compare it with ANY OTHER.

ASSORTMENTS OF PEERLESS WHITE GRANITE WARE—*SHIPPED DIRECT FROM POTTERY.*

For the convenience of buyers we have had packed up a few assortments of our "Peerless" ware. Assortment No. 1 gives a fairly complete variety of the most staple sellers, and Nos. 2 to 5 are intended to supply those items which naturally sell out first. By having a large number of cases packed at one time, in advance of orders, we can afford to sell any of these assortments at lowest net prices (which are figured at 60, 5 and 5 per cent off the regular W. G. List).

Our No. 1 Assortment—*Shipped from Pottery*—$30.39 Complete.

		Doz.	Total.
4 doz.	5-inch Plates—Size 7-inch	$0 32	$1 28
2 "	6-inch Plates— " 8 "	40	80
8 "	7-inch Plates— " 9 "	48	3 84
1 "	8-inch Plates— " 10 "	54	54
2 "	8-inch Soups— " 9 "	48	96
3 "	Fruits—Actual size 5 inches	18	54
1 "	Individual Butters—Size 3 in	18	18
4 "	Handled Teas (4 doz. cups, 4 doz. saucers)	58	2 32
2 "	Unhandled Teas (2 doz. cups, 1 doz. saucers)	49	98
1 "	Unhandled Coffees (1 doz. cups, 1 doz. saucers)	58	58
1 "	Handled Coffees (1 doz. cups, 1 doz. saucers)	68	68
½ "	2½-inch Bakers—Size 5-inch	51	51
½ "	6-inch Bakers— " 8 "	72	36
½ "	7-inch Bakers— " 9 "	87	45
¼ "	8-inch Bakers— " 10 "	1 30	65
¼ "	8-inch Dishes— " 11 "	72	18
¼ "	10-inch Dishes— " 13 "	1 30	33
¼ "	12-inch Dishes— " 15 "	2 17	54
¼ "	14-inch Dishes— " 17 "	3 03	51
½ "	3-inch Dishes— " 6 "	44	44
¼ "	8-inch Covered Dishes	3 47	87
¼ "	8-inch Casseroles	3 90	98
¼ "	Sauce Boats	$1 16	$0 29
	Pickles	87	22
½ "	Covered Butters	2 60	65
½ "	Jugs, No. 42—Size 1 pint	62	31
½ "	Jugs, No. 30— " 2 "	72	36
½ "	Jugs, No. 36— " 3 "	87	44
½ "	Jugs, No. 24— " 4 "	1 01	51
½ "	Jugs, No. 12— " 6 "	1 73	43
1-6 "	Tea Pots	1 95	33
¼ "	Sugars	1 74	43
¼ "	Creams—Actual size 1 pint	81	20
¼ "	Individual Creams	46	23
¼ "	Bowls, No. 36—Size 1 pint	48	24
½ "	Bowls, No. 30— " 1½ "	58	29
¼ "	Bowls, No. 24	72	38
½ "	Oyster Bowls	58	58
½ "	Nappies, No. 5— " 6-inch	58	29
¼ "	Nappies, No. 6— " 7 "	72	36
¼ "	Nappies, No. 7— " 8 "	88	44
¼ "	Nappies, No. 8— " 9 "	1 30	65
¼ "	Ewers and Basins	5 58	1 40
¼ "	Covered Chambers	3 47	87
¼ "	Slabs	3 47	11
¼ "	Mugs	54	14
	Extra charge for cask		1 75
	Total for Assortment, $30.39 Complete.		

Our "No. 2" Assortment—*Shipped from Pottery*—$20.52 Complete.

		Doz.	Total.
4 doz.	5-inch Plates—Size 7-inch	$0 32	$1 28
3 "	6-inch Plates— " 8 "	40	1 20
10 "	7-inch Plates— " 9 "	48	4 80
2 "	Handled Teas (6 doz. cups, 6 doz. saucers)	58	3 48
		Doz.	Total.
4 "	Unhandled Teas (4 doz. cups, 4 doz. saucers)	49	1 96
½ "	8-inch Bakers—Size 10 inches	1 30	65
½ "	Mugs, No. 30	54	27
½ "	Jugs, No. 24—Size 4 pints	$1 01	$0 51
½ "	Jugs, No. 36— " 3 "	72	36
½ "	Bowls, No. 30—Size 1½ pints	58	29
½ "	Bowls, No. 36— " 1 "	48	24
½ "	Nappies, No. 7—Size 8-inch	88	44
¼ "	Nappies, No. 8— " 9 "	1 30	65
½ "	Ewers and Basins	5 58	1 40
½ "	Covered Chambers	3 47	1 74
	Extra charge for cask		1 25
	Total for Assortment, $20.52 Complete.		

Our "No. 3" Assortment—*Shipped from Pottery*—$15.54 Complete.

		Doz.	Total.
3 doz.	5-inch Plates—Size 7-inch	$0 32	$0 96
2 "	6-inch Plates— " 8 "	40	80
6 "	7-inch Plates— " 9 "	48	2 88
6 "	Handled Teas (6 doz. cups, 6 doz. saucers)	58	3 48
½ "	Jugs, No. 24—Size 4 pints	$1 01	$0 51
¼ "	Bowls, No. 30—Size 1½ pints	58	29
½ "	Oyster Bowls— " 1 "	58	29
½ "	Nappies, No. 7—Size 8-inch	88	44
¼ "	Nappies, No. 8— " 9 "	1 30	65
¼ "	Covered Chambers	3 47	1 74
	Extra charge for cask		1 10
	Total for Assortment, $15.54 Complete.		

Our "No. 4" Assortment—*Shipped from Pottery*—$6.86 Complete.

6 doz.	7-inch Plates—Size 9-inch	$0 48	$2 88
6 "	Handled Teas (6 doz. cups, 6 doz. saucers)	58	3 48
	Extra charge for tierce		$0 50
	Total for Assortment, $6.86 Complete.		

Our "No. 5" Assortment—*Shipped from Pottery*—$6.32 Complete.

6 doz.	7-inch Plates—Size 9-inch	$0 48	$2 88
6 "	Unhandled Teas (6 doz. cups, 6 doz. saucers)	49	2 94
	Extra charge for tierce		$0 50
	Total for Assortment, $6.32 Complete.		

"PARIS WHITE" C. C. WARE.
SHIPPED DIRECT FROM THE POTTERY.

Shipped direct from our central warehouse near Bellaire, Ohio. You can have this and "Peerless" White Granite or "Bee Hive" decorated ware packed together, but in that case please be very explicit in stating your wants. Packages will be charged according to the never broken rule among crockery makers.

Positively warranted not to craze. Superior make, worth ten per cent more than most lines. We guarantee it superior both in strength and finish to any other C. C. ware produced in America. We name net prices figured at exactly 55 per cent from the standard C. C. list, adopted July 1st, 1895. No charge for cartage.

Bakers, Oval—		Doz.
5-inch (actual size 7-inch)		$0 50
6 " " 8 "		50
7 " " 8¼ "		70
8 " " 9½ "		90
9 " " 10¼ "		1 04
Bowls—		
St. Denis, 30s (actual size 5⅜-inch)		45
Plain, 42s (actual size 5¼-inch)		29
" 36s " 5¾ "		32
" 30s " 6½ "		38
" 24s " 7 "		45
" 18s " 8¼ "		79
" 12s " 10 "		1 17
" 9s " 11 "		1 74
" 6s " 12 "		2 30
" 4s " 12½ "		3 15
Bed Pans, French—		
No. 2		4 86
No. 1		5 40
Chambers, Fluted and Plain—		
12s uncovered (actual size 7¼-inch)		1 26
9s " " 9 "		1 80
12s covered		1 98
9s "		2 81
6s open		2 25
6s covered, 9½-inch		3 49
Cospadores—		
3s unh'd and uncov'd (actual 11¾-inch)		5 56

Dishes—		
2½, 3 and 4-inch		36
5-inch		45
6-inch		47
7-inch flat oval (actual size 9¼-inch)		68
8 " " 11¼ "		68
9 " " 12½ "		81
10 " " 13¼ "		1 13
11 " " 14¼ "		1 49
12 " " 15¾ "		1 80
14 " " 18¼ "		2 93

Sauce Boats		$1 16	$0 29
	Pickles	87	22
Covered Butters		2 60	65
Ewers and Basins—			Doz.
Cable, 12s			$4 50
" 9s			5 18
Ewers only, 12s			2 48
" 9s			2 93
Basins only, 12s (actual size 13¼-inch)			2 25
" 9s " 14 "			2 48
Fruit Saucers—			Gross.
4-inch French (actual size 4⅜-inch)			$2 16
Ice Creams—			
4-inch (actual size 4⅜-inch)			2 14
Jugs, Cable—			Doz.
42s (actual size 1-pint)			$0 63
36s " 2 "			68
30s " 3 "			81
24s " 4 "			1 01
12s " 6 "			1 69
6s " 7 "			2 52
Mugs—			
30s (actual size 3⅜-inch)			50
Nappies, Fluted, New—			
5-inch (actual size 6⅜-inch)			56
6 " " 7⅜ "			71
7 " " 8¼ "			86
8 " " 9½ "			1 13
9 " " 10¼ "			1 58
Plates—			
5-inch flat (actual size 7¼-inch)			27
6 " " 8¼ "			36
7 " " 9½ "			45
8 " " 10¼ "			50
7 " deep " 9¼ "			45
Teas, St. Denis—			Gross.
Unhandled			$2 70
Handled			3 15
Baltimore, unhandled			2 48
" handled			2 93
Tulip, unhandled only			2 25

THE "BEE-HIVE" LINE SHIPPED DIRECT FROM POTTERY.

A Gold Edge Line of Semi-Porcelain Ware, Embossed Pattern, Elegantly Painted Floral Decoration, Gold Edges.

After twelve months of pattern making we are at last prepared to supply in any quantity any of the items mentioned below in this marvellously pleasing "Bee-Hive" pattern. Do not think because the prices are low that the ware is not the very best. We not only guarantee it in every way, but warrant every piece against "crazing." *These net prices named below are subject to our regular terms—2 per cent 10 days, net 60 days.*

N. B. You can have the "Bee-Hive" goods packed together with either the "Peerless" or "Paris White."

A REQUEST!—Will you kindly order a few pieces of the staples in this line in order that you may see the ware. We assert that these are the best and cheapest offerings ever made in tableware.

Bakers—	Doz.
Oval, 5-inch	$0 78
" 7 "	1 21
" 8 "	1 56
Berry Saucers—Festooned, 5-inch	47
Bowls— St. Denis, 30s	78
Butters— Covered, loose drainer	4 29
	Gross.
Butters— Individual	$4 54
	Doz.
Cake Plates—9-inch	$1 87
Casseroles—8-inch	5 00
Covered Dishes—8-inch	5 00
Creams—30s	1 33
Dishes—	
4-inch	63
8 "	1 17
10 "	1 95
12 "	3 12
14 "	5 07
Egg Cups—Double	78
	Gross.
Fruits—4-inch	$4 10
Ice Creams—Plain, 4-inch	3 71

Jugs—	Doz.
Pressed, 42s	
36s	1 17

Jugs—	Doz.
Pressed, 30s	$1 41
" 24s	1 70
" 12s	2 93
Nappies—	
Scalloped, 5-inch	89
" 6 "	1 17
" 7 "	1 48
" 8 "	1 95
Oatmeal Saucers	47
Pickles	1 45
Plates—	
Flat, 5-inch	47
" 6 "	63
" 7 "	78
" 8 "	86
Plates—Deep, 7-inch	78
Sauce Boats	1 95
Slop Bowls	78
Soup Tureens—	
Complete, 4 pieces	21 84
Tureens only	13 46
Stands	4 68
Ladles	4 21
Sugars—Cable, 30s	2 81
	Gross.
Teas (72 cups and 72 saucers)—	
St. Denis and Chinese, handled	$5 46
	Doz.
Tea Pots—Pressed, 24s	$3 90

Cast your eye over the prices of some of the every day staples in this line. We simply ask that you order a small quantity for comparison. We shall then be certain of your future orders.

COMBINATION DINNER AND TEA SET—106 Pieces.

Comprising 106 pieces. This set is so desirable as to assortment, being arranged for a complete breakfast, dinner and supper service, that it is one of the most popular items from our entire crockery department. One needs only to read to understand our ability to dispose of a hundred sets per week of this assortment. N. B.—Please note the absence of small pieces useful for counting purposes only.

12	7-inch Plates.	1	Handled Sauce Boat.	1	9¼-in. Oblong Vegetable Dish and Cover (h'ndl'd)
12	8 " "	1	Sugar Bowl and Cover.	1	9-in. Pickle Dish.
12	9 " "	1	Large Bowl.	1	Handled Butter Dish, Covered, with Drainer.
12	Individual Butter Plates.	1	10-in. Bread Plate.		
12	5¼-in. Sauce Plates.	12	Handled Cups and Saucers.	1	Tea Pot and Cover.
1	8½-in. Oval Dish (covered and handled).	1	11¼-inch Platter.	1	Milk Pitcher.
2	10-inch Vegetable Dishes.	1	13 " "	1	10-in. Cake Plate.
		1	17 " "		

(*Shipped from pottery. 106 pieces in pkg. Sold only by pkg. Bbl. 35c.*) **Price, $4.35 per Set.**

The Phenomenal Growth of Our Crockery Sales is a Standing Marvel Among the Makers.

We Offer Values Never Before APPROACHED in This Honest and Beautiful American Ware.

DECORATED AMERICAN TEA AND DINNER SETS---Shipped from Pottery.

Of course you know that many Dinner Sets in the market contain *small size pieces* to bring down the cost, and that some of them *omit covers* on dishes which ought to have them. Our pottery doesn't turn out that kind of goods. All our sets *are honest throughout*. *Quality considered* our prices get right down to the roots of things.

Our "EVERY DAY" 101-Piece Dinner Set.
Speaking of Bargains---How is This Sightly and Serviceable Set for $6.50.

New shape, plain print decoration in handsome floral designs. Made of semi-porcelain. Order one package and you will see this is a very special bargain. The pieces are the ones needed in every household—regular 101-piece outfit.

12 8-inch Dinner Plates.
12 9-inch Dinner Plates.
12 9-inch Deep Soup Plates.
12 5-inch Square Fruit Dishes.
12 Individual Butters.
12 Tea Cups and Saucers, regular size.
1 Butter Dish, cover and drainer.
3 Platters. 1 each 11-inch, 13-inch and 15-inch
1 9-inch Square Covered Vegetable Dish, handled
1 8-inch Oblong Covered Vegetable Dish, han'dled.
2 8-inch Deep Dishes.
1 Soup Tureen and Cover, handled.
1 Sauce Boat, handled.
2 Pickle Dishes.

Each set in bbl. (Bbl. 35c.)   **Price, $6.50 per Set.**

Our "STYLISH AND SERVICEABLE" Dinner Set.
101 Pieces---New Shape and Hand-Painted Rose Spray Decoration.

This is a truly elegant dinner set made in one of the handsomest of shapes and more desirable at the price than any we have ever before shown. It comprises 101 pieces, with filled-in hand-painted decorations in tasty designs; all decorations burnt in. A single set put on exhibition in your store will sell many for you. Same list of pieces as in Every Day Set.
(*Each set in bbl.* Bbl. 35c.)   **Price, $8.50 per Set.**

Our "GOLD CLOUDED" 101-Piece Dinner Set.
A Most Fascinatingly Beautiful Set. Gold Clouds, Edges and Handles.

The richness of this decoration is only comparable to the choice French designs which are always so much admired. White and gold makes a combination which pleases every artistic taste. The pieces in this set are the same in size and number as are contained in the Every Day Set.
(*Each set in bbl.* Bbl. 35c.)   **Price, $10.75 per Set.**

Our "ROYAL BLUE" 101-Piece Dinner Set.
Underglazed Gold and Blue Decoration. Rich Enough for the Richest.

We have never before dared to enter the domains of the Tiffany trade in any article so thoroughly practical as a dinner set. But opportunities having been presented whereby we could contract for an aristocratic "swell" set at less than one-half the ordinary swell price, we are able to show our friends this gem of table ware decorated in the richest of that wealthy Royal Blue. Underglazed decoration, with gold trimmings and also the leaves and vines traced in gold.
The set comprises the same pieces as shown in the Every Day Set.
(*Each set in bbl.* Bbl. 35c.)   **Price, $15.00 per Set.**

Our "GOLD EDGE" 101-Piece Dinner Set.

Identically the same shape as "Every Day" set above, but with gold edge. Silver gray plain print with gold edges and handles. Same pieces as in the "Every Day" set.
Each set in bbl. (Bbl. 35c.)   **Price, $8.25 per Set.**

Our "FORGET-ME-NOT" 101-Piece Dinner Set.
A Set That Will Daily Grow More Beautiful in the Eyes of its Fortunate Possessor.

A magnificent set with a filled-in hand-painted decoration in a most natural forget-me-not design with an all-over scroll work pattern.
The same list of pieces as shown in the Every Day Set.
(*Each set in bbl.* Bbl. 35c.)   **Price, $12.75 per Set.**

Our "UTILITY" Tea Set—(56 Pieces).
As Staple as Sugar. As Handsome as a Tea Set.

Tasteful printed decorations in beautiful tints. A special bargain for the money. 2 full 56-piece sets in barrel, one blue tinted and one brown.
Printed decoration in assorted blue and brown tints. Very pretty and wonderfully salable. Full 56-piece set.
2 sets in bbl. (Bbl. 35c.)
Price, $2.60 per Set.

Our "GOLDEN ROD" Tea Set—(56 Pieces).
Painted Decorations Very Handsome.

Filled-in golden rod decoration in carmine and turquoise with gold clouded handles. Each set is full 56 pieces, and will sell as soon as opened out. Total 2 sets in bbl.
(Bbl. 35c.)
Price, $3.60 per Set.

Our "WHITE AND GOLD" Tea Set—(56 Pieces).
Heavy Gold Clouded Edges and Gold Striped Handles.

White and gold is rich enough for the rich, tasty enough for the tasteful and modest enough for the modest. It is a combination never out of style and always "right" in any place.
The first customer that sees it will buy a set (if she has the money. 56 pieces in set. 2 sets in bbl. (Bbl. 35c.)
Price, $4.40 per Set.

Our "PURITAN" 56-Piece Tea Set.
Pure White Ware.
A Bargain at $1.78.

Regular 56-piece tea set in plain pure white ware. A good thing for you to advertise with.
Put up 2 sets in bbl. (Bbl. 35c.)
Price, $1.78 per Set.

Keen Buyers Are Always Ready for Low Quotations—Whether Named by a Talking Salesman or a Catalogue.

Our Only Trouble in Selling Crockery to Any Buyer Is to Get the First TRIAL ORDER.

DECORATED TOILET SETS.
SHIPPED DIRECT FROM THE POTTERY.

Our "GENERAL USE" Toilet Set.
Print Decoration in Blue and Red Tints.

Full size and best ware, bowl being 14½ inches in diameter and extra deep—not the ordinary small one. Neatly decorated in floral pattern in blue and red. Set comprises ewer and basin, quart pitcher, covered soap dish with drainer, tooth brush vase, handled mug, chamber and cover. *Shipped from pottery. 2 sets in bbl. Sold only by pkg. (Bbl. 35c.)* **Price per Set, $1.38.**

Our "COTTAGE" Toilet Set.
All Extra Size Pieces in Real Oil Color Decoration.

Full size pieces, neatly and artistically decorated in a rich floral pattern. Set comprises ewer and basin, quart jug, covered soap dish with drainer, tooth brush vase, handled mug, chamber and cover. *Shipped from pottery. 2 sets in bbl., 1 blue, 1 pink. Sold only by bbl.* (Bbl. 35c.) **Price, $2.20 per Set.**

Our "NEW HOME" Toilet Set.
"One for the Blue Room—One for the Pink Room."

Elegant and elaborate pattern of raised decoration. Gold traced leaves and gold edges. A set heretofore sold at much above this price. "If you can sell anything seems as though this should sell." Set of 10 pieces, full size, same pieces as mentioned in above. *Shipped from pottery. 2 sets in bbl., 1 pink, 1 blue. Sold only by bbl.* (Bbl. 35c.) **Price, $2.50 per Set.**

Our "GUEST ROOM" Toilet Set.
A Popular Addition to Our 1896 Offerings.

Profuse green floral decoration all over, gold clouded edges and handles. Full 12-piece set and a beauty. Set comprises bowl and pitcher, extra large covered slop bowl, chamber with cover, tooth brush vase, soap dish with cover and drainer, hand pitcher and handled mug. *Shipped from pottery. Each set in bbl. Sold only by pkg.* (Bbl. 35c.) **Price per Set, $4.10.**

Our "ANNIVERSARY" Toilet Set.
A Taking Set at a Taking Price.

Comprising 12 full size pieces, gold edges, colored filled-in decoration in beautiful tints, half hand work, tastefully colored flowers and leaves, gold edges. Comprises bowl and pitcher, extra large covered slop bowl, chamber with cover, tooth brush vase, soap dish with cover and drainer, hand pitcher and handled mug. *Shipped from pottery. Each set in bbl. Sold only by pkg.* (Bbl. 35c.) **Price per Set, $4.75.**

☛ *Please note that all Toilet Sets on this page are shipped from pottery, whereas Yellow and Rockingham packages are shipped from our house.* ☚

Our "BEST ROOM" Toilet Set—(Shipped from Pottery).
Basket Pattern in White and Gold—A Beauty.

This is a 12-piece set, full size, and of course richly decorated in gold clouds on a basket pattern of ware. All the pieces are very handsome, the slop bowl being handled. The set comprises bowl and pitcher, extra large covered slop bowl, chamber with cover, tooth brush vase, soap dish with cover and drainer, hand pitcher and handled mug. *Shipped from pottery. Each set in bbl. Sold only by pkg.* (Bbl. 35c.) **Price, $4.90 per Set.**

☛ *Please note that the following assortments are shipped from our house, whereas Toilet Sets preceding are shipped from pottery.* ☚

PACKAGE LOTS OF
YELLOW AND ROCKINGHAM WARE.
Carried in Stock at Both Our Houses.

"KITCHEN FAVORITE" 5c Assortment (Yellow and Rockingham).
A Very Attractive Assortment of Genuine Necessities.

These goods will stand as among the best of the captures in our history. To buy a package costs but little. Try one.

THE ASSORTMENT COMPRISES 1⅓ DOZ. EACH OF THE FOLLOWING:

Yellow Bowls—6¼-inch in diameter.　　Yellow Pie Plates—8½-inch in diameter.
Yellow Bakers—8-inch in diameter.　　Rockingham Nappies—5½-inch in diameter.
Yellow Nappies—6½-inch in diameter.　Rockingham Bowls—5¼-inch in diameter.
Rockingham Mug—Good size.　　　　　Rockingham Pie Plates—7¼-inch in diameter.

(Shipped from our house. Total of 12 doz. to pkg. Sold only by pkg. Bbl. 35c.) **Price, 39c Doz.**

Our "USEFUL" Yellow Ware Assortment.
A Bargain Lot of Big 10-Cent Trade Winners.

Nothing so appeals to the customer as a kitchen article. What other kitchen article is so clean, so wholesome, so healthful as a yellow ware dish?

THE ASSORTMENT COMPRISES 1 DOZ. EACH OF THE FOLLOWING:

Milk Boilers—With spout and handle, outside Rockingham, inside yellow.　　Bakers—10 inches in diameter.
Nappies—9 inches in diameter.　　Rustic Pitchers—Hold 3 pints.
Extra Deep Bowls—8½ inches wide.　　Large Milk Pans—9½ inches in diameter.

(Shipped from our house. 6 doz. to pkg. Sold only by pkg. Barrel 35c.) **Price, 78c Doz.**

Our "UTILITY" Large Dish Assortment (Yellow Ware).
What Every Housekeeper Wants for Mixing, Baking, etc.

If a customer will, on our recommendation, order a package of this assortment, he will find it one of the *most attractive* and best selling lines he ever added.

THE ASSORTMENT COMPRISES 1-3 DOZ. EACH OF THE FOLLOWING:

Deep Bowls—10¼ inches in diameter.　　Nappies—11¼ inches in diameter.
Deep Bowls—11 inches in diameter.　　Fluted Nappies—10 inches in diameter.
Nappies—10⅜ inches in diameter.　　Fluted Nappies—11¼ inches in diameter.

(Shipped from our house. Total of 2 doz. to pkg. Sold only by pkg. Bbl. 35c.) **Price, $1.30 Doz.**

Our Rockingham "TEA POT ASSORTMENT."
All Choice and Staple Sellers.
The assortment comprises the following:

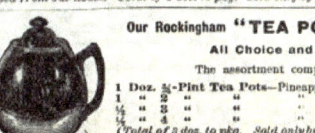

1 Doz. ¾-Pint Tea Pots—Pineapple shape		$0 96
1 " 2 " " " "		1 40
½ " 3 " " " at $1.60		80
¼ " 4 " " " at $1.80		90

(Total of 3 doz. to pkg. Sold only by pkg. Barrel 35c.)
Shipped from our house. **Total for Package, $4.06**

ETERNAL PUSHING is the Price of Success in These Days of Stirring Competition.

No Other Line Than Glassware Offers Such a Tempting Array of "LEADERS."

DEPARTMENT OF GLASSWARE.

Our plan of selling Glassware in "assorted packages" has revolutionized the glass business. Why buy a barrel of each item when you can get six or twelve items in a package at equally low prices per dozen? No overstocking—no money needlessly tied up—goods sold almost as soon as in—and something fresh always on the way.

We originated and introduced the "assortment plan" of selling Glassware, and have forced the exclusive jobbers and many of the factories to follow us in sheer self-defense. But as yet the assortments of these would-be imitators are "juggled"—they contain dozens of the small-cost goods and half-dozens of the higher-cost, as well as a sprinkling of small or undesirable pieces put in to "help out the average." By and by, may be, when they learn how to make up assortments of uniform value throughout, and of equal-selling qualities, they may produce packages which will bear some sort of comparison with ours.

We charge 35 cents each for all glassware packages (though some of them cost us upwards of 60 cents each), except two cask packages at 90c each and chimney boxes which are charged at 30, 40 and 50 cents. We charge for no packages aside from glassware and crockery.

☞ The never-broken combination between glassware manufacturers compels all factories to charge for packages, and, accordingly, *every jobber must pay for them*. Therefore, if we did not charge directly for the barrel we should be obliged to add it to the price of the goods.

Wash your glassware frequently. Nothing can injure its attractiveness and salableness except a careless coating of dust and dirt.

Our assortments are all made up and packed by professional packers at the factory before being shipped to us, and are not opened until they reach our customers' stores.

CAUTION! When Opening Glassware Barrels **DO NOT DRIVE IN THE HEADS.**

Our "WINNER" Assortment.

While All "3-CENT POSSIBILITIES," Yet This Assortment Will Compare Favorably with the 5-Cent Assortments of Our Imitators Among the Glass and Crockery Jobbers.

This assortment ranks high among our 1896 capture. There is not a piece in the lot but would hold its own against the articles offered by our followers in their 5-cent assortments.

The "Winner" Assortment Comprises 2 Doz. Each of the Following:
Round Deep Dishes—6¼ inches in diameter—very bright.
A B C Plates—6-inch. One of the most popular of 5-cent sellers.
Handled Mugs—A full size mug of very attractive pattern.
Fan-Shaped Nappies—A popular pattern and a rapid seller.
Long Dishes with Handles—7 inches long. For preserves, pickles, etc.
Family Table Salts—Rich plain pattern of family size.
Scalloped Table Dishes—7-inch oblong dish. Rich and useful.
Cut Pattern Wine Glasses—A very elegant wine.
Tumblers—A heavy, attractive, finished pattern.
Goblets—One of the most attractive of cut pattern designs.

(Total of 20 doz. to pkg. Sold only by pkg. Barrel 35c.) Price, 35c Doz.

Our "SENSATION" 5-Cent Assortment.

An Assortment Particularly Recommended to Customers Who Sell Glassware at Wholesale.

If a customer is doing a jobbing business he will find this assortment will outrank any 4½c package offered by his competitors.

The "Sensation" Assortment Comprises 1 Doz. Each of the Following:
7-Inch Square Diamond Plates—A regular 10-center in value.
Cream Pitchers—A gem of the glassmakers' art.
Cups and Saucers—Of the heart shape "Trilby" pattern.
7-Inch Oval Dishes—Convenient for a hundred uses.
Sugar Bowls and Covers—Dart pattern, full size and good value.
Spoon Holders—Dart pattern, always staple.
Butter Dishes and Covers—Dart pattern, ever breaking, always wanted.
Milk Pitchers—Dart pattern, sure and prompt seller.
High Footed Jelly Dishes—Stands up high, very useful.
6-Inch Round Dishes—Useful for table purposes.
Deep Scalloped Nappies—For sauces, preserves, olives, etc.
Full Size Goblets—New pattern of pretty design.

(Total of 12 doz. to pkg. Sold only by pkg. Tierce 35c.) Price, 36c Doz.

New 25-Cent "SALVER ASSORTMENT."

For 1896 we offer two entirely new and rich salvers in one package, thereby enabling our customers to get two patterns instead of one.
¾ Doz. 10-Inch Plain Salvers. ¾ Doz. Fancy Scalloped Edge Salvers.
(Total 1½ doz. to pkg. Sold only by pkg. Bbl. 35c.) Price, $1.67 Doz.

CARE OF GLASS. To get best results out of your glass stock you must keep it always clean and bright. Do this and name fair prices and your glass will not require any pushing—It will sell itself.

Our "CHARM" 5-Cent Assortment.

All Large—All Finished—All Individual Bargains.

An assortment consisting of what should properly be termed 5 and 10-cent goods. If our customers do not find this a rare bunch of quick-selling attractions, then we are not prophets.

The "Charm" Assortment Comprises 1 Doz. Each of the Following:
7-Inch Oblong Dishes—A large, rich and practical piece.
Sugar Bowls and Covers—Large size bowl with foot, covered.
Cut Pattern Tumblers—Rich, heavy, full finished article.
7-Inch Square Diamond Plates—Useful for a hundred purposes.
Milk Pitchers—To match the sugar and butter.
Butter Dishes and Covers—Always a ready seller at 10 cents.
Large Handled Mugs—A new full handled pattern of elegant proportions.
8½-Inch Oblong Dishes—For cheese, pickles, etc., etc.
Round Deep Dishes—A heavy, fancy pattern 6-inch dish.
Cut Diamond Goblets—A full size, heavy goblet, fire polished.

(Total of 10 doz. to package. Sold only by package. Barrel 35c.) Price, 42c Doz.

Our "BIG VALUE" 5-Cent Assortment.

Cast Your Eye Over These Values and Send for a Sample Package.

One-half of these articles are really 10-cent goods. If you will try a barrel of these goods you'll buy many more during the season.

The "Big Value" Assortment Comprises 1 Doz. Each of the Following:
7-Inch Oblong Dishes—Heavy square edge dish, very useful.
7-Inch Plates—A most attractive pattern, a real custom winner.
Flanged Foot Tumblers—One of the heaviest of brilliant tumblers.
7-Inch Oval Dishes—Useful for forty purposes.
Deep Low Footed Dishes—Size 5½-inch. One of the most practical of dishes.
Tankard Cream Pitchers—High, beautiful and salable.
Deep Round Dishes—Measuring full 5½ inch in diameter.
Round Deep Dishes—5½ inch, footed, scalloped edge.
Cups and Saucers—Both cup and saucer together constitute one piece. Worth double.
Table Goblets—Of artistic design and finish.
High Footed Jellies—Measures 4¾-inch in diameter. Another 10-center.
Low Sugar Bowls and Covers—This 4½-inch sugar bowl and cover are counted as one piece.

(Total of 12 doz. to bbl. Sold only by bbl. Barrel 35c.) Price, 42c Doz.

Our 1896 SUGAR BOWL Assortment.

All Telling Bargains at a 10-Cent Price.

Comprising 1 doz. each of four styles, of which we have room here to show but three. They are of such size and shape as to appeal to the demands of all classes. Bright and attractive in design and finish. The assortment comprises 1 doz. each of the 4 styles.

(Total of 4 doz. to bbl. Sold only by bbl. Barrel 35c.) Price, 79c Doz.

A SUGGESTION: Next time you get hold of one of the illustrated assortment sheets put out by the glassware factories or handed you by some traveling man, put same alongside one of our assortments at same price. Note the uniform good value of the items in our assortment and the absence of small pieces. Then see if the other will stand the test!

Glassware Barrels and Boxes Are the ONLY Kind of Packages for Which We Make Any Charge.

QUANTITIES In Our Assortments Will Suit the Smallest Buyers and Prices the Largest.

Our "RADIANT" 10-Cent Assortment.
The Richest of High Finished Ware at a Marvelously Low Price.

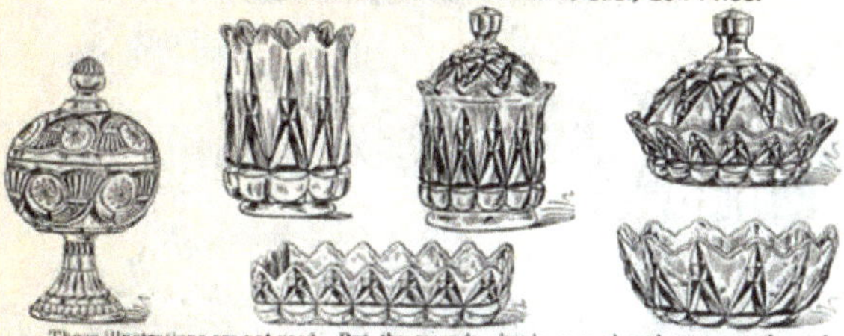

These illustrations are not good. But the ware is simply as good as glassware can be made. All the pieces are of one pattern.

The "Radiant" Assortment Comprises 1 Doz. Each of the Following:
High-Footed Covered Bowls—For sweetmeats, preserves, etc. Measures 5 inches in diameter.
Round Scalloped Dishes—7¼-inch, very deep, very beautiful, very useful.
High Celery Dishes—Stands 6 inches high, of artistic pattern and proportions.
Flanged Butter Dishes and Covers—A 7-inch flanged butter that any lady would buy.
High Sugars and Covers—A very handsome sugar bowl that will sell when first shown.
Oblong Heavy Dishes—8 inches in length. Useful for forty purposes.
(Making a total of 6 doz. to bbl. Sold only by bbl. Bbl. 35c.)   **Price, 81c Doz.**

Our "ALARM" 10-Cent Assortment.
EVERY ONE of These Pieces Would be CHEAP AT A QUARTER.

The biggest of the big—the brightest of the bright—the finest of the fine. This assortment is actually worth 25 per cent more at the factory than we are charging for it in New York and Chicago. Will you send for one package?

The "Alarm" Assortment Comprises 1 Doz. Each of the Following:
Full Half-Gallon Pitchers—Elegant pattern.
9-Inch Salvers—Plain, rich and useful.
9¼-Inch Bread Plates—Useful at every meal.
6¼-Inch High Footed Bowls—A splendid table dish for sauces, etc.
8¼-Inch Deep Round Dishes—Heavy, with a scalloped edge.
9-Inch Oblong Dishes—Fully 6 inches wide, very serviceable.
(Total of 6 doz. to pkg. Sold only by pkg. Barrel 35c.)   **Price, 83c Doz.**

Our "EXHIBITION" 10-Cent Assortment.
An Exhibition That Will Prove Most Attractive to Bargain Seekers.

There is not a piece in this lot but is fire polished and superbly finished. If a customer will order a sample package we can promise that 'twill not be the only one.

The "Exhibition" Assortment Comprises 1 Doz. Each of the Following:
Large Quart Water or Milk Pitchers—Brilliant and of full size.
6½-Inch High Footed Bowls—A beautiful, square-shaped, scalloped utility dish.
7½-Inch Footed Dishes—A footed round dish with scalloped edge.
Large Flanged Butters and Covers—A deep and splendid dish of large capacity.
7½-Inch Round Dishes—A dish that the people are buying every minute.
9-Inch Deep Plates—A rich, serviceable plate for bread, cake or fruit.
(Total of 6 doz. to pkg. Sold only by pkg. Barrel 35c.)   **Price, 83c Doz.**

Our "X RAYS" Assortment.
Of 10-Cent Custom Getters.

This assortment is one of the very best lots of glass ever offered by us and we predict for it a royal welcome among the bargain seekers during the fall and winter of '96.

The "X-Rays" Assortment Comprises 1 Doz. Each of the Following:
8-Inch Round Dishes—Large, deep and beautiful.
7-Inch Footed Dishes—Usually sold from 15 to 25 cents.
Stuck Handled Milk Pitchers—A large and elegant table necessity.
7¼-Inch Flared Butter Dishes and Covers—An every day necessity.
5-Inch High Footed Bowls with Covers—For sauces or preserves.
8x10-Inch Oval Bread Plates—An attractive, self-selling item.
(Total of 6 doz. to pkg. Sold only by pkg. Bbl. 35c)   **Price, 80c Doz.**

Our "MAMMOTH" 10-Cent Cask Assortment.
Note the Absence of Small Pieces Among These Bouncing Bargains.
(16 of these pieces are actually 25-cent goods.)

Important. The crockery and glass jobbers and glass manufacturers have always been famous for their "old fogyism." But within the last year they have aroused themselves to the fact that Butler Brothers' *original* method of selling glassware (by package only) has pretty nearly taken all their business away from them. Now, therefore, instead of working out some new plan, they have gone heels over head into the "assortment" (?) business—and, of course, *without* putting up goods that *will sell off evenly.* In order to show our customers that we can furnish "cask" assortments as well as barrel lots, we here offer one *by way of comparison* with our would-be competitors. We leave the verdict to the intelligent minds of our customers.

The "Mammoth" Assortment Includes 1-2 Doz. Each of the Following:
Half Gallon Pitchers—The famous "Trilby" jug.
9¾-Inch Deep Footed Bread Plates—9½ inches long and 4½ inches deep.
10½-Inch Round Bread Plates—A brilliant pattern, very attractive.
High Tankard Milk Pitchers—Stands 7½ inches high.
10½-Inch Celery Dishes—Is 5 inches wide, with bent sides. Very brilliant.
Extra Heavy Double Foot Banded Goblets—One of the unbreakables, engraved band.
Flower Vases—8 inches high. Beautiful cut glass pattern.
Round Dishes and Covers—For sugar, honey, etc.
Molasses Pitchers—With metallic snap top.
8½-Inch Round Dishes—An elaborate pattern and a useful dish.
Handled Vinegar Bottles with Stoppers—For vinegar, oil, etc.
High Footed Bowls—5½ inches in diameter. Cut pattern.
Footed Sugars and Covers—One of the best of these staple utensils.
6-Inch Flaring (High Footed) Bowls—Rich and elegant design.
9½-Inch Cake Salvers—This footed cake salver is large and of diamond pattern.
2-Bottle Casters—Has glass stand with handle, containing salt and pepper bottles.
7½-Inch Flaring Round Dishes—Large, rich, beautiful and useful.
Flanged Butters and Covers—Large size, elegant pattern.
7½-Inch Deep Scalloped Dishes—Everybody wants one.
6½-Inch High Footed Bowls and Covers—This large dish needs no encouragement to make it go.
(Total of 10 doz. to the cask. Sold only by the cask. Cask 90c.)   **Price (for Glass), 76c Doz.**

Our "DIME SYRUP PITCHER" Assortment.
Look First at These Patterns, Then at the Price. Every One is Worth a "Quarter."

Fitted with the patent "tight-top" collars. *No cement, no plaster.* The tops are of a very superior grade. Send for one assortment and you will thank us for advising it. Assortment consists of 1 dozen each of 5 patterns as shown by the illustrations.
(Total of 5 doz. to pkg. Sold only by pkg. Barrel 35c.)   **Price, 89c Doz.**

Our "10-CENT BUTTER DISH" Assortment.

An attractive assortment of handsome and quick-selling Butter Dishes. The ware is of the highest grade, the pieces good size and the patterns genuinely beautiful. Send for a barrel, and your sales will surprise you. The assortment consists of 1 doz. each of 4 styles, making a *total of 4 dozen to pkg.* Sold only by pkg. (Barrel 35c.)   **Price, 79c Doz.**

STORE SHELF JARS (Crystal Glass).

Just what every storekeeper wants and so cheap he can't afford to be without them.

"Squat" Pattern Jars—The low round shape. 7½ inches high. 6½ inches wide. ½ gallon. Japanned tops.
(Packed 1 1-4 doz. in bbl. Sold only by pkg. Barrel 35c.)
Price, 95c Doz.

Square Corner Jars—½ gallon size, with heavy ground glass stoppers, wide opening. 11 inches high including cover. Very handsome.
(Packed 1 doz. in bbl. Sold only by pkg. Barrel 35c.)
Price, $2.75 Doz.

These Attractive and Useful Home Needs in Glass Will Sell When All Other Business is Stagnant.

Study Our Assortments—Note the UNIFORM VALUE and the ABSENCE OF SMALL PIECES.

Our "WAR CRY" 25-Cent Assortment.
Just Note the Sizes of These Mammoth Pieces.

Truly the best 25c assortment yet put together. Of course these pieces are all of highly finished ware and are of sizes usually found in the half-dollar assortments. Study these descriptions.

The "War Cry" Assortment Comprises 1-2 Doz. Each of the Following:
Tankard Water Pitchers—Large, beautiful, and at a marvelously cheap price.
7-Inch High Footed Bowls and Covers—Standing 11¼ inches high.
8½-Inch Deep Dishes and Pitchers—Extra large, extra deep, extra beautiful.
9-Inch High Footed Bowls—A splendid fruit dish for center table.

(Total of 2 doz. to pkg. Sold only by pkg. Barrel 35c.) **Price, $1.80 Doz.**

Our "PERFECTION" 25-Cent Assortment.
Superb Specimens of High-Grade Glass-Making.

All of one pattern. There is satisfaction to ourselves as well as to you and your customers in showing these splendid articles of everyday utility.

The "Perfection" Assortment Comprises 1-2 Doz. Each of the Following:
10-Inch Deep Cake or Fruit Plates—Useful three times a day for bread, cake, fruit, etc.
7½-Inch High Footed Fancy Bowls—Beautiful square pattern with scalloped edge.
6-Inch High Footed Deep Bowls and Covers—Rich and elegant table dish.
9¼-Inch Deep Round Dishes—With scalloped edge—a rich offering for 25 cents.

(Total of 2 doz. in pkg. Sold only by pkg. Barrel 35c.) **Price, $1.78 per Doz.**

Our "GREAT" 25-Cent Assortment.
Not Only Great in Value and Size, but Great in Richness and Splendor.

These pieces are all fully finished, and in richness are unsurpassed by anything made of glass.

The "Great" Assortment Comprises 1-2 Doz. Each of the Following:
7-Inch High Footed Bowls and Covers—Extra high cover—extra deep bowl.
9½-Inch High Footed Salvers—A rich cake salver.
9-Inch High Footed Flaring Deep Bowls—A useful article and a sharp seller.
Half Gallon Water Pitchers—Extra heavy, and of "taking" design.

(Total of 2 doz. to barrel. Sold only by barrel.) **Price, $1.85 Doz.**

Our "PRIZE WINNER" 25-Cent Assortment.
Each of These Four Bargains "Will Prove Useful Three Times a Day and Ornamental All the Time."

Adjectives prove entirely inadequate in describing the richness and splendor of truly high-class crystal ware. Therefore we here refrain—but with the suggestion that you send for a sample package. (All of one pattern.)

The "Prize Winner" Assortment Comprises 1-2 Doz. Each of the Following:
Square Deep Scalloped Dishes—Averaging 9¼ inches in diameter.
High Tankard Water Pitchers—Regularly sold at a half dollar.
7-Inch Deep Dishes with High Covers—Of the same exquisite pattern as the other pieces.
8¼-Inch High Footed Dishes—Extra deep, of scalloped pattern, as above.

(Total of 2 doz. in pkg. Sold only by pkg. Bbl. 35c.) **Price, $1.79 Doz.**

"SPARKLING GLASSWARE" Won't sparkle its way into your customers' favor one-fifth as fast when dust-coated as when bright and clean. You can't afford *not* to wash your glass stock often.

Our "CROWN JEWEL" 50-Cent Assortment.
Heroic Products of the Glassmakers' Art.

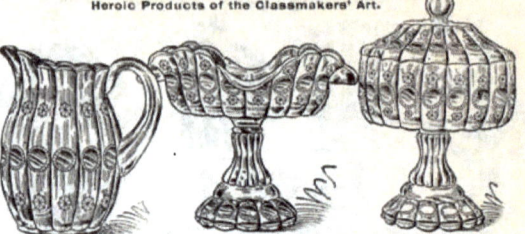

These three splendid articles will not only prove magnetic attractions, but will exert such a hypnotic influence over the art-loving public as to prove themselves sellers as well.

The "Crown Jewel" Assortment Comprises 1-3 Doz. Each of the Following:
8-Inch High Footed Covered Bowls—High art article of every-day use.
Large 2-Quart Pitchers—Very heavy, very large, very beautiful.
10-Inch Square Flared Dishes—Measures 11¼ inches at corners. For fruit, etc., etc.

(Total of 1 doz. to barrel. Sold only by barrel. Barrel 35c.) **Price, $3.35 Doz.**

PATENT TOP SYRUP PITCHER ASSORTMENT.

With plated brittania top with patent hinge. Has an inside glass lip. No dripping possible.

The Assortment Comprises:
1 doz. fluted pattern.... } Making a total of 2 doz. in package.
1 " plain ....

Sold only by pkg. (Box. 25c.) **Price, $1.50 Doz.**

"STANDARD" JELLY TUMBLERS.
Best quality—not the small sizes sold by many.

"Jelly Tumbler Assortment"—Packed in equal selling quantities of the two popular sizes and of two popular patterns. These jelly tumblers are of the best standard quality, large sizes, and are packed safely in a barrel, assorted as follows: 12 doz. of the medium or regular size in equal quantities of plain and fluted, and 6 doz. of the large size of these two popular shapes, making a total of 18 doz. to pkg.—12 doz. at 17c, $2.04, and 6 doz. at 19c, $1.14, or a total of $3.18. Sold only by pkg. (Barrel 35c.)....**Total for 18 Doz. $3.18.**

"Medium Size" Jelly Tumblers—Some of our customers in "sorting up" require only one size, and we have accordingly put up some packages of solids.... 24 doz. to pkg., half plain and half fluted. Sold only by pkg. Barrel 35c........... **Price, 17c Doz.**

"Large Size" Jelly Tumblers—Same as largest size shown in our "jelly tumbler" assortment, and packed 18 doz. to pkg., in equal quantities of plain and fluted. Sold only by pkg. Barrel 35c. **Price, 19c Doz.**

New Pattern Glass "TABLE OUTFIT."
Our 1896 Pattern—A Complete Dining Room Service—85 Pieces for $3.38.

We first introduced the idea of selling a dining-room outfit of glass some six years ago, and from the very start our merchant friends proved their ability to sell package lots to their customers. We have an entirely new pattern for 1896—every piece fire polished and full finished. The assortment comprises 85 pieces (not counting spoons) including large and small pieces—such as bowls, dishes, salver, butter, sugar, spoon holder, pitchers, tumblers, goblets, etc., etc., etc. Try one and buy many. All safely packed in a barrel. Sold by package only. (Barrel 35c.)

Price for the Assortment, $3.38.

Our "GAS SHADE" Assortment.

Those customers who live in gas-lighted cities and have never sold gas shades will at once appreciate this opportunity to furnish household necessities (usually retailed at "war prices") at a reasonable popular price.

The assortment comprises ⅓ doz. each of 6 styles, viz.: Crystal rib, cone shape, scalloped top; etched cone shape, plain top; etched bowl shape, plain top; etched cone shape, scalloped top; No. 2 etched cone shape, plain top; tulip shape, scalloped top.

(Total of 4 doz. to bbl. Sold only by bbl. Barrel 35c.) **Price, $1.50 Doz.**

OUR PRICES BACK UP EVERY CLAIM WE MAKE.

Why is it we can sell you glassware cheaper than the factories themselves can afford to do it? Simply because our expense for selling (by *catalogue only*) is next to nothing, whereas a factory which seeks to enter the retail trade direct must employ high-priced salesmen whose salaries and expenses eat up profits as a prairie fire eats up dry grass.

Whenever any competing jobbing concern has acquired an equally great output with which to sledge-hammer down prices in buying goods, and has found an equally efficient and inexpensive way of disposing of their product, then—and not till then—shall we feel that we have any real competition in the glassware business.

You Can Readily Sell Any of This Glassware at DOUBLE the Price Suggested.

WE HAVE NO COMPETITION Worthy the Name in This Department of Glassware.

PACKAGE LOTS OF TUMBLERS.

Our "SPECIAL" Tumbler Assortment.
"Three staples in glassware."

This assortment is made up of the regular size (large third pint) plain tumbler in three different bottoms as follows: "Star," "Plain" and "Horse Shoe." 8 doz. each of 3 styles, making a total of 24 doz. to bbl. Sold only by bbl. (Bbl. 35c.)
Price, 16c Doz.

Our 1896 "NICKEL Assortment."
A new lot of "high grades" at a low price.

Six splendid patterns of the very best of crystal glass, standard size, table tumblers, all sure sellers.
3 doz. each of 6 styles, making a total of 18 doz. to bbl. Sold only by bbl. (Bbl. 35c.)
Showing only four of the patterns to save space. The other two are fully as good. Illustrations should be larger.
Price, 18c Doz.

Our "RIBBED BAND" Tumbler Assortment.
Quick-selling every-day necessities.

The illustrations show four tumblers, which although offered at a low price are yet good enough for use anywhere. Full size, good quality, 4 doz. each of 4 different styles of bands.
(Total 16 doz. to bbl. Sold only by pkg. Barrel 35c.)
Price, 20c Doz.

LARGE "CRYSTAL" Tumbler Assortment.
As staple as sugar—as good as can be made.

Four attractive patterns of large size table tumblers that will be appreciated for quality and finish. One of these patterns has an engraved band.
3 doz. each of 4 patterns, making a total of 12 doz. Sold only by bbl. (Barrel 35c.)
Price, 28c Doz.

"LEADER ENGRAVED" 5-Cent Assortment.

All hand engraved work—a bargain!
Four patterns of excellent engraving on four different popular shape tumblers. You will sell them by the dozen.
4 doz. each of 4 styles, making a total of 16 doz. to bbl. Sold only by bbl. (Bbl. 35c.)
Price, 32c Doz.

Our "BARGAIN" ENGRAVED
5-Cent Tumbler Assortment.

An opportunity to sell a splendid clear, sparkling tumbler, with a genuine hand engraving, for 5 cents each. Here is an assortment of them. They need no commendation.
4 doz. each of 4 different patterns of decoration.
(Total of 16 doz. to bbl. Sold only by pkg. Bbl. 35c.)
Price, 34c Doz.

Our "SPARKLING" Tumbler Assortment.
Full Finished—Ground Bottom—Fire Polished—Crystal Beauties for 5 Cents.

Here is a bunch of tumblers never before shown outside of the 10-cent assortments. They need no description.
3 doz. each of four different patterns. Total of 12 doz. to pkg. (Barrel 35c.)
Price, 36c Doz.

Our "PLAIN AND BANDED" Assortment.
Of Lead Glass BLOWN TUMBLERS "Firsts."

Positively the best goods made in America to-day. Assortment comprises:
12 doz. Full Size, Plain Blown "Lead Glass" Tumblers @ 29c $3 48
8 doz. " Engraved Band " Tumblers @ 36c 2 88
Total of $6.36 for pkg. Sold only by pkg. (Bbl. 35c.) **Total, $6.36.**

"ENGRAVED" BLOWN GLASS Tumbler ASSORTMENT.

If you want something with which to startle the community and keep up the excitement for more than a single day, buy some of these and sell them cheap. Genuine lead glass (10 oz.) elegantly engraved. You will sell them by the dozen. Put up 3 doz. each of 6 different engravings in bbl.
(Total 18 doz. in bbl. Sold only by pkg. Bbl. 35c.) **Price, 42c Doz.**

"NEEDLE ETCHED BAND" Blown Tumbler.
New York city stores get 25 cents for these.

Best of 9-ounce genuine lead blown glass, modest pattern of beautiful needle etching. A high grade lead blown tumbler like this will be appreciated by your patrons at a dime.
Put up 12 doz. in bbl. Sold only by bbl. (Bbl. 35c.) **Price, 80c Doz.**

Our "BARGAIN" Berry Set.
A Rich 25-Cent Possibility.

A rich and attractive pattern of pure glass to sell at a remarkably winsome figure. Each set comprises 1 8-inch round deep berry dish, and 6 4-inch nappies to match.
(Packed 24 sets in bbl. Sold only by bbl. Bbl. 35c.)
Price, 13c Set.

Our "JEWEL" Sauce or Berry Set.
A Rich and Rare 25-Cent Offering.

This new set comprises one 8-inch berry dish of most brilliant pattern and six 4½-inch sauce dishes to match. Pattern, ware and size make it one of the best values we ever offered in 25c glass.
Put up 24 sets in bbl. Sold only by bbl. (Barrel 35c.) **Price, 14c Set.**

Footed "ROSETTE" Table Set.
A Splendid Set to Run at a "Quarter."

Another 25-cent leader to offer the trade, and one that will be appreciated. Quality, size and pattern are high standard.
Put up 24 sets in barrel. Sold only by barrel. (Barrel 35c.)
Price, 13c per Set.

Our "FINE FLUTED" Table Set.
A New 25-Center and a Good One.

This is the latest conquest in "quarter" possibilities. A bright and attractive full size set.
Put up 24 sets in barrel. Sold only by barrel. (Bbl. 35c.) **Price, 14c Set.**

Our "BON TON" Table Set.

This is an exact reproduction of genuine cut glass, and can hardly be distinguished from the same. Full size pieces—fire polished—full finished.
Put up 12 sets in barrel. Sold only by barrel. (Barrel 35c.) **Price, 24c Set.**

"BRIGHT AND HEAVY" Table Set.
A Mammoth Set of Richest Crystal. A Bargain if Sold at 50c.

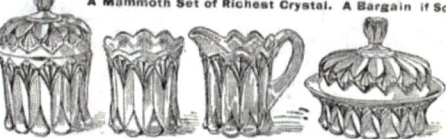

Large — brilliant—beautiful—heavy — and most important of all, salable. If this set does not prove a seller then 'twill be because our friends don't order the first barrel.
Put up 12 sets in barrel. Sold only by barrel. (Barrel 35c.) **Price, 25c Set.**

Our "HIGH FOOTED" Table Set.

A new and good one as a "50-center."
This is a fully finished set of unusual brilliancy and of magnificent properties.
1 doz. sets in barrel. (Sold only by barrel. Bbl. 35c.)
Price, 28c Set.

Our "CROWN JEWEL" Table Set.
Positively the Richest of All Rich Sets.

There are some articles which, when we endeavor to portray them either by word or picture seem to mock us with their indescribable beauty and brilliancy. This set is one of those items. Send for a package and you will understand us.
12 sets in a bbl. Sold only by bbl. (Barrel 35c.) **Price, 33c Set.**

QUICK-SELLING GOBLETS.
(In Barrel Lots.)

Each Style Packed in Barrel by Itself. Barrels 35c.

	Doz.
"Fine Flute" Goblet—Full size. Bright and shapely. 10 doz. in bbl. Sold only by bbl.	$0 26
"Plain" Goblet—A standard favorite. Rich and tasteful. 10 doz. in bbl. Sold only by bbl.	28
"Optic Flute" Goblet—One of the prime favorites, and deservedly so. 10 doz. in bbl. Sold only by bbl.	29
"Huber" Goblet—As bright as a new silver dollar, as salable as a gold one. 10 doz. in bbl. Sold only by bbl.	29
"Cut Pattern" Goblet—Attractive, brilliant and shapely. One of the best of the good sellers. 10 doz. in bbl. Sold only by bbl.	30
"Leader Hotel" Goblet—A clear, extra heavy, full size, hotel goblet. 8 doz. in bbl. Sold only by bbl.	36
"Cup Foot" Hotel Goblet—Seamless. Extra heavy. Full size, full finished, and a beauty 8 doz. in bbl. A business making bargain at 5 cents.	40
"Double Thick" Hotel Goblet—Seamless. Double thick throughout, even to the foot. One of the can't-break-'em sort. 7 doz. in bbl. Sold only by bbl.	48

IT IS NOT POSSIBLE to Make a Better Grade of Glassware Than That Offered Here.

Our Glassware Assortments Contain no Small Pieces Put in to "HELP OUT THE AVERAGE."

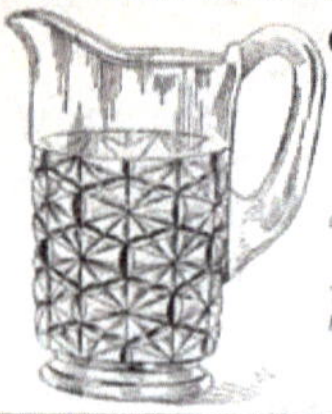

Our "DAZZLING" HALF-GALLON PITCHER.

Bright, large and attractive.

(Packed 2 doz. in bbl. Sold only by bbl. Bbl. 35c.)

Price, 95c Doz.

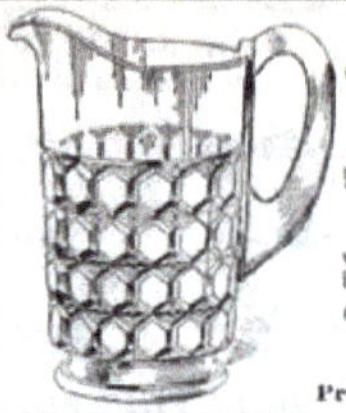

Our "BLOCK DIAMOND"

½ Gallon Pitcher.

Exceptional value. First quality.

(2 doz. in barrel. Sold only by bbl. Bbl. 35c.)

Price, $1.00 Doz.

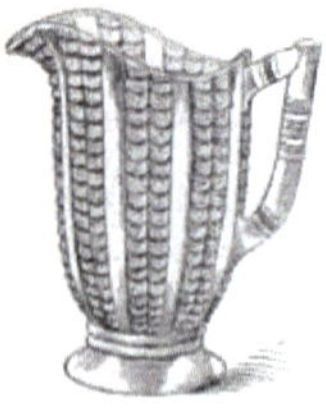

Our "JUMBO" PITCHER.

Half-Gallon.

Handsome pattern. Handy shape. Large size.

(2 doz. in barrel. Sold only by bbl. Bbl. 35c.)

Price, $1.15 Doz.

See pages 88 to 91 for Glass Specialties in "open stock."

"ENTERPRISE" WATER SET.

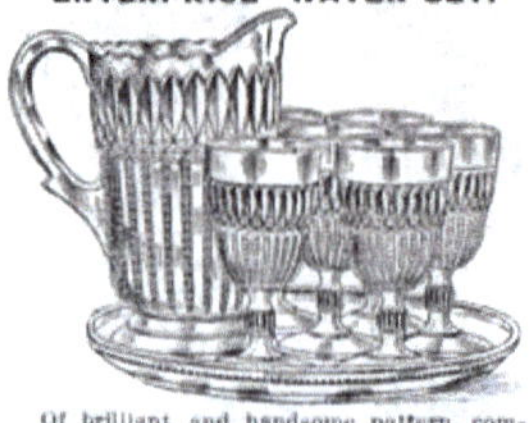

Of brilliant and handsome pattern, comprising 1 large ½-gallon pitcher, 1 11½-inch glass tray and 6 full size goblets to match.

(12 sets in bbl. Sold by bbl. only. Bbl. 35c).

Price, 33c Set.

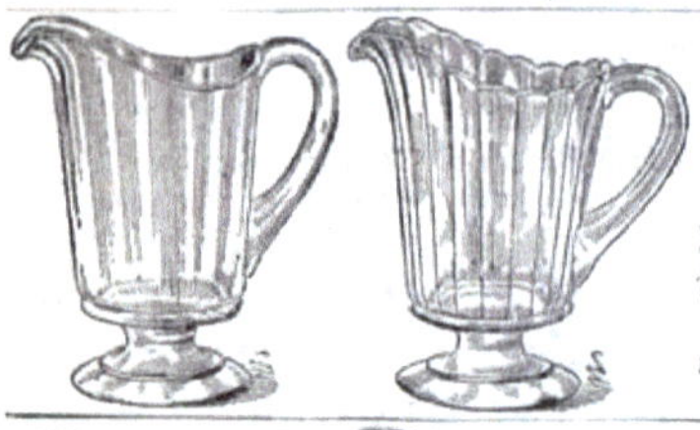

"PLAIN AND FLUTED" Pitcher Assortment.

Two ready-selling, full size, brilliant bargains.

Here is a little 2 dozen assortment of ½ gallon pitchers. *If you buy one barrel of them you will wire back for more!* 1 doz. each of two patterns.

Total 2 doz. in bbl. Sold only by pkg. (Barrel 35c.)

Price, $1.30 Doz.

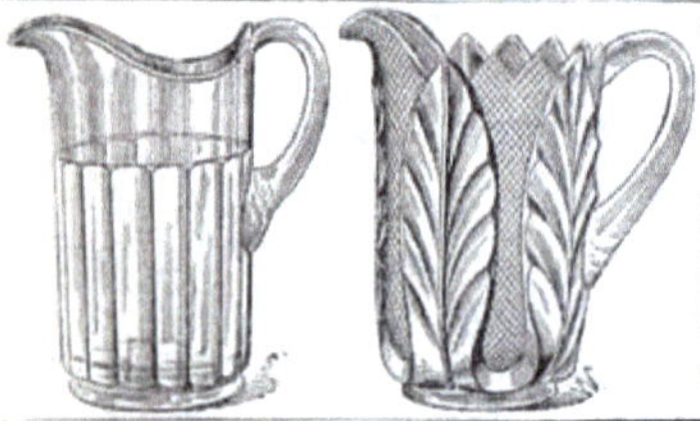

Our "HIGH CLASS" 25c Pitcher Assortment.

Two useful "every day" articles at "once-a-week" prices.

Some trade demand a superior grade of goods, and to all such we recommend these two magnificent specimens of the glass workers' art brought down to prices within the reach of the masses (one optic pattern, one "wide mouth" shape). 1 doz. each large ½-gallon pichers.

(Total of 2 doz. to pkg. Sold only by pkg. Barrel 35c.)

Price, $1.75 Doz.

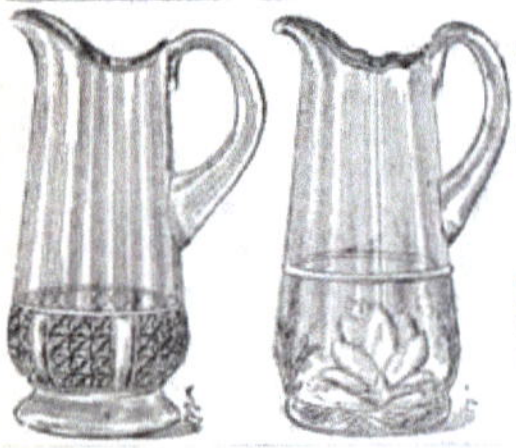

Our "TANKARD" Pitcher Assortment.

Full Tankards to Offer as "Leaders" at Common Jug Prices.

Will readily bring 50c if you wish.

Two patterns of finest finish and of aristocratic shape. Put up in a ready selling assortment, comprising 1 doz. each of 2 patterns, large ½-gallon size.

(Total of 2 doz. to pkg. Sold only by pkg. Barrel 35c.)

Price, $2.10 Doz.

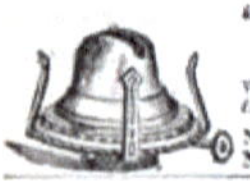

"QUEEN ANNE" BRASS LAMP BURNERS.

Positively the best burners in America. Best polished brass with all improvements. Standard weight and strength. *Do not confuse these with the light weight burners.* 1 doz. in box.

	Doz.		Doz.
No. 0—	$0 37	No. 2 or "B"—	$0 60
No. 1 or "A"—	40		

"UTILITY" Assortment of Lamp Globes.

Would Be Bargains at 15 per Cent More.

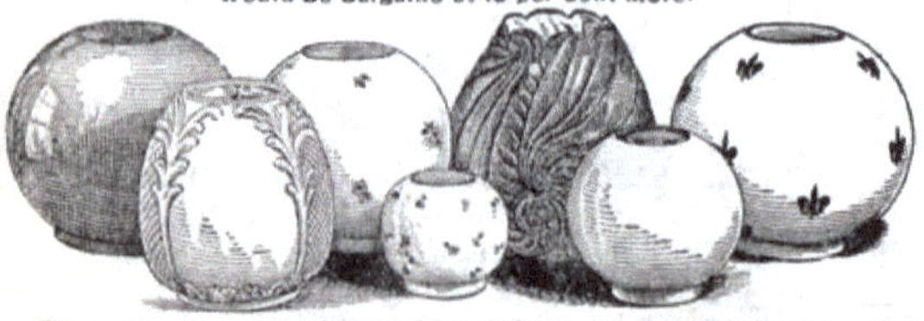

This assortment comprises only those globes which seem to appropriately fit most any lamp. Made up in the beautiful solid color tints and the staple floral Dresden and gilt Fleur-de-lis decoration. Put up in the best selling sizes.

		Doz.	Total.
1-6 doz.	**4-inch Globes**—In Dresden and rich canary, to fit Princess lamps	$ 3 25	$0 54
1-12 "	**6-inch Globes**—In ruby rose	6 00	50
⅓ "	**8-inch Globes**—Canary, ruby rose, gilt Fleur-de-lis and floral Dresden	9 00	3 00
1-6 "	**9-inch Globes**—In ruby rose and gilt Fleur-de-lis	12 00	2 00
1-12 "	**Semi-Globes**—Standing 7½ inches high, in ruby rose	8 00	67
1-12 "	**Rich Canary Globes**—Standing 8½ inches high	9 50	79

Total for Assortment, $7.50.

N. B.—All the above globes, with the exception of first three, are made to fit 4-inch rings, the three smaller ones to fit 3-inch rings.

Shipped from our house. Total of 11 Globes to barrel. Sold only by barrel. (Barrel 35c.)

LAMPS AND LAMP GOODS.

All Goods on This and Opposite Pages are Shipped from Our Houses.

Our "HAND" Lamp Assortment.

Two Excellent 10-Cent Hand Lamps at a Possible "5c Give-away Price."

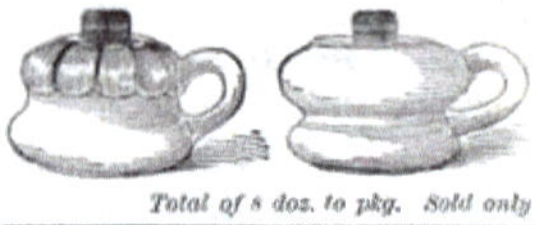

This assortment contains two of the very best selling and handsomest shaped patterns of the very useful hand lamps. The assortment is as follows:

4 Doz. **Optic Pattern Hand Lamps**—With large size handles.
4 Doz. **Plain Pattern Hand Lamps**—With large size handles.

All above with collars to fit No. 1 burner.

Total of 8 doz. to pkg. Sold only by pkg. (Barrel 35c.) **Price, 45c Doz.**

Our "WONDER" Patent Collar Lamp Assortment.

While Possible 10-Cent Leaders "Would Be Cheap at Double the Price."

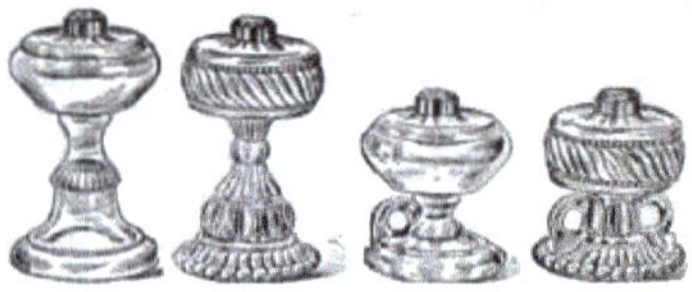

These are not only of superior quality and of extra large size but have the patent shrunk-on collar which cannot be taken off without breaking the lamp—no plaster, no cement, no oil can get through the collar, absolutely non-explosive. The top of each lamp is so shaped as to serve as an oil drip. If any customer will order a barrel of these lamps on our 'say so' and is not entirely satisfied with them we will gladly take them back at our expense. The assortment comprises the following:

1½ doz. **Plain Stand Lamps**—With wide base 8½ inches high.
1½ doz. **Brilliant Stand Lamps**—Beautiful pattern, with wide base, 8½ inches high.
1½ doz. **Plain Footed Hand Lamps**—With wide base and large handle.
1½ doz. **Fancy Pattern Hand Lamps**—With two handles and wide bottom.

Total of 6 doz. to pkg. Sold only by pkg. (Barrel 35c.) **Price, 85c Doz.**

Our "HONEST VALUE" 25-Cent Lamp Assortment.

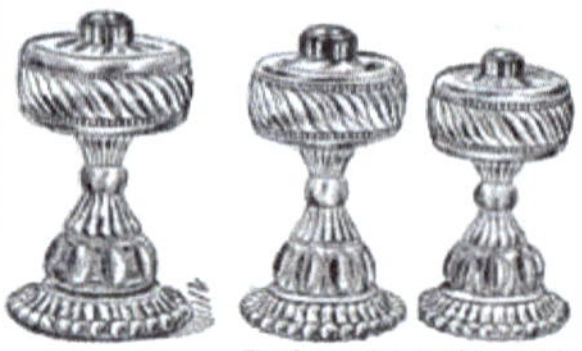

Fitted with the same patent shrunk-on collar as above assortment. This new and beautiful "crown" pattern is positively the handsomest thing that has been produced in crystal glass. The assortment comprises the 3 largest sizes in same pattern and will give any merchant the choicest bunch of popular priced lamps we have ever offered. All with No. 2 collars. The assortment consists of:

1 doz.	**9-Inch Crown Pattern Stand Lamps**	$1 20	$1 20
1 doz.	**9½-Inch Crown Pattern Stand Lamps**	1 68	1 68
½ doz.	**10-Inch Crown Pattern Stand Lamps**	1 90	95

Total 2 1-2 doz. to pkg. Sold only by pkg. (Barrel 35c.) **Total, $3.83**

Our "TABLE LAMP" Assortment.

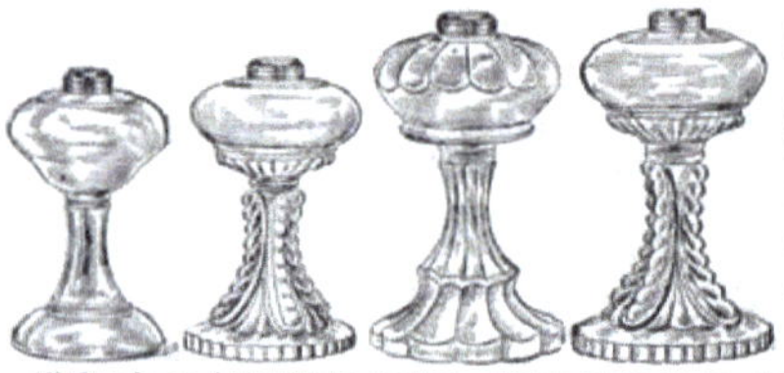

Popular patterns at popular prices and of quality unsurpassed.

The assortment comprises ½ doz. each of the following:

High standing, plain pattern, $1.30	$0 65
High standing, feather pattern, $1.30	65
Large and high, umbrella pattern, $1.78	89
Large and high, fancy pattern, $1.78	89

Total, $3.08

All above lamps fitted with No. 2 collars. (Total of 2 doz. to pkg. Sold only by pkg. Barrel 35c.)

Our "ALL LEADERS" 10-Cent Lamp Assortment.

Staple as Nails and Sugar and Cheaper Than Either.

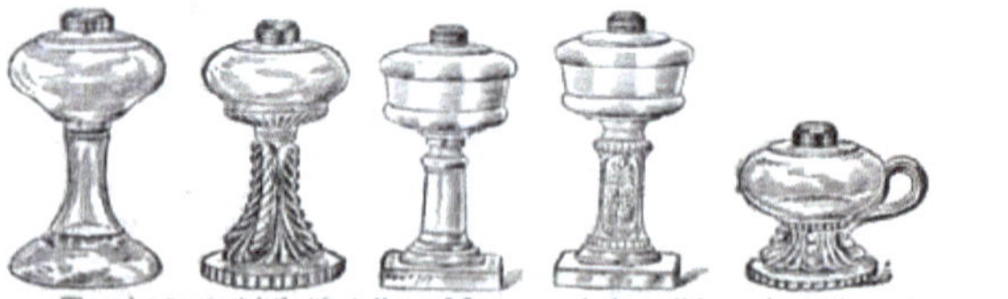

These lamps are strictly "firsts," are of finest crystal glass, all large sizes and are 10 per cent below regular jobbers' rates. The assortment comprises 1 doz. each of the following:

High Plain Pattern Lamp.
High Feather Pattern Lamp.
High Plain Pattern Lamp—Square Base.
High Fancy Pattern Lamp—Square Base.
Footed and Handled Stand Lamp, fancy pattern.

All above with No. 1 collars. (Total of 5 doz. to pkg. Sold only by pkg. Barrel 35c.)

Price, 72c Doz.

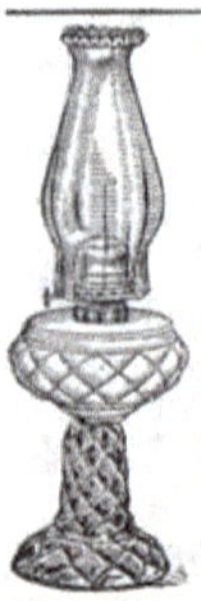

Our "LIVING ROOM" Lamp.

In Rich Ruby.

A complete lamp from chimney to base—A seller.

One of the cheapest and handsomest lamps ever offered. Stands 19 inches high, pineapple pattern body in double finish, assorted ruby and deep canary. Has brilliant crystal column and footing all complete with lead glass chimney and best brass burner.

1½ doz. in pkg. Sold only by pkg. (Barrel 35c.)

Price, $4.35 Doz.

Our "SEWING" Lamp Asst.

All Wide Base Low Stand Lamps.

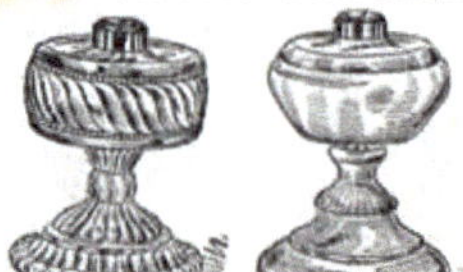

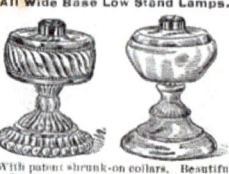

With patent shrunk-on collars. Beautiful design of purest crystal glass, of large oil capacity and arranged for large burner, wide base and low enough to make them absolutely safe from the danger of tipping. The assortment consists of 1 doz. beautiful plain pattern and 1 doz. fancy "Crown Jewel" pattern.

Total 2 doz. to pkg. Sold only by pkg. (Bbl. 35c.)

Price, $2.25 Doz.

TEN DOLLARS' WORTH of Attractive Glassware Will Help to Sell Fifty Dollars' Worth of Other Goods.

Glassware Barrels and Boxes Are the ONLY Kind of Packages for Which We Make Any Charge.

LAMP CHIMNEYS AND LANTERN GLOBES.

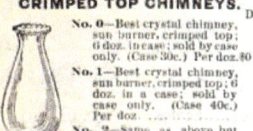

The Genuine "VESUVIUS" BRAND
of Fire-Proof Lead Chimneys.

Have won the highest award against all other chimneys in the most severe fire-test competitions. If anyone wants the best chimney they will have the "Vesuvius." None genuine without the word "Vesuvius" neatly etched on each chimney. Sold only by case.

	Doz
No. 1—"Vesuvius," crimped top, 6 doz. in case. (Case 40c.)	$0 39
No. 2—"Vesuvius," crimped top, 6 doz. in case. (Case 50c.)	53
No. 1—"Vesuvius," plain top, 6 doz. in case. (Case 40c.)	39
No. 2—"Vesuvius," plain top, 6 doz. in case. (Case 50c.)	53

CRIMPED TOP CHIMNEYS.

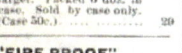

	Doz.
No. 0—Best crystal chimney, sun burner, crimped top; 6 doz. in case; sold by case only. (Case 50c.) Per doz	$0 18
No. 1—Best crystal chimney, sun burner, crimped top; 6 doz. in a case; sold by case only. (Case 40c.) Per doz	19
No. 2—Same as above, but larger. Packed 6 doz. in case. Sold by case only. (Case 50c.)	29

"FIRE PROOF" LEAD CHIMNEYS.

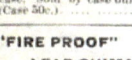

High-grade almost unbreakable chimneys, offered at our usual low prices.

	Doz.
No. 1—6 doz. in case. Sold only by case. (Case 40c.)	$0 36
No. 2—6 dozen in case. Sold only by case. (Case 50c.)	48

"Tubular" LANTERN GLOBES.

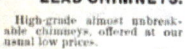

Best goods. Ground top and bottom. Fitting any of the tubular lanterns.

Put up 5 doz. in bbl. Sold only by pkg. (Barrel 35c.)
Price, 30c Doz.

"Electric" LANTERN GLOBES.

For our famous "Electric" lantern. Packed 6 or 7 doz. in bbl. Sold only by pkg. (Barrel 35c.)
Price, 44c Doz.

"ELECTRIC" CHIMNEYS.

A very necessary chimney for use on the Climax and other burners where globes are used. These are "lead" glass.

	Doz.
No. 2—(Lead.) 6 doz. in box. Sold only by box. (Box 40c.)	$0 58

"ROCHESTER" LEAD CHIMNEYS.

This chimney has become a standard. Here we have it in best "lead" glass.

	Doz.
No. 2—(Lead.) 6 doz. in bbl. Sold only by bbl. (Barrel 25c.)	$0 58
No. 3—(Lead.) 6 doz. in bbl. Sold only by bbl. (Barrel 35c.)	1 20

New 10c Assortment Engraved Globe Chimneys.

If you have never sold these try a barrel and you will sell many.

Assortment consists of 1 doz. each of 3 designs of engraved and banded chimneys, all large No. 2 size and swelled center globe shape. Regularly sold at 20 cents. 3 doz. in pkg., sold only by pkg. (Bbl. 35c.)
Price, 79c Doz.

FLETCHER'S LAMP WICKS.

	Gross
No. E—Fletcher's, the best made. 8-inch, cut ready for use	$0 18
No. 1 or A—8-inch, as above	26
No. 2 or B—8-inch, as above	37
No. D—8-inch as above, for large lamps	58
No. E, Full Length—32 yards to roll, equal to 1 gross	18
No. 1 or A, Full Length—As above	26
No. 2 or B, Full Length—As above	37

BRASS TABLE LAMPS.

Richest offerings at prices within the reach of the masses. Sold in quantities as wanted, regular charge for packages. N. B.—These are shipped from our houses in *New York* and *Chicago*.

No. B, 80c Each.   No. F, $2.95 Each.   No. G, $3.95 Each.   Each

No. B, Cupid Standard Brass Lamps—Standing 18 inches high, with embossed head and openwork base. The cupid is in silver, balance of the lamp in gilt. Burner has patent rod-lifting wick action. This is not one of the breakable cupids.................... $0 80

No. F, Gold Inlaid Column Lamp—With real inlaid cloissonne column, gold on royal blue ground work. The head is on heavy openwork cast pattern, containing movable fount, base also openwork and very large. Pittsburg burner with screw movement. Stands 20 inches high, base and head is a beauty... 2 95

No. G, Richest Onyx Brass Lamp—4-inch Mexican onyx column with onyx ball between column and base, heaviest openwork head with movable font, large openwork base, all gilt except onyx. Pittsburg burner with screw lift. Handsomest lamp in America.   3 95

Above are shipped from our house. Sold in quantities as wanted (regular charge for pkgs.)

LANTERNS AND REFLECTOR LAMPS.

Lanterns.

Each style put up ½ doz. in case. Sold only by case. No charge for case.

Tubular, $4.10 Doz.   Crank Tubular, $4.20 Doz.   Electric, $4.50 Doz.

Our "Tubular" Lantern—*The king of tubular lanterns*. The most desirable one in the market. Has solid stamped base firmly attached. The globe portion raises the burner with a spring which is secured by a very ingenious contrivance at the top. First class brass burner. A style that is a favorite with all farmers and liverymen. ½ doz. in case................. $4 10

Our "Crank Tubular" Lantern—A first-class tubular lantern which is opened and closed merely by turning a crank or lever at side. The handiest lantern in the world to get at. Made in the strongest and most thorough manner. ½ doz. in case, no less sold............ 4 20

Our "Electric" Lantern—*Best in the world*. This lantern has stood the test of 12 years' trade with steadily increasing sales. A good, reliable article in every respect. Planished stand, 12 inches high, opening at top and bottom, so that it can be readily lighted and cleaned. Doubly guarded and well braced. Altogether the best lantern in the market. ½ doz. in case.. 4 50

Stable or Dash Board Lantern—With reflector. A tubular lantern with automatic lift, the same as our "Tubular" above, with reflector at the back of which is a strong wire spring hook. Made to attach to the dash board of wagon or to hang up in the stable, throwing a bright light over a large space. ½ doz. in case............................. 6 00

Candle Lantern and Reflector Lamp.

Run-about, 72c Doz.   Jaxon, $1.45 Doz.

"Run-about" Lantern—For candles. Entirely new, not a toy but an article of merit. 5-inch heavy corrugated tin base, made for No. 2 chimney which is held securely in place by springs, will not blow out. Can be retailed for 10 cents or complete with chimney for 15 cents. Each in box. 1 doz. in carton...................... (3 doz. or more, 69c.)   72

"Jaxon" Reflector Lamp—Made from one piece of 7-gauge steel wire, very strong and springy, complete with 7-inch bright tin reflector and 4½-inch fount, made for No. 2 burner. Entirely new and a seller. Safely packed, 1 doz. in case, no less sold... 1 45

FANCY LAMP SHADES.

BEAUTIFUL GOODS—Ranging from 43 Cents per Dozen to $2.25 Each.

A few years ago these goods were classed with "fancy goods"—now they are staple all the year and every lamp must have a shade. We have a good line and prices are emphatically "right."

5 and 10-Cent Lamp Shades.

No. 659, 43c Doz.   No. 4, 85c Doz.

	Doz
No. 659, Table Lamp Shade—10¾ inches in diameter, pasteboard in assorted colors, gilt trimmed and figured. A beauty 5-center. (6 doz. or more, 43c.)	$0 43
No. 4, "Augusta" Table Lamp Shade—Fancy fold, pointed, edges with swell top, 13 inches in diameter. Assorted red, green and yellow in box of 3 dozen, complete with holders, sold only by box	85

Linen Lamp Shades.

7-Inch Linen Table Lamp Shade—Pleated pattern, fringed edge, in leading colors. Complete with holders	1 50
9-Inch Linen Table Lamp Shade—Same style as above. Complete with holders	2 40
No. 101, 10-Inch Linen Banquet Lamp Shade—Same style and colors as above. Complete with holders	3 00
No. 102, 12-Inch Linen Lamp Shade—For banquet or parlor lamp. Same style as above. Complete with holders	3 60

Isabella, $4.50 Doz.   No. 1753, $4.50 Doz.

"Isabella" Dresden Banquet Lamp Shade—Fancy shape, folded pattern, fringed edge, figured material. Complete with holders...... 4 50

No. 1753, Linen Banquet Lamp Shade—Fancy shape, pleated design, fringed edge, popular colors. Complete with holders............ 4 50

Silk Shades for Central Draft Lamps.

No. 111, Banquet Shade.   No. 210, $2.25 Each.

	Each
No. 111, China Silk Banquet Shade—14-inch, soft top effect, 6-inch lace flounce, fancy shape. For banquet or parlor lamp. Complete with central draft holder	$0 85
No. 111, China Silk Banquet Shade—16-inch, soft top effect, 8-inch lace flounce, fancy design. Complete with central draft holder	1 10
No. 111, China Silk Banquet Shade—18-inch, soft top effect, 8-inch lace flounce, fancy design. Complete with central draft holder	1 45
No. 210, China Silk Banquet Shade—18-inch, soft top effect, 10-inch fancy chiffon flounce. Complete with central draft holder	2 25

N. B.—We carry the following colors in stock: White, pink, corn, nile and red. The following can be supplied on short notice: Old rose, sky-blue and heliotrope.

We Can Save You Enough on Every Barrel of Glassware to MORE THAN PAY THE FREIGHT.

These Fine Lamps Are No Longer for the "Classes"—They Are Now in Reach of THE PEOPLE.

DECORATED LAMPS—SHIPPED FROM FACTORY NEAR PITTSBURGH.

The Decorated Lamps on these two pages are shipped from factory near Pittsburgh. This is to your benefit in two ways—danger of breakage is lessened, and by saving one handling we are enabled to name much lower prices. Freight from Pittsburgh on these light goods is very small.

The Lamps here listed are not merely equal to any other—they are positively **the finest lamps produced in America.** You may think this a strong statement when you note that we quote prices as low as you can buy the common grade goods, but if any buyer will send for one sample package he will find we have not claimed a grain too much. *A hint:* You may be offered these same lamps by other jobbers—if so **compare prices.**

N. B. We have a few copies of an elaborate Catalogue of Decorated Lamps, containing large illustrations showing goods in exact colors, and will on request send one to any merchant who may wish to investigate further before placing orders.

LAMP NO. 600.

One to advertise with. All glass body, 7-inch dome shade, assorted decorations. Height 14 inches. Takes No. 2 sun burner and 7-inch ring. 12 in bbl.

Sold only by pkg. of 12 lamps. (Bbl. 35c.)
Price, 48c Each.

LAMP NO. 610.

Same style as No. 600 with globe instead of dome. All glass body, 7½-inch globe shade, assorted in pink, Nile-green, yellow, etc. 8 in bbl.

Sold only by pkg. of 8 lamps. (Barrel 35c.)
Price, 64c Each.

LAMP NO. 620.

A fine "dollar" lamp to retail for less.

Stands 14½ inches high, all glass body with 7-inch dome shade, embossed glass with pink and yellow tints and embossed floral decorations. No. 2 sun burner and 7-inch ring. Packed 8 in barrel.

Sold only by pkg. of 8 lamps. (Barrel 35c.)
Price, 55c Each.

No. 660 Assortment of Blue and Brown "DELFT" Lamps

Standing on elegant gilt bases.

16 inches high. 7-inch Vienna dome shades, both founts and shades decorated in beautiful Delft scenes. Two styles of founts and assorted blue and brown decoration. No. 2 burners and 7-inch rings. Packed 8 in barrel, 4 of each pattern.

Sold only by pkg. of 8 lamps. (Bbl. 35c.)
Price, 70c Each.

LAMP NO. 640.

A 7-inch lamp, standing 16 inches high, metal base, assorted decorations, dome shape globe with 7-inch ring. No. 2 sun burner. 12 in barrel.

Sold only by pkg. of 12 lamps. (Bbl. 35c.)
Price, 60c Each.

LAMP NO. 650.

Same as No. 640 in every respect except that it is fitted with 7½-inch globe shade instead of the dome shape pattern. 8 in bbl.

Sold only by pkg. of 8 lamps. (Bbl. 35c.)
Price, 72c Each.

Lamp Assortment No. 710.

Half with dome shades and half with globe shades. Elegant glass fount lamps standing 17¾ in. high, handsome open-work metal bases, decorated with colored bands and beautiful floral scroll and Delft spray designs. Fine blending of delicate shades of pink and green. Assorted, 3 with 10-inch dome shades, as shown above, and 3 with globe shades.

Sold only by pkg. of 6 lamps. (Barrel, 35c.)
Price, 89c Each.

No. 770 Assortment of Decorated "Central Draft" Lamps.

No better lamps—no finer decoration—at any price.

This fine line of No. 2 central draft lamps speaks for itself. A very popular shape. 10-inch dome shade with tripod, fount brass lined. Height 18¼ inches. Two styles of fount and base, both shades and founts embellished and tinted in delicate green and blue, in floral sprays and in Delft effect. Provided with "Royal" central draft with ratchet wick-lift and lighting lift. Put up 4 lamps in bbl., 2 each of the patterns shown.

Sold only by pkg. of 4 lamps. (Bbl. 35c.)
Price, $1.70 Each.

Lamp Assortment No. 740.

This assortment consists of two patterns, of which we have space to show but one. The one illustrated has 10-inch dome shade with tripod, lift-out oil pot, metal base, assorted elegant decorations, height 16½ inches, takes climax burner. The other lamp also has metal base, lift-out oil pot, handsome assorted decorations and takes climax burner with 4-inch ring, globe pattern shade. Height 18 inches. Packed 6 lamps in bbl., assorted 3 of each pattern.

Sold only by pkg. of 4 lamps. (Barrel 35c.)
$1.12 Each.

IRON BASE LAMP NO. 810.

One of the richest lamps in the line.

An elegant iron base lamp with oxidized brass fittings to match. This is one of the most effective designs we offer. Height 17½ inches, globe and fount beautifully decorated in assorted patterns. Put up 4 lamps in bbl.

Sold only by pkg. of 4 lamps. (Bbl. 35c.)
Price, $1.35 Each.

Decorated Lamp No. 700.

A lamp for which you could ask $2.00 with good grace.

This is a very handsome lamp, full size, with metal base, large 10-inch dome shade, height 16½ inches, handsome decorations assorted in assorted bbl. Takes No. 2 sun burner and 10-inch tripod. Packed 6 lamps in bbl.

Sold only by pkg. of 6 lamps. (Barrel 35c.)
Price, 80c Each.

Decorated Lamp No. 670.

One of the prettiest lamps and one of the best bargains.

Fancy moulded body with 7-inch dome shade, assorted tints and decorations. Height 16 inches. Takes No. 2 sun burner and 7-inch ring. Packed 8 in barrel.

Sold only by pkg of 8 lamps. (Bbl. 35c.)
Price, 79c Each.

No. 760 Assortment of DECORATED GLOBE LAMPS.

Illustrations cannot do justice to these beautiful art lamps.

These superb lift-out oil pot lamps have 8-inch globes and stand 19¾ inches high. They are designed in Colonial and Louis XV. styles and are markedly characteristic of these two periods. Decorations are in blue and brown Delft effects, fancy metal bases, supplied with climax burner and ring. Put up 4 lamps in bbl., 2 each of the patterns shown.

Sold only by pkg. of 4 lamps. (Barrel 35c.)
Price, $1.65 Each.

Lamp Assortment No. 750.

Half with globes and half with dome shades.

Elegantly decorated in assorted tints, assorted, half with globe shades, as shown in illustration, height 19 inches, and half with 10-inch dome shades, height 17½. Lift-out oil pots, brass lined. Packed 6 in bbl., 3 of each, as above specified.

Sold only by pkg. of 6 lamps. (Barrel 35c.)
Price, $1.25 Each.

It is *unquestionably* best for the retailer to have his fine Lamps shipped direct from factory, as not only can we quote better prices, but risk of breakage is reduced to the smallest possible point, the packing at the factory being done by professionals.

There are reasons why we are selling these very fine lamps at prices at least as low as you can buy much less desirable lines. We hope no lamp buyer will fail to sample our line before placing his orders.

We Have Gone into Fine Lamps in Earnest and Name Prices to Get Our Share of the Business.

Here Are the Finest Lamps Made—but NOT at the "Fancy Prices" Usually Charged.

DECORATED LAMPS Shipped from Factory.

No. 630 Assortment of Blue and Brown "DELFT" Lamps.

Comprising equal quantities of the two rich patterns illustrated, both in the now-so-popular "Delft" decoration, one brown and one blue.

All glass bodies, blue and brown Delft decorations, standing with 7-inch Vienna dome shade 14½ inches high, take No. 2 sun burner and 7-inch ring. Packed 8 in bbl., 4 of each pattern.

Sold only by pkg. of 8 lamps. (Bbl. 35c.)
Price, 62c Each.

No. 680 Assortment of DECORATED PARLOR LAMPS.

High class lamps to retail at prices that will advertise you.

Comprising equal quantities of the two patterns illustrated, one artistically decorated in blue and brown Delft, and the other in pink and yellow tints with Dresden flowers. Handsome metal bases, beautifully embossed, bodies and special shape 7-inch shades. Height 16¾ inches. 4 of each pattern in bbl.

Sold only by pkg. of 8 lamps. (Barrel 35c.)
Price, 90c Each.

No. 690 Assortment of DECORATED PARLOR LAMPS.

You can retail these for what similar lamps have heretofore sold at wholesale.

These lamps, with richly polished brass bases, ornate and highly embossed bodies and large 7-inch dome shades, are striking novelties. They stand 15 inches high and are decorated in pink and Nile-green and wild rose sprays and in rich blue and brown Delft effects. Assorted, 3 lamps each of the 2 patterns shown.

Sold only by pkg. of 4 lamps. (Barrel 35c.)
Price, 95c Each.

No. 780 Assortment of DECORATED BANQUET LAMPS.

No. A.   No. B.   No. C.

A fine assortment of banquet lamps, comprising 3 styles: Pattern "A" stands 26 inches high, 9½-inch globe, beautifully decorated in ivory and Nile-green with wild rose and scroll designs. Pattern "B" stands 27 inches high, 9-inch globe, decorated in artistic blue and brown Delft effects. Both A and B are supplied with climax burners and 4-inch rings. Pattern "C" stands 28 inches high, 9-inch globe and No. 2 central draft burner, elegantly decorated in Delft designs. 4 lamps in bbl. as follows:

1 No. "A," $1.58 .... $3 16 | 1 No. "B," $2.65 .... $2 65 | 1 No. "C," $3.25 .... $3 25

Sold only by pkg. of 4 lamps. (Barrel 35c.) **Price, $9.06 for the Assortment.**

DECORATED LAMPS Shipped from Factory.

Assortment No. 730 of DECORATED GLOBE LAMPS.

In the rich and tasty "Delft" ornamentation.

These very beautiful globe lamps are the richest ones for the money ever shown. They stand 17 inches high, have 7½-inch globes and are very handsomely embossed in Colonial and Louis XV. styles, elegantly decorated in blue and brown Delft effects, gilt metal bases. Put up 4 in bbl., 2 each of the two patterns shown.

Sold only by pkg. of 4 lamps. (Barrel 35c.)
Price, $1.30 Each.
(Shipped from Factory.)

DECORATED PARLOR LAMP No. 790.

One of the richest lamps produced—of the grade heretofore sold at such prices that none but the rich could own them.

A splendid example of the Louis XV. models adapted to modern wants. Beautifully tinted in ivory and pink and faithfully decorated, this number leaves but little to be desired in the way of a high grade artistic lamp. Height 22 in. Fitted with 8-inch globe and "Royal" central draft fount. Put up 2 lamps in bbl.

Sold only by pkg. of 2 lamps. (Barrel 35c.)
Price, $3.55 Each.
(Shipped from Factory.)

Decorated GLOBE LAMP No. 800.

Our retail "fine art" stores get $15.00 for a lamp like this.

A large and imposing lamp with 10-inch globe, height 24½ inches, elegantly decorated in raised work and colors in "Empire" effect. "Royal" central draft fount, including ring. Each lamp in barrel.

(Barrel 35c.)
Price, $5.75 Each.
(Shipped from Factory.)

Do not judge these lamps by price alone. These are without exception the finest lamps in the country.

NIGHT LAMPS IN "OPEN STOCK." Shipped from Our House.

Carried in Stock at Each of Our Houses. No Charge for Package.

Our No. 41 TINTED NIGHT LAMP.

Daintiest lamp ever produced to sell at 50c.

Glass fount and special design chimney, both moulded in ornate pattern and richly tinted. Complete with burner. Assorted colors, cream, pink, blue and chocolate. Stands 10 inches high. A real work of art. Each in pasteboard box. *(No charge for box.)*
(Shipped from our house.)
Price, $3.25 Doz.

Our No. 42 TINTED NIGHT LAMP.

You would buy this if you could see it.

Similar to No. 41, but different pattern. Designed in the colonial school. 10 inches high. Each in pasteboard box with burner. Four rich tints, Delft blue, pink, cream and chocolate. *(No charge for box.)*
(Shipped from our house.)
Price, $3.25 Doz.

THE FOLLOWING ARE SHIPPED FROM OUR HOUSE.

PARISIAN SUSPENSION LAMP—72-Candle Power.

A Competitor of the Electric Arc Light.

One of these will brilliantly illuminate a room 16 feet square.

A magnificent lamp, having a beautifully hand-painted are globe 12x14 inches in diameter. With patent extension and automatically balanced extension chains. Has a No. 2 electric fount and is unquestionably the best lamp in the U. S. Each lamp complete with fixtures, burner, chimney and wick carefully packed in a barrel. *(Bbl. 25c.)*
Price, $4.40 Each.
(Shipped from our house.)

THE "PITTSBURG" STORE OR HALL LAMP.

Thirty-two candle power stronger than the next best lamp in existence—equal to an electric street lamp.

Beyond all question the best lamp for store or hall use ever put on the market. Absolutely non-explosive. Burns over 10 hours without refilling. Perfect draft, no dirt, no odor. Smallest wick exposure of any lamp made. Has patent drip indicator showing quantity of oil in fount.

The only lamp made with extra feeder wick and oil drip cup on handle of tube to carry any over-flow back to the wick. 20-inch tin shade. Fitted with No. 3 burner, fount, wick and chimney. Each lamp complete ready for use and in box. *(Shipped from our house.)*
Price Each, $2.25.
(No charge for case.) *(4 or more, $2.17 Each.)*

Include a Few Lamps with Your Next Order and TEST OUR VALUES.

...dy Consider Sugges. *...ciency of "Our Drummer" in Any*

...DEX TO D... ARTMENTS.

...ordions+ ... 61
...ount Books+ ... 109
...Rifles+ ... 163
...num Department+ .58 & 59
...bums+Autograph ... 56
...lbums+Scrap ... 57
...lmond Dishes+China ... 34
Ammunition+ ... 163
Aprons+ ... 124
Armlets+ ... 148
Ash Receivers+China ... 45
Atomizers+ ... 114
Augers+ ... 168
Autoharps+ ... 60
Axes+ ... 168
Axle Grease+ ... 121

Baby Carriage Robes+ ... 135
Bags+Paper ... 120
[illegible] ... 100
[illegible] ... 86
[illegible] ... 91
[illegible] ... 121
[illegible] ... 8
[illegible] ... 11
[illegible] ... 8
[illegible] ... 60
[illegible] ... 12
...nd Shears 177
[illegible] ... 115
...+ ... 109
[illegible] ... 120
[illegible] ... 46
[illegible] ... 50
...sons+ ... 165
...Spreads+ ... 124
Bells+Hand and Call ... 164
Belt ...kles+ ... 78
Belts and Belting ... 146
Belts+Men's ... 139
Berry Sets+China ... 38
Bibs+ ... 146
Bicycle Miscellanies+ ... 171
Bicycles+ ... 157
Bill Heads, etc+ ... 106
Bird Cage Hooks+ ... 165
Bird Cages+ ... 175
Bird Seed+ ... 121
Bisque Figures+ ... 47
Blank Books+ ... 109
Blankets+Bed ... 139
Blankets+Horse ... 156
Blocks+ ... 17
Blotting Papers+ ... 109
Bluing+ ... 121
Board Clips+ ... 101
Bolts+Carriage, etc ... 171
Bolts+Miscellaneous ... 170
Bone Dishes+China ... 35
Book and Shawl Straps+ ... 99
Book Department+ ... 92 to 99
Books+Juvenile ... 64 and 65
Books+Music ... 95
Bowls+Wood ... 119
Boxing Gloves+ ... 109
Box Papers+ ... 57 and 105
Brackets+Iron ... 166
Braids+ ... 148
Bread and Butter Plates+ ... 33
Bread and Milk Sets+ ... 37
Bread Boxes+Tin ... 160
Brooms+ ... 117
Brush Department+116 to 118
Burners+Lamp ... 188
Butter Molds, Ladles, etc. 119
Butter Plates+China ... 35
Buttons+ ... 148
Buttons+Automatic ... 150
Button Hooks+ ... 151

Cake Turners+ ... 164
Candies+ ... 121
Candles+Wax ... 7
Candy Boxes+ ... 120
Canes+ ... 147
Can Openers+ ... 165
Cap Department+ ... 141 to 143
Caps+Children's Winter ... 126
Cards+Playing ... 103
Carpets+ ... 135
Carpet Sweepers+ ... 167
Carpet Sweepers+Toy ... 15
Carving Sets+ ... 177
Cash Sales Checks+ ... 100
Ceiling Hooks+ ... 166
Celery Trays+China ... 37
Celluloid Novelties+ ... 11
Chafing Dishes+ ... 160
Chairs+Dining ... 99
Chairs+Rocking ... 99
Chair Seats+ ... 119
Chalk+Carpenters' ... 170

Chamber Sets+ ... 183
Chamois Skin+ ... 114
Checkers and Boards+ ... 17
China Novelties+ ... 46
Chinaware+Impt'd ... 32 to 49
Chinaware+Japanese. 28 to 31
Chinaware+Fancy ... 46 & 47
Chisels+ ... 169
Chocolate Pots+China ... 36
Chocolates+ ... 120
Christmas Cards+ ... 65
Christmas Tree Candles+ ... 19
Christmas Tree Ornam'ts+ 19
Chromos+Embossed ... 7
Cigars+ ... 123
Clocks+ ... 74 and 75
Clothes Lines+ ... 119
Clothes Lines+Wire ... 174
Clothes Wringers+ ... 172
Clothing+Oiled ... 140
Clothing+Waterpr'f. 140 & 141
Coffee Mills+ ... 172
Collar & Cuff Boxes+Fancy 53
Collar Buttons+ ... 150
Collars and Cuffs+ ... 139
Combs+ ... 152 and 153
Comfortables+ ... 139
Compasses+ ... 168
Composition Books+ ... 107
Copy Books+Spencerian ... 101
Copying Books+ ... 108
Copying Outfit+ ... 105
Copying Press+ ... 101
Cork Screws+ ... 164
Cornets+Brass ... 61
Corset Laces+ ... 149
Corsets+ ... 133
Corticelli Silk+ ... 149
Cotton+Ball and Spool ... 149
Cotton Bats+ ... 124
Cracker Jars+China ... 36
Crashes+ ... 125
Crayons+Checking ... 103
Crayons+Colord & Drawing 109
Crayons+School ... 100
Crockery+ ... 179 to 183
Crumb Trays & Brushes+ ... 159
Cups & Saucers+China ... 42-44
Cups, Saucers and Plates+ 37
Curling Irons+ ... 147
Curry Combs+ ... 166
Curtain Fixtures+ ... 167
Curtains+Chenille ... 134
Curtains+Lace ... 134
Cushion Covering+ ... 126
Cuspidors+China ... 47
Cuspidors+Lava ... 99
Cuspidors+Metal ... 159
Cutlery+Pocket ... 176 and 177
Cutlery+Table ... 177 and 178
Cyclometer+ ... 171

Diamond Jewelry+ ... 85
Dice+ ... 17
Dinner Sets+American 181-182
Dinner Sets+Imported ... 49
Display Stands+ ... 157
Dog Chains, etc (Metal)+ ... 165
Dog Collars+Leather ... 109
Dog Collars+Steel ... 164
Doll Department+ ... 20 to 27
Doll Heads+ ... 20
Dolls+Japanese ... 29
Dolls+Rubber ... 8
Doll Stands+ ... 24
Doll Sundries+ ... 22
Dominoes+ ... 17
Door Bell+ ... 171
Drawer Pulls+ ... 167
Drawing Books+ ... 105
Dress Braid+ ... 148
Dress Shields+ ... 148
Dress Stays, etc+ ... 148
Drug Miscellanies+114 and 115
Drums+ ... 9
Dry Goods+ ... 124 to 140
Duck Clothing+ ... 140
Dusters+Feather and Wool 117

Ear Muffs+ ... 124
Easels+Floor ... 69
Easels+Wire ... 175
Egg Cups+China ... 35
Electric Battery+ ... 123
Envelopes+ ... 107
Erasers+Blackboard ... 100
Erasers+Rubber ... 100
Eye Glasses+ ... 115
Face Cloths+Turkish ... 125
Face Powder+ ... 114
Fan Cases+Celluloid ... 55
Faucets+Wood ... 119

Files and Rasps+ ... 169
Files+Letter ... 101
Files+Paper ... 100
Fire Shovels+ ... 164
Fishing Tackle+ ... 173
Flags+ ... 109
Flat Irons+ ... 172
Flavoring Extracts+ ... 121
Fleisher's Worsted and Yarn 149
Flower Pots+Lava ... 99
Flute Accordions+ ... 61
Fry Pans+ ... 165
Furniture Polish+ ... 121
Furniture+Toy ... 14
Galvanized Ironware+ ... 162
Games+ ... 16 and 17
Garters & Hose Supporters ... 148
Gimlets+ ... 168
Glassware Dept+ ... 184 to 191
do Imported+ ... 50 and 52
do Open Stock+ ... 88 to 90
Gloves and Mittens+144 to 146
Glove and Hdkf. Boxes+ ... 55
Glue+ ... 104
Granite Ironware+ ... 162
Graphoscopes+ ... 8
Grindstones+ ... 166
Grocers' Sundries+ ... 121
Guitars+ ... 60
Gum+Chewing ... 121
Guns and Revolvers+ ... 163
Guns+Toy ... 17
Hair Oil, Bay Rum, etc+111
Hair Pin Boxes+China ... 46
Hair Pins+ ... 151
Hair Pins+Fancy ... 153
Hammers+ ... 168
Hammock Hooks+ ... 164
Handkerchief Boxes+ ... 55
Handkerchiefs+ ... 128 and 129
Hardware+ ... 164 to 172
Harmonicas+ ... 62
Harness+ ... 155
Harness Snaps & Horse Bits 166
Hasps, etc+ ... 165
Hat and Coat Racks+Wood 119
Hatchets+ ... 168
Hats and Caps+ ... 141 to 143
Heminway Silks+ ... 149
Hinges+ ... 170
Hooks and Eyes+ ... 150
Horns+Tin ... 160
Horse Goods+ ... 154 to 156
Hose Supporters, etc.+ ... 148
Hosiery Department+ ... 130-131
Ice Cream Sets+China ... 38
Indian Clubs+ ... 109
Inks+ ... 104
Ink Stands+ ... 101
Invoice Books+ ... 108
Ironing Wax+ ... 121
Jackets+Ladies' Knit ... 124
Jack Stones+ ... 17
Japanese Goods+ ... 28 to 31
Jewel Cases+Plush, etc ... 56
Jewelry+ ... 76 to 80
Jews' Harps+ ... 63
Jump Ropes+ ... 17
Juvenile Books+ ... 64 and 65
Kettles+Iron ... 172
Key Rings, Chains, etc+ ... 151
Kites+ ... 17
Knit Goods+ ... 133
Knives and Forks+ ... 178
Labels+Gummed ... 104
Laces, etc+ ... 127
Lamp Department+ ... 188 to 191
Lamps+Night ... 88 and 101
Lamps+Reflector ... 162
Lamps+Store ... 191
Lamp Burners, etc.+ ... 188
Lamp Chimneys+ ... 189
Lamp Shades+ ... 189
Lamp Stoves+ ... 162
Lamp Wicks+ ... 149
Lanterns+ ... 162
Lap Robes+ ... 156
Leather Clothing+ ... 140
Leatherette Novelties+ ... 18
Leather Goods+Fancy ... 55
Levels+ ... 169
Linen Goods Department+125
Locks+ ... 170
Lunch Boxes+ ... 120
Machine Oil+ ... 121
Mackintoshes+ ... 141
Magic Lanterns+ ... 9
Mandolins+ ... 60
Manicure Sets+ ... 53

Marbles+ ... 18
Masks+ ... 7
Matches+ ... 119
Match Safes+China ... 45
Match Safes+Pocket ... 123
Match Safes+Tin ... 160
Mathematical Instrum'ts+ ... 100
Matting+Floor ... 135
Mats+Cocoa, etc ... 135
Mats+Wire ... 175
Medallions+ ... 68 and 69
Medicines+ ... 114 and 115
Meerschaum Goods+122 & 123
Memorandum Books+ ... 108
Metal Novelties+ ... 6
Mica+ ... 162
Microscopes+ ... 115
Mincing Knives+ ... 165
Mirrors+Silver Plated ... 73
Mirrors+Toilet ... 113
Mirrors+Wall ... 113
Mittens+ ... 144 to 146
Money Banks+ ... 12
Money Drawer+ ... 166
Mucilage+ ... 104
Mufflers+ ... 129
Mugs+China ... 46
Musical Goods+ ... 60 to 63
Music Boxes+ ... 60
Music+Sheet ... 95
Mustard Pots+China ... 35
Nail Puller+ ... 175
Nails+Boot and Shoe ... 163
Napkins+ ... 125
Napkins+Paper ... 107
Necklaces+ ... 13
Necktie Cases+Celluloid ... 56
Neckwear+ ... 138
Needles+ ... 150
Notes and Receipts+ ... 100
Notions+Dry Goods 148 & 149
Notions+Staple ... 150 and 151
Nursing Bottles, etc+ ... 114
Nut Dishes+China ... 34
Oatmeal Bowls+China ... 33
Oil Cans+ ... 161
Oil Cloth+ ... 124
Oiled Clothing+ ... 140
Oil Heaters+ ... 160
Opera Glasses+ ... 27
Optical Goods+ ... 115
Order Books+Manifold ... 108
Organs+ ... 60
Overall Department+ ... 140
Overshirts+Men's ... 136
Oyster Plates+China ... 34
Padlocks+ ... 170
Paints+Oil & Decorative ... 114
Pants+Men's ... 140
Paper Novelties+ ... 17
Paper+Shelf ... 120
Paper+Tissue ... 107 and 120
Paper+Toilet ... 119
Paper+Wrapping ... 120
Paper+Writing ... 107
Pencil Boxes+ ... 101
Pencil Holders+ ... 100
Pencils, Pen Holders+102 & 103
Pens+ ... 103
Pens+Gold ... 78
Perfume Bottles+Silvered ... 73
Perfume Dept+ ... 111 and 112
Phonoharps+ ... 61
Photo Frames+Fancy ... 63
Photo Frames+Silver 56 & 72
Photo Frames+Wood ... 68
Photo Holders+Celluloid ... 55
Pianos+Toy ... 11
Picture Cord, Knobs, etc+ ... 167
Picture Department+ ... 66 to 69
Pincers+ ... 168
Pins+Belt and Skirt ... 147
Pins+Hat and Trimming ... 151
Pins+Toilet and Safety ... 150
Pin Tickets, etc+ ... 104
Pin Trays+China ... 45
Pipes+ ... 122 and 123
Pitchers+China ... 36
Planes+ ... 169
Plates+China ... 32 to 34
Playing Cards+ ... 103
Pliers+ ... 168
Plush Goods+ ... 53 to 59
Pocket Books+ ... 86 and 87
Poker Chips+ ... 17
Pokers+Stove ... 164
Price Tickets+ ... 104
Printing Outfits+ ... 104
Pudding Sets+China ... 39
Purses+ ... 86 and 87

Quilts+ ... 124
Rattles+Rubber ... 8
Rattles+Toy ... 10 and 11
Razors+ ... 177
Razor Strops and Hones+ ... 115
Reading Glasses+ ... 115
Reed Furniture+ ... 90
Revolvers+ ... 163
Ribbons+ ... 124
Rifles+ ... 163
Rockingham Ware 179 and 183
Rocking Horses+ ... 3
Rose Bowls+Glass ... 50
Rubber Balloons+ ... 8
Rubber Balls+ ... 8
Rubber Bands+ ... 100
Rubber Goods+Druggists' 114
Rugs+Floor ... 135
Rulers+Wood ... 100
Rules+Boxwood ... 150
Rustic Baskets and Vases ... 11
Saddles+ ... 155
Sad Irons+Toy ... 15
Safes+ ... 157
Salad Dishes+China ... 35 & 37
Satchels and Bags+ ... 91
Satchet Powder+ ... 111
Sauce Dishes+China ... 33
Sauce Sets+China ... 38
Saws+ ... 169
Scales+ ... 172
Scholars' Companions+ ... 101
School Bags+ ... 100
School Supplies+ ... 100 to 108
Scissors+ ... 178
Screw Drivers+ ... 168
Screw Hooks and Eyes+ ... 167
Screws+ ... 171
Scythe and Whet Stones+165
Sewing Machines+ ... 192
Shades+Window ... 135
Shaving Mugs+China ... 46
Shaving Sets ... 56
Shawl and Book Straps+ ... 99
Shawls+ ... 124
Shears ... 178
Shears+Tinners' & Pruning 173
Shell Boxes+ ... 6
Shirts+Men's ... 136
Shoe Blacking and Dressing 121
Shoe Laces+ ... 149
Shopping Bags+ ... 86
Shovels, etc+ ... 172
Show Cases+ ... 91
Show Window Pieces+ ... 9
Sieves+Wood Rim ... 119
Silver Polish+ ... 121
Silverware+ ... 70 to 73
Slate Pencils+ ... 103
Slates+School ... 101
Slates+Transparent ... 2
Sleigh Bells+ ... 163
Smokers' Goods ... 122 and 123
Smokers' Sets and Tables+ 15
Smokers' Sets+China ... 45
Smokers' Sets+Plush, etc. 55
Soap Department ... 110 and 111
Soldering Sets+ ... 164
Spalding's Sporting Goods 109
Spectacles, etc+ ... 115
Spelling Blanks+ ... 101
Spices+ ... 121
Sponges+ ... 114
Spoon Holders+China ... 35
Spoons and Forks+Metallic 178
Spring Balances+ ... 164
Squares+Carpenters' ... 169
Stamping Outfit+ ... 150
Stationery Dept+ ... 100 to 109
Stereoscopes and Views+ ... 8
Stove Boards+ ... 162
Stove Cover Lifters+ ... 164
Stove Paste and Polish+ ... 121
Stove Pipe Dampers+ ... 162
Stoves+Lamp ... 162
Stoves+Toy ... 9
Sugar and Cream Sets+ ... 35
Sugars and Salts+China ... 35
Surprise Boxes+ ... 6
Suspenders ... 136 and 137
Sweaters+ ... 140
Syringes+Rubber ... 114
Syrup Pitchers+China ... 37
Table Cloths+ ... 125
Table Covers+ ... 125
Table Sets+China ... 38
Tables+Parlor ... 99
Tables+Folding Work ... 109
Tablets+Writing ... 106
Tacks+ ... 171

Tags and Labels+ ... 104
Tape Measures+ ... 151
Tea Kettles+Brass ... 161
Teapots+China ... 36
Tea Pot Stands+China ... 35
Tea Sets+American ... 182
Tea Sets+Imported ... 48
Tea Sets+Toy ... 45
Teas+ ... 121
Thermometers+ ... 115
Thimbles+ ... 151
Threads+ ... 149
Ticket and Card Holders ... 104
Tidies+Turkish ... 126
Tinware Department 158 to 162
Tobacco Boxes+ ... 123
Toilet Paper, etc+ ... 119
Toilet Preparations+ ... 114
Toilet Sets+Plush, etc 54 & 55
Tool Chests+Toy ... 15
Tools+Farm and Garden ... 172
Tools+Mechanics, etc 168-169
Tooth Pick Holders+China 47
Tooth Picks+Wood ... 119
Tops+American ... 17
Tops+Imported ... [illegible]
Towel Racks & Rollers 119 & 166
Towels+ ... 125
Toys+Celluloid ... 11
Toys+China ... 46 and 47
Toys+Iron ... 12
Toys+Leatherette ... 18
Toys+Misc. Imported ... 2 to 6
Toys+Musical ... 10 and 11
Toys+Pewter ... 13
Toys+Roaming ... 13
Toys+Rubber ... 8
Toys+Steam ... 8
Toys+Steel ... 19
Toys+Tin ... 13
Toys+Wood ... 14 and 15
Tracing Wheels+ ... 164
Traps+Mouse and Rat 119 & 174
Traps+Steel ... 165
Traveling Bags+ ... 91
Trays+Japanese ... 30
Truck+Store ... 175
Trumpets+Toy ... 10 and 11
Trunks+ ... 91
Trunks+Toy ... 11
Trunk Straps+ ... 91
Twine+ ... 120
Umbrellas+ ... 147
Underwear Dept+ ... 132
Underwear+Muslin ... 127
Upholstery Specialties+ ... 16.
Valises+ ... 91
Vases+China ... 47 and 52
Vases+Glass ... 50 and 51
Vases+Japanese ... 30 and 31
Veilings+ ... 124
Velveteens+ ... 33
Views+Photographic ... 8
Violin Miscellanies+ ... 63
Violins+ ... 60
Vises+ ... 169
Visiting Cards ... 100
Wagons+Toy ... 19
Waiters and Trays+ ... 158
Wall Pockets+ ... 67
Wardrobe Hooks+ ... 167
Wash Boards+ ... 119
Washing Machines+ ... 172
Watches+ ... 81 to 85
Watches+Ansonia ... 157
Watches+Toy ... 7
Waving Irons+ ... 147
Wheelbarrows+Toy ... 19
Whips+ ... 154
Whips+Toy ... 4
Whisk Holders+Fancy ... 56
Whistles+Toy ... 151
White Goods+Piece ... 134
White Granite Ware 180 & 181
Window Shades+ ... 135
Wine Sets+Glass ... 52
Wire Goods Dept+ ... 174 & 175
Woodenware+ ... 119
Work Boxes+Plush, etc ... 53
Work Boxes+Wood ... 57
Wrapping Paper+ ... 120
Wrenches+ ... 168
Wringers+Clothes ... 172
Writing Desks+Leather ... 57
Writing Desks+Wood ... 57
Writing Paper+ ... 107
Writing Tablets & Pads+ ... 100
Yellow Ware+ ... 179 and 183
Zithers+ ... 61

Our Drummer Now is and We Aim to Keep It the Foremost Wholesale Catalogue in the World.

Keep This Catalogue for Ready R... Copy of the N...

Two LEADING ESTABLISHMENTS ... LEADING CITIES OF A...

CHICAGO: Looking west on Adams street from a point opposite Marshall Field & Co.'s famous wholesale building, showing Butler Brothers' massive new seven story and basement store, between Franklin and Market streets and running through to Quincy street.

NEW YORK: Looking up Broadway (north) from the corner of Broome street, showing Brothers' giant building, eight stories above ground and two below, which runs through to Mercer street. Our illustration is an exact reproduction from a photograph.

INSTRUCTIONS FOR ORDERING.

BY OBSERVING THESE SUGGESTIONS YOU FACILITATE THE FILLING OF YOUR ORDERS AND LESSEN THE POSSIBILITY OF ERRORS.

In ordering from us for the first time please give us as reference the names of a few houses with which you have an established credit.

Write your order on separate sheets from any other communication you have to make. This permits both being attended to at once.

Use only one side of the paper, if possible, in ordering (except when using our order sheets), as this sometimes prevents items being overlooked.

Our order sheets are put up in pads of 25. If you haven't a pad mention in your next order or drop us a card.

Write name and address plainly. A doubtful word in the middle of a sentence can be guessed at, but a bad signature is an unsolvable puzzle. Avoid fancy signatures.

Shipping directions. Be sure to mention your nearest shipping point if you are not located on a railway or water route. If there are competing transportation companies, name your preference. If express shipments specify which company serves your town.

One item only on a line. Never write more than one item on a line, and carry out the price at which we have catalogued it. This helps us to identify the exact article wanted.

In using our order blank write nothing upon it except the order. If you have other matters to communicate or a remittance to enclose mention same on your own letter paper.

Orders for less than $5.00 will not be filled. This is for your economy as well as ours. Transportation charges on such bills eat up your profits, and our expense for filling is as great as on larger orders.

Goods cannot be returned, except for cause. We guarantee every item as described and are always ready to rectify errors. If goods received are not as ordered, notify us and await instructions. Never return them without notice.

Avoid ordering goods to be packed with those of other houses. Some houses absolutely refuse to receive such packages, and nothing causes more annoying delays and misunderstandings. It costs you no more to ship separately, and saves trouble and delays.

Do not ask us to purchase goods outside our stock. We naturally wish to be accommodating, but so much difficulty has been experienced in endeavoring to even approximate such requests, often from very meagre directions, we have been compelled to refuse them.

Examine all cases, barrels, etc., and see that they are in good condition before accepting same from transportation company. All shipments made by us are in good order when taken by transportation lines and so receipted for. Our responsibility then ceases.

TERMS AND REQUIREMENTS.

Our regular terms are two per cent 10 days—and 11 days. **Net 40 days.** No longer time. Be sure to send references with your first order.

Special terms on Holiday Goods. These goods will be found only on the pink pages of this catalogue and the special terms on same are given at top of page 1.

A deposit must accompany every C. O. D. order. If you desire goods sent C. O. D. you will please send us a deposit of at least 10 per cent of the presumable amount of the order, and on orders of any amount less than $50 you will please send at least $5 as a guarantee of your acceptance of the goods. The amount of the deposit will be deducted from the draft. No C. O. D. shipments for less than $10 will be made.

We can send goods C. O. D. by freight, marked "Butler Brothers." The invoice is mailed direct to you, and the bill of lading (indorsed over to you), accompanied by a draft on you for the amount of invoice (less your deposit), is sent to your nearest bank for collection. Upon the payment of this draft you can secure the bill of lading and thus get your goods from the railroad agent.

C. O. D. Crockery Shipments.—C. O. D. customers ordering Crockery shipped from factory, in the same order with goods to be shipped from our house, should send **separate deposit for each shipment**—at least $5.00 each or $10.00 in all.

Do not send us checks on country banks. It is to your interest as well as ours that you observe this rule, as a debtor is liable until his obligation has been paid in cash, and he should remit so that currency can be realized quickly. Therefore, in remitting, send us a bank draft on New York or Chicago, or if that is not convenient send an express or post office money order. We pay no exchange or express charges on money.

Never send money by mail unregistered. Notwithstanding Uncle Sam's vigilance money letters disappear in transit every day.

No charge for case or cartage. Glass and crockery packages are the only ones we charge for. All manufacturers and jobbers charge for these.

Goods by mail. All packages sent by mail are absolutely at the expense and risk of purchaser. They may be registered, but while that costs 8 cents extra for each parcel it does not guarantee delivery. We therefore advise our patrons to instruct us to have their mail shipments insured. The Home Insurance Co. furnishes us printed blanks, which when filled out by us will insure you against loss. The cost of this insurance (which we charge for with goods and postage on invoice) will average about 5 cents for each $5.00 of insurance. This will positively protect you against loss. Shall we insure your mail shipments?

We sell to merchants only. Consumers into whose hands this catalogue may accidentally fall will save labor and stamps by remembering this.

We cannot break packages. All our goods are put up in as small packages as possible consistent with safe shipping. We will not furnish less quantities than indicated.

Merchants wishing to learn concerning our business standing are respectfully referred to the following: Chemical National Bank, New York; Ninth National Bank, New York; and Corn Exchange Bank, Chicago

BUTLER BROTHERS,

IMPORTERS AND WHOLESALERS OF "DEPARTMENT STORE" GOODS.

| NEW YORK: | "TWO MAMMOTH HOUSES." | CHICAGO: |
| 495 & 497 BROADWAY. | | 230, 232, 234 & 236 ADAMS ST. |

ALWAYS Send Your Orders to Our Nearest House. ... R Fail to State Your Name and Address Plainly.

What are you in business for? If to make money then you ought to be as quick to recognize good values when offered by a catalogue as by a salesman. Are you?

This catalogue is the sole medium by means of which we sell nearly ten millions a year. The many thousand merchants who give us their trade do so because they find it pays them.

We ask no favors. All we want is an even chance. The fact that we here quote net wholesale prices (less 2% 10 days) makes it easy for you to decide whether or not we merit a trial.

Note the "Special Offer to New Trade" on next page and test us with an order.

...will be put on our ...ing ... You will at once receive a copy of complete number and all printed matter thereafter.

Our complete catalogue is about four times as large as this "CONDENSED" and contains illustrations of nearly every article. Our customers not only receive the complete number regularly, but are kept advised through frequent circulars of price changes and of the many good bargains which come to us between seasons.

* * *

WATCH THE LITTLE THINGS.—If your business today is on a profitable basis don't overlook the little leaks which if not stopped in time may undermine your whole business. Insist that each department and each little sub-department and on its own basis as a profit payer. See to it that every clerk you have makes you a profit on his sales. Don't count a profit as made until you have the cash in hand; therefore, give as little credit as you can and on what you just give, watch collections closely.

It is very well to talk about "letting well enough alone" but the man who is satisfied with his present condition is not apt to improve it.

* * *

OUR "ADAMS" AND "BUTLER" BICYCLES.—Did you know that during 1897 we sold more wheels than ever before handled by any American jobbing concern in a single season?

Think what it means that it costs us *less than 50 cents* to sell bicycles. Contrast this with the selling expenses ...ch weights down most wheel handlers and requires them to ask $40.00, $50.00 and $60.00 for wheels not one whit better than ours.

Our "ADAMS" wheel ($26.00) is guaranteed absolutely high-grade with high-grade equipment, whereas the usual moderate priced wheel has cheap fittings throughout.

Our "BUTLER" bicycle ($34.00) is as good a wheel as it is possible to build—equal in riding qualities, in strength, in durability, in ease of running and in finish to any wheel in the world at no matter what price. Its factory cost is as great as that of any wheel in the market; we sell it to you for $34.00 simply because we handle bicycles as we do dry-goods, at a small jobbing advance over first cost.

We should like to have you order a sample of either of our wheels. If you don't care to do that, then be sure to ... us for circulars describing and illustrating our bicycles, but quoting no prices, so that same can be shown to your customers without exposing your cost. It is easy in this manner to sell bicycles without a penny invested.

Going into business? Thinking of changing your business? Any of your friends looking for an opening?

If so, write us. We can help you to find a location and to get started right. We make it our business to keep posted on promising openings over the country, and our long experience fits us to give helpful advice to beginners.

The "department store" business is booming. It is safer than Klondike and as promising a field. Though here are not today as many "nings" as there are same, yet we find ry day for inquir...

Whatever may have been his success in a one-line store, he realizes that present conditions make it necessary for him to handle many lines of goods. He, therefore, with that quickness that has contributed so materially to his success in the past, loses no time in adjusting himself to the new conditions.

In the conduct of his store the successful merchant is continuously watchful of little things. Little leaks are promptly stopped. Little rudenesses are not permitted. Little courtesies are observed. No part of his business is so little that it is not made to pay at least a little profit.

The successful merchant keeps faith with his customers. If he advertises bargains, he gives bargain values. In every action, every representation, he guards against every appearance of wishing to mislead.

The successful merchant keeps his stock well-balanced. He does not tie up money in too big a lot of any one line. While he aims to make every line sell freely he tries to carry just enough goods in each line to keep pace with the demand for them.

The successful merchant knows that lower prices mean more trade, and that the dealer who does a cash business can safely sell at lower prices than the one who gives credit. Hence the successful dealer is doing or preparing to do a cash business.

* * *

ONE PRICE, ONE DISCOUNT TO ALL.—When you see a price quoted in "OUR DRUMMER" you may know it is the lowest given by Butler Brothers to the largest customer on our books and that the best discount he gets is 3 per cent for cash. In order that we may get business in competition with other houses whose prices are elastic, it is necessary that we name our best quotation the first time, for we have no second chance.

We know it serves to strengthen the confidence of the trade that they may feel sure our first price to them is our final price, and that no time-taking, unsatisfactory haggling is necessary before rock-bottom has been reached.

* * *

"DIRECT FROM THE FACTORY"—You are probably besought every day or two to place orders direct with the factory and doubtless have some very attractive prices named on this basis. But even though you save 5 per cent in price when buying "direct," is there any *net* economy in so doing?

Take the strongest possible case in favor of the factory—goods shipped by them and by us in original packages—for instance, lamp chimneys. It is almost certain that one of our three houses is closer to you than the factory, and therefore you would not only lose time but pay something more in freight, and in bulky, low-priced goods like these it is astonishing what difference a slight advance in freight makes. Take a case of six dozen No. 1 chimneys at 17 cents per dozen plus case 40 cents, making a total of $1.42. Even if you can buy No. 1 chimneys for less than 17 cents per dozen do you not actually lose more in freight than you save in the goods themselves?

The standing temptation in buying direct from the mill is to buy more goods than one really needs, and we want to say, too, that a price is not *necessarily* cheap merely because it is named from the mill. We have known more than one instance where a customer (taking for granted that any price named "from the factory" must be cheap) has actually *paid more* for goods in large lots than we quoted in our catalogue. Next time you get a tempting quotation direct from the factory, first put it alongside of our *quantity price* on the same thing and see whether we do not offer you at least as low a price on an investment of considerably less.

* * *

DEPENDABLE MERCHANDISE—Price alone never makes an article cheap. Trustworthy quality is equally necessary. We feel that we cannot *afford* to sell our customers any goods which will not give satisfaction, therefore we make it our business to sift over the thousands of new items offered to us every year and to reject those which do not come up to the standard of RELIABLE QUALITY.

The confidence our customers have in us is the best part of our capital. We want them to feel that any article listed by us must be of safe quality or we would not offer it. Sometimes we lose business because we will not sell "seconds" or "job lots," but we can better afford to lose a great many...

Any merchant not now a customer may send us one first trial order from this catalogue with the privilege of returning any or all of the goods if not satisfactory, provided such return is made within five days after receipt.

We are opposed *on principle*, as a general rule, to the idea of allowing customers to order goods with the privilege of returning them except for some fault in the goods themselves. We seek the trade of *business men*, who know what they want and keep what they order. At the same time we recognize the fact that a merchant may properly wish to see what our goods are like before giving us his trade, and as an inducement to that end we make this special offer on one trial shipment. It is of course understood that this offer holds good only with one *first* order from this catalogue.

* * *

THE STORE THAT PAYS—That's the store every merchant wants to run. That's the store any merchant can run. It won't be a one-line store, though. One-liners used to pay. They won't now. The store of many lines is the money-maker of the present. Quit selling the single line of goods you like to sell. Begin selling anything the people want. Watch developments intelligently and profits will be yours.

Don't load up too heavily in any one line. Buy some things in many lines. Let every article be one that's a ready seller in your neighborhood. Make prices low enough to sell goods quickly. Use the proceeds to buy more goods to be similarly treated. Keep up this process. Never mind the per cent of profit.

That per cent of profit is a rock that has wrecked many a merchant. Of course, he who ties up his capital for six months or a year in a "complete" one-line stock must have a big per cent. The man with a representative many-line stock can let per cents take care of themselves. Low prices sell out a line for him again and again. Each time his per cent may be small. But the several profits together make him richer at the end of the year than his one-line neighbor who may have had big per cents but not so many profits.

* * *

WHAT $600 WILL DO IN THE DEPARTMENT STORE BUSINESS—See final pages of this book for a representative $600 stock of department store goods. We are often asked by merchants just starting in business to pick for them, and this assortment represents just such a variety as we advise for the purpose. It has been very carefully prepared to give the widest possible variety with the smallest capital investment in each item.

From this assortment we have eliminated every slow moving article—it is boiled down to a net lot of practical, everyday sellers, so that this $600 worth of goods can be turned over two or three times as fast as the usual one line stock.

Whether you intend to invest more or less than $600 you will find this assortment helpful. If, for instance, you wish to invest only $400 you can reduce the total either by running through every department and striking out items here and there, or you can omit entire lines if you choose. If, however, you desire to invest say $1,000, then you can take this assortment as a basis, running through our catalogue, and adding additional items in every line you can increase the quantities of individual items.

The assortment is offered entirely for your benefit, and may be varied to suit the requirements of your particular case. The only limitation is that of course we cannot sell less of an item than the quantity stated in catalogue as in package.

The right plan to pursue in running a department store is to buy every article in small quantity but often. The smaller the investment in each item the larger the variety you can show with a given number of dollars. The best advertising you can do (after giving bargains) is to have something always on the road so that you can be opening up every day or so, something new, fresh and attractive.

In the last twenty years we have started into business ...nt store merchants. We therefo... ...nd...

Boxed Tumblers.

All put up in spaced display boxes of 1 doz. each.

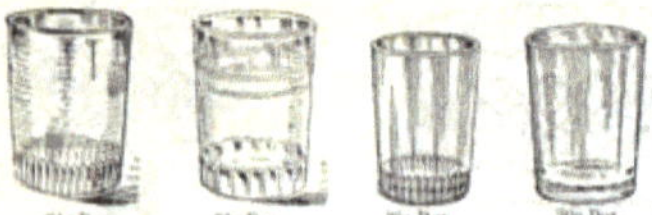

24c Doz. 21c Doz. 28c Doz. 30c Doz.

Doz.

420, "Leader" Boxed Tumbler—Full size, pure crystal............(6 doz. or more, 23c) $0 24

"Mold Banded" Tumbler—Double band. (6 doz., 26c) 27

421, "Rich and Strong" Tumbler—.......(6 doz., 27c) 28

422, Heavy Bottom Tumbler—Smooth bottom, nearly ½-inch thick, almost indestructible.......(6 doz., 29c) 30

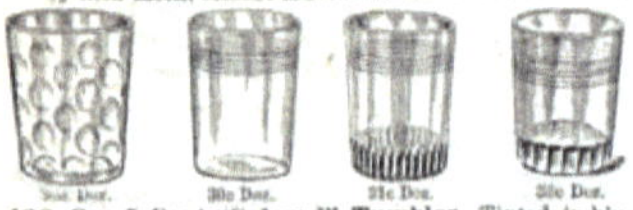

30c Doz. 30c Doz. 31c Doz. 33c Doz.

428, Our 5-Cent "Colored" Tumbler—Tinted in blue and amber, full size. 1 doz. in box.......(6 doz., 29c) 30

423, Our "Four-Band" Tumbler—Rich, plain pattern with a 4-band hand engraving. 1 doz. in box. (6doz., 29c) 30

424, "Flute Banded" Tumbler—Engraved (6 doz., 30c) 31

425, "Banded Service" Tumbler—A strong, handsome table tumbler with hair line engraved band.......... (6 doz., 31½c) 33

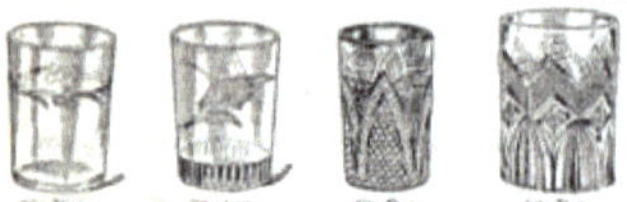

38c Doz. 38c Doz. 42c Doz. 42c Doz.

426, "Floral Engraved" Tumbler—Full size, pretty engraving........................(6 doz. or more, 36½c) 38

427, "Fern Engraved" Tumbler—Full size, fluted bottom, fern engraved decoration..(6 doz. or more, 36½c) 38

431 "Rich and Rare" Small Table Tumbler—Imitation rich cut glass.........(6 doz. or more, 41c) 42

430, "Cut Pattern" 5-Cent Tumbler—Another imitation cut, very heavy.................................. 42

Blown Glass Tumblers.

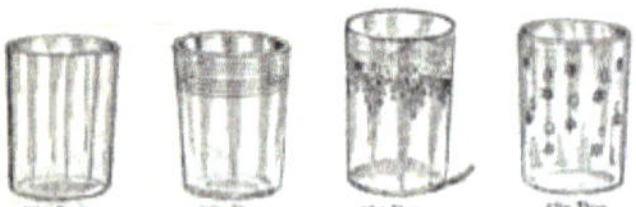

30c Doz. 36c Doz. 41c Doz. 43c Doz.

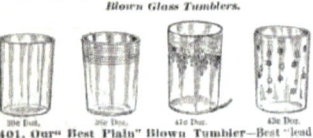

401, Our "Best Plain" Blown Tumbler—Best "lead glass," shapely and staple. Full size, 9-oz. (6 doz., 29c) 30

402, Our "Banded" Blown Tumbler—Genuine engraved band, best lead glass......(6 doz. or more, 35c) 36

407, "Leader Engraved" Blown Tumbler—Lead glass, 3 floral engravings. 1 doz. of pattern in box. (6 doz., 40c) 41

404, Our "Star Engraved" Blown Tumbler—Superfine lead glass, star engraving............(6 doz., 42c) 43

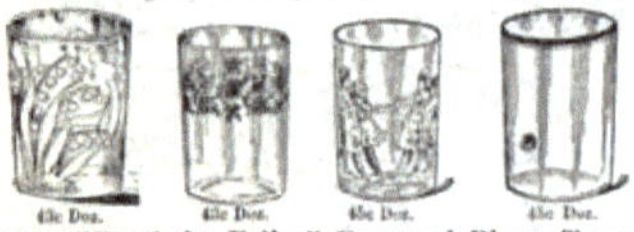

43c Doz. 43c Doz. 45c Doz. 45c Doz.

405, "Lily of the Valley" Engraved Blown Tumbler—Lead glass. Lily of Valley engraved. (6 doz., 42c) 43

406, Our "Floral Engraved" Blown Tumbler—Pure lead glass, richly engraved.......(6 doz. or more, 42c) 43

413, Enamel Etched "Scene" Tumbler—Designs from famous paintings on lead glass blown 9-ounce tumblers. 45

414, "Gold Edge" Tumbler—Lead blown glass, gold edge, 9-oz.. 45

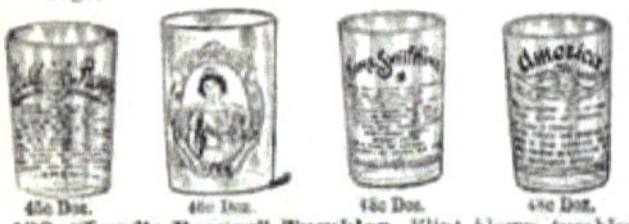

45c Doz. 46c Doz. 48c Doz. 48c Doz.

409, "Lord's Prayer" Tumbler—Flint blown tumbler with the Lord's Prayer etched on side.....(6 doz., 44c) 45

412, "Beautiful Women" Tumblers—Blown lead glass, etched figures. 2 each of 6 actresses in box. (6 doz., 45c) 46

410, "Home Sweet Home" Tumbler—Flint glass, one verse of "Home Sweet Home" etched on side...... 48

411, "Patriotic" Tumbler Assortment—Flint. One verse each "Star Spangled Banner," "Yankee Doodle" and "America', etched on side. 1 doz. in box.......... 48

NIGHT LAMPS AND CHIMNEY.

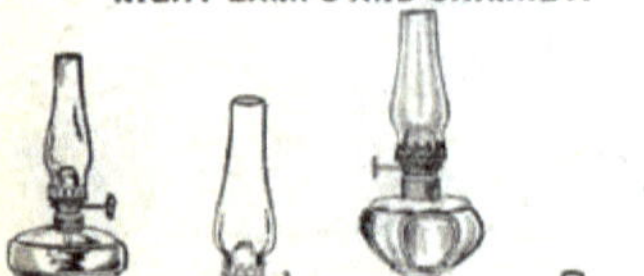

300, 89c Doz. 301, 95c Doz. 302, $1.20. 12c Doz.

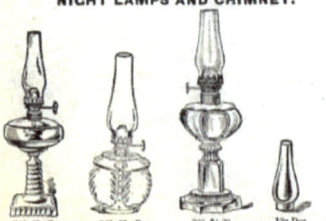

Doz.

300, "Little Handy" Lamp—Body, chimney, burner and wick. Purest crystal. ¼ doz. in box............ $0 89

301, "Little Puck" Lamp—*In opal and turquoise.* Burner, chimney, wick. ½ doz. in box.................. 95

302, Our "Pretty" Night Lamp—9½-inch. Burner, chimney, wick and patent clinch collar. ½ doz. in box. 1 20

Night Lamp Chimney—Fits ordinary night lamps...... 12

"Emerald Green" Glass Offerings.

The latest fad in bric-a-brac is this new green.

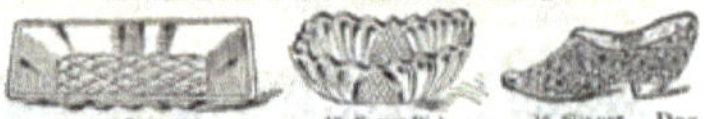

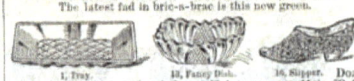

1, Tray. 13, Fancy Dish. 16, Slipper.

Doz.

1, Tray—4½x6 in. 1 doz. in box. (6 doz. or more, 41c). $0 42

13, Fancy Dish—Lines of beauty. 4½-inch. 1 doz. in box...............................(6 doz. or more, 41c) 42

16, Slipper—A decorative and useful piece. 1 doz. in box. (6 doz. or more, 41c) 42

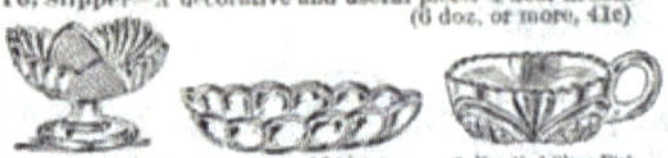

15, High Footed Dish. 14, Leaf Dish. 2, Handled Olive Dish.

15, High Footed Dish—For jelly or preserves. Top 3½ inches. 1 doz. in box............(6 doz. or more, 41c) 42

14, Leaf Dish—6 inches long. 1 doz. in box. (6 doz., 41c) 42

2, Handled Olive Dish—A choice pattern. 1 doz. in box. (6 doz. or more, 41c) 42

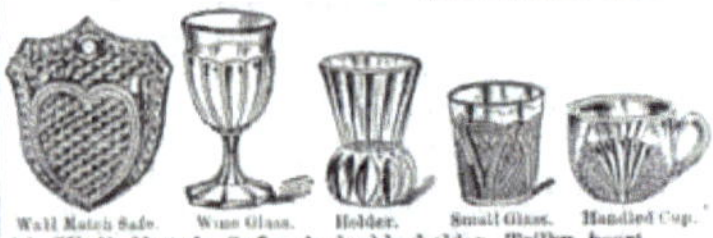

Wall Match Safe. Wine Glass. Holder. Small Glass. Handled Cup.

12, Wall Match Safe—A double holder, Trilby heart shape. 1 doz. in box..............(6 doz. or more, 41c) 42

4, Wine Glass—Neat for table decoration.... (6 doz., 41c) 42

7, Holder—Very pretty design. 1 doz. in box. (6 doz., 41c) 42

10, Small Glass—Size about 3½ oz. 1 doz. in box....... (6 doz. or more, 41c) 42

8, Handled Cup—For table or mantel. 1 doz. in box.... (6 doz. or more, 41c) 42

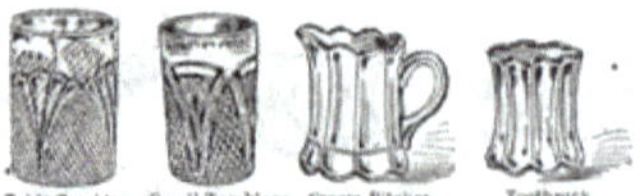

Table Tumbler. Small Tumbler. Cream Pitcher. Toothpick.

3, Table Tumbler—A full size. 1 doz. in box. (6 doz., 41c) 42

11, Small Table Tumbler—Imitation cut. 1 doz. in box (6 doz. or more, 41c) 42

6, Cream Pitcher—Heavy panel effect. 1 doz. in box.... (6 doz. or more, 41c) 42

5, Toothpick—Heavy panel effect. 1 doz. in box......... (6 doz. or more, 41c) 42

"Ruby Stained" Specialties.

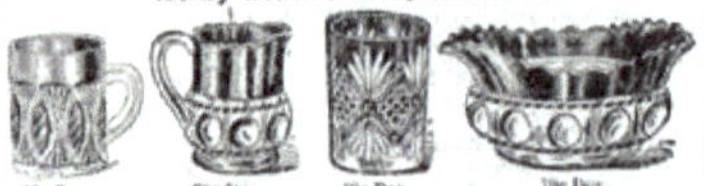

77c Doz. 78c Doz. 80c Doz. 79c Doz.

279, Mug—Gold ruby stain..........(4 doz. or more, 75c) 77

181, Cream Pitcher— ....(4 doz. or more, 76c) 78

429, Table Tumbler—...............(4 doz. or more, 78c) 80

154, Scalloped Dish—Scalloped and flared dish for preserves, bonbons, etc..............(4 doz. or more, 77c) 79

"Green and Gold" Art Ware.

The latest and richest combination. It is the "talk of the town" wherever shown. N.B.—The gold used on this line of goods is absolutely pure.

26, Olive Dish. 27, Round Plate. 29

26, Olive Dish—A 5¼-inch dish, exquisite pattern. 1 doz. in box.......................(4 doz. or more, 78c) 80

27, Round Plate—6¼ inches in diameter, rich gold edging. 1 doz. in box.................(4 doz. or more, 78c) 80

29, Toothpick Holder—A regular little nugget. 1 doz. in box..................................(4 doz. or more, 78c) 80

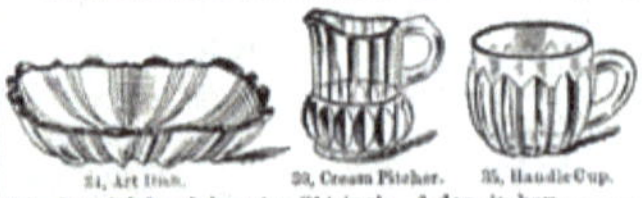

34, Art Dish. 30, Cream Pitcher. 35, Handle Cup.

34, Art Dish—A beauty, 6¼-inch. 1 doz. in box........ (4 doz. or more, 78c) 80

30, Cream Pitcher—Very attractive article. Rim of gold.................................(4 doz. or more, 78c) 80

35, Handle Cup—Gold edge and beading. 1 doz. in box. (4 doz. or more, 78c) 80

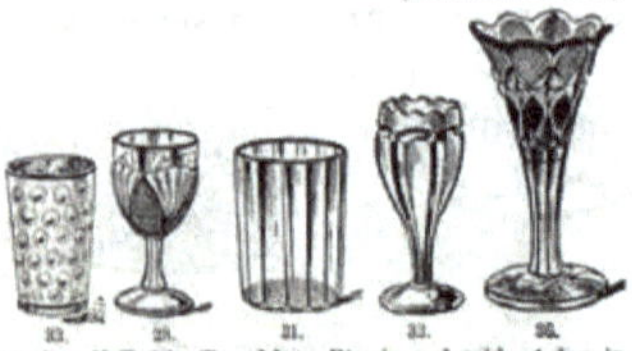

33. 28. 31. 32. 36.

33, Small Table Tumbler—Rim in real gold. 1 doz. in box...............................(4 doz. or more, 78c) 80

28, Wine Glass—Very beautiful effects. 1 doz. in box. (4 doz. or more, 78c) 80

31, Table Tumbler—A choice pattern, edged in gold. 1 doz. in box.......................(4 doz. or more, 78c) 80

32, Flower Vase—5½-inch, gold rim and foot. 1 doz. in box...............................(4 doz. or more, 78c) 80

36, Cut Pattern Vase—Top and foot edged with gold. 1 doz. in box.......................(4 doz. or more, 78) 80

2 PER CENT 10 DAYS—

We never charge for cartage, and for cases only on Crockery and Glassware.

"Crystal and Gold" Glassware.

The gold used on these articles is positively genuine. Send for sample boxes of these and you'll sell quantities.

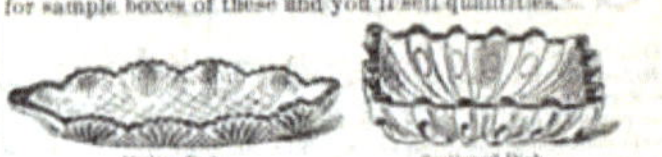

Utility Dish. Scalloped Dish.

Doz.

55, Utility Dish—8-inch including handle, wide gold scalloped edge.. $0 80

58, Scalloped Dish—Almost square.......................... 80

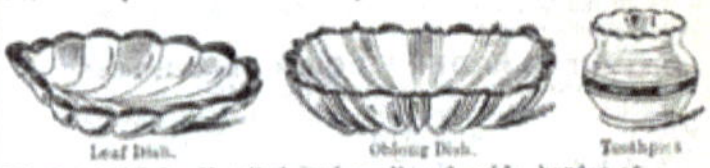

Leaf Dish. Oblong Dish. Toothpick.

54, Leaf Dish—Handled and scalloped, wide border of real gold, 4x5½ inches.................................... 80

61, Rustic Oblong Dish—Gold edge.......................... 80

52, Toothpick—Gold band and edge.......................... 80

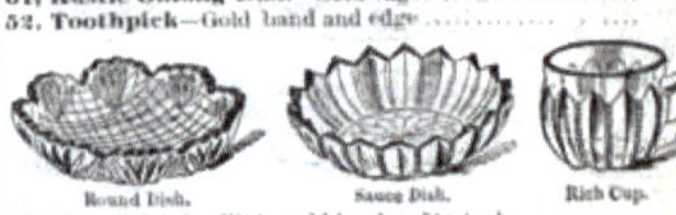

Round Dish. Sauce Dish. Rich Cup.

57, Round Dish—Wide gold border, 5¼-inch 80

59, Sauce Dish—Gold beaded decoration and gold edge, 5-inch.. 80

53, Rich Cup—Gold rim and beads.......................... 80

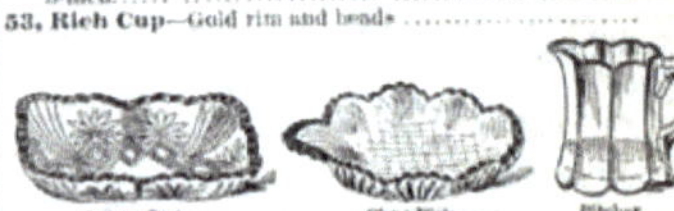

Oblong Dish. Olive Dish. Pitcher.

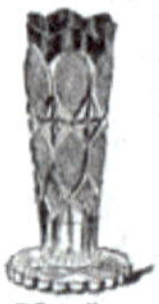

Tiffany Vase.

56, Oblong Dish—Rolled up edges, 6¼-inch, gold on edges.................................... 80

60, Olive Dish—5¼-inch, gold edges...... 80

51, Footed Pitcher—Gold on edge....... 80

50, Tiffany Vase—Like real cut glass. 6 inches high. Band of gold on edge. ½ doz. in box ......(4 doz. or more, 78c) 80

Get out your last bill from the other house and see how much saving these prices mean.

BRASS AND NICKEL LAMPS.

No charge for packages on the following.

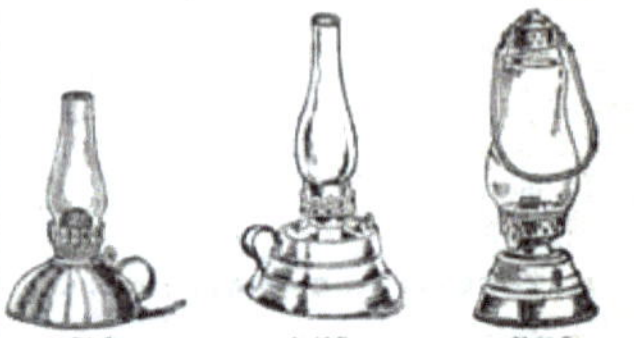

98c Doz. $1.25 Doz. $1.90 Doz.

Doz.

Full Nickel Plated Night Lamp—Nickeled, with handle, burner to match, complete with chimney and wick. 1 doz. in box...................................... $0 98

Genuine Brass Night Lamp—Lacquered. 7-inch, body 4-inch. Burner, wick and large chimney. ½ doz. in box.. 1 25

"Klondike" Handy Lantern, Brass—A perfect lantern in every detail, swinging handle, complete with wick and glass globe; height, not including handle, 7¼ inches. All brass ventilated top. ½ doz. in box (no charge for box)...................................... 1 90

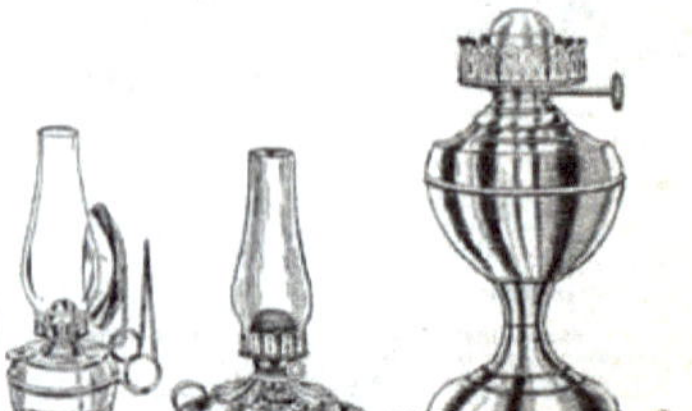

$2.00 Doz. $2.10 Doz. 48c Each.

"Bridgeport" Nickel All-Night Lamp—Full nickel plated throughout. Adjustable reflector, burner, chimney, finger holder and hanger. 8-inch. 1 doz. in box. 2 00

"Wide Base" Night Lamp—Bright lacquered brass, outside filler, base 4½-inch. Burner, wick, chimney, ½ doz. in box.. 2 10

Nickel Table or Sewing Lamp Each.—Full nickel plated, large No. 2 nickel plated burner, 10-inch without chimney, outside filling device, extension wick raiser. Each in pasteboard box....................Each 48

Table or Sewing Lamp—As above, 7-inch nickel plated ring for shade.......................................Each. 55

Thousands of America's best merchant's are Butler Brothers' best customers. It is worth your while to spend a few minutes studying the reason why. You won't have to look long. Inferior merchandise is cheap at any price. Remember always that our quotations are on goods of dependable grade.

GLASSWARE.

Our plan of selling Glassware in "assorted packages" has revolutionized the glass business. Why buy a barrel of each item when you can get six or twelve items in a package at equally low prices per dozen? No overstocking—no money needlessly tied up—goods sold almost as soon as in—and something fresh always on the way.

We charge 35 cents each for all glassware packages (though some of them *cost us* upwards of 60 cents each), except cask and tierce packages, and chimney boxes, which latter are charged at 30, 40 and 50 cents. We charge for no packages aside from glassware and crockery.

Our "LEADER" 3-Cent Assortment.

Study these 3-cent possibilities!—While we call these "3-cent goods," yet we are willing to put this assortment against any of the 5-cent assortments of our competing friends.

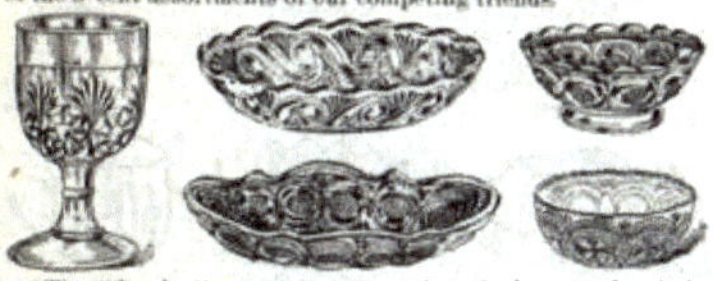

The "Lender" assortment comprises **2 doz. each** of the following:

6¼-inch Round Plate.
4½-inch Footed Dish.
Brilliant Pattern Tumbler.
Wine Glass.
6-inch Round Dish.
Sauce or Preserve Dish.
Goblet.
7-inch Scroll Dish.
Handled Mug.
8-inch Table Dish.

20 doz. to bbl.
Sold only by pkg.
Bbl. 35c.
Price 25c Doz.

Our "INVINCIBLE" Assortment.

Cast your eye over these sizes, remembering that the quality is first-class. All finished ware.

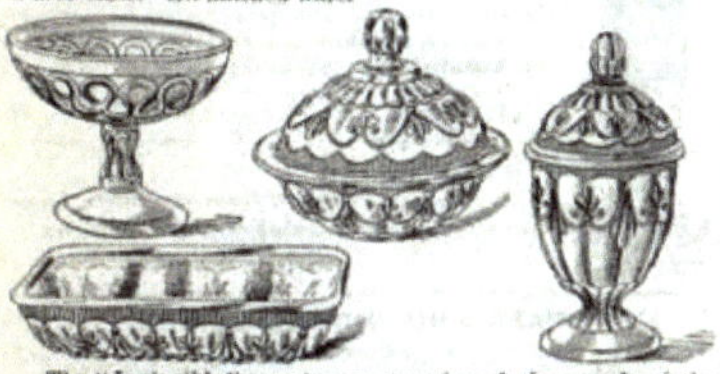

The "Invincible" assortment comprises **1 doz. each** of the following:

6¼-Inch Footed Deep Dish.
Heavy Oblong Dish—5¼x8 inches.
Large Butter Dish and Cover—6¼-inch.
Bent Up Sauce Salver—6-inch.
Bread and Cake Plate—Full 8-inch.
Deep and Heavy Dish—7-inch.
High Footed Bowl—5-inch, extra deep
Quart Water or Milk Pitcher.
High Sugar Bowl and Cover.
High Footed Dish—5¼-inch.

10 doz. to pkg.
Sold only by pkg.
Tierce, 60c.
Price, 40c Doz.

Our "MATCHLESS" 5-Cent Assortment.

A brand new assortment. All pieces fire polished and of the most attractive of new patterns.

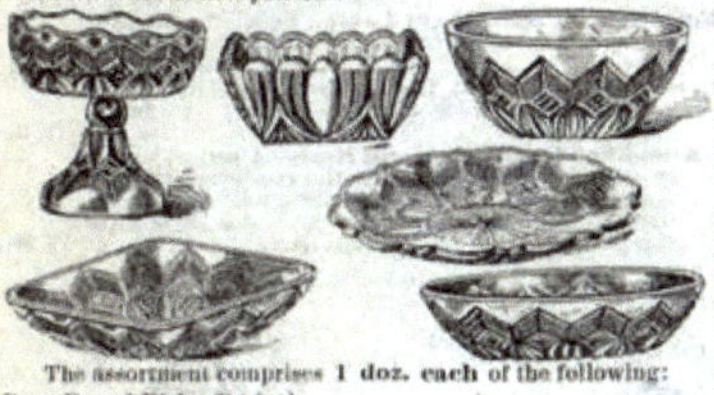

The assortment comprises **1 doz. each** of the following:

Deep Round Dish—6¼-inch.
7½-Inch Oval Dish—Large and beautiful.
7¼x5¼ Deep Square Dish.
8-Inch Diamond Square Dish.
8-Inch Round Bread Plate.
High Footed 5-Inch Dish.
Handled Olive Dish—5¼ inches.
7¼x6¼ Platter—Flared up edges.
6-Inch High Footed Bowl.
9-Inch Kite Shaped Dish—Handled.
5¼ Extra Deep Extra Heavy Dish.
6¼-Inch Square Dishes—Turned up edges.

12 doz. in tierce.
Sold only by pkg.
Tierce, 50c.
Price 40c Doz.

Our "CONQUEST" 10-Cent Assortment.

Six large pieces—Six bright pieces—Six sellers.

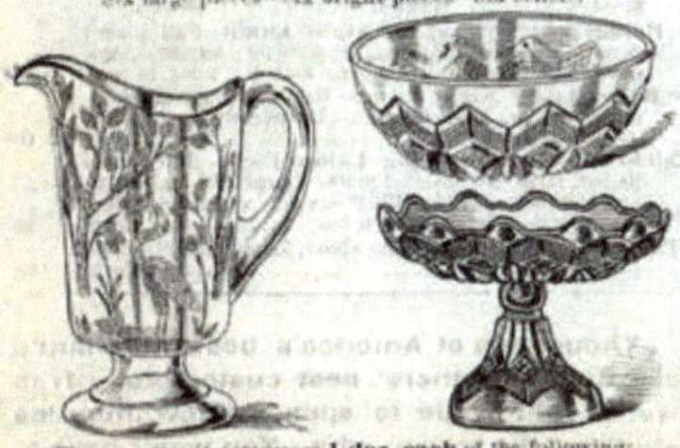

The assortment comprises **1 doz. each** of the following:

Half Gallon Pitcher—Stork pattern.
8-Inch Large Dish—8x4-inch, circle pattern dish.
10-Inch Bread or Cake Plates.
Large Flanged Butter Dishes and Covers.
High Fruit Bowl—7½-inch.
8½-Inch Deep Round Dishes.

6 doz. in bbl.
Sold only by bbl.
Barrel 35c.
Price, 79c Doz.

Our "STARTLING" 5-Cent Assortment.

A 36-cent assortment, comparing favorably with the 42-cent ones of our followers.

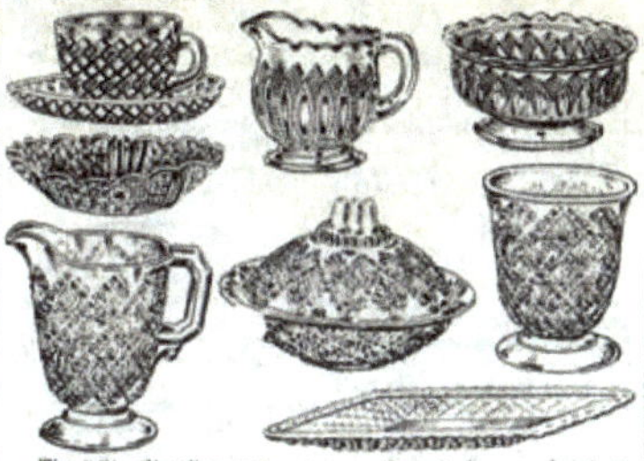

The "Startling" assortment comprises **1 doz. each** of the following:

Sugar Bowl and Cover.
Milk Pitcher—matches sugar bowl.
Butter Dish and Cover.
Spoon Holder.
High-Footed Jelly Dish.
7-inch Square Diamond Pattern Plates.
Handled Cup and Saucer.
Large handled Cream Pitcher.
6½-inch Heart Shaped Dish.
Footed Comport.
Rich Table Tumbler.
6-inch Clover Leaf Dish.

12 doz. to pkg.
Sold only by pkg.
Tierce, 35c.
Price 36c Doz.

Our "BON TON" 5-Cent Assortment.

A rich opportunity for 1898. All extra heavy polished ware.

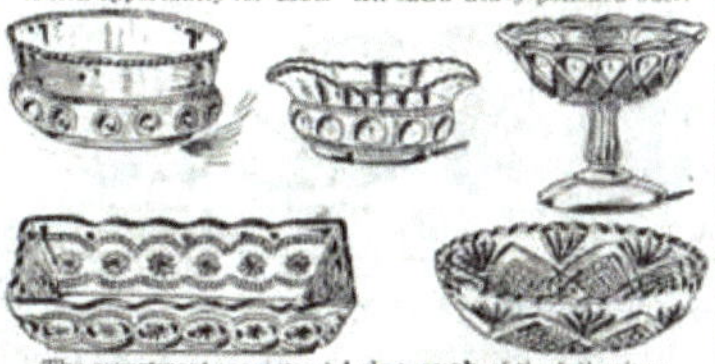

The assortment consists of **1 doz. each** of the following:

6¼-Inch Round Deep Plate.
Handled Olive or Bon Bon Dish.
Bell Body Crimped Top Dish—Extra deep. 5-inch.
6¼-Inch Round Deep Dish.
High Footed Jelly Dish—5¼-inch.
7¼-Inch Oval Dish.
Extra Heavy Table Tumbler.
Flaring Edge Fancy Dish—5-inch
Handled Cup and Sauser.
7¾-Inch Clover Shape Dish.
7¾-Inch Heavy Deep Plate.
8-Inch Oblong Deep Dish.

12 doz. in pkg.
Sold only by pkg.
Tierce 35c.
Price, 39c Doz.

Our "CHAMPION" 5-Cent Assortment.

These are *not* "5-cent goods"—*but* goods *worth 10c, 15c* and 20c, which we here offer for a possible "5-cent sale." Look at these sizes, remembering that every piece in the lot is fire polished. These pieces are all of one pattern.

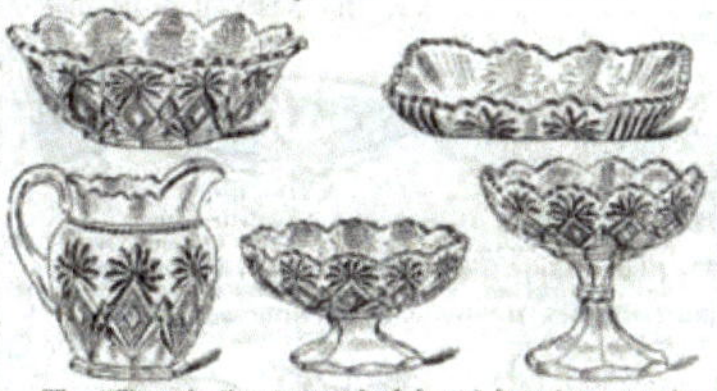

The "Champion" assortment of 5-cent bargains comprises **1 doz. each** of the following:

7½-inch Scalloped Edge Dish.
7¾ " Olive or General Table Dish.
6 " Bent-up Edge Dish.
Large and Heavy Sugar and Cover.
Large Swell Center Milk Pitcher.
5¼-inch High Footed Bowl.
5½-inch Double Handle Bonbon Dish.
7x4½-inch Oblong Dish.
Scalloped Footed Dish.
7¾-inch Scalloped Plate.

10 doz. in pkg.
Sold only by pkg.
Tierce, 60c.
Price, 40c Doz.

Our "EXHIBITION" 10c Assortment.

There is not a piece in the lot but is fire polished and superbly finished. Order a sample package.

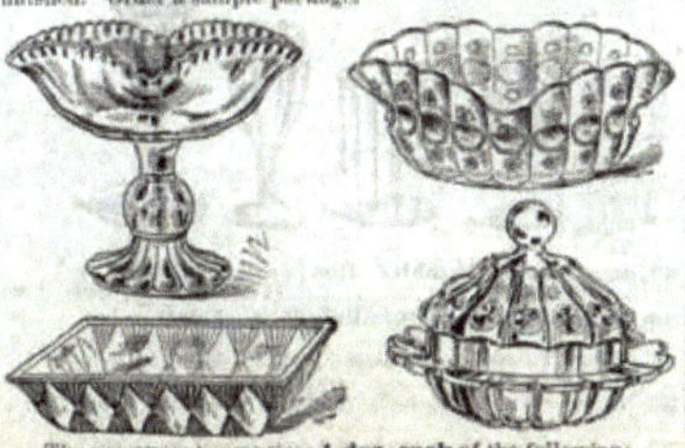

The assortment comprises **1 doz. each** of the following:

Half-gallon Water Pitchers—Full size.
6½-Inch High Footed Bowls—Scalloped.
7½-Inch Footed Dishes—Round, scalloped.
Large Flanged Butters and Covers.
8-Inch Deep Dishes.
8¼-inch Oblong Dishes—New, serviceable.

6 doz. to pkg
Sold only by pkg.
Barrel 35c.
Price, 80c Doz.

Our "VICTORY" 10-Cent Cask Assortment.

Remember that these pieces are all finished fire polished ware.

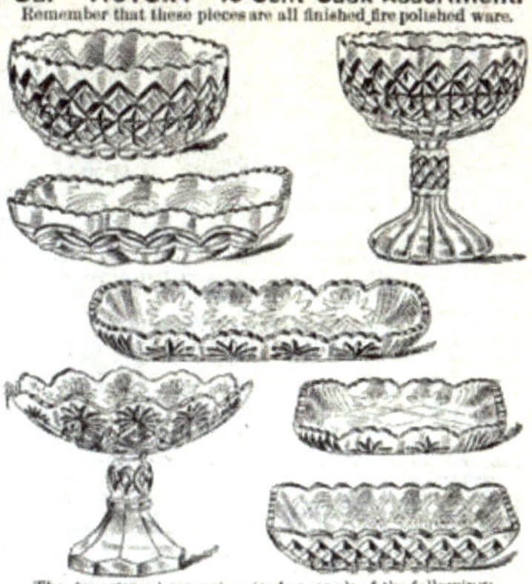

The Assortment comprises ½ **doz. each** of the following:

8½-Inch Round Deep Scalloped Dish—Extra deep.
7½-Inch High Footed Scalloped Bowl.
7-Inch Square Rolled Up Edge Dish.
8½-Inch High Footed Flared Bowl.
9-Inch Slender Vase.
Square Bent-in Dish—Measuring 7x7.
11-Inch Celery Tray.
9¼-Inch Salver or Cake Stand.
Vinegar or Oil Pitcher with Stopper.
7½-Inch Scalloped Deep Dish.
Extra Heavy Sugar Bowl and Cover.
Extra Deep and Extra Heavy Dish—7-inch.
8x6 Utility Dish.
Extra Heavy Butter Dish and Cover.
Deep High Footed Bowl—6-inch.
10-Inch Bread Plate—Heavy pattern.
High Footed Dish—5½-inch high.
9-Inch Oval Utility Dish.
Water Pitcher.
9x6¾ Deep Dish.

10 doz. to pkg.
Sold only by pkg.
Cask 90c.
Price, 74c Doz.

Our "ALL STARS" 10-Cent Assortment.

All of these pieces are of the same pattern.

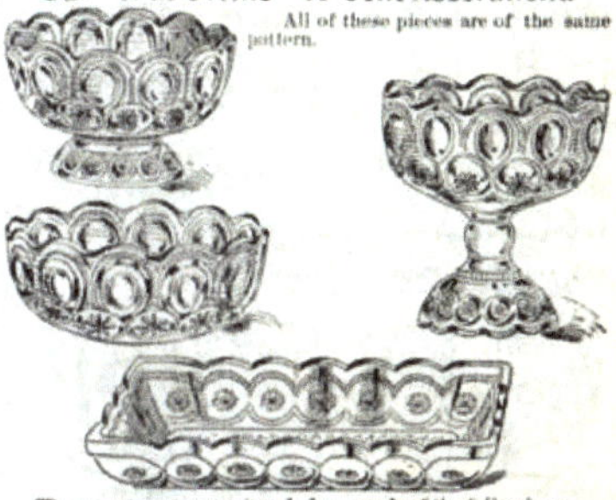

The assortment comprises **1 doz. each** of the following:

High Footed Bowl—6¼-inch.
11-Inch Bread Tray.
7¼-Inch Deep Footed Dish.
7-Inch Extra Deep Dish.
6¼-Inch Footed Extra Deep Dish.
High Celery Dish—6¼-inch.

6 doz. in pkg.
Sold only by pkg.
Tierce 35c.
Price, 80c Doz.

Miscellaneous Assortment of ART GLASS.

The nearest approach to real cut glass ever produced.

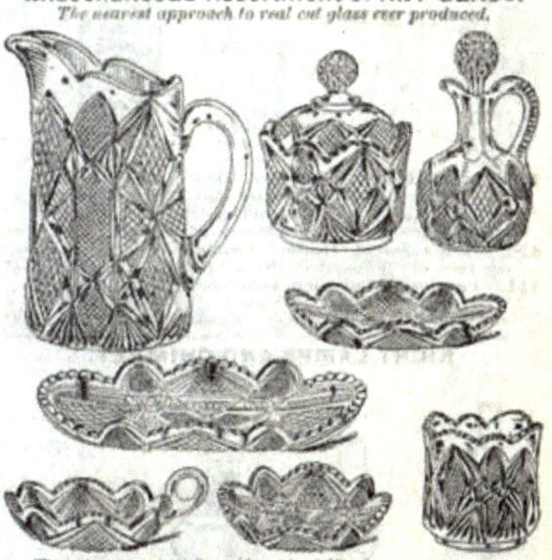

The "Assortment" Comprises the following:

2	only	Four-Piece Table Sets	$0 33	$0 66
2	"	Half Gallon Tankard Pitchers	30	60
2	"	8½-inch Extra Deep Round Dish	17	34
2	"	Glass Lip Syrup Pitchers—Silver plated top	17	34
2	"	Oil or Vinegar Pitchers—Ground stoppers	15	30
2	"	10½-inch Celery Trays	9	18
¼	dozen	Handled Olive Dishes	80	20
1	"	Goblets		48
1	"	Tumblers		45
1	"	Wines		33
2	"	4½-inch Round Deep Nappies	33	66
1	"	7-inch Pickle Dishes		44
1	"	5½-inch Olive Dishes		45

Sold only by pkg. (Bbl. 35c.) **Total for Assortment, $5.43**

We Can Save You Enough on Every Barrel of Glassware to MORE THAN PAY THE FREIGHT.

Our "MONSTER" 10-Cent Cask Assortment.

We refer to these as "10-cent goods." They are really 25-cent articles.

The assortment comprises ⅓ doz. each of the following:
8-inch Footed Table Dish.
High Footed Sugar Bowl and Cover.
High Celery Dish.
10¼-inch Bread Plate.
Handled Syrup Pitcher.
Half Gallon Water Pitcher.
Heavy Butter Dish and Cover.
High Bowl and Cover—Full 6-inch.
Extra Deep Footed Dish—7½-inch.
Handled Butter and Cover—Full 6-inch.
8-inch Flower Vase.
8   "   Sauce or Berry Dish.
8½ "   Footed Dish.
8   "   Deep Dish—Nearly 4 inches deep.
Oil or Vinegar Bottle with Stopper.
New Quart Water or Milk Pitcher.
11-inch long Celery Dish.
Heavy Handle Olive Dish—6-inch.
7-inch High Footed Bowl.
9   "   Cake Salver.

10 doz. in pkg.
Sold only by pkg.
Cask, 90c.

Price, 74c Doz.

Our "HURRAH" Dime Assortment.

Actually worth 25 per cent more at the factory than we are charging for it in New York and Chicago.

The assortment comprises 1 doz. each of the following:
Full Half-Gallon Pitchers.
9-Inch Salvers.
Mammoth Fluted Dishes—10¾x8 inches.
9¼-Inch High Footed Bowls.
8½-Inch Deep Round Dishes—Scalloped.
9-Inch Oblong Dishes—6 inches wide.

6 doz. to pkg.
Sold only by pkg.
Barrel 35c.

Price, 82c Doz.

Our "HALF DOLLAR" Big Variety Assortment.

These six pieces of one pattern are so large, so heavy and so rich that we will not attempt to describe their beautiful proportions, but instead hope that you may order a sample package.

The assortment comprises ½ doz. each of the following:
Extra Large Water Pitcher.
Large and Deep Fruit Bowl—9 inches high.
Extra Large Cracker Jar and Cover—9 inches high.
Mammoth Bowl an 1 Cover—12½ in. high.
Water Bottle and Tumbler.
Extra Deep Covered Footed Bowl—8 inches wide at base.

1 doz. to pkg.
Sold only by bbl.
(Bbl. 35c.)

Price, $3.25 Doz.

"RICH AND RARE" Assortment of 5 and 10 Cent Ware.

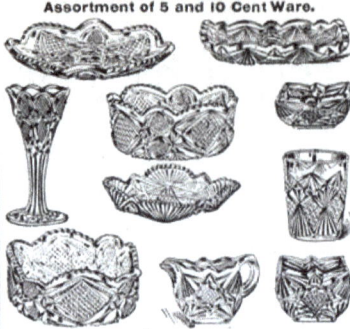

The assortment comprises:
1 doz. 6-Inch Fancy Olive Dish.
1   "   3½-inch Extra Deep Bonbon.
1   "   7-inch Round Plates.
1   "   Beautiful Table Tumbler.
1   "   6-Inch Diamond Flower Vase.
½ "   6-inch Square Deep Dish—Fancy edge.
½ "   8-inch Rolled Up Edge Plate.
½ "   Square   Pattern Heavy Cream Pitcher.
½ "   Square Shape Heavy Open Sugar.
½ "   7½-inch Oblong Heavy Dish.
½ "   9½-inch Round Extra Deep and Heavy Dish.

8 doz. to pkg.
Sold only by pkg.
Total for pkg.
(Bbl. 35c.)   **$4.24**

Summary of above: 5 doz. 5c goods at 35c, $1.90; 3 doz. 10c goods at 78c, $2.34.

Our "PRIZE WINNER" 25-Cent Assortment.

Large and splendid, high-class crystal glass. All of one pattern. The assortment comprises 1-2 doz. each of the following:
Square Deep Scalloped Dishes—9¼-inch.
High Tankard Water Pitchers.
7-In. Deep Dishes with High Covers
8¼-In. High Footed Dishes—Extra deep, scalloped.

2 doz. in pkg   Sold only by pkg
(Barrel 35c.)   **Price, $1.65 Doz.**

Our "WELCOME" 25-Cent Assortment.

The "Welcome" Assortment is made up of four of the richest of the art glass productions of 1898. Our customers will make no mistake in ordering a barrel in order to sample these popular, pleasing pieces.

The "Welcome" 25c Assortment Comprises 1-2 doz. each of the following:
Stuck Handle Water Pitcher.
9-Inch Deep Round Dish.
7-Inch Extra Deep Covered Dish.
8¼-In. High Footed Scalloped Dish.

2 doz. in pkg.   Sold only by pkg.   (Bbl. 35c)   **Price, $1.75 Doz.**

Our "ELITE" 25-Cent Assortment.

If You Want Big Pieces, and Bright Pieces, and Beautiful Pieces, Here They Are!

In this assortment quality has not given way to size, although one never before saw such large pieces per dozen in a "quarter" assortment.

The "Elite" Comprises 1-2 doz. each of the following:
9-Inch High Footed Fruit Bowls.
Large Tankard Water Pitchers.
10-Inch Heavy Footed Dishes.
10½-Inch High Footed Salvers.

2 doz. to pkg.   Sold only by pkg. (Barrel 35c.)   **Price, $1.78 Doz.**

Our "WAR CRY" 25-Cent Assortment.

Just note the sizes of these mammoth pieces. All pieces in same pattern as the one shown, all highly finished ware.

The assortment comprises 1-2 doz. each of the following:
Tankard Water Pitchers — Large and beautiful.
7-Inch High Footed Bowls, Covered—11½ inches high.
8½-Inch Deep Dishes and Covers—Extra large.
9-Inch High Footed Bowls—Splendid fruit dish.

2 doz. in pkg.   Sold only by pkg.
(Barrel 35c.)   **Price, $1.80 Doz.**

WE LEAD IN GLASSWARE.

Our "assorted package" plan of selling Glassware is best for the retailer because he need carry but a small stock, and because he can buy at as little price per dozen as the large buyer gets at the factory in barrel lots of each item.

Merchants who have never tried our assortments sometimes say: "I do not like your assortments because some goods sell out faster than others." What if they do? If covers a tumbler or a goblet will sell faster than a butter dish or a spoon holder, and for that very reason we sell you tumblers and goblets in solid packages.

Outside of these two items the rest of the goods in our glass assortment are so nearly equal in selling qualities that he must be indeed a little resourceful merchant who cannot clean out the last half dozen pieces in a week.

The merchant who tries to buy glassware at the factory in package lots of each item is the man who has reason to wince because he finds himself overstocked on certain items.

Our "PRINCELY" Salver Assortment.

Two full finished 25c beauties of which we have room to show only one. The assortment comprises:
⅔ doz. Crimped Edge 10-inch Salvers.
⅔ doz. Scalloped Edge 10½-inch Salvers.
Total of 1⅓ doz. to bbl.
Sold only by bbl. (Bbl 35c.)   **Price, $1.65 Doz.**

Our 10-Cent "Butter Dish" Assortment.

Ware is of the highest grade, pieces good size and patterns genuinely beautiful. The assortment consists of 1 doz. each of 4 styles, making total of 4 doz. to pkg. Sold only by pkg. (Barrel 35c.)

Price, 79c Doz.

Patent Top Syrup Pitcher Asst.

With plated britannia top with patent hinge. Has an inside glass lip. No dripping possible. The assortment comprises 1 doz. fluted pattern and 1 doz. plain pattern, making a total of 2 doz. in pkg. Sold only by pkg. (Box 25c.)

Price, $1.30 Doz.

When you study these prices do you wonder that we are doing the glass business of America.

Our 1898 Sugar Bowl Asst.

Comprising 1 doz. each of four styles all as good as the one shown. They are of such size and shape as to appeal to the demands of all classes. Total of 4 doz. to pkg. Sold only by bbl. (Barrel 35c.)

Price, 79c Doz.

Our "1898 DIME SYRUP PITCHER" Assortment.

Fitted with the patent "tight top" collars. No cement, no plaster. The tops are of a very superior grade. Assortment consists of 1 doz. each of 5 patterns. Total of 5 doz. to pkg. Sold only by pkg. (Barrel 35c.)

Price, 89c Doz.

"Tall Molasses Pitcher" Assortment.

Patent nickel plated tops, clinch collars. No plaster—no cement—easily cleaned. Top cannot come off without breaking the pitcher.

The assortment comprises:
½ doz. plain.
½ doz. plain ribbed.
½ doz. fluted.
½ doz. diamond pattern.

2 doz. in case. Sold only by case. (Case 25c.)

Price, $1.25 Doz.

4-Piece Glass Table Sets.

Comprising sugar bowl, spoon holder, cream pitcher and butter dish, all in same pattern as the one piece illustrated. Sold only by barrel. Barrels 35c.

Mascot.   Electric.   Floral.
Per Set.
"Mascot"—Rich in quality, rich in pattern and rich in self-selling qualities. Put up 24 sets in pkg. $0 13
Our Footed "Electric"—A good handsome set of a most attractive and desirable pattern. Put up 24 sets in bbl. ... 13
Our "Floral"—A splendid, shapely, handsome, every day set. Put up 24 set in bbl. 13½

Diamond.   Two Pattern.   Jewel.
Our "Diamond"—A fire polished set of most desirable size and of richest pattern. Packed 24 setsin bbl. 14
"Two Pattern" Assortment—Both patterns of rich finished glass. The assortment comprises 6 sets of the Bon Ton and 6 sets of the Infanta. Total of 12 four-piece sets to pkg. 22
Our "Jewel" Assortment—Made up from two of the very best of table sets, the "Crown Jewel" and "Sussex" (illustration shows Sussex). Total of 12 sets to pkg. 39

"Variety" Assortment—Made up of 3 of the richest of patterns, all very heavy and full finished. Assorted, 4 sets Bright and Heavy; 4 sets Sparkling; 4 sets Radiant.
Variety.
Total of 12 sets to bbl. 25

These Useful Glass Items Are Always "Sellers"—They Know No Season.

Sauce or Berry Sets.

Each set comprising large dish (as illustrated), and 6 sauce dishes in pattern to match.

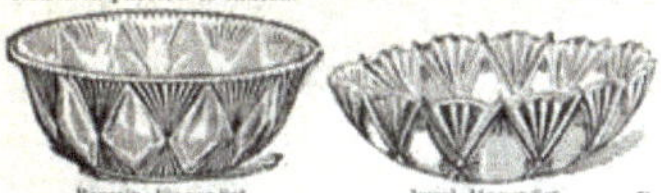

Bargain, 13c per Set. Jewel, 14c per Set.

Per Set.

Our "Bargain"—A rich and attractive pattern of pure glass. Each set comprises 1, 8-inch round deep berry dish, and 6, 4-inch nappies to match. 24 sets in bbl. Sold only by bbl. Bbl. 35c. $0 13

Our "Jewel" 8-inch berry dish of brilliant pattern and six 4¼-inch sauce dishes to match. Pattern, ware and size make it one of the best values we ever offered. 24 sets in bbl. Sold only by bbl. Barrel, 35c 14

Glass Pitchers and Water Sets.

Sold only by barrel. Barrels 35c.

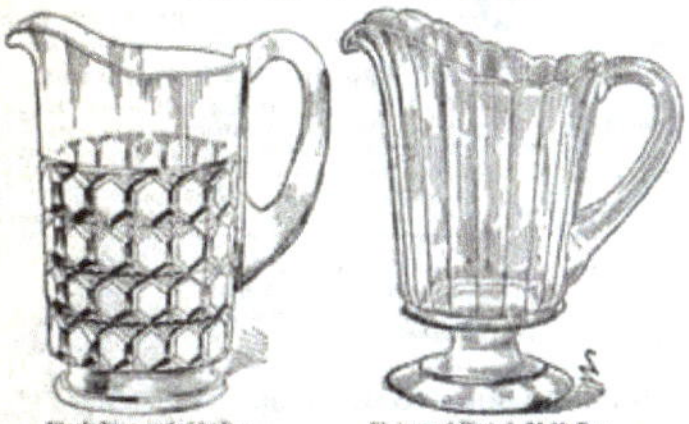

Block Diamond, 96c Doz. Plain and Fluted, $1.15 Doz.

Doz.

Our "Block Diamond" Half-Gallon Pitcher—Exceptional value. First quality. 2 doz. in bbl $0 96

"Plain and Fluted" Pitcher Assortment—1 doz. each of two patterns of full size ½ gallon pitchers, plain and fluted. 2 doz. in bbl.......... 1 15

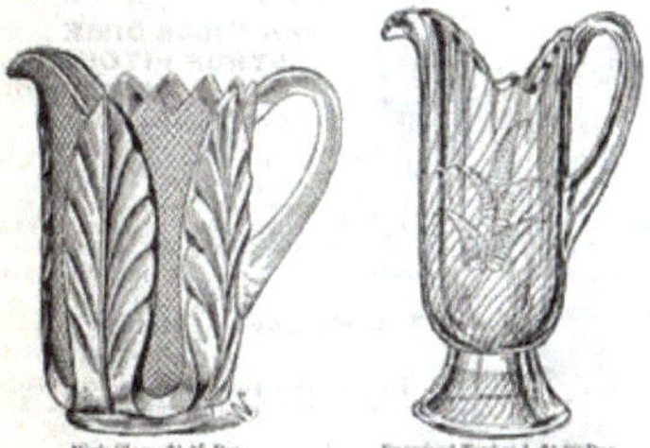

High Class, $1.55 Doz. Engraved Tankard, $1.90 Doz.

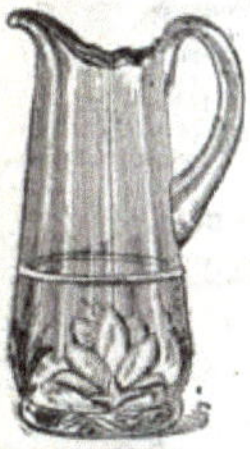

Tankard, $2.00 Doz.

Our "High Class" 25c Pitcher Assortment—A superior grade of goods. Large ½-gallon size, 2 patterns, one optic pattern, one "wide mouth" shape. 2 doz. to pkg.......... 1 55

"Engraved Tankard" Pitcher Assortment—*Think of it! A real engraved tankard jug to sell on "Friday from 1 to 4" at 25c each.* 1 doz. each of plain and flute patterns—both having fern engraving on two sides. Half gallon size. 2 doz. to bbl.......... 1 90

Our "Tankard" Pitcher Assortment—Finest finish and aristocratic shape. 1 doz. each of 2 patterns—one as per cut, the other about same shape but different style fancy bottom. Large ½ gallon size. 2 doz. to pkg.... 2 00

Glass Water Sets.

These are the freshest, choicest, most salable patterns produced in crystal, engraved and opalescent ware.

Per Set.

"Shapely" Tankard Water Set—While made in the newest of shapes and of finished glass, yet the price is low enough to make it attractive to all classes. The "Shapely" tankard water set consists of 1 tankard water pitcher and 6 tumblers to the set. Packed 12 sets in bbl. (*Bbl. 35c*).......... $0 30

"Emerald Green" Water Set—A luminous design, made up in this new 1898 color (emerald green). Each set comprises 1 high water pitcher and 6 tumblers to match. Total 12 sets in pkg. (*Bbl. 35c*).......... 30

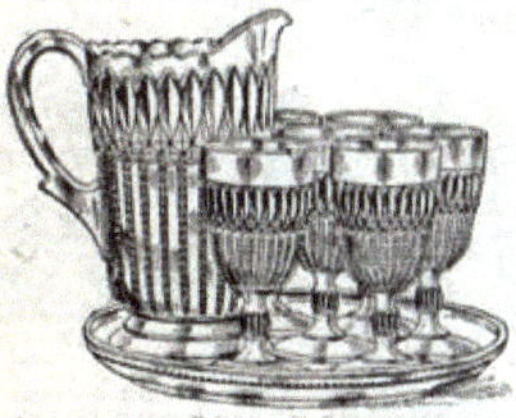

Enterprise, 33c Set.

"Enterprise" Water Set — Of brilliant and handsome pattern, 1 large ½-gallon pitcher, 1, 11½-inch glass tray and 6 full size goblets to match. 12 sets in bbl. 33

"Engraved" Blown Glass Water Set—In purest of blown lead glass, and embellished with rich and elaborate hand engravings in floral designs. Each set comprising 1 stuck handle half-gallon England blown pitcher and 6 blown engraved tumblers to match. Two sets each of 3 patterns. Making a total of 6 sets in pkg. (*Bbl. 35c*).......... 58

"Opalescent" Water Set—You know this indescribable opalescent dot ware. Therefore we need only to say that each set comprises: 1 water pitcher and 6 tumblers to match. They are packed 3 sets, each of flint opalescent, blue opalescent and ruby opalescent. Total of 9 sets to pkg. (*Bbl. 35c*).......... 67

Package Lots of Tumblers.

We have room to show but one style in each assortment. *Sold only by barrels. Barrels 35c.*

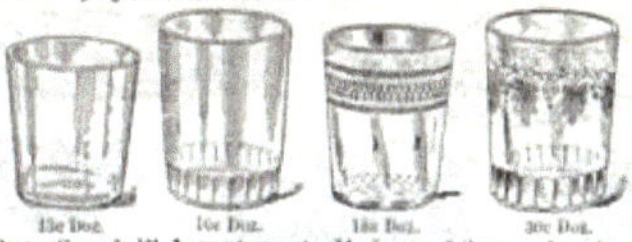

13c Doz. 16c Doz. 18c Doz. 30c Doz.

Doz.

Our "Special" Assortment—Made up of the regular size (large third pint) plain tumbler in three different bottoms as follows: "Fancy," "Plain" and "Horse Shoe." 8 doz. each of 3 styles, total 24 doz. to bbl.......... $0 13

Our 1898 "Tumbler Assortment"—Six splendid patterns of best crystal glass, standard size. 3 doz. each of 6 styles, total 18 doz. to bbl.......... 16

Our 1898 "Ribbed Band" Assortment—Full size, good quality. 4 doz. each of 4 different styles of bands. Total 16 doz. to bbl.......... 18

"Rich Engraved" Assortment—Four patterns of excellent engraving on four different popular shape tumblers. 4 doz. each of 4 styles, total 16 doz. to bbl.......... 30

Tall Lemonade Glass.

The Staple of the Staples.

Full size 12-oz. glass. The standard shape, heavy and first quality. Packed 6 doz. in case. (Case 30c.)

Price, 35c Doz.

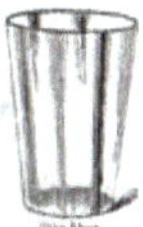

39c Doz.

"Lemonade and Soda" Blown Tumbler Assortment.

"Firsts" in full size pure lead glass.

3 doz. 12-oz. tall flared (bell top) glasses and 3 doz. 12-oz. taper glasses—making a total of 6 doz. to case.

(*Sold only by case. Case 30c.*)

Price, 39c Doz.

Goblets—*In Barrel Lots.*

Each style packed in barrel by itself. Barrels 35c.

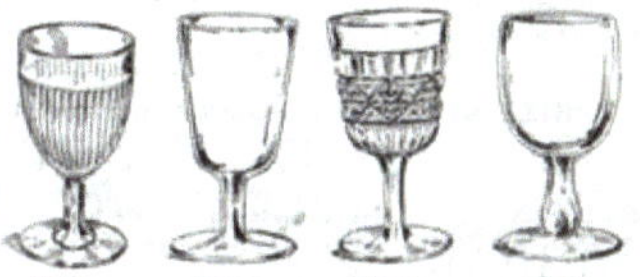

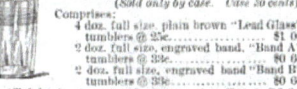

26c Doz. 28c Doz. 30c Doz. Hotel.

"Fine Flute" Goblet—Full size. 10 doz. in bbl.......... 26

"Plain" Goblet—A standard favorite. 10 doz. in bbl.... 28

"Cut Pattern" Goblet—10 doz. in bbl.......... 30

"Leader" Hotel Goblet—A clear, extra heavy, full size. 8 doz. in bbl.......... 35

"Cup Foot" Hotel Goblet—*Seamless.* Extra heavy, full size, full finished. 8 doz. in bbl.......... 39

"Double Thick" Hotel Goblet—Seamless. Double thick throughout, even to foot. 7 doz. in bbl.......... 47

Our "Plain and Banded" Assortment.

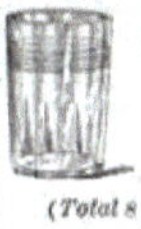

Lead glass blown tumblers ("Firsts"). (*Sold only by case. Case 30 cents*).

Comprises:

4 doz. full size, plain brown "Lead Glass" tumblers @ 25c.......... $1 00

2 doz. full size, engraved band, "Band A" tumblers @ 33c.......... $0 66

2 doz. full size, engraved band "Band B" tumblers @ 33c.......... $0 66

(*Total 8 doz. to case. Case 30c.*) **Total, $2.32**

"Standard" Jelly Tumblers.

Best quality—not the small sizes sold by many. (*Sold only by pkg. Bbl. 35c.*)

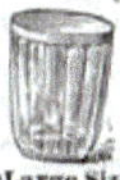

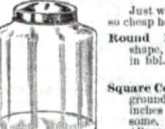

"Jelly Tumbler Assortment"—Equal quantities of plain and fluted. 12 doz. medium size and 6 doz. large size, total of 18 doz. to pkg. (*Bbl. 35c.*) 12 doz. at 13½c, $1.62, and 6 doz. at 15½c, 93c. Total for 18 Doz., $2.55.

"Medium Size"—24 doz. to pkg., half plain and half fluted. Sold only by pkg. Bbl. 35c 13½

"Large Size"—18 doz. to pkg., equal quantities of plain and fluted. Sold only by pkg. Barrel 35c.......... 15½

Store Shelf Jars—*Crystal Glass.*

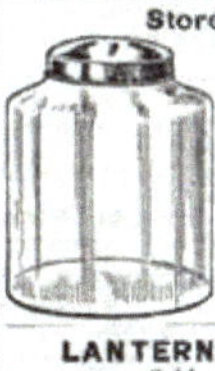

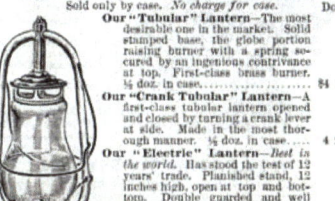

Just what every store keeper wants and so cheap he can't afford to be without them.

Round Pattern Jar—Popular round shape, ½ gallon, japanned tops. 1½ doz. in bbl. Sold only by pkg. (*Barrel 35c.*) **Price, 95c Doz.**

Square Corner Jar—½ gallon, with heavy ground glass stopper, wide opening. 11 inches high including cover. Very handsome. 1 doz. in bbl. Sold only by pkg. (*Barrel 35c.*) **Price, $2.75 Doz.**

LANTERNS AND REFLECTOR LAMPS.

Sold only by case. *No charge for case.* Doz.

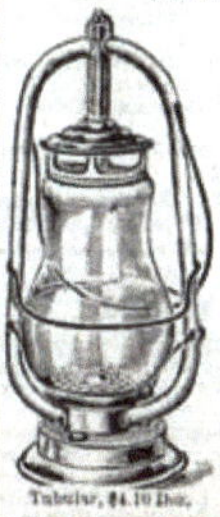

Tubular, $4.10 Doz.

Our "Tubular" Lantern—The most desirable one in the market. Solid stamped base, the globe portion raising burner with a spring secured by an ingenious contrivance at top. First-class brass burner. ½ doz. in case.......... $4 10

Our "Crank Tubular" Lantern—A first-class tubular lantern opened and closed by turning a crank lever at side. Made in the most thorough manner. ½ doz. in case.... 4 20

Our "Electric" Lantern—*Best in the world.* Has stood the test of 12 years' trade. Planished stand, 12 inches high, open at top and bottom. Double guarded and well braced. ½ doz. in case.......... 4 50

Stable or Dashboard Lantern—A tubular lantern with automatic lift and reflector, at the back of which is a strong wire spring hook. ½ doz. in case.......... 6 00

"Jaxon" Reflector Lamp—One piece of 7-gauge steel wire, with 7-inch bright tin reflector and 4½-inch fount, made for No. 2 burner. 1 doz. in case.......... 1 45

Keep your glass bright and clean. There is nothing more attractive in your store than bright, sparkling glassware.

Lamp Chimneys.

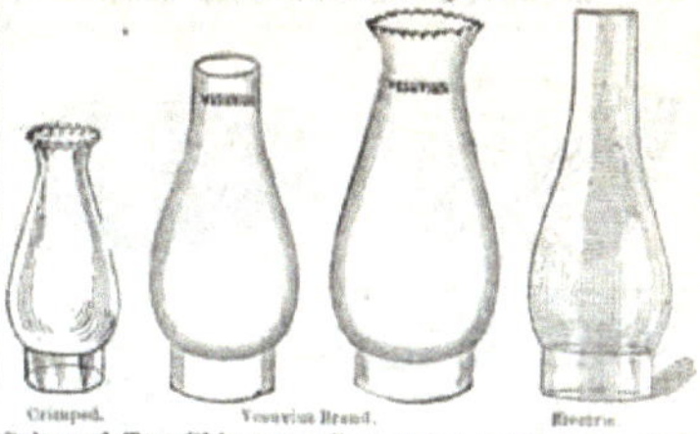

Crimped. Vesuvius Brand. Electric.

Doz.

Crimped Top Chimneys—Best crystal chimney, sun burner, crimped top. Sold only by case.

No. 0—6 doz. in case.......... (Case 30c) $0 16

No. 1—6 " " .... " 40c) 17

No. 2—6 " " .... " 50c) 27

"Fire Test" Bead Top Chimneys—Made from German glass—a mixture of lime and lead. Will not break when put into hottest fire.

No. 1—Bead top chimney. 6 doz. in case. (Case 30c).. 27

No. 2— " " 6 " " " 40c) 36

"Fire-Proof" Lead Chimneys—High grade almost unbreakable chimneys, bead tops. Sold only by case.

No. 1—6 doz. in case.......... (Case 40c) 36

No. 2—6 " " .... " 50c) 48

The Genuine "Vesuvius" Brand *of fire-proof lead chimneys.* Have won the highest award against all other chimneys in the most severe fire-test competitions. None genuine without the word "Vesuvius" etched on each chimney. *Sold only by case.*

No. 1—Crimped top, 6 doz. in case.......... (Case 40c) 38

No. 2— " " 6 " " .... " 50c) 52

No. 1—Plain top.... 6 " " .... " 40c) 38

No. 2— " .... 6 " " .... " 50c) 52

2, **"Electric" Chimneys**—A very necessary chimney for use on the Climax and other burners where globes are used. "Lead" glass, narrow plain top. 3 doz. in box. Sold only by box.......... (Box 40c) 58

2, **Slim-Shape "Electric" Chimneys**—For globes with 4-inch openings. 3 doz. in box. Sold only by box.......... (Box 40c) 58

"Wellsbach" Lead Chimneys—8-inch. Genuine lead glass. 6 doz. in case.......... (Case 40c) 60

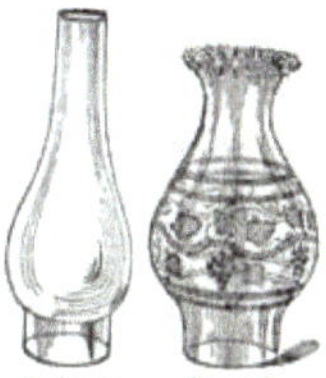

Rochester. Engraved.

"Rochester" Lead Chimneys—This chimney has become a standard. Best "lead" glass, plain top. Sold only by bbl.

No. 2—6 doz. in barrel.. 58 (*Barrel 35c*)

No. 3—2 doz. in barrel. 1 20 (*Barrel 35c*)

Assortment Engraved Globe Chimneys—1 doz. each of 3 designs of engraved and banded chimneys, all large No. 2 size and swelled center globe shape. 3 doz. in pkg. Sold only by pkg. 79 (*Barrel 35c*). *Sold only by pkg.*

Lantern Globes.

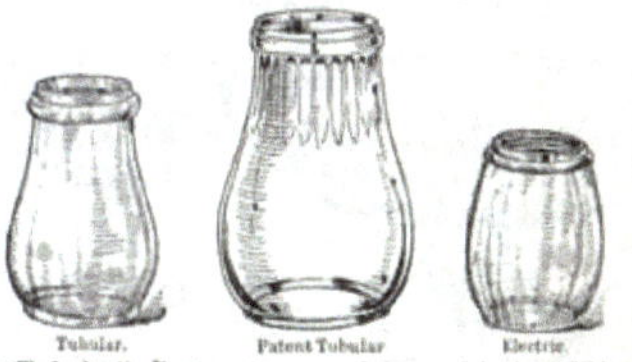

Tubular. Patent Tubular Electric.

"Tubular"—Best goods, *ground top and bottom*, fitting any tubular lantern. 5 doz. in barrel. (*Barrel 35c*)... 29

"Patent" Tubular—Pressed and blown from best of crystal glass. Finished tops and bottoms. 5 doz. in bbl. 35 (*Barrel 35c*)

"Electric"—For our famous "Electric" lantern. 6 or 7 doz. in bbl. (*Barrel 35c*).......... 44

STORE OR SUSPENSION LAMPS.

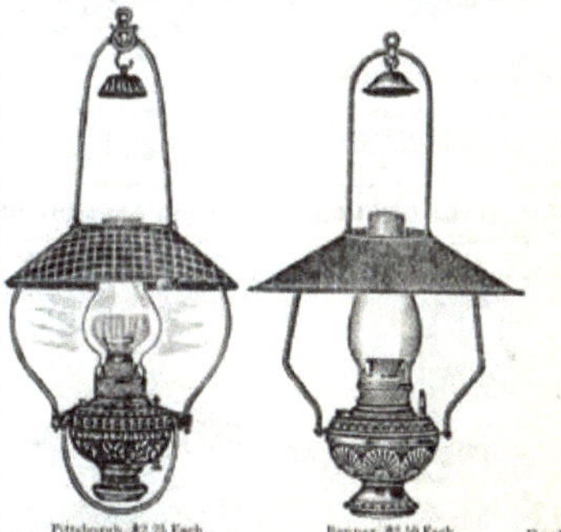

Pittsburgh, $2.25 Each. Banner, $2.50 Each

Each.

"Pittsburgh" Store or Hall Lamp—Absolutely non-explosive. Burns over 10 hours without refilling. Perfect draft, no dirt, no odor. Smallest wick exposure, patent dial indicator showing quantity of oil in lamp, extra feeder wick and oil drip cup on handle of tube to carry any over-flow back to the wick. 20-inch tin shade. Fitted with No. 3 burner, fount, wick and chimney. Each in box. (*No charge for case*). (4 or more, $2.17) $2 25

Famous "Banner" Store Lamp—Has extra feeder wick and oil drip cup on inside of tube to carry any overflow back to the wick. 20-inch tin shade. Fitted with No. 3 burner, fount, wick and chimney. Each in box complete. (*No charge for case*).......... 2 50

Study Our Assortments—Note the UNIFORM VALUE and the ABSENCE OF SMALL PIECES.

New "Hand" Lamp Assortment.

Comprising 2¼ doz. each of three patterns. **Price, 45c Doz.**

Total of 6 1-4 doz. to bbl. (Barrel 35c.)

Our "All Leaders" Lamp Assortment.

Comprising 1 doz. each of 5 patterns, 4 stand and 1 hand. All strictly "firsts," finest crystal glass, all large sizes. 1 doz. each of the following:
High Cut Lamp.
High Octagon Pattern Lamp.
High Square Foot Pattern Lamp—Square Base.
High Ball Center Lamp.
Footed and Handled Stand Lamp, staple.
All above with No. 1 collars. Total of 5 doz. to pkg. Sold only by pkg. (Barrel 35c.)
Price, 65c Doz.

"Wonder" Patent Collar Lamp Assortment.

Superior quality and extra large size. Patent shrunk-on collars, no plaster, no cement, no oil can get through the collar, absolutely non-explosive, shape to serve as an oil drip. The assortment comprises 1½ doz. each of the following:
8½-inch plain stand lamps, wide base.
8½ " brilliant stand lamps, wide base.
Plain footed hand lamps, wide base.
Fancy pattern hand lamps, two handles, wide base.
Price, 85c Doz.
Total of 6 doz. in pkg. (Barrel 35c.)

WE DO NOT ASK YOUR BUSINESS unless we can benefit you. If we can demonstrate a saving, will you give us your business?

"All Sizes" Lamp Assortment.

Best selling pattern shown in years. All best sizes, worth 10 per cent more. The assortment comprises the following:

1 doz.	OOA.	No. 1 collar		$0 55	$0 55
¼ "	OA.	" 1	"	65	33
¼ "	A.	" 2	"	75	25
¼ "	B.	" 2	"	85	21
¼ "	C.	" 2	"	1 15	29
¼ "	D.	" 2	"	1 25	21
¼ "	¼A.	Flat hand lamp, No. 1 collar		55	37
¼ "	¼A.	Footed hand lamp, No. 1 collar		65	22

3½ doz. in pkg. Sold only by pkg. *(Barrel 35c.)* **Total, $2.43**

Our "Honest Value" 25c Lamp Assortment.

Fitted with patent shrunk-on collars, 3 largest sizes of stand lamps all in new and beautiful "crown" pattern. All with No. 2 collars. The assortment consists of:

1 doz.	9-inch Stand Lamps	$1 20	$1 20
1 "	9¼ " "	1 68	1 68
½ "	10 " "	1 90	95

Total, $3.83
Total 2 1-2 doz. to pkg. (Barrel 35c.)

"Table Lamp" Assortment.

Popular patterns at popular prices and of quality unsurpassed. All fitted with No. 2 collars. The assortment comprises ½ doz. each of the following:

High standing cut pattern	$1.20	$0 60
" " octagon "	1.20	60
Large and high, square foot, plain pattern	1.60	80
Large and high, ball center	1.60	80

Total, $2.80
Total of 2 doz. to pkg. (Barrel 35c.)

Miscellaneous Lamps.

"Ready-for-Use" Lamp Assortment: A complete family lamp on a possible 25-center. Assortment comprises 1 doz. high standing 17-inch lamps and 1 doz. low standing handled 14-inch lamps, completely fitted with No. 1 brass burner, crimped top chimney and wick. Total of 2 doz. in pkg. Sold only by pkg. *(Barrel 35c.)* **Price (complete), $1.85 Doz.**

"Big and Safe" Complete Lamp Assortment: All with patent clinch collars. Assortment comprises ½ doz. each of two patterns of high stand lamps, 19¼ inches to top of chimneys, and ½ doz. sewing lamps, 18 inches in height. Complete with No. 2 burners, chimneys and wicks. 1 doz. in pkg. Sold only by pkg. *(Barrel 35c.)* **Price (complete), $3.60 Doz.**

GLASSWARE FROM PITTSBURGH.

The following goods are shipped direct from our Pittsburgh warehouse. This method suits the many buyers who thereby save freight to New York, Chicago or St. Louis and receive their goods with the least possibility of breakage. N. B.—We urge buyers so far as possible to order two or more of these packages at one time although, we will gladly ship a single package if desired.

Our "FURORE" 5-Cent Assortment.

An assortment consisting of what should properly be called 5 and 10-cent goods. All large, all fine polished, all self-selling.

The assortment comprises **1 doz. each** of the following:
8-Inch Handled Dishes.
Sugar Bowls and Covers, Footed.
Rich Table Tumblers.
8-Inch Round Plates.
Milk Pitchers—To match sugar and butter.
Butter Dishes and Covers.
4½-inch Footed Nappy.
7¼-inch Heavy Preserve Dishes.
Round Deep Dishes—Fancy, 6-inch.
Cut Pattern Goblets.

10 doz. to pkg. Sold only by pkg. Cask 35c.
Price, 37c Doz.

Our "FULL FINISHED" 10-Cent Assortment.

Six rich and elegant articles, all of the same shapely pattern, here offered at a price 20 per cent below the price paid for by the regular crockery and glass jobber.

The assortment comprises 1 doz. each of the following:
8-Inch High Footed Salvers.
8-Inch Round Deep Dishes.
10-Inch Bread or Cake Plates.
7-Inch High Footed Dishes.
7¼-inch Scalloped Footed Dish.
Mammoth Butters and Covers.

6 doz. to bbl. Sold only by bbl. (Bbl. 35c.)
Price, 74c Doz.

Two Good Leaders in Glass.

25-Cent Salver Assortment—½ doz. each of two entirely new and rich salvers—one 11-inch, scalloped edge as shown in cut, the other 10-inch, plain. 1½ doz. in pkg. Sold only by pkg. *(Bbl. 35c.)* **Price, $1.40 Doz.**

Our "Big" Finished ½-Gallon Pitcher—A splendid, heavy, fire polished pitcher. Worth two of the common sort. 2 doz. in bbl. Sold only by bbl. *(Bbl. 35c.)* **Price, 84c Doz.**

SHIPPED FROM PITTSBURGH.

Our "EXCITEMENT" 10c Cask Assortment.

Twenty different articles, fifteen of which would be cheap at a "quarter." Take into consideration *size, quality and finish* and see if you do not say that Butler Brothers can and do sell glassware cheaper by 20 per cent than any other house in America.

The assortment comprises ½ doz. each of the following:
11½-inch Celery Trays.
New Half Gallon Water Pitchers.
7-Inch Extra Deep Dishes.
7-Inch Footed Dishes—Scalloped.
10-Inch Oval Bread Plates.
Large and Rich Milk Pitchers—Serviceable.
6-inch Utility Dishes—All want it.
9-Inch Cake Salvers—Scalloped edge.
8-Inch High Footed Bowls—Rich, deep.
5-Inch High Footed Jellies.
8-Inch Olive Dishes—Extra heavy.
Double Handle Dishes—Cut pattern, 6-in.
Large Sugar Bowls and Covers.
10-Inch Round Plates—For cake or fruit.
1898 High Celery Dishes—6 inches high.
5-Inch Handled Jellies or Olives.
7¼-inch Oblong Dishes—Square corners.
Wide Flanged Butter Dishes and Covers.
New Cut Pattern Flower Vase—9½-inch.
8¼-Inch Deep Round Dishes—Berries, etc.

10 doz. to cask. Sold only by cask. Cask 30c.
Price, 65c Doz.

Our New "WALDORF" Asst. of 5c Gems.

The "Waldorf" is a late capture of a new pattern in the richest of cut glass imitation. Every piece is fire polished and full finished. All pieces are same pattern as those illustrated.

The assortment comprises 1 doz. each of the following:
7¼-Inch Oblong Dish.
7-Inch Square Plate—Heavy.
Jelly Dish with Handle.
Stuck Handle Milk Pitcher.
8¼-Inch Oblong Dish.
Bent-in Tumbler—A good one.
6-inch Round Scalloped Dish.
Oatmeal Bowl or Utility Dish.
Rich Spoon Holder.
4½-inch Fancy Table Dish.
Open Handle Mug.
Handled Sugar Bowl and Cover.

12 doz. in bbl. Sold only by bbl. (Bbl. 35c.)
Price, 38c Doz.

"BRIGHT AND HEAVY" Table Set.

A rich one to run at 50 cents per set.
A rich set of purest crystal, Large—brilliant—beautiful—heavy. 12 sets in barrel. Sold only by barrel. *(Bbl. 35c.)*
Price, 24c Set.

SHIPPED FROM PITTSBURGH.

Our "X RAYS" Assortment.

One of the best lots of glass ever offered by us.

The assortment comprises 1 doz. each of the following:
8-Inch Round Dishes—Large and deep.
7-Inch Footed Dishes.
Stuck Handled Milk Pitchers.
7½-Inch Covered Butter Dishes.
5-Inch High Footed Bowls, Covered.
8x10-Inch Deep Oval Plates.

6 doz. to pkg. Sold only by pkg. Barrel 35c.
Price, 74c Doz.

Our "WEDDING TABLE OUTFIT."

A new and choice complete dining room service—85 pieces for $2.95.

In this new lot every piece is fire polished and full finished. And all pieces match *exactly* even to the smallest article. The assortment comprises 85 pieces (not counting covers) including large and small pieces—such as bowls, dishes, salver, butter, sugar, spoon holder, pitchers, tumblers, goblets, etc., etc., etc. All safely packed in a barrel. Sold only by barrel. *(Barrel 35c.)*
Price for the Assortment, $2.95.

Our "GREAT" 25-Cent Assortment.

Not only great in value and size but great in richness and splendor. All fully finished and in richness unsurpassed by anything made of glass.

The assortment comprises 1-2 doz. each of the following:
7-Inch High Footed Bowls and Covers.
9½-Inch High Footed Salvers.
9-Inch High Footed Flaring Bowls.
Half Gallon Water Pitchers—Extra heavy.

2 doz. to bbl. Sold only by pkg. (Barrel 35c.)
Price, $1.63 Doz.

Our "Peerless" Ware Is Not Merely Equal to Any Other—It is Positively THE BEST.

CROCKERY SHIPPED FROM POTTERY.

All goods on this page are shipped from pottery near Bellaire, Ohio.

"PEERLESS" WHITE GRANITE WARE—Shipped from Pottery.

Every piece absolutely warranted not to craze. New pattern of matchless finish and unequaled strength. Positively worth 10 to 20 per cent more than some well known lines. Send for a package and if the ware is not equal to any other we will refund it subject to our offer. All "run-of-the-kiln" firsts, absolutely guaranteed not to craze.

60, and 5 per cent from W. G. List. The net prices given below are figured at exactly 60, and 5 per cent from the standard White Granite List, adopted by all the potters of America. In order to make possible the prices here named we have made arrangements to fill all orders for "Peerless" ware direct from our warehouse near Bellaire, Ohio, from which point we have obtained advantageous freight rates. Sold only in barrel lots (no less than $10.00). Packages will be charged according to never-broken rule among crockery manufacturers. No charge for cartage.

All sizes here given are so-called "trade sizes" and pieces actually measure a good deal more. N. B.—Any merchant who has been in the habit of buying at a certain discount (W. G. or A.) from regular list can buy from us at best terms to be obtained from any pottery.

[Extensive price list for Peerless White Granite Ware items including Bakers or Vegetable Dishes, Bone Dishes, Bowls, Footed Oyster, Footed Punch, Brush Vases, Butters, Cracker Jars, Casseroles, Celery Trays, Chambers, Coffees, Comports, Cuspadores, Creams, Covered Dishes, Dishes or Platters, Cup Plates, Egg Cups, Ewers and Basins, Fruit Saucers, Ice Creams, Jugs, Mugs, Nappies, Pickles, Plates, Salads, Sauce Boats, Slop Pails, Slop Jars, Soaps, Soup Ladles, Oval Soup Tureens, Spittoons, Sugars, Tea Pots, Teas, Tea Sets, Toilet Sets]

"PARIS WHITE" C. C. WARE.

Shipped direct from our central warehouse near Bellaire, Ohio. You can have this and "Peerless" or "Bee Hive" ware packed together. Regular charge for packages.

Positively warranted not to craze. We guarantee it superior both in strength and finish to any other C. C. ware produced in America. We name net prices figured at exactly 55 per cent from the standard C. C. list, adopted by all potters of America. No charge for cartage.

[Price list for Paris White C. C. Ware items]

MOSAIC MOTTLED WARE.

In mottled blue, brown and yellow.

[Price list: Emmett Tea Pot, Cuspidor, Cracker Jar, Jardinieres, etc.]

YELLOW AND ROCKINGHAM WARE—From Pottery.

Of Matchless Quality—Shipped Direct from Pottery.

50 per cent off list—The list below is the net list after deducting the 50 per cent. These are the prices the goods will cost you—subject, of course, to our usual cash 2 per cent. Freight rates from the pottery district on this ware average very low. We cannot afford to make any shipment amounting to less than $5.00. Packages will be charged as charged by all jobbers and potteries. No charge for cartage.

Customer dealing with us on a C. O. D. basis, when ordering a bill of Crockery to be shipped from factory in the same order with goods to be shipped from our house, should send separate deposit for each shipment.

Yellow Ware.
[Price list: Bakers Square shape, Bakers Oval, Bed Pans, Bird Baths, Bowls, Covered Jars, Bed Pans Large, Chambers, Custard Cups, Nappies Corrugated bottom, Fluted Rice Nappies, Pie Plates]

Rockingham Ware.
[Price list: Bakers, Bed Pans, Bowls, Mugs, Cuspidors Wicker, Jugs, Milk Boilers, Fluted Rice Dishes, Nappies, Pie Plates, Soap Drainers, Tea Pots—Emmett individual, Tea Pots—Pineapple shape, Tea Pots—Rebecca]

THE "BEE-HIVE" DECORATED LINE—From Pottery.

Shipped from pottery near Bellaire, Ohio. A gold edge line of semi-porcelain ware, embossed pattern, elegantly painted floral decoration, gold edges. Can be packed with "Peerless" or "Paris White" ware. Prices below are net, subject to our usual terms—2 per cent 10 days. Regular charge for packages. We not only warrant but warrant every piece against "crazing."

[Price list: Bakers, Berry Saucers, Bowls, Butters, Cake Plates, Casseroles, Covered Dishes, Creams, Cups and Saucers, Dishes, Egg Cups, Jugs, Oatmeal Saucers, Nappies, Pickles, Plates, Sauce Boats, Slop Bowls, Soup Tureens, Soup Ladles, Sugars, Tea Pots]

Our "Introduction" 10-Cent Assortment of "Bee Hive" Ware.

Same handsome decorated ware as above. Assortment comprises the following:
- ½ doz. 9-inch (actual size) Bakers.
- ½ " 11½ " Platters.
- ½ " Fancy Cups and Saucers (24 pieces).
- 2 " Cups and Saucers (48 pieces).
- 1 doz. Milk Pitchers (42's).
- 3 " Plates, 8-inch (actual size).
- 3 " Plates, 9-inch.
- 1 " Deep Plates (soup), 9-inch, actual size.

All of the above in embossed pattern—richly decorated in floral design with gold edges.
(Shipped from pottery.) Total of 12 doz. to bbl. Sold only by bbl. Bbl. 25c.) **Price, 77c Doz**

Assortments of "Peerless" W. G. Ware—From Pottery.

Representative assortments put up for the convenience of buyers. Figured at 60 and 5 from regular W. G. list.

No. 1 Assortment—Comprising a large variety of the staple items, giving a good outfit for any retail stock, properly proportioned as to quantities—for instance, 8 doz. 7-inch plates and 4 doz. handled tea cups and saucers, ranging down to 1-6 doz. teapots. Assortment is very carefully proportioned and we believe will be found to sell out evenly. Price complete, including cask ... **$32 50**

No. 2 Assortment—Intended to supply the goods which would naturally sell out first from No. 1 assortment above. Including the biggest selling items only—plates, cups and saucers, jugs, bowls, etc. Price complete, including cask ... **21 73**

No. 3 Assortment—Mainly as above, smaller quantities. Price complete, including cask ... **16 45**

No. 4 Assortment—6 doz. 7-inch plates and 6 doz. handled teas. Complete, including tierce ... **7 22**

No. 5 Assortment—6 doz. 7-inch plates and 6 doz. unhandled teas. Complete, including tierce ... **6 62**

Our Only Trouble in Selling Crockery to Any Buyer Is to Get the First TRIAL ORDER.

DECORATED TEA AND DINNER SETS—Shipped from Pottery.

Not only do we give you lowest prices, but remember our sets are *just what they claim to be. Very many* in the market are cheapened in cost by slipping in small size pieces, and by omitting covers on some of the dishes which ought to have them. You may depend on it that all sets bought from us will be honest *throughout.*

101-Piece Dinner Sets—*Regular 101-Piece Outfit.* Per Set.

Our "Every Day"—New shape, plain print decoration in handsome floral designs. Made of semi-porcelain. Order one package—this is a bargain. Each set in bbl. (Bbl. 35c) $6 50

Our "Illuminated Gold Decorated"—Each piece handsomely decorated in colored flowers, illuminated in gold clouds, all handles with heavy bands of gold. Fancy shaped cups and large size soup tureen. Each set in bbl. (Bbl. 35c) 8 15

Our "Hand Decorated"—Floral decoration in beautiful colors on each 101 pieces, stippled gold handles. Extra large pieces, including soup tureen. Each set in bb, (Bbl. 35c) 8 75

Our "Gold Traced Embossed"—Rich white ivory ground, embossed edges on every piece, traced with rich gold decoration on all flanges, each piece gold edged. All handles have fancy gold work. Each set in bbl. (Bbl. 35c) 9 50

Our "Floral and Gold Decorated"—Fancy shape dishes, odd designs footed cups, elaborately decorated in delicate colored shaded flowers with fancy gold tracings over each of the 101 pieces, artistic gold decorated handles on all covers. Each set in bbl. (Bbl. 35c). 11 50

56-Piece Tea Sets—*Regular 56-Piece Outfit.*

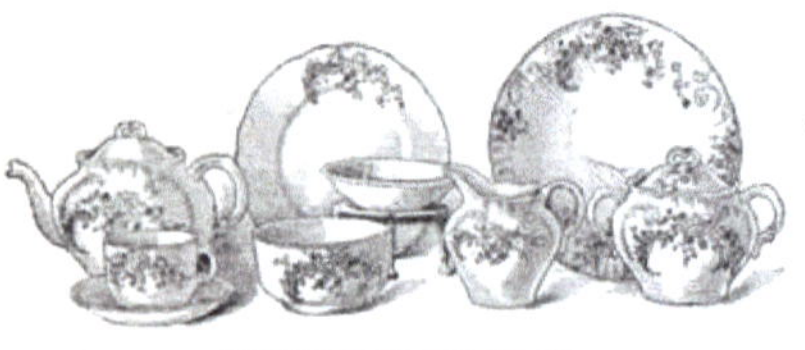

Our Utility 56-Piece Tea Set, $2.60 per Set.

Our "Utility"—A special bargain. Print decoration in blue and brown. 2 sets in bbl. (Bbl. 35c). 2 60

Our "Decorated and Gold"—All good size pieces. Fancy cups stippled gold handles, decoration on each piece in profuse natural color flowers. 2 sets in bbl. Sold by pkg. only. (Bbl. 35c) 4 00

Our "Embossed Gold"—Richly embossed gold work on every one of the 56 pieces. Good body and graceful shapes. 2 sets in bbl. Sold by pkg. only. (Bbl. 35c) 4 10

PURE WHITE TEA AND DINNER SETS—*From Pottery.* Per Set

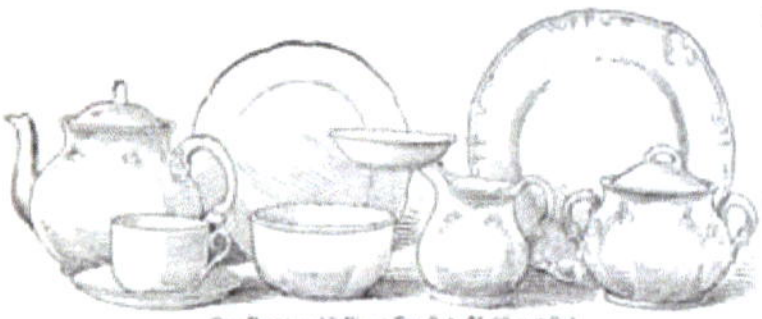

Our Puritan 56-Piece Tea Set, $1.88 per Set.

Our "Puritan" 56-Piece Tea Set—Regular 56-piece tea set in plain pure white ware. A good thing for you to advertise with. 2 sets in bbl. (Bbl. 35c) $1 88

Combination Dinner and Tea Set—Comprising 106 pieces. Pure white ware. Complete breakfast, dinner and supper service. Each set in bbl. (Bbl. 35c) 4 65

100-Piece Semi-Porcelain Dinner Set—*From Pottery.*

Our "Department Advertiser" Semi-Porcelain Dinner Set—"Most anything" would be cheap at $5.75 for 100 pieces of decorated semi-porcelain, but when you get these in you will find they are nice goods as well as cheap. Good grade semi-porcelain, print decoration in foliage green. We can also furnish (when specially mentioned) in fog blue. Each set in bbl. (Bbl. 35c) 5 75

65-Piece Combination Breakfast, Dinner and Tea Set.—*From Pottery.*

Our "Honeymoon" Combination Set—A new combination in dinner ware, embracing a complete outfit for all occasions, comprising 65 pieces. It furnishes just the lot of pieces wanted by those starting housekeeping. Each piece profusely decorated in natural color rosebuds, fancy gold edges and gold clouded handles. Each set in bbl. (Bbl. 35c) 6 75

DECORATED TOILET SETS—Shipped from Pottery. Per Set.

Our "Immense Decorated" 10-Piece Set—The pieces in this set are all of extra large size and are decorated to match. Comprises ewer and basin, quart pitcher, covered soap dish with drainer, tooth brush vase, handled mug, chamber and cover. In each cask are 4 colors assorted, such as brown, red, green and blue. 4 sets in cask. Sold by pkg. only. (Cask 60c) $1 45

Our "Floral" 10-Piece Set—Same enumeration of pieces as in "Immense Decorated," all extra size. Artistically decorated in floral designs with gold edges. 2 decorations. 2 sets in bbl. Sold by pkg. only. (Bbl. 35c) 2 35

Our "New Home" 10-Piece Set—Elegant and elaborate pattern of raised decoration. Gold traced leaves and gold edges. A set heretofore sold at much above this price. 10 pieces, full size, as above. 2 sets in barrel, 1 pink, 1 blue. (Bbl. 35c) 2 35

Our "Anniversary" 12-Piece Set—Full size pieces, gold edges, colored filled in decoration in beautiful tints, half hand work, tastefully colored flowers and leaves, gold edges. Extra large covered slop bowl. Each set in barrel. (Bbl. 35c) 4 50

Our "Clouded Gold Decorated" 12-Piece Set—Comprising covered slop jar, bowl and pitcher, covered chamber, covered soap dish with drainer, tooth brush vase, hand pitcher and handled mug. Each piece decorated all over and with extra heavy gold clouded edges and handles. Each set in bbl. (Bbl. 35c) 4 00

Our "Green-Room" 12-Piece Set—Large handsome pieces, each in molded pattern, filled in, in the natural green effect, traced and edged with gold. This makes a very rich and elaborate effect. Set comprises covered slop jar, bowl and pitcher, covered chamber, tooth brush vase, covered soap dish with drainer, hand pitcher and handled mug. Each set in barrel. (Bbl. 35c) 4 95

All goods on this page except Yellow and Rockingham Ware are shipped only from factory.

Assortments of YELLOW AND ROCKINGHAM WARE.

Carried in Stock at All of Our Houses.

"Kitchen Favorite" 5c Assortment—*(Yellow and Rockingham).*

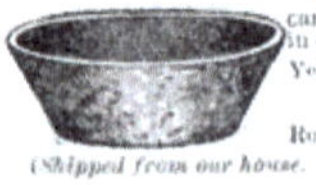

Comprising 1½ **dozen each of 8 items** as named below, of which we can illustrate but one. These goods stand among the best of the captures in our history.

Yellow Bowls—6¾-inch.	Yellow Pie Plates—8½-inch.
" Bakers—8-inch.	Rockingham Nappies—5½-in.
" Nappies—9½-inch.	Rockingham Bowls—5½-inch.
Rockingham Mugs—Good size.	" Pie Plates—7¾-in.

(Shipped from our house. 12 doz. to pkg. Sold only by pkg. Bbl. 35c.) **Price, 41c Doz.**

Our "Useful" Yellow Ware Assortment.

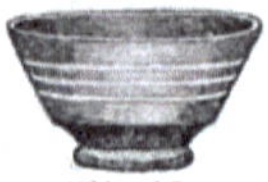

Comprising **1 doz. each of the 6 items below.**

Handled Milk Boilers—Outside Rockingham, inside yellow.	Bakers—10-inch.
Nappies—9-inch.	Rustic Pitchers—3-pint.
Extra Deep Bowls—8½-inch.	Large Milk Pans—9¾-inch.

(Shipped from our house. 6 doz. to pkg. Sold only by pkg. Barrel 35c.) **Price, 81c Doz.**

Our "Utility" Large Dish Assortment—*(Yellow Ware).*

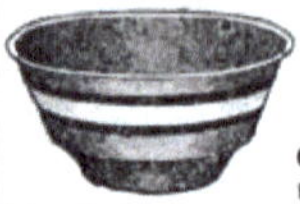

The assortment comprises ½ **doz. each of the 6 items below.**

Deep Bowls—10¾-inch.	Nappies—11¼-inch.
" " —11-inch.	Fluted Nappies—10-inch.
Nappies—10⅝-inch.	" " —11¼-inch.

(Shipped from our house. 2 doz. to pkg. Sold only by pkg. Barrel 35c.) **Price, $1.48 Doz.**

Our Rockingham "Tea Pot Assortment."

Popular "pineapple" shape. The assortment comprises the following:

1 doz. ¾-pint	$1 00	½ doz. 3-pint at $175	$0 88
1 " 2 "	1 50	½ " 4 " at $2.13	1 07

(Shipped from our house. 3 doz. to pkg. Sold only by pkg. Barrel 35c.)

Total, $4.45

DECORATED LAMPS—SHIPPED FROM FACTORY.

IMPORTANT—The following Lamps are **shipped from warehouse near Pittsburg.** This is to your benefit in two ways—danger of breakage is lessened, and by saving one handling we are enabled to name much lower prices.

The lamps here listed are not merely equal to any other—they are positively the **finest lamps produced in America.** You may think this a strong statement when you note that we quote prices as low as you can buy the common grade goods, but if any buyer will send for one sample package he will find we have not claimed a grain too much. Prices are for complete lamp except chimneys. *In our complete catalogue these Lamps are illustrated.*

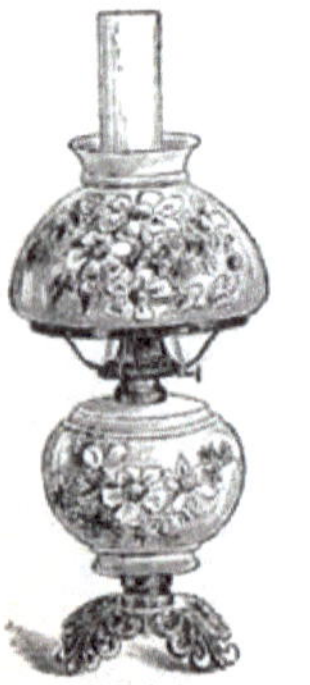

401, 58c Each.

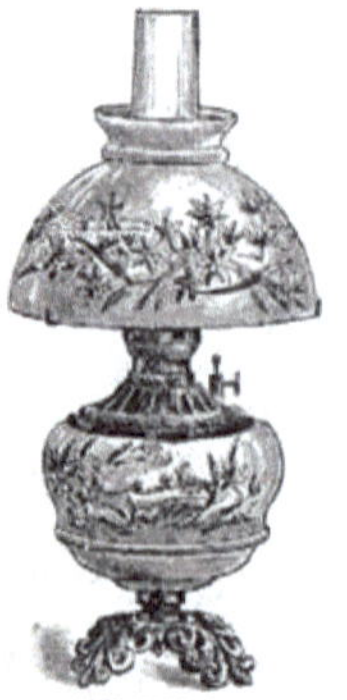

411, $1.42 1-2 Each.

401, "Dome Shade" Lamp—Handsome table lamp with 7-inch shade, artistic metal base, No. 2 burner, 15½ inches to top of shade. Decorations are elaborate, being in heavy floral designs in anemones and daisies, with color combinations of purple, yellow, red and blue. Assorted in pkg. 8 lamps in bbl. Sold only by bbl. (*Bbl.* 35c.) ..... Each $0 58

411, Central Draft Lamp—16½ inches high, removable central draft oil fount, dome 10 inches in diameter, assorted decorations of yellow, orange and pink narcissus with daintily colored landscape background, pink or green tint at top of shade and lower edge of body. 4 lamps in bbl. Sold only by bbl. (*Bbl.* 35c.) ..... Each 1 42½

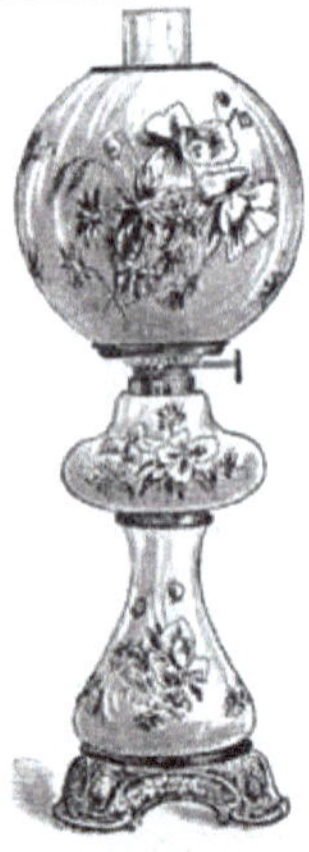

414, $2.40 Each.

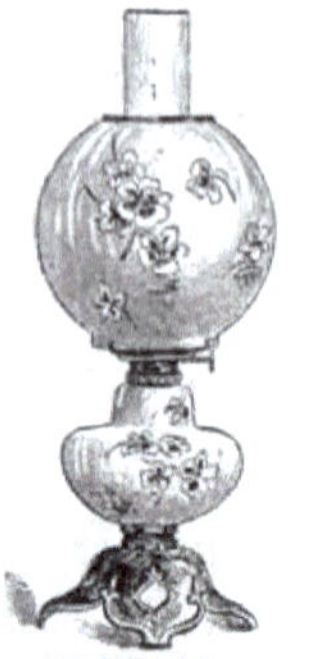

One Style, Asst. C.

414, Banquet Lamp—9-inch globe shade, broad metal base, complete with burner and 4-inch ring, 22¾ inches high. Two decorations, assorted poppies, daisies, etc., prevailing colors being scarlet, yellow, blue and pink. Sold only by bbl. of 3 lamps. (*Bbl. 35c*) ..... Each 2 40

Assortment "C"—Comprising four of the newest and richest of 1898 shapes. 6 lamps in pkg. Two 15½ inches high with 7-inch globe, fancy decorations in blue, purple, etc. Two 14½ inches high, 7½-inch globe, assorted decorations in scrolls and violets. One 15 inches high, 7½-inch globe, popular squat shapes, decorated in elaborate and beautiful designs. One 12½ inches high, 7½-inch globe, new squat pattern, decorations in Louis XVI style in design of yellow ribbons and masks. All with metal base and fitted with No. 2 burners. Total of 6 lamps in pkg. Sold only by pkg. (*Bbl.* 35c.) ..... Total for pkg., 6 80

10-CENT LAVA CUSPIDOR. Doz.

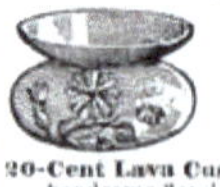

10-Cent Lava Cuspidor—*A genuine surprise.* A genuine lava cuspidor, 6½ inches in diameter and 4¼ high. Assorted colors, each with hand painted floral decoration on either top or side. Nicely assorted, packed 4 doz. in crate, no less sold. No charge for crate $0 72

20-Cent Lava Cuspidor—7 inches in diameter, 4½ high, handsome floral decoration on both top and side, assorted colors in each crate of 2 dozen, no less sold, no charge for crate 1 20

GLAZED CUSPIDOR. Doz.

"Dime Leader" Cuspidor—Buff color, glazed, diameter about 7¾ inches, 5¾ high. Figured body, well made and finished, large opening, making easy to clean. 2 doz. in crate, sold only by crate *(no charge for crate)* $0 92

GLAZED JARDINIERES.

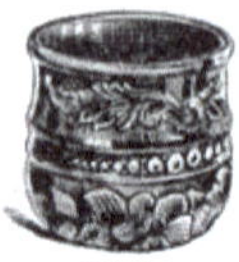

79, 89c Doz.

79, Large Glazed Jardiniere—Height 5½ inches, diameter 5½, circumference 17¾, glazed inside and out. Assorted colors in each package, such as pea green, royal blue, chocolate, canary, orange, etc. Packed 2 doz. in crate, sold only by crate (no charge for crate) ..... Doz. $0 89

50-Cent Glazed Jardiniere—Glazed inside and out, large size, diameter 7 inches, height 6½, assorted colors in each pkg., such as royal blue, chocolate, pea green, canary, orange, etc. 1 doz. in crate, sold by crate only *(no charge for crate)* 2 25

CROWDED OUT FOR LACK OF ROOM.

We have been compelled to omit from this **condensed catalogue** the following entire departments:

Ladies' Trimmed Hats.
Baby Carriages.
Reed Furniture.
Easels.

If you are interested in any of the above lines send for our complete catalogue.

As soon as you are a customer we shall make it our business to keep you supplied with bargain offerings right along. You will get the best we have.

Whenever We Call an Item a "Bargain" the Word Means Something.

"LEADERS FOR BARGAIN DAY."

CONTINUED—*Prices Subject to Our Regular Terms: 2 per cent 10 days. Net 40 days.*

MEN'S SUMMER CRASH HAT.

Cool—comfortable—light weight—will outlast a half dozen straw hats.

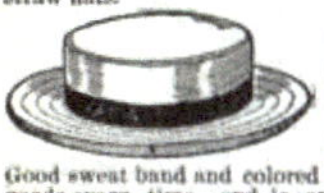

B1106—Made of good quality crash, curled brim, properly quilted and pressed, brim interlined with heavy canvas so will not lose its shape when wet, like common paper lined goods. Lined throughout with ventilated cloth. Good sweat band and colored band. This will outsell the straw goods every time, and is an attractive bargain at a quarter. ½ doz. in box, assorted. Price per dozen, **$2.25**

"Dime Leader" in MEN'S CRASH CAPS.

A cap that would easily fetch a quarter, but ours is a 10-cent price.

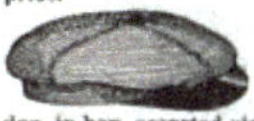

B1109—Made of nice quality brown crash, golf yacht style, black enameled visor and sweat band. It took good buying, backed up by a little good luck, to effect this price. 1 doz. in box, assorted sizes. Price per dozen, **96c**

OUR GREAT "SPECIAL" in LADIES' VESTS.

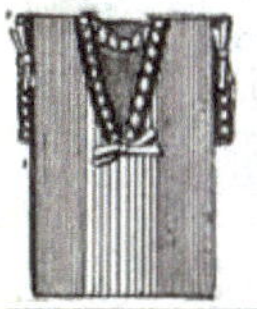

Real Egyptian yarn and full silk taped—in fact a regular $1.25 vest to run at 10 cents.

B153—Egyptian combed yarn, ecru color, combination 1-and-1 and 4-and-1 ribs, V-shape front, handsomely crocheted and silk taped neck and armholes. The only full silk-taped Egyptian vest in the market that can be retailed for a dime, and our lot is limited to 200 cases. Price per dozen, **95c** (10 doz. or more, 93½c) (Case lots of 50 doz., 92c)

TO BUY UNDERWEAR without studying our spring '98 line is an unwise policy. We have fought our way to the front in underwear until today we control many lines which you need. Our opportunities for securing "leader" values in this line are second to those of no other house in the trade. If you will study our this season's offerings in underwear we know we will get a share of your business.

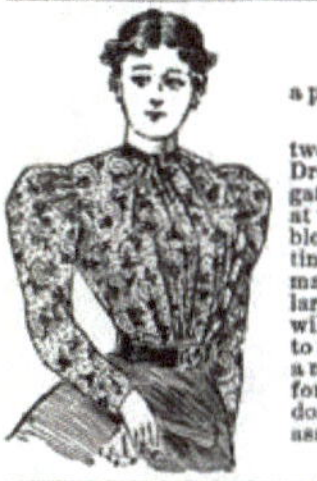

LADIES' SHIRT WAIST.

Unmatchable in America at so low a price.

B500—Fine quality goods, two assorted patterns in fancy Dresden and stripes. Full set-in yoke, gathered back and front with tie string at waist. Can be worn as a loose-fitting blouse front, or tailor-made tight-fitting style. Laundried cuffs to match material, white laundried standing collar. This is the best $4.50 waist that will be shown this season — made to sell at $7.50. We bought them from a manufacturer who wanted money before the shirt waist season began. 1 dozen in box, assorted patterns and assorted 32 to 42. Price per dozen, **$4.50**

"Scarborough" BED SPREAD.

If you want to see how cheap this is, send for a sample lot and *compare with the values of other houses.*

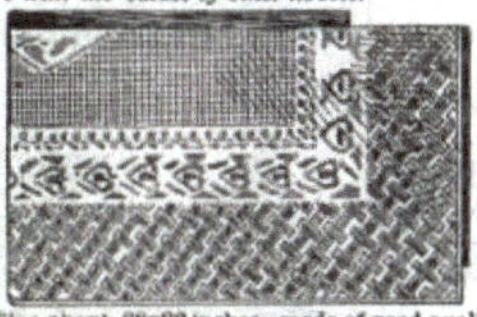

B38—Size about 68x82 inches, made of good quality cotton in handsome Marseilles pattern, hemmed ready for use. This price is the result of an order placed months ago when the mill wanted orders mighty bad. 6 in pkg., no less sold. Price each, **48c**

THE HAMMOCK BARGAIN OF THE SEASON.

A dollar "leader" that will make your competitors hungry to buy of you.

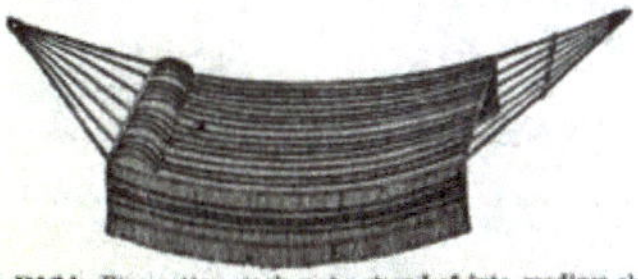

B124—Fine cotton stock, not a strand of jute, medium close weave, full size pillow, metal head stretcher and foot adjustment, 12-inch valance sides, effective combination colorings in red, green, gold, etc., heavy cord ends and metal hangers. Size of bed 34x74, extreme length 10½ feet. It took the biggest order in hammock history to pound this down to a possible "dollar" price. Price each, **77c**

See colored pages in back of this book, also page 184, for additional "LEADERS FOR BARGAIN DAY."

MANY "LEADERS" IN GLASS.

Though we have in the past offered many rare bargains in Glassware, those grouped on this page and next are *easily first in competitionless good value.*

"Pearl Opalescent" ART WARE ASSORTMENT.

Beautiful beyond description. Yet at popular price figures.

Look to be worth $1.00 each. You buy them at 84c doz. We are used to offering unusual values—but here we have some of the choicest impossible-to-describe pieces of rich and useful pearl opalescent art glass ware that can be imagined—and best of all at a price seemingly one-fourth its value. Assortment comprises:

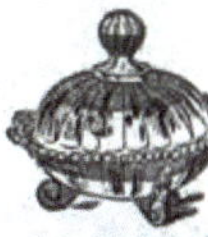

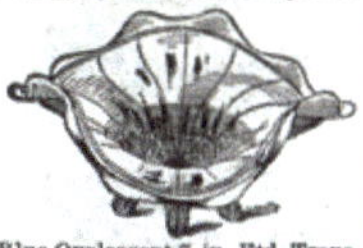

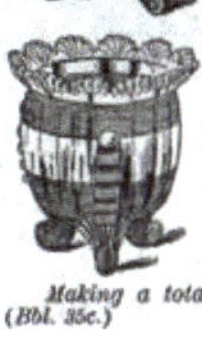

1 doz. Pearl Blue Opalescent 7-in. Ftd. Trays.
1 " Pearl Yellow " " "
1 " Pearl Flint " " "

These "Trays" or "Card Receivers" are exquisitely shaped with flared and scalloped edge and stand on three little artistic feet.

1 doz. Open Sugar or Flower Bowl. Assorted blue, yellow and flint. These also have three feet.

1 doz. 5-inch covered Jewel or Puff Tray. Assorted blue, yellow and flint. These also have three feet.

Making a total of 5 doz. to pkg. Sold only by bbl. (Bbl. 35c.) Price per dozen— **84c**

Pearl Footed TRAYS.

—Same as above assortment. Packed in barrels of 1¼ doz. each pearl blue, pearl yellow and pearl flint, making a total of 3¾ doz. to bbl. *Sold only by bbl. (Bbl. 35c.)* Price per dozen, **89c**

"ENGRAVED BLOWN TUMBLER" ASST.

2 doz. each of 4 rich engravings, safely packed in case.

Here is one of the best 5-cent bargain day offerings it is possible to suggest.

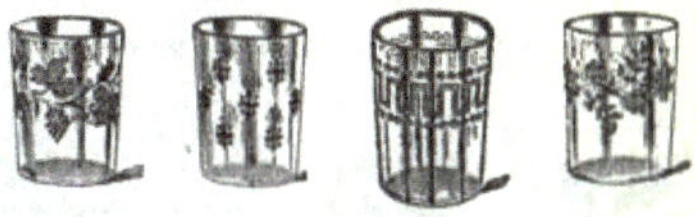

—The heading tells almost the whole story. Four rich engravings on full size (9 oz.) genuine lead glass table tumblers. Packed 2 doz. of each in a case—*making a total of 8 doz. to case.* (Case 30c.) Sold by case only. Price per dozen, **36c**

"Bargain Sheet" LAMP ASSORTMENT.

A tempting bunch of lamps at tempting prices.

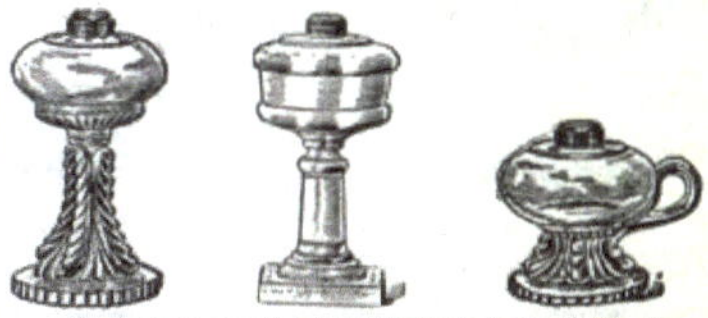

—These lamps are absolutely high grade and "firsts." These are all standard lamps, which take No. 1 burners. The assortment comprises 1 doz. each of 4 high lamps and 1 doz. low stand lamps, making a total of 5 doz. to pkg. Sold only by pkg. (Bbl. 35c.) Price per dozen, **48c**

The Following Are in Pasteboard Boxes, No Charge for Packages.

"Dew Drop" SALT SHAKER.

A staple favorite at a winning price.

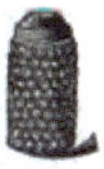

—The greatest of all "sellers" among the many "cellars." The dew drop or dot pattern in crystal. Best nickel top. 1 doz. in box. Price per dozen, **20c**

"Dew Drop" Pepper Shaker.

As above. Price per dozen, **20c**

"Green and Gold" JEWEL TRAY.

Your customers will fairly fight for these at a *10-cent price. It looks to be worth 50 cents.*

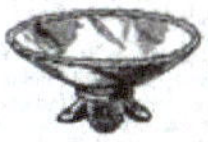

B25—A rich emerald green receptacle for cards, jewels, hairpins, etc., on cute little feet. Has real gold edge and gold feet. 1 doz. in box, no charge for box. Price per dozen, **80c** (4 doz. or more, 78c)

SPECIAL OFFERING IN NEST EGGS.

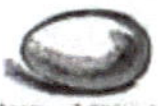

—A special lot of standard nest eggs, made up by special contract during the dull season. These are of the very best grade. No rough edges, uniform in size. Consider how cheap these are when the wooden case costs us 20 cents at factory. *1 gross in case.* Price per gross (including case), **$1.60**

"10-Band" ENGRAVED BLOWN TUMBLER.

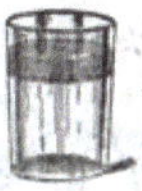

Best of lead glass. Full 9-oz. table tumblers. *A sure enough trade stimulator.*

—Full size table tumbler of genuine lead glass. All firsts. Having a rich and delicate 10-band engraving. 1 doz. in box. Price per dozen, **33c**

Special Factory Purchase

ART VASE SALTS AND PEPPERS

at one-third cost value.

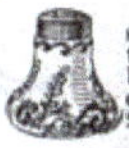

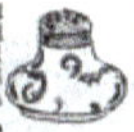

B15—Hand painted, gold decorated salts and peppers. Having real gold plated tops. In rich display boxes. Formerly sold by factory for 25c goods. Sold in equal quantities salts and peppers (in less than 2 doz. lots) assorted patterns. Price per dozen, **75c**

"American Beauty" CRYSTAL VASE.

A rich 10-cent bargain day offering.

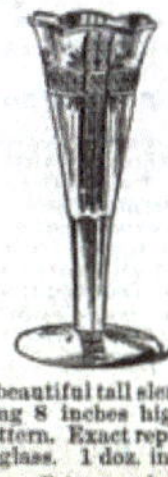

—A beautiful tall slender vase, standing 8 inches high, exquisite pattern. Exact reproduction of cut glass. 1 doz. in box. Price per dozen, **80c**

Hand Painted

SALT AND PEPPER SET—With Tray.

A great 10-center.

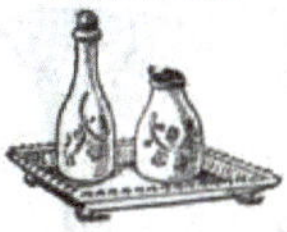

—Comprising salt and pepper in vine pattern, rich opal with tasty colored decoration, also plain opal tray. A rich offering and a bargain at 10 cents. Each set in pasteboard box, no pkg. charge. Price per dozen sets— **89c** (4 doz. sets or more, 87½c)

"Enameled Etched" FLORAL BLOWN TUMBLERS.

These etchings usually found on 25c tumblers.

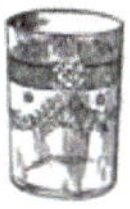

These etchings are not comparable with the usual simple floral affairs, but are of rich and elaborate design. The tumbler is a full 9-oz. pure lead glass. Put up 1 doz. of a pattern in spaced box.

408A—Rose bouquet design. Per dozen, **40c**
408B—Arbor festoon design. Per dozen, **40c**
408C—Lily of the Valley design. Per dozen, **40c**

"Emerald Green" FLOWER VASE.

A rich 5-cent sales' opportunity.

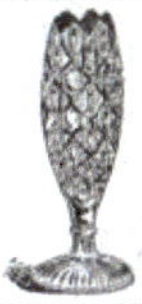

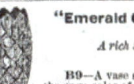

B9—A vase standing 6¾ inches high in the all-the-rage color of "Emerald Green." You will sell all you can get of these if you dare name this small figure. You'll sell quarter as many 10 cents. 1 doz. in pasteboard box, no charge for box. Price per dozen, **43c** (6 doz. or more, 41c)

"Pearl Opalescent" JEWEL TRAY.

The richest of the new things at a 10c price.

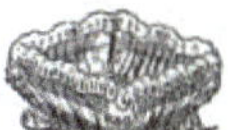

—We can't describe the ever varying yet exquisite coloring, but they are extra heavy and unique shape, 4 inches in diameter, 2 inches deep, with footed corners. Assorted pearl blue, pearl yellow, and pearl flint in a box of 1 doz. (*No charge for box.*) Price per dozen, **80c** (4 doz. or more, 78c)

"Crystal and Gold" BON BON DISH.

The queen among the new 10-cent offerings.

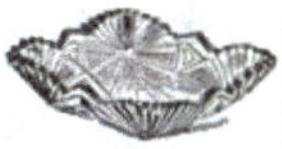

B62—Imagine the richest of crystal with a wide band in genuine gold, and this in connection with the most shapely of receptacles measuring 5½ inches in diameter, and you have it. *Send for sample dozen* and buy many. 1 doz. in box. Price per dozen, **80c**

"RICH AND RARE" 5c CRYSTAL TRAY.

For hairpins, pins, jewels, etc.

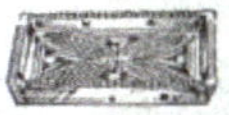

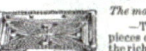

The most beautiful of all cut glass patterns.

—This is positively one of the choicest pieces of ware ever produced and will adorn the richest home. 1 doz. in box. Price per dozen, **39c**

"DIAMOND PURE" MUG.

A rich 5-cent attraction.

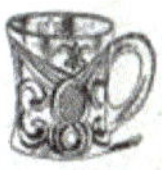

—Of exquisite design in fleur-de-lis pattern, purest of glass. Just right size. 1 doz. in box. Price per doz. **37c** (6 doz. or more, 36c)

Though we group here on the colored pages a few best "leaders" from each department, you must study the fine type offerings on every page in this book if you want to get a right idea of the bargains with which our line abounds.

ONE GOOD BARGAIN Will Sell for You Twenty Items on Which You Make Money.

"LEADERS FOR BARGAIN DAY."—Continued.
Prices Subject to Our Regular Terms: 2 per cent 10 days, net 40 days.

Our "WAREHOUSE" 5-Cent Assortment.
Here is a Sample of What We Can Do When Quoting Pittsburgh Prices.

Our customers when looking at samples from glass factories sometimes overlook the item of freight which has been paid on glassware before it reaches either of our three distributing houses. Here is a chance to compare prices on an even basis. Tell the factory fellow to "match 'em, if he can."

The "Warehouse" 5-Cent Assortment Comprises 1 Doz. Each of the Following:
7-Inch Deep Round Dish—Serviceable for forty purposes.
Celery Dish—A large and heavy dish.
Heavy Table Tumbler—One of the always staple sort.
Heavy Handled Olive Dish—Large 5-inch dish with heavy practical handle.
Extra Deep Preserve Dish—Measures 4½ inches in diameter, 2 inches deep. Cut glass pattern.
Square Diamond Plate—Measures 7½ inches square. Very useful.
8-Inch Oblong Dish—Always wanted. Always a seller.
High Footed Bowl—Measures scant 5 inches in diameter. Stands 5¼ inches high.
Flanged Butter Dish and Cover—Bottom 7 inches. Has a knob top cover.
8-Inch Extra Heavy Oval Dish—Large and shapely.
(Shipped from Pittsburgh. Total of 10 doz. to pkg. Sold only by pkg. Bbl. 35c.) **Price—34c Doz.**

N. B.—For other warehouse glassware opportunities see page headed Direct Shipments from Pittsburgh.

Our "BARGAIN" 10-cent Cask Assortment.
You Will Wonder How We Can Offer These 20 and 25-cent Goods at a Possible 10-cent Figure! We Want You to Wonder; That's Why We Do It.

We delight most of all in giving our customers something to offer their customers at prices which will call forth exclamations of surprise. This is one of the rarest of opportunities to give bargains which will call forth such exclamations. The pictures are here, the sizes are given. Neither do the pieces more than justice. Here is one of the real opportunities of 1898.

SIX RICH "BARGAIN DAY LEADERS."—(Shipped from Pittsburgh.)
Any of these goods would be cheap at a quarter, but we offer them here as possible 10-cent articles.

☞ **Special Requirement.**—To get this price customers must order no less than 3 packages of these goods. Either 3 packages of one lot or 3 packages of different lots.

LOT NO. 1.

9½-inch Plain Salver. Best crystal glass. scalloped edge. 2½ doz. in bbl. (Bbl. 35c.) **Price—82c Doz.**

LOT NO. 2.

10-inch Footed Dish. Best goods. Newest pattern. 3½ doz. in bbl. (Bbl. 35c.) **Price—82c Doz.**

LOT NO. 3.

9½-inch Fancy High Finish salver. 2½ doz. in bbl. (Bbl. 35c.) **Price—82c Doz.**

LOT NO. 4.

High Footed Bowl, 8½-inch large table dish. 3 doz. in bbl. (Bbl. 35c.) **Price—82c Doz.**

LOT NO. 5.

10-inch Fancy High Finished Dish. 4 doz. in bbl. (Bbl. 35c.) **Price—82c Doz.**

LOT NO. 6.

Large 8-inch flanged Butter Dish with High Cover. 4 doz. in bbl. (Bbl. 35c.) **Price—82c Doz.**

All the above six lots shipped only from our Pittsburgh warehouse and in no less than 3 pkg. shipments.

The "Bargain" 10c Assortment Comprises 1-2 Doz. Each of the Following:
8-inch Deep Round Dish—One of the heavy patterns.
High Footed Bowl—A high table dish 6¼ inches in diameter.
Heavy Sugar Bowl and Cover—A big, bright every-day seller.
10-inch Oval Heavy Dish—25 cents would be cheap for it.
Oil or Vinegar Bottle—A handled vinegar jug with glass stopper.
Tall Flared Vase—A 7-inch tall, slender vase of exquisite pattern.
7-inch Extra Deep Footed Dish—This splendid dish has a low foot and has scalloped edges.
8-inch Square Deep Heavy Plate—A staple, "taking" table necessity.
Half Gallon Water Pitcher—A great, big, splendid jug.
7-inch High Footed Bowl—Of the crimped pattern, big and good.
10-inch Oval Heavy Dish—A bouncer, and one that sells at sight.
7-inch Extra Deep Round Dish—An every-day necessity.
9-inch Salver on High Foot—For cake, etc., etc.
7-inch Deep Square Platter—Everybody wants it.
8-inch Oblong Dish—Show it and it will belong to another.
7-inch High Footed Bowl—A gem of a pattern.
Heavy Butter Dish and Cover—A big, strong butter dish, bright and beautiful.
9½-inch Fancy Oval Dish—One that's good for bread or other purposes.
13-inch Celery Tray—A large one, but a beautiful one.
High Flared Footed Bowl—A rich 7-inch high-footed dish for sauces, berries, etc.
(Total of 10 doz. to pkg. Sold only by pkg. Cask, 30c.) **Price per dozen—74c**
(Shipped from our house.)

Our "Big VALUE" 5-cent Tierce Assortment.
Ten Great, Big, Brilliant Beauties, Worth from 10 to 20 Cents Each.

And still another—Here is another assortment made up of goods which really belong in the 10-cent lots, but which *if you want to* you can *run on a "nickel" apiece.*

The "Big Value" 5c Tierce Assortment Comprises 1 Doz. Each of the Following:
6½-inch Footed Salver—The newest and richest of cut glass patterns.
Quart Water or Milk Pitcher—This large piece is of the rich "Astor" pattern.
6½-inch Round Deep Dish—An every day useful table dish—"Astor" pattern.
7-inch Round Plate—For cheese, etc., etc.—"Astor" pattern.
Heavy Sugar Bowl and Cover—Of the same rich "Astor" pattern.
Flanged Butter Dish and Cover—Another of the good things of the same pattern.
5-inch High Footed Bowl—For sauces, preserves, etc.—"Astor" pattern.
8½-inch Handled Dish—For pickles, etc. "Astor" pattern.
7½-inch Footed Bowl—A large table dish of the same pattern.
8¼-inch Deep Oval Dish—Always salable. Always useful. "Astor" pattern.
Total of 10 doz. to pkg. (Tierce 60c.) **Price per dozen—40c**
(Shipped from our house.)

Note that "Bargain" and "Big Value" Assortments are shipped from our house, whereas "Warehouse" Assortment and Lots 1 to 6 are shipped from Pittsburgh.

Remember, This Catalogue Quotes **WHOLESALE PRICES.** Keep It Out of Your Customers' Hands.

THREE LEADING HOUSES IN AMERICA'S THREE DISTRIBUTING CENTERS.

CHICAGO — Looking west on Adams street from a point opposite Marshall Field & Co.'s famous wholesale building, showing Butler Brothers' mammoth seven story and basement store between Franklin and Market streets and running through to Quincy street.

NEW YORK — Looking up Broadway north from the corner of Broome street, showing Butler Brothers' great building, eight stories above ground and two below, which extends through. An accurate representation from a photograph.

ST. LOUIS — Looking east from Twelfth street, showing Butler Brothers' seven story and basement building at Nos. 1115, 1117, 1119 and 1121 Washington avenue, running through to Lucas avenue.

TERMS AND REQUIREMENTS.

Our terms are 2 per cent 10 days—net 41 days. Net 40 days or longer time.

No charge for case or cartage. Glass and crockery packages are the only ones we charge for. All manufacturers and jobbers charge for these.

A deposit must accompany every C. O. D. order. If you desire goods sent C. O. D. you will please send as a deposit of at least 25 per cent. of the presumable amount of the order, and on orders of any amount less than $50 you will please send at least $5 as a guarantee of your acceptance of the goods. The amount of the deposit will be deducted from the draft. No C. O. D. shipments for less than $10 will be made.

We can send goods C. O. D. by freight, marked Butler Brothers. The invoice is mailed direct to you, and the bill of lading (insured over $100), accompanied by a draft on you for the amount of invoice (less your deposit), is sent to your nearest bank for collection. Upon the payment of this draft you can secure the bill of lading and thus get your goods from the railroad agent.

C. O. D. Crockery Shipments. C. O. D. customers ordering Crockery shipped from factory, in the same order with goods to be shipped from our house, should send separate deposit for each shipment — at least $5.00 each or $10.00 in all.

Do not send us checks on country banks. It is to your interest as well as ours that customers observe this rule, as a debtor is liable until his obligation has been paid in cash, and he should remit so that currency can be realized quickly. Therefore in remitting send us a bank draft on New York, Chicago or St. Louis, or if that is not convenient send an express or post office money order. We pay no exchange or express charges on money.

Goods by mail. All packages sent by mail are discounts at the expense and risk of purchaser. They may be registered but, while that costs 8 cents extra for each parcel it does not guarantee delivery. We therefore advise our patrons to instruct us to have their mail shipments insured. The **Home Insurance Co.** furnishes us printed blanks, which when filled out by us will insure you against loss. The cost of this insurance, which we charge up with goods and postage on invoice, will average about 3 cents for each $5.00 of insurance. This will positively protect you against loss. Shall we insure your mail shipments?

We sell to merchants only. Consumers into whose hands this catalogue may accidentally fall will save labor and stamps by remembering this.

We cannot break packages. All our goods are put up in as small packages as possible consistent with safe shipping. We will not furnish less quantities than indicated.

SUGGESTIONS TO CUSTOMERS.

Never send money by mail unregistered. Notwithstanding Uncle Sam's vigilance, money letters disappear in transit every day.

Examine all cases, barrels, etc., and see that they are in good condition before accepting same from transportation company. All shipments made by us are in good order when taken by transportation lines and so receipted for. Our responsibility then ceases.

Goods cannot be returned, except for cause. We guarantee every item as described and are always ready to rectify errors. If goods received are not as ordered, notify us and await instructions. Your return them without notice.

Orders for less than $5.00 will not be filled. This is for your economy as well as ours. Transportation charges on such bills eat up your profits, and our expense for filling is as great as on larger orders.

INSTRUCTIONS FOR ORDERING.

By Observing these Suggestions You Facilitate the Filling of Your Orders and Lessen the Possibility of Errors.

In ordering from us for the first time please give us as reference the names of a few houses with which you have an established credit.

Write your order on separate sheets from any other communication you have to make. This permits both being attended to at once.

Use only one side of the paper, if possible, in ordering, except when using our order sheets, as this sometimes prevents items being overlooked.

Our order sheets are put up in pads of 20. If you have not a pad mention it in your next order or drop us a card.

Write name and address plainly. A doubtful word in the middle of a sentence can be guessed at, but a bad signature is an unsolvable puzzle. Avoid fancy signatures.

Shipping directions. Be sure to mention your nearest shipping point if you are not located on a railway or water route. If there are competing transportation companies name your preference. If express shipments, specify which company serves your town.

One item only on a line. Never write more than one item on a line, and never put the price at which we have catalogued it. This helps us to identify the exact article wanted.

In using our order blank write nothing except the order. If you have other matters to communicate or a remittance to enclose, mention same on separate letter sheet.

Avoid ordering goods to be packed with those of other houses. Some houses absolutely refuse to receive such packages, and in doing causes us no annoying delays and misunderstandings. It costs you no more to ship separately, and saves trouble and delays.

Do not ask us to purchase goods outside our stock. We naturally wish to be accommodating, but so much difficulty has been experienced in endeavoring to even approximate such requests, often from very meager directions, we have been compelled to refuse them.

Our principal banks of deposit are the following, to which we refer:
Chemical National Bank, New York.
Corn Exchange National Bank, Chicago.
State Bank of St. Louis, St. Louis.

BUTLER BROTHERS,
IMPORTERS AND WHOLESALERS OF GENERAL MERCHANDISE.

| NEW YORK: | CHICAGO: | ST. LOUIS: |
| 495 TO 497 BROADWAY | 230, 232, 234 & 236 ADAMS ST. | 1121 TO 1127 WASHINGTON AVE. |

"Our Drummer"

If you were in our place and Knew you were selling goods for less than market, what would you do to impress that fact upon your trade?

Send men to their stores with samples? But if we do that our cost of selling will be so swollen that we will be *forced* to raise our prices.

Pay railroad fares to bring buyers to us? That's equally bad—in either event we shall lose the single advantage that makes it possible for us to quote the lower prices.

It seems to us there is one way and only one way open to us. We send you a catalogue that shows our goods just as they are and quotes our best prices in plain black and white. Will you not meet us half-way by sending to us for sample lots for the only satisfactory test of value— *comparison in your own store?*

One thing sure, we never before sent out a catalogue that so well deserved the close heed of buyers who know values when they see them and are open to buy where a dollar buys most.

THE REVOLUTION IN BUYING.

Twenty-five years ago the retailer bought all his wares from travelling men except on his infrequent trips to market.

...we venture the strong assertion that *eighty per cent* of the goods purchased by retailers are bought without seeing samples, and that the merchant who buys even *half* his goods from samples is very much the exception.

It is commonly figured among houses with drummers that mail-order and house sales amount to as much as the direct sales of road men.

Nearly every jobbing house nowadays sends out a catalogue and circulars as well as men.

Half the drummers one meets carry no more than a grip in which are borne photographs and printed matter, possibly a few samples of specialties.

The retail dry goods man buys probably two-thirds of his wares, barring piece goods, either "as last" or from catalogue, or from simple mention of an item to the salesman without submission of sample. The dry goods drummer seldom lumbers his trunks down with samples of plain black hose or common towels or notions.

The grocery road man may carry a few samples of teas and profitable specialties, but probably ninety-five per cent of his sales are from a printed price list.

Hardware salesmen usually carry a big catalogue and a lot of loose circulars and discount sheets, but mighty few samples. No doubt ten per cent would more than cover their sales from samples.

The drug man carries a little grip containing price lists and possibly a few specialties, but no more.

Yet drummers were never so thick as they are today. They grow keener after trade all the time. The intervals between trips get shorter each year, the territory a man can cover smaller.

Is it any wonder that sales from catalogues are growing when all the road man does is to write down the order?

One can understand why a salesman should accompany samples, but when he bears simply photographs and price lists it is hard to see what good purpose he serves that the catalogue does not serve BETTER.

The salesman names a high price and comes down if you force him. The catalogue names its bottom price the first time.

The salesman tries to persuade you to buy this item or that. The catalogue lays its line before you and awaits *your* pleasure.

The salesman urges you to buy grosses. The catalogue gives you a right price in single dozens.

The salesman asks you to suit your convenience to his—to give him a quick audience that he may catch a train. The catalogue waits until *you* are ready.

The salesman gives you a copy of the order, mentioning simply numbers and prices. The catalogue stays with you until goods come in, shows a cut, gives size or weight, enables you to know that you get what you bought.

A high-priced man sent in a high-priced way to do the clerical work of writing down an order—to do that which a catalogue does BETTER—is waste, sheer waste.

As a man gets to know merchandise better he has less and less need of samples. If he has learned that our catalogue tells the truth, when we tell him that a certain number in 84-needle half-hose has a ribbed top and weighs 24 ounces to the dozen, price 48 cents, we have told him all he wants to know.

There are some goods that will always be sold from samples—wall paper, carpets, dress goods, etc. But the great bulk of the goods sold over the retail counter, at least the great bulk of the goods shown in this catalogue, are the sort where to the man who knows merchandise a cut and a brief description tell all the sample can tell on the brief scrutiny a busy man gives each item when looking over a line.

Jobbing goods by catalogue is just in its infancy. It is bound to grow because it means economy in time, labor and expense.

EXPANSION ON EXPANSION.

As we have told you before, our Chicago house has just moved into its permanent home, which is the "largest continuous wholesale premises in America".

January 1st of this year our New York house gained a number of additional floors in the adjoining building at 491 and 493 Broadway.

Since our February catalogue was mailed, our St. Louis house has closed the contract for a huge new warehouse building located within a stone's throw of their present structure, which will give them nearly three hundred thousand additional feet of floor area. The building is to be hastened to completion and possession is promised by July 1st of this year, in season for the heavy fall trade.

We are not paying additional rent for fun. We are simply keeping in shape to take care of our business, which is growing by leaps and bounds — *faster to-day than ever before.*

SPRING 1903

Prices go into effect March 6th, and take precedence over all others. We guarantee them during March or until our April catalogue is out.

PRESERVE THIS CATALOGUE as there will not be another Unabridged edition until September.

UNABRIDGED CATALOGUE No. 456

BUTLER BROTHERS St. Louis

THE GOODS WE SELL—AND WHY.

We are not ashamed to say that we make a specialty of low priced goods.

Eighty per cent of our offerings are identical in grade with those offered you by the exclusive houses. The other twenty per cent of our line consists of popular priced goods—those that are commonly hardest to buy because there is least profit in them for maker or jobber.

The other twenty per cent of the exclusive houses' lines is in goods that appeal to the classes rather than to the masses.

There are firms enough to push the more expensive goods, to tell you how much better linen is than cotton, and how much longer a XXXX tin pan will outlast a common IC one; which you probably know already.

It seemed to us there was room for *one* wholesale house that made a specialty of low-priced goods—that should make it easy for the trade to buy such at right prices. Our success would seem to show that we were right in that opinion.

Good value means something more than quality. It means a fair price as well.

We will not sell a high priced article if we can find something in the market equally good at a lower price. We do not care to contribute to someone else's advertising bills nor to pay too much for a name unless it stands for a fair price as well as quality.

The retailer who means to serve all classes requires 5-cent articles as well as 50-cent ones. He cannot buy them of the drummer at right prices, for it costs him too much to sell. He cannot buy them of the drummer at any price without meeting the sneer "cheap goods."

It takes a salesman as long to sell a dozen $2.25 underwear, on which he makes perhaps 15 cents, as it does a dozen at $18, on which he makes maybe three dollars. Small wonder he encourages the sale of the latter.

In the early days of our business we sold nothing but low priced goods. As our business grew our standard of quality rose. We added higher priced goods as well as more departments, and each year our proportion of the more expensive goods grows larger.

But we would feel that we fell short of our duty to our trade if we did not supply them with goods of every *worthy* grade, from best down to the cheapest.

Nothing delights an exclusive jobber quite so much as to buy some fairly good article, put on it his own brand, and then make you retailers pay ten to twenty per cent more than actual value.

Nothing delights us more than to have some well known maker sell us his standard brand of goods, possibly without labels, but *absolutely the same* in all other respects, at a price so we can sell them at a quarter or a third less than usual rates.

A TERM THAT NEEDS DEFINITION.

What *are* "cheap goods" anyway?

They say the stables of certain millionaire horsemen in New York have marble floors and porcelain bathtubs. Yet we know of some very worthy people who would not on that account relish a sneer at the less expensive furnishings which adorn their own houses, meant for people not beasts.

Possibly the finest goods on your shelves would be relegated to the bargain basement of Field's in Chicago or Wanamaker's in New York.

The rich man's son who pays five to ten dollars per pair for Parisian half hose probably has no words strong enough to tell his contempt of 50-cent goods. Chances are that most retail merchants even of the high toned sort think a 50-cent pair of socks pretty good. And it is certain if there were no such thing as half hose to retail at five and ten cents, a lot of men would emulate the example of a certain western statesman and go sockless.

Of course a sheer linen towel is better than a slimsy cotton one. *Of course* sterling silver knives and forks are nicer than common iron handled ones. *Of course* there is more satisfaction in a 75-cent steel hammer than in a 10-cent cast iron one.

But the fact remains that a great many men must work for $1.50 per day. They too would prefer sheer linen and sterling silver and the good steel tools, but the few dollars they have left when rent and grocery bills are paid forces them to buy what they can afford and not what they might like.

And if some good woman in your town that you think could afford the higher priced goods, prefers to buy the cheaper in order that she may spend more elsewhere, be sure she will do it. What do you profit by forcing her to go to another store to buy that for which she naturally looks to you?

The sure penalty of selling only high priced goods is that you limit your trade to the well-to-do.

There is more money to be made in serving all the people than in serving one single class. Sell only high priced goods and you drive the masses away. Sell all grades and you can serve the entire public, *including* the well-to-do.

WE WILL NOT SELL TRASH.

In each line we strive to buy the lowest-cost article to be had anywhere that is worth selling and worth using. We will not knowingly sell any article that will not give satisfaction to the man who uses it and to the merchant who sells it.

There are few articles in this book of which there are not cheaper imitations in the market. We violate no confidence when we say that many of those cheaper goods were produced for the express purpose of getting something to "beat Butler's price."

When our competitors go below the trash line we do not follow. You may usually be safe in figuring, when you get a lower price than we name, that it stands for trash. If the goods were what they should be we would have them.

We have no sympathy with that silly fear of "cheap goods" which judges an article by price alone. Nothing is too cheap for our buyers to look at. If the quality is right, the cheaper the price the better we like it. We think we can tell trash better when we see the goods than we can from price alone.

For many years the following words were painted on the wall of our Chicago house in its old home on Adams Street: "NO MATTER HOW LOW THE PRICE OUR STANDARD OF QUALITY WILL BE MAINTAINED." That sign could not be moved to our new home, but the spirit it expresses is maintained more rigidly than ever.

We do not and will not sell job lots or auction goods or trash of any sort.

WHAT COUNTS.

When hucksters put their small potatoes on top of the basket and the big ones below—when country lads go courting in jeans and ploughing in broad cloth—when circuses are advertised in monosyllables—then and not until then will it be safe to judge that *all* a salesman's prices are low because he names a low quotation on nails or sheetings or breakfast foods.

There are certain "staples" in your line that you know all about. So does every other merchant. The drummer knows these as well as you do. They are used as a "football" by every seller. No jobber makes any money on them. If a salesman be found high on these he is ruled out at the start. They are priced in every catalogue. Of necessity the prices of all sellers must be about the same on goods like these.

But, Mr. Merchant, when you buy "staples" at your own price the game has just begun and you don't hold the best cards.

The drummer is no chicken and no chump or he wouldn't be on the road for a living. He is of value to the house, not because he can sell you Amoskeag gingham or plain cedar lead pencils at a loss, but because, after getting you good natured by selling you those goods at a low price, he can get enough more for other items so the whole bill shall show a satisfactory profit.

Be fair to yourself. Don't let your conceit as a buyer fog your good sense. You know, when you stop to think, that you are not and cannot be sure of the value of more than one article out of ten in your store within from five to ten per cent.

If you think otherwise, have one of your clerks bring you twenty articles from stock at random, without cost or selling marks. Lay aside those whose precise cost you remember. Put down your "guess" as to values, then go look at costs and see how close you came.

Or try it on the next line of samples you look over. Take some entire line, "leaders" and staples and all, and note down your estimate of prices. Then have the salesman give you his real prices, item by item.

We shall take off our hats to you as a judge of values if the result does not prick your pride. Demonstrate that you can, on more than nine items out of ten, habitually guess within five per cent of market value and you can pick your job with any of the big wholesale houses in the country. They are anxious to pay ten thousand a year to men who can do that.

The only thing that counts is a seller's prices on NON-COMPETITIVE goods—the odd nine items out of ten whole values no one knows accurately.

IF YOU WERE A DRUMMER.

Put yourself in the drummer's place. Tax yourself with an expense of five to ten dollars per day and then make your own salary dependent, not merely on your sales, but on the *profit* your sales show, and see what you would do.

If you found a man who had his mind made up to buy some certain item at a certain price wouldn't you oblige him if you saw the order hinged on so doing? And then wouldn't you get that lost profit back something else before you got through or know the reason why?

If you found a man running over with the conceit that he was a cracker jack buyer, wouldn't you take a fall out him just for fun if you could?

If you run across a man who didn't know value would you give him your lowest price or make him pay your highest? Honor bright, now.

If the head of the house wrote you a personal letter saying they were badly stuck on so-and-so, wouldn't you try your best to include same in every sale whether your customer needed it or not?

If you had a real "snap" would you give it to your good friend Brown who always has an order ready for you, or would you hold it for Jones who still keeps you at arm's length?

If you found a good-credit buyer in a pliant mood, would you urge him to cut down a quantity when you felt he was going in too deep, or would you coax him along?

It's poor fun and bad business to fool one's self. Buy of the drummer when he has goods you need and sells them at a right price, but *don't* permit yourself to believe that the drummer begins to look after your interests until he has gotten through with his own.

What you would do if you were on the road the drummers do now who call on you.

PROFIT-SHARING WITH OUR EMPLOYEES

For three years past we have distributed a part of our earnings each January among those employees who have been with us more than a year. The letter of explanation which accompanied the che[que] [receiv]ed by each employee this year contained th[e follo]wing paragraph:

"Our people have been divided into four classes "and this classification has been made upon as fair a "basis as possible. In these individual estimates we "have taken into account Reliability, Industry, Willing-"ness, Carefulness, Conduct, Punctuality, Originality "and Ability."

A messenger boy who shows exceptional zeal may be placed in the highest class, whereas the head of a department who has grown tired in the service or energy may go in the lowest.

We are now perfecting plans for making the profit-sharing plan with our employees a permanent feature of our policy. We propose to set aside in perpetuity one thousand shares of our capital stock (par value one hundred thousand dollars) which shall be used solely for the benefit of the privates and minor officers in our concern.

Two things are necessary to make a business *permanently* great and strong:

First, an ever-fresh supply of new blood—of active, capable young men who will help develop the countless opportunities that open up before a growing concern.

Second, enlisting the best efforts of all employees so that each may be as much interested in the welfare of the business as though it were his own.

We hope and believe profit-sharing will help to accomplish these ends for our business. For the country and the world we hope it may help to solve the knotty problem of the relations between capital and labor.

Our Splendid Business in Glassware (Largest in America) Has Not Come By Chance.

GLASSWARE at Under-Market Rates.

Buyers who know the state of the glass market—how costs at the factories have been rising steadily for the past year—will be pleasantly disappointed when they scan the following pages. *Costs are often determined by combinations but we make our own selling prices.*

We here present what are, in view of all conditions, **the best values we have ever shown in glassware.** There is no "mystery" about them. The simple explanation is that we buy more glass than any one else in America, and it costs us less than two per cent to sell, where it costs others ten to fifteen per cent. *This catalogue makes glassware prices for America.*

We call special attention to the quality of our ware and the large size of our pieces. The glassware we sell is of high standard quality—selected patterns of leading makers—and will prove better value in your store than it looks on paper.

☞ The never-broken combination between glassware manufacturers compels all factories to charge for packages, and accordingly, *every jobber must pay for them.* Therefore, if we did not charge directly for the barrel, we should be obliged to add it to the price of the goods.

CAUTION! When Opening Glassware Barrels DO NOT DRIVE IN THE HEADS.

We charge 35 cents each for all glassware packages (though some of them cost us upwards of 60 cents each), except a few cask and tierce packages and chimney boxes, which latter are charged at 30, 40 and 50 cents. We charge for no packages aside from glassware and crockery.

Our assortments are all made up and packed by professional packers at the factory before being shipped to us, and are not opened until they reach our customers' stores.

Our "BARGAIN DAY" 3c Assortment.

30 Possibilities, but Comparable Only with the 5-Cent Assortments Offered by Our Neighbors.

C106—Although these *can* be sold for 3 cents, they are all large pieces which have never before retailed for less than 5c. All brilliant cut glass patterns, most of them full finished and fire polished.

Assortment Comprises 1 Doz. Each of the Following:

5½-Inch Footed Scalloped Edge Tray—Brilliant and attractive.
Large Handled Mug—Shapely and rich.
Medium Size Cut Pattern Salt and Pepper—Extra heavy with good tops.
4½-Inch Deep Footed Sauce Dish—Fancy scalloped edge.
Large Fancy Goblet—Brilliant and shapely.
5½-Inch Fancy Olive or Bonbon Dish—Footed, with turned-up sides.
Extra Heavy Rich Table Tumbler—Deep cut pattern.
4½-Inch Footed Comport—Extra deep, full finished.
Full Finished Wine Glass—Brilliant rich pattern.
4½-Inch Beaded Edge Nappy or Sauce Dish—Extra deep, extra bright.
Rich and Heavy Toothpick Holder—A 5c gem.
6½-Inch Fancy Finished Plate—Always useful.

(Total 12 doz. in bbl., Bbl. 35c.) **Per dozen, 25c**

Our "SUNRISE" 5-cent Assortment.

A Rare Collection of Crystal Gems.

C117—All exceptionally rich and fancy shaped pieces—all of exceptionally beautiful pattern, full finished and fire polished.

Assortment Comprises 1-2 Doz. Each of the Following:

5½-in. Fancy Tulip Shape Vase—Dainty and rich.
4½-in. Footed Comport or Sauce Dish—Fancy scalloped edge.
5½-in. Footed Bon-Bon Tray—With bent-up sides.
5½-in. Footed Deep Round Dish—Useful for many purposes.
4½x4½-in. Comport or Sauce Dish—Fancy square shape.
6-in. High Footed Bon-Bon Dish—An artistic and beautiful piece.
5½-in. Footed Tray or Receptacle—Fancy star design.
6-in. Tray Plate—Fancy star design.
5½-in. Salver on High Foot.
8½-in. Extra Long Deep Oval Dish—Cheap at 10c.
4½-in. High Footed Jelly Dish—Extra deep and fancy shape.
5-in. Round Footed Nappy—Fancy shape and extra brilliant.

(Total of 12 doz. in barrel. Bbl. 35c.) **Per dozen, 40c**

Our "CHALLENGE" 5-Cent Assortment.

Although Offered as a 5c Assortment, Nearly all of These are TEN-Centers in Size and Quantity

C109—One of the best assortments ever offered, all pieces extra large size. New and brilliant patterns, nearly all being richly finished and fire polished. Order a few barrels and mark them "Your choice for 5 cents" and your customers and your competitors alike will be surprised.

Assortment Comprises 1-2 Dozen Each of the Following:

7-Inch Extra Large Flanged Butter Dish with Cover—An invariable 10-center.
Extra Heavy Footed Spoon Holder—Height 4½ inches. Matches butter dish.
Extra Heavy Sugar Bowl and Cover—Same beautiful pattern. A 10-cent beauty.
Extra Large and Heavy Milk or Cream Pitcher—Matches sugar bowl.
6-Inch Extra Deep Round Berry Dish—A bargain at a dime.
6¼-Inch Crystal Flaring Vase—Always useful. A bargain.
7¼x5¼ Deep Oval Table Dish—With heavy scalloped edge.
5½-Inch Extra Deep Round Footed Bowl—A full finished gem.
5½-Inch Footed Tray Plate With Scalloped Edge—Richest pattern.
4½-Inch Footed Comport—Useful for many purposes.
8½-Inch Deep Oval Dish—Extra heavy. Always a 10-center.
5-Inch Extra Heavy Deep Bonbon or Olive Dish—With large open handle.
Extra Heavy Full Size Table Tumbler—Deep cut design.
7-Inch Round Deep Footed Fancy Dish—Of brightest pattern.
Extra Brilliant Footed Mug—With large convenient handle.
5½x4½-Inch Footed Fancy Dish—With bent-up sides.
7¼-Inch Round Bread or Cake Tray—Footed, cheap at 10 cents.
Large Size Brilliant Goblet—With plain finished mouth edge.
7x5¼-Inch Extra Deep Oval Utility Dish—Of new rich pattern.
8-Inch Bread or Cake Tray—Round shape with elaborate scalloped edge.

(Total 10 dozen in tierce. Tierce 45c.) **Per dozen, 43c**

"3 TABLE NECESSITIES" Assortment.

3 staple dime sellers at price which leaves you a profit.

C338. All in richest of plain crystal glass, full finished and fire polished. Prices lower than usually sold in barrel lots. Assortment Comprises:

1 doz. medium size Oil or Vinegar Bottle with stopper and graceful handle.
1 doz. tall Mustard Pot, smooth ground bottom and convenient knob handle cover with opening for spoon.
1 doz. extra heavy and rich Salt and Pepper Shaker with heavy nickel plated cast dome top.

Total 3 doz. in box, *no charge for box.* **Per dozen, 72c**

IT IS NOT POSSIBLE to Make a Better Grade of Glassware Than That Here Shown.

Look Over Every Line of Glassware in the Trade and Then Come Here and Save Money.

Our "BIG SURPRISE" 5c Assortment.
Invariable Dime Articles at a 5c Figure That Leaves a Profit for You.

C105. All large pieces, best staple sellers, new patterns, brilliantly finished and polished.

Assortment Comprises 1 Doz. Each of the Following:
Extra Large Handled Cream Pitcher—Brilliant pattern, fancy footed.
Large Footed Spoon Holder—To match creamer.
7-inch Extra Deep Flanged Butter Dish and Cover—Same rich pattern.
6½-inch Deep Round Table Dish—Always a 10-center.
8½-inch Deep Oblong Dish—Fancy scalloped edge.
5½-inch Deep Handled Bonbon Dish—Always a seller.
9½-inch Extra Long Fancy Pickle—or Small Celery Tray—Bright pleasing pattern.
5½-inch Bonbon Dish—Artistic 3-corner shape.
7½-inch Round Scalloped Edge Plate—Cheap at 10-cents.
Extra Large Full Finish Goblet—Rich beaded panel pattern, plain finished edge.
5½-inch Extra Deep Round Bowl or Table Dish—A useful piece.
Rich and Shapely Wine Glass—Beaded panel design with plain flaring top.
(Total 12 doz. in bbl. Bbl. 35c.) Per dozen, **41c**

Our 5c "OPALESCENT" Assortment.
Order a Package—You'll be Pleased with the Goods and Amazed at the Value.

C108—This superb assortment of richest opalescent ware is in entirely new patterns, most of them being in a brilliant ribbed basket design. Equally assorted in 3 colors, flint, blue and canary opalescent. Every piece full finished and fire polished. You'd expect to pay a toc-price for everyone of these.

The Assortment Comprises 1 Doz. Each of the Following:
5-Inch High Footed Fancy Tray or Bonbon Dish—With elaborate crimped edge.
4x4 Extra Deep Bonbon Dish—Fancy square shape, rich beaded edge.
Rich Full Size Table Tumbler—Ribbed pattern, very brilliant.
Fancy Shape Bud Vase—Beautiful serpentine twist pattern.
Heavy Ribbed Salt and Pepper Shaker—Good top.
Fancy Footed Handled Sherbet Cup—Always a 10-center.
5¼-Inch Footed Tray or Plate—With beaded edge.
Fancy Footed Toothpick Holder—Serpentine pattern.
Large Footed Spoonholder or Open Sugar—A handsome piece.
4-Inch Extra Deep Footed Trinket Tray or Sauce Dish.
4½-Inch Deep Bonbon Dish—Scalloped edge, standing on 3 handsome feet.
6½-Inch Tall Flower Vase—Beautiful lily shape.
(Total 12 doz. in bbl., wt. 82 lbs. Bbl. 35c.) Per dozen, **43c**

Our "ALL FINISHED" Bowl and Salver Assortment.
Extra heavy rich plain pattern.

C383—All extra large pieces and staple all the year sellers, full finished and fire polished.

Assortment comprises:
⅓ doz. 7¼-in. extra deep high footed bowls with high dome cover........ @ $2 10 $0 70
⅓ doz. Extra large 10-in. high footed cake salvers........................... " 2 10 70
⅓ doz. Mammoth 8-in. extra deep footed bowls with high dome cover........ " 2 40 80
(Bbl. 35c.) Total for asst. of 1 doz. **$2.20**

"NEW VICTORY" 5-Cent Assortment.
Half of Them Belong to the 10-Cent Class.

C103—The assortment is made up of the most staple selling items in glassware. All in bright patterns, most of them being full finished and fire polished.

Assortment Comprises 1-2 Doz. Each of the Following:
Handled Measuring Mug—Graduated spaces for cups and ounces.
6-in. Fancy Shape Plate—Cut diamond pattern.
Shell Pattern Salts and Peppers—With high dome tops.
Banded and Fluted Table Tumbler—Full finish, smooth edge.
Fancy Stem Wine Glass—Rich and elegant.
Extra Large Footed Sugar Bowl and Cover—Brilliant pattern.
Large Footed Spoonholder—Matches sugar bowl.
Large Handled and Footed Cream Pitcher—In the same pattern.
7-in. Flanged Butter Dish with High Cover—Always a 10-center.
Optic Fluted Table Tumbler—Rich and brilliant.
4½-In. Extra Deep Nappy—With fancy scalloped edge.
Large 6½-In. Berry Dish—With fancy scalloped edge.
4½-In. Deep Nappy or Bon-Bon Dish—Square shape.
Footed Toothpick Holder—Fancy twist pattern.
Large Milk or Cream Pitcher—Handled or footed.
Large Fancy Handled Mug—Bright, attractive seller.
5-In. High Footed Dish—For jellies, preserves, etc.
5-In. Extra Heavy Bowl—A useful piece.
4½-In. Fancy Sauce Dish—All brilliant patterns.
8¼-In. Utility Table Dish—Fancy oblong shape.
(Total 10 doz. in tierce. Tierce 45c.) Per dozen, **39c**

Our "WELCOME" 5-Cent Assortment.
All Big Bright Pieces. Extraordinary Values.

C113—A choice collection of staple sellers in new and bright patterns, all of which can be retailed at 5 cents, though most of them are worth more.

Assortment Comprises 1-2 Doz. Each of the Following:
6-in. Flanged Butter Dish and Cover—*Worth 10 cents.*
Medium Size Cream Pitcher—Fancy foot and handle.
Fancy Footed Sugar Bowl and Cover—Matches cream pitcher.
Fancy Footed Spoon Holder—Of the same pattern.
5½-in. Extra Deep Round Dish—Double open handles.
8¼x4½-in. Oblong Utility Dish—Fancy beaded edge.
Handled and Footed Lemonade or Sherbet Cup—Always a seller.
5x5-in. Fancy Square Shape Tray Plate—With turned up corners.
4½-in. Extra Deep Bonbon Dish—Footed and with open handle.
Shapely Wine Glass—Rich beaded and paneled design.
6¼x4½-in. Extra Deep Oblong Table Dish—A useful piece.
Round Footed Mustard Pot and Cover—A brilliant 5c bargain.
5½-in. Extra Large Round Deep Olive or Bonbon Dish—Large open handle.
5½-in. Fancy Tulip Vase—A crystal beauty.
Full Finished Table Tumbler—With fancy fluted bottom.
4½-in. Extra Deep Round Bowl—Footed and with fancy scalloped edge.
6-in. Fancy Shape Handled Dish—Rich cut diamond pattern.
Large Handled Mug—Dot mirror pattern on fancy foot.
5¼x5½-in. Extra Heavy Square Deep Dish—Heavy scalloped edge.
Tall Tankard Cream Pitcher—Footed, ht. 5½-in.
(Total 10 doz. in bbl. Bbl. 35c.) Per dozen, **39c**

It Costs Us 1 Per Cent to Sell Glass—It Costs the Factories 10 to 15—The Difference Is YOUR SAVING.

Our New "BRILLIANT" Assortment of 5c Gems.

Although Possible 5-Centers Many of These Retail Regularly at Double That Price.

C110 — 12 of the most staple quick selling articles in crystal table ware—bright new patterns. *Will compare favorably with many 10-cent assortments offered by others.*

The Assortment Comprises 1 Doz. Each of the Following.

Extra Large Footed Sugar Bowl—With cover—Dot mirror pattern.
Large Footed Spoon Holder—Dot mirror pattern.
7-Inch Flanged Butter Dish—With cover and fancy knob handle.
Large Handle Cream Pitcher—Fancy footed.
4¾-Inch Extra Deep Footed Bowl—Rich cut diamond pattern, fancy scalloped edge.
6x6 Square Brilliant Plate—Rich dew-drop pattern.
7x5 Large Oblong Table Dish—Useful for many purposes.
4½-Inch Footed Comport—Extra deep and extra brilliant.
4½x4½ Olive or Bonbon Dish—With large open handle.
8½-Inch Spoon Tray or Pickle Dish—Fancy shape and pattern.
Handled and Footed Mug—Dot mirror pattern.
5½-Inch High Footed Deep Bowl or Comport—For jellies, etc.
(Total 12 dozen in bbl. Bbl. 35c.)

Per dozen, **41c**

Floral "HAND DECORATED" 10-Cent Assortment.

A Matchless Collection of 10-Cent Leaders.

C221 — All in pure crystal, full finished and fire polished in rich plain and fluted design, each and every piece being decorated with white enameled bands and hand painted floral designs in carnations with green leaves. All the decorations are burnt-in and will not wear off.

Assortment Comprises 1-2 Doz. Each of the Following:

7¼x5¾-in. Extra Large Deep Oval Tray—Both useful and beautiful.
Fancy Footed Toothpick Holder—With flaring crimped edge, elaborate decorations.
4½-in. Extra Deep Round Sauce Dish—Especially attractive in this ware.
Extra Large Footed Spoonholder—Ht. 4¼-in., fancy swell shape, wide fluted edge. *Worth 25c.*
4¾-in. Round Fancy Footed Tray—For trinkets or jewelry.
Fancy Footed Sherbet or Lemonade Cup—Genuine stuck handle.
Shapely Stuck Handled Cream Pitcher—Fancy footed, with good pouring lip.
Fancy Footed Open Sugar—Ht. 2¾-in. Matches cream pitcher.
5-in. Extra Deep Fancy Dish—Footed, with fluted edge.
Full Size Shapely Table Tumbler—Also useful as a spoonholder.
4¼-in. Extra Deep Footed Comport—Fancy crimped edge. Useful for many purposes.
Extra Large Rich Goblet—Flaring edge and imitation cut stem, beautifully decorated as above.
(Total 6 doz. in bbl. Bbl. 35c.)

Per dozen, **77c**

Our "PEERLESS" Gold Decorated Assortment.

12 Matchless 10c Bargains in this Ever Popular Ware.

C219 — All in richest of full finished and fire polished crystal in newest and most beautiful patterns and all with elaborate decorations and extra wide bands of pure gold, decorations being burnt-in and will not wear off.

Assortment Comprises 1-2 Doz. Each of the Following:

7¼x5 Extra Large Deep Oval Dish—Rich scalloped edge.
Open Footed Sugar Bowl—Ht. 2¾-in., diam. 3¾, brilliant panel design, wide gold edge.
Tall and Shapely Cream Pitcher—Footed, with large handle. Matches sugar bowl.
5-in. Fancy Tray Plate—Rich cut diamond pattern with scalloped and decorated edge.
7½-in. Fancy Bonbon or Olive Dish—A large piece of brilliant design.
Large Fancy Handled Mug or Lemonade Cup—Footed, ht. 4¾-in., ¾-in. gold band.
4¾-in. Fancy Shape Extra Deep Heavy Bonbon Dish—Footed, fancy flaring sides.
Tall Shapely Table Tumblers—Also used as a spoonholder.
Round Deep Footed Sauce Dish—Diam. 4-in., rich beaded panel pattern with wide gold band.
6-in. Tall Shapely Flaring Vase—Beautiful floral design with gold band more than 1-in. wide.
Massive Round Deep Dish—Diam. 4¾-in., extra heavy bull's eye pattern, fancy beaded edge.
Large Brilliant Goblet—Beautiful panel pattern, ¾-in. gold band.
(Total 6 doz. in bbl. Bbl. 35c.)

Per dozen, **78c**

OUR "THUNDERBOLT" 10c Cask Assortment.

Extra Large, Extra Heavy and Extra Brilliant Pieces as Dime Possibilities.

C259—An unsurpassed and exceptionally desirable assortment of large pieces, nearly all of them being full finished and fire polished. The smallest one of them would be a 10c leader—*more than half of them would be cheap at 15c to 20c.*

The Assortment Comprises 1-2 Doz. Each of the Following:

Large Footed Quart Water Pitcher—Plain but rich.
8x3¾ Celery or Utility Tray—Extra deep, beautiful pattern.
Extra Heavy Cut Panel Pattern Spoonholder—A gem, looks like cut glass.
Extra Heavy And Large Sugar Bowl—With cover. Of same pattern.
Large and Heavy Stuck Handled Cream Pitcher—Matches sugar bowl.
6¼-Inch Round Deep Table Dish—Fancy scalloped edge.
Rich Plain Quart Decanter—With stopper, ht. not including stopper 8 in. *Worth 25c.*
7½-Inch Scalloped Edge Berry Bowl—Footed, full finished and fire polished.
8½x4¼-Inch Spoon Tray—Fancy shape, deep cut pattern.
Tall Molasses Pitcher—With spring top.
7¼-Inch Flanged Butter Dish and Cover—New all-over etched design.
7-Inch Extra Deep Round Berry Bowl—Extra heavy and rich pattern.
6-Inch Olive or Bonbon Dish—Extra large and deep, large open handle
8¼x4¼ Celery or Spoon Tray—Very brilliant.
Handled Oil or Vinegar Bottle—With stopper. Plain rich pattern.
7x7 Deep Table Dish—With fancy edge.
4¾x3¾ High Footed Deep Jelly Dish—Finished, bright pattern.
7¼x7¼ Extra Deep Berry Bowl—Square shape, fancy scalloped edge.
18-Inch Combination Vase or Water Bottle—New shape. A handsome piece.
8-Inch Brilliant Salad Bowl—Crimped and fancy scalloped edge.
(Total 10 doz. in cask. Cask 90c.)

Per dozen, **77c**

Our "CHOCOLATE IVORY" 5c Assortment.

One of the best collections of every-day selling novelties we have ever offered.

C102 :. This 5-cent assortment in this new and beautiful ware is one of the best offerings of the season. Rich chocolate color in artistic shades, elaborately embossed.

Assortment Comprises 1 Doz. Each of the Following:

5¼-Inch Extra Deep Covered Butter—Fancy edge and feet. Extra heavy and rich.
Fancy Footed Sugar Bowl—Cover to match.
Handled and Footed Cream Pitcher—To match Butter Dish.
Footed Fancy Scalloped Edge Spoon Holder—Same pattern.
4½-Inch Handled Bonbon Dish—Fancy 3-corner shape on 3 dainty feet.
5-Inch Tall Tankard Cream Pitcher—With large handle and fancy feet, richly embossed.
Fancy Salt and Pepper Shaker—Footed, good nickel top.
4-Inch Round Deep Footed Nappy—Always salable.
Extra Large Fish Shape Bouquet Holder—A 10c bargain.
4½-Inch Extra Deep Scalloped Large Nappy—Standing on 3 feet.
4-Inch Tall Flaring Tumbler or Spoon Holder—Richest coloring and embossing.
4¾-Inch Round Bonbon or Utility Dish—With open handle.
(Total 12 dozen in bbl. Bbl. 35c.)

Per dozen, **43c**

We Not Only Meet But We BEAT ALL PRICES Quoted on This Staple Glassware.

Pay as Much as You Wish You Cannot Get Better Glassware Values Than These.

Our "UP-TO-DATE" Asst. of COLORED and GOLD DECORATED Table Ware.

Although offered as a 10c assortment they retail regularly at double the price.

C269—Beautiful mirror and feather panel pattern, all of the pieces being brilliantly finished the panels of every piece elaborately decorated alternately in red, green and canary colors and all profusely traced in gold bronze giving a rich peacock effect, decorations are not burnt-in but will wear a long time.

The Assortment Comprises 1-2 Doz. Each of the Following:

7-Inch Extra Deep Table Dish—With fancy scalloped edge.
Extra Large 7-Inch Flanged Butter Dish and Cover—Both pieces being decorated. Worth 25c.
Large Footed Spoonholder—Scalloped top.
Extra Large Footed Sugar Bowl with Cover—Both pieces decorated to match.
Large Footed and Handled Cream Pitcher.
5¼-Inch Extra Deep High Footed Bowl or Jelly Dish.
8½-Inch Extra Deep Oval Utility Dish—Fancy edge, richly decorated.
6¼-Inch Deep Flaring Bowl—Standing on handsome foot.
6¼-Inch Round Deep Table Dish—A useful piece.
7-Inch High Footed Comport or Fruit Bowl.
8¼-Inch Oblong Deep Tray—Scalloped fancy edge.
7½-Inch Bread or Cake Tray—Fancy shape, artistic foot.
(*Total 6 doz. in bbl. Bbl. 35c.*) **Per dozen, 78c**

Our "RECORD MAKER" 10-Cent Cask Assortment.
All Big, All Bright Pieces. Most of Them Will Bring Twice 10c.

C273—Notice especially that this assortment contains only the most desirable pieces and will sell out evenly. All are brilliant and well finished.

Assortment Comprises 1-2 Doz. Each of the Following:

8¼x6-in. Oblong Deep Table Dish—Attractive shape and beaded edge.
6¼-in. Tall Flower Vase—Fancy flaring shape.
5¼-in. Deep Round Butter Dish and Cover—With double open handles.
Extra Large Footed Celery Holder—Ht. 6¼ in.
Large Handled and Footed Milk or Cream Pitcher—Wide top and beaded edge.
Extra Large Footed Spoonholder—Matches cream pitcher.
Extra Large High Footed Sugar Bowl and Cover—Of the same pattern.
5½-in. High Footed Jelly or Preserve Dish—Extra deep round shape.
Tall Handled Syrup Pitcher—Rich beaded panel design with spring top.
7½-in. Utility Bowl—Footed, flaring shape.
10¼x3¼-in. Extra Long Deep Celery Tray—Useful for many other purposes.
Extra Large Brilliant Sugar Shaker—Nickel dome top.
5¼-in. High Footed Jelly Bowl—Extra deep, with beaded edge.
Tall Graceful Shape Oil or Vinegar Bottle—Large handle, fancy glass stopper.
6¼-in. Oval Footed Bonbon Dish—Extra large, with double open handles.
Large, Brilliant Water Pitcher—Rich beaded panel design.
6¼-in. Extra Deep High Footed Comport—A brilliant and useful piece.
7¼-in. Extra Deep Round Berry Bowl—Beautiful pattern, fancy edge.
8¼-in. Extra Large High Footed Fruit Dish—Fancy flaring shape.
9-in. Extra Large High Footed Cake Salver—Cheap at 25c.
(*Total 10 doz. in cask. Cask 90c.*) **Per dozen, 75c**

Our "CENTURY" Glassware Asst. of All Leaders.
Positively the Richest Cask Assortment Ever Offered by Any House.
Every piece full finished and fire polished.

C242—The several patterns represented are of striking excellence. As shown in cuts, one is a heavy pattern showing four large heart-shaped panels, filled with very fine cutting resembling a mass of brilliant cut jewels, each panel separated by deep-cut band. Another is the large deep-cut design so popular in the costly cut glass.

It is a simple matter for any thinking merchant to sell five or six of these items at higher prices so as to cover cost of freight, package and possible breakage.

The "Century" Assortment Comprises 1-2 Doz. Each of the Following:

9-Inch Extra Large Flaring Deep Table Dish—Genuine cut glass pattern.
8¼-Inch Round Scalloped Platter—A bargain among all bargains.
8-Inch Flared-side Oblong Dish—Cut-jewel paneled pattern.
8-Inch Fancy Square Tray—Almost a 25-center.
Handled Sugar and Cover—Fire polished, full finished.
Handled Spoon or Celery—Heavy and handsome.
Handled Milk Pitcher—In the pretty paneled pattern.
8-Inch Flanged Butter and Cover—Full size, heavy.
8¼-Inch Extra Heavy and Extra Deep Flaring Bowl—With fancy scalloped edge. Heavy cut pattern.
6¼-Inch Extra Deep Heavy Round Dish—This style dish always sells.
6¼-Inch Extra Deep Heavy Square Dish—Of surpassing value.
10¼-Inch Celery Tray—Heavy, serviceable.
7¼-Inch Extra Deep and Extra Heavy Fruit Bowl—Of brilliant design.
8¼-Inch Spoon Tray—A seller and worth more than 10 cents.
8¼-Inch High Footed Cake Salver—20 cents is usual retail price.
8¼-Inch Cut Pattern Vase—A new cut design.
Oil or Vinegar Bottle—With fancy stopper. A crystal gem.
5¼-Inch Olive Dish—With two handles.
5¼-Inch High Footed Preserve Dish—Good size, rich value.
9¼-Inch Optic American Beauty Vase—Looks worth a quarter.
(*Total of 10 doz. to cask, wt. 203 lbs. Cask 90c.*) **Per dozen, 78c**

The Comprehensive Line of Glassware in the Trade Is That Here Shown.

Our "MOSAIC" 10-cent Assortment.

One of Our Newest and Best Offerings in 10c Bargains of Unequaled Beauty.

C285—This entirely new and beautiful ware is one of the most artistic ever produced, being made in a combination of light and dark blended colors, giving a beautiful marbleized effect. It is beautiful beyond description and will sell on sight. While they would readily retail at 25c each, you can advertise yourself by offering the entire assortment, your choice for 10c.

Assortment Comprises 1-2 Doz. Each of the Following:

8½-Inch Extra Large Footed Fancy Shape Tray—Elaborate crimped edge.
Extra Large Round Deep Open Sugar Bowl—Standing on three feet.
6¼-Inch High Footed Tray or Jelly Dish—Useful for many purposes.
Extra Large Tall Flower Vase with Wide Base—Height 7 inches.
6-Inch Fancy Rustic Footed Bonbon Dish—Turned up sides.
Extra Large Footed Rose Bowl—Height 4¾-in., circumference 15-in.
Large Fancy Footed Cream Pitcher—Large handle and wide top.
Large Spoonholder—Matches the cream pitcher.
Tall Rustic Flower Vase—Fancy 3 corner foot. Height 6¾-in.
5-Inch High Footed Jelly Dish or Card Receptacle—Artistic and useful.
7⅝Inch Deep Footed Fancy Dish—Fancy and crimped edge.
8½-Inch Extra Large Fancy Shape Basket—Large open handles.

(Total 6 doz. in barrel. Barrel 35c.) Per dozen, **79c**

Our "ALL STARS" 10-Cent Assortment.

Another Group of Magnificent Dime Possibilities. All of the Same Pattern.

C288—This assortment is made up of 10 rapid selling items—all in the same pattern which is a rich, almost plain and colonial flute design with small all over pressed stars that are exceptionally attractive.

Assortment Comprises 1-2 Doz. Each of the Following:

7-Inch Deep Flanged Butter Dish—Fancy handled high dome top cover.
Large Footed Spoon Holder—Bright and rich.
Large Footed Milk or Cream Pitcher—With wide top and good pouring lip.
Extra Large Footed Sugar Bowl and Cover—Always a seller.
2-Bottle Caster Set with Handled Glass Stand—One of the best staple sellers.
5½-Inch High Footed Jelly Dish—Deep round shape. For jellies, etc.
6½-Inch Extra Heavy and Extra Deep Round Bowl—With high dome cover.
7½-Inch Large Round Berry Bowl—Extra heavy and extra deep.
Large Fancy Shaped Syrup Pitcher—With large finished handle and good top.
Richly Finished ½-Gal. Water Pitcher—With heavy fluted base and convenient handle.

(Total of 5 doz. in bbl. Bbl. 35c.) Per dozen, **76c**

Our "FLORAL ETCHED" 10c Assortment.

The Latest Novelty in Decorated Classware. Your Loss if You Do Not Sample These Attractive Possibilities.

C266—This entirely new and beautiful ware is etched all-over in rich satin frosted effect, artistically embossed, each piece profusely decorated in elaborate colored floral and gold bronze designs. Decorations in cold colors.

Assortment Comprises 1-2 Doz. Each of the Following:

7½-Inch Round Table Dish—Extra deep. Worth twice 10c.
Full Size Table Tumbler—Richly decorated.
Round Footed Puff Box With Cover—Extra large. Both pieces decorated to match.
6½-Inch Round Tray or Plate—Beautiful chrysanthemum and gold decorated.
Large Tall Shape Salt and Pepper—With good top.
4½-Inch Sauce or Berry Dish—Extra deep, fancy scalloped edge.
4½-Inch Covered Trinket or Jewel Box—Fancy shape, footed. An artistic piece.
4½-Inch High Footed Deep Dish—Six panel decorations.
Large Footed Spoon Holder—Elaborate decorations, scalloped edge.
Extra Large Footed Sugar Bowl with Cover—Of same beautiful pattern.
Large Footed and Handled Cream Pitcher—Fancy top, gold lip. Matches sugar bowl.
7½-Inch Flanged Butter Dish with Cover—A beautiful piece, elaborately decorated.

(Total 6 doz. in bbl. Bbl. 35c.) Per dozen, **80c**

Our "COLDEN SUNSET" Assortment.

Although Offered as 10c Possibilities, They Would as Readily Retail at Double the Price.

C283—One of the latest and most beautiful productions of the glass-maker's art, being of a rich golden agate color, delicately shaded and blended, giving an exceptionally beautiful effect. No cuts could do justice to this ware, and it must be seen to be appreciated.

Assortment Comprises 1-2 Doz. Each of the Following:

7½-In. Extra Deep Round Bowl—*Worth 25c.*
4¾-In. High Footed Jelly Dish—Artistic and useful.
Large Milk or Cream Pitcher—Handled, fancy shape.
7½-In. Long Utility Tray—Deep oval shape.
4¾-In. Deep Bon-Bon Dish—With fancy handle.
7¼-In. Round Tray Plate—Extra deep and extra heavy.
Large Spoonholder or Open Sugar.
Large Tall Shape Handled Stein or Mug.
Tall Fancy Flower Vase—Height, 6 inches.
7½-In. Round Utility Dish—Will sell always.
4¾-In. Deep Footed Comport—Useful and salable.
5-In Extra Deep Butter Dish—With high cover.

(Total 6 doz. in barrel. Barrel 35c.) Per dozen, **77c**

Our Special "GOLDEN" ASSORTMENT.

A Collection of Pure Cold Decorated Crystal Gems. None so Beautiful Ever Before Offered at a 10-Cent Price.

C260—All in the same deep cut pattern, one of the latest genuine cut glass designs, every piece full finished and fire polished, very brilliant. All elaborately decorated with wide band of pure gold burnt in. Half of these do not belong in the 10-cent class, but *will readily retail from 15 to 20 cents.*

Assortment Comprises 1-2 doz. Each of the Following:

6¼-inch Footed Flaring Vase—Extra large, extra heavy, very elaborate.
Large and Shapely Goblet—⅜-inch band of gold round top.
Heavy Ground Tumbler—⅜-inch gold band. Will sell as readily for a spoon holder.
6½-inch Oval Olive or Bonbon Dish—Very brilliant.
Fancy Cut Stem Wine Glass—¼-inch gold band.
Heavy Rich Salt and Pepper Shaker—Wide spread base, richly decorated.
Extra Large Cream Pitcher—Handled and footed. Ht. 3¾-in. A beauty.
Large Fancy Shape Open Sugar—Worth 20 cents.
Fancy Shape Cream Pitcher—Matches open sugar.
Fancy Shape Oval Dish—6¼-in., extra deep, footed, beautiful scalloped edge, elaborately decorated.
4½-inch Deep Footed Flaring Nappy—or Sauce Dish—a gem.
4¼-inch Round Bonbon Dish—Extra deep, footed, with fancy scalloped edge.
Footed Toothpick Holder—Heavy and rich, artistic pattern.
Oil or Vinegar Bottle—Brilliant and shapely, with stopper. *Worth 25c.*
Glass Lip Syrup Pitcher—With patent britannia top, solid gold decorated handle.

(Total 7½ doz. in bbl., wt. 82 lbs. Bbl. 35c.) Per dozen, **78c**

Perhaps You Have No Glassware Department—Better Add It—Diversified Merchandising PAYS BEST.

Merchants Who Are "Up to the Times" Never Know a Dull Season.

Our "LUMINOUS" Assortment.
Excels in Quality and Price. Will Sell on Sight.

Every Piece Large, Every Piece Fire Polished and Full Finished.

C251—An assortment of "all leaders." Pieces are all of generous size. In this, as in all our 10c assortments, there are pieces that you can sell for more than a dime to make up for freight and possible breakage.

The "Luminous" Assortment Comprises 1-2 Dozen Each of the Following:
8-inch Extra Deep Fruit Bowl—Generous size and generous value.
8-inch Flanged Butter Dish, Dome Cover—Showy patterns, good size.
5½-inch High Footed Fancy Jelly Dish—Most useful size.
6½-inch Extra Deep Footed Berry Bowl—Specially desirable in this pattern.
Brilliant Stuck Handle Milk Pitcher—With shapely lip.
10½-inch Footed Bread Plate—A seller in any store at 10c.
7-inch Round Utility Dish—A bargain on any 10-cent counter.
7½-inch Large Bottom Vase—Large and pretty and cheap.
9-inch Extra Large Footed Bowl or Comport—Regular 25 center.
8½-inch High Footed Fancy Bowl—You can sell it for 25c to help pay freight and breakage.
(Total 5 doz. in bbl., wt. 100 lbs. Bbl. 35c.) **Per dozen, 74c**

Our NEW "FANCY SHAPE" Bowl Assortment.
Every one Full Finished and Fire Polished.

C378. This unusually attractive assortment comprises the newest and most artistic productions in crystal glassware. Nearly all of them footed and of exceptionally handsome shapes.

Assortment Comprises ½ Doz. Each of the Following:
7-in. High Footed Flaring Bowl—Rich panel design.
10¾x6¼-Inch Celery or Bread Tray Fancy Shaped—Dot mirror pattern.
8¼-Inch Flaring Footed Bowl or Comport Fancy Shaped—Standing on handsome foot.
6½-in. Fancy Footed Bowl—With roll up edges.
7¼-Inch Footed Deep Comport—Of endless utility.
7½-in. Deep Fancy Shape Dish—Richly finished.
8½-Inch 3-corner Footed Cake or Fruit Dish—Fancy rolled-up edges.
8½-Inch Footed Flaring Table Dish—Beautiful reflector pattern.
9½-Inch Footed Fancy Celery or Cake Tray—Rolled-up sides.
7-in. High Footed Comport—Fancy 3-corner shape.
(Total 5 doz. in tierce. Tierce 50c.) **Per dozen, 76c**

Our "WORLD BEATER" 10c Cask Asst.
Twenty Crystal Beauties, the Smallest One of Which Will Be a Rare 10c Leader.

C252—Every piece full finished and fire polished and all in the most brilliant new cut patterns. More than half of them are actually worth more than double the price here named.

The "World Beater" Assortment Comprises 1-2 Doz. Each of the Following:
High Footed Cake Salver—9¼ in., worth easily 25c.
7-in. Footed Bowl—Of most brilliant pattern.
Extra Heavy Spoonholder—Ht. 4½-in.
8-in. Deep Oval Dish—Fancy scalloped edge.
5¼-in. High Footed Jelly Dish—Dainty and rich.
Large Handled Milk or Cream Pitcher—Ht. 4½-in.
11-in. Oval Celery Tray—Extra large, heavy rolled up edges.
Footed Flaring Flower Vase—6½-in., all want it.
Footed Jelly or Utility Dish—6½-in., fancy shape.
Vinegar or Oil Bottle—Extra large, with stopper.
Extra Deep Round Berry Bowl—7-in. general utility beauty.
Flange Butter Dish and Cover—7-in. handsome pattern.
Square Bread and Cake Tray—10¼-in., fancy scalloped edge.
Sugar Bowl with Cover—Extra heavy, extra handsome.
7¼-in. Footed Comport—Plain but rich.
Heavy Deep Celery Tray—10½-in., as useful under any other name.
Footed Jelly or Preserve Dish—Diam. 5½-in. ht 5.
¼-gallon Water Pitcher—Extra heavy and extra large, wide top, large handle.
8-in. High Footed Bowl—Big size and a *bargain*.
6½-in. Deep Footed Bowl—A handsome piece.
(Total 10 dozen in cask. Cask 50c.) **Per dozen, 77c**

Our New "DIME OPALESCENT" Assortment.
The Latest and Richest Offering in This Popular and Beautiful Ware.

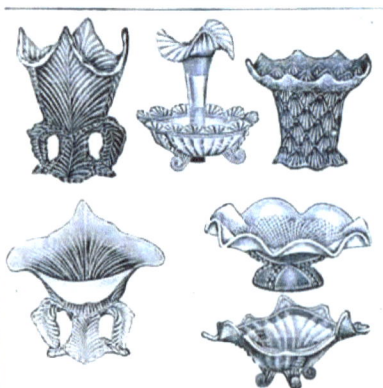

C284—1½ large and beautiful pieces equally assorted in the best selling colors—canary, blue and crystal opalescent. You ought to get from 15 to 20 cents for many of the pieces in this assortment.

The Assortment Comprises 1-2 Doz. Each of the Following:
7¼-in. High Footed Hair Receiver—An art store 25-center.
6-in. High Footed Card Tray or Jelly Dish—With fancy scalloped edges.
7¼-in. Footed Fancy Flared Dish—For many uses.
7½-in. Fancy Flared Dish—Standing on three feet.
Fancy Square Cream Pitcher—Will sell when shown.
6-in. Large Open Vase—Extra wide top with double handles.
Combination Flower Vase of Two Pieces—Rich lily pattern, footed. Height 6-in.
Fancy Open Bowl—Height 4½-in., diameter 5½. An artistic piece.
5¼-in. Fancy Shape Dish—With double handles.
6½-in. Fancy Double Handle Dish—Rich shell design.
5⅜-in. Openwork Edge Footed Dish—A beautiful piece.
Large Open Bowl—Fancy 3-corner shape.
(Total 6 doz. in barrel. Bbl. 35c.) **Per dozen, 78c**

A Plainly Marked Price Ticket Is a Low-Priced and Effective Salesman.

Our "CHARMER" 10-Cent Assortment.

Dime Possibilities of Large Size, Possessing Exceptional Selling Qualities.

C286—All the same pattern, which is a very attractive, plain and frosted beaded panel effect—all pieces also having rich beaded edges, giving an unusually bright appearance.

Assortment Comprises 1-2 Doz. Each of the Following:

Extra Large 7¼-in. Berry Bowl—Extra deep, round shape.
7-In. High Footed Flaring Dish—Fancy 3-cornered shape.
Extra Large Sugar Bowl and Cover—Footed, extra tall.
Extra Large Footed Milk or Cream Pitcher—Large handle and wide top.
Large Footed Spoon-Holder—Rich, beaded edge.
7¼-In. Extra Large Flanged Butter Dish and Cover—Exceptionally rich in this pattern.
5¼-In. Extra Deep High Footed Bowl—Useful and salable.
6¼-In. Extra Deep Round Bowl—High dome cover.
8¼x6-In. Extra Deep Oblong Table Dish—Of endless utility.
Extra Large ½-Gal. Water Pitcher—Footed with large handle. **A regular 25-center.**
(*Total of 5 doz. in tierce. Tierce 50c.*) Per dozen, **75c**

Our "OPALESCENT" Novelty Assortment.

Nothing Better Ever Shown to Retail at 10c.

C593—All fancy shaped pieces and all extra large sizes, equally assorted in blue, canary and flint opalescent. Each piece being richly finished and fire polished. It is your loss if you do not sample this assortment.

Assortment Comprises 1-2 doz. Each of the Following:

7¾-in. Fancy Shape Dish—Rich scalloped crimped edge.
High Footed Deep Fancy Dish—Extra heavy and brilliant. Diameter 4½-in.
6½-in. High Footed Card Tray—Useful also for many other purposes.
7¾-in. Fancy Shape Dish or Card Receptacle—Of beautiful design, 3 dainty feet.
Large Milk or Cream Pitcher—Footed with fancy handle and wide top.
7½-in. Fancy Shape Basket—Large Handle and fancy scalloped edge.
Tall Flaring Flower Vase—Rich crimped edge. Height 6½-in.
Extra Large and Extra Deep Open Sugar Bowl—Diameter 5¾-in. Beautiful dew drop pattern.
Extra Large Fancy Shape Bonbon Receptacle—Footed, rustic design. Diameter 5¾-in.
6½-in. Extra Large Rustic Vase—Of beautiful design.
5¼-in. High Footed Receptacle or Jelly Dish—Fancy embossed pattern, with scalloped edge.
8¼-in. Footed Tray or Receptacle—Heavy dew drop pattern, fancy crimped edge.
(*Total 6 doz. in barrel. Barrel 35c.*) Per dozen, **79c**

Our "DIME OPALESCENT" Assortment.

A Ten-Cent Price will Sell These Fast in Any Store in the Land.

Assorted in the selling colors: Canary, blue, crystal or opalescent.

—If you will send for one barrel of this assortment we think you will find the goods better than you ever bought from any other source for a 10-cent price.

Opalescent ware continues its hold on public favor. It is nice ware to sell over the retail counter. It pays a profit. For example, you *ought* to get 15 to 20 cents for certain of the pieces below.

The "Dime Opalescent" Assortment Comprises 1-2 Doz. Each of the Following:

7¼-Inch High Footed Tray Receiver—An art store 25-center.
Extra Large Rose Bowl—Beautiful pattern, crimped top.
9¼-Inch Fancy Salad Dish—With turned up sides.
6-Inch High Footed Card Tray or Jelly Dish—Fancy scalloped edge.
7½-Inch Tall Flaring Vase—New pattern.
6-Inch Large Crackle Vase—Just as good for celery.
7¼-Inch Fancy Flared Dish—Footed. For many uses, decorative always.
8-Inch Deep Scalloped Dish—In "crackle" glass effect.
7¼-Inch Fancy Flared Dish—3 feet. Something out of common.
7-Inch Footed Card or Spoon Tray—Fluted edge, turned up sides.
Open Sugar, Spoon or Flower Vase—A true art piece.
Fancy Square Cream Pitcher—Will sell if shown.
(*Total 6 doz. in bbl., wt. 100 lbs. Sold only by pkg. Bbl. 35c.*) Per dozen, **80c**

Our "ARTISTIC" Asst. of 10-Cent "Leaders."

12 Possible "10-Centers," Whose Usual Retail Price is Double 10 Cents.

C225—All of one pattern, every piece, full finished and fire polished, each with three jeweled feet, and jewel beaded edge. The simplicity of this old colonial pattern appeals to people who appreciate beautiful plain crystal glassware. These pieces are really **remarkable value, and will** be great attractions in your store.

The "Artistic" Assortment Comprises 1-2 Doz. Each of the Following:

6-Inch Deep Round Dish—Plain and rich.
6¼-Inch 3-Cornered Dish—With stuck handle.
6¾-Inch Card Tray—Footed. A 15-center.
7¼-Inch Rolled-up Side Dish—A rich and rare beauty.
7-Inch Useful Dish—Fancy crimped sides.
6½-Inch 3-Cornered Turned-up Dish.
7-inch High Footed Crimped Dish—Worth 20 cents
1¼-Inch Deep Table Bowl—Rich in this ware.
Rich and Beautiful Milk Pitcher—On three feet.
Sugar Bowl and Cover—Extra large size.
Spoonholder—Used as an open sugar.
Butter Dish and Cover—Splendid value.
(*Total 6 doz. in tierce, wt. 113 lbs. Tierce 50c.*) Per dozen, **79c**

GLASS CANDY TRAYS.

C75 — Pure crystal goods. Size 5x8-in. Plain sides and smooth bottom. Per dozen, **84c**
(*Total 2 doz. in box, wt. 35 lbs. Case 25c.*)

We Never Sacrifice Quality to Gain a Point—If an Article Is Not Good We Do Not Sell It.

Add That New Line Today—Your Neighbor May Get Ahead of You Tomorrow.

Our "MIGHTY" 10-Cent Cask Assortment.
Mighty in Name and Mighty in Value. Comparable Only with the Assortments Offered by Others at 25 Per Cent More.

Our "MONARCH" 10-Cent Cask Assortment.
20 Peerless Beauties of Extra Large Size.

C274—An unusual collection of ready selling staples, the smallest one of which is a 10-cent bargain, and most of them you would expect to find in the 25-cent assortments. All are in brilliant new patterns and all are extra well made and finished.

Assortment Comprises 1-2 Doz. Each of the Following:

8-in. Extra Large High Footed Fruit Bowl—Round flaring shape. Worth 20c.
6¼-in. Fancy 3-cornered Turned-up Dish. Standing on high foot.
Fancy Handled Lemonade or Sherbet Cup and 5¼-in. Saucer. The 2 pieces counting as one.
7-in. Footed Flaring Bowl or Comport—For fruit, etc.
7¼-in. Extra Deep Round Berry Bowl—Brilliant paneled design.
Extra Heavy Footed and Covered Pickle Jar—Full ht. 6 in. *Useful and beautiful.*
8¼-in. Extra Large High Footed Cake Salver—Never too many in stock.
8¼-in. Deep Table Dish—Fancy oval shape.
Tall Shapely Syrup Pitcher—With good spring top.
7¼-in. Flanged Butter Dish—With high dome cover.
Large Family Shape Milk or Cream Pitcher—With fancy handle and good lip.
Extra Large Footed Spoonholder—Matches butter dish.
Large Footed and Covered Sugar Bowl—Of the same pattern.
5¼-in. Extra Deep High Bowl—For jellies and preserves.
10⅜x4¾ in. Extra Large Oval Bread or Cake Tray—With handsome scalloped edge.
7¼-in. Extra Deep Footed Bowl—Round flaring shape.
8¼x6¼-in. Fancy Shape Deep Oval Dish—Useful for many purposes.
Large Handled and Footed Cream Pitcher—With wide top.
Extra Large and Extra Deep 8½-in. Berry Bowl—Brilliant pattern. Worth 25c.
Large Footed Water Pitcher—So-called ½ gal. Wide top and good handle.
(Total of 10 doz. in cask. Cask 90c). **Per dozen, 75c**

C253.—This assortment is composed of the most staple sellers in crystal table glassware, and although offered as a 10c assortment, most of the pieces are usually retailed at DOUBLE the price.

The Assortment Comprises 1-2 Doz. Each of the Following:

Large Footed Jug—So-called ½ gallon, with good lip and large handle.
Fancy Oil or Vinegar Bottle—With stopper. Always a seller.
12-Inch Extra Deep Celery or Bread Tray—Large and handsome.
4¾-Inch Round Bowl—Extra deep.
8¼-Inch Deep Oval Dish—A useful piece.
Tall Syrup Pitcher—Good top and handle.
6¼-Inch Deep Fancy Dish—Footed. For jellies, etc.
Covered and Footed Sugar Bowl—Extra large and bright.
7-inch Flanged Butter Dish—With cover. Matches sugar bowl.
7¼-Inch Footed Fruit or Jelly Dish—Same pattern as above.
7¼-Inch Deep Round Dish—Always useful.
8½-Inch High Footed Cake Salver—Worth 25c.
8-Inch Footed Table Dish—Fancy 3-corner shape.
8-Inch High Footed Bowl—Not the 10c kind.
7¼-Inch Flower Vase—Rich and shapely.
Footed High Celery Holder—Large and brilliant.
11½x8 Plate—For bread or cake.
7¼-Inch Flanged Butter Dish—With cover. Extra deep.
Extra Large Sugar Bowl—Footed and with cover.
Large Milk Pitcher—Good pouring lip.
(Total 10 doz. in cask. Cask 90c.) **Per dozen, 78c**

Our Dime "CHOCOLATE IVORY" Assortment. 12 Items.
A Record Breaking Offer in This All-the-Rage Ware.

C265.—One of the latest and most popular productions of useful and rich table ware, being of a rich chocolate color shading to dark ivory in almost exact imitation of the old and extremely popular Holland Ivory Ware. All in elaborately embossed patterns, giving an unusually rich and attractive effect. *All the pieces would retail readily at from 15 to 25c.*

The Assortment Comprises 1-2 Doz. Each of the Following:

½-Gal. Footed Jug—Beautiful embossed squirrel and vine pattern. *Easily worth 25c.*
Large Fancy Spoon Holder—Embossed edge and standing on 3 feet.
Tall Tankard Cream Pitcher—Footed and shapely.
4½-Inch Tall Flaring Vase or Iced Tea Tumbler—Richly colored and embossed.
6-Inch Oval Footed Table Dish—Fancy scalloped edge.
8½-Inch High Footed Comport or Jelly Dish—A handsome piece.
5½-Inch Extra Deep Round Bowl—With fancy foot.
7½-Inch Extra Large Butter Dish—Flanged and footed with high dome cover.
6¼-Inch Tall Flower Vase—Artistic flaring top.
Large Covered Sugar Bowl—Standing on 3 feet.
Large Handled Milk or Cream Pitcher—Matches sugar bowl.
8½-Inch Berry Bowl—Extra large, extra deep, footed. An extremely rich piece. (*Total 6 doz. in bbl., bbl. 35c.*) **Per dozen, 82c**

Goods of Merit Will Sell More Goods of Merit, But to Sell Them You Must Advertise.

Our Position on This Staple Glassware Is Right Next to the ACTUAL COST OF PRODUCTION.

Our "RICH RUBY" Dime Assortment.

An Unusual Collection of Quick Sellers in this Popular and Attractive Ware.

C230—All large pieces in new and attractive patterns, all with extra wide bands of pure rich ruby which will not wear off, every piece full finished and fire polished. *Many pieces you would not expect to find in assortments at double the price.*

Assortment Comprises 1-2 Doz. Each of the Following:

Extra Large Square Cream Pitcher—Stuck handle, footed, 1¼-in. ruby band.
Full Size Fluted Table Tumbler—Ground bottom. 1¾-in. ruby band.
4½x3¼ Square Comport—Extra deep, footed, fluted pattern, ¾-in. ruby band.
Square Toothpick Holder—Medium size, footed, extra wide ruby band.
Handled Sherbet Cup—Smooth ground bottom, ½ fluted and ½ ruby.
Square Salt and Pepper Shaker—Tall, bright pattern with 1½-in. ruby band, heavy plated cast top.
5-Inch Fancy Shape Cup—Imitation cut pattern. Scalloped edge and rich ruby decorations.
Medium Size Handled Mug—Smooth ground bottom, 2-in. extra wide ruby band.
4¼-Inch 3-Corner Bonbon Dish—Extra deep, brilliant pattern, elaborate ruby decorations.
4½-Inch Round Sauce Dish—Extra deep and heavy. Beaded panel pattern, wide ruby decorated edge.
Beaded Panel Wine Glass—Rich and shapely, 1-in. band of ruby.
Extra Heavy Ground Bottom Table Tumbler—Beaded panel pattern with deep solid ruby band.

(Total 6 doz. in bbl. Bbl. 35c.) Per dozen, **78c**

Our "TOP NOTCH" Asst. of Leaders.

Twenty large crystal beauties which can be retailed at a dime.

C244—All extra large full finished pieces, many of which will readily retail at from 15 to 25 cents each. All of the most brilliant crystal pattern, to which no pictures could do justice.

Assortment Comprises 1-2 Doz. Each of the Following:

8-Inch High Footed Berry Dish—Fancy scalloped edge.
10¼-Inch Large Oval Dish—Very heavy cut pattern.
Heavy Cut Pattern 2-quart Jug—Easily worth a quarter.
8-Inch Deep Oval Dish—A popular seller.
7-Inch Beaded Panel Flaring Vase—Looks like cut glass.
7-Inch High Footed Bowl—Always in demand.
6¼-Inch Fancy Square Shape Table Dish—Very brilliant cut pattern
8-Inch Heavy Flanged Butter Dish and Cover—Not a 10-center.
Extra Large Covered Sugar Bowl—Matches butter dish.
Good Size Milk or Cream Pitcher—Matches sugar and butter.
Fancy Scalloped Edge Spoonholder—This also matches.
5¼-Inch High Footed Jelly Dish—Very artistic.
7¼-Inch Square Bread Plate—Beautiful pattern.
11¼-Inch Oval Celery Tray—Heavy rolled up edges.
9½-Inch Footed Cake Salver—Easily worth 25 cents.
Heavy Footed 1-qt. Jug—Brilliant banquet pattern.
8x5-Inch Footed Tray—Fancy bent-up edges. Useful for many purposes.
7-Inch Footed Comport or Berry Dish—Fancy scalloped edges.
7-Inch Extra Deep Round Bowl—Very heavy and brilliant.
10¼x8-Inch Oval Cake or Bread Tray—Scalloped edges, rich and showy.

(Total 10 doz. in cask. Cask 90c.) Per dozen, **76c**

Our "SUPERIOR" 10-cent Cask Assortment.

A Marvellous Group of Dime Possibilities.

C275—An assortment of all staples and all exceptional bargains. Contains a large variety of pieces, all in rich and beautiful patterns, every piece being full finished and fire polished. Notice especially the extra large size of most of them and the absence of small pieces. Nearly all of them would retail readily at from 15 to 25c.

Assortment Comprises 1-2 Doz. Each of the Following:

7-in. Extra Large Deep Round Berry Bowl—Scalloped edge.
9-in. Extra Long Olive or Utility Dish—Fancy open stuck handle.
Large and Heavy Cream Pitcher—Heavy cut diamond pattern.
5½-in. Extra Heavy Deep Bon Bon Dish—With open handle.
8¾-in. Extra Large High Footed Cake Salver—Big and brilliant.
Extra Large 7½-in. Butter Dish—With high dome cover.
Large Footed Sugar Bowl and Cover—Fancy pearl panel pattern.
Large Footed Spoonholder—Matches sugar bowl.
7¼-in. Flanged Butter Dish and Cover—Of the same pattern.
Large Milk or Cream Pitcher—Handled and footed.
7½-in. Fancy Shape Deep Dish—With turned up sides.
7-in. Round Deep Bowl—Fancy scalloped edge.
Tall Tankard Oil or Vinegar Bottle—With glass stopper.
6-in. Fancy Deep Dish—Artistic 3-corner shape.
8-in. Extra Deep Round Berry Bowl—Worth 20c.
6-in. Extra Deep High Footed Comport—Useful for many purposes.
11x7 Extra Large Tray or Plate—For bread or cake.
7½-in. Extra Heavy Deep Table Dish—Richest pattern and finish.
Large Quart Pitcher—Brilliant optic plain pattern.
7¼x7¼ Square Extra Deep Table Dish—Brilliant cut glass pattern.

(Total 10 dozen in cask. Cask 90c.) Per dozen, **79c**

Our "GOLD PANEL" 25-Cent Assortment.

Big, Heavy and Beautiful Pieces at a Bargain Price.

C247 — Extra heavy, extra large and exceptionally rich pieces in a beautiful genuine cut glass pattern with elaborate 18-karat gold decorated panels and wide bands of gold around edges. *Gold will not wear off, being burnt-in.*

Assortment Comprises 1-2 Doz. Each of the Following:

6½-Inch Extra Deep Round Bowl—Fancy footed. A regular 50-center.
6¾-Inch High Footed Tray or Dish—Rich beaded gold edge and gold panels. An artistic piece.
Large Handled Cream Pitcher—With gold band almost 1 inch wide around top, gold decorated panels.
Extra Large Footed Spoon Holder—Decorated to match cream pitcher.
Extra Large Footed Sugar Bowl with Cover—Both pieces elaborately decorated.
8¼x5¾ Shapely Deep Table Dish, Extra Large and Heavy—Massive and rich.

(Total 3 doz. in bbl. Wt. 80 lbs. Bbl. 35c.) Per dozen, **$1.79**

The Only Better Thing Than Quality About Our Glassware Is the Price—BOTH ARE RIGHT.

Your Money Is as Safe Invested in This Staple Glassware as in Government Bonds.

Our New "HIGHEST AWARD" 10c Cask Asst.
All Fire Polished, Full Finished and All Big Sellers.

Many wise merchants select a few of these pieces to sell at higher prices, making an additional profit to cover freight, package and breakage.

C245—This assortment comprises many of the latest and most brilliant cut patterns, all of purest crystal, and many of them you would not expect to find in an assortment short of double the price.

The Assortment Consists of 1-2 Doz. Each of the Following:
- 9-Inch Large Footed Fruit Bowl—Beautiful fleur-de-lis pattern.
- 8-Inch Extra Heavy Oblong Dish—For preserves, jellies, etc.
- 5-Inch Handled Deep Olive or Jelly Dish—Very salable.
- 9¼-Inch Fancy Cake Salver—Would be cheap at 25c.
- 7¾-Inch Footed Tray Plate—One of the newest patterns.
- Rich Cut Pattern Spoon Holder—Very heavy and bright.
- Large Covered Sugar Bowl—Of the same brilliant pattern.
- Good Size Handled Cream Pitcher—To match sugar bowl.
- 8-Inch Extra Heavy Flanged Butter Dish and Cover—Of the same rich pattern.
- 6½-Inch High Celery Holder—A handsome piece.
- 7-Inch Round Deep Berry Bowl—Always in demand.
- 9½-Inch Fancy Slender Flower Vase—Standing on a handsome foot.
- 7¼x5¼-Inch Deep Oblong Dish—Plain but rich.
- 8-Inch High Footed Fruit Dish—Another of the latest patterns.
- 9½-Inch Square Bread or Cake Tray—Very popular pattern.
- Extra Heavy Footed 2-Quart Water Pitcher—Worth a quarter.
- 6½-Inch High Footed Card Receiver or Bonbon—Useful and ornamental.
- 8½-Inch Round Deep Bowl—Big seller.
- 11-Inch Extra Large Oval Celery Tray—25-cent value.
- 9¾-Inch High Footed Cake Salver—Brightest of patterns.

(Total 2 dozen in cask, wt. 230 lbs. Cask 30c.)
Per dozen, **77c**

Our "PERFECTION" 25-Cent Assortment.
Four Big Brilliant Pieces, Comparable Only with the 50 Centers Offered by Competitors.

C291—All of the same pattern, which is a new and beautiful optic mirror panel design, finest crystal glass, full finished and fire polished. Positively the highest grade glass that can be made.

Assortment Comprises 1-2 Doz. Each of the Following.
- Extra Large and Extra Heavy ½-gal. Footed Water Pitcher—Large imitation cut handle, fancy scalloped top. A full finished beauty.
- 8¾-in. Extra Heavy and Extra Deep Round Footed Fruit Bowl—With elaborate scalloped edge. A handsome piece.
- 9½-in. Extra Large and Extra Heavy High Footed Fruit Bowl—Full ht. 8½ in. A rich and massive piece. Worth 50c.
- 10-in. Extra Large Footed Round Deep Bowl. Same beautiful pattern. Always a staple seller.

(Total 2 doz. in bbl. Wt. 107 lbs. Bbl. 35c.)
Per dozen, **$1.80**

Our MISCELLANEOUS "RUBY" Assortment.
Regular 35c and 50c Sellers to Retail at 25c.

C294—All extra large and extra heavy, elaborate cut glass patterns, extra well finished and fire polished. Each piece profusely decorated in **pure burnt-in ruby** which will not wear off. All are staple every-day sellers, and in this exceptionally beautiful ware are unusually attractive and desirable.

The Assortment Comprises 1-4 Doz. Each of the Following:
- Extra Large and Heavy Butter Dish—7¾-inch, flanged, both pieces decorated.
- Extra Heavy Footed Cream Pitcher—1¼-inch band of ruby around top. Matches butter.
- Extra Large Heavy Sugar Bowl—In same pattern, both pieces decorated.
- Extra Heavy Footed Spoonholder—Matches above.
- 7¼-inch Tall Flaring Flower Vase—Beaded panel pattern, 1-inch ruby band around top.
- 7½x4½ Oblong Table Dish—Extra heavy, extra deep, elaborate ruby decoration.
- Massive Celery Holder—Large and heavy, 2-inch ruby band around top.
- Large Wide Base Syrup Pitcher—With nickel-plated dome top.
- 5½-inch Open Handle Bonbon Dish—Extra deep, deep cut pattern, profuse decorations.
- 5-inch High Footed Jelly Bowl—Deep, fancy edge, rich cut diamond pattern.
- 9x3½-inch Footed Utility Dish—1-inch band of ruby around entire edge.
- Large Oil or Vinegar Bottle—Cut panel pattern, with stopper, alternating panels in solid ruby.

(Total 3 doz. in bbl. Bbl. 35c.)
Per dozen, **$1.75**

Our "MISCELLANEOUS" Asst. of FULL FINISHED WARE.
An Assortment of Staple Sellers, Every One of Which Can Be Retailed at a "Leader" Price.

C779—All of the same beautiful pattern, which is an entirely new beautiful cut diamond design, every piece full finished and fire polished and all except three being footed. Will sell off evenly and pay you a handsome profit. Assortment comprises the following:

⅓ doz. four piece table sets (Butter Dish, Sugar Bowl, Spoon Holder and Cream Pitcher)	$1 85	$0 62
¼ doz. 2-qt. Water Pitchers—Fancy Shape	1 25	31
¼ " 8-inch High Footed Fancy Bowls	1 20	30
¼ " 9½-inch High Footed Cake Salvers	1 20	30
¼ " Extra Large High Celery Holder	96	24
¼ " 9-inch Footed Flaring Salad Bowl	66	16
¼ " 9½-inch Footed Cake Plates	80	20
¼ " 7¼-inch Extra Deep Footed Round Bowl	80	20
¼ " 6-inch High Footed Salver	60	15
¼ " 5¼x5¼ High Footed Fancy Shape Deep Jelly Dish	60	15
1 " Heavy Rich Table Tumblers	33	33
⅓ " 4½-inch Footed Compote	36	36
¼ " Heavy Cut Pattern Salt Shakers	20	15
¼ " Heavy Cut Pattern Pepper Shakers	20	15
¼ " 8x4½-inch Oval Utility Dish	20	15

(Total 5¼ doz. in bbl. Wt. 100 lbs. Bbl. 35c.)
Total for assortment, **$3.36**

A PROPERLY KEPT Glassware Stock Makes THREE TIMES the Sales of an Ill-Kept One.

Our Glassware Department Is One Full of Usefulness—Every Article Is One In Constant Demand.

Our New "JUMBO" 25-Cent Assortment.
Full Finished, Fire Polished, Extra Large Pieces.

C302—Every one of these four pieces is larger than the usual 25-cent goods, and the ware is of the highest possible grade.

The "Jumbo" Assortment Comprises 1-2 Doz. Each of the Following:
9-Inch Full Finished Deep Bowl—High footed scalloped edge.
7-Inch Extra Deep High Footed Bowl—With cover, rich and heavy.
Extra Heavy and Bright Half Gallon Tankard Jug—Full finished fire polished.
11-Inch High Footed Cake Salver—Extra bright, extra heavy.
(Total 2 doz. in bbl. Bbl. 35c.)
Per dozen, **$1.75**

Our "EXHIBITION" 5c Assortment.
Four Mammoth Pieces of Exceptional Selling Qualities.

C295—All of brilliantly rich, almost plain pattern of purest crystal. Every piece full finished and fire polished. *Note specially the extra large size of pieces.*

The Assortment Comprises 1-2 Doz. Each of the Following:
Extra Large Swell Shape 1-2 Gal. Pitcher—Heavy, footed, large and finished stuck handle crimped top. A 50c beauty.
7x7 4-Corner Comport or Berry Bowl, Extra Deep, Footed—Fancy edge.
11-Inch Extra High Cake Salver—Beaded foot and fancy edge.
8½-Inch High Footed Deep Bowl—Brilliant and beautiful.
(Total 2 doz. in bbl. Wt. 108 lbs. Bbl. 35c.)
Per dozen, **$1.87**

Our "BEAUTY BRIGHT" Assortment.
Six Fine "Leaders." Every Piece Full Finished and Fire Polished.

C311—This good assortment includes six large heavy pieces that are *supposed* to be retailed at 25 cents. Of course you will do as you choose, but we would suggest that you make a profit and an advertisement by selling them for less.

The "Beauty Bright" Assortment Comprises 1-2 Doz. Each of the Following:
6½-Inch Flared Fruit Bowl—Unites bigness with beauty.
8½-Inch High Footed Fancy Dish—Easy to get 25 cents for this.
8½-Inch Deep Round Utility Dish—A dish of a sort that always sells.
8-Inch High Footed Round Bowl—Good seller, better ware, best bargain.
9-Inch Fancy Square Corner Table Dish—Showy Dish for a "leader."
9½-Inch High Footed Cake Salver—Usually retails for a quarter.
(Total 2 doz. to bbl. Sold only by bbl., wt. 105 lbs. Bbl. 35c.)
Per dozen, **$1.15**

Our "PRIZE WINNER" 25c Asst. of Crystal Beauties.
Mammoth and Brilliant Pieces to Retail at 25c or More.

C305—The assortment is composed of 6 staple sellers, all of the same pattern, which is a beautiful genuine cut glass design, all are extra heavy and brilliantly fire polished.

The Assortment Comprises 1-3 Doz. Each of the Following:
10½-in. Extra Heavy Footed Comport or Cake Dish.
9-in. High Footed Flaring Fruit Bowl—Beautiful and shapely.
Extra Large 12x8½-in. Fancy Shapely Dish—Extra deep and very useful.
Extra Large and Extra Heavy ½-gal. Water Pitcher—Richly finished with fancy handle.
8-in. High Footed Deep Bowl—Extra heavy and extra brilliant.
10-in. Extra Large Footed Flaring Bowl—Massive and very deep. Scalloped edge.
(Total 2 doz. in tierce. Tierce 45c.)
Per dozen, **$1.69**

Our "PLAIN PATTERN" Set Assortment.
4 Staple Sellers in Rich Plain Pattern and Shapely Design to Retail at Popular Prices.

C339—This assortment is made up of four every-day-selling sets in crystal ware, thereby enabling you to secure a large assortment in one package. Assortment comprises the following:

4 Four-Piece Table Sets—Consisting of 7¼-inch flanged butter with cover, large footed and handled cream pitcher, spoonholder, extra large sugar bowl and cover @ 16½c $0 66
2 Covered Berry or Sauce Sets—Comprising 7½-inch extra deep footed berry bowl with high dome cover and six 4-inch footed nappies or comports @ 32c. 64
2 Uncovered Berry or Sauce Sets—Comprising 7½x7½ extra deep and heavy square corner berry bowl and six 4-inch square nappies @ 22c. 44
4 only Water Sets—Comprising so-called ½-gal. jug and six tumblers @ 30c 1 20
(Bbl. 35c. Wt. 95 lbs.) Total for assortment of 12 sets, **$2.94**

Our "LATEST AND RICHEST" Set Assortment.
Massive and brilliant high grade sets as possible 50-centers, although worth regularly 75c.

C511—These beautiful sets are all of the same pattern, which is an exceptionally beautiful and heavy wide colonial flute design, made of purest crystal, full finished and fire polished. The assortment comprises:

4 only 4-piece table sets. Each consisting of extra large and extra heavy flanged butter dish and cover, extra large fancy shape sugar bowl and cover, large spoon holder and handled and footed milk or cream pitcher.
8 only 7-piece berry sets. Each consisting of 8½-in. large footed fancy shape bowl and six 4½-in. deep nappies to match.
(Total of 12 sets in bbl. Bbl. 35c.)
Average price per set, **35c**

Glassware Like Chinaware Sells When Other Lines Are Dull, and Always Pays a Good Profit.

You May Search the Market as Close as You Wish—You'll Find No Values to Equal These.

Our New "COLOSSAL BEAUTIES" Assortment.

4 Extra Large and Beautiful Pieces Which, Although Offered as Possible 50-Centers, Usually Retail at 75c.

C293—All of the same beautiful pattern, which is entirely new and in exact imitation of genuine cut glass being of a rich cut diamond and flute design. Every piece brilliantly finished and fire polished.

Assortment Comprises 2 Pieces Each of the Following:

Extra Large ½ Gal. Water Pitcher. Extra heavy and brilliantly finished.
10½-inch Extra Large High Footed Comport or Fruit Bowl—Rich scalloped edge. An exceptionally handsome piece.
Extra Large and Extra Heavy Cracker Jar with Handled Cover—Full height 9 inches circumference 19.
Extra Large High Footed Cake Salver—Diameter 10¼ inches, fancy prism pattern edge. (*Total 8 pieces in barrel. Wt. 66 lbs. Bbl. 35c.*)   Each, **29c**

Our "PLAIN STAR" Set Assortment.

Two Every Day Selling Sets in Bright New Pattern to Retail at Popular Prices.

C778—Attractive almost plain pattern in all over star design, best crystal glass, full finished and fire polished. Assortment comprises:

6 only 7-piece Water Sets, consisting of large footed ¼-gal. jug with wide top and convenient handle, and 6 tall tapering tumblers to match, @ 24c set........ $1 44
12 only 4-piece Table Sets, consisting of 7-in. large flanged butter dish and cover, large footed covered sugar bowl, footed spoonholder, handled and footed cream pitcher, @17½c. 2 10

(*Total 18 sets in bbl. Bbl. 35c.*)   Total for 18 sets, **$3.54**

"HEAVY CUT CRYSTAL" Dining Set Assortment.

Beautiful Sets to Retail at Bargain Prices.

C351—Looks like genuine cut glass, all being of the same pattern, which is an exceptionally heavy rich and beautiful design in purest of crystal, and all richly full finished and fire polished.

Assortment Comprises 2 Sets Each of the Following:

7-Piece Berry Set—Consisting of extra large and extra heavy 8¾-in. deep fancy shape berry bowl and six 5-in. fancy shape deep nappies to match.
4-Piece Table Set—Consisting of extra heavy and massive 8-in. flanged butter dish with high dome cover; extra large and extra heavy sugar bowl and cover; handled milk or cream pitcher and spoon holder.
7-Piece Water Set—Consisting of 1 large and heavy footed tankard shape jug with fancy handle and 6 heavy straight shape table tumblers to match.
(*Total 6 sets in bbl. Bbl. 35c.*)   Per set, **39c**

Our Decorated "OPALESCENT" Set Assortment.

Three Beautiful Sets to Retail With Profit at $1.00.

C826—This new and beautiful ware is of rich opalescent glass in elaborate panel and beaded scroll design. All of the pieces are profusely decorated in enameled hand painted floral designs in bright and natural colors, edges being decorated in gold bronze.

Assortment comprises 2 sets each of the following—One of each being in pearl flint and the other in blue opalescent:

7-Piece Water Set—Each consisting of one extra large fancy shape ½-gal. footed jug with fancy flaring top and large handle. 6 full size fancy tumblers to match.
7-Piece Berry Set—Each consisting of one mammoth 9-in. extra deep footed fruit bowl and six 5-in. deep footed nappies or comports to match.
4-Piece Table Set—Each consisting of extra large flanged and footed butter dish and cover, footed and covered sugar bowl, handled cream pitcher and fancy footed spoonholder.
(*Total 6 sets in bbl. Bbl. 35c.*)   Wt. 76 lbs.   Per set, **60c**

Our "MASSIVE GOLD BANQUET" Dining Outfit.

Richest of the Rich. Beautiful Beyond Description.

C818—All the pieces are the same pattern, which is the newest and most beautiful one ever produced in pressed glass, being of elaborate wide colonial panel design, purest crystal, extra heavy and brilliantly fire polished. Each piece is elaborately decorated with bands of pure burnt in gold, some of them being ½ inches wide. The 23 pieces make a complete outfit for the table, or can be retailed separately. The complete outfit would make a beautiful wedding present.

Each Outfit Comprises the Following:

1 only 7-piece Berry Set, consisting of extra large and extra deep 7½-in. fancy footed berry bowl and six 4½-in. deep footed nappies to match. *A bargain to retail at 80c per set.*
1 only extra large and shapely Oil or Vinegar Bottle and stopper, with solid gold handle and gold decorated lip. *Cheap at 25c.*
1 only 4-piece Table Set, comprising extra large 8-in. scalloped flanged butter dish and fancy high cover; extra large fancy footed sugar bowl and cover; fancy footed spoon holder; handled footed wide deep cream pitcher. *A regular $1.50 set which can be retailed at $1.00.*
1 only extra large fancy footed Celery Holder of beautiful design, ht. 8¼-in. *Cheap at 50c.*
1 only 8¼-in. extra large and extra deep oval Table Dish with rich scalloped edge. *A bargain to retail at 25c.*
1 only tall heavy Salt Shaker with nickel dome top. *A 10c beauty.*
1 only Pepper Shaker to match salt.
1 only 7-piece Water Set, comprising tall tankard shape jug, fancy footed with rich scalloped edge, ht. 8¼-in., and 6 fancy footed table tumblers to match. *A regular $1.50 set as a possible dollar seller.*
(*Total 23 pieces in outfit. 2 outfits in bbl. Bbl. 35c.*)   Per outfit, **$3.10**

WASH YOUR GLASSWARE

The difference between "washed" and "unwashed" glass is the difference between *showy, brilliant, self-selling goods* and *cheap-looking, unsatisfactory, pass-without-seeing-it merchandise.*

Every Dollar Invested Here Buys Full Value in Glassware—No Inflated Prices Creep Into This Book.

There is Not a Busier Glassware Department in the World Than This One of Ours.

Our "EGYPTIAN" Set Assortment.
Three Popular Selling Sets in a New Pattern and Elaborate Decoration.

C346—All of the same pattern which is very attractive, being alternating frosted and plain beaded panels with numerous stars and crescents decorated in richest bright red which is obtained only in cold colors, unusually elaborate and beautiful.

The Assortment Comprises 4 Sets Each of the Following:

7-piece Berry Set—Consisting of 8¼-in. extra large and extra deep berry bowl and six 4¼-in. deep nappies to match.
4-piece Table Set—Comprising 7-in. flanged extra deep butter dish and cover, extra large footed covered sugar bowl, large footed spoon holder, and handled and footed cream pitcher to match.
7-piece Water Set—Comprising extra large and heavy ½-gal. pitcher and 6 shapely table tumblers to match.
(Total 12 sets in bbl. Bbl. 35c.) Average price per set, **32c**

Our "GOLDEN SPLENDOR" Dining Set Assortment.
These Sets of Richest Finish and Decoration. Can be Retailed with a Profit at $1.00.

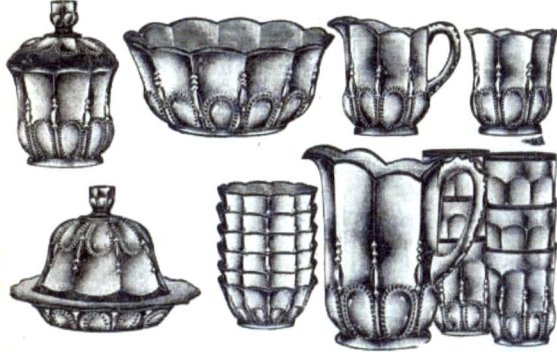

C358—All extra large sizes, all in same pattern, which is a beautiful mirror panel design, extra heavy, brilliantly finished and fire polished, all with pure gold decorations in wide bands, decorations being burnt-in and will not wear off.

Assortment Comprises 3 Sets Each of the Following:

7-piece Water Set—Consisting of extra large and heavy footed ½-gal. jug and 6 full size heavy rich table tumblers to match.
4-piece Table Set—Comprising extra large 8-in. flanged butter dish with extra high dome cover, elaborate gold decorations; heavy footed sugar bowl and cover; handled and footed cream pitcher; footed spoon holder.
7-piece Berry Set—Consisting of mammoth extra deep 8½-in. round footed berry bowl and six 4¼-in. deep footed nappies to match.
(Total 9 sets in bbl. Bbl. 35c.) Per set, **67c**

"PURE GOLD" Dining Set Assortment.
The Gem of the Collection. No One Ever Saw Better Value.

C355—The gold on all these pieces is genuine. Handsomest of crystal patterns, profuse and heavily decorated with genuine gold. All these pieces not only have gold band edges but are otherwise decorated as shown in the illustrations.

Assortment Comprises Two Sets Each of the Following.

7-Piece Berry or Sauce Set, Composed of one 7½-inch extra deep scalloped footed dish and six 4¼-inch nappies to match.
Water Set, Comprising wide top water pitcher and six table tumblers to match.
4-Piece Table Set, Composed of creamer, spoonholder, butter dish and cover, sugar bowl and cover. (6 sets complete in bbl. Wt. 75 lbs. Bbl. 35c.) Per set, **78c**

"GOLD BAND" Dining Set Assortment.
Among the richest of patterns. Because of their unusual attractiveness you can make an extra profit on every one of these items.

C345—The following sets are all one pattern in perfect imitation of cut glass. Extra heavy, each piece with heavy gold band around top, in some places 2 inches wide. Large size, fire polished.

The Assortment Comprises 2 Sets Each of the Following:

2 only. **7-Piece Berry Sets**, comprising 8-inch fancy round shape deep berry bowl and six 4½-inch deep nappies to match. At 65c, $1.30.
2 only. **7-Piece Water Sets**, comprising 9-inch jug with heavy stuck handle and 6 full size, extra heavy tumblers. At 96c, $1.92.
2 only. **4-Piece Table or Tea Sets**, comprising creamer, sugar bowl and cover, spoonholder and butter dish and cover. At 87c, $1.74.
(6 sets complete in bbl. wt. 74 lbs. Bbl. 35c.) Total for 6 sets. **$4.96**

Our "FRENCH CRYSTAL" Dining Outfit.
A New and Beautiful Combination on Which you Can Make a Handsome Profit.

C819—All the same pattern, made of heavy seamless mirror plate glass, richly finished and fire polished and all with fancy heavy crimped edges. The entire 23 pieces make a complete table outfit and can be retailed as such or by the piece. Pattern is an exceptionally beautiful one and price here named is extremely low considering quality and finish.

Outfit Comprises the Following:

1 only **7-piece Berry Set**, consisting of 1 extra large and extra deep 8¼-in. round footed berry bowl and six 4½-in. deep nappies to match.
1 only extra large round footed **Cracker Jar** with cover, ht. 9½-in.
1 only 8½-in. **Deep Oval Bread or Cake Tray**.
1 only extra large and heavy **Oil or Vinegar Bottle** with glass stopper.
1 only **4-piece Table Set**, consisting of 6¼-in. extra large and extra deep footed butter dish and cover; extra large footed and covered sugar bowl; large stuck handled and footed cream pitcher; large footed spoon holder.
1 only fancy tall **Salt Shaker** with wide fluted base and high dome top.
1 only **Pepper Shaker** to match salt.
1 only **7-piece Water Set**, each set consisting of ½-gal. extra large tall tankard shape footed Jug and 6 full size tumblers to match.
(Total 23-pieces in outfit. 2 outfits in bbl. Bbl. 35c.) Per outfit, **$1.65**

New "MANSION" Assortment of Richest Gems.
All Large Full Finished and Bright Pieces to Sell at 25c or More.

C304—This assortment is composed of staple every day items and is one that will sell out clean. Observe the extra large size of the pieces.

The "Mansion" Assortment Comprises 1-2 Doz. Each of the Following:

7-Inch Round Footed Dish with Cover—For berries, sauces, etc.
9¼-Inch High Footed Bowl—Very handsome design.
9½-Inch Footed Round Scalloped Bowl—Very deep and heavy.
Wide Top Water Pitcher—Extra heavy and artistic.
Total of 2 doz. in bbl., wt. 105 lbs. Sold only by bbl. Bbl. 35c.) Per dozen, **$1.85**

The Selling Prices We Occasionally Mention Are Merely Suggestions—YOU CAN OFTEN GET DOUBLE.

Any Merchant Can Sell Glassware—It's Only a Question of "I WILL."

Our "ROSE PINK" SET Assortment.
Elegant, Refined, Massive and Beautiful.

C340—This latest production of the glass art is of rich solid rose pink color. Exceptionally rich and brilliant. All of the pieces are new pattern in alternating wide and narrow panels, and all of fancy shapes, every piece being full finished and fire polished. All **extra heavy**. Will be a valuable addition to your glass department.

The Assortment Comprises 2 Sets Each of the Following:

7-Piece Water Set—Rich cut panel pattern ½-gal. jug, large stuck handle, ground bottom, and 6 large ground bottom tumblers.
7-Piece Berry Set—8-inch deep fancy shape berry bowl and 6 4-inch nappies.
4-Piece Table Set—8-inch flanged butter and cover, heavy ground bottom stuck handle cream pitcher, ground bottom spoonholder, large ground bottom sugar bowl and cover. *(Total 6 sets in bbl. Wt. 75 lbs. Bbl. 35c.)* Average price per set, **69c**

Our "ROYAL" Berry Bowl Assortment.
Four big and beautiful pieces as 25-cent profit payers.

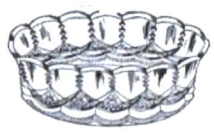 

C392—These extra large and heavy bowls are all of new and beautiful patterns, being among the richest ever produced in pressed glass. Assortment comprises ½ doz. each of 4 styles as illustrated, all extra large and extra deep, the average size being about 9½-inches in diameter. *(Total 2 doz. in bbl. Bbl. 35c.)* Per dozen, **$1.60**

OUR 'PLAIN SALVER" ASST.
Superior quality — the most staple sellers in the salver line.

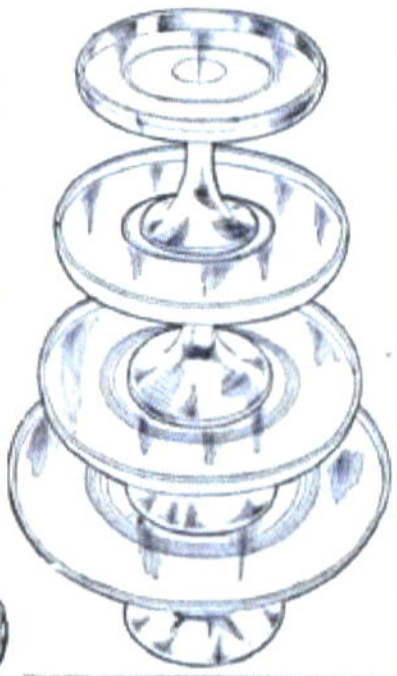

C483—All full finished, very best quality ware, superior finish. Assortment comprises:
¼ doz. 8-in. @ 79c. .. $0 27
¼ doz. 9-in. @ $1.32 .. 44
⅓ doz. 10-in. @ $2.10 .. 70
⅙ doz. 11-in. @ $2.50 .. 42

Total for the 1⅙ doz...**$1.83**
(1 1-6 doz. in bbl., wt. 65 lbs. Bbl. 35c.)

"FOUR SIZES" SALVER ASST.
Possible 10c, 15c, 20c and 25c sellers that commonly retail for more than that.

C482—A new good assortment. Four sizes. All are in a splendid fancy pattern that makes selling easy.
¼ doz. 6½-in. @ 76c .. $0 38
⅙ doz. 9-in. @ $1.25 .. 42
⅙ doz. 10¼-in. @ $1.60 .. 80
⅙ doz. 11-in. @ $2.10 .. 35

Total for the 1½ doz...**$1.95**
(Total 1½ doz. in bbl. only, wt. 61 lbs. Bbl. 35c.)

Our "PRINCELY" Salver Assortment.
Two full finished 25-cent beauties.

C481—There cannot be better glass made than is here found in these richest of salvers. The assortment comprises:
⅙ doz. Crimped Edge 10-inch Salvers, ⅙ doz. Scalloped Edge 10¼-inch Salvers.
(Total of 1⅓ doz. to bbl., wt. 75 lbs. Bbl. 35c.) Per dozen, **$1.72**

No Cartage Charge.

Our "NEW ELEGANT" Bowl Assortment.
Four mammoth size bowls—all newest patterns—as 25c profit payers.

C384—Extra large, extra heavy, all new and elaborate patterns, full finished and fire polished. An exceptionally desirable assortment. Pieces that will sell every day in the year. Assortment comprises ⅙ doz. each of the following:
9¼-Inch Extra Deep Footed Flared Bowl—Elaborate pattern in alternating plain and optic beaded panels, fancy scalloped edge.
7½-Inch Footed Bowl—Extra deep and extra heavy square. Very brilliant new pattern, massive and rich.
7-Inch Extra Deep High Footed Bowl—Height 7½-in., same beautiful pattern.
7½-Inch Round Footed Salad Bowl—Extra deep, being 4½-in. in depth, elaborate panel pattern. A massive piece.
(Total 2 doz. in bbl. Bbl. 35c.) Per dozen, **$1.60**

Our "COLONIAL" Covered Bowl Assortment.
Splendid big pieces to retail at popular prices.

C381—Covers and bowls full finished, fire polished. All in the richest of patterns. Each piece on high foot.
⅙ doz. 6-inch @ $1.70 .... $0 65
⅙ " 7 " @ 2.25 .... 1 13
⅙ " 8 " @ 3.60 60

Total for the doz. **$2.38**
(Total 1 doz. in bbl., wt. 73 lbs. Bbl. 35c.)

Our PLAIN" Covered Bowl Asst.
This assortment contains only the best selling sizes at prices which will make sales lively.

C385—All footed and of heavy rich plain pattern and all with high dome top covers. Assortment comprises—
⅓ doz. 7½-inch low footed bowls 6/ $1.70 .... $0 57
⅓ doz. 8½-inch low footed bowls @ $2.25 75
⅓ doz. 7½-inch high footed bowls @ $1.95 65
⅓ doz. 8½-inch high footed bowls @ $2.65 80

(Bbl. 35c.) Total for asst. of 1⅓ doz. **$2.86**

Our "HIGH FOOTED" Colonial Bowl Assortment.

One of the richest of the almost plain full finished patterns.

C395—These are among the best sellers made in glassware, being extremely useful and popular. The assortment comprises 3 sizes, all being high footed and extra deep, and all brilliantly fire polished, as follows:
⅙ doz. 6½-in. @ $1.30 $0 65
⅙ " 7 " " 1.80 90
⅙ " 8 " " 2.20 55
Total for 1¼ doz. **$2.10**
(Bbl. 35c.)

"COMPETITION" Table Set Asst.
Extra large sets, extra small price.

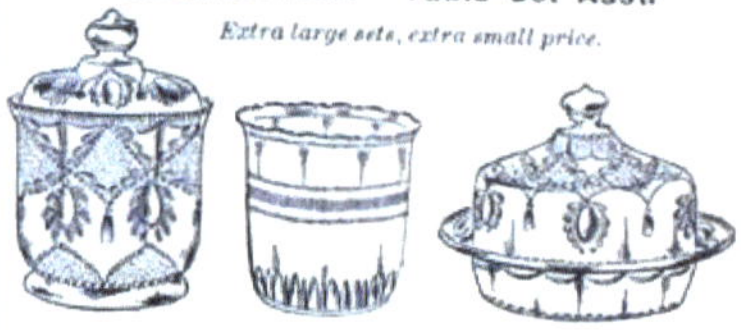

C523—Two bright new patterns, one satin etched frosted design with brilliant stars; the other attractive deep cut pattern. All pieces extra large. 12 sets each of two styles, total 24 sets in bbl. *(Bbl. 35c.)* Per set, **15c**

Sell Good Goods—Sell Them Cheap—Be Honest in All Dealings and PROSPERITY WILL BE YOURS.

Bargain Specialties in COMPETITION GLASSWARE.

Splendid Items Which We Offer to Compete Against the Offerings of Glassware Factories.

While this ware is not *fully* equal to our regular lines we guarantee it to be as good as most of the ware coming from those factories whose representatives call upon you. *All rare opportunities for "bargain day" sellers. All handsome patterns.*

"LEADER" TANK Glass Tumbler Asst.

With these you can meet and defy all competition.

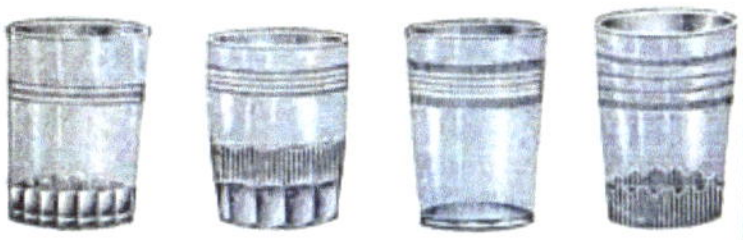

C554—Although not equal in quality and finish to our regular line, yet they are not as cheap in quality as many in the market offered at more money. All regulation ½ pint size. **5 doz. each of 4 patterns,** all with neat mold bands, 3 with fancy fluted bases. Total 20 doz. in bbl. (*Bbl. 35c.*) Per dozen, **17c**

"OUR STAPLE" Tumbler Asst.

All full finished, all good shapes.

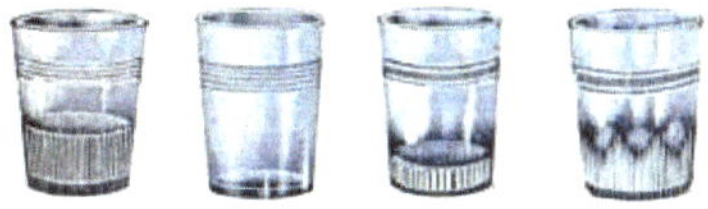

C555—Not quite as good as our best, but superior to the best of some. Full table size, well finished. Assortment comprises 5 doz. each of four styles—one plain, two with flute and neat mold bands, one plain and flute. (*Total 20 dozen in bbl. Bbl. 35c.*) Per dozen, **19c**

Our "COTTAGE SIZE" Berry Set Assortment.

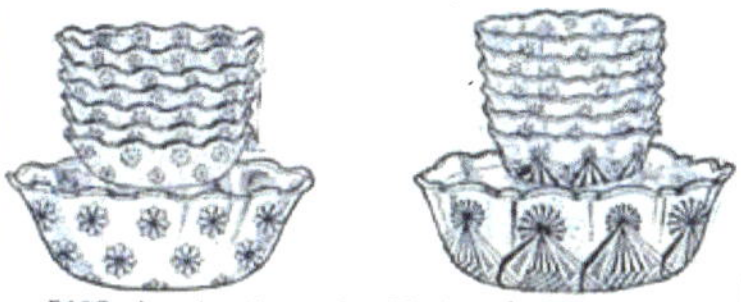

C408—Assortment comprises 12 sets each of 2 patterns—one in all over frosted design with numerous cut stars, the other fancy frosted and drapery pattern. Each set consists of one 7½-in. deep berry bowl and six 4-in. deep nappies to match. (*Total 24 sets in bbl., Bbl. 35c.*) Per set, **12½c**

Our "STAR AND CRESCENT" Water Set.

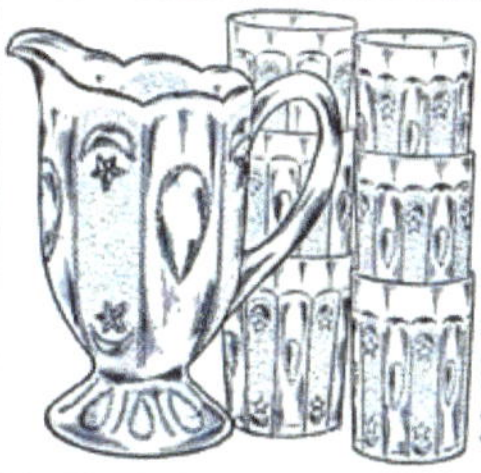

A big and brilliant set as a 50c profit payer.

C672—Entirely new and attractive pattern, being of an alternating plain frosted and beaded panel design with numerous beaded stars and crescents, full finished and fire polished. Each set comprises one large half-gallon footed jug with wide top and convenient handle, 6 heavy full size table tumblers to match. *12 sets in barrel.* (*Bbl. 35c.*) Per set, **28c**

Our "BRILLIANT" Jug Assortment.

Two big bright ones only $1.18 per dozen.

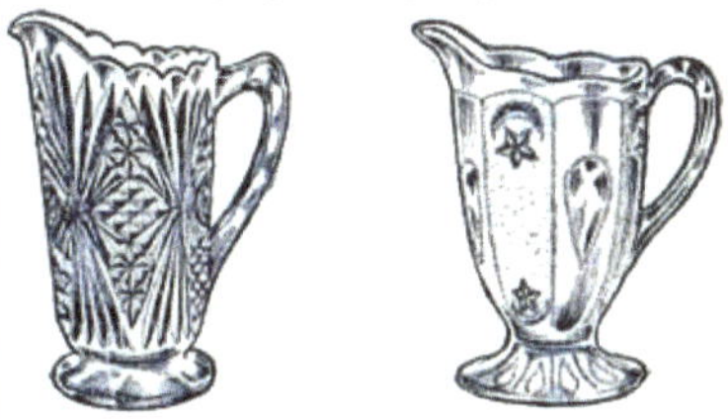

C474—Assortment comprises 1 doz. each of 2 styles, both so-called ½-gal. size, one being extra large and heavy, frosted and plain panel design, with numerous beaded stars and crescents, wide top and fancy foot; the other rich brilliant cut pattern with fancy scalloped edge. (*Bbl. 35c.*) *Total 2 dozen in bbl.* Per dozen, **$1.18**

Our "WIDE TOP" Pitcher Asst.

Only $2.25 per dozen for these two "big fellows."

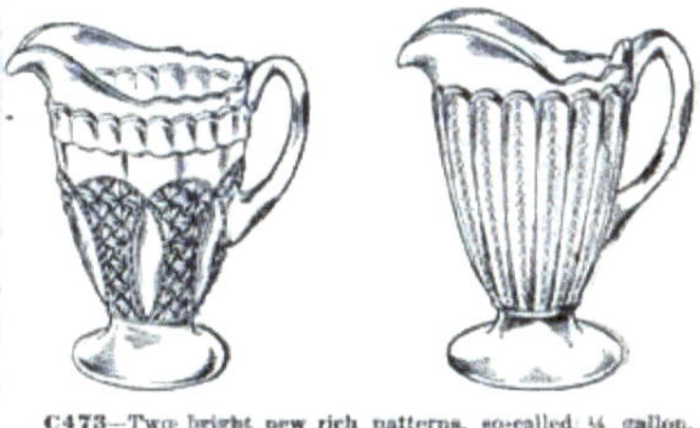

C473—Two bright new rich patterns, so-called ½ gallon, both footed, extra wide fancy tops, good lips and handles, full finished. 1 doz. each of two styles. Total 2 doz. in bbl. (*Bbl. 35c.*) Per dozen, **$2.25**

Our New "BARGAIN BOWL" Assortment.

Four extra large and heavy 10-cent leaders.

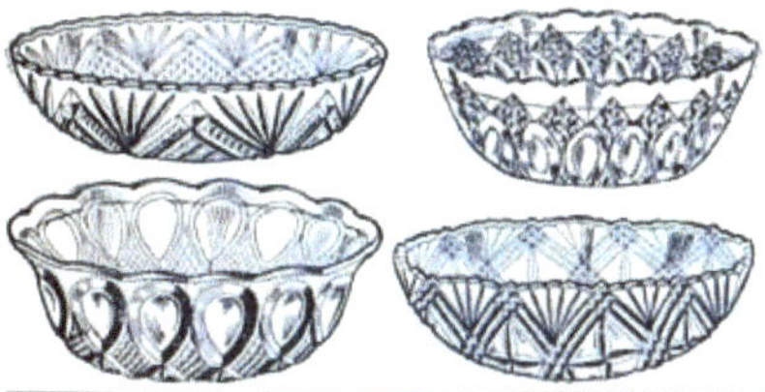

C377 — Illustrations do not do these big, handsome bowls justice. You can *easily* get 15 cents for two out of the four. Assortment comprises **1 doz. each** of the following:

8¼-in. extra deep and heavy berry bowl, fancy flaring scalloped edge.

7½-in. deep bright optic pattern bowl.

8½-in. extra large deep mirror pattern bowl with scalloped edge.

7½x7½-in. square deep vine pattern bowl.

(*Total 4 doz. in bbl. Bbl. 35c.*)

Per dozen. **76c**

Our "ALL SELLERS" Assortment.

Bouncing Big 10-cent Leaders. Most of Them Worth 15c or 20c.

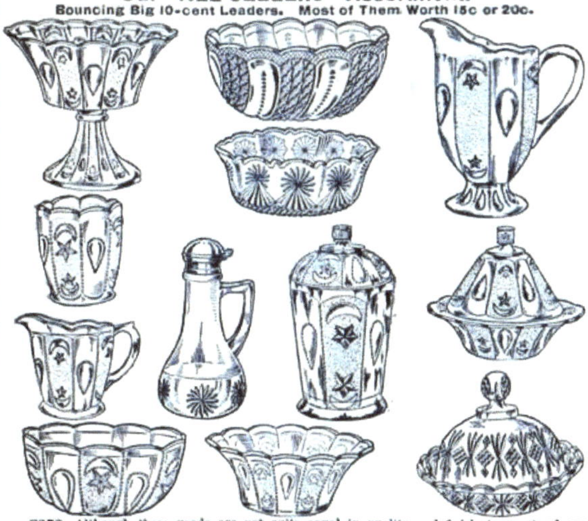

C272—Although these goods are not quite equal in quality and finish to most of our assortments, the pieces are all extra large and will make exceptional leaders for Bargain Day.

Assortment Comprises 1-2 Doz. Each of the Following.

7½-inch Extra Deep Round Berry Bowl—Star and crescent pattern.
Extra Large Footed Sugar Bowl and Cover—Of the same rich pattern.
Large Handled Milk or Cream Pitcher—Footed, with wide top.
Large Footed Spoonholder with Scalloped Edge.
7-in. Deep Flanged Butter Dish and Cover—Rich and bright.
7½-in. Extra Deep High Footed Fruit Bowl—Extra large and brilliant.
7½-in. Scalloped Edge Nappy or Table Dish—Fancy flared shape.
Large ½-gal. Water Pitcher—Wide top, footed, large finished handle.
7½-in. Extra Deep Round Berry Bowl—Fancy frosted design.
7-in. Extra Large Butter Dish—With high dome cover.
Tall Shapely Molasses Pitcher—With wide base and good spring top.
8½-in. Mammoth Extra Deep Berry Bowl—Of brilliant twisted designs with scalloped edge.
(*Total 6 doz. in tierce. Tierce 50c*). Per dozen, **74c**

"Our 10-CENT BERRY BOWL Assortment."

All big leaders and of bright patterns.

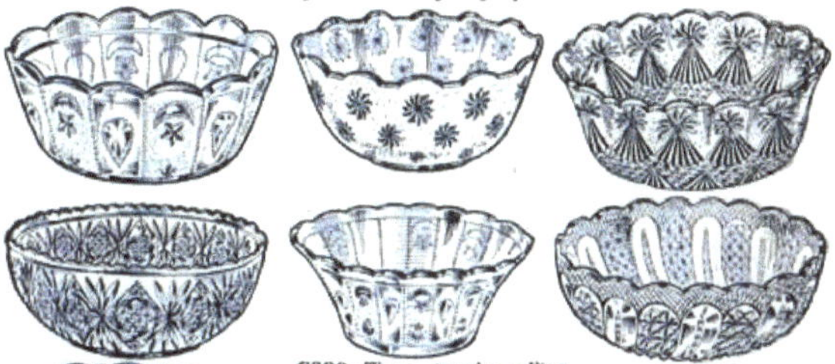

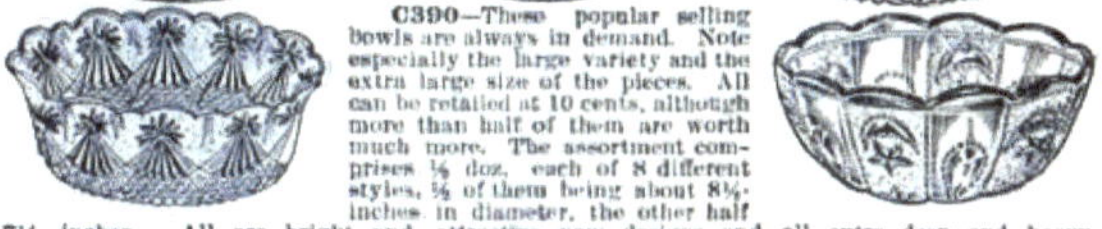

C390—These popular selling bowls are always in demand. Note especially the large variety and the extra large size of the pieces. All can be retailed at 10 cents, although more than half of them are worth much more. The assortment comprises ½ doz. each of 8 different styles, ½ of them being about 8½-inches in diameter, the other half 7¼ inches. All are bright and attractive new designs and all extra deep and heavy. (*Total 2 doz. in barrel. Bbl. 35c.*) Average price per doz. **75c**

Our "BIG SPECIAL" 10-Cent Asst. Competition Ware.

10-cent Possibilities of Mammoth Size.

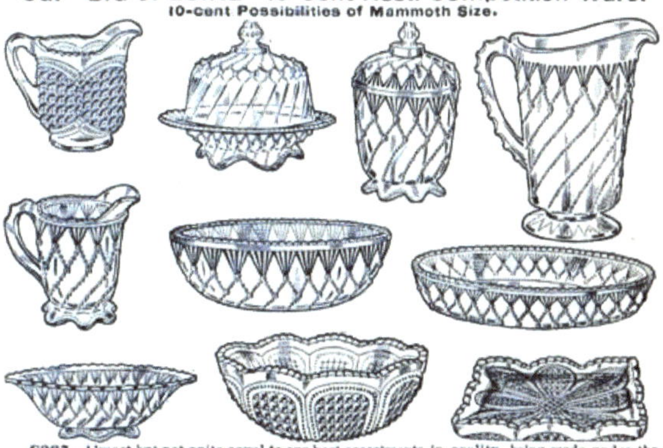

C287—Almost but not quite equal to our best assortments in quality being made under the new tank process. However, with these you can meet and defy all competition.

Assortment Comprises 1-2 Doz. Each of the Following:

7¼-in. Extra Heavy Bread or Cake Plate—Square shape, rich cut diamond pattern.
8-in. Extra Heavy Round Deep Fruit Bowl—Massive and rich.
Heavy Brilliant Cream Pitcher—Handled and footed.
7¼-in. Round Flaring Bowl—On fancy foot.
9¼-in. Extra Large and Extra Heavy Utility Table Dish—Extra deep oval shape.
8¼-in. Extra Large, Extra Deep Berry Bowl—Cheap at 20c.
Extra Large 7-in. Flanged Butter Dish—Dome cover and on fancy foot.
Handled and Footed Cream Pitcher—Good size. Matches butter dish.
Extra Large Footed Sugar Bowl and Cover—Of the same bright pattern.
Large Footed so-called ½ gal. Water Pitcher—Wide top and fancy handle.
(*Total of 5 doz. in Bbl. 35c.*) Per dozen, **75c**

The Retailer Who Does Not Carry a Line of Popular Glassware Rejects a ROYAL OPPORTUNITY.

Our "COTTAGE BRIDE" Table Set.

One of the newest and best of the popular medium size sets.

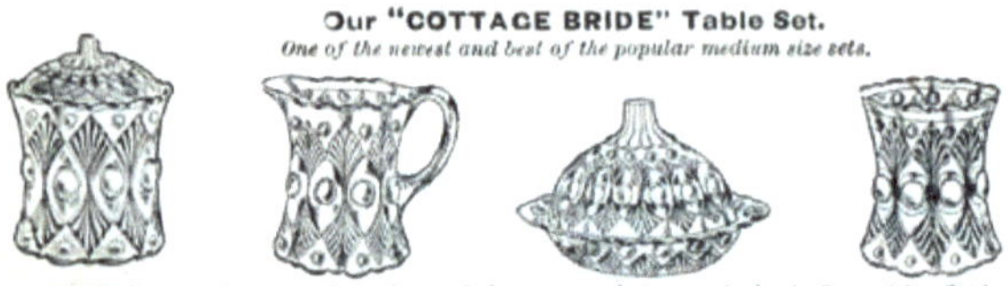

C533—Richest of patterns, best of crystal glass (not made from tank glass). Comprising 6¼-in. flanged butter and cover, shapely footed creamer, large handled footed spoon holder, footed sugar and cover. *(24 sets in bbl., wt. 107 lbs. Bbl. 35c.)* Per set, **14½c**

Our "OPTIC MIRROR" Table Set.

Bountifully big—beautifully bright.

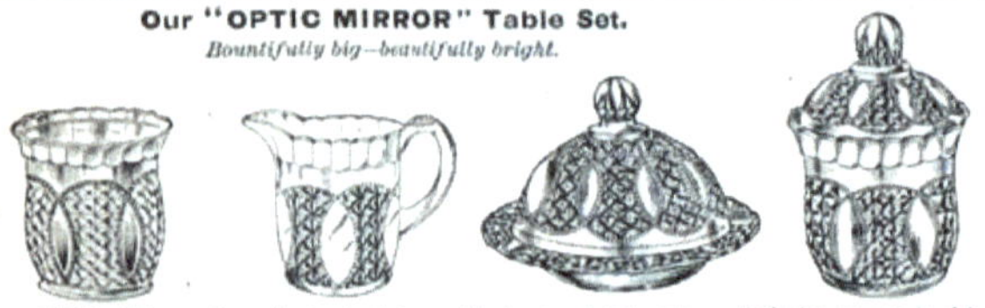

C522—Not one of our best sets, but excellent value for the price. Full size, pieces in rich and pleasing "optic mirror" pattern. The set comprises sugar and cover, 7½-inch butter and cover, spoonholder and milk pitcher. *(Total 24 sets in bbl., wt. 142 lbs. Bbl. 35c.)* Per set, **16½c**

Our "STAPLE" Plain Table Set Asst.

Sets that are popular everywhere.

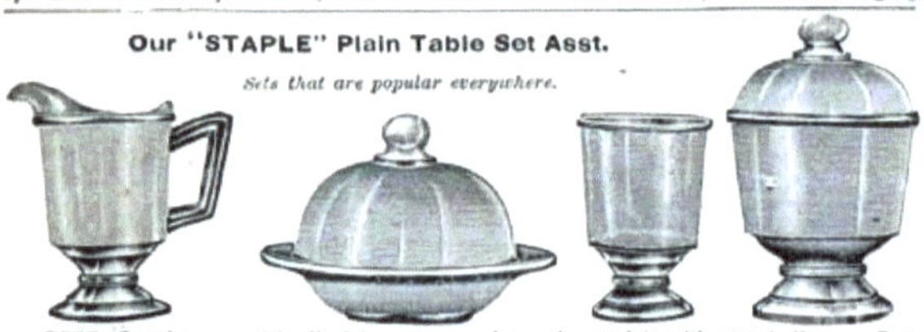

C525—2 styles—one rich all plain pattern, and one almost plain with optic bull's eye effect. Well finished and not to be compared with the unfinished goods usually sold at this price. 12 sets each of 2 patterns. *(Total 24 sets in bbl., wt. 134 lbs. Bbl. 35c).* Per set, **16½c**

Our "SUBSTANTIAL" 4-Piece Table Set Assortment.

Possible 25c sets of extra size and rare brilliance.

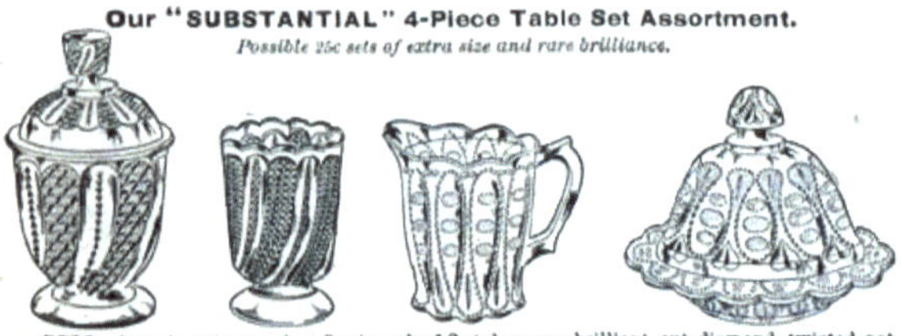

C510—Assortment comprises 9 sets each of 2 styles—one brilliant cut diamond twisted pattern, the other fancy embossed and frosted design. Each set consists of one extra large flange butter dish with high dome cover. Sugar bowl with cover. Cream pitcher and spoonholder. All pieces footed. *(Total 18 sets in barrel. Bbl. 35c.)* Per set, **17c**

Our "PLAIN AND COLONIAL FLUTE" 4-Piece Table Set.

An extra large and heavy set at a small price

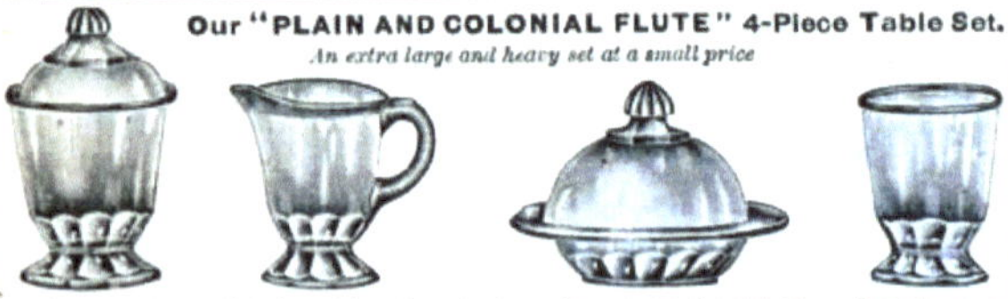

C507—Almost plain but rich pattern, having wide colonial fluted bottoms, fancy knob on cover of sugar bowl and butter dish. Each set comprises one 7-in. flange butter dish with cover. One extra large footed sugar bowl with cover. One fancy handled and footed milk or cream pitcher. One footed spoonholder. *(24 sets in barrel. Bbl. 35c.)* Per set, **17c**

Our "LATEST YET" Table Set Assortment.

Two bouncing big sets as 25-cent Bargain Day Leaders.

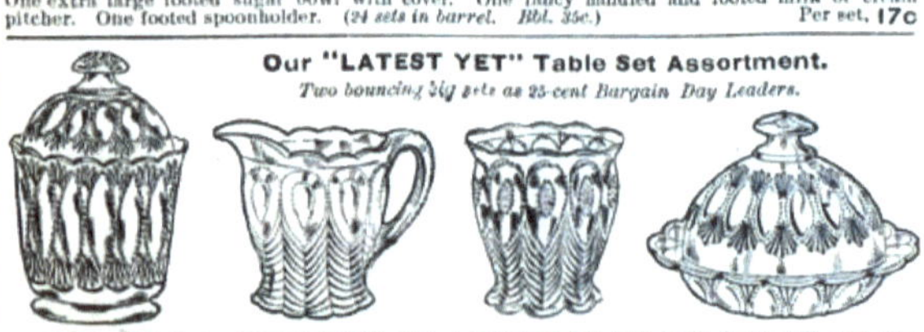

C526—Not the small ones usually sold at this price, but both extra large full size sets. Assortment comprises 12 sets each of two entirely new and brilliant patterns, both footed and well finished. Total 24 sets in bbl., wt. 145 lbs. *(Bbl. 35c.)* Per set, **17½c**

Our "THREE WINNERS" 4-Piece Table Set Assortment.

Three large and brilliant sets at a small price.

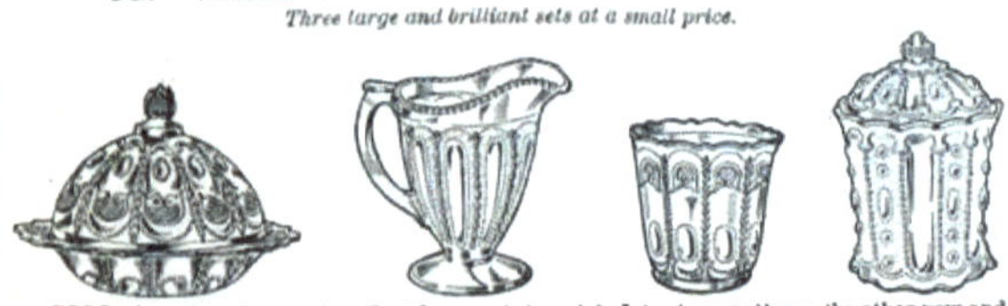

C508—Assortment comprises 3 styles, one being rich dot mirror pattern; the other new and artistic panel design; the other fancy feather panel pattern. Each set comprises: One extra large 7¼-in. deep flanged butter dish and cover. One extra large sugar bowl and cover. One handled milk or cream pitcher. One spoonholder. All pieces being of extra large size and all footed. 8 sets each of 3 styles. *(Total 24 sets in bbl. Bbl. 35c)* Set, **18c**

Our "FANCY FOOTED" Heavy Table Set.

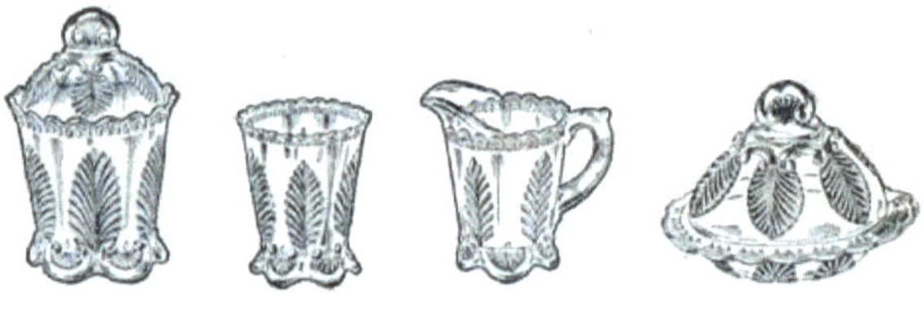

C501. The upright fern leaves on the plain background are very effective and mark this above the average low-priced set. *(24 sets to bbl., wt. 130 lbs. Bbl. 35c)* Per set, **21c**

Our "HEAVY BRIGHT" 4-Piece Table Set Assortment.

"Big and brilliant 50c sets at a price which leaves you a profit."

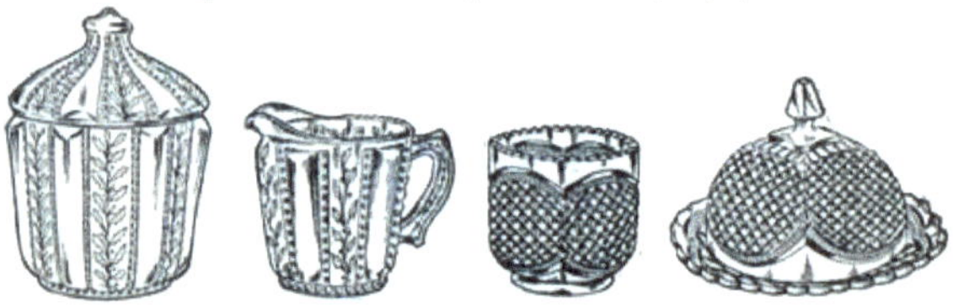

C530—Comprises 2 styles—one the fancy bead panel and vine pattern, extra heavy and rich; the other a brilliant cut diamond design, both being full finished and fire polished. Each set comprises one extra large flanged butter dish and cover, one covered sugar bowl, one handled cream pitcher, one spoon holder. 9 sets of each pattern. *(Total 18 sets in bbl. Bbl. 35c.)* Set, **24c**

Our "BEAUTEOUS" 4-piece Table Set Assortment.

Two magnificent crystal beauties to retail at 50c.

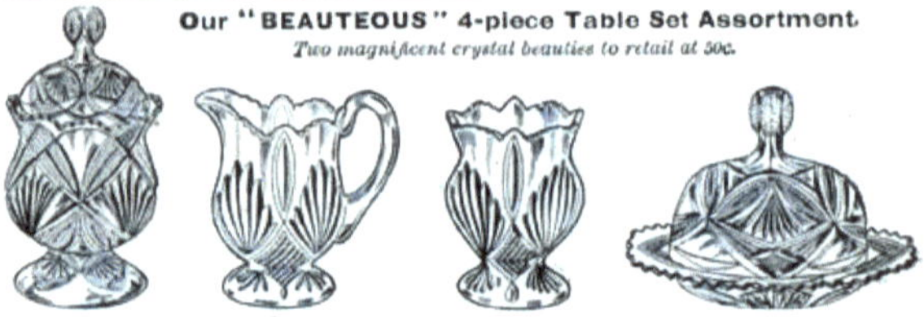

C506—Assortment comprises 6 sets each of 2 patterns as illustrated, both being of richest genuine cut glass design, both brilliantly finished and fire polished. Each set comprises: One extra large 8¼-in. flange butter dish with high dome cover. One extra large fancy shape footed sugar bowl and cover. One large footed spoon holder with fancy scalloped edge. One handled and footed cream pitcher. *(Total 6 sets in bbl. Bbl. 35c.)* Per set, **30c**

Our "HANDLED AND FOOTED" Table Set.

A bargain at 50c or more.

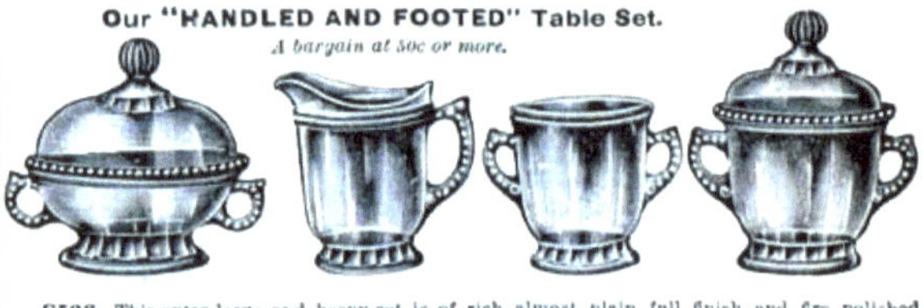

C528—This extra large and heavy set is of rich almost plain full finish and fire polished crystal. All pieces footed, with brilliant beaded pattern handles and edge, giving extremely rich effect. All except creamer have double handles. *(12 sets in bbl., wt. 100 lbs. Bbl. 35c.)* Per set, **31c**

Our "MAGNIFICENT" 4-Piece Table Set Assortment.

Positively the most beautiful sets ever offered at a 50c price.

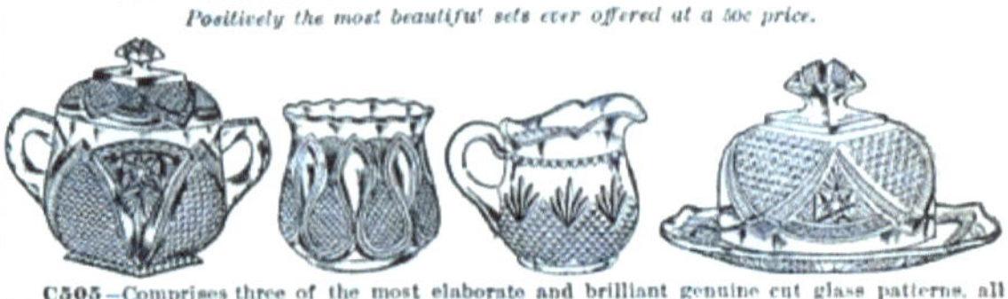

C505—Comprises three of the most elaborate and brilliant genuine cut glass patterns, all being extra large and extra heavy and massive, and all richly finished and fire polished. Each set consists of covered butter dish, covered sugar bowl, cream pitcher and spoon holder. 4 sets of 3 patterns. *(Total 12 sets in bbl. Bbl. 35c.)* Per set, **32c**

Our "CHOCOLATE IVORY" Table Set.

A beautiful set in this popular ware to retail at 50c.

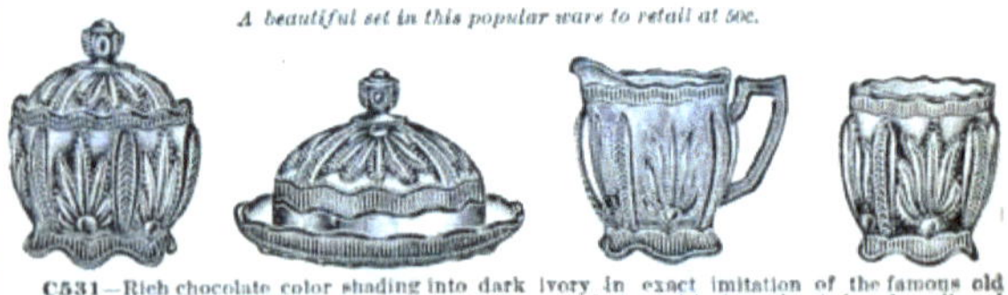

C531—Rich chocolate color shading into dark ivory in exact imitation of the famous old Holland ivory ware, elaborately embossed, relief panel design with fancy beaded and scalloped edges. All pieces extra large and footed. *(12 sets in barrel, wt. 110 lbs. Bbl. 35c.)* Per set, **31c**

Our Glassware Is All of the Very Best Quality and Finish Possible for the Prices Named.

Don't Let Your Neighbor Set the Pace—Set It Yourself and Make Him Hustle.

Our New "BERRY" Nappy Assortment.
3 new styles to retail with a profit at 3 for 5.

C374—These exceptionally low priced berry or sauce dishes are in three attractive patterns, extra deep, beaded edges, all bright and finished. 6 doz. each of 3 patterns. Total 18 dozen in bbl. (Bbl. 25c.) Per dozen, **15½c**

"Our VINE PATTERN" Sauce Set.

C403—A well finished, large size crystal set, pearl beaded edge with embossed grapevine pattern around sides. Set comprises 7¼x7¼ deep heavy dish and six 4-inch nappies to match. (24 sets in bbl., wt. 115 lbs. Bbl. 35c.) Per set, **14c**

New "VARIETY" Asst. Sauce Sets.
Two quick-selling 25-cent sets at a bargain price.

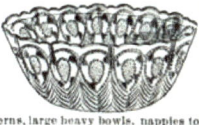

C404—Two brilliant patterns, large heavy bowls, nappies to match. Each set includes one 8-inch deep round dish and six 4½-in. nappies. 12 sets of each pattern in package. (Total 24 sets in bbl., wt. 117 lbs. Bbl. 35c.) Per set, **15½c**

Our "EXCELLENT" Berry Set Assortment.
Two extra large and brilliant 25-cent possibilities although actually worth much more.

C416—Assortment comprises 12 sets each of 2 beautiful patterns both being extra heavy and brilliantly fire polished. One style comprises 9¼-in. extra large footed flaring bowl, brilliant cut diamond design, and six 4½-in. deep nappies to match; the other 8-in. fancy shape deep berry bowl, beaded prism pattern and six 4½-in. fancy shape nappies to match. (Total 24 sets in bbl., Bbl. 35c.) Per set, **17c**

Our "SPECIAL SALE" Berry Set Assortment.
Two bouncing big sets to retail at popular prices.

C414—Comprising 2 styles as illustrated—one a rich beaded panel design; the other fancy shape pattern with scalloped sides and beaded edge. Each set consists of 1 extra large 8¼-in. deep round berry bowl and six 4½-in. deep nappies to match. 12 sets each of 2 patterns. (Total 24 sets in bbl., Bbl. 35c.) Per set, **18c**

Our "CHOICEST" Berry or Sauce Set Asst.
The richest and most beautiful sets ever offered to retail with a profit at 50 cents per set.

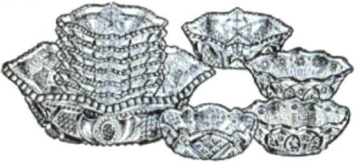

C413—3 sets each of 4 extra large, extra heavy and rich patterns in exact imitation of genuine cut glass designs. All full finished and fire polished in fancy and round shapes with beaded and scalloped edges. Set consists of extra large deep berry bowl, about 9¼-in. and six 4½-in. sauce dishes. (Total 12 sets in bbl., wt. 88 lbs. Bbl. 35c.) Per set, **29c**

TIN TOP CANDY OR SHELF JARS.
Plain crystal, full finished.

C759—Round squat shape, ground top, japanned tin cover, capacity ½ gallon, ht. 6½ inches. 1 doz. in case. (Case 25c.) Doz. **$1.45**

C760—Tall round shape, ht. 9¼ in., capacity ½ gallon, ground top, japanned tin cover. 1 doz. in case. (Case 25c.) Doz. **1.45**

Our "BOUNTEOUS" Sugar Bowl Assortment.
Four big ones to retail at 10c each.

C543—Comprising four styles, all except one being footed and all extra large and brilliantly finished. (1 doz. of each style. Total 4 doz. in bbl.) Per dozen, **72c**

Our "1903 SUGAR BOWL" Assortment.
A barrel will convince you that we are indeed bargain givers.

—One doz. each of four different patterns in sugar bowls, all bright and finished. The package gives you a good variety of shapes and sizes. Not one of these is regularly retailed for less than 15 cents. (Total 4 doz. to bbl., wt. 197 lbs. Bbl. 35c.) Per dozen, **73c**

OUR 10c BUTTER DISH ASSORTMENT.
All big splendid shapes. Big 10c leaders.

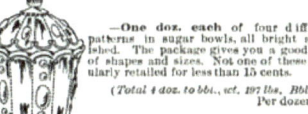

C421—The assortment comprises the following: 2 doz. extra large and extra heavy with dome top and round knob handles. 1 doz. extra large fleur-de-lis pattern. 1 doz. large beaded prism pattern. All being very brilliant and with large high covers. (Total 4 doz. in bbl.) Per dozen, **74c**

"BIG FOUR" Butter Dish Assortment.
Every day sellers. All large and all bright.

C424—All of pure crystal, extra heavy and well finished comprising four styles, all with wide flanges, extra deep and with high covers. 6 doz. each of four patterns. (Total 4 doz. in barrel. Bbl. 35c.) Per dozen, **75c**

"ENAMEL DECORATED" WINE SET
Richest $1.00 set of the year.

C685—Comprises 11½-in. round footed tray with fancy glass stopper, elaborate white enamel decorations in leaf and vine effect, 6 fancy shape wine glasses decorated to match. 6 sets in case. Wt. 60 lbs. (Case 30c.) Per set, **57c**

Our "UNIQUE" Vase Assortment.
Fancy shape, rich colors, rare bargains.

C781. Average ht. about 8¼-in., all in rich opalescent colorings, beautiful beyond description, equally assorted in 3 beautiful colors; canary, blue and flint opalescent. Positively the best assortment of vases we ever offered at a 10c price. 1 doz. each of 6 beautiful shapes, such as flaring panel, lily, tulip and serpentine. Total 6 doz. in bbl. (Bbl. 35c. Wt. 90 lbs.) Per dozen, **82c**

Our "MAMMOTH" Crystal Vase Assortment.
Four magnificent and sparkling beauties to retail at popular prices.

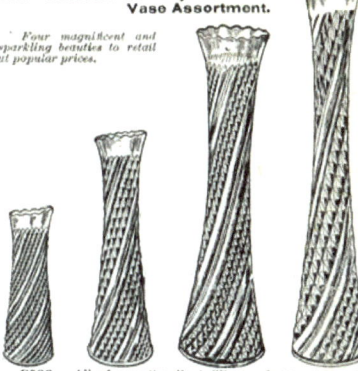

C590—All of exceptionally brilliant and attractive twist column design, wide spread heavy bases and fancy scalloped shaped tops. All in purest and most elaborately full finished crystal, brilliantly fire polished. These extra large vases are not only useful but exceedingly ornamental and are everywhere the rage. You can retail them with a profit at about half usual price.

2 only (ht. 15 inches, circumference about 14. To retail at 50c), at 29c	$0.58
2 only (ht. 18 inches. To retail at 75c), at 48c	.96
2 only (ht. 21 inches. To retail at $1.00), at 69c	1.38
2 only (ht. 28 inches. To retail at $1.50), at 95c	1.90
(Total 8 vases in bbl. 35c.) Total for assortment	$4.28

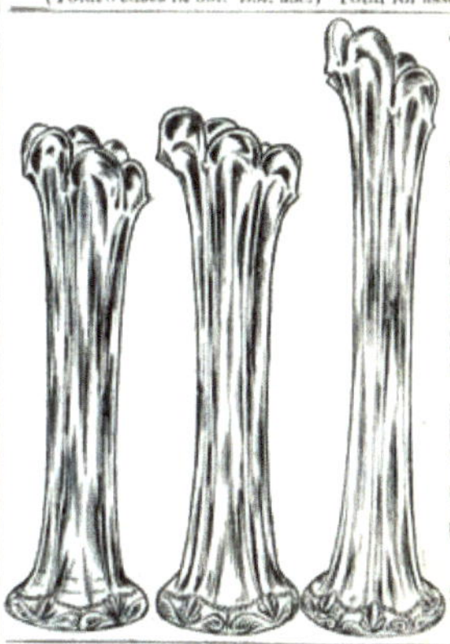

"AMERICAN BEAUTY" Vase Asst.
Three rich ones to retail at from 15 to 25c.

C583—Entirely new and beautiful wide panel or fluted design in fancy new shapes having extra heavy bases, extra tall and with floral design tops. The Assortment Comprises the following:

½ doz. 11¾-in. at $1.25, $0 63
½ doz. 13¾-in. at $1.75, 87
½ doz. 15½-in. at $2.00, 1 00

Total **$2.50**

Total 1½ doz. in bbl. 35c.

"BIG" MOLASSES PITCHER ASST.
All with clinch collars. No plaster, no cement.

C436—Comprising ½ doz. each of the three styles. All extra large sizes, fancy shapes, dome tops. Rare bargains at this price. (Total 2 doz., wt. 44 lbs.) (Case 25c.) Per dozen, **1.45**

We Furnish Our Customers the Ammunition With Which to Advertise.—See Colored Pages.

We Have One Price and That One is Named in Plain Figures—It's the Same for Big and Small Buyers.

"PLAIN AND FLUTED" Pitcher Assortment.
Two ready-selling, full finished, brilliant bargains.

C451—Here is a little 2 dozen assortment of ½-gallon pitchers. *If you buy one barrel of them you will wire for more!* 1 doz. each of two patterns. (*Total 2 doz. in bbl., wt. 107 lbs. Bbl. 35c.*) Per dozen, **$1.30**

Our "NEWEST" High Tankard Jug.
A jug of quarter quality for a bargain price.

C458—With large handle and wide base. Full finished. Regular so-called half gallon. Just the jug to run at any 15c or "Star Day." (2 dozen in bbl., wt. 103 lbs. Barrel 35c.) Per dozen, **$1.30**

Our "BIG AND HEAVY" Jug Assortment.
Rich 25c profit payers.

C476—Comprising 2 styles, both extra large and heavy, richly finished, fire polished jugs, one tall tankard shape, ht. 10 in., the other an attractive star pattern with extra wide top and scalloped edge. 1 doz. of each style. (*Total 2 doz. in bbl. Bbl. 35c.*) Per dozen, **$1.65**

Our "FANCY AND PLAIN" Jug Assortment.
Big and bright quarter leaders.

C470—Two extra large ½ gallon jugs. One of low massive and rich panel design with fancy feet and large handle. The other extra large, footed, almost plain pattern with good handle and lip. Both full finished with wide tops. Especially adapted for ice water, etc. 1 doz. of each pattern. (*Total 2 doz. in bbl. Bbl. 35c.*) Per dozen, **$1.69**

"HIGH CLASS" Pitcher Assortment.
Two useful "every-day" articles at "once-a-week" prices.

C455—Some trade demands a superior grade of goods, and to all such we recommend these two magnificent **full finished** specimens of the glass worker's art. 1 doz. each large ½-gallon pitchers. (*Total of 2 doz. to pkg. Bbl. 35c.*) Per dozen, **$1.75**

Our "MODERN SHAPE" Vase and Jug Assortment.
Possible 25-centers although worth regularly much more.

C466—The assortment comprises 1 doz. extra large and extra heavy wide top half gallon jugs with heavy base in beautiful rich reflecting panel design, and ¼ doz. ½ doz. extra tall and heavy panel pattern vases, ht. 12-in., both being of purest crystal, richly finished and fire polished. Average price per dozen, **$1.78** (*Total 1¼ doz. in bbl. Bbl. 35c.*)

Our "FIRE POLISHED" Pitcher Assortment.
Three sparkling full finished beauties to retail at popular prices.

C464—Assortment comprises:

1 doz. medium size, tankard shape footed, with fancy handle, so-called quart size, beautiful genuine cut glass pattern $0.87
1 doz. large fancy shape, so-called ½-gallon size, footed, fancy handle, wide top, brilliant pattern 1.25
½ doz. extra large and extra heavy massive ½-gallon ice water jugs, extra wide top, brilliant reflecting prism pattern .... @$2.75, 1.38
(*Bbl. 35c.*) Total for 2½ doz. in bbl. **$3.50**

"FANCY OPALESCENT" Blown Jug Asst.
(All in beautiful opalescent.)
Four styles of splendid 50-cent pitchers.

C461—Assortment comprises 3 each of 4 patterns, richly assorted in richest flint, blue and green opalescent. (*Total 1 doz. in bbl. Barrel 35c.*) Per dozen, **$3.50**

Our "STAR" Water Set.
A set well named—it will prove a "star" seller.

C673½—This set comprises one-half gallon rich, plain water pitcher with indented stars all over same, and SIX shapely table tumblers to match.
(*Total 12 sets in bbl. Bbl. 35c.*) Per set. **25c**

No cartage charge on any goods.

Our "WIDE FLUTE" Tankard Water Set.
One of the biggest and best 50c sets ever offered.

C683—Unusually brilliant design in purest crystal, being of an attractive wide flute pattern. Each set comprises one extra large and extra heavy half gallon jug, ht. 9½-in. with wide top and large handle and 6 only double thick fluted tumblers to match. (12 sets in bbl. Bbl. 35c.) Per set, **29c**

Our "BARGAIN COUNTER" Water Set.
A rare value at this exceedingly low price.

Bought too late to make cut.

C659—A bright and attractive 7-piece set comprising one tall fancy shape so-called half gallon jug with fancy wide scalloped top, flint molded bands, and tumblers to match. (*Total, 15 sets in bbl. Bbl. 35c.*) Per set, **19c**

Our "DOT MIRROR" Water Set.
The brightest of the bright.

C675—A set that will always sell at sight. Has alternate panels of plain mirror and etched panels with bull's-eye effects, all panels framed in delicate dew-drop effects. Set comprises footed wide top water pitcher with 1-quart size, and six tumblers to match. (12 sets in bbl. Bbl. 35c.) Per set, **30c**

Our FLORAL AND GOLD DECORATED Water Set Assortment.
A regular one-dollar set which you can retail with a profit at 65c.

C656—These sets being entirely new and very attractive are sure to sell on sight. The assortment comprises 6 sets each of two styles, one with heavy gold edges, the other with elaborate hand painted enamel decorations in natural colored floral and leaf designs, both floral and gold decorations being burnt in and will not wear off. Each set consists of one large so-called half-gallon optic pattern jug and 6 full size optic tumblers to match. (*Total 12 sets in bbl. Bbl. 35c.*) Per set, **42c**

Our "CHOCOLATE IVORY" Water Set.
A regular $1.00 set which you can retail with a profit at say 69c.

C663—This new and attractive ware, so much in demand is of a rich blended chocolate ivory color in almost exact imitation of the famous and popular old Holland ivory ware. Set comprises extra heavy, massive ½-gal. footed jug, elaborately embossed in beautiful panel pattern, and six 4-inch tall flaring tumblers to match. (12 sets in bbl., wt. 107 lbs. Bbl. 35c.) Per set, **39c**

KEEP HUSTLING—The Merchant Who Hustles for More Business Usually Gets More Than His Share.

The Foundation Stones of Success in the Department Store Business Are CASH and LOW PRICES.

OUR FANCY COLORED BLOWN WATER SET ASST.

Beauties to retail at 75c or more if you choose.

C655—Comprising 3 extra large fancy shape jugs, all in brilliant optic design, one being a tall tankard shape, height 11¼-in., with wide base, one extra large swell shape with fancy crimped edge, and the other a low tankard shape with the extra wide base, full height 9¼-in., with flaring crimped edge. All have large genuine stuck handles, each with 6 tall optic pattern tumblers to match. 3 sets each of 3 shapes equally assorted in 3 colors, namely, wine ruby, blue and light green. (Total 9 sets in bbl. Bbl. 35c.) **Per set, 45c**

OUR "LATEST" OPALESCENT WATER SET ASSORTMENT.

New and handsome shape. Exclusively our own.

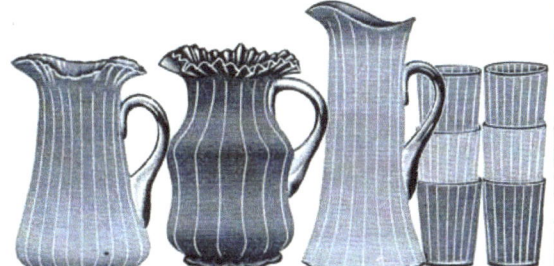

C666—This new water set in beautiful and always popular opalescent glassware consists of 1 extra large swell shape ½ gal. jug with fancy crimped and scalloped top and heavy twist stuck handle and 6 full size tall shape tumblers to match. 3 sets each of three patterns, each pattern being in 3 colors—namely, flint, ruby and blue opalescent. (Total 9 sets in bbl. Bbl. 35c.) **Per set, 67c**

Our Enamel Decorated Satin Etched BLOWN LEMONADE OR WATER SETS.

A regular $1.50 set as a $1.00 bargain day leader.

C669—This is one of the most beautiful sets ever produced, being of rich all over satin etched glass with elaborate decorations in large and highly colored floral design, the decorations being hand painted and richly enameled. The edges of both jugs and tumblers are decorated with wide bands in pure gold, each set comprising one extra large and extra tall half gallon jug, beautiful tankard shape, height 13-inches, with large fancy genuine stuck handle and 6 tall tapered full size tumblers to match, 2 crystal and 2 blue. (Total 6 sets in bbl. Bbl. 35c.) **Per set, 75c**

STANDARD "OPALESCENT" WATER SET.

Indescribably rich opalescent ware.

C665—Everybody knows it. Therefore we need only to say that each set comprises 1 water pitcher and 6 tumblers to match. They are packed 2 sets each of ruby, green, blue and flint opalescent. (Total 8 sets in bbl., wt. 74 lbs. Sold only by bbl.) **Per set, 66c**

OUR TANKARD OPALESCENT WATER SET ASSORTMENT.

Popular sellers in new and handsome shapes.

C667—These very popular selling opalescent sets are in two fancy shapes, one being an extra tall half gallon tankard shape, ht. 12¾-in.; the other a large half gallon fancy twist pattern, wide top and fancy twist handle. Each set comprising one jug and 6 tumblers to match. The assortment contains one set of each shape in four colors, namely, ruby, blue, green and flint opalescent. (Total 8 sets in bbl. Bbl. 35c.) **Per set, 69c**

OUR "PUREST GOLD" WATER SET

Best one-dollar bargain ever offered.

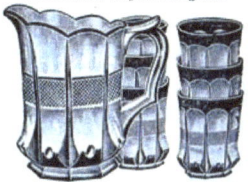

C678—Entirely new and beautiful shape, elaborate cut panel and cut diamond banded design elaborately decorated with wide bands of pure burnt-in gold importing an extremely rich and brilliant effect. Each set comprises 1 extra large and extra heavy footed ½-gallon pitcher with large fancy shape handle and fancy scalloped top and 6 full size tumblers to match. (Total 8 sets in bbl. Bbl. 35c.) **Per set, 75c**

Our "RICHEST COLORED" Water Sets.

Rich in color and rich in finish. One of our newest and best offerings.

C681—These beautiful sets are in an elaborate scroll and bull's-eye beaded pattern, extra heavy, massive, and very brilliant. They need only to be shown to be sold and will retail readily at from 75c to $1.00 per set. Each set comprises one extra large and extra heavy half gallon jug on fancy foot, with wide top and large fancy handles and 6 full size tumblers to match. Assortment comprises 6 sets of amethyst or wine ruby, 3 blue and 3 green. (Total 12 sets in bbl. Bbl. 35c.) **Per set, 44c**

TALL TANKARD ENGRAVED BLOWN WATER SETS.

A regular $1.00 seller as a 75c leader.

C657—Each set comprises extra large tall half-gallon tankard jug, large stuck handle, elaborately engraved floral fern and leaf patterns and six 9-oz., lead-blown table tumblers to match. An exceptionally beautiful and attractive set. 2 sets each of 3 patterns—lilies of the valley, fern and banded leaf engraving. (Total 6 sets in case, case 25c). **Per set, 57c**

BLOWN ENGRAVED WATER SET.

New rich patterns. Will be big sellers if offered for a dollar.

C671—High tankard shape, ½-gallon lead blown jug, good stuck handle profusely engraved in beautiful leaf and vine effect pattern, each set comprises 1 jug and six 9-oz. lead blown tumblers to match. 3 sets each of 3 patterns. (Total 9 sets in bbl., wt. 76 lbs. Bbl. 35c.) **Per set, 62c**

ENAMELED DECORATED BLOWN WATER SET ASSORTMENT.

A new and rich dollar leader.

C668—Comprising 3 styles, one a tall fancy fluted shape jug with hand painted enamel decorations in a beautiful delicate vine pattern, and one a tall wide flare top jug with elaborate floral and leaf decorations; the other an extra large swell shape jug with fancy crimped edge, with rich decorations and a wide etched band and floral enameled design. Each set consisting of one jug and 6 tumblers decorated to match, all the decorations being burnt in. The three styles being equally assorted in 3 colors, namely, green, blue and amethyst. (Total 9 sets in bbl. Bbl. 35c.) **Per set, 65c**

"CROWN TOP" SHELF JARS.

—The best of all fine finished, fire polished goods. They pay for themselves on the retail shelf by selling more goods.

C761, Round Shelf Jar—Capacity 4½ lbs. Roomy shape, cut top and rich. ½ dozen in case. Wt. 45 lbs. (Case 25c.) **Per dozen, $2.85**

C762, Square Jars—Capacity 4½ lbs. ½ doz. in case. Wt. 45 lbs. (Case 25c.) **Per dozen, $2.85**

The Man Who Rises Rapidly Is the Fearless One Who Constantly and Thoughtfully Undertakes New Things.

We Could Not Afford to Name Prices Like These With Any Other Salesman Than Printer's Ink.

For lower priced Tumblers see page 318.

Our "SPECIAL" Tumbler Asst.

Do not judge these by price alone. They are "firsts."

C557—Extra quality, full finished. Not the dull goods or those with rough mouth edge. Full size 8 oz., being 6 doz. each of *star, round plain, flat plain and horseshoe* bottoms. *(24 doz. in bbl., wt. 165 lbs. Bbl. 35c.)* Per dozen, **21c**

Our "NICKEL" Tumbler Asst.

Buy a barrel for trial, the goods will do the rest.

C558—Rich quality, bright goods, handsome patterns, regular table size. Goods of this grade are worth, *at Pittsburgh*, more than the price we name, 4 dozen each of 6 patterns. Per dozen, **22c**

(Total 24 doz. to bbl., wt. 160 lbs. Bbl. 35c.)

"FANCY PATTERN" Tumbler Asst.

C559—Excellent quality, large size, assorted, 4 doz. each of six styles. 4 with neat bands. Order a sample package and compare with goods that cost you 10 per cent more. Per dozen, **23c**

(Total 24 doz. in bbl., wt. 145 lbs. Bbl. 35c.)

"RICH ENGRAVED" Tumbler Asst.

If you can sell anything you can sell these beautiful goods.

C563—Four patterns of excellent engraving on four different popular shape medium weight pressed glass tumblers. *(4 doz. each of 4 styles, making a total of 16 doz. to bbl., wt. 101 lbs. Bbl. 35c.)* Per dozen, **36c**

Our "GROUND BOTTOM" Hotel Tumbler.

Large size, full finished.

C577 — Medium heavy weight, almost straight shape with fancy fine fluted base and smooth ground and polished bottom, capacity 9-oz. Full finished and fire polished. 6 doz. in case. *(Case 30c.)* Per dozen, **34c**

HEAVY HOTEL Tumbler.

Tall, almost straight shape.

C571—Full large size, heavy, finished goods. A seller. The price is right. *(6 doz. in case, wt. 69 lbs. Case 30c.)* .... Per dozen, **41c**

"DOUBLE THICK" Table Tumblers.

One you need, the price is right.

C573—Plain large hotel tumblers. Very heavy, double thick, almost unbreakable, just the one for hotel or restaurant use. *(6 doz. in case, wt. 68 lbs. Case 30c.)* Per dozen, **42c**

Our "HEAVY BOTTOM" Hotel Tumbler.

An extra good one to retail at 5c.

C576—Made of best quality crystal glass, extra heavy and with double thick bottom, extra large size regular hotel style. 6 doz. in case. *(Case 30c)*. Per dozen, **33c**

"SPECIAL" LEMONADE OR ICED TEA TUMBLER.

A big 5-cent leader and a profit payer.

C634—Capacity about 12-oz., medium heavy bottom, long flat flute, neat mold bands. Size most universally used for lemonade, iced tea, etc. 1 doz. in case. *(Case 30c.)* Per dozen, **33c**

TALL LEMONADE GLASS.

Superior goods.

C631—13-oz. goods, pressed glass, shapely and strong, 5¾-in. high. A staple seller at a right price. *(6 doz. in wood case, wt. 83 lbs. Case 30c.)* Per dozen, **48c**

Standard SODA OR LEMONADE Tumbler Asst.

Four of the best selling sizes with ground bottoms, assorted in one barrel. To retail at 5 and 10 cents.

C633 — Standard goods, all full finished and with ground bottoms which will not scratch bar or table. The assortment comprises the following: 3 doz. 11 oz. Medium Soda or Lemonades, 4 doz. 12-oz. just the size for Iced Tea, etc., 3 doz. 13-oz. Tall Lemonades, 2 doz. 14-oz. Extra Tall Lemonades. *(Total 12 doz. in bbl. Wt. 120 lbs. Bbl. 35c.)* Average price per dozen, **52c**

Standard 8-oz. "ST. LOUIS" Beer Mug.

C673—This 8-oz. beer mug has the ground bottom, so will not scratch table or bar. Standard goods. *(6 doz. in case, wt. 98 lbs. Case 30c.)* Per dozen, **48c**

GOBLETS in Original Packages.

Finest quality and very best finish for the prices named. Only the best selling styles are here offered. *Sold only by bbl.*

C606, 34c Doz. C607, 35c Doz. C602, 38c Doz. C608, 43c Doz.

	Doz.
C606, "Plain" Goblet—A standard favorite. Rich and tasteful. *(9 doz. in bbl., wt. 100 lbs. Bbl. 35c.)*	$0 34
C607, "Banded" Goblet—New smooth pressed band, with appearance of French hand etching. Extra large, above average weight. A good seller either for family or hotel use. *(10 doz. in bbl., wt. 128 lbs. Bbls. 35c.)*	35
C602, "Low Shape" Hotel Goblet—Full size, heavy crystal glass, well finished, good heavy foot, smooth mouth edge. *9 doz. in bbl., wt. 117 lbs. (Bbl. 35c)*	38
C608, "Mold Band" Hotel Goblet.—Large size, low hotel shape, extra heavy crystal, well finished with 3 wide mold bands, heavy fancy foot. A new one and one that will be a seller. *(Total 10 doz. in bbl. Bbl. 35c)*	39
C603, "Large Size" Hotel Goblet—Extra heavy and large finely finished hotel goblet. Always a staple seller. *(9 doz. in bbl., wt. 130 lbs. Bbl. 35c.)*	43
C605, "Railroad" Double Thick—Hotel shape. Very best quality, flat foot. *(8 doz. in bbl., wt. 123 lbs. Bbl. 35c.)*	45
C610, Double-Thick Hotel Goblet. Very heavy. Large size. Double thick. Heavy foot. *(7 doz. in bbl. wt., 150 lbs. Bbl. 35c.)*	45

C605, 45c Doz.

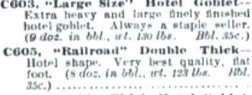

C610, 45c Doz.

"1903" GOBLET Assortment.

3 styles in one package.

—Three new and attractive patterns at a price that leaves you a good profit. Assortment includes **3 doz. each** of the 3 styles. Per dozen, **36c** *(9 doz. in bbl., wt. 105 lbs. Bbl. 35c.)*

Our "STAR" Goblet and Tumbler Assortment.

Two popular sellers assorted in one package.

C600—Rich almost plain pattern with numerous small pressed stars, both in pure crystal, full finished and fire polished.

Assortment comprises the following:

6 doz. full size fancy shape goblets with imitation cut stem @ 37c. $2 22

6 doz. 9-oz. flaring table tumblers with fancy fluted bottom @ 23c. Wt. 98 lbs. 1 38

Total, **$3.60**

(Total 12 doz. in bbl. Wt. 98 lbs. Bbl. 35c.)

EXTRA FINE BLOWN Glass Tumblers.

C564—Plain, full size 9-oz. blown water tumbler, lead glass, clear as crystal. *(6 doz. in case, wt. 31 lbs. Case 30c.)* Per dozen, **37½c**

Our "FOUR BAND" Blown Tumbler.

C565—Best quality flint glass, 4 heavy engraved bands, full size 9 oz. *(6 doz. in case, wt. 31 lbs. Case 30c.)* Per dozen, **43c**

"ENGRAVED AND PLAIN" Blown Tumbler Asst.

Purest lead glass. Strictly firsts.

C570—All regulation 10-oz. table size in plain, engraved band and engraved floral designs. Assortment comprises:

6 dozen Plain .... @	$0 37½	$2 25
2 " Engraved Four Band .. @	43	86
1 doz. Engraved Band—one wide and two narrow .... @	43	43
1 doz. Engraved All-over Floral Pattern .... @	48	48
1 doz. Engraved Oak Leaf Band Effect .... @	48	48
1 doz. Feather Fern Engraved all over Pattern .... @	48	48
(Bbl. 35c.) Total for assortment of 12 dozen		**$4.98**

ENGRAVED BLOWN Tumblers.

C567, 48c Doz. C566, 48c Doz. C568, 48c Doz.

C567, "Band and Sprig"—Latest pattern, engraved band of scattered shamrock leaves with 4-line band engraving above and below, full 9 oz. pure lead glass. *(6 doz. in case, wt. 31 lbs. Case 30c.)* Per dozen, **48c**

C566, "Wreath Band" — Engraved flint glass, very deep, floral engraving forming wide band, extra quality pure lead glass, 9 oz. *(6 doz. in case, wt. 31 lbs. Case 30c.)* Per dozen, **48c**

C568, Fancy "Spray Engraved"—Floral spray decoration, covering both sides, full size, 9 oz. flint glass. *(6 doz. in case, wt. 31 lbs. Case 30c.)* Per dozen, **48c**

BELL SHAPE BLOWN TUMBLER ASSORTMENT.

Five sizes of these popular selling staples assorted in one package.

C569—All of the purest thin lead blown glass, all in the flaring bell shape. Note that the assortment contains only the most staple sellers. Assortment comprises the following:

1 doz.,	5-oz.	at 39c	$0 39
2 "	8 "	" 44c	88
1 "	9 "	" 48c	48
1 "	10 "	" 55c	55
1 "	11 "	" 65c	65

(Total 6 doz. in case. Case 30c.) Total, **$2.95**

JELLY TUMBLERS—"Firsts."

Superior quality—large sizes—guaranteed "Firsts." There are cheaper tumblers in the market than the following, but they are cheaper in quality as well as in price. Note that our ½ pint jelly tumblers are full 6-oz. size—not the 5-oz. commonly sold as ½ pint and worth fully 1 cent per doz. less. *Sold only by pkg.*

"STANDARD" JELLIES—Plain.

C552—½-pint, regular medium size. 24 doz. to pkg., wt. 160 lbs. *(Bbl. 35c)* ..... Doz. $0 18¾

C553—Large half pints, really holding full 9 ounces. Tin tops. *(18 doz. in bbl., sold by pkg. only, wt. 143 lbs. Bbl. 35c)* .... Doz. 20

C545, "Extra Size" Asst.—Comprises:

9 doz. ½-pint medium size plain @ 17½c. $1 58

9 " 10-oz. @ 19½c. 1 75

(Bbl. 35c.) Total, **$3.33**

TUMBLER SHAPE" JELLY TUMBLERS.

C547—8-oz. tumbler shape, neat mold bands and fine cut flute. Asst. comprises 5 doz. each of four patterns, total 20 doz. in bbl. Wt. 145 lbs. *(Bbl. 35c)* .... Doz. 19¼

TUMBLER OFFERING EXTRAORDINARY.

C400:.Deep prism cut pattern, star bottom. Good quality—good enough for any one. We shall be glad if our purchase, large as it is, lasts us through the month. 1 doz. in pasteboard box. *No pkg. charge.* Per dozen, **24c**

In bbl. lots of about 18 doz. *(Bbl. 35c.)* Per dozen, **20c**

You Have the Satisfaction of Guaranteed Prices When Buying Here—We Never Advance Prices Without Notice.

Page 60

If You Have an Idea, Utilize It—Every New Method of Doing Things Advertises You.

GLASSWARE IN OPEN STOCK— No Package Charge.

A still larger showing of these quick-selling bargain specialties, which sell themselves if given half a chance. If we were to tell here the plain truth as to how *very much more* the exclusive jobbers get for these same goods, you would set it down as an exaggeration. We would prefer that you buy a few sample dozens and COMPARE.

This is one of the few lines in which a retailer may **double his money** and still give values that make fast friends. Very many of the following items, though so priced that they can be sold at 5 cents, commonly retail at ten. **All the following are in pasteboard boxes.**

"PLAIN PATTERN" SAUCE DISH.

A 3-cent bargain.

C147—Round shape, diameter 4¼-in., extra heavy, deep, plain pattern with star bottom. 1 doz. in box. Per dozen, **22c**

"CUT DIAMOND" SAUCE DISH.

An exceptional 3c bargain.

C160—Round shaped diameter 4¼ inches, brilliant genuine cut glass pattern, extra deep scalloped edge. 1 doz. in box. Per doz., **25c**

"STRAWBERRY AND FAN" SAUCE DISH.

Bright and useful and cheap.

C161 — Diam. 4¼ in., round shape, extra deep, scalloped edge. Unusually rich in this popular pattern. 1 doz. in box. Per dozen, **26c**

"BEADED HEART" SAUCE DISH.

A large and brilliant 5-center on which you can double your money.

C146—Round, extra deep, diam. 4½ in., richest of new brilliant patterns, fancy scalloped edge. 1 doz. in box. Per dozen, **27c**

CRYSTAL "PURE" SAUCE DISH.

A 5-cent profit payer or rare bargain to run "3 for 10c."

C152:. Round shape, diam. 4¾-in., extra deep and heavy, deep cut diamond pattern with fancy scalloped edge. 1 doz. in box. Per dozen, [illegible]

OUR "PLAIN PATTERN" FOOTED COMPORT.

Always a staple 5-cent seller.

C148—Round shape, extra deep, diameter 4¼-in., on fancy foot. Especially desirable for ice cream, etc. 1 doz. in box. Per dozen, **33c**

"RADIANT" SAUCE DISH.

A sparkling crystal beauty.

C168—Extra heavy brilliant pattern, diameter 4½-in., extra deep and with fancy scalloped edge. Full finished and fire polished. 1 doz. in box. Per dozen, **36c**

"CROWN JEWEL" SAUCE DISH.

Not a prettier pattern made.

C150—A regular magnet at a "nickel." Fancy deep 4½-inch dish. Suitable for table use or bonbons. 1 doz. in box. Per dozen, **37c**

"ASTORIA" BERRY OR SAUCE DISH.

Extra bright and extra brilliant.

C175—Diameter 4¼-in., extra deep, round shape, footed, with fancy scalloped edge. Brilliant pattern in all-over cut glass design. 1 doz. in box. Per dozen, **37c**

FANCY DECORATED NAPPY.

A new and rich 5-center.

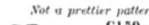

C171—Round shape, diam. 4¼ in., attractive beaded heart and plume design in pure crystal, panels being decorated alternately in ruby, green, canary and gold bronze, giving an unusually attractive effect. 1 doz. in box. Per dozen, **37c**

"BELL RIMMED" SAUCE DISH.

Attractive 5-center.

C162 — Diam. 4¼-in., extra deep, round shape, footed, brilliant genuine cut glass pattern, fancy edge. 1 doz. in box. Per dozen, **38c**

"HOLLAND HOUSE" SAUCE DISH.

Another 5-cent gem.

C173 — Fancy square shape, footed, extra deep, 4¼x4¼-in., fancy scalloped edge, richly finished and fire polished. 1 doz. in box. Per dozen, **38c**

"ARTISTIC SHAPE" SAUCE DISH.

An unequalled 5-center.

C156—Diameter 4¾ in., fancy scalloped flaring shape, richest cut diamond and star pattern, extra heavy and brilliantly finished with fancy scalloped edge. 1 doz. in box. Per dozen, **39c**

"SWELL SHAPE" SAUCE DISH.

A full finished beauty.

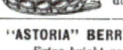

C163:. Diam. 4¾-in., fancy pointed and scalloped edge. Order a sample dozen and see how they sell. 1 doz. in box. Per dozen, **39c**

"PRISM" NAPPY OR SAUCE DISH.

A rich and rare 5-center.

C158 — Round, diam. 4½-in., deep flaring shape, diamond cut base and fancy bull's eye pattern edge. 1 doz. in box. Per dozen, **40c**

OUR "TOURAINE" BERRY DISH.

Artistic shape, richest design.

C174 — Extra deep fancy round flaring shape, diameter 4¾-in., footed, with rich scalloped edge. A brilliant pattern, and a fire polished gem. 1 doz. in box. Per dozen, **39c**

"FANCY SHAPE" SAUCE DISH.

Looks like cut glass.

C166—Diam. 4½-in., beautiful pattern, extra heavy, 4-corner shape, heavy brilliant edge. 1 doz. in box. Per dozen, **41c**

"FRENCH PLATE" SAUCE DISH.

One of the best 5-centers ever produced.

C153—Round shape, diam. 4½ in., extra heavy and extra deep, rich block diamond pattern with scalloped edge, full finished and fire polished, very brilliant. 1 doz. in box. Per dozen, **41c**

DEEP "SCALLOPED EDGE" SAUCE DISH.

Finest dish ever offered at a 5c price.

C165—Fancy round shape, diam. 4¾-in., rich genuine cut glass pattern, purest crystal, fancy scalloped edge. 1 doz. in box. Per dozen, **40c**

"BEADED PANEL" SAUCE DISH.

Extra heavy and extra brilliant.

C164 — Diam. 4¼ in., round shape, footed, rich beaded panels and fancy edge. A fire polished gem. 1 doz. in box. Per dozen, **42c**

Scalloped and Footed Beaded Edge Nappy.

The finest finished dish ever shown for 5c.

C155—Pure crystal glass, beaded edge, tripod shaped foot. 1 doz. in box. Per dozen, **43c**

"BON TON" BERRY NAPPY.

A beauty—looks like cut glass.

C172 — Diameter 5½-in., large size, fancy shape, richest of cut glass patterns with elaborate scalloped edge, brilliantly fire polished. Will sell if shown. 1 doz. in box. Per dozen, **42c**

"PRISM" BONBON DISH.

A value unapproachable.

C151—Round shape, diam. 3¾-in., extra deep, rolled-in edges. Made of purest crystal in genuine cut glass pattern. 1 doz. in box. Per dozen, **39c**

FANCY LONG CRYSTAL DISH.

A 5-center on which you can make a profit.

C149 — Oval shape, 7½x3¾-in. brilliant mirror panel pattern with fancy scalloped edge. 1 doz. in box. Per dozen, **33c**

"RUBY AND CRYSTAL" UTILITY DISH.

A sparkling 10-cent beauty.

C170—Diam. 5 in. Attractive cut pattern, scalloped edge, decorated in pure burnt-in ruby, ornamental and useful. 1 doz. in box. Per dozen, **77c**

HANDLED TRINKET RECEPTACLE.

Brilliant and artistic. A rare 5-center.

C159—Diam. 5 in., footed, rolled up side, open handle, purest finished crystal, bright new pattern. Will be a great seller. 1 doz. in box. Per dozen, **43c**

"BEAUTY" MATCH OR TOOTHPICK.

Staple as wheat—5-cent seller.

C350 —A dainty little item in pure crystal glass. 1 doz. in box, no charge for package. Per dozen, **29c**

5-CENT GLASS HAT.

"Fine as silk"—a nickel seller.

C317—Of the best flint glass made up to illustrate the good old grandfather's hat. For matches, toothpicks, etc. 1 doz. in box. Per dozen, **29c**

COMMON SENSE MATCH SAFE or TOOTHPICK.

One of the things that SELL.

C364—Beaded panel pattern, panels forming numerous scratchers, wide base. 1 doz. in box. Per dozen, **33c**

"DOT MIRROR" TOOTHPICK HOLDER.

New and rich 5-center.

C343—Good size, fancy shape, rich reflecting panel design with fancy foot. 1 doz. in box. Per dozen, **35c**

"RADIANT" TOOTHPICK.

A seller—a bargain.

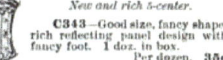

C352—Good size, richly finished, solid and heavy. Will not tip over easily. Very brilliant. 1 doz. in box. Per dozen, **37c**

"PRISM" TOOTHPICK HOLDER.

Looks like a 10-center.

C360 — Ht. 2¼-in., rich cut diamond base, fine flutes and optic bull's eye effect. A full finished beauty. 1 doz. in box. Per dozen, **39c**

"SIX PANEL" TOOTHPICK HOLDER.

A 5-cent gem.

C347—Of purest crystal, extra heavy and rich panel design, fancy flaring base and scalloped top. 1 doz. in box. Per dozen, **39c**

Our "Bon Ton" Toothpick Holder.

Exact reproduction of genuine cut glass. Looks like a 10-center.

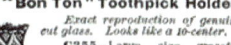

C355—Large size, graceful shape, footed, fancy scalloped and flared top, extremely rich and beautiful pattern. Will be an exceptional 5-center. 1 doz. in box. Per dozen, **40c**

GYPSY KETTLE.

A 5-cent crystal beauty.

C316—The prettiest and best size kettle made. Very handy for hanging up or for mantel use for matches, picks, etc. 1 doz. in box. Per dozen, **39c**

Our "SURE THING" NEST EGG.

—Most natural of all nest eggs. Heavy opal glass. "Firsts." Safely packed. 1 doz. in spaced box. Per dozen, **18c**
(Case of gross, *no pkg. charge*, $2.00 gross.)

"RICHEST AND BRIGHTEST" TOOTHPICK HOLDER.

Shapely and brilliant.

C341—Purest crystal, beautiful new genuine cut glass pattern, artistic fancy square shape. A 5-cent bargain. 1 doz. in box. Per dozen, **40c**

"OPTIC" PANEL TOOTHPICK HOLDER.

At 5c will sell every day in the year.

C354:. Medium size, almost plain, optic panel pattern, purest finished crystal to which no picture could do justice. 1 doz. in box. Per dozen, **41c**

DECORATED OPAL TOOTHPICK HOLDER.

New and attractive 5-center.

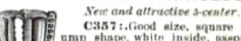

C357:. Good size, square column shape, white inside, assorted colored heavy panels on outside. Very unique pattern. 1 doz. in box. Per dozen, **41c**

OUR "BRILLIANT" TOOTHPICK HOLDER.

A bargain at 5 cents or more.

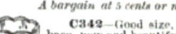

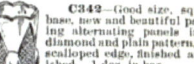

C342—Good size, square shape base, new and beautiful pattern, having alternating panels in rich cut diamond and plain pattern, with fancy scalloped edge, finished and fire polished. 1 doz. in box. Per dozen, **41c**

OUR "HEAVY CUT" TOOTHPICK HOLDER.

Would be cheap at 10 cents.

C344—Large size, extra heavy, deep, rich cut glass pattern, with heavy plain edge, brilliantly finished and fire polished. 1 doz. in box. Per dozen, **42c**

"LOVING CUP" TOOTHPICK HOLDER.

A dazzling production of best crystal glass.

C353—Imitation cut glass pattern, 3 handles, scalloped top. 1 doz. in box. Per dozen, **42c**

"ROSE PINK" TOOTHPICK.

At 10 cents every lady will want one.

C358—Extra heavy cut panel design in rich solid rose pink color, heavy smooth ground and polished bottom. Rich and attractive 1 doz. in box. Per dozen, **75c**

"RUBY AND CRYSTAL" TOOTHPICK.

Rich and brilliant. A pleasing 10-center.

C348—Graceful flaring shape, rich genuine cut pattern with fancy scalloped edge, edge and panels decorated in pure burnt-in ruby. 1 doz. in box. Per dozen, **78c**

"DAINTY" GOLD BAND TOOTHPICK HOLDER.

A little 10-cent gem.

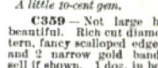

C359 — Not large but very beautiful. Rich cut diamond pattern, fancy scalloped edge, 1 wide and 2 narrow gold bands. Will sell if shown. 1 doz. in box. Per dozen, **79c**

"ROSE RED" TOOTHPICK —With Gold Edges.

At 10 cents will sell always.

C374—Medium size, footed, fancy shape, deep cut panel design in imitation of genuine cut glass, solid burnt-in rose red color with rich band, gold edge. An unusually rich piece. 1 doz. in box, *no pkg. charge.* Per dozen, **82c**

Better to Buy in Small Lots and Prosper Than Gain Repute as a Buyer and Tie Your Profits Up in Goods.

The Price-Informed Merchant Can Tell at a Glance That Our Prices Are Rock Bottom.

Our "Cut Pattern" SHERBET.
At 5c a leader—a profit-payer.
C26—Handy handled glass in brilliant cut design. 1 doz. in box. Per dozen, **35c**

GRADUATED COOKING CUP.

Every housewife will want one.
C281—Heavy and well finished with good handle, capacity one cup, has graduated spaces measuring ¼, ⅓, ½ and ¾ cups. 1 doz. in box. Per dozen, **45c**

FANCY GLASS CUP.
Your customers will want them by the half dozen.
C28—For custard, punch or sherbet. Purest finished crystal. 1 doz. in box. Per dozen, **43c**

OUR "PLAIN AND RICH" SHERBET CUP.
Always a staple seller.

C36—Good size and shape, made of purest crystal with smooth ground and polished bottom, large handle, plain except with neat fine flute around base. 1 doz. in box. Per dozen, **69c**

Our Footed "Ground Bottom" SHERBET CUP.
A popular 10-cent seller.

C39—Regulation size, rich plain pattern, star bottom and fancy ground and polished foot, large handle. Richly finished and fire polished. 1 doz. in box. Per dozen, **72c**

"CUT PATTERN" LEMONADE OR SHERBET CUP.

Buy a sample dozen and see how they sell.
C32—Large size, beautiful cut satin diamond pattern, good handle, brilliant, full finished, ground bottom. 1 doz. in box. Per dozen, **75c**

"CUT PANEL" SHERBET CUP.
A price ticket "10 cents" will sell these rapidly.

C37—Large size, good shape, rich cut diamond panel design, smooth ground and polished bottom. A fire polished beauty. 1 doz. in box. Per dozen, **75c**

GROUND BOTTOM SHERBET CUP.
A finished gem.

C31—Extra large, full finished, pure crystal, good handle and smooth ground bottom, rich optic panel pattern. A profit paying 10-center. 1 doz. in box. Per dozen, **78c**

"ROSE PINK" SHERBET CUP.

A 10c beauty—a charming seller.
C30—Ht. 2½-in., ground bottom, large handle, fancy cut panel pattern, solid rich color. 1 doz. in box. Per dozen, **82c**

"Bell Shape" FRENCH BLOWN SHERBET.
Regular 15c value, but 10c can be named.

C29—Best selling size, purest crystal lead glass, flaring bell shape ground top, good stuck handle. 1 doz. in box. Per dozen, **$1.08**

Our "French Blown" SHERBET.
High class—you can sell this for $1.75 a dozen.

C27—Ground tops, purest lead glass, stuck handle. This rich plain pattern is always preferred. 1 doz. in box. Per dozen, **$1.20**

GENUINE CUT GLASS SHERBET CUP
Beautiful and shapely.

C34—Rich plain lead blown ground top and stuck handle with genuine cut stars all over pattern. *A regular 25c seller* which you can retail at say 19c. 1 doz. in box. Per doz., **$1.65**

Our "OPAL" SOAP DISH.

A 5-cent pure white dish.
C631—*Cheap at a dime anywhere.* You can sell a lot of them at this popular figure. 1 doz. in box. Per dozen, **45c**

TURQUOISE SOAP SLAB.
Everybody will want one at 5c.

C632 — Handsome turquoise colored soap dish that you cannot keep in stock long. 1 doz. in box. Per dozen, **45c**

3-CENT GLASS MUG.

A regular 5-cent mug to run as a 3-cent leader.
C272—Medium size, good pattern. A bargain at this price. 1 doz. in box. Per dozen, **24c**

OUR "FANCY FOOTED" MUG.

Good 5-center at a price which leaves you a profit.
C271 — Good size, height 3¼-in., footed, with large handle, fancy beaded drapery pattern. Capacity 5-oz. 1 doz. in box. Per dozen, **33c**

"UTILITY" GLASS MUG.

A bargain at 5c or more.
C279—Pure crystal glass, large size, arch dot pattern, with large shapely handle. 1 doz. in box. Per dozen, **39c**

OUR "UNIQUE" HANDLED MUG.
Shapely rich pattern.

C277 — Large size, on fancy foot with convenient handle, elaborate frosted and dew-drop pattern — *entirely new.* Would be a 10-center if we had paid the regular price. 1 doz. in box. Per dozen, **42c**

"TIFFANY" Mug.
A very pretty 5-center.
C276—A full finished gem. Especially cheap at this little price. 1 doz. in box. Per dozen, **43c**

"CRYSTAL PURE" MUG.
Extra good at this price.
C275—Full size diamond pattern, very brilliant, with plain rim. 1 doz. in box. Per dozen, **43c**

OUR "ELITE" MUG.
Richest of cut glass patterns.
C280—Full size, a perfect beauty. Fire polished. 1 doz. in box. Per dozen, **47c**

OUR "PATRIOTIC" ETCHED AND DECORATED MUG.
New and beautiful 10-center.

C285—Extra large footed, ht. 3½-in., fancy handle, all-over etched glass giving frosted effect. Elaborately embossed and decorated sides—one side colored floral and gold design, the other stars and stripes in relief. 1 doz. in box. Per dozen, **75c**

DECORATED COVERED STEIN.

C286 — Extra large size, full ht. including cover 6½-in. made of pure opal in beautiful all-over embossed designs with ancient figures and mottoes, footed, with large fancy handle and fancy shaped cover, elaborately decorated all-over in combination of bright and attractive colors and silver and gold bronze. Asstd. colors, such as red, brown, green and blue in box of 1 doz., no pkg. charge. Per dozen, **96c**

GLASS LEMON SQUEEZER.
Needed in every household.

C1—A hat shaped piece of glass, rough jagged crown upon which half the lemon is to be forced and turned. 1 doz. in box. Per dozen, **35c**

GLASS LEMON SQUEEZER.
A staple 5-center.

C3 — Extra large, with high cone and deep saucer for holding juice, good lip, handled. 3 doz. in case. Per dozen, **40c**
1 doz. in pasteboard box. Per dozen, **43c**

"MANNY" LEMON JUICE EXTRACTOR.
Best in the market.

C2—The large saucer holds the juice of a number of lemons and the little pillars retain all the seeds. 1 doz. in box. Per dozen, **72c**

BLOCK DIAMOND GLASS CREAM PITCHER.

A brilliant new 5-cent profit payer.
C178—Medium size, ht. 3-in., extra heavy rich block diamond pattern in pure crystal, good handle and fancy scalloped top. A full finished fire polished gem. 1 doz. box. Per dozen, **42c**

"TIFFANY" CREAM PITCHER.
A self-selling 5-center.
C177—Pretty beyond compare. Useful as it is pretty. 1 doz. in box. Per dozen, **42c**

"MIRROR" CREAM PITCHER.

You need bargains like this.
C181 — Perfectly plain, full polished. Scallop footed, rich pattern, 3 inches high. 1 doz. in box. Per dozen, **42c**

OUR PEARL TOP DECORATED CREAM PITCHER.
A regular 10-center as a possible 5-center.
C179—Large size, ht. 5¼-in., rich almost plain pattern, footed, fancy tankard shape with large handle, wide top and fancy beaded edge. 1 doz. in box. Per dozen, **45c**

"STUCK HANDLE" CREAM PITCHER.

No prettier 10-center ever shown.
C180—Tall tankard shape in purest crystal, exceptionally rich pattern, ht. 4½-in., footed, large genuine stuck handle. Full finished and fire polished. 1 doz. in box. Per dozen, **75c**

HANDLED SAUCE OR CREAM PITCHER.

An all the year seller in a fancy new shape.
C176 — Good size, rich half fluted and half plain pattern, fancy footed, large handle and good lip. Finished and brilliant. 1 doz. in box. Per dozen, **78c**

"GEM" VINEGAR OR OIL BOTTLE.
Not cut glass, but looks like it.
C312—An artistic 3-oz. bottle; 5 inches high, with glass stopper. Very fine imitation of genuine cut glass. 1 doz. in box. Per dozen, **72c**

"SMALL" VINEGAR OR OIL BOTTLE.
To retail at 10c and pay you a profit.
C503 — Capacity about 4 oz., imitation cut glass pattern in extra heavy block diamond design, gold glass stopper, fire polished, rich and attractive. 1 doz. in box. Per dozen, **75c**

"COTTAGE" VINEGAR OR OIL BOTTLE.
A shapely 10-center.
C315 — Extra heavy rich pattern, capacity about 5 oz., large handle and fancy stopper. Full finish and very brilliant. 1 doz. in box. Per dozen, **77c**

RICH PLAIN OIL OR VINEGAR BOTTLE.
An attractive 10c offering.
C314—Ht. 4¾-in., medium size, capacity about 5-oz., rich plain body with fluted neck, and stopper, gracefully shaped handle. A full finished and fire polished gem. 1 doz. in box. Per dozen, **79c**

BLOCK DIAMOND VINEGAR or OIL BOTTLE.
A brilliant 10-cent offering.
C313 — Pretty deep cut pattern, medium size 14-oz., glass stopper. 1 doz. in box. Per dozen, **80c**

"DIAMOND CUT" VINEGAR JUG.
Deep cut pattern, price very attractive.
C502—Fine imitation cut glass. Very heavy and brilliant. Glass stopper, will hold 5 ounces. 1 doz. in box. Per dozen, **82c**

GLASS LIPPED "CRYSTAL JEWEL" SYRUP PITCHER.

Greatest 15c item of the season.
C384 — Extra heavy, 6 inches high, heavy britannia top. Band of large crystal jewels around bulb vase, with smaller imitation cut flute neck. Finely finished. ½ doz. in neatly labeled pasteboard box. Per dozen, **$1.25**

Our "TIFFANY" SYRUP PITCHER.

Good 25-center, or a big leader at 19 cents.
C386—Large size, large swell shape, extra heavy. In the beautiful strawberry and fan cut glass pattern, with large convenient handle and heavy nickel plated dome top. Richly fire polished and very brilliant. ½ doz. in box. Per dozen, **$1.65**

"TINTED OPAL" SYRUP PITCHER.
Rich opal in beautiful tints. A splendid seller.
C381—Melon shape, shell embossing, decorated with sprays of roses, gold stripe around top, green handle. Nickel plated dome top with drip lid inside. ½ doz. in box. Per dozen, **$2.00**

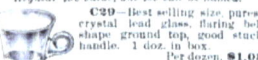

"BIG DECORATED" OPAL SYRUP PITCHER.
An exceptionally rich one to retail at 25c.
C385 — Large attractive melon shape, beaded panels, decorated in gold bronze, elaborate hand painted floral decorations on both sides, decorations fired and will not wear off. fancy handle and best nickel plated dome top. ½ doz. in box, no pkg. charge. Per dozen, **$2.25**

"ROSE BLUSH DECORATED" CRYSTAL GLASSWARE.

A splendid new line of rich, quick-selling glassware specialties. Entirely new delicate rose color decoration, being very elaborate and burnt-in. Will not wear off. You can retail all of them at 10c, although they are actually worth much more.

"ROSE BLUSH" TOOTHPICK HOLDER.
Something fine. A matchless value.
C463—Good size, footed, fancy shape, panels and edges decorated as above, fire polished. 1 doz. in box. Per dozen, **82c**

"ROSE BLUSH" SHERBET CUP.
Brilliantly bright—exceedingly rich.
C461—Fancy shape, footed, beautiful pattern, flaring top, convenient handle, brilliantly fire polished, decorated as above. 1 doz. in box. Per dozen, **82c**

"ROSE BLUSH" FLOWER VASE.
Pretty as the flowers it was made to hold.
C465—Ht. 6 in., footed, tall flaring shape with long deep cut panels, scalloped top, decorated as above. 1 doz. in box. Per dozen, **82c**

"ROSE BLUSH" TANKARD CREAM PITCHER.
Strikingly attractive—wonderfully cheap.
C462—Tall tankard shape, ht. 4 in., footed, with large handle, good lip, reflecting panel design, panels and edge decorated as above. 1 doz. in box. Per dozen, **82c**

"ROSE BLUSH" UTILITY DISH.
As beautiful as it is useful.
C464 — Oval shape, length 6¾ in., extra deep, rich panel and cut diamond design with scalloped edge, elaborate decoration as above. 1 doz. in box. Per dozen, **82c**

"ROSE BLUSH" TUMBLER.
An every-day seller.
C460 — Extra heavy fancy flaring shape, heavy cut panel design, richly finished, fire polished, decorated as above. 1 doz. in box. Per dozen, **82c**

Our Standard of Quality is Always Maintained--Poor Goods Find No Market Here.

BOXED TUMBLERS.

All full finished and fire polished.

The following tumblers are put up in neat display spaced boxes of 1 doz. each as in adjoining illustration. (*No charge for boxes.*) Each pattern is shown in connection with the description.

C434. C419. C436.

Doz.

C434, "Flat Flute" Table Tumbler — One of the staple patterns in tumblers. This price in *open stock* is exceedingly low. 1 doz. in display box. $0 27

C419, Our "Plain and Serviceable" Table Tumbler—Rich plain pattern, popular almost straight shape with medium heavy bottom. extra well made and full finished. 1 doz. in box....... 29

C436, "Plain and Finished" Tumbler — Bright crystal, large 9-oz.; good shape, smooth mouth edge. 1 doz. in pasteboard box.......... 29

C449, "Tapered" Table Tumbler — *Sells every day in the year.* Tall, tapered shape, just fits the hand, well finished, deep fine flute base, 3 mold bands. 1 doz. in box.... 29

C421, "Fine Flute" — Handsome table pattern, fluted bottom. This attractive, sight selling, serviceable tumbler will *retail by the dozen* at 5c each. 1 doz. in box..... 30

C442, "Plain and Shapely" Table Tumbler—Bright crystal, tall, almost straight shape, extra well finished, medium heavy bottom. A rich plain tumbler that always sells. 1 doz. in box........... 30

C428, Our "Rich Optic" Table Tumbler—Large size, good shape, made of purest full finished crystal in rich reflecting optic pattern. Exceptionally good 5-center. 1 doz. in box 31

C438, "Fan Flute"—Regulation table size and shape, upper half plain, lower half with rich flute and fine ribbed combination, making fan design. 1 doz. in box...... 31

C433, "Prism Cut" Table Tumbler:. Full size, best ware, deep prism cut pattern, star bottom. This price would be cheap in barrel lots. 1 doz. in spaced box 31

C416, "French Plate" Table Tumbler—Well named "French plate." Very heavy table tumbler with fire polished narrow paneled straight sides. Looks like plate glass, clear as a crystal. 1 doz. in box.. 31

C447 — "Molded Band and Flute" Table Tumbler — Regulation table size, well finished, medium heavy star bottom and neat flutes, 2 wide bands. An attractive and serviceable tumbler. 1 doz. in box...... 31

C453, Our "Wide Flute" Table Tumbler—Regulation table size in new pattern, having alternating wide and deep cut flutes and four neat mold bands. An everyday seller. 1 doz. in box..... .. 32

C443, "Molded Four Band" Table Tumbler — Regulation table size, rich finished plain pattern, smooth mouth edge. 4 neat mold bands. Would be cheap at the price in barrel lots. 1 doz. in box....... 32

C435, "Mold Band" — Five mold bands and finely finished. A full size, shapely tumbler that is an attraction in any store. 1 doz. in box. 32

Doz.

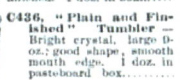

C450, "Long Knife Flute Tumbler" — Regular 8-oz. table size, purest crystal, medium heavy bottom, exceptionally rich design, alternating long knife cut and wide flutes, smooth mouth edge. Full finished and fire polished. 1 doz. in box............ $0 32

C448—"Four Band" plain table tumbler. Full table size, extra well finished, medium heavy star bottom, 2 wide and 2 narrow mold bands. *Will be a marvelous 5-cent seller.* 1 doz. in box 32

C439, "Star" Table Tumbler—Regular 8-oz. table size, tall shape, allover star pattern, fancy flute and star bottom, full finished and shapely. 1 doz. in box............ 32

C441, "5-Band and Fine Flute"—Regular 8-oz. table size, finely finished smooth edges, 5 mold bands and fine flute bottom. A rich and attractive tumbler. 1 doz. in spaced box............. 32

C441½, "6-Band and Fine Flute" — Regular 8-oz. table size, finely finished smooth edges, 5 mold bands and fine flute bottom. A rich and attractive tumbler. 1 doz. in spaced box, no pkg. charge.!............ 33

C444, Rich "Engraved Band" Tumbler—Regulation table size, full finished and fire polished, with 1 wide and 2 narrow engraved bands. An exceptionally rich and attractive 5-center. 1 doz. in box.............. 36

C423, Our Engraved "Four-Band" Table Tumbler — Rich, plain pattern with a 4-band hand engraving. A tumbler that always sells at 5c. 1 doz. in spaced box 37

C452, Engraved "Floral Band" Tumbler—8-oz., regulation table size, full finished, smooth mouth edge, attractive fluted base, neat floral engraving. 1 doz. in box........ 42

C427, "Fern Engraved" Table Tumbler—A full size table tumbler full finish, rich fern engraved decoration. 1 doz. in box 43

C445, "All over Engraved" Table Tumbler— Most popular engraving in glassware. Full table size. Note this price is *in open stock*—not in barrel lots. 1 doz. in box 43

C446, "Gold Band" Table Tumbler — Regulation table size, rich plain pattern, well finished, burnt-in wide band of gold on edge. A regular 10-center at a possible 5-cent price. 1 doz. in box............. 46

Bear in mind: These prices are for goods in pasteboard boxes. **No package charge. No cartage charge.**

WIDE GOLD BAND CHAMPAGNE TUMBLER.

Rich pattern, beautiful shape.

C70½—Height 3½-inches, flaring shape, rich cut glass design, with ¾-in. wide gold band. 1 doz. in box. Per dozen, **82c**

"Floral Wreath Engraved" TABLE TUMBLER.

Rare value.

C426 — A rich, plain, full size table tumbler with delicate floral engraving on same. *Makes a strong window attraction at 5c.* 1 doz. in box. Per dozen, **42c**

TALL LEMONADE GLASS.

With ground and polished bottom.

C331—13-oz. goods shapely and strong, 5¾ inches high. A staple seller at a right price. 1 doz. in a box. (For price in 6 doz. lots see original pkg. glassware.) Per dozen, **55c**

"STRAWBERRY AND FAN" GOLD DECORATED TUMBLER.

A 10 cent beauty.

C430—Large size, straight shape, purest crystal in strawberry and fan pattern with wide gold edge. Ornamental and useful as a spoon-holder and for other purposes. 1 doz. in box. Per dozen, **82c**

TAPERED CIDER OR BEER GLASS.

A popular and staple seller.

C323—Ht. 4-in., capacity about 6½ oz., bright finish crystal with star bottom and neat flute. 1 doz. in box. Per dozen, **37c**

"RUBY AND CANARY" DECORATED TUMBLER.

C495—Full size tumbler in pure crystal in new and beautiful embossed pattern with plain mouth edge. The lower part of tumbler being enameled in rich frosted effect with floral decorations in canary and ruby tints, all the decorations are burnt-in and will not wear off. 1 doz. in box. Per dozen, **80c**

"STUCK HANDLE" TUMBLER.

Large, shapely and beautiful.

C284:. Ht. 3¾-in., brilliant new genuine cut pattern in bull's-eye and flute design, large genuine stuck handle, full finished and fire polished. Useful for many purposes. 1 doz. in box. Per dozen, **78c**

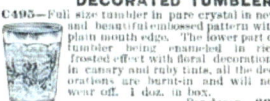

BLOWN TABLE TUMBLERS IN BOXES.

C401.

Doz.

C401, Our "Best Plain"— Best 9 oz. lead glass, popular shape. This is the most staple of all blown tumblers and our price is right. 1 doz. in box.....$0 46

C334.

C334, "Bell Shape" Tumbler — For soda or lemonade. Regular full 9-oz. size, best of lead blown glass. This tumbler invariably retails at 10 cents. You can sell on bargain day at 5c and make a profit. 1 doz. in box...................... 48

C402.

C402, "Four Band" Blown Tumbler—Best quality flint glass, with four heavy, genuine engraved bands. Full size, 9 oz. 1 doz. in display box.... 50

C333.

C333, "Cylinder Shape" Tumbler—For beer, ale or water. Large 10-oz. size. Purest of lead blown glass. No better goods made. This shape is always salable. 1 doz. in box...... 52

C403.

C403, "Floral Band' Blown Tumbler—Regular 9-oz. table size, straight shape, purest lead blown glass, with rich floral and leaf engraving in band effect. 1 doz. in box............ 55

C406.

Doz.

C406, "Wreath Band" Blown Tumbler — Very deep, handsome floral engraving forming a neat, wide band entirely around. Full size, extra quality pure lead glass. 1 doz. in box.....................$0 55

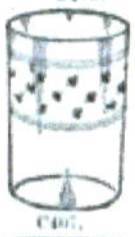

C407.

C407, "Band and Sprig" Engraved Blown Tumblers — Engraved band of scattered shamrock leaves with a four-line band engraving above and below. Full 9-oz., pure lead glass. 1 doz. in box.......... 56

C404

C404, "Fleur-de-Lis Band" Blown Tumbler — Full 9-oz. size, pure thin lead blown glass, with neat etched fleur-de-lis in wide band design. Specially attractive pattern and one that is sure to be a seller. 1 doz. in box.............. 57

C408.

C408, "Spray Engraved" Blown Tumblers — Floral spray decoration, covering both sides. This is superior engraving, and is the best full-size, 9-oz. flint glass tumbler we can buy. 1 doz. in box. ... 57

No package charge on any goods on pages 316 to 324. No cartage charge on any goods.

BLOWN MINERAL WATER OR PONY BEER GLASS.

C324—Capacity 7 oz., pure lead blown glass, flaring bell shape. The most staple size. Universally used for many purposes. 1 doz. in box. Per dozen, **45c**

BLOWN MINERAL WATER OR PONY BEER GLASS.

A staple all-the-year seller.

C324½:— Capacity 7-oz., straight shape, purest lead blown glass. A size that is a universal favorite. 1 doz. in box. Per dozen, **44c**

CHILDREN'S "GOLD EDGE" BLOWN TUMBLER.

A regular 10-center. Retail 3 for 25c.

C306—Best lead blown glass with burnished gold band around top, inside and out. 5-oz. size. 1 doz. in box. Per dozen, **54c**

"LORD'S PRAYER" BLOWN TABLE TUMBLER.

Big selling 10-center.

C409—Flint glass blown tumbler with the Lord's prayer etched on side. 1 doz. in box. Per dozen, **57c**

"GOLD BAND" BELL SHAPE BLOWN SODA TUMBLER.

A popular 10-center which you can retail with a profit at "3 for 25c."

C336—8-oz., pure lead blown, flaring shape, 2 burnt-in gold bands—one wide and one narrow. Will not wear off. Universally used for soda, lemonade, etc. 1 doz. in box. Per dozen, **67c**

"GOLD BAND" MINERAL WATER TUMBLER.

Your loss if you do not sample this exceptional 5c possibility.

C338—Pure lead blown, tall flaring shape, capacity 4 oz., 2 burnt-in bands of gold, 1 wide and 1 narrow. Retails regularly at 10c. 1 doz. in box. Per dozen, **48c**

"GOLD EDGE" BLOWN TABLE TUMBLER.

Richest of all "dime" offerings.

C414—An extremely neat and handsome tumbler for table use. Large 10-oz. size, best blown lead glass, burnished gold band at top, inside and out. 1 doz. in box. Per dozen, **65c**

GENUINE CUT GLASS TABLE TUMBLERS.

Never before offered as a 10-center.

C410 — Regulation 9-oz. table size, lead blown with heavy cut bottom, 1-in. deep genuine cut flutes. Exceptionally rich and attractive. 1 doz. in box. Per dozen, **86c**

FINE BLOWN SODA TUMBLER.

Extra fine goods.

C635:. Standard size, 12-oz., full finished, bell shape top an extremely popular style. 2 doz. in box. Per dozen, **67c**

TAPERED BEER OR TABLE TUMBLER.

C12. Purest thin lead blown glass, absolutely firsts, capacity 8 ounces, tall tapered shape. A size that is a universal seller. 1 doz. in spaced box. Per dozen. **36c**

Keep Your Stock Constantly Freshened Up With New Goods—It Keeps People "Coming Your Way."

Page 63

The Retail Stock That Omits These Popular Priced Glassware Specialties Is Robbed of Cream Profit Payers.

OUR "BEADED" WINE GLASS.

A rapid seller.

C86—Small size, fancy beaded pattern with plain finished edge, cut stem. 1 doz. in box. Per dozen, 28c

OUR "STAR" WINE GLASS.

A "Star" bargain also.

C97—Medium size, bright new pattern, being almost plain with numerous small pressed stars. Pure crystal, well finished. Worth more than this price, in barrel lots. 1 doz. in box. Per dozen, 30c

OUR "DIAMOND" WINE.

You've paid double for one not so good.

C75—Imitation cut pattern of good shape and finish. 1 doz. in box. Per dozen, 30c

OUR "BRIGHT" WINE.

Pretty—useful—salable.

C79—A very attractive dot mirror pattern, equally desirable for wine and mantel. 1 doz. in box. Per dozen, 31c

OUR "POPULAR" WINE.

Needs no pushing—sells itself.

C83—A wine that you can double your money on and still give the full of good value. 1 doz. in box. Per dozen, 31c

OUR "MIRROR" WINE GLASS.

A dainty and rich 5-center.

C76—Beautiful dot mirror pattern. One on which you can make a handsome profit and yet give exceptional 5c value. 1 doz. in box. Per dozen, 32c

OUR "PLAIN" WINE GLASS.

Rich and staple.

C73—Medium size, well finished, cut stem. 1 doz. in box. Per dozen, 33c

"BEADED PANEL" WINE GLASS.

Rich in beauty—rich in selling quality.

C82—Brilliant, full size slightly flared top. 1 doz. in box. Per dozen, 34c

OUR "PRESSED BAND" WINE GLASS.

An attractive graceful shape.

C80—Medium size, well finished, three mold bands, nicely shaped stem. 1 doz. in box. Per dozen, 36c

OUR "CUT DIAMOND" WINE GLASS.

Good size, brilliant pattern.

C74—Made of purest crystal in fancy cut diamond and plain panel design with smooth plain edge and fancy cut stem, brilliantly fire polished. 1 doz. in box. Per dozen, 36c

FLARED SHERRY WINE GLASS.

Would be cheap at this price in barrel lots.

C96—Medium size, ht. 4½-in., new and beautiful flaring shape, rich beaded heart pattern, imitation cut stem. A fire polished beauty. 1 doz. in box. Per dozen, 37c

OUR "SATIN CUT" WINE GLASS.

A 5-cent gem.

C87—Medium size, beautiful genuine cut glass pattern, fancy cut stem, cut star pattern base. Will sell at sight. 1 doz. in box. Per dozen, 37c

OUR "SHAPELY" WINE GLASS.

Plain but rich.

C88—Bright full finished panel pattern, graceful flaring shape, fancy cut stem. 1 doz. in box. Per dozen, 38c

OUR "ELITE" WINE GLASS.

Rich and attractive.

C89—Medium size, fancy deep cut panel pattern with plain edge, fancy cut stem. A full finished beauty. 1 doz. in box. Per dozen, 42c

OUR "BAND ENGRAVED" WINE GLASS.

Always in demand.

C101—Plain but rich pattern, with fancy cut stem, 1 wide and 2 narrow engraved bands. 1 doz. in box. Per dozen, 40c

"CUT PATTERN" WINE GLASS.

Hard to equal it elsewhere—even as a 10-center.

C81—Cut stem, purest crystal glass. 1 doz. in box. Per dozen, 41c

"SOFT DRINK" GLASS.

A nickel profit payer.

C307—5-ounce, thin glass, ground bottom finely finished. 1 doz. in box. Per dozen, 41c

"ENGRAVED BAND" WINE GLASS.

An attractive 5-center.

C90—Medium size, rich plain pattern, full finished crystal with one wide and two narrow engraved bands. 1 doz. in box. Per dozen, 42c

"FLORAL ENGRAVED" WINE.

A cheap barrel price in open stock.

C84—Regular size crystal wine with delicate old floral engraving. 1 doz. in box. Per dozen, 43c

CUP FOOT WINE GLASSES.

Five quick sellers in superior ware offered at right prices.

C91, 41c Doz. C92, 42c Doz. C94, 42c Doz. C93, 43c Doz.

C91, Cut Stem Cordial Glass—New and beautiful shape. Plain finished pattern with fancy imitation cut stem, genuine cup foot. 1 doz. in box............$0 41

C92, Cut Stem Wine Glass—New at a 5-cent price. Medium size, plain pattern, fancy cut stem, full finished and fire polished. 1 doz. in box............. 42

C94, Plain Wine Glass—The one always in demand. Rich finished crystal, shapely and unique stem. Used everywhere. 1 doz. in box................ 42

C93, "Hoffman House" Wine Glasses—Finest of crystal. Regulation low shape, plain rich pattern, bright finish, slender stem, genuine cup foot. 1 doz. in box.... 43

C77, Our "Banded" 5-cent Wine Glasses—Who can match this price when we consider that it is the very highest grade of crystal glass? 1 doz. in box........ 43

HEAVY GROUND BOTTOM WHISKY GLASSES.

Most popular selling patterns.

C319—1½ oz., rich plain pattern, heavy ground bottom, will not scratch bar nor table. Full finished rich and bright. 1 doz. in box......................$0 37
C320—As above, 2-oz..................... 38
C321—As above, 2½-oz..................... 40
C322—As above, 3½-oz..................... 42

"TAPERED CAMPAGNE" GLASS.

Blown lead glass.

C308—A ready-selling 5-center. One of our best selling glasses. Useful for many purposes. Pure goods, rounded edges. Per dozen, 41c

"SPECIAL SALE" OF PURE LEAD BLOWN WHISKY GLASSES

C860—Purest thin lead blown glass, capacity 1½-oz., popular almost straight shape. Per dozen, 22c
C861—As above, capacity 2-oz. Per dozen, 23c
C862—As above, capacity 2½-oz. Per dozen, 24c
C863—As above, capacity 3-oz. Per dozen, 25c
C864—As above, capacity. Per dozen, 26c

LEAD BLOWN WHISKY GLASSES.

C300—1½-oz. This little pure lead blown glass is made for a bar whisky tumbler, but it is especially salable as a toothpick or matchholder. 1 doz. in box. Per dozen, 32c
C301—2- oz. As above. Per dozen, 33c
C302—2½- oz. As above. Per dozen, 34c
C303—3- oz. As above. Per dozen, 35c
C304—4- oz. As above. Per dozen, 36c

STANDARD PONY BEER or SOFT DRINK GLASS.

A staple—a very low price.

C337—Capacity 4 oz., full finished heavy ground bottom, will not scratch bar or table. 1 doz. in box................... 40c

"SATIN DIAMOND" SMALL GLASS

Beautiful pattern and ground bottom. Makes 5c look cheap.

C361½. Ht. 2½-in., beautiful and brilliant pattern with plain edge and smooth ground bottom, full finished and fire polished. Commonly called a "whisky" glass, but useful for many purposes. 1 doz. in box. Per dozen, 39c

---

No package charge on any goods on pages 319 to 324.

"CANARY AND CRYSTAL" HAND DECORATED WARE.

A new line of decorated ware which is exceptionally beautiful, the lower half of each piece in solid canary color and the upper part in clear crystal with profuse hand painted carnation decoration in natural colors giving an exceptionally rich effect. The decorations are burnt-in and will not wash off. Will prove great sellers at the popular 10-cent price.

"CANARY AND CRYSTAL" TOOTHPICK HOLDER.

Exceedingly rich.

C853—Medium size, rich panel design, footed, scalloped flaring top. A dainty and beautiful piece. 1 doz. in box. Per dozen, 80c

"CANARY AND CRYSTAL" HANDLED CUP.

A Quick Seller.

C854—Fancy flare shape, diam. 3-in., footed, good handle, brilliant pattern. 1 doz. in box. For lemonade, sherbet, etc. Per dozen, 80c

"CANARY AND CRYSTAL" TRAY.

This will always sell.

C851—Diam. 5½-in., round shape, scalloped edge. Every lady will want one of these. 1 doz. in box. Per dozen, 80c

"CANARY AND CRYSTAL" ROUND DISH.

Ornamental and useful.

C850—Diam. 5-in., footed, scalloped edge, richly finished. 1 doz. in box. Per dozen, 80c

"CANARY AND CRYSTAL" HANDLED MUG.

A pretty piece—a pleasing price.

C852—Large size, 4-in. high, diam. 2¾. New and beautiful reflecting mirror, panel pattern, plain smooth flaring edge, footed, fancy handle. 1 doz. in box. Per dozen, 80c

"CANARY AND CRYSTAL" CREAM PITCHER.

A gem of value.

C856—Good size, ht. 3-in., diam. 2½, brilliant panel design, footed, fancy handle, good lip, finished scalloped edge. 1 doz. in box. Per dozen, 80c

HAND DECORATED SALT AND PEPPER.

C855—Lower half in canary colors, upper part in clear crystal with hand-painted carnations in natural colors. Extra heavy, tall shape, wide spread base, ht. 3½-in., brilliant fleeting pattern, high dome tops, 6 salts and 6 peppers in box of 1 doz. Dozen, 80c

The Very Popular "HOLLAND IVORY" WARE.

This newest and richest ware is an almost exact reproduction of the expensive old Dutch earthen ware. Artistic and attractive, being of a rich brown chocolate color on the outside and soft yellow glaze on the inside. In large demand.

"Holland Ivory" Match or Toothpick.

An artistic 5-center.

C356—Ht. 2¾-in., embossed ribbed panel pattern with fancy foot. Everybody will want one. 1 doz. in box. Per dozen, 41c

"Holland Ivory" Salt and Pepper.

Exceptionally rich in this beautiful ware.

C236—Ribbed pattern, embossed, ht. 3¼-in., footed, good screw top, 6 salts and 6 peppers in box of 1 doz. Per dozen, 43c

"Holland Ivory" Smoker's Set.

A rare bargain—makes 25c look small.

C693—Ware as above. Comprises 7½-in. round tray fancy beaded and scalloped edge; 4-inch high tumbler shape cigar holder; 4-inch footed ash receiver; ribbed and footed to match holder. Total 4 pieces in set. ½ doz. sets in box, no charge for box. Dozen sets, $2.25

"Holland Ivory" Trinket Tray.

Will sell every day if offered for 5c.

C169—Round shape, diam. 4-in., elaborately embossed, fancy scalloped edge and fancy foot. 1 doz. in box. Per dozen, 43c

"Holland Ivory" Stein and Mug, Assorted.

Two bargain leaders in this new and beautiful ware to retail at 5 and 10c.

C692—This new and rich ware is an almost exact reproduction of the famous Old Holland Ivory, being of a rich chocolate color shading into a light yellow. Assortment comprises:
1 doz. extra large and heavy 4½-inch handled steins with ribbed panel sides and smooth edge.............................$0 82
1 doz. 3½-inch large handled mugs elaborately embossed and colored...... 43
Total 2 doz. in box, *no charge for box.* Price complete, $1.25

Many of the Cheap Counter's BRISKEST SELLERS and BRIGHTEST BARGAINS are Gleaned from This Page.

Our Ability to Save You a Tidy Per Cent on Glassware Is Signally Shown in the Following Prices.

CRYSTAL GLASS SALTS AND PEPPERS.

"LARGE TWIST" SALTS AND PEPPERS.

Genuine blown glass.

C222 — Large swell shape, serpentine flute pattern, good top. 6 salts and 6 peppers in box of 1 doz. Per dozen, **26c**

"STAR" SALT AND PEPPER SHAKERS.

A regular 5-center as a 3c possibility.

C203, Salt: Medium size, fluted bottom, with all-over neat pressed stars and good top. Finished and brilliant. 1 doz. in box, no pkg. charge. Per dozen, **25c**

C203, Peppers: As above, 1 doz. in box, no pkg. charge. Per dozen, **25c**

"DOT MIRROR" SALTS AND PEPPERS.

Big and brilliant 5-centers here offered as possible 3-centers.

C245 — Large size artistic shape with wide spread base, new and brilliant pattern, good screw tops. A bargain sure enough. 6 salts and 6 peppers in box of 1 doz. Per dozen, **29c**

"LARGE BRILLIANT" SALTS AND PEPPERS.

Good 5-centers that pay a fine profit.

C228—Extra large swell shape, new beaded panel design, pure finished crystal. Exceptionally attractive. Good tops. 6 salts and 6 peppers in box of doz. Per dozen, **29c**

"FLUTED BASE" SALTS AND PEPPERS.

Large size, fancy pattern. Splendid 5-centers.

C209—Extra large, blown glass, attractive pattern with wide fluted base, nickel plated tops. Exceptional value. 6 salts and 6 peppers in box of 1 doz. Per dozen, **30c**

"DOME TOP" SALT AND PEPPER SHAKERS.

A 5c bargain at a price which leaves you a profit.

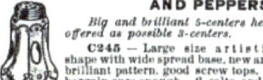

C246, Salts: Extra large swell shape in new beaded panel design, pure crystal, high dome caps. Well finished and exceptionally attractive. 1 doz. in box, no pkg. charge. Per dozen **30c**

C246, Peppers: As above. 1 doz. in box, no pkg. charge. Per dozen **30c**

OUR "CRYSTAL FLUTE" SALTS AND PEPPERS.

Large size, attractive new pattern.

C211 — Good size, fancy new fluted pattern, purest crystal, with extra heavy nickel plated top. 6 salts and 6 peppers in box of 1 doz. Per dozen, **32c**

"WIDE BASE" SALTS AND PEPPERS.

Double your money and yet give value.

C232—Fluted, large bottom, nickel top. Sensible pattern. 7 salts and 5 peppers in box of 1 doz. Per dozen, **33c**

"French Plate" SALTS AND PEPPERS.

As good a 5-center as you want.

C233—Plain, heavy mirror pattern. The price is low for this grade. Assorted 7 salts, 5 peppers in box of 1 doz. Per dozen, **34c**

"COLONIAL CRYSTAL" SALTS AND PEPPERS.

New and pleasing 5-centers.

C225—Fancy colonial fluted design, neat and attractive, footed vase shape, made of pure crystal with smooth finished edge, extra heavy nickel plated top. 6 salts and 6 peppers in box of 1 doz. Per dozen, **35c**

OUR "RADIANT" SALTS AND PEPPERS.

Look like 10-centers.

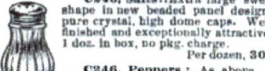

C260 — Tall square column shape, extra heavy, fancy cut diamond and mirror panel design, nickel plated tops. 6 salts and 6 peppers in box of 1 doz. Per dozen, **39c**

"DOUBLE THICK" SALTS AND PEPPERS.

Beautifully plain and rich—large tops.

C234 — This is different from any other in that it has a larger and better nickel top, and the glass is extra heavy and richly plain. 6 salts and 6 peppers in box of 1 doz. Per dozen, **39c**

LARGE PLAIN SALTS & PEPPERS.

A bountifully big 5-center.

C244, Salt—Ht. 4-in., tall square shape, best blown crystal glass, good screw top. An especially good one for family use. 1 doz. in box. Per dozen, **42c**

C244, Pepper — As above. 1 doz. in box. Per dozen, **42c**

"Extra Bright" SALTS & PEPPERS.

Extra bright and extra rich 5-centers.

C230, Salt—Extra heavy, tall, shape, brilliant twist pattern, full finished, pure crystal, good top. 1 doz. in box. Per dozen, **41c**

C230, Pepper — As above. 1 doz. in box. Per dozen, **41c**

"BIG FAMILY" SALTS AND PEPPERS.

A large one and a seller.

C221—4½ inches high, fluted pattern, plain sides. Packed 8 salts and 4 peppers in box. Per dozen, **42c**

"FAVORITE" SALTS AND PEPPERS.

Rich and heavy 5-centers.

C219, Salt—Large tall shape, extra heavy, deep cut panel pattern, well finished, good screw top. 1 doz. in box. Per dozen, **41c**

C219, Pepper—As above. 1 doz. in box. Per dozen, **41c**

"ILLUMINATED PATTERN" SALTS AND PEPPERS.

Dime beauties to retail at a nickel.

C235 — Beautifully cut pressed pattern, column shape, 1¾x3½, nickel cap. 6 salts and 6 peppers in box of 1 doz. Per dozen, **43c**

"BRIGHT AND HEAVY" SALTS AND PEPPERS.

Exceptionally rich. Look like cut glass.

C263—Extra heavy and extra brilliant, rich genuine cut pattern, fire polished beauties, good nickel plated tops. 6 salts and 6 peppers in box of 1 doz. Per dozen, **41c**

"HEAVY TWIST" SALTS AND PEPPERS.

Usual 10-centers.

C229—Extra large, ht. 4-in., extra heavy brilliant twist pattern, full finished, best nickel dome tops. 6 salts and 6 peppers in box of 1 doz. Per dozen, **45c**

HIGH GRADE SALTS & PEPPERS.

"Regular 10-centers as 5-cent advertisers."

C220: Salts. Good size, ht. 3¾-in., extra heavy brilliant crystal in rich cut pattern, genuine heavy cast plated tops. Jobs regularly at 75c per dozen. 1 doz. in box, *no pkg. charge.* Per dozen, **45c**

C220: Peppers. As above. Per dozen, **45c**

OUR "BIG PLAIN" SALTS AND PEPPERS.

Regular 10-centers as 5-cent leaders.

C265—Extra large size, extra tall with wide spread base and attractive fancy flute pattern. Exceptionally good one for restaurant or hotel use. Extra heavy nickel plated tops. 6 salts and 6 peppers in box of 1 doz. Per dozen, **42c**

"BEADED PANEL" SALTS AND PEPPERS.

Extra heavy and brilliant. Look like 10-centers.

C218 — Large size, deep cut beaded panel pattern of exceptional brilliancy, footed, and with good screw top. 6 salts and 6 peppers in box of 1 doz. Per dozen, **43c**

OUR "HEAVY BASE" SALTS AND PEPPERS.

Artistic shape. Rare 5-cent leaders.

C254—Extra heavy and rich, full finished crystal in new and beautiful plain panel design with wide flaring base. One that will always sell. Good nickel plated tops. 6 salts and 6 peppers in box of 1 doz. Per dozen, **43c**

"DIAMOND CUT" SALTS AND PEPPERS.

Extra good 10c profit payers.

C261—Extra heavy tall shape, rich deep cut and diamond panel pattern. A beauty and very brilliant. Heavy cast nickel plated tops. 6 salts and 6 peppers in box of 1 doz. Per dozen, **72c**

"PRISM" SALTS AND PEPPERS.

Unusually attractive in looks as well as price.

C213—Crystal prism pattern, brilliant gems, heavy plated tops. 1 doz. in box, 6 salts and 6 peppers. Per dozen, **80c**

OUR "HEAVY RICH" SALTS AND PEPPERS.

10-cent crystal gems.

C267 — Fancy tall shape, extra heavy full finished crystal in new and beautiful cut and plain panel pattern. Looks like genuine cut glass. Heavy cast plated tops. 6 salts and 6 peppers in box of 1 doz. Per dozen, **79c**

"BEADED CUT PATTERN" SALTS AND PEPPERS.

Exceptional 10-centers.

C214—Rich banded panel pattern, exact imitation of genuine cut glass, tall shape with wide base, heavy plated tops. 1 doz. in box, 6 salts and 6 peppers. Per dozen, **77c**

"MAMMOTH" CAST TOP SHAKER.

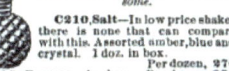

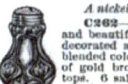

A 10c bargain. Can be used for either salt or sugar.

C243—Ht. 4-in., extra heavy, deep cut beaded panel pattern, heavy nickel plated top. Just the thing for restaurant or hotel use. 1 doz. in box. Per dozen, **78c**

COLORED GLASS AND DECORATED OPAL SALTS AND PEPPERS.

"COLORED LEADER" SALTS AND PEPPERS.

Exceedingly cheap yet very handsome.

C210, Salt—In low price shaker there is none that can compare with this. Assorted amber, blue and crystal. 1 doz. in box. Per dozen, **27c**

C210, Pepper—As above. Per dozen, **27c**

"SCROLL PATTERN" SALTS AND PEPPERS.

Possible 3-centers.

C223—Large tall shape, wide base, fancy all-over embossed pattern, good tops. 6 salts and 6 peppers in box of 1 doz. Per dozen, **28c**

ELABORATELY DECORATED OPAL SALTS AND PEPPERS.

Regular 10-center as a 5-cent profit payer.

C248.—Large size, tall shape, fancy embossed scroll pattern, elaborately decorated in rich colors and gold bronze, extra well made, heavy nickel tops. Assorted colors such as red, blue and green (6 salts and 6 peppers), in box of 1 dozen. *(no pkg. charge.)* Per dozen, **36c**

OUR "EGYPTIAN" SALTS AND PEPPERS.

New and attractive 5-centers.

C227 — Tall column shape, fancy beaded and frosted design with stars and crescent decorations in rich ruby, good nickel plated dome tops. 6 salts and 6 peppers in box of 1 doz. Per dozen, **42c**

"Floral Opal" SALTS AND PEPPERS.

Worth 10-cents at retail any day.

C224—Good size, melon shape, opal body, delicate red and blue, corn flower decoration. Patent satin nickel top, 3x2¼ inches. 6 salts and 6 peppers in box of 1 doz. Per dozen, **42c**

LARGE COLORED SALTS & PEPPERS.

You've paid double for some not as good.

C226—Tall square shape, embossed good screw tops. 3 assorted colors, blue green and amethyst in box of 1 doz. Asstd. 6 salts and 6 peppers. Per dozen, **43c**

"High Class" SALTS AND PEPPERS.

Richly hand decorated.

MC231, Salt—Beautiful opal panel pattern, rich hand decoration of colored flowers and gold bronze, nickel plated top. Assorted decorations. 1 doz. in box. Per dozen, **43c**

MC231, Pepper—As above. Per dozen, **43c**

"ARTISTIC" DECORATED OPAL SALTS AND PEPPERS.

You will think 10c a low retail price. A 5c bargain.

C204—Perfection in artistic designing. Very fine opal ware with attractive colored floral and gold bronze decoration, patent satin nickel top, 3¼-inch high. 6 salts and 6 peppers in box of 1 doz. Per dozen, **43c**

"MOSAIC" SALTS AND PEPPERS.

Cheap at a dime.

C258 — Entirely new, being in combination of variegated light and dark colors richly embossed in elaborate floral design, altogether making a very beautiful effect. Tall, good shape, with nickel plated tops. 6 salts and 6 peppers in box of 1 doz. Per dozen, **43c**

"RELIEF DECORATED" SALTS AND PEPPERS.

10-centers at a 5-cent price.

C249 — Pure opal, low swell shape, elaborate embossing in floral and leaf design. Decorated in bright natural colors. Extra heavy nickel plated top. 6 salts and 6 peppers in box of 1 doz. Per dozen, **44c**

"RAINBOW DECORATED" SALTS AND PEPPERS.

A nickel seems too cheap for this.

C262—Fancy tall shape in new and beautiful embossed pattern, decorated all over in rich, solid blended colors and elaborate clouds of gold bronze, good nickel plated tops. 6 salts and 6 peppers in box of 1 dozen. Per dozen, **44c**

OUR "VASE SHAPE" DECORATED OPAL SALTS AND PEPPERS.

Regular 10-centers as 5-cent advertisers.

C266 — Large size, tall, fancy footed, vase shape in pure white opal with elaborate decorations in bright colors and gold bronze, smooth finished edges and extra heavy nickel plated tops. 6 salts and 6 peppers in box of 1 doz.......Per dozen, **44c**

"FLEUR-DE-LIS" SALTS AND PEPPERS.

A mammoth 5-center.

C237: Extra large, wide spread base, rich opal with embossed fleur-de-lis decorated in colors and gold, good screw tops, 6 salts and 6 peppers in box of 1 doz. Per dozen, **45c**

"EMBOSSED DECORATED" SALTS AND PEPPERS.

You'd think them 10-centers if you didn't know the price.

C238—Extra large, tall shape ht. 3½ in., wide spread base, rich opal embossed decorated in bright colors. 6 salts and 6 peppers in box of 1 doz. Per dozen, **45c**

"ALL-OVER DECORATED" SALTS AND PEPPERS.

They retail regularly at 10 cents. Here offered as possible 5-centers.

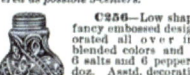

C256—Low shape, good size, fancy embossed design richly decorated all over in artistically blended colors and gold bronze. 6 salts and 6 peppers in box of 1 doz. Asstd. decorations. Per dozen, **45c**

"BOW-KNOT EMBOSSED" SALTS AND PEPPERS.

Unequaled 5-centers.

C253—Pure white opal, extra large tall fancy shape, embossed and decorated in attractive bow-knot design. Asstd. decorations in box of 1 doz. 6 salts and 6 peppers. Per dozen, **45c**

OUR "FRENCH FLORAL DECORATED" SALTS AND PEPPERS.

Large rich ones at an exceedingly small price.

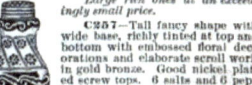

C257—Tall fancy shape with wide base, richly tinted at top and bottom with embossed floral decorations and elaborate scroll work in gold bronze. Good nickel plated screw tops. 6 salts and 6 peppers in box of 1 doz. Per dozen, **48c**

GENUINE RUBY RED SALTS AND PEPPERS.

New and rich 10-centers.

C239—Extra large, wide spread base, brilliant optic fluted and embossed pattern in solid ruby red. Must be seen to be appreciated. 6 salts and 6 peppers in box of 1 doz. Per dozen, **72c**

"FLORAL PANEL" S. & P.

Shapely and rich 10-center.

C215: Good size, footed, new panel pattern, in rich flint opalescent, embossed and decorated on both sides in gold and colored floral designs, extra heavy plated tops. 1 doz. in box, 6 salts and 6 peppers. Per dozen, **84c**

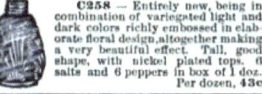

It Is Our Unequaled Consumption of These Specialties Which Enables Us to Name Such Unequaled Prices.

Not an Item in This Line But That WE KNOW to Be of SUPERIOR DESIRABILITY.

No package charge on any goods on pages 316 to 324.

"RUBY AND CRYSTAL" SALTS AND PEPPERS.

One of our newest and best 10c offerings.

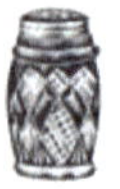

C216—Extra heavy and rich cut diamond pattern, elaborately decorated in pure ruby, genuine plated cast tops. 6 salts and 6 peppers in box of 1 doz. Per dozen, **80c**

"ROSE RED" SALTS & PEPPERS.

Richest of the rich.

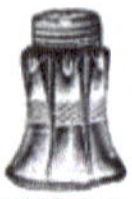

C208—Ht. 3¼-in., extra heavy cut panel pattern with wide base, rich solid burnt-in rose red color with elaborate gold decorations, good top. A pleasing 10-center. 6 salts and 6 peppers in box of 1 doz. Per dozen, **82c**

"BEADED" INDIVIDUAL SALT CELLAR.

An extra good one to retail "3 for 5."

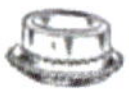

C199—Medium size, round shape, footed, with smooth edge, full finished and fire polished. 1 doz. in box. Per dozen, **15c**

INDIVIDUAL SALTS—Six in Box.

A "dime a box" will sell 'em all.

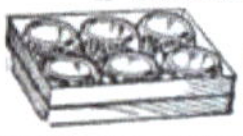

C250—Entirely new plan of packing 6 salts of choice pattern in a box to run at 10 cents per box. Per dozen boxes, **80c**

OUR "HEAVY TWIST" INDIVIDUAL SALT CELLAR.

Extra good. To retail "2 for 5."

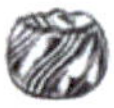

C200—Large size, extra heavy, fancy twist shape with scalloped edge, made of pure crystal, richly finished and fire polished. 1 doz. in box. Per dozen, **18c**

"STAR" 2-BOTTLE CASTER SET.

An old staple seller in a bright new pattern.

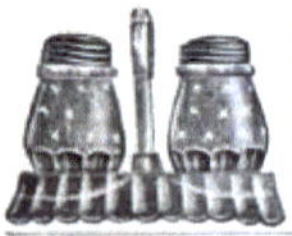

C54—Good size fancy shape caster, containing large salt and pepper shaker, neat star pattern and convenient glass handle. Each set in carton, 1 doz. in pkg. *No pkg. charge.* Per dozen, **87c**

"TRAY" CASTER SET.

Four popular fancy pieces to sell at 10c.

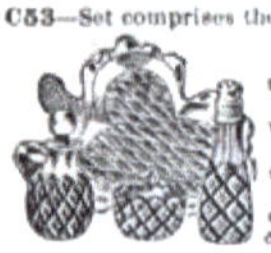

C53—Set comprises the following—
Open salt cellar.
Tall pepper shaker, nickel top.
Small oil or vinegar with glass stopper.
4-inch handled, leaf shaped tray.
Each in pasteboard box complete. *(No pkg. charge.)* Per dozen sets, **88c**

"ROSETTE" HANDLE CASTER SET.

At 10 cents will sell always.

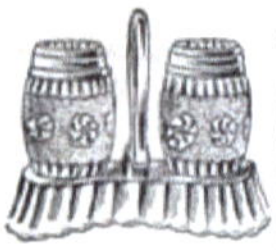

C55:. Rosette pattern caster combination set comprising good size glass caster containing large salt and pepper shaker and with convenient handle. Each set in carton, 1 doz. sets in pkg. Per dozen, **87c**

OPAL OPENWORK PLATE.

One of the very best of sellers.

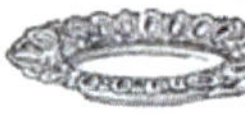

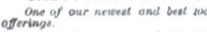

C695. The enormous quantities we sell prove the popularity of this item. Rich white opal with rim of artistic openwork pattern. ½ doz. in box. Per dozen, **45c**

CHILDREN'S "PICTURE" PLATE.

A little 5-cent gem—a seller if shown.

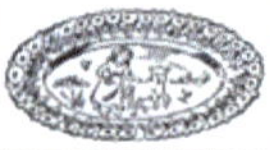

C699—Round; diam. 5½ in., fancy scalloped openwork edge, etched picture center in asstd. subjects, such as, Mary and her little Lamb, Children at Play, etc. 1 doz. in box, asstd. subjects. Per dozen, **43c**

"PARIAN" MEDALLION PLATE.

Striking imitation of wedgewood. The plate novelty of the season.

C696—6½-inch opal plate with beautiful embossed white border, raised white figures in center. Backgrounds tinted, 2 rich blue, 5 sage green and 5 dark maroon. Can be used as a tray or window transparency. 1 doz. in pasteboard box, no charge for box. Per dozen, **75c**

PRISM TRAY PLATE.

A brilliant 5c gem.

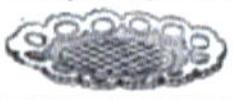

C157:.Round shape, diameter 5¼-in., beautiful cut diamond and bull's eye pattern, neat scalloped edge. Just the thing for ice cream and many other purposes. Looks like cut glass. 1 doz. in box. Per dozen, **36c**

DECORATED OPAL PLAQUE.

A 10-center of extra size and rare beauty.

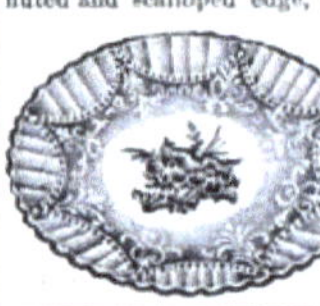

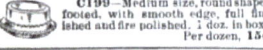

C694.—Fancy round shape. Diam. 8 in., fluted and scalloped edge, embossed in fancy design with wide tinted flange and hand painted floral decorated center, embossed work and edges being decorated in gold bronze. 1 doz. in box. Per dozen, **92c**

"Combination" OPAL TABLE SET.

Always a retailer at 25c.

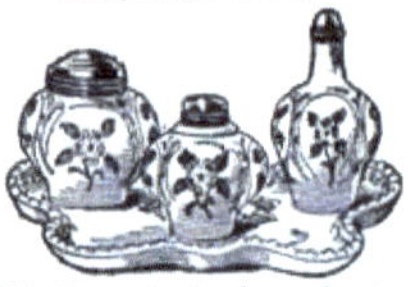

C400:.Comprising handsome glass tray with mustard, salt and pepper, each richly decorated in opal, best nickel tops. Each set in box. Per dozen sets, **$2.10**

Our "FOOTED TRAY" CRUET SET.

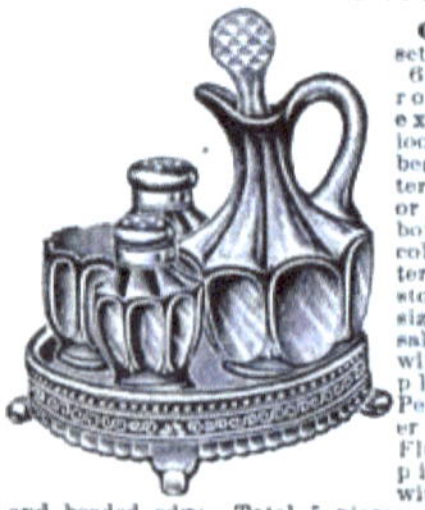

C56—Each set comprises: 6¾-inch round deep extra heavy footed tray in beaded pattern. Large oil or vinegar bottle, fluted colonial pattern, ground stopper. Large size footed salt shaker with heavy plated top. Pepper shaker to match. Fluted toothpick holder with scallop'd and beaded edge. Total 5 pieces. 3 colors—amethyst, blue and green. Each set in pkg., *no pkg. charge.* Set, **39c**

We suggest that customers order at least three sets and thereby get the full asst. of colors.

"RICH AND DAINTY" TOY TABLE SET.

A full finished beauty to retail for 25c.

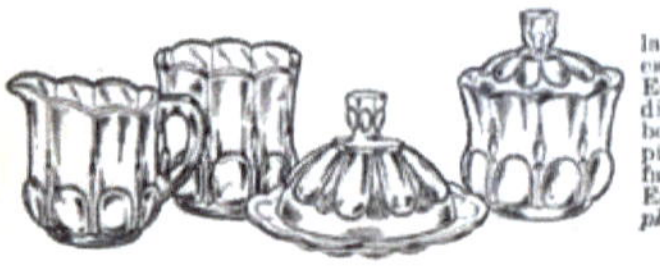

C508—Although a toy set it is almost large enough for table use. Made of purest crystal, full finished and fire polished. Each set consists of 5¼-in. flanged butter dish with cover, covered and footed sugar bowl, fancy footed and handled cream pitcher and footed spoonholder. All with fancy scalloped top and in panel design. Each set in box. ½ doz. sets in pkg, *no pkg. charge.* Per doz. sets, **$1.95**

DECORATED OPAL FLOWER VASE.

A rich and rare 10-center.

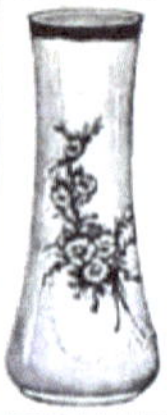

C144.—Extra size. Height 8½-in., opal-ware with wide band of gold bronze around top and elaborate and assorted decoration in hand painted floral designs. Assorted decorations in box of 1 doz. *(No charge for box.)* Per dozen, **96c**

"VASE OF MANY COLORS."

For picks, flowers or matches.

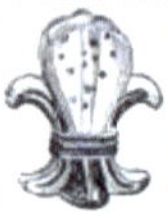

C137—Send for a dozen of these and you'll be glad we asked you. They are worth double this price. 1 doz. in box. Per dozen, **43c**

"Crystal Panel" FLOWER VASE.

Full finished and dainty 10-cent profit payer.

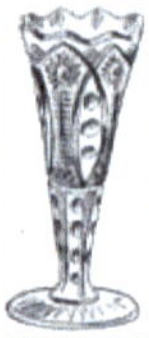

C140—Ht. 6¼-in., richest and most beautiful of cut glass patterns, fancy scalloped flaring top. 1 doz. in box. Per dozen, **62c**

"TINTED" 10-CENT VASE.

Your loss not to sample this.

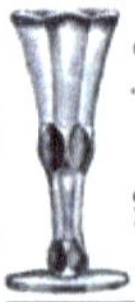

C143—6¼-inch, varied colored decorations in center and near base. Pretty and cheap. ½ doz. in box. Per dozen, **67c**

OUR "MIRROR" VASE OR SPOONHOLDER.

Positively one of the biggest bargains on this page.

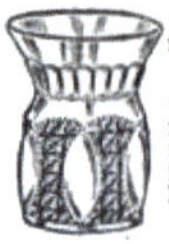

C282—Ht.3¼-in.,artistic shape, wide flare top, one of the latest and most brilliant crystal glass patterns, richly finished and fire polished. At 5c will make things lively. 1 dozen in box. Per dozen, **41c**

OUR "CUT DIAMOND" FLOWER VASE.

A 10-center of exquisite pattern.

C138—Height about 8 in., slender shape with wide flaring top and fancy fluted base, beautiful strawberry and fan pattern, brilliantly finished and fire polished. ½ doz. in box. Per dozen, **75c**

CRYSTAL CANDLESTICK.

Tall and shapely. Looks like cut glass.

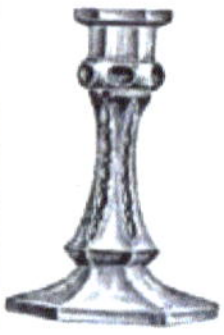

C290—Ht. 6 in., fancy tall shape, wide base, elaborate pattern, full finished and fire polished. A beautiful and useful ornament. 1 doz. in box. Per dozen, **82c**

OUR "FOOTED" EGG GLASS.

An exceptional 5-center.

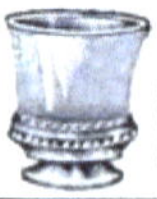

C20—Good size, height 3¼-in., fancy flaring shape, footed, rich plain pattern with beaded band. Full finished and fire polished. 1 doz. in box. Per dozen **39c**

PURE GOLD DECORATED CRYSTAL GLASSWARE.

"GOLD PRISM" SALT AND PEPPER.

The richest 10-center in the salt line.

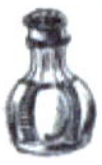

C212—Genuine silver plated screw tops, solid burnt in gold neck, 6 salts and 6 peppers in box. Per dozen, **83c**

Most of these lively sellers in glass can be retailed at **double** the selling prices we suggest, if you wish to use them as **profit** payers instead of business getters.

NO PACKAGE CHARGE. NO CARTAGE CHARGE.

"GOLD EDGE" SMALL GLASS.

In large demand.

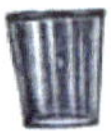

C305—Lead blown glass with band of gold around top, 3-oz. 1 doz. in box. Per dozen, **45c**

"GOLD BAND" CHAMPAGNE TUMBLER.

Very elaborate. Supremely good value.

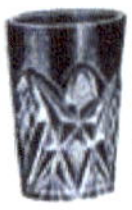

C70—Tall flaring shape, height 3½-in., beautiful deep cut jewel pattern, ground and polished bottom, 1¼-in. extra wide and heavy gold band around top. 1 doz. in box. Per dozen, **83c**

"GOLDEN PRISM" TUMBLER.

A general utility glass of extreme beauty.

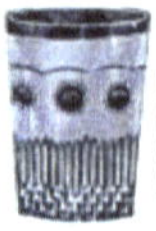

C482—Rich cut diamond, fine flute and bull's-eye design in purest crystal, being an exact imitation of genuine cut glass, elaborately gold decorated bulls' eyes and edge. Can also be used as a spoon holder. 1 doz. in box. Per dozen, **83c**

"GOLD DECORATED" FRENCH CRYSTAL VASE.

A new brilliant pattern that will sell on sight.

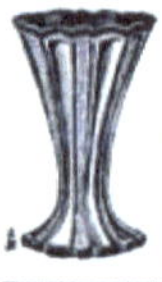

C141—Heavy gold band, scalloped top, 5½ inches high, large opening at top. ½ doz. in box. Per dozen, **83c**

Our "Six Panel" CRYSTAL & GOLD VASE.

Shapely and bright.

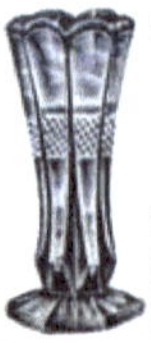

C142—Ht. 6¾ in., rich panel design in new cut pattern, fancy wide foot, scalloped flaring top, edges elaborately decorated in burnt-in gold. Easily worth 15 cents—a rare bargain at a dime. 1 doz. in box. Per dozen, **83c**

"Crystal and Gold" TABLE TUMBLER.

This will sell till dimes go out of fashion.

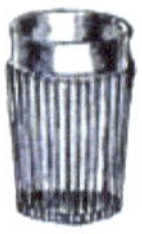

C67:.Ribbed pattern, wide gold band. This also makes a fine spoonholder. 1 doz. in box. Per dozen, **80c**

"CRYSTAL AND GOLD" TIFFANY VASE.

Richest of high art glassware cleverly reproduced.

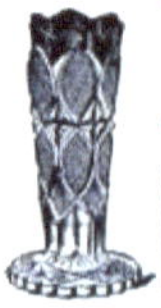

C50—A vase of the most exquisite fineness. So exactly like real cut glass that only an expert could discover the difference. Stands 6 inches in height and has a rich band of real gold on the mouth edge. ½ doz. in box. Per dozen, **83c**

"WIDE GOLD BAND" TUMBLER.

A 10-center of exceedingly rich pattern.

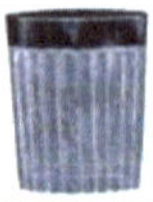

C431—Regular 8-oz., table size, medium heavy weight, pure crystal in beautiful optic panel design, ⅝-in. wide gold band. A popular seller everywhere. 1 doz. in box. Per dozen, **82c**

BRILLIANT WIDE GOLD BAND TUMBLER.

A brilliant glass and a brilliant bargain.

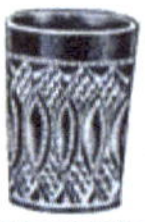

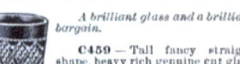

C459—Tall fancy straight shape, heavy rich genuine cut glass pattern with extra wide ¾-in. band of pure burnt-in gold, brilliantly finished and fire polished. 1 doz. in box. Per dozen, **82c**

"GOLD DECORATED" COMBINATION RING AND JEWEL RECEPTACLE.

An ornamental and useful piece for the bureau.

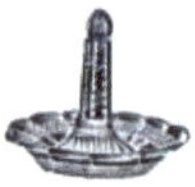

C489—Fancy round shape, diam. 3¾-in., footed, with scalloped and gold decorated edge, solid gold decorated post 2¼ in. in height, for holding rings. 1 doz. in box. Per dozen, **80c**

Courteous Treatment, Painstaking Attention, Good Goods and Low Prices Will Bring You Lasting Success.

Don't Be Too Greedy for Profit or You'll Kill the Goose That Lays the Golden Egg.

RICHEST PURE GOLD DECORATED CRYSTAL GLASSWARE.

An extensive, carefully selected line. Strikingly beautiful, exceedingly popular—the choicest, quickest-selling glassware made. An attractive window display of this beautiful ware will fill your store with eager buyers.

"GOLD BAND AND PANEL" UTILITY DISH.

Unmatchable at a 10c price.

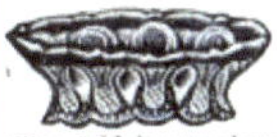

C66—Extra large round flaring shape diam. 5-in., fancy footed, beautiful jeweled panel design with heavy gold band edge and numerous gold decorated panels showing both inside and outside. 1 doz. in box. Per dozen, **80c**

"GOLDEN PRISM" BONBON DISH.

Shapely and beautiful.

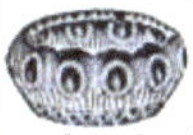

C475—Diam. 4-in., round shape, extra heavy rich cut diamond and bull's eye design with fancy rolled-in edges, richly finished and fire polished, elaborate decorations in pure burnt-in gold. 1 doz. in box. Per dozen, **80c**

"GOLD PRISM" HANDLED TRINKET TRAY.

Every lady will want one.

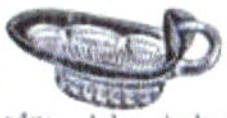

C476—Fancy shape, diameter 4¾-in., with turned-up sides and large open handle with rich cut diamond center and wide gold edge. 1 doz. in box. Per dozen, **82c**

"GOLDEN PRISM" ROUND DISH.

Another striking 10-center.

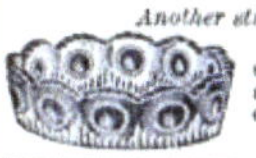

C477—Diam. 4¾-in., scalloped edge, diamond and bull's eye pattern. 1 doz. in box. Per dozen, **82c**

"GOLDEN PRISM" FLARING DISH.

A fire polished gem.

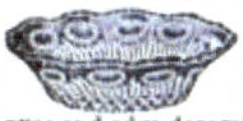

C478—Round shape, diam. 5 in., brilliant cut diamond center with flaring sides in attractive bull's eye design, bull's eyes and edge decorated in gold. 1 doz. in box. Per dozen, **80c**

"GOLD DECORATED" DOUBLE HANDLED DISH.

Brilliant addition to the dime counter.

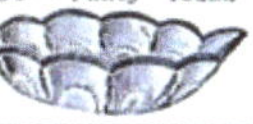

C484—Fancy round shape, diam. 6-in. rich panel design with scalloped edge, decorated in pure gold. 1 doz. in box. Per dozen, **83c**

"CRYSTAL AND GOLD" RICH SQUARE BONBON.

Massive and rich 10-center.

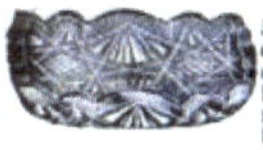

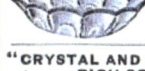

C496—Square shape, 5x5 in., extra heavy and deep cut glass design with scalloped edge, decorated in pure gold. Useful for many purposes. 1 doz. in box. Per dozen, **82c**

"GOLD DECORATED" EXTRA LONG DISH.

Extra value for a dime.

C485—Length 8-in., fancy scalloped shape in full finished almost plain crystal, with small beaded panels and edge decorated in pure burnt-in gold. 1 doz. in box. Per dozen, **83c**

"GOLD EDGE" UTILITY DISH.

Large and brilliant 10-center.

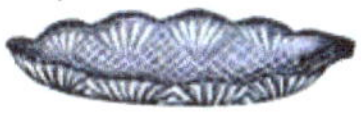

C492—8 inches long, oval shape, rich strawberry and fan pattern in pure crystal with fancy scalloped gold decorated edge. 1 doz. in box. Per dozen, **82c**

"GOLD BAND" UTILITY DISH.

One of our best 10c offerings.

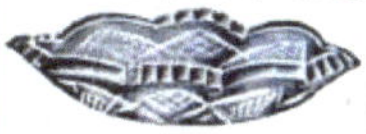

C65—Fancy shape, length 6¾ in., diam. 4¼, beautiful cut pattern, full finished and fire polished, extra heavy gold decorated edge. For bonbons, etc. Will sell always. 1 doz. in box. Per dozen, **83c**

"Crystal and Gold" BONBON DISH.

A queen among 10-cent offerings.

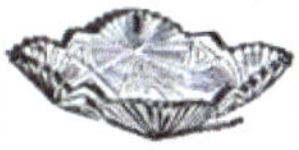

C62:.Richest of crystal with a wide band in genuine gold, most shapely of receptacles, 5½ inch. 1 doz. in box. Per dozen, **80c**

"GOLD BAND" FOOTED TRAY FOR JELLY.

Makes a dime look cheap by comparison.

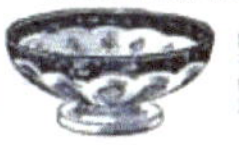

C552—5-inch diameter, fire polished, panel design, ½-inch gold band around top, purest crystal. 1 doz. in box. Per dozen, **80c**

"GOLD BAND" FANCY DISH.

Richest of the rich.

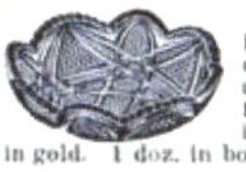

C483.—Diameter 5½-in., extra deep, of pure crystal in unusually rich and brilliant pattern with fancy scalloped edge heavily decorated in pure burnt-in gold. 1 doz. in box. Per dozen, **80c**

MASSIVE "GOLD DECORATED" OBLONG DISH.

Useful for many purposes.

C491—7¼x4, oblong shape, extra heavy and deep, rich brilliant cut glass pattern, fancy scalloped and heavy decorated gold edge. Will sell on sight if offered for 10 cents. 1 doz. in box. Per dozen, **82c**

"GOLDEN PRISM" ROUND DISH.

Few in the 10c class can equal this.

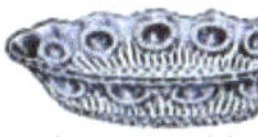

C59—Fancy round shape, diam. 6 in., extra heavy and deep with flaring sides, beautiful cut diamond pattern, gold decorations. 1 doz. in box. Per dozen, **82c**

"CRYSTAL AND GOLD" OBLONG TOILET TRAY.

A new and beautiful dime possibility.

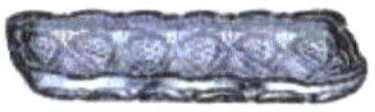

C493—Oblong shape, extra large, length 8-in., width 4, brilliant jewel pattern with elaborate gold decorated edge, richly fire polished. 1 doz. in box. Per dozen, **82c**

"CRYSTAL AND GOLD" FOOTED RECEPTACLE.

An artistic and handsome piece.

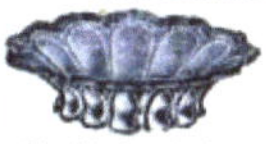

C494—Fancy round shape, diameter 5¼ in., new reflecting panel pattern, fancy foot, scalloped edge decorated in pure burnt-in gold. Need only be shown to sell. 1 doz. in box. Per dozen, **82c**

"CRYSTAL AND GOLD BAND" NAPPY.

A seller at 15 cents or a bargain at 10 cents.

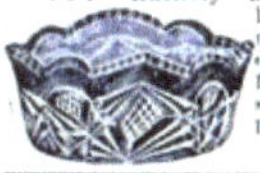

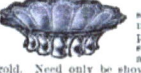

C64—Entirely new fancy oval shape, length 5-in., extra deep and heavy, full fancy, elaborate cut pattern with fancy gold band edge. A shapely and useful receptacle. 1 doz. in box. Per dozen, **83c**

"CRYSTAL AND GOLD" FANCY DISH.

Buy a dozen, sell a gross.

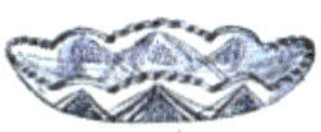

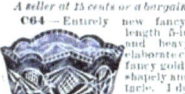

C68—7-inch wide, gold band scalloped edges. 1 doz. in box. Per dozen, **83c**

"Crystal and Gold" OVAL DISH.

Useful in many ways.

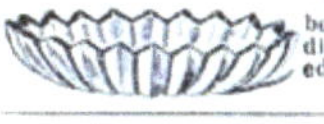

C63:. A 7-inch beautifully patterned dish having gold edges. 1 doz. in box. Per dozen, **80c**

GOLD DECORATED FANCY LONG DISH.

A general utility dish of real beauty.

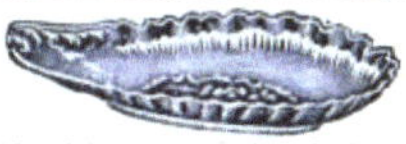

C485:.8 in., fancy scalloped shape with small beaded panels decorated in gold. 1 doz. in box. Per dozen, **83c**

"GOLDEN PRISM" OVAL TRAY.

Useful for mans purposes.

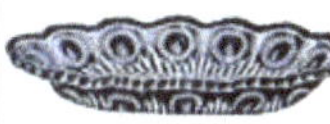

C60. 7½x6-in., diamond and bull's eye pattern, burnt-in gold. 1 doz. in box. Per dozen, **82c**

"GOLD NUGGET" TOOTHPICK HOLDER.

Striking design, likewise a striking price.

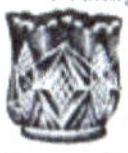

C71—Large size, footed, elaborate pattern with fancy nugget edge, profusely decorated in genuine gold. Every lady will want one. 1 doz. in box. Per dozen, **83c**

"GOLD BAND" TUMBLER TOOTHPICK.

A bargain for a dime anywhere—any time.

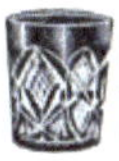

C69—Not large but very beautiful, purest crystal in deep cut pattern, smooth ground bottom, ¾-inch heavy gold band around top, very brilliant. Useful for toothpicks, matches and many other purposes. 1 doz. in box. Per dozen, **83c**

"GOLD BAND" PANEL TOOTHPICK.

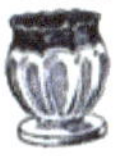

A 10-center of rare beauty.

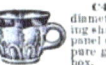

C349—Very bright, ⅜-inch gold band around top. 1 doz. in box. Per dozen, **83c**

"CRYSTAL and GOLD" Loving Cup Toothpick.

The daintiest of 10-cent leaders.

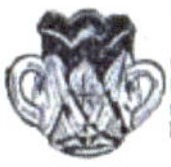

C362—A tasty little cup with three handles and heavy gold band around top. An art item that will sell quick. 1 doz. in box. Per dozen, **83c**

"BRILLIANT" GOLD BAND CUP.

Will not linger long in any store.

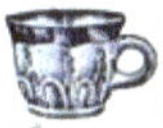

C486.—Good size, 2¼-in. diameter 3-in., footed fancy flaring shape with large handle, rich panel design with ½ in. band of pure gold around top. 1 doz. in box. Per dozen, **80c**

"CRYSTAL AND GOLD" CUT STAR SHERBET CUP.

A sparkling gem.

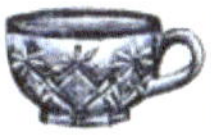

C497—Large size, footed, large handle, diameter 3¼ inches, height 2¾, purest of crystal, rich cut pattern, brilliantly finished, fire polished, gold decorated edge. 1 doz. in box. Per dozen, **82c**

"Crystal and Gold" RICH CUP.

Make a table of these at "10 cents" and see them go.

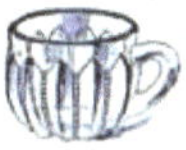

C53:.This most beautiful piece so desirable for punch, sherbet, or for table or mantel use, is exquisitely decorated with gold rim. 1 doz. in box. Per dozen, **80c**

BEAUTY "COLD BAND" SHERBET CUP.

None more popular than this.

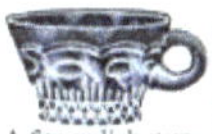

A fire polish gem.

C372—Medium size, flaring shape, rich jewel pattern base. Optic, bull's eye and fluted design sides, bull's eye and edge being richly decorated in gold convenient handle. 1 doz. in box. Per dozen, **82c**

CRYSTAL AND GOLD "DELMONICO" SHERBERT CUP.

Large size beautiful pattern.

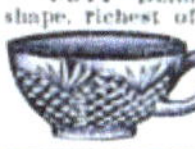

C371—Diam. 3¾-in., footed, fancy flaring shape, richest of cut glass patterns, being the popular strawberry and fan design, with large handle and rich gold edge. Brilliantly fire polished. 1 doz. in box. Per dozen, **82c**

MASSIVE "GOLD DECORATED" CUP.

Size and richness combined.

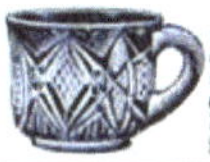

C370—Large size, rich pattern, footed, large fancy handle with gold band around top. A fire polished gem. Not only useful for many purposes but ornamental as well. 1 doz. in box. Per dozen, **83c**

"WIDE COLD BAND" HEAVY MUG.

A bargain at 10c anywhere.

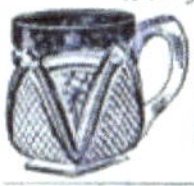

C274—3¼ inches high, square shape, heavy handle, beautiful cut jewel effect on the sides. ⅜-inch heavy wide gold band around top. ½ doz. in box. Per dozen, **83c**

DEEP "GOLD BAND" MUG

A bargain among bargains.

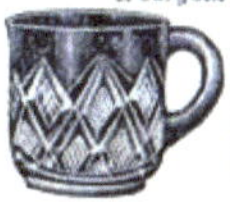

C72. Large size, extra heavy and massive, ht. 3¼ in., footed, large fancy fluted handle, elaborate cut glass pattern, 1-in. extra wide gold band around top. 1 doz. in box. Per dozen, **80c**

GOLD BAND CRYSTAL SUGAR AND CREAMER.

Splendid sellers by the set.

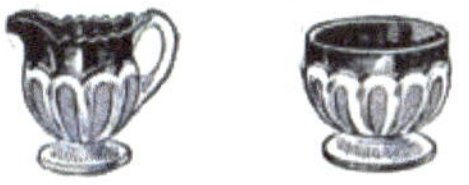

C182, Creamer—3½-in. high, 1-in. gold band around top, neat foot. Per dozen, **83c**

C474, Sugar—3-in. across top, ½-in. gold band around top. Per dozen, **83c**

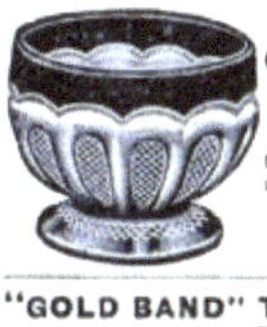

GOLD BAND SUGAR BOWL.

C475. 3-in. across top, ½-in. gold band around top. 1 doz. in box. Per dozen, **82c**

"GOLD BAND" TANKARD CREAM PITCHER.

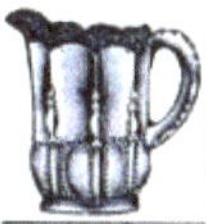

Although a 10-center, is worth 15c.

C184—Fancy tall tankard shape, height 4 in., rich optic panel design, footed, with fancy handle, fancy scalloped wide gold band edge. 1 doz. in box. Per dozen, **82c**

"GOLDEN PRISM" CREAM PITCHER.

Popular shape, attractive design.

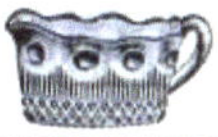

C479—Fancy oval shape, length 3¾-in., with convenient handle and good lip, gold decorated bull's eyes and edge. 1 doz. in box. Per dozen, **83c**

"RICH CUT GOLD BAND" CREAM PITCHER

An ornamental and useful dime seller.

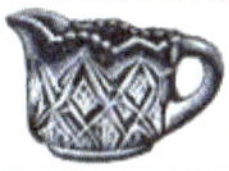

C183. Large low shape, exquisite pattern, good handle, footed, fancy edge elaborately decorated in gold. A queen among 10-cent offerings. 1 doz. in box. Per dozen, **80c**

"GOLDEN PRISM" OPEN SUGAR.

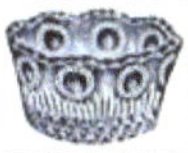

Matches C479 cream pitcher.

C480—Round shape, diam. 3¾ in., ht. 2 in., full finished and fire polished, pure gold edge and bull's eyes. 1 doz. in box. Per dozen, **82c**

'GOLD BAND" CUT PATTERN WINE GLASS.

Will sell to all who see it.

C367—Extra heavy deep cut pattern in purest crystal with fancy imitation cut stem and ¼-in. band of 18-karat gold around top. A rich and rare 10-center. 1 doz. in box. Per dozen, **83c**

"Crystal and Gold" Reflector Wine Glass.

A bargain reflected in the price.

C366—Medium size, symmetrical shape, popular style. Burnished gold band. 1 doz. in box. Per dozen, **83c**

OUR "GOLD PRISM" WINE GLASS.

One of our best 10-centers.

C85:.Gold line on top and bottom, six wide gold prism panels. Richest of 10c wines. 1 doz. in box. Per dozen, **80c**

No package charge on any goods on pages 316 to 324.

Economy Is One Great Source of Revenue—"Our Drummer Is An Economizer of Time and Money.

WE RECOGNIZE NO COMPETITION in This Department of Popular Priced Glass Specialties.

No package charge on any goods on pages 316 to 324.

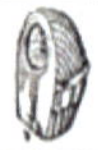

BIRD CAGE CUP.

MC325—*5-cent necessity.* Beautiful crystal glass. Will fit all cages. 1 doz. in box. Per dozen, **29c**

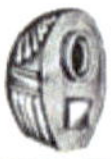

OPAL KNOB SEED CUP.

A chance for you to make a profit.

C326¼—Rich white opal, fluted pattern, patent knob for fastening to cage. 1 doz. in box. Per dozen, **32c**

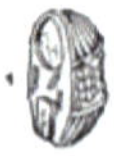

PATENT CAGE CUP.

A brisk 5-center.

C326—Has a projection on the back by which it is held between the wires of the cage. Fits any cage. 1 doz. in box. Per dozen, **37c**

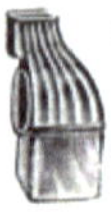

PATENT CRYSTAL CAGE CUP.

Staple and a good profit-payer.

C327½ — Large size, 3-corner shape, crystal glass with patent knob at top to fit any cage. 1 doz. in box. Per dozen, **39c**

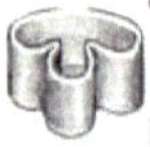

OPAL SEED OR WATER CUP.

Always in demand.

C327—Pure opal, the largest patent shape, fits all cages. 1 doz. in box. Per dozen, **39c**

5-INCH OPAL BIRD BATH.

The largest size and the smallest price.

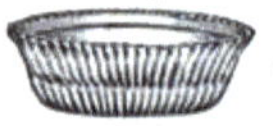

C330—Handsome pattern, high quality. 1 doz. in box. Per dozen, **40c**

REGULATION OPAL BIRD BATHS.

Your stock incomplete without them.

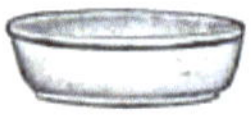

C328—Plain oval shape, 4¾ x 4 ¼, footed and fancy pressed bottom. 1 doz. in box. Per dozen, **39c**

C329—As above, much larger, 5¼x3¾, extra deep. 1 doz. in box. Per dozen, **42c**

LIPPED MEDICINE GLASS.

Always a seller—here a bargain.

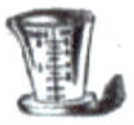

C318—Has measuring scales for tea spoon, table spoon, etc. 1 doz. in box. Per dozen, **37c**

MEASURING GLASS—With Lip.

An all the year 5c seller.

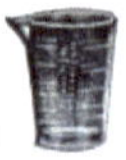

C283—Medium size, ht. 2¾, good lip, graduated scale for measuring teaspoon, tablespoon, ounce, etc. 1 doz. in box. Per dozen, **39c**

OUR "CRYSTAL" COVERED JEWEL BOX.

Beautiful and useful.

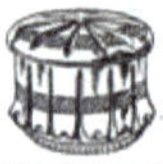

C289—Round shape, diam. 2¾-in., rich panel and cut diamond banded design, footed and with deep cut glass cover. 1 doz. in box. Per dozen, **42c**

"COLD DECORATED" JEWEL BOX.

A dime wonder.

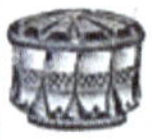

C487 — Round shape, diam. 2½-in., footed beautiful panel and cut diamond banded design with glass cover elaborately decorated in pure burnt-in gold. 1 doz. in box. Per dozen, **83c**

OUR "CRYSTAL AND GOLD" JEWEL BOX.

A dime item of rare beauty.

C61—Medium size, round shape, diam. 2¼-inches, extra deep, brilliant crystal pattern with solid burnt-in gold decorated cover in rich green jeweled effect. A beautiful ornament for bureau or dressing table. 1 doz. in box. Per dozen, **82c**

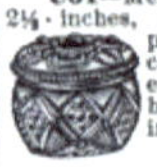

MASSIVE "GOLDEN" PUFF BOX.

A profit paying 25 center which is sure to sell rapidly.

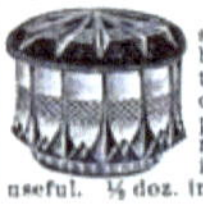

C488—Extra large round shape, ht. 3 in., diameter 3¼, brilliant deep cut panel pattern, footed, with fancy deep cut cover, both in purest fire polished crystal, cover being richly decorated in pure burnt-in gold. Ornamental and very useful. ¼ doz. in box. Per dozen, **$2.10**

DECORATED OPAL JEWEL BOX.

Extra good at this price.

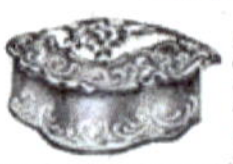

C803.—Diam. 4-in., new and artistic design, richly embossed in fancy scroll design with fancy shaped cover, both cover and box richly tinted and decorated, all embossed work elaborately traced in gold bronze. 1 doz. in box. Per dozen, **92c**

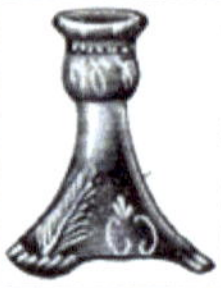

FANCY OPAL CANDLESTICK.

A rich 10-center at a profit-paying price.

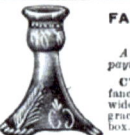

C700:-Plain white opal in fancy embossed pattern with wide spread base, 5-in. tall, graceful shape. 1 doz. in box. Per dozen, **70c**

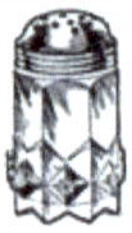

"DIAMOND PANEL" SUGAR SHAKER.

A profit-paying 10-cent leader.

C202—Large size, extra heavy, rich reflecting panel pattern, brilliantly finished and fire polished, high dome top. ½ doz. in box. Per dozen, **80c**

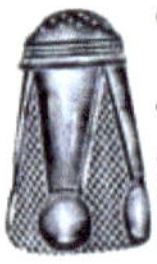

OUR "REFLECTOR" SUGAR SHAKER.

Will be an advertiser if retailed at 10c.

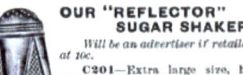

C201—Extra large size, ht. 5¼-in., with wide base, rich brilliant but diamond and mirror panel pattern, extra heavy and brilliantly fire polished, nickel plated dome top. 1 doz. in box. Per dozen, **89c**

GLASS SPECIALTIES IN WOOD CASES. No Package Charge.

"DIME CREAM PITCHER" Asst.

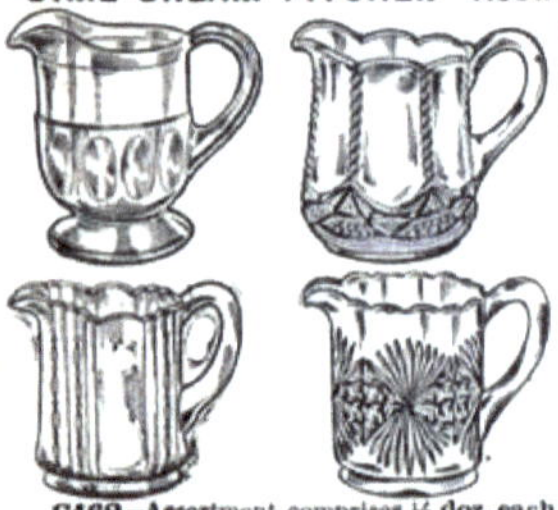

C469—Assortment comprises **¼ doz. each** of 4 patterns all full finished and fire polished. 2 doz. in box, *no charge for box.* Dozen, **75c**

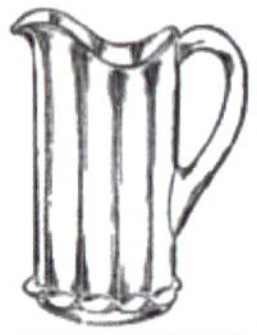

"BEADED TANKARD" MILK OR CREAM PITCHER.

A profit-paying dime bargain.

C468 — Tall tankard shape, 6¼-in., rich beaded panel pattern, heavy base, large handle, full finished and fire polished. A size that sells always. 2 doz. in box, *no pkg. charge.* Dozen, **74c**

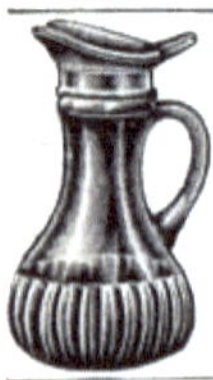

"SPREAD BASE" SYRUP PITCHER.

A possible 10-cent wonder.

C440—Ht. 6¼-in., new and beautiful shape, rich plain and fluted pattern in purest crystal, wide spread base, large handle and good spring top. 2 doz. in wood box—*no charge for box.* Per dozen, **95c**

HIGH GRADE "GLASS LIP" SYRUP PITCHER ASST.

Two brilliant 15 centers.

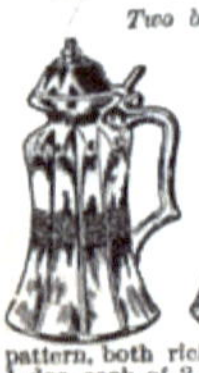

C429—Medium size, ht. about 7 in., large fancy handle, glass lip and patent britannia top, 2 styles, both with wide spread bases, one in rich panel design, the other rich cut diamond pattern, both richly finished and fire polished. 1 doz. each of 2 sizes. *Total 2 doz. in case, no charge for case.* Per dozen, **$1.20**

OUR "DELMONICO" OIL OR VINEGAR BOTTLE ASSORTMENT

Dime leaders unexcelled.

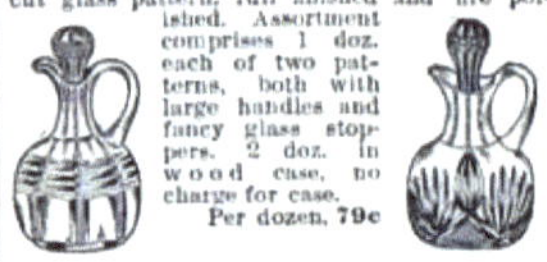

C653—Medium size, purest crystal, genuine cut glass pattern, full finished and fire polished. Assortment comprises 1 doz. each of two patterns, both with large handles and fancy glass stoppers. 2 doz. in wood case, no charge for case. Per dozen, **79c**

NEW "GEM" GLASS LIP SYRUP PITCHER ASSORTMENT.

Two brilliant 15-centers which will pay you a profit.

C441—Comprising 2 styles, both medium size, extra heavy, pure crystal glass in 2 bright new patterns, with glass lips and heavy nickel plated britannia tops. 1 doz. each of 2 styles. Total 2 doz. in case. No charge for case. Per dozen, **$1.20**

Our "DAZZLING" Oil or Vinegar Bottle Assortment.

Four good ones to retail at 10 and 15c each.

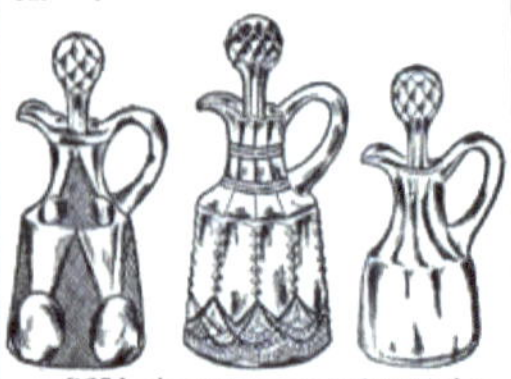

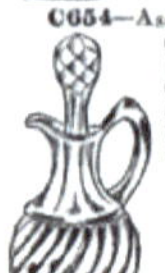

C654—Assortment comprises ¼ doz. each 4 extra brilliant and fancy patterns, 2 being of 4 oz. and 2 of 6 oz. capacity, all purest crystal and all richly finished and fire polished. Asstd. as follows:

1 doz. 4-oz....at $0 79
1 doz. 6-oz....at 1 25
Total for box of 2 doz.... **$2 04**

(No charge for box.)

OUR "PERFECTION" SYRUP PITCHER AND VINEGAR CRUET ASST.

Profit paying 15-centers — really worth 25 cents.

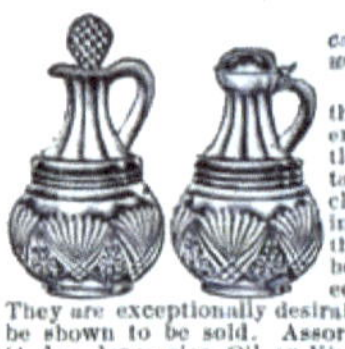

C766—These are the well known patent separable bottles, which can be taken apart for cleaning, etc. Made in pure crystal in the popular strawberry and fan pressed glass patterns. They are exceptionally desirable and need only be shown to be sold. Assortment comprises: ½ doz. large size Oil or Vinegar Cruets, with glass stoppers, full ht. 5¼-in.; ½ doz. handled Syrup Pitchers, with glass lips and heavy nickel plated tops. Ht. 5½-in. Total 1 doz. in wood case. No charge for case. Per dozen, **$1.25**

DECORATED OPAL GLASS LIPPED SYRUP PITCHER.

A 25-center possessing exceptional selling qualities.

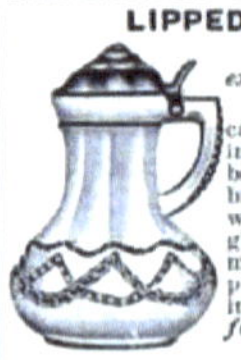

C427—Extra large size, capacity 16-oz., fancy shape in pure opal attractively embossed and decorated in bright colors and gold bronze, with large fancy handle and glass lip, fancy heavy top made of brass and full nickel plated. Assorted decorations in case of 1 doz., *no charge for case*... Per dozen, **$2.25**

BOMER GLASS BUTTER MOLD.

A staple 25-cent seller.

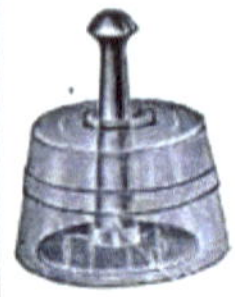

C735—Full finished crystal bowl shape mold, diam. at top 3¾ in., bottom 4¼, height 3, with 5-inch hardwood handle and 3½-in. glass stamp, which imprints cow or fleur-de-lis on butter and forces same from mold. 2 stamps with each. 1 doz. in case. Per dozen, **$1.34**

GLASS BOWL DIPPER.

Just the thing so many housewives want. They will buy it at 10c.

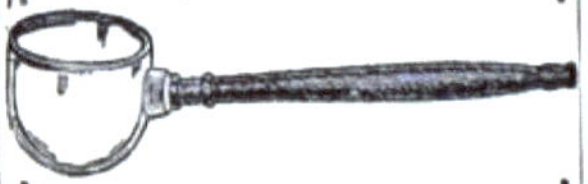

C—Glass dipper. 13 in. long, bowl about the size of a tea cup, black enamel handle extra heavy. For use in soups, punches, lemonade, fruit canning, etc. *Easily cleaned, will not leak or corrode.* 1 doz. in wood box, *no charge for box.* Per dozen, **69c**

Our "BIGGEST AND BEST" SOAP DISH.

A regular dime seller as a 5-cent possibility.

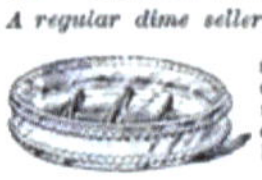

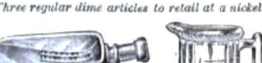

C333—Heretofore considered cheap as a 10-center. Largest size, splendid pattern. Sells on sight. 2 doz. in wood box., *no charge for box.* Per dozen, **44c**

GLASS KITCHEN UTENSIL ASST.

Three regular dime articles to retail at a nickel.

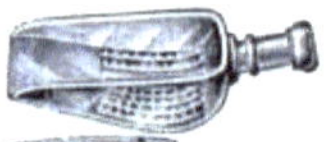

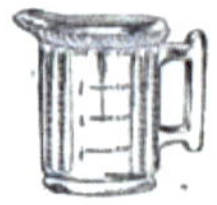

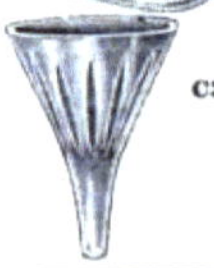

C556—2 doz. graduated measuring pitchers, good lip and handle, 4x4¼, 1 doz. handle glass scoops, 3x6½. 1 doz. glass funnels, 3¼ in. in diam. 4 doz. in box. *No charge for case.* Per dozen **43c**

"MATCHLESS" Asst. of Syrups and Vinegars.

Four full finished 25-centers to retail at 15c.

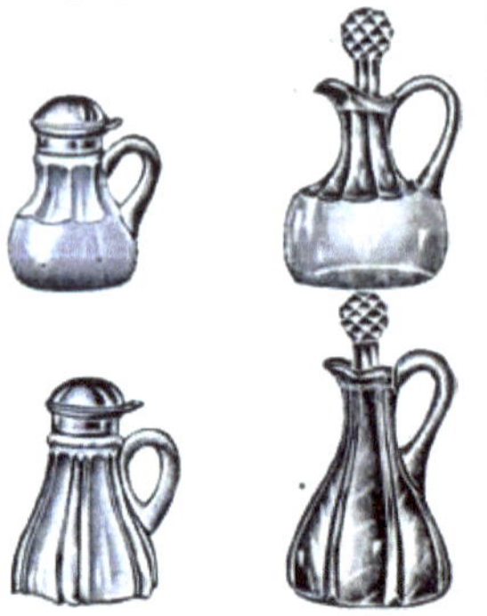

C336—Assortment comprises **¼ doz. each** of the following:

Extra heavy plain rich Syrup Pitcher—Nickel dome top.

Extra large Oil or Vinegar Bottle—Heavy, with stopper and large graceful handle.

Large fancy panel pattern Syrup Pitcher—With wide spread base and large handle, heavy nickel plated britannia top.

Large heavy Vinegar or Oil Bottle—With stopper, fancy panel pattern, wide spread base, large handle.

Total 2 doz. in box—*no charge for box.* Per dozen, **$1.30**

We Buy in Such Unprecedented Quantities That Our Prices Defy Those of the Auction Flag.

WASH YOUR GLASSWARE OFTEN—Nothing but Dust and Dirt Can Lessen Its Salableness.

GLASS SPECIALTIES IN WOOD CASES. No package charge.

"FANCY" Wine Glass Asst.
Four sparkling beauties. To retail with a profit at 5c.

C640—These beautiful stem glasses are all of the richest cut patterns, finished and fire polished. Assortment comprises 1 doz. each of 4 patterns. 4 doz. in wood case, no charge for case.
Per dozen, 31c

"STAPLE" Wine Glass Asst.
Four crystal beauties as 5-cent profit payers. 

C641—Assortment comprises 1 doz. each of four bright patterns as follows: colonial flute, bead panel, plain flute and diamond band. Total 4 doz. in box, no charge for box.
Per dozen, 30c

Our "SPARKLING" Full Finished Berry Nappy Asst.
None more beautiful ever made. Rare 5-centers.

C372—Comprising 4 styles, 2 being fancy round shape and 2 fancy square shape, all footed, all with fancy scalloped edges, diameter 4½ inches, richest of genuine cut glass patterns, brilliantly fire polished. 1 doz. each of 4 styles. (*Total 4 doz. in case. No charge for case.*)
Per dozen, 36c

OUR "FIFTH AVENUE" NAPPY AND TRAY ASST.
Three dazzling crystal beauties to retail at 5 cents.

C375—All full finished and fire polished. The richest of rich patterns. Sample these on your 5-cent bargain counter—they will make sales lively on the dullest days. Assortment comprises 1 doz. each of 3 styles.
5½-Inch Round Footed Tray.
5-Inch Footed Fancy Square Comport.
4½-Inch Footed Sauce Dish—Fancy edge.
(*3 doz. in box. No charge for box.*) Doz., 39c

THE "TWO WONDERS" TUMBLER ASST.

An every day bargain in the richest of staples.

C550, 3 doz. extra large mirror pattern, and 3 doz. double thick bottom. Good at very low price. 6 doz. in case.
Doz., 32c

"HAND DECORATED" OPAL SYRUP PITCHERS.
Bouncing 25-centers of attractive shape and rich decoration.

C428—All extra large, full 16-oz. size. 2 new and fancy shapes, both being embossed and elaborately decorated all over in rich colors and gold bronze clouded effect. 1 doz. of each shape in assorted decorations. Total 2 doz. in box. *No charge for box.*
Per dozen, $2.20

"DECORATED OPAL" SYRUP PITCHER Asst.
25-centers on which you can reap a handsome profit and yet give rare value.

C430—Three entirely new shapes, one wide spread base, one deep cut panel design, one swell shape. All profusely decorated in assorted bright colors, all with new plated dome tops. ⅓ doz. each of 3 shapes. Total 2 doz. in box, no charge for box.
Per dozen, $1.69

"BELL SHAPE" SODA TUMBLER.
A big seller. The size which fits the silver holders.

C578—Capacity 11-oz., popular flaring bell shape, purest thin lead blown glass. The one universally used for soda fountains. 2 doz. in case, no charge for case.
Dozen, 72c

OUR "5-CENT" MUG ASST.
Three staple all-the-year sellers.

C780—Extra large size, most brilliant patterns in pure crystal, large handles, all full finished. Assortment comprises ⅓ dozen each of 3 styles. Total 2 doz. in box—*no charge for box*.
Per dozen, 43c

DECORATED "KITTEN PLAQUE."
An exceedingly popular item.

C805—Pure opal ware with openwork edge. Diam. 7 in., upper edge in embossed relief effect with three kittens, 1 black, 1 white and 1 maltese. Openwork edge beautifully tinted, centre part of plaque decorated in assorted hand painted floral designs. 1 doz. in box. (*No charge for box.*)
Per dozen, 87c

OWL AND KITTEN PLAQUE ASSORTMENT.
Rich 10 centers always in demand.

C783—Pure opal ware, diameter 7¼ in. fancy openwork edges. Two styles—one with 3 owls and the other with 3 kittens on upper edge in embossed relief effect; lower part in hand painted assorted floral, landscape and water scenes. Owls, kittens and edges decorated in solid gold bronze and green shading. 2 doz. of each style, total 4 doz. in case. (*No charge for case.*)
Per dozen, 87c

OUR "GOLDEN SUNSET" 4-PIECE CONDIMENT SET.
Especially rich in this new and beautiful ware.

C398—This attractive seller is entirely new, being of rich golden agate or amber color in combination of light and dark shades.
One extra large deep 8½-in. fancy long tray. Footed, beaded edge.
One tall fancy shape Vinegar Bottle with fancy glass stopper. Panel and vine pattern.
One fancy column shape Salt Shaker.
One Pepper Shaker to match.
Total 4 pieces in set. 6 sets in case. *No charge for case.*
Set, 28c

SLENDER FLOWER VASE ASSORTMENT.
— Brilliant Crystal. 
Beauties to retail at 10c.

C585—Comprising 4 beautiful patterns—plain colonial flute, flute twisted, rich cut diamond and strawberry and fan designs, tall and slender with wide flaring tops, height about 9 inches, made of the purest crystal, full finished and fire polished. ½ doz. each of 4 styles.
Per dozen, 84c
(*Total 2 doz. in case. No charge for case.*)

Showing 3 of the 4 styles C585, 84c Doz.

Our "Stylish and Serviceable" 4-PIECE CONDIMENT SET.
One of the best 25-centers we have ever offered.

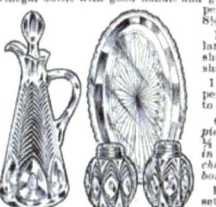

C399—New and beautiful mirror and plume design in pure and brilliantly finished crystal.
1 only 8-in. extra deep oval shape tray with fancy scalloped edge.
1 only tall and graceful shape tankard oil or vinegar bottle with good handle and glass stopper, full ht. 8½-in.
1 only large swell shape salt shaker.
1 only pepper shaker to match.
(*Total 4 pieces in set. ¼ doz. sets in box, no charge for box.*)
Per dozen sets, $2.25

The Famous "BANNER STORE" LAMP.
$2.25 for this lamp known by every merchant.

—Has extra feeder wick and oil drip cup on inside of tube to carry any overflow back to the wick. 20 inch tin shade. Fitted with No. 3 burner, fount, wick and chimney. Each in box complete.
One tin shade only sent in box.
Each, $2.25

OUR EXTRA LARGE CRYSTAL VASE ASSORTMENT.
Exceptionally rich 25-centers.

C581—Comprising two styles, both being extra tall flaring shapes, height 12 inches, one with extra heavy block diamond base and fancy diamond cut pattern with scalloped top, the other a full fluted design with scalloped top. ½ doz. of each style. (*Total 1 doz. in case. No charge for case.*)
Per dozen, $1.95

"SCALLOPED EDGE" CANDY TRAY.
Never before at a price so low.

C76—Oblong shape, square corners, 8x5¼ extra deep, heavy bright attractive pattern fancy scalloped edge. 2 doz. in box.
Per dozen, 79c

PERFECTION WATER BOTTLES.
A good seller for 25c. A bargain for a quarter. 

C765—One of the best and most practical water bottles ever made. Can be taken apart for cleaning, capacity 1 full quart, made of pure crystal in brilliant cut glass pattern, with fancy fluted neck, fitted with nickel-plated screw ring which fastens neck to bottle. 1 doz. in case. (*No charge for case.*)
Per dozen, $2.00

C764— As above. ½ doz. in case. Doz., $2.10

BRACKET LAMP.
A good return for your investment. Retails everywhere for 75 cents.

C446—French bronze bracket lamp. Complete with No. 2 filler founts, 8-inch silvered glass reflector and No. 2 Sun burner, but *without chimney*. Sold only in lots of 1 doz. *No charge for case.*
Per dozen, $4.75

THE "PITTSBURGH" STORE OR HALL LAMP.

No package charge.
—Absolutely non-explosive, burns over 10 hours without refilling. Perfect draft, no dirt, no odor. Smallest wick exposure of any lamp made. Has patent dial indicator showing quantity of oil in lamp.
Has extra feeder wick and oil drip cup on handle of tube to carry any overflow back to the wick. 20-inch tin shade. Fitted with No. 3 burner, fount, wick and chimney. Each lamp complete ready for use and in box, wt. 26 lbs.
(*No charge for case.*)
Each, $2.25

There is Nothing that Stimulates Trade So Well as the Systematic Giving of Bargains.

You Ought to Sell Lamps—Those Here Listed Are the Best Values Any Firm Will Offer You.

A LAMP DEPARTMENT That Dares to Cut Prices.

There is profit for you, Mr. Merchant, in looking us over carefully in this line. We have goods you want and prices you won't match elsewhere. When you buy lamps here you have a chance to make more profit for yourself than when you pay market prices. So far as quality is concerned, if you will order sample packages you will find that when there are two or more grades of an article in the trade ours is *never the poorest* and USUALLY THE BEST.

GENUINE "VESUVIUS"

Fireproof Lead Chimneys.

Each chimney packed in attractive pasteboard carton. Reduces breakage to a minimum—clean and convenient to handle—no dust nor straw.

Have won the highest award against all other chimneys in the most severe fire-test competitions. If anyone wants the best pure lead chimney he will have the "Vesuvius." None genuine without the word "Vesuvius" neatly etched on each chimney. Sold only by case.

*Impossible to make a better chimney than our "VESUVIUS," which is made from purest lead glass under a **secret formula.***

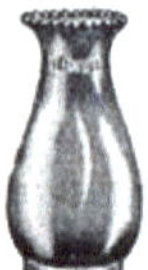
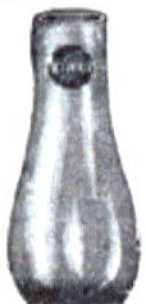

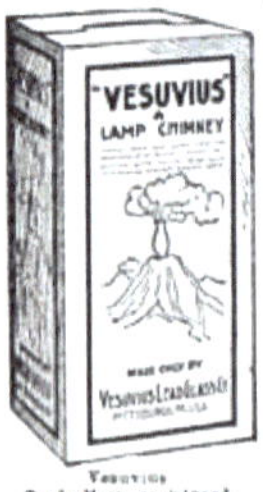

Vesuvius Trade-Mark, registered May 1, 1900.

"Vesuvius" Crimped Bead Top— Doz.

No. 1—Each in carton, 6 doz. in case, wt. 41 lbs. (*Case 40c*). $0 48

No. 2—Each in carton, 6 doz. in case, wt. 57 lbs. (*Case 50c*). 63

"Vesuvius" Plain Top—

No. 1—Each in carton, 6 doz. in case, wt. 41 lbs. (*Case 40c*). 48

No. 2—Each in carton, 6 doz. in case, wt. 57 lbs. (*Case 50c*). 63

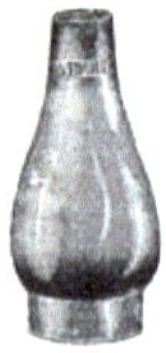
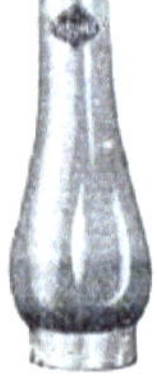

"Vesuvius" Rochester—

No. 2—Diameter at bottom 2⅝-inch. Each in carton, 6 doz. in case, wt. 62 lbs. Sold only by case (*Case 50c*) ... 75

No. 2—12-inch, extra long, for use with large globes. Diameter at bottom 2⅝ inch. Each in carton ... 1 44

No. 2—12-inch, as above, each in carton, 3 doz. in case, wt. 42 lbs. (*Case 40c*) ... 1 20

No. 3—Diameter at bottom 4-inch. Each in carton, 2 doz. in case, wt. 46 lbs. Sold only by case. (*Case 50c.*). 1 50

Vesuvius" Electric—For use on the Climax and other burners where globes are used—

No. 2—Diam. at bottom 3 in. Each in carton, 3 doz. in box, wt. 36 lbs. Sold only by box. (*Box 40c*) ... 75

No. 2—Diameter at bottom 3-inch. Each in carton. Slim shape, for globes with 4-inch openings. 3 doz. in box, wt. 37 lbs. Sold only by box. (*Box 40c.*) ... 75

Why you should sell "Vesuvius" Chimneys: Freights same, boxes same, no wrapping to be done by you when selling. Can be **guaranteed** against breaking from heat. One of them will outlast 50 lime chimneys.

LIME CHIMNEYS—*First-class quality.*

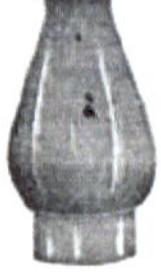

No. C0—Best crystal chimney, sun burner, crimped top; 6 doz. in case, wt. 37 lbs. (*Case 30c.*) ... Doz $0 22

No. C1—Best crystal chimney, sun burner, crimped top; 6 doz. in case, wt. 41 lbs. (*Case 40c.*) ... 22

No. C2—Same as above, but larger. Packed 6 doz. in case, wt., 50 lbs (*Case 50c.*) ... 32

"FIRE-TEST" LEAD CHIMNEYS.

These are strictly "firsts" and while not equal in quality and quantity of lead to the "Vesuvius," yet will compare in fire or melting test with any other lead chimney offered at ten per cent higher prices.

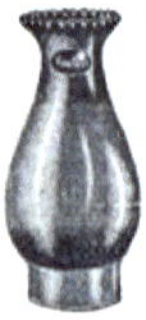

"Fire Test" Bead Top— Made from German glass. Will not break when put into hottest fire. Absolutely "firsts." *Each wrapped. A saving of expense when selling.*

No. 1—6 doz. in case, wt. 41 lbs. (*Case 40c*) Doz. $0 27

No. 2—6 doz. in case, wt. 51 lbs. (*Case 50c*) 39

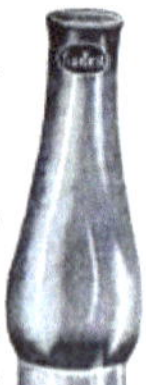

"Fire Test" Rochester Lead—Satisfactory in every particular. Doz.

No. 2—Diameter at bottom 2⅝-inch. 6 doz. in bbl., wt. 62 lbs. Sold only by bbl. (*Barrel 35c*) ... $0 60

No. 3—Diameter at bottom 4-inch. 2 doz. in bbl., wt. 46 lbs. Sold only by bbl. (*Barrel 35c*) ... 1 05

NOTE—No. 3 fits Rochester, Banner, Yale and Aurora mammoth lamps.

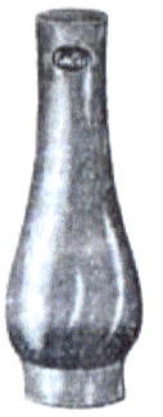

"Fire Test" Electric—For use on the Climax and other No. 3 wick burners.

No. 2—Diameter at bottom 3-inch. 3 doz. in box, wt. 30 lbs. Sold only by box. (*Box 40c*) ... 60

No. 2 Slim Shape—Diameter at bottom 3-inch. For globes with 4-inch openings 3 doz. in box, wt. 37 lbs. Sold only by box. (*Box 40c*) ... 60

ENGRAVED GLOBE CHIMNEYS.

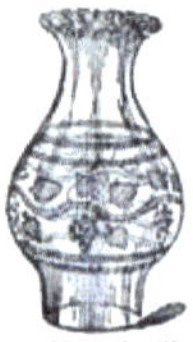

Try these 10-centers and you'll make them one of your staples.

No. 2—Assortment consists of equal quantities, each of 3 designs of engraved and banded chimneys, all large No. 2 size and swelled center globe shape. Regularly sold at 20 cents. 3¼ doz. in pkg., wt. 55 lbs. (*Bbl. 35c.*) Sold only by pkg. Per dozen. **80c**

No. 1 Size—As above. 5 doz. in bbl. (*Bbl. 35c.*) Per dozen. **67c**

MAMMOTH "SATIN ETCHED" GLOBE CHIMNEY.

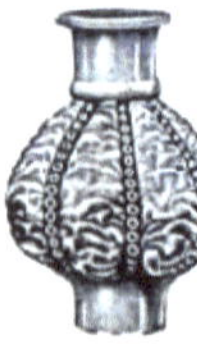

New 25-center and very beautiful.

C2—Made of pure lead glass, ht. 9 in., crimped top, extra large swell shape bulb, circumference 21 in., bulb having beautiful alternating panels of rich satin etching and beaded crystal, giving a rich frosted effect. Fits regular No. 2 Sun burner. Will be an ornament to any lamp. 1½ doz. in bbl. *Bbl. 35c.* Weight 46 lbs. Per dozen. **$1.95**

"STERLING" GLOBE OR CHIMNEY.

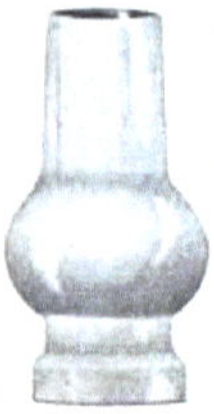

Fits the Pittsburg store lamp.

—Made of pure lead glass, mammoth size, ht. 11 in., diam. at base 4½-in. 1¼ doz. in bbl. Bbl. 35c. ... Doz. $1 75

(Less than barrel lots, $2.10 doz.

CHIMNEYS FOR GAS LAMPS.

8-Inch "Fire Test" Welsbach Gas Chimneys—Lead glass, best quality, not comparable with the cheaper goods. 3 doz. in case. (Case 30c.) ... Doz. $0 57

8-Inch "Vesuvius"—Etched base gas chimney. Each in corrugated carton. ½ doz. in pkg ... Doz. 78

C210, "Vesuvius" Etched Base Combination Gas Chimney Asbestos Ringed—A new popular chimney suitable for all incandescent gas lamps and our new "Suns-Ray" lamp. Goes over outside of burner upright and rests on springs at bottom of burner. Made from purest of lead glass, and being large does not break easily. **In carton.** Doz. 89

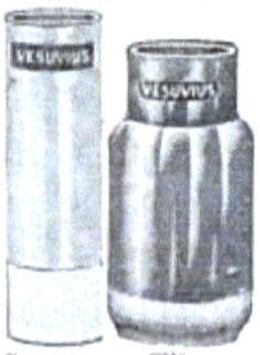

Vesuvius C210

C210—As above, 6 doz. in case, (Case 50c.) Doz. 75

GLOBES FOR "WELSBACH" GAS BURNERS.

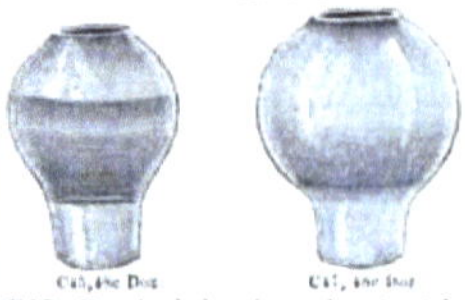

C45, 48c Doz. C47, 48c Doz

C45—Pure lead glass (pear shape), etched top and bottom, clear crystal center. 3 doz. in case (*Case 25c*) ... Doz. $0 48

C46—Plain opal, shape as above. 3 doz. in case (*Case 25c*) ... Doz. 48

C47—Pure lead (apple shape). Etched all over. 3 doz. in case (*Case 25c*) ... Doz. 48

TUBULAR LANTERN GLOBE.

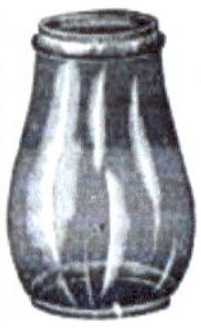

C0—Best goods, *ground top and bottom*, fitting any tubular lantern. 5 doz. in pkg. (*Pkg. 35c.*) Per dozen, **33c**

COLD BLAST LANTERN GLOBE.

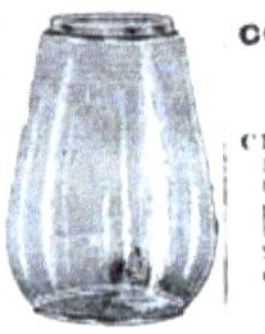

C1217: Large size for cold blast lanterns, best glass, ground tops and bottoms, fine goods. 2 doz. in box, no charge for pkg. Doz. $0 57

LAMP SUNDRIES.

Wicks ... Page 3
Burners ... " 248
Shades ... " 146
Brackets ... " 248

Our "FANCY PATTERN" Hand Lamp Assortment.

Best quality, cream patterns, lowest price

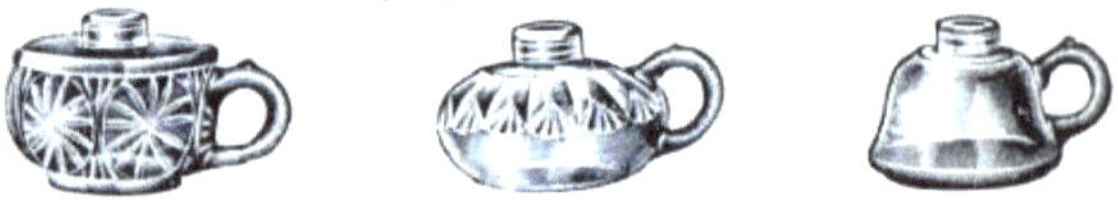

C704 Three all the year staple sellers in bright attractive, new patterns, all with large strong handles and best No. 1 brass collars. Can be fitted complete and retailed at a popular price. **2¾ doz. each** of the 3 styles—total 8¼ doz. in bbl. (*Wt. 105 lbs. Bbl. 35c.*) Per dozen. **65c**

GROOVED FLAT. FILLER FOUNT.

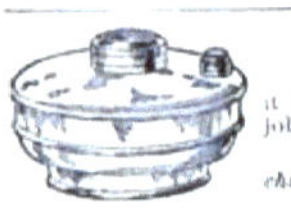

You can fit with bracket, reflector, chimney and burner, and then *sell* it for about what you would pay for complete lamp from the lamp jobbers.

C2—No. 2 size, superior goods. 1 doz. in case, wt. 40 lbs., *no charge for case* Per dozen. **98c**

Our "BRACKET FOUNTS" Assortment.

Clinch collar founts at the price of the common goods.

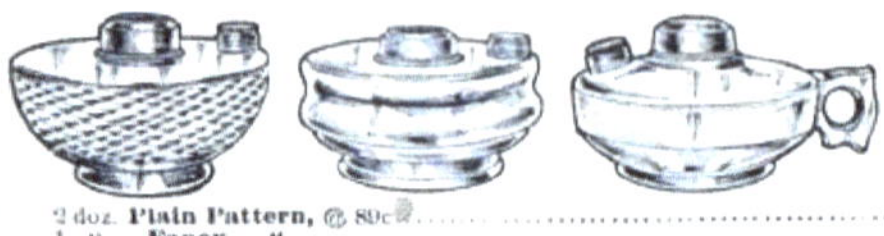

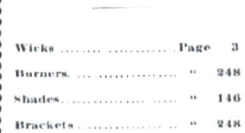

C717—Each having clinch collar—no plaster, no dirt, coming loose. Good large sizes, each having OUTSIDE FILLER. Assortment comprises:

2 doz.	**Plain Pattern,** @ 89c ...	$1 78
1 "	**Fancy** " ...	95
1 "	**Handled Pattern** ...	1 10
	Total for the 4 dozen.	**$3.83**

(*Total 4 doz. in bbl., wt. 94 lbs. Bbl. 35c.*)

"ALL SIZES" Lamp Assortment.

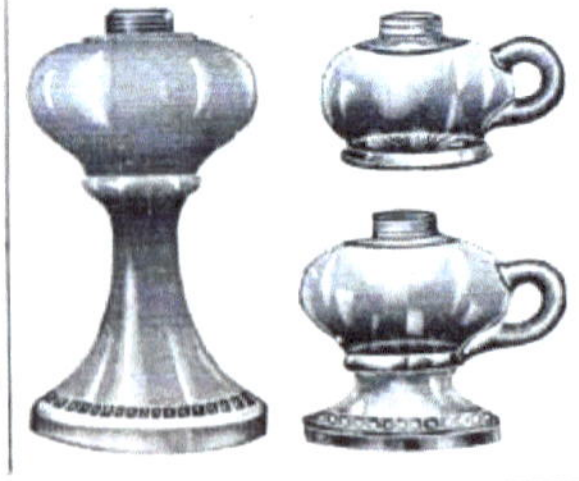

All of bright new patterns—all extra large sizes.

C731—Best selling pattern shown in years. Here is an assortment of all best sizes at prices 10 per cent below market. Remember, these sizes are "extra large," and none marked up.

The assortment comprises the following:

1 doz.	OOA, No. 1 collar ...	$0 87	$0 87
½ "	OA, " 1 " ...	95	48
⅓ "	A, " 1 " ...	1 20	40
¼ "	B, " 2 " ...	1 60	40
¼ "	C, " 2 " ...	1 92	48
⅙ "	D, " 2 " ...	2 10	35
⅔ doz.	½A. Flat hand lamp. No. 1 collar ...	65	44
⅓ doz.	½A. Footed lamp. No. 1 collar	87	29
	Total.		**$3.71**

(*Total of 3 1-2 doz. in pkg., wt. 80 lbs. Barrel 35c.*)

Nothing Pulls Trade Like VALUE—It Is That Which Pulls So Great a Business to Our Lamp Department.

Our "DEFIANCE" Lamp Assortment.

High footed handled lamp assortment. New patterns. Heavy, extra well made and finished. *Always popular sellers.*

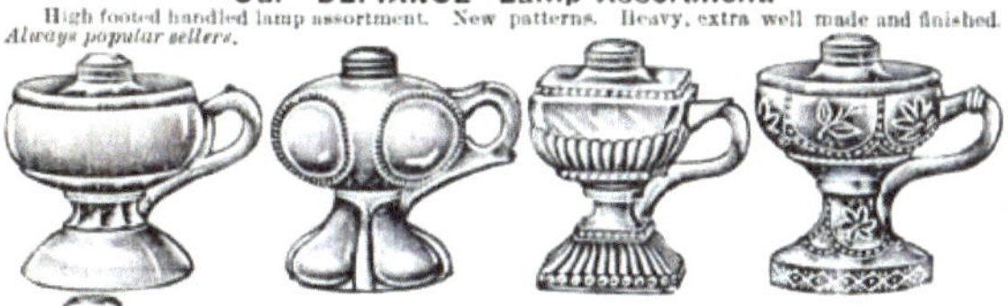

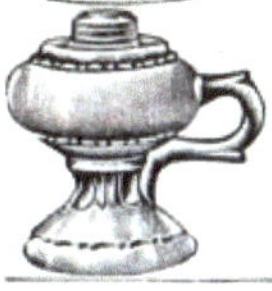

C705—Comprising 5 styles all in pure crystal and in best new patterns, height 5¼ inches. All with large convenient handles and all fitted with No. 1 brass collars. 1 doz. each of the five styles as illustrated. (*Total of 5 doz. in bbl. Bbl. 35c.*) Per dozen. **87c**

OUR "TABLE LAMP" ASSORTMENT.

Popular in pattern, unsurpassed in quality, unequaled in price.

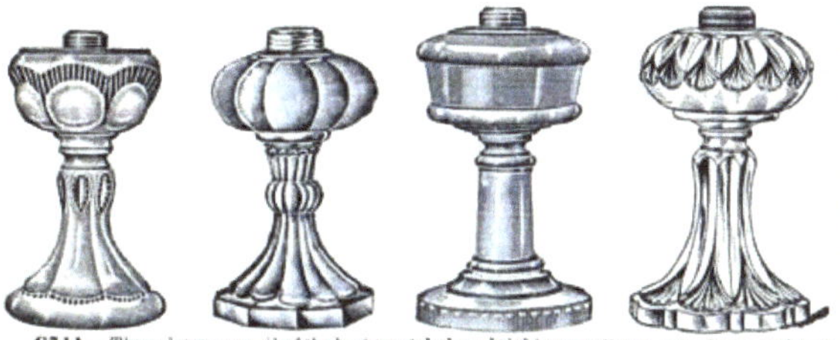

C711 — These lamps are all of the best crystal glass, bright new patterns, extra heavy and well finished. *No "tank glass" in our lamps.*

Large size, ½ doz. @ $1.40 .... $0 70	Extra large, ½ doz. @ $1.95 .... $0 98
Large size, ½ doz. @ $1.50 75	Extra large, ½ doz. @ $2.10 .... 1 05

All with No. 2 collars. (2 doz. to pkg., wt., 95 lbs. Bbl. 35c.) Total, **$3.48**

Our "BARGAIN" Lamp Assortment.

Brilliant new patterns. Well made and finished. Exceptionally good value at this price.

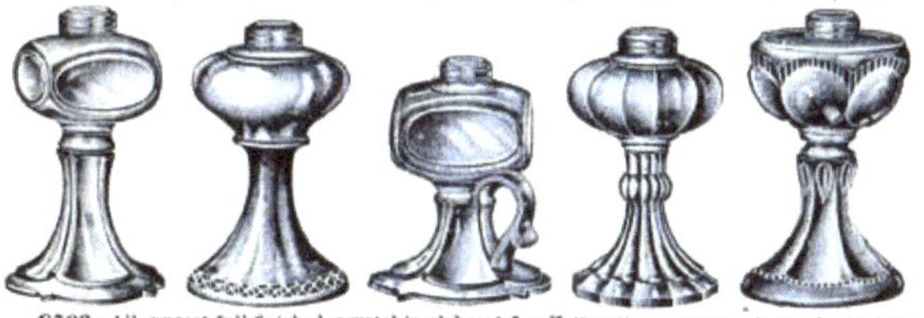

C703—All purest full finished crystal in elaborate and attractive patterns, all fitted with best No. 1 brass collars. None better made at any price.

Assortment Comprises 1 doz. Each of the Following:

6¾-in. high, footed handled stand.
7½-in. high, footed stand, fluted pattern.
7¾-in. high, footed stand, cut panel pattern.
7¼-in. high, footed stand, almost plain pattern.
7¾-in. high, footed stand, rich optic pattern.

(*Total of 5 doz. in bbl. Wt. 110 lbs. Bbl. 35c.*) Per dozen, **84c**

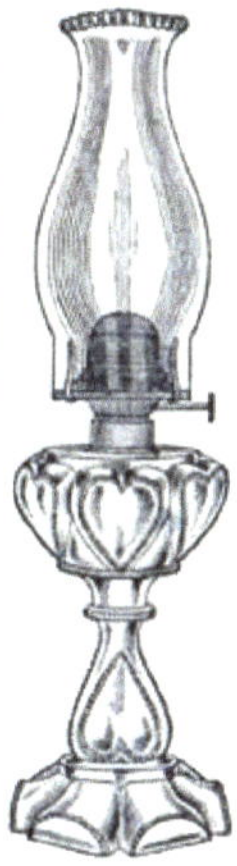

"BIG AND SAFE" Complete Lamp Assortment.

The best 50c complete lamps ever offered. All with patent clinch collars. No plaster, no cement, no dirt, no working loose.

C714—The assortment comprises ⅓ doz. each of two patterns of high stand lamps, measuring 19¼ inches to top of chimneys and ⅓ doz. of large sewing lamps measuring 18 in. in height. *All complete with No. 2 burners, chimneys and wicks.*

(*Total of 1 doz. in pkg., wt. 70 lbs. Barrel 35c.*) Per dozen complete, **$3.75**

Our "ALL FITTED" Green Lamp Assortment.

Complete—ready to pour the oil in.

C716—Comprising identically same lamp as "Big and Safe" Assortment, but in green instead of crystal, all having the PATENT CLINCH COLLAR. (*Total 1 doz. in bbl., wt. 70 lbs. Bbl. 35c.*) Per dozen, **$3.80**

Our TINTED" Complete Lamp Assortment.

A great 50c offering. All clinch collar lamps.

C715—Comprising ⅓ doz. each of 3 extra large lamps, all with No. 2 collars and with stems decorated in royal blue, bases in ruby. ⅓ doz. each of 3 styles fitted complete with burners, chimneys and wicks.

(*Total 1 doz. in bbl., wt. 75 lbs. Bbl. 35c.*) Per dozen, **$3.75**

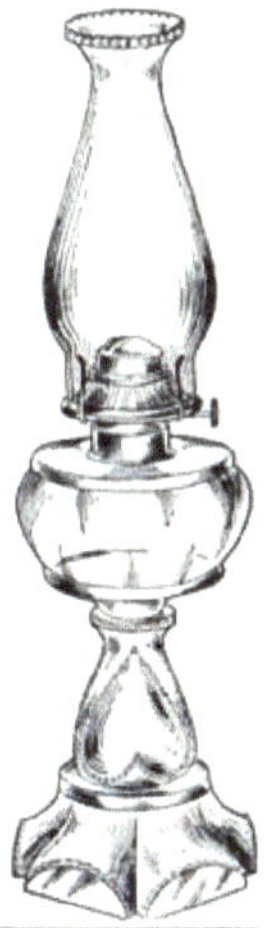

The "ALL READY" Lamp Assortment.

Full rigged ready to pass over the counter for a quarter.

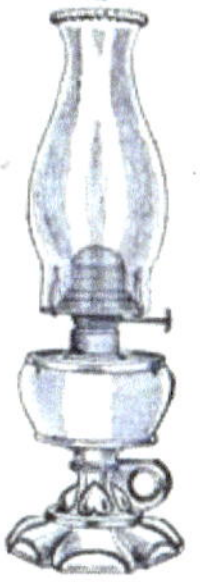

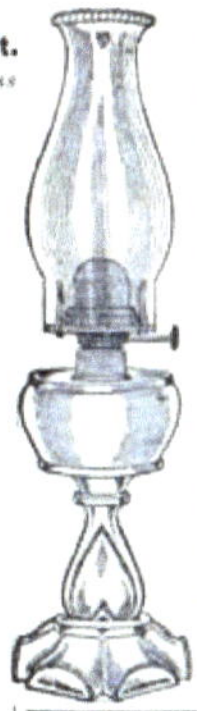

C734 — Comprising **1 doz. each** of hand and high stand lamps as illustrated. Clinch collar — no plaster. Complete with chimney, burner and wick. Per dozen, **$2.10**
(*Total 2 doz. in bbl., wt. 80 lbs. Bbl. 35c.*)

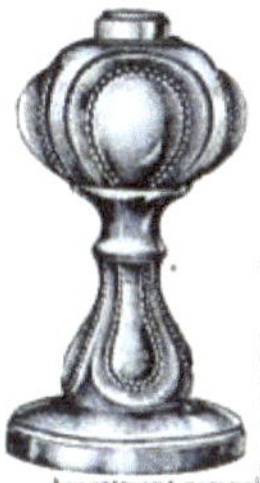

OUR MAMMOTH "CLINCH COLLAR" LAMP ASSORTMENT.

Positively the best glass lamps ever made.

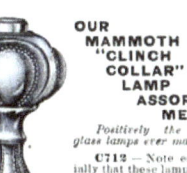

C712 — Note especially that these lamps are extra heavy and made of one piece of solid glass and are almost unbreakable, all fitted with best shrunk on brass clinch collars, no plaster or cement used.

Assortment comprises the following:

¼ doz.	C, plain pattern,	ht. 10½-in.,	at $2.25	$1 13
½ "	C, fancy	" 10½ "	" 2.30	1 15
¼ "	D, plain	" 11¾ "	" 2.95	74
¼ "	D, fancy	" 11¾ "	" 3.00	75

(*Total 1½ doz. Bbl. 35c.*) Total, **$3.77**

OUR NEW TUBULAR LANTERNS.

Standard crank tubular. Positively the best ever made. *Far superior to any heretofore offered at these prices.*

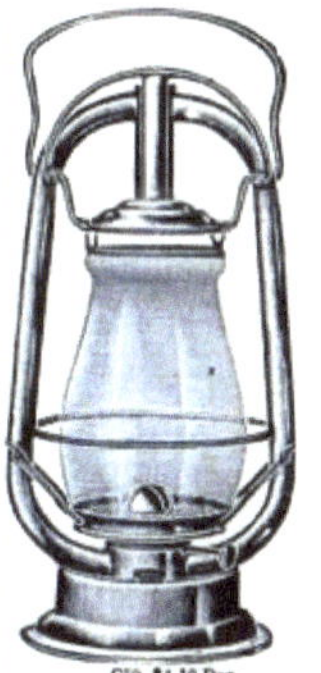

C50, $4.10 Doz.

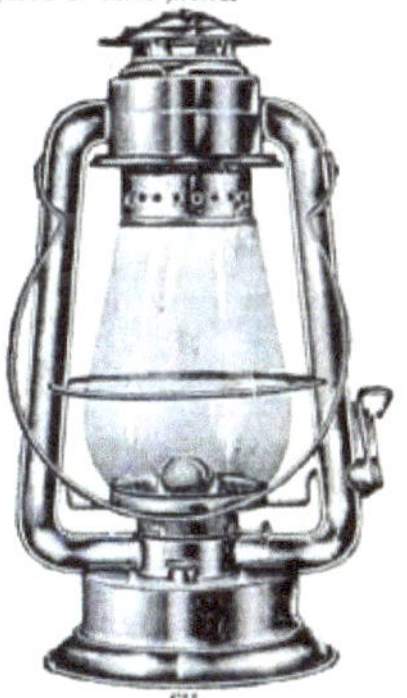

C55.

C50— Heavy base, oil fount with outside filler, concaved top wire-guard and bail handle, brass burner. AUTOMATIC LIFT Complete with globes. 1 doz. in case, no charge for case. Per dozen, **$4.10**

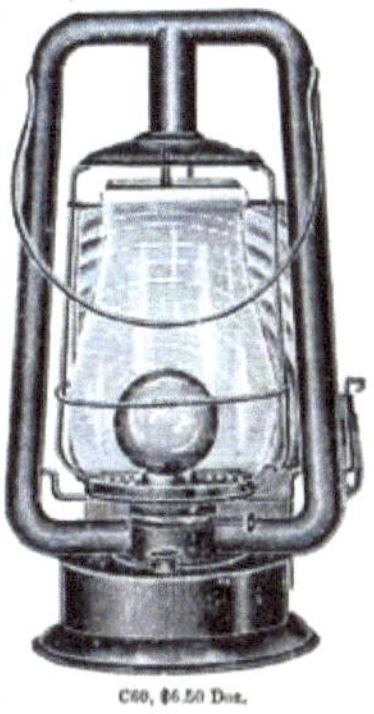

C60, $6.50 Doz.

C55—The best, most convenient and substantial lantern ever offered, having solid stamped base, extra large oil fount with outside filler, best brass locked burner, extra strong tubes made from one piece of heavy tin, strong bail handle and guard. Globe is raised by the popular and improved side lift crank which throws globe upward and outward, giving easy access to burner. Complete with globe. 1 doz. in case, no charge for case. Per dozen, **$4.35**

C60, Stable or Dash board Lantern — Same size and style as our C55 above only made of best blued japanned tin with reflector and firmly attached wire spring hook. Made to fit the dash board of wagon or carriage or to hang up in the stable. Fitted with bull's eye globe for magnifying and concentrating the light. ½ doz. in case, no charge for case. Per dozen, **$6.50**

Our "HONEST VALUE" Lamp Assortment.

Patent clinch collar lamps at price of common ones.

C713 — Fitted with the patent CLINCH COLLAR. The assortment comprises the 3 largest sizes and will give any merchant the choicest bunch of popular priced lamps we have ever offered. All with No. 2 collars. The assortment consists of:

1 doz. medium size fancy	$1 55
½ " large size plain @ $1.60	80
1 " large size fancy	1 95
Total for 2½ doz	**$4.30**

(*Total 2 1-2 doz. to pkg., wt. 104 lbs. Bbl. 35c.*)

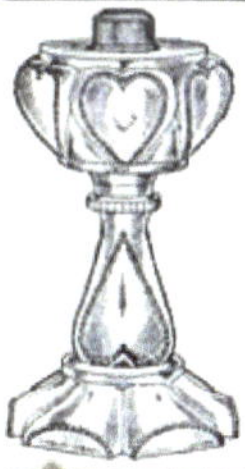

Our "TINTED STAND" Lamp Assortment.

☞ *A very striking combination. Will sell if simply shown and ticketed.*

C735—Clinch collar, no plaster. Ruby base with royal blue stem, or vice versa. Very best goods. Assortment comprises:

1 doz.	medium.	No. 1	collars	$0 88	$0 88
½ "	large,	" 1	"	1 35	67
½ "	"	" 2	"	1 85	93
½ "	"	" 2	"	2 10	1 05
½ "	"	" 2	"	2 25	1 13

Total, **$4.66**

(*Total 3 doz. in bbl., wt. 105 lbs. Bbl. 35c.*)

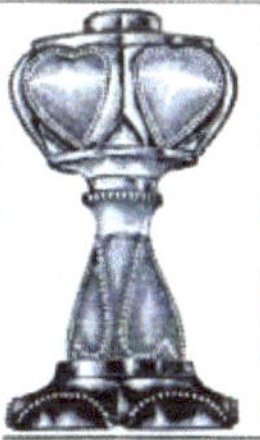

Our "SEWING LAMP" Assortment.

Very popular sellers at exceptionally low prices.

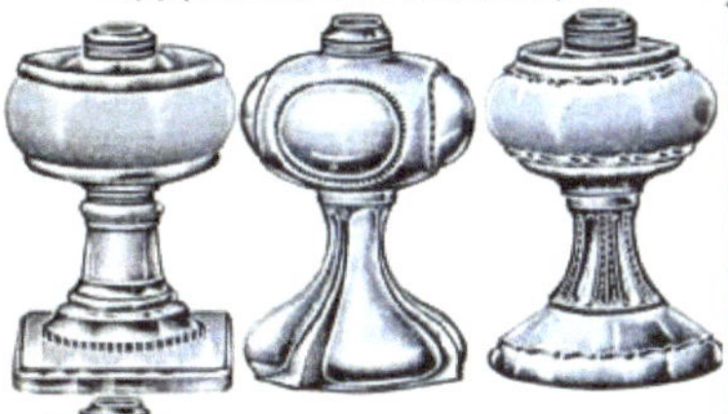

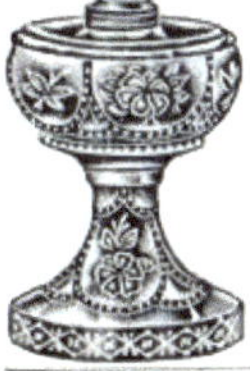

C710—Comprising 4 styles, all with No. 2 brass collars and of extra large low shape, with large founts. All of pure crystal brilliantly finished and brightest new patterns. ½ doz. of each style. (*Total 2 doz. in bbl. Bbl. 35c.*) Per dozen, **$1.87**

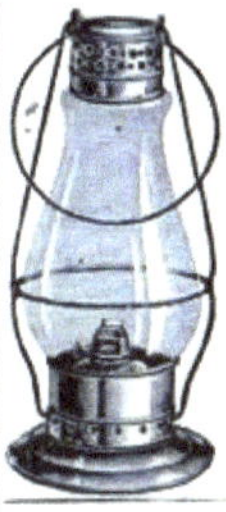

"FULL SIZE" 25c LANTERN.

C5—Heavy tin and 10-gauge wire, ht. 11¾ in., base and oil cup detachable. Good burner, fitted with No. 0 tubular globe. 1 doz. in case, *no charge for case.* Per dozen, **$2.10**

Our Celebrated COLD BLAST LANTERN.

C65 — Perfect combustion, flame being wind-proof. Ht. without handle 15 in. heavy block tin, oil tank with outside filler. No. 2 brass burner, crank lift for raising and lowering globe, bail handle and guard. ½ doz. in case, complete with globes. *No charge for case.* Per dozen, **$7.95**

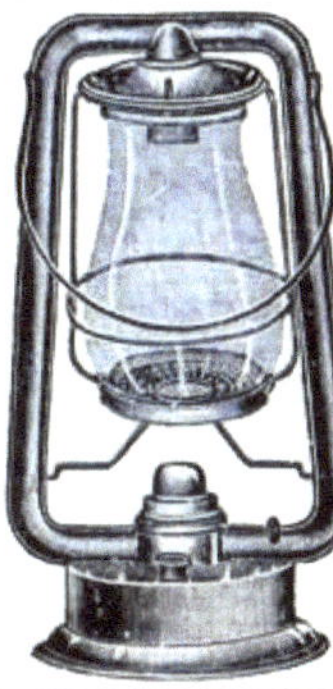

BULL-DOG PERSEVERANCE Will Ofttimes Win Out When All Other Means Have Failed.

NO PACKAGE CHARGE on any Goods on this Page.

MANTLES—*For gas fixtures, etc.*

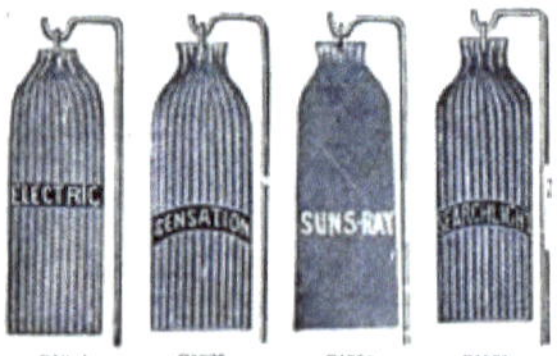

C1924, 6½c Each. C1925, 8c Each. C1926, 12c Each. C1931, 14c Each.

C1924, "Electric": The best mantle for the money. Suitable for either gas or gasoline. Gives a bright, white, high candle power light, is strong and durable. 25 in box.......... Each $0 06½
(In lots of 100 or more, 6¼c)

C1925, "Sensation": Perfect in shape and construction, unusually strong, and giving an intense incandescent light for either gasoline or ordinary gas. 25 in box.......... 08
(In lots of 100 or more, 7½c)

C1926, "Sun's-Rays": Treated by special process which greatly increases the incandescence and strength, extra coated at the top. Expressly adapted for gasoline or gas. Our own copyrighted brand. Manufactured by the Welsbach Co. 25 in box.......... 12
(In lots of 100 or more, 9c).

C1931, "Searchlight": *Copyrighted.* A perfect double thread mantle made from finest chemicals by the Welsbach Company exclusively for us. Special double woven net permits double the absorption of chemicals, producing a heavier and stronger mantle. 12 in showy case.......... 14
(In lots of 100 or more, 12c).

C114, "Starlight".—Double weave mesh. Gives 125 candle power light. Mounted on cap with twin support. 12 in box. 16

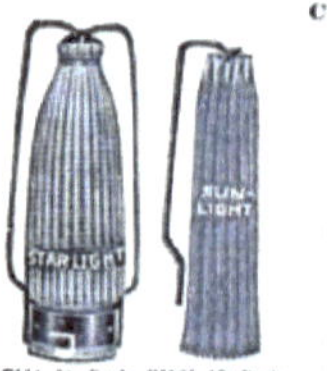

C114, 16c Each. C1927, 17c Each.

C1927, "New Sun Like": For pressure lamps only. 5 in., red color. We guarantee this to be the best pressure mantle made. Double weave, extra strong, best chemicals, gives a clear, brilliant light. It will stand the pressure. 1 doz. in box.......... 17
(In lots of 100 or more 16c)

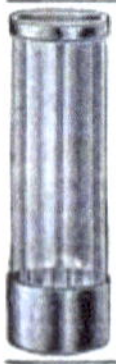

MICA CHIMNEY FOR GAS LAMP.

7-Inch Mica Chimney—6-piece. Fits all incandescent gas burners, made of the finest and most transparent mica, does not break, so saves your mantle bill. Clean with vinegar and hot water. Packed in neat pasteboard carton.... Doz. $0 76

SHADES FOR GAS LAMPS.

No package charge.

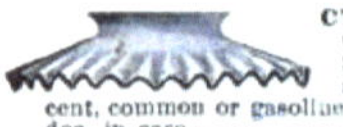

C74, 8-inch Opal Gas Shade—Fits all incandescent, common or gasoline burners. 2 doz. in case.......... Doz. $0 90

"BRILLIANT" REFLECTOR LAMP.

10c leader of leaders.

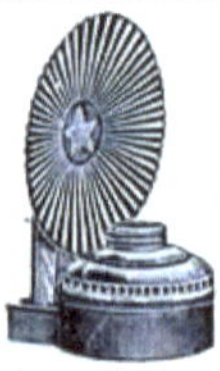

C99: Frame of heavy block tin, handsomely painted, tin reflector, 4¼ inch glass fount made for No. 2 burner. Packed 3 doz. in case. *No charge for case, wt. 52 lbs.* Per dozen, 85c

"JAXON" REFLECTOR LAMP. With Burner.

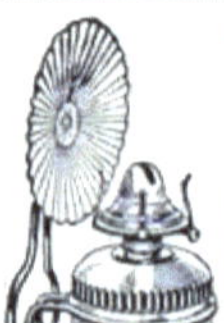

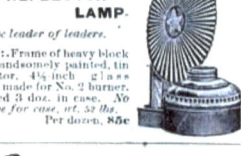

C98 — Made from one piece of 7-gauge steel wire, very strong and springy, complete with 7-inch bright tin reflector and 4¼-inch fount, fitted with No. 2 burner. 1 doz. in case, wt. 26 lbs. *No charge for case.* Per dozen, $1.89

DECORATED OPAL NIGHT LAMP.

An unequaled dime possibility.

C724 — Full height 6¾-in., body of pure white opal in fancy embossed design, rich decorations in bright colors and gold bronze, complete with burner, chimney and wick. ½ doz. in box. Per dozen, 96c

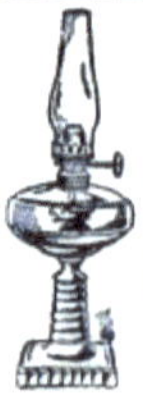

THE "LITTLE HANDY" NIGHT LAMP.

Will make a most popular "special."

C300—A complete lamp-body, chimney, burner and wick. Handsome pattern of purest crystal. ½ doz. in box. Per dozen, $1.08

"ALL GREEN" NIGHT LAMP.

Offer it at 15 cents and hear your competitors growl.

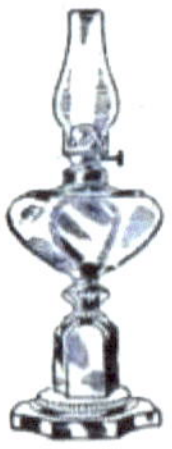

C1380—Large night lamp of peculiarly pleasing shape, 9½ inches in height. Patent clinch collar. Complete with burner, chimney and wick. ½ doz. in pasteboard box. Per dozen, $1.25

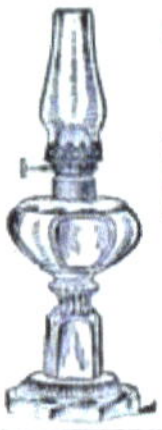

HEART PATTERN NIGHT LAMP.

With patent clinch collar.

C302—A large pure crystal night lamp of rare lines of beauty. 9½ inches high. Has burner, chimney and wick complete. ½ doz. in box. Per dozen, $1.25

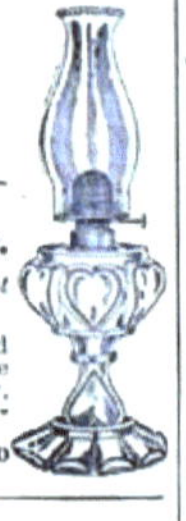

"DOUBLE TINT" NIGHT LAMP.

New and rich combination that will please.

C721—Assorted red base and blue stem, and red stem and blue base. Complete with chimney, burner and wick. *Worth a quarter.* ½ dozen in box. Per dozen, $1.30

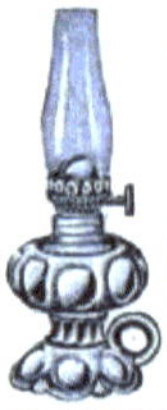

OUR "SHAPELY" HANDLED NIGHT LAMP.

C720: An attractive little lamp in entirely new crystal pattern. Footed and with fancy open handle, and fitted with nutmeg burner, chimney and wick. Full ht. to top of chimney 7 in. Will sell every day in the year. 1 doz. in box. (No pkg. charge.) Per dozen, $1.15

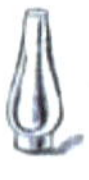

NIGHT LAMP CHIMNEY.

Always in demand and sells at a big profit.

—A chimney to fit ordinary shape night lamps. Diameter at bottom 1½ in., height 3½. Put up 1 doz. in box. Per dozen, 12c

GEM NIGHT LAMP CHIMNEY.

—One of the necessities. *Quick sellers at 2 for 5.* Fits any metal night lamp. Diameter at bottom 1½-inch, height 4¼-inch. 1 doz. in box. Per dozen, 17c

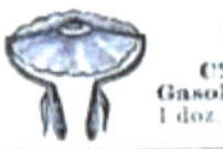

MICA CANOPY.

C352, Mica Canopy for Gasoline Lamp—Two supports. 1 doz. in pkg. Doz., 36c

ALUMINUM CROWN MICA CANOPY.

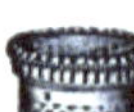

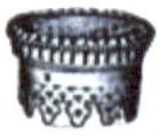

MC353. Not only a protection against smoke, wind and insects, but an attractive ornament to the lamp. Each in carton. 1 doz. in box. Doz., 84c

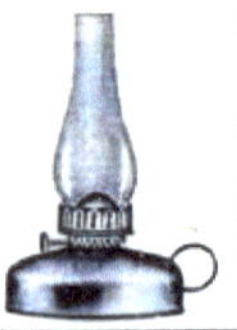

BRASS FINISHED NIGHT LAMP.

A splendid 10-cent bargain.

C48— Full height 7 in. extra wide fount, almost impossible to upset, fitted with best brass gem burner, wick and large chimney. 1 doz. in box. Per dozen, 89c

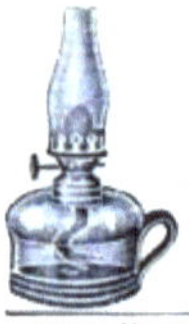

HANDLED METAL NIGHT LAMP.

A seller and a profit paying 10-center.

C298: Height 6¾ in. glass fount in blue, opal and crystal, patent brass finished combination metal base and handle, burner, wick and chimney. Assorted colors in box of 1 doz. Per dozen, 96c

THE "SOUTHERN" BRASS HAND LAMP.

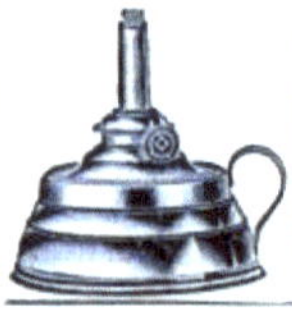

One of the best of 10-centers.

C47—Large size, brilliantly lacquered brass fount, good handle, fitted with brass fluid ratchet burner and round wick, requires no chimney. 1 doz. in box complete with wicks. Per dozen, 96c

FULL NICKEL PLATED NIGHT LAMP—*Complete.*

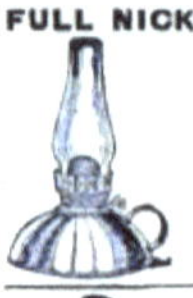

One of the best of our offerings.

C41—Full nickel on brass, with liberal handle. Has nickel burner to match, and complete with chimney and wick. 1 doz. in box. Per dozen, 96c

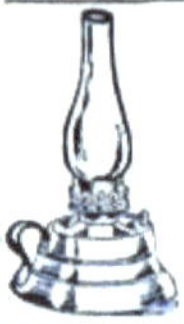

GENUINE BRASS NIGHT LAMP

Brilliant lacquered brass.

C42—A large size lamp. Stands 7 inches high, body of lamp 4 inches. Complete with burner, wick and large chimney. ½ doz. in box. Per dozen, $1.08

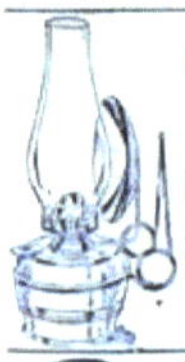

"BRIDGEPORT" ALL-NIGHT NICKEL LAMP.

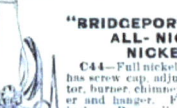

C44—Full nickel plated, fount has screw cap, adjustable reflector, burner, chimney, finger holder and hanger. Full height 8 inches. Burns all night without odor. 1 doz. in pkg. Per dozen, $2.00

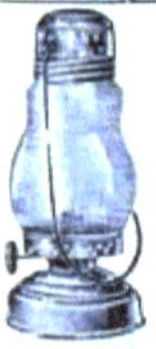

"THE JEWEL" DIME LANTERN.

Biggest seller on the market. Specially packed 1 dozen in spaced box.

C46—Same size and style as the brass lantern which costs twice as much, only made of heavy tin, height not including handle 7 inches. A complete lantern in every particular. 1 doz. in box, complete with wick. Per dozen, 96c

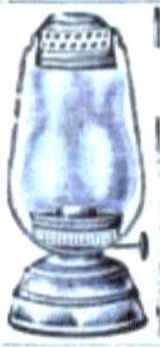

"KLONDIKE" LANTERN—Brass Trimmed.

A splendid 25-cent bargain.

C43—A perfect lantern in every detail, swinging handle, complete with wick and glass globe. Full height, not including handle, 7¼ inches. All brass ventilated top. Of endless utility and just the thing for bicycles, as it can be swung on handle bar or carried in hand. ½ doz. in box. Per dozen, $1.80

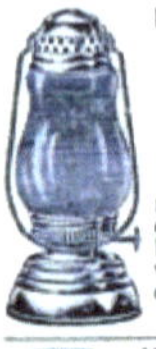

BRASS TRIMMED LANTERN with Red, White and Blue Globes.

A quick seller at 25c.

C45—A perfect lantern in every respect, full height including handle 11½ inches. Complete with burner, wick and assorted red white and blue glass globes. Colors equally assorted in box of ½ doz. Per dozen, $2.10

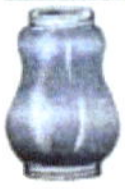

"KLONDIKE" LANTERN GLOBES.

—To fit "Klondike" lanterns. 1 doz. in pkg. Securely packed in paste board box for safe shipment. Per dozen, 40c

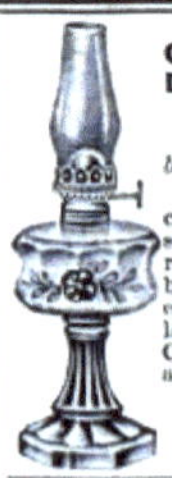

OUR "FLORAL DECORATED" ETCHED NIGHT LAMP.

Regular 25-center to retail on bargain day at, say, 19c.

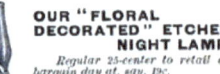

C725—Full height including chimney 9-in., new and fancy shape, stand being decorated in rich red with satin edge fount, embossed and decorated in rich colored floral designs. A dainty little lamp that is sure to be a seller. Complete with burners, chimneys and wicks. ½ doz. in box. Per dozen, $1.60

DECORATED ETCHED GLOBE NIGHT LAMP.

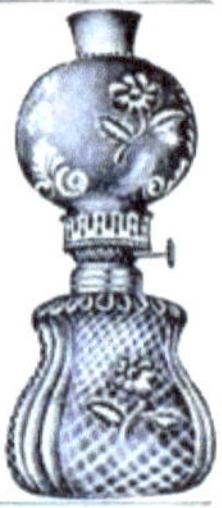

C723—Full height 9¼ in., large and shapely fount, fitted with best brass collar, "Gem" burner and wick, large globe. Both fount and globe of satin etched glass embossed and profusely decorated in gold and rich colored floral designs. 3 colors, blue, green and amethyst. Each in carton. ½ doz. in pkg. Per dozen, $2.25

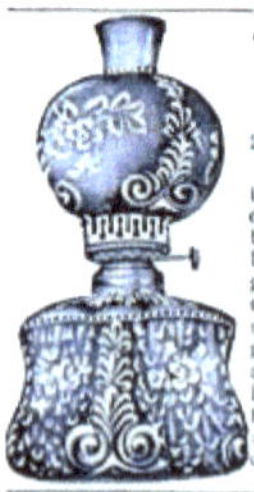

"OUR BOUDOIR" GLOBE NIGHT LAMP.

A regular 50-center at a 25-cent price.

C722—Full ht. 9 in., extra large square front or oil receptacle, fitted with best brass collar, "Gem" burner and wick, large globe chimney in 3 rich colors, blue, green and amethyst, both lamp and globe artistically embossed and elaborately decorated in gold and natural color floral designs. Each in carton. ½ doz. in pkg., asstd. colors. Per dozen, $2.25

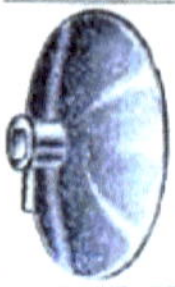

8-INCH SILVERED GLASS REFLECTOR.

C2—No. 2. Brightly silvered—not the dull goods. 1 doz. in case. Sold by case only. *no charge for case.* Doz., $1.75

The Sawyer-Man HIGH GRADE INCANDESCENT ELECTRIC LAMPS.

You can make a good profit on these and at the same time save your customers a big per cent over the prices charged by the electrical supply dealers.

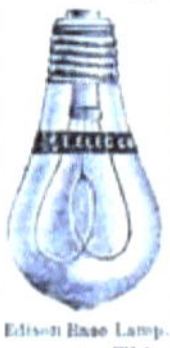

Edison Base Lamp.

. Made by the Sawyer-Man Electric Co.—the Incandescent Lamp Department of the Westinghouse Electric & Mfg. Co. We have tested all the different makes of lamps on the market and have found the Sawyer-Man Lamp to be the best for the following reasons: *First.* All bulbs are mold blown and made of the best lead glass. *Second:* Because the filaments are by electrically deposited carbon, not unreliable paste cement. *Third.* Because filaments are securely anchored rendering injury by jarring impossible. *Fourth.* Because lamps are carefully selected as to voltage and are absolutely uniform.

The Sawyer-Man lamps are longer lived than any other. They maintain rated candle power longer than any other. They use **less current** and give **more light** than any other. We guarantee every one to be mechanically and electrically perfect.

The standard candle powers most in use are 8 and 16. The 16 candle power is the one in common use for house and store purposes. Ninety per cent of the electric light companies run on a 110-volt circuit which is the voltage we carry in stock. **When ordering be sure and state the style of base wanted as the different bases are not interchangeable. Always order by our title number.**

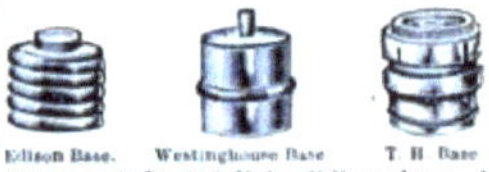

Edison Base. Westinghouse Base. T. H. Base

C302. 8 C. P., 110 Volt, Edison base. 1 doz. in box.......... Each	$0 20
C304. 16 C. P., 110 Volt, Edison base. 1 doz. in box.......... Each	20
C402. 8 C. P., 110 Volt, Westinghouse base. 1 doz. in box.......... Each	20
C404. 16 C. P., 110 Volt, Westinghouse base. 1 doz. in box.......... Each	20
C502. 8 C. P., 110 Volt, Thompson Houston base. 1 doz. in box..... Each	21
C504. 16 C. P., 110 Volt, Thompson Houston base. 1 doz. in box..... Each	21

NOTE—We can supply 10, 25 and 32 candle power in 110 volts on special orders.

Orders for **200 or more** shipped direct from factory at a discount of **2 cents** each from above prices.

That Customers Find Our Prices Low on Lamps Is Attested by Largely Increased Sales.

DECORATED TABLE LAMPS.

NOTICE! All of our lamps having fancy metal crowns are also fitted with a thin brass spun crown, which prevents the heavy metal from coming in contact with the glass—thus preventing breakage. All are complete INCLUDING CHIMNEYS. All our founts are of solid brass, not the cheap tin affairs used by some makers.

Artistic lamps below common lamp prices. One might expect to pay a premium for these masterly decorations, but we *never overlook the selling price*, and are able, therefore, to offer these truly artistic lamps *at prices below* the market on common goods. If you don't know our lamps order one package at random and you will then understand why we do the lamp business.

Assortment No. C2.
DECORATED GLOBE AND DOME TABLE LAMPS.
A rare assortment of $1.00 profit payers.

1:—An assortment of 8 lamps. 4 with dome shades, and 4 with globes, 1 each of 4 tints, namely: ruby, pink, green and white. Decorations are profuse and include such as wild roses and narcissus. Fitted complete, including No. 2 burner and chimney, full ht. 15-in. 4 with 7-in. dome shades, 4 with 7¼-in. globe shades. Total 8 in bbl., no two exactly alike. Sold only by assortment of 8 lamps. (Bbl. 35c.) Wt. 63 lbs.   **Each, 57c**

Assortment No. C7.
DECORATED GLOBE LAMPS.
An attractive and ornamental lamp at a price lower than usually charged for the common sort.

1:—This assortment consists of 4 lamps, all with 9-in. globes—2 ruby, 1 green and 1 yellow, all elaborately decorated in beautiful rose designs in bright colors which harmonize with the tints. All have large semi-squat shaped bodies and the best gilt finished openwork metal bases. Fitted with best No. 3 Climax burners, 4-in. shade ring. Full ht. to top of chimney, 19½ in. 4 lamps in bbl. (complete with chimney), wt. 56 lbs. Sold only by the bbl. (Bbl. 35c.)   **Each, $1.40**

Assortment No. C13—PARLOR GLOBE LAMPS.
Lamps which for genuine good value have no equal.

1:—Assortment comprises 2 lamps, both with 10-in. globes. One, the popular low squat shape, extra wide body, diam. about 10-in. globe and body tinted in combination light and dark green with extra large chrysanthemum decorations in lavender and white, hand painted and heavily enameled, full height to top of chimney 21½ in. The other, a tall artistically-shaped lamp in rich ruby tint shading to pale yellow, elaborate wild rose decorations in purple and yellow with dark green leaves. Full ht. 24½-in. Extra heavy gilt finish metal bases and removable brass founts, fitted with No. 2 Royal center draft burners, 4-in. shade rings and chimneys. 2 lamps in barrel complete with chimneys. Sold only by barrel. (Bbl. 35c.)   **Each, $2.95**

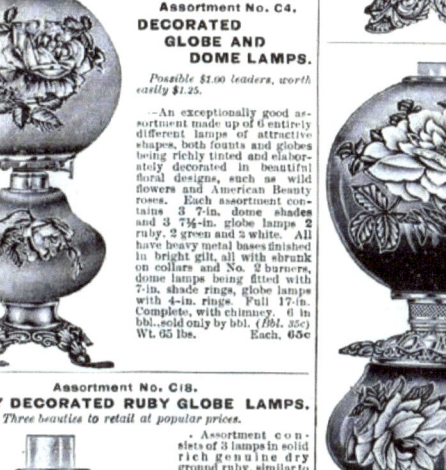

Assortment No. C4.
DECORATED GLOBE AND DOME LAMPS.
Possible $1.00 leaders, worth easily $1.25.

—An exceptionally good assortment made up of 6 entirely different lamps of attractive shapes, both founts and globes being richly tinted and elaborately decorated in beautiful floral designs, such as wild flowers and American Beauty roses. Each assortment contains 3 7-in. dome shades and 3 7¼-in. globe lamps, 2 ruby, 2 green and 2 white. All have heavy metal bases finished in bright gilt, all with shrunk on collars and No. 2 burners, dome lamps being fitted with 7-in. shade rings, globe lamps with 4-in. shade rings. Full 17-in. Complete, with chimney. 6 in bbl., sold only by bbl. (Bbl. 35c.) Wt. 65 lbs.   **Each, 65c**

Assortm't No. C15.
SUPERBLY DECORATED GLOBE LAMPS.
Two beautiful specimens of decorative art.

Assortment comprises 2 lamps, each with 10-in. globe. One an extra tall vase shape full height to top of chimney 25½ in., fancy swell body, limoges ground in combination of ivory, pink and green, giving rich mottled effect, very profuse decorations in dark red and white chrysanthemums richly enameled. The other a semi-tall lamp, full height 24-in., extra large swell shape body tinted in rich blended ruby and carmine forming solid ground, decorations in large and heavily enameled ten roses in handpainted design being in a combination of white, yellow and green. Extra large and heavy gilt finish metal bases, elaborate crowns, removable brass founts, fitted with No. 2 Royal center draft burners, 4-in. shade rings and No. 2 Rochester chimneys. 2 in barrel complete, with chimneys. Sold only by barrel. (Bbl. 35c.)   **Each, $3.40**

Assortment No. C18.
RICHLY DECORATED RUBY GLOBE LAMPS.
Three beauties to retail at popular prices.

—Assortment consists of 3 lamps in solid rich genuine dry ground ruby, similar to the popular Crown Derby maroon. One style has white and pink shaded roses decoration, one with large rose and leaf design in delicate yellow tint, one with large white poppy decoration. All decorations hand painted and enameled. Gilt finish metal open work bases and crowns, removable brass founts, fitted with No. 2 Royal center draft burners, 4-in. shade rings and No. 2 Rochester chimneys. Assortment comprises the following: Each.
1 only Medium tall lamp, with 9-inch globe. Full ht. to top of chimney 21½-in. . $2 65
1 only Swell shape lamp with 9-inch globe. Full ht. to top of chimney 22½ inches. . 2 95
1 only Extra large lamp with 10-inch globe. Full ht. to top of chimney 26 inches. . 3 65
Total for assortment. . $9.25
Sold only by assortment of 3 lamps complete, including chimneys. (Bbl. 35c.)

Assortment No. C29.
SAMPLE CASK Assortment of DECORATED LAMPS.
Special 5 per cent reduction to induce you to test our values.

:—For the small merchant this is an ideal assortment, for it gives large variety for a very small outlay. For the large merchant it is emphatically his best opportunity to test the best line in America with but small investment to himself. All lamps are complete, including chimneys, and are *fully described elsewhere* on these pages.

Assortment comprises the following:
One only Combination Globe shade, pink, as in Asst. No. 1 . . . . $0 39
One only 7¼-in. Globe, green, as in Asst. No. 2. .   57
" 7-in. Dome Shade, ruby, as in Asst. No. 2. .   57
" 7¼-in. Globe, white, as in Asst. No. 4 . .   67
" 8¼-in. Dome Shade, ruby, as in Asst. No. 6   84
One only Center Draft, 8-in. Globe, vignette, as in Asst. No. 8 . . . . 1 50
One only Center Draft, 10-in. Globe, green, as in Asst. No. 10 . . . . 1 95
One only Center Draft, 10-in. Globe, ivory, pink and green mottled, as in Asst. No. 15 . . . . 3 40
Total at regular prices. $9 89
Less special 5 per cent.   50
Net total for 8 lamps. $9.39
Sold only by assortment of 8 lamps complete, with chimneys. (Wt. 83 lbs., Cask 75c.)

TALL PARLOR OR BANQUET GLOBE LAMP.
Note the extra large size and the exceedingly small price.

C171. 27-in. high to top of chimney, swell shape body, 11-in. globe. Globe and body tinted in a combination dark red and green artistically blended, large chrysanthemum decorations in red and white with yellow center, hand painted and heavily enameled, heavy elaborate gilt finish metal base and crown, removable brass fount, fitted with No. 2 Royal center draft burner, 4-in. shade ring, No. 2 21-in. Rochester chimney. One of the handsomest medium priced lamps ever produced. Each in barrel complete, including chimney. (Bbl. 35c.)   **Each, $3.60**
Wt. 45 lbs.

If in Doubt Where to Buy Lamps, Send For a Few Sample Packages and Compare.

We Could Not Afford to Name Prices Like These With Any Other Salesman Than Printer's Ink.

"BIG BARGAIN" PARLOR GLOBE LAMP.

An extra large lamp at an exceptionally small price.

C16—Popular squat shape, having massive low shape body and 11 in. globe. The color is a beautiful shade of pink, decorations are large wild flowers in pink and white with delicate green leaves. Lamp is fitted with extra large and extra heavy gilt finished metal base and crown with removable brass fount, fitted with No. 2 Royal center draft burner, 4-in. globe ring and chimney. Full ht. of lamp to top of chimney 24¾-in., complete with chimney. (Bbl. 35c.) Each, **$3.75**

"MAGNIFICENT" RUBY GLOBE LAMP.

One of the best values we offer.

C20. Extra large and unusually attractive. Semi-squat shape body, diam. about 11½ in., 11-in. globe, both body and globe in solid genuine dry ground ruby decorated with cosmos in white with green and delicate blue shaded tints, not the usual scant decorations but very elaborate and hand painted, also richly enameled. Very heavy gilt finish, metal openwork base and fancy scalloped design crown, removable brass fount, fitted with No. 2 Royal center draft burner, 4-in. shade ring, No. 2 Rochester chimney. Full ht. to top of chimney 24¾-in. Will prove a rapid seller. Each in barrel complete, including chimney. (Bbl. 35c.) Each, **$4.45**

Assortment C14 OUR BIG "SPECIAL" DECORATED GLOBE LAMPS.

Largest and most attractive lamps ever offered at so low a price.

Asst. C14;. 2 lamps—one in green tint, the other in pink and yellow shaded effect, extra tall, full ht. to top of chimney 26¾-in., large fancy swell shape bodies, extra large 11-in. globes. Tinted in entirely new mottled effect, elaborate and over decoration of wild roses in deep pink and light yellow with green leaves, extra large heavy gilt finish metal bases and fancy crowns, removable brass founts fitted with No. 2 Royal center draft burners, 4-in. shade rings, and No. 2 Rochester chimneys. 2 lamps in bbl. complete, including chimneys. Sold only by bbl. wt. 58 lbs. Each, **$3.60**

Assortment No. C19. BEAUTIFUL 10-INCH GLOBE LAMPS.

Two elegant lamps on which you can realize a fine profit.

1. Assortment consists of 2 lamps, both of the same shape. Exceptionally beautiful design, having large swell shape bodies. Extra large, 10-in. globes. One is solid genuine dry ground ruby, the other with entirely new limoges mottled ground in pink, green and yellow effect; both having elaborate enameled decorations in rich carnation design in pink and white. Heavy and artistic gilt finish metal bases and crowns, removable brass founts. fitted with No. 2 Royal center draft burners, 4-in. shade rings, and No. 2 Rochester chimneys. Full ht. to top of chimney 24¾-in. Sold only by asst. of 2 lamps complete, including chimneys, wt. 55 lbs. (Bbl. 35c.) Each, **$3.75**

"EXHIBITION" GLOBE LAMP.

Beautiful beyond description. The illustration fails to do it justice.

C26;. This extra large and beautiful lamp is one of the richest ever produced, has extra large vase shape body, circumference 30¼ in., extra large globe, diam. 12-in., circumference 38½. Both lamp and globe have the rich limoges ground, which is a combination of delicate pink and green shaded tints, producing an unusually beautiful effect. Decorations are in large roses in deep pink and white with green leaves, hand painted, richly enameled and very elaborate, being on both sides of the lamp. Large and artistically designed gilt finished metal base and crown, removable brass fount. Fitted with No. 2 Royal center draft burner, 4-in. globe ring and No. 2 12-inch Rochester chimney. Full ht. of lamp to top of chimney 30-in. Each in barrel complete including chimney. (Bbl. 35c.) Each, **$6.50**

OUR "RICH RUBY" PARLOR GLOBE LAMP.

Another beauty possessing matchless selling qualities.

C24;. Extra large, the popular and beautiful low shape, mammoth squat shape body circumference about 38-inch, mammoth 12-in. globe, both lamp and globe in solid genuine dry ground ruby. Richly enameled and hand painted chrysanthemum decorations in a combination of white and heliotrope with delicate green leaves, the decorations being very profuse and beautiful. Fitted with heavy fancy design gilt finished metal base and crown, removable brass fount. No. 2 Royal center draft burner, 4-in. globe ring and No. 2 Rochester chimney. Full ht. to top of chimney 25½-in. Each in bbl complete with chimney. Wt. 45 lbs. (Bbl. 35c.) Each, **$5.50**

OUR "EXQUISITE METAL HANDLED" GLOBE LAMP.

C25—Large round swell shape body and 10-in. globe in combination of delicate green and pink, giving a rich mottled effect. Decorations are in hand painted wild roses in white and pink with green leaves, richly enameled. Old English brass and verde finished metal base, crown and frame with double handles, removable fount finished to match crown. Fitted with No 2 Royal center draft burner, 4-in. globe ring, No. 2 Rochester chimney. Full ht. to top of chimney 23-in. Each in small bbl. complete with chimney. (Bbl. 25c.) Wt. 30 lbs. Each, **$5.75**

Our "SUSPENSION" Brass Hall Lamp.

A staple $1.50 seller at a dollar bargain price.

C150.—Genuine brass trimmed, adjustable brass chains for lowering lamp, large twist pattern globe in 3 rich colors. Ht. of globe 7½-in. circumference 22. Complete with fount, burner and chimney, 2 ruby 2 blue and 2 opalescent. total 6 complete lamps in bbl. Wt. 50 lbs. (Bbl. 35c.) Each, **72c**

NICKEL PLATED TABLE LAMP.

Fitted With Center Draft Burner.

An extra large lamp at a price which makes it one of the rarest bargains we have ever offered.

C32;. Made of solid brass, heavily nickel plated, good wide base, fount with outside fillers, complete with nickel plated tripod, 10-in. dome and Rochester chimney. Full height of lamp to top of chimney 19¼ in. 4 complete lamps in bbl. Wt. 45 lbs. (Bbl. 35c.) Each, **$1.15**

These High-Grade Decorated Lamps Are the Most Artistic in Design and Description on the Market.

We Drum Up Trade by Clear Statements, Low Prices and Goods of Honest Quality.

NICKEL TABLE OR SEWING LAMP.

Ordinarily you would pay 65c for a lamp as good as this one.

C1824—Full nickel plated, No. 2 nickel plated burner, 10 inches high without chimney. Outside filling device, extension wick raiser, broad safety base. Each in pasteboard box. Each, **45c**

We have found it—just what you have been looking for.

IMPROVED "AMERICAN" ARC PRESSURE LAMP.

New and improved style, splendid illuminators, reasonable in cost.

C540:.For indoor use. About 800-candle illuminating power—more than 5 times that of the ordinary gravity gasoline lamps. The best substitute for electric arc light yet devised and perfectly safe, being approved by the National Board of Fire Insurance Underwriters. When the gasoline in the reservoir is renewed it is put under an arc pressure by means of a pump. Handsomely finished in oxidized copper, height 30 in., wt. 10¾ lbs., 3½-qt. reservoir, fitted with nickeled reflector, mantle, chimney and extra quality 16-in. pump complete. Each in case, no charge for case............Each **$8 25**

C541:.Fitted with pressure gauge as shown on cut..................Each **9 50**

C542:.For outdoor use. As above, except fitted with a heavy hood and globe, thus protecting the generator and mantle. Each in case, no charge for case... Each **9 00**

Note:.We can furnish a pressure gauge with which you can tell the exact pressure on your lamp..............................Each **1 25**

> The "American" Arc Pressure Lamp — better than any other—absolutely safe and costs ridiculously little to run.

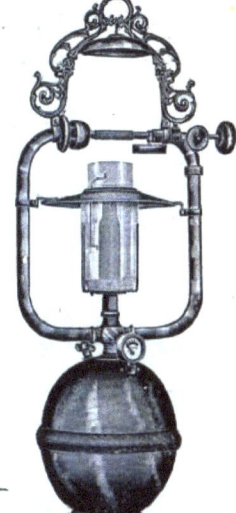

THE NEW "POWERFUL" ARC PRESSURE LAMP.

C543:. 600 candle power, 3½-qt. reservoir, nickel plated. So constructed that they are absolutely proof against leakage and explosion. Each reservoir tested to 150 lbs. pressure to square inch. With the new sub-flame generator used in this lamp flame can be turned nearly out and allowed to burn as long as desired. Fitted with an eccentric cleaning needle, which operates independent of the stop valve, polished metallic shade, safety filler plug. Each lamp complete with mantel, pump, alcohol can, wrench and torch. Each in box, no charge for pkg. Wt. complete 12 lbs. Each, **$6.20**

C544:. As above, only fitted with finely adjusted gauge, which shows the exact amount of pressure in reservoir. Each, **$7.50**

"UNIVERSAL" COMPLETE READING or SEWING LAMP.

A big dollar article.

C31:. Best brass fount with outside filler, full nickel plated, height 8 inches, fitted with best No. 2 nickel burner, 7 in. nickel shade ring, best imported opal dome shade and No. 2 crimped top chimney. Full height to top of chimney, 16½-in. Each, **62c** (*Total 8 complete lamps in bbl. Bbl. 35c.*)

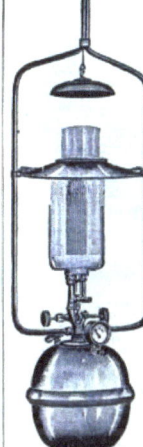

"BEACON" ARC PRESSURE LAMP.

Underneath Generator.

Simple in construction and easy to operate, safe and economical, needs no glass, globe nor shade, thus eliminating breakage.

APPROVED BY THE NATIONAL BOARD FIRE INSURANCE UNDERWRITERS.

C550, For indoor use, 600 candle power:. Guaranteed mechanically perfect. Will brilliantly light a room 30 feet square. Height 34 inches, full nickel plated, removable polished metal reflector, 3½-quart reservoir. Complete with 16-in. pump for pumping in air, wrench, torch funnel and mantle. Do not use chimney unless lamp is in a draft. Manufacturer's guarantee and full instructions for operating accompanying each. Each in case, no pkg. charge. Each, **$5.75**

Mantels for "Beacon" Lamp.

C1928:.Made specially for above lamp. Each, **15c** (In lots of 50 or more 14c.)

Assortment C105. NICKEL PLATED ROYAL CENTER DRAFT READING LAMPS.

Staple lamps at less than staple prices.

—Complete, including 10-inch dome shades, chimneys and tripods. Height to top of shade, 17 inches. All finely nickel plated and best grade. Center draft, 3 styles. Each

One No. 1, plain **$1 25**
One No. 2, fleur-de-lis embossed **1 35**
One No. 3, fancy cast metal foot. **1 50**

Total **$4.10**

(3 complete lamps in case. Case 25c.)

The New "ECLIPSE" ALL BRASS GASOLINE GAS LAMPS.

The best and most economical lighting device ever offered. The approximate cost of operating this lamp is only one-seventh of a cent per hour, or about 25 cents per month for each 100-candle power burner. The "ECLIPSE" GASOLINE GAS LAMPS are the most perfect lamps of their kind. They are superior to and more economical than either gas or electricity. Made entirely of brass of the heaviest desirable weight and highest quality, finished in best possible manner.

Latest improved under-generator type, the gas being generated immediately below point of combustion, insuring perfect generation and obviating the necessity of a sub-flame, with a consequent saving in fuel of at least 20 per cent. They are positively non-explosive and absolutely safe, though exceedingly simple throughout. Strongly made, and will last a lifetime. Our prices for these all-brass lamps cannot be equaled.

C300:.All polished brass, harp pattern, 100-candle power, 3-pint reservoir of 24-gauge brass. Length 35-in., wt. complete 3 lbs. A very popular style, suitable for every kind of indoor lighting. We recommend it for residences..............Each **$3 60**

C302:.Polished brass, double pendant, 200-candle power, 5-pint reservoir. Length 41 in., spread of arms 30, wt. complete 4 lbs. Especially designed for stores, halls and churches.... Each **4 75**

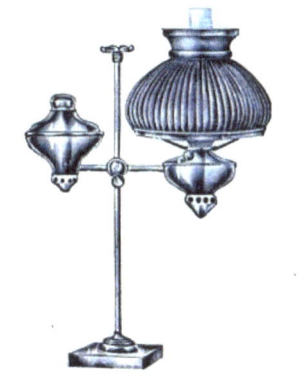

STUDENT LAMP.

One of the most staple sellers in the entire lamp department.

C35. Made of brass, bright copper plate, extra heavy metal base, fancy shaped fount and screw attachment for raising and lowering lamp, fitted with the best burner, 7-in. shade ring, fancy fluted green shade and chimney. Each in complete case. Each, **$2.87**

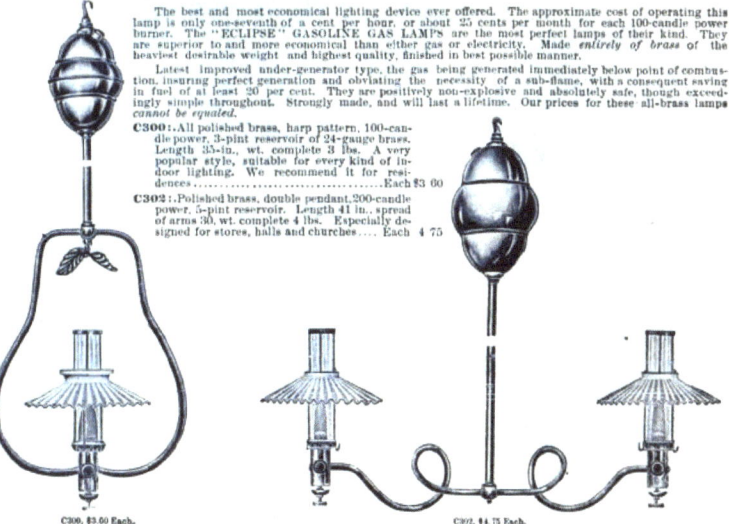

C300, $3.60 Each. C302, $4.75 Each.

Every Penny We Are Able to Save Through Close Buying Is at All Times Shared With Our Customers.

We Have Tested Every Make of Gasoline Store Lamp Made—THIS IS THE BEST.

Improved "SUNS=RAY" Incandescent Gasoline Gas Lamp

We invite comparison of "Suns-Ray" with any lamp made no matter how much greater the price.

We offer the "Suns-Ray," not merely as the best for the price, but **THE BEST AT ANY PRICE**. We know whereof we speak. We tested every gasoline gas lamp in America before we settled on the "Suns-Ray." It is no experiment. It has stood the test of use. Buy one to use in your store. It will advertise itself and you.

All the following "SUNS-RAY" VAPOR LAMPS (excepting Nos. C50, C150 and C250) are equipped with removable safety tanks holding about one quart, which is sufficient to keep one burner burning about 16 hours with one filling; the cleanest, most convenient and safest device ever invented. Finished in first-class shape and workmanlike manner and **elegantly nickel-plated**. ONE RATCHET only to be operated, to be turned on full and let alone, just like ordinary gas. Thumb screw at bottom has needle attached at top and only screwed up and down occasionally to clean hole in the burner nipple. Fill pan below burner with wood alcohol, burn this entirely out, heating burner sufficiently to generate gas, turn on gasoline, then light at top of chimney. A small bent-spout oil can for the wood alcohol accompanies each lamp. Throws a steady and even light of about one hundred candle power for each burner—more light for less money than any other device. Desirable as well in the farm house as in the city residence, store, office or hall. Gas and electricity are outdone, as a much cheaper and very much better light is now placed within the reach of all. The cost is moderate and there is nothing you can put into your home, store or office that will yield greater returns.

Illustration to left shows burner of the SUNS-RAY with chimney gallery raised.

C50: Wall or bracket lamp. A popular store or hall fixture, can be raised or lowered with thumb screw. Japanned tubing, maroon enameled cast metal work, stationary polished brass reservoir......Complete **$3.00**

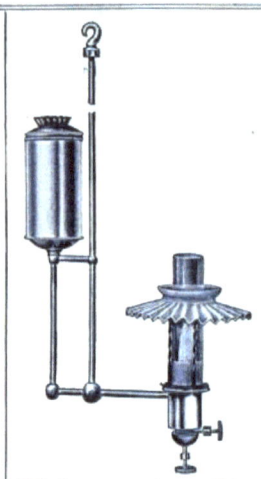

C100: One-light pendant. Full nickel plate, with removable reservoir. Length 40 inches, spread over all 16.....Complete **$3.95**

C150: One-light pendant. A good practical gas lamp. Stationary polished brass reservoir, japanned tubing, maroon enameled cast ornament. Length 33 inches. Complete **$3.00**

THE "SUNS-RAY" 100-Candle Power **STUDENT LAMP.**

C500: Elegant desk or table lamp. Height 26¾ inches, spread over all 16 inches, elaborately nickel plated. Removable reservoir. Complete (ready to light) with opal glass shade, chimney and mantle. Would be good value at $5.00 wholesale and should retail from $6.00 to $8.00. The ideal lamp for reading and needlework. Complete **$4.20**

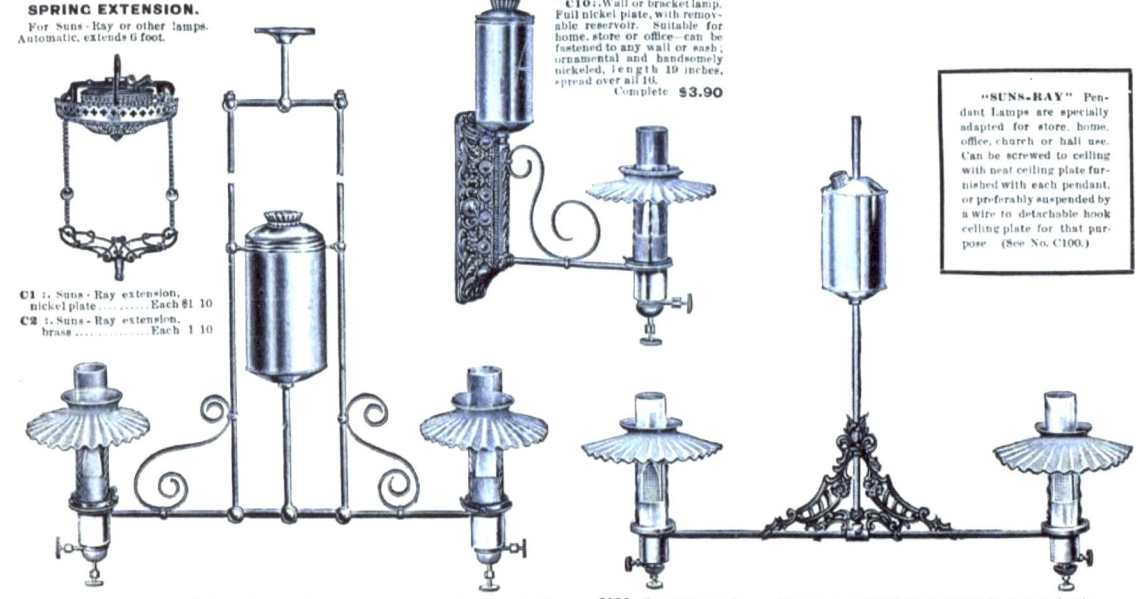

SPRING EXTENSION. For Suns-Ray or other lamps. Automatic, extends 6 foot.

C1: Suns-Ray extension, nickel plate..........Each $1.10
C2: Suns-Ray extension, brass..............Each 1.10

C10: Wall or bracket lamp. Full nickel plate, with removable reservoir. Suitable for home, store or office—can be fastened to any wall or sash; ornamental and handsomely nickeled, length 19 inches, spread over all 16. Complete **$3.90**

C200: Two-light pendant. Full nickel plate with removable reservoir. Complete **$6.00**

C250: Two-light pendant. Stationary, polished brass reservoir, japanned tubing, maroon enameled cast ornament. Length 33 inches......Complete **$4.40**

"SUNS-RAY" Pendant Lamps are specially adapted for store, home, office, church or hall use. Can be screwed to ceiling with neat ceiling plate furnished with each pendant, or preferably suspended by a wire to detachable hook ceiling plate for that purpose. (See No. C100.)

The Best Store Lamp Ever Invented—Good Strong Light and Perfectly Safe.

"New PEERLESS" WHITE GRANITE WARE

SHIPPED FROM POTTERY.

FINEST QUALITY, light weight, new and attractive shapes. **Every piece absolutely warranted not to craze.** It is positively worth **10 to 20 per cent more** than some well known lines. Send for a package and if the ware is not **equal to any other** hold it **subject to our order.** All of these are "run-of-the-kiln" goods, but *after the thirds have been taken out.* In pattern, in finish and in strength "Peerless" ware has no equal. *Order a sample lot and compare with any in the market.*

60 PER CENT FROM W. G. LIST—The net prices given below are figured at exactly 60 per cent from the standard White Granite List, adopted by all the potters of America.

Shipped Direct from Our Central Warehouse. **"Peerless" ware is shipped direct from our warehouse near Bellaire, Ohio, from which point we have obtained advantageous freight rates.**

NOTE—Packages will be charged according to the never broken rule among crockery manufacturers. **No charge for cartage.**

☞ *We are now making unusually prompt shipments.*

Fancy Echo Shape—"NEW PEERLESS" WHITE GRANITE WARE.

To assist customers in ordering we give actual measurements of some items which are occasionally misunderstood. IN ORDERING BE SURE TO ONLY GIVE THE FIRST OR TRADE SIZE.

Bakers' or Vegetable Dishes—	Doz.
6 - inch (actual size 8 inch)	$0 80
7 " " 9 "	96
8 " " 9¾ "	1 44
Butters—	
Individual, 2½-inch (actual size 3-in.)	16
Covered, loose drainers, 5-inch	2 88

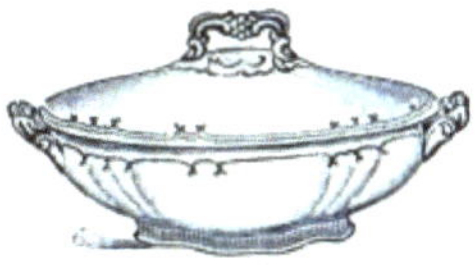

Casserole.

Casseroles (Covered Vegetable Dishes)— Round, 8-inch (actual 10½ inch)	4 32

Covered Dish.

Covered Dishes—Oval shape. 8-inch, oval (actual size 10-inch)	3 84
Cake Plates— Actual size 10¾-in.	1 20
Cups and Saucers—Each doz. comprises 12 cups and 12 saucers.	
Teas, handled fancy ovide shape	64
" cups only, handled	37
" saucers only	27
Coffees, handled, fancy ovide shape	75
" cups only, handled	43
" saucers only	32
Coupe Soups— 7-in. (actual size 7¾-in.)	52

Cream.

Sugar.

Creams— 24s (actual size 1½-pint)	96
Sugars— Round, 24s	2 16
Sauce Tureens Only	2 64

Oval Soup Tureen.

Oval Soup Tureens	8 96
Oyster Tureens	6 40
Pickle Dishes	96
Sauce Boat— Single	1 28
Slop Bowl	64

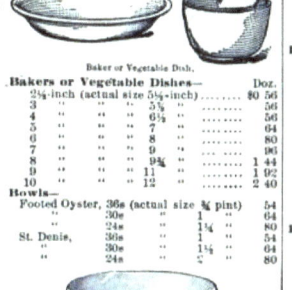

Teapot

Teapots—	Doz.
24s	$2 56

Plate.

Plates—	
Flat, 4 - inch (actual size 6-inch)	28
" 5 " " 7½ "	36
" 6 " " 8¼ "	44
" 7 " " 9½ "	52
" 8 " " 10½ "	60
Deep 7-inch (actual size 9-inch)	52
Dishes or Platters—	
Single thick, 4- inch (actual 7 - in.)	48
" " 6 " " 10 "	56
" " 7 " " 11 "	64
" " 8 " " 12 "	80
" " 10 " " 13¾ "	1 44
" " 12 " " 16 "	2 40
" " 14 " " 19 "	3 36
" " 16 " " 20½ "	5 28
Fruit Saucers—	
Round, 4 -inch (actual size 5-inch)	24
" 4½ " " " 5½ "	26
Jugs—	
42s (actual size ½-pint)	69
36s " 1 "	80
30s " 2 "	96
24s " 3 "	1 12
12s " 4 "	1 92
6s " 6 "	2 88
Nappies—	
Scalloped, 3-inch (actual size 4½-in.)	56
" 4 " " 5½ "	56
" 5 " " 6¾ "	64
" 6 " " 7 "	80
" 7 " " 8¾ "	96
" 8 " " 9 "	1 44
" 9 " " 10¾ "	1 92

Combinet or Slop Pail.

C59, Combinet or Slop Pail— Ht. 11 in., circumference 32¼ in. Each $0 67

"PEERLESS" WHITE GRANITE NESTED NAPPIES—*From Pottery.*

C35—A nest comprises one each of eight sizes of deep nappies in regulation sizes from 4½ to 11-in. in diameter (actual size). *At regular prices these nests would figure 77c.*

Per nest, **75c**

(6 nests or 48 nappies in bbl. Bbl. 40c.)

"PLAIN PEERLESS" WHITE GRANITE WARE.

Same grade as "New Peerless" only in the standard regulation plain pattern.

Baker or Vegetable Dish.

Bakers or Vegetable Dishes—	Doz.
2½-inch (actual size 5½-inch)	$0 56
3 " " " 5¾ "	56
4 " " " 6½ "	56
5 " " " 7 "	64
6 " " " 8 "	80
7 " " " 9 "	96
8 " " " 9¾ "	1 44
9 " " " 11 "	1 92
10 " " " 12 "	2 40
Bowls—	
Footed Oyster, 36s (actual size ¾ pint)	54
" 30s " 1 "	64
" 24s " 1¼ "	80
St. Denis, 36s " 1 "	54
" 30s " 1½ "	64
" 24s " 2 "	80

Footed Punch or Soup Bowl.

Footed Punch or Soup Bowls—	
7-inch (actual size 8½-inch)	2 40
8 " " 9¾ "	3 20
9 " " 10½ "	3 60
10 " " 12 "	4 80
Butters— Individual, 2½-in. (actual 3-in.)	16
Cake Plates— Actual size 10¾-inch	1 20
Coffees—Each dozen comprises 12 cups and 12 saucers.	
St. Denis, handled	75
" unhandled	64
" cups only, handled	43
" " unhandled	32
" saucers only	32
Creams— Individual Restaurant	50
Fruit Saucers—	
Round, 4 in. (actual size 5 in.)	24
" 4½ " " " 5½ "	26
Ice Creams—	
3½ in. (actual size 4½ in)	20
4 " " " 5 "	22

Jugs.

Jugs—	
42s (actual size ½ pint)	69
36s " " 1 "	80
30s " " 2 "	96
24s " " 3 "	1 12
12s " " 4 "	1 92
6s " " 6 "	2 88
4s " " 7 "	4 32
Nappies, Scalloped—	
3-inch (actual size 4½-inch)	56
4 " " " 5½ "	56
5 " " " 6¾ "	64
6 " " " 7 "	80
7 " " " 8¾ "	96
8 " " " 9 "	1 44
9 " " " 10¾ "	1 92
10 " " " 11 "	2 40
Egg Cups—Double	56
Mugs—	
36s (actual size ½-pint)	50
30s " " ¾ "	61
24s " " 1 "	76

Platter.

Dishes or Platters—	Doz.
Double thick, 2½ in. (actual 5¾ in.)	$0 48
" " 3 " " 6½ "	48
" " 4 " " 7 "	48
" " 5 " " 8 "	52
" " 6 " " 9 "	56
Single " 5 " " 9 "	52
" " 6 " " 10 "	56
" " 7 " " 11 "	64
" " 8 " " 12 "	80
" " 9 " " 12¾ "	96
" " 10 " " 13¾ "	1 44
" " 11 " " 14½ "	1 92
" " 12 " " 16 "	2 40
" " 14 " " 19 "	3 36
" " 16 " " 20½ "	5 28
Plates—	
Flat, 3-inch (actual size 5- inch)	24
" 4 " " " 6 "	28
" 5 " " " 7½ "	36
" 6 " " " 8¼ "	44
" 7 " " " 9½ "	52
" 8 " " " 10½ "	60
Deep, 6 " " " 8¼ "	44
" 7 " " " 9 "	52
Plates—Flat, double thick.	
5-inch (actual size 7¼-inch)	36
6 " " " 8¼ "	44
7 " " " 9¼ "	52
Soup Ladles—	
No. 2	2 40
No. 1	2 88

Baltimore, Unhandled.

St. Denis, Handled.

Teas—Each dozen comprises 12 cups and 12 saucers.	
St. Denis, unhandled	54
" handled	64
" cups only, handled	37
" " unhandled	27
" saucers only	27
Baltimore, unhandled	44
" handled	54
" cups only, handled	32
" " unhandled	22
" saucers only	22
Soap Slabs—	48
Square, fast drainer	1 00
Chambers—	
Uncovered, 12s	1 92
" 9s	2 56
" 6s	2 88
Covered, 12s	2 88
" 9s	3 84
" 6s	4 32
Slop Jars—3's	11 52
" 2's	15 36
Slop Pails— Handled, funnel top	9 60

Ewer and Basin.

Ewers and Basins—	
Complete, 9s	6 88
Ewers only— 9s	3 84
Basins only— 9s	3 04
Spittoons—Low parlor cuspidor	2 40

SCHEDULE OF PACKAGE CHARGES.

Following is the scale of package charges as provided by the Association of Crockery Manufacturers. If any customer thinks he has been overcharged he can readily settle the matter for himself by measuring the cask or barrel and referring to this scale for the proper charge. If an over-charge has been made please report same to us with all necessary facts, and we will bring the matter to the attention of the pottery.

Cask No. 0—Head 40- inch, stave 42- inch	$2 25	Half Bbl. Head 14½-in., stave 24 - in.	$0 35
" 1 " 38 " " 42 "	2 00	Small " " 17½ " " 28½ "	40
" 2 " 35 " " 40 "	1 90	Bbl. No. 1 " 18½ " " 30 "	40
" 3 " 33 " " 40 "	1 75	" 2 " 19½ " " 30 "	50
" 4 " 29½ " " 34 "	1 50	" 3 " 20½ " " 30 "	50
" 5 " 25½ " " 34 "	1 25	" 4 " 21½ " " 32 "	50
" 7 " 21½ " " 34 "	1 10	Tierces. 24 "	75
" 6 " 25½ " " 30 "	90	" 22 "	60

Our Tender of Potential Cash for Great Quantities Makes Makers Figure to the Closest Notch.

DON'T BE SATISFIED With the Business You Now Have—Be On the Lookout for More.

ASSORTMENT OF "PEERLESS" WHITE GRANITE WARE.

Shipped direct from pottery.

For the convenience of our customers we have arranged the following assortments of our "Peerless" W. G. ware. Asst. No. 30 gives a fairly complete variety of the most staple sellers. Assts. Nos. 31, 32, and 33 are intended to supply the items which naturally sell out first. We will carry these in stock at the pottery, packed ready for shipment at all times, and by having a large number packed at one time we are enabled to offer them at the same net prices which are figured at the same discounts as the regular line.

Assortment No. C30—All in the fancy "Echo" shape.

					Doz.	
2 doz.	5-in. plates (actual size 7¾-in.)				36	$0 72
2 "	6 "	"	"	8¼ "	44	88
4 "	7 "	"	"	9¼ "	52	2 08
1 "	8 "	"	"	10¼ "		60
2 "	7 " deep plates(actual size 9¼-in.)				52	1 04
6 "	handled teacups and saucers				64	3 84
1 "	" coffee " "					75
1 "	6-in. bakers (actual size 8 -in.)					80
"	7 " " " 9 "					96
½ "	8 " " " 9¾ "				1 44	72
¼ "	Sauce boats				1 28	32
1 "	5-in. nappies (actual size 6½-in.)					64
1 "	6 " " " 7 "					80
1 "	7 " " " 8¼ "					96
1 "	8 " " " 9 "					1 44
½ "	36's bowls, capacity ⅜ pint				54	27
¼ "	30's " 1 "				64	32
¼ "	8-in. covered dishes (actual 10-in.)				3 84	96
¼ "	36's jugs (capacity 1 pint)				80	40
¼ "	30's " 2 "				96	48
¼ "	8-in. dishes (actual 12-in.)				1 44	72
¼ "	10 " " 13 "					
Extra charge for cask						1 50
Total for 28 doz. in assortment						**$21.60**

Assortment No. C31—Fancy "Echo" shape.

					Doz.	
4 doz.	7-in. plates(actual size 9¼-in.)				52	2 08
4 "	Handled teacups and saucers				64	2 56
1 "	5-in. nappies (actual size 6½-in.)					64
"	6 " " " 7 "					80
½ "	7 " bakers " 9 "				96	48
½ "	8 " " " 9¾ "				1 44	72
8 "	dishes " 12 "				80	40
¼ "	30's jugs (capacity 2 pints)				96	48
Extra charge for cask						60
Total for 12 doz. in assortment						**$8.76**

Assortment No. C32—Regulation plain shape.

			Doz.	
6 doz. Baltimore handled tea-cups & saucers.			54	3 24
6 " 6-in. (actual size 8½-in.) plates			44	2 64
Extra charge for pkg				40
Total for 12 doz. in assortment				**$6.28**

Assortment No. C33—Regulation plain shape.

			Doz.	
6 doz. St. Denis handled tea-cups and saucers.			64	3 84
6 " plates (actual size 9½-in.)			52	3 12
Extra charge for tierce				50
Total for assortment of 12 dozen (complete)				**$7.46**

"All Sizes" Decorated LA BELLE CHINA JUG ASSORTMENT.

Shipped direct from pottery near Bellaire, O.

Matchless bargains to retail at from 15 to 50c.

C57 — Extra well made, good pure white La Belle china bodies in asstd. new and fancy shapes in 6 sizes from 1 to 5 pints. All are elaborately decorated in rich hand painted floral designs in natural colors, decorations being on both sides and also on the lips, all have rich gold clouded handles and edges, altogether making an exceptionally desirable asst. and one that will sell wherever shown. Total 2 doz. in pkg. pkg. 40c. Average price Per dozen, **$2.35**

DECORATED SEMI-PORCELAIN JUG ASST.

Regular 50-centers to retail at 25 cents. Shipped direct from pottery.

C55—Extra strong and well made, semi-porcelain body, in rich cream color, tall tankard shape, ht. 8-in., capacity 3 pints, large handle and good lip, profusely embossed and decorated in daffodils in natural colors. Assorted decorations in bbl. of 2 doz. Sold only by bbl. Bbl. 35c. Doz., **$1.95**

No cartage charge on any goods.

50% Off List On "PARIS WHITE" C. C. WARE

Shipped Direct from Pottery.

Positively warranted not to craze. Superior make, worth ten per cent more than most lines. We guarantee it superior, both in strength and finish, to any other C. C. ware produced in America. We name **net prices** which, when reduced by our cash discount, figure at exactly 50 per cent from the standard C. C. list, adopted by all the potters of America.

Shipped direct from our central warehouse near Bellaire, Ohio. You can have this and "Peerless" White Granite or "Bee Hive" decorated ware packed together, but in that case please be very explicit in stating your wants. Packages will be charged according to the never broken rule among crockery makers.

To assist customers in ordering we have given the actual measurements of some items which are occasionally misunderstood. In ordering, however, be sure to enter ONLY THE FIRST OR TRADE SIZE.

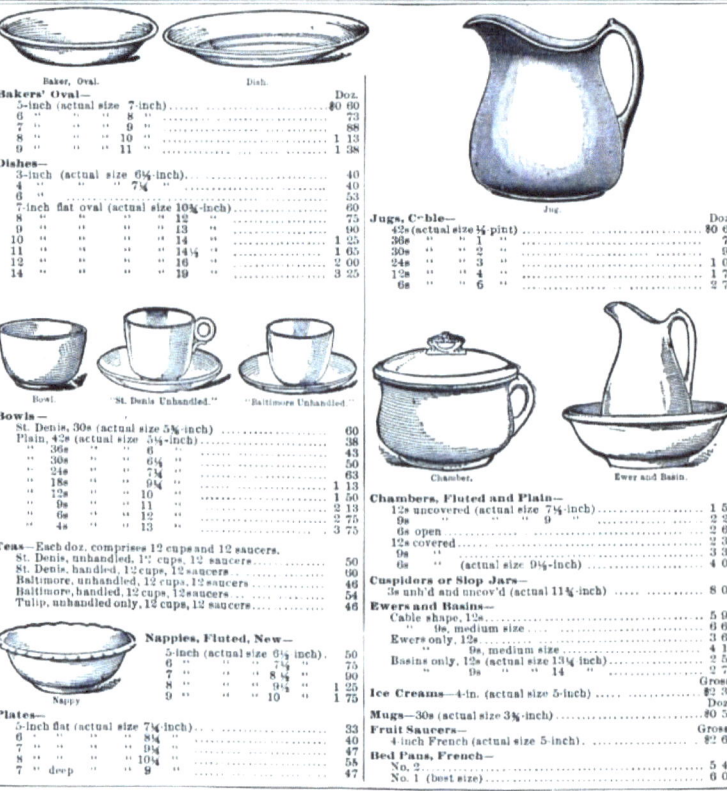

Bakers' Oval—

				Doz.
5-inch (actual size 7-inch)				$0 60
6 " " 8 "				73
7 " " 9 "				88
8 " " 10 "				1 13
9 " " 11 "				1 38

Dishes—

3-inch (actual size 6½-inch)			40
4 " " 7¼ "			40
6 " " 9¼ "			53
7-inch flat oval (actual size 10¼-inch)			60
8 " " 12 "			75
9 " " 13 "			90
10 " " 14 "			1 25
11 " " 14½ "			1 65
12 " " 16 "			2 00
14 " " 19 "			3 25

Bowls—

St. Denis, 30s (actual size 5⅞-inch)				60
Plain, 42s (actual size 5¼-inch)				38
" 36s " 6 "				43
" 30s " 6½ "				50
" 24s " 7¼ "				63
" 18s " 9¼ "				1 13
" 12s " 10 "				1 50
" 9s " 11 "				2 13
" 6s " 12 "				2 75
" 4s " 13 "				3 75

Teas—Each doz. comprises 12 cups and 12 saucers.

St. Denis, unhandled, 12 cups, 12 saucers	50
St. Denis, handled, 12 cups, 12 saucers	60
Baltimore, unhandled, 12 cups, 12 saucers	46
Baltimore, handled, 12 cups, 12 saucers	54
Tulip, unhandled only, 12 cups, 12 saucers	46

Nappies, Fluted, New—

5-inch (actual size 6½-inch)			50
6 " " 7¼ "			75
7 " " 8¼ "			90
8 " " 9¼ "			1 25
9 " " 10 "			1 75

Plates—

5-inch flat (actual size 7¼-inch)			33
6 " " 8¼ "			40
7 " " 9¼ "			47
8 " " 10¼ "			55
7 " deep " 9 "			47

Jugs, C'ble—

			Doz.
42s (actual size ½ pint)			$0 63
36s " "			75
30s " "			90
24s " 3 "			1 00
12s " 4 "			1 75
6s " 6 "			2 70

Chambers, Fluted and Plain—

12s uncovered (actual size 7¼-inch)		1 58
9s " " 9 "		2 20
6s open " "		2 65
12s covered		2 38
9s "		3 33
6s " (actual size 9½-inch)		4 00

Cuspidors or Slop Jars—

3s unh'd and uncov'd (actual 11¾-inch)	8 00

Ewers and Basins—

Cable shape, 12s	5 90
" 9s, medium size	6 65
Ewers only, 12s	3 65
" 9s, medium size	4 15
Basins only, 12s (actual size 13¼-inch)	2 50
" 9s " 14 "	2 75

	Gross.
Ice Creams—4-in. (actual size 5-inch)	$2 38

	Doz.
Mugs—30s (actual size 3¾-inch)	$0 55

	Gross.
Fruit Saucers—	
4-inch French (actual size 5-inch)	$2 63

Bed Pans, French—

No. 2	5 40
No. 1 (best size)	6 00

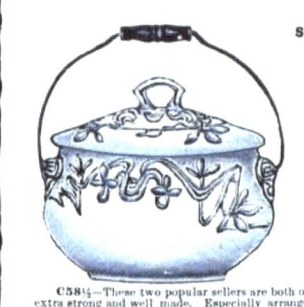

SEMI-PORCELAIN CHAMBERETTE AND CUSPIDOR ASSORTMENT.

Shipped direct from pottery.

One of the best values we offer.

C58½—These two popular sellers are both of a rich ivory colored semi-porcelain body, extra strong and well made. Especially arranged for economy in packing. A cuspidor packed inside of each chamberette. Assortment comprises:

½ doz. chamberettes. A new and very useful piece, being a combination chamber and slop jar. Artistic embossed design, extra large size, ht. 6½ in., diam. 9½, circum. 34. Fancy handled cover and strong bail handle. At 50c will be a *phenomenal seller*. ½ doz. @ $3.95... **$1 98**

½ doz. extra large and shapely cuspidors. Diam. 7½ in., ht. 5. Elaborately embossed and decorated in assorted colors in an entirely new and beautiful modern art effect. *A splendid quarter item.* ½ doz. @ $2.00... **1 00**

(Pkg. 50c.) Total for assortment of 6 chamberettes and 6 cuspidors **$2.98**

Monday, Tuesday and the Four Following Days Are the Days to Push Trade.

OUR "ADVERTISER" GREEN PRINT DECORATED WARE. Shipped direct from Pottery.

—All of good white granite or semi-porcelain and all decorated in beautiful floral and leaf design in delicate green. Decorations are not scant but very profuse, all open pieces being not only decorated on the outside but on inside as well. Every piece positively guaranteed against crazing. No line of decorated dinner ware has ever been offered at such exceedingly low prices, and the opportunity it affords you for offering irresistible bargains should not be overlooked.

Special Notice: While the "Advertiser" line does not comprise all strictly "Firsts" it is equal to many lines sold by others as such. On account of the heavy demand which is sure to be made on us for this line, we may at times be unable to furnish it all in the same shape, and at such times will substitute another shape equally good, decorations being exactly the same. We also request customers not to order less than a barrel or about $5.00 worth of these good, as this will facilitate prompt shipment. To assist customers in ordering we have given actual measurements of items which are occasionally misunderstood but in ordering *be sure to enter only the first or trade size.* Prices subject to 1 per cent 20 days, net 40 days. Regular charge for packages.

Baker.

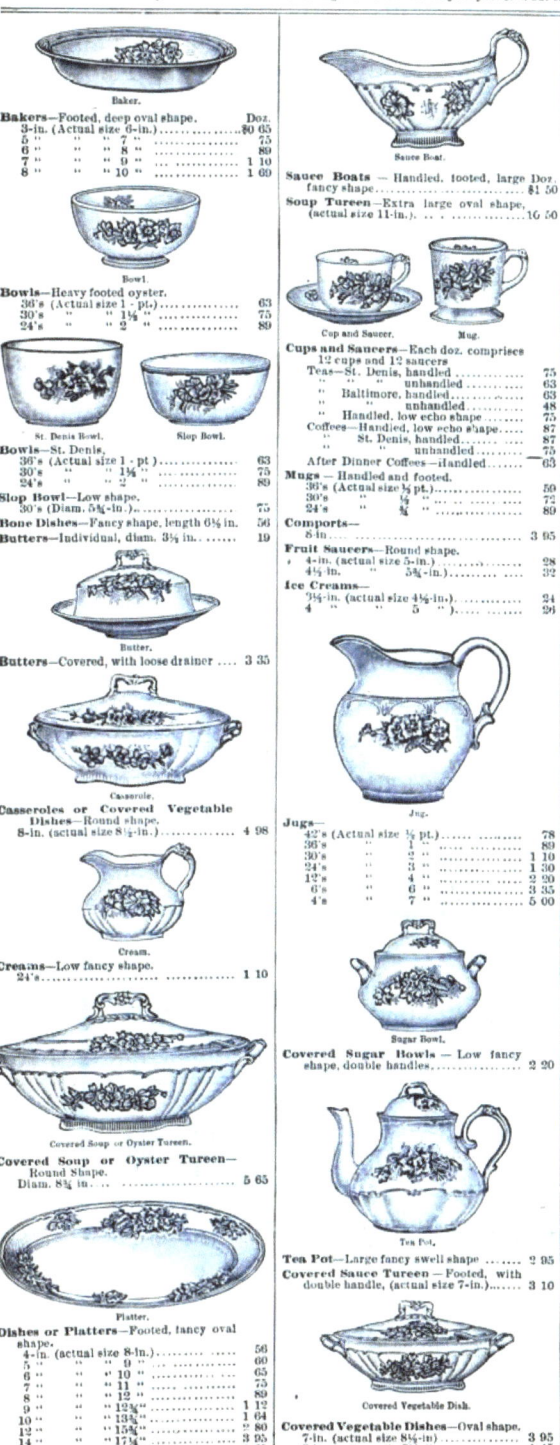

Bakers—Footed, deep oval shape. Doz.
3-in. (Actual size 6-in.) $0 65
5 " " " 7 " 75
6 " " " 8 " 89
7 " " " 9 " 1 10
8 " " " 10 " 1 69

Bowl.

Bowls—Heavy footed oyster.
36's (Actual size 1 - pt.) 63
30's " " 1½ " 75
24's " " 2 " 89

St. Denis Bowl.

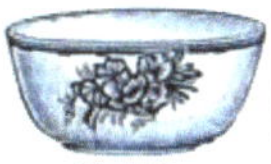

Slop Bowl.

Bowls—St. Denis.
36's (Actual size 1 - pt) 63
30's " " 1½ " 75
24's " " 2 " 89

Slop Bowl—Low shape.
30's (Diam. 5¾-in.) 75

Bone Dishes—Fancy shape, length 6½ in. 56

Butters—Individual, diam. 3½ in. 19

Butter.

Butters—Covered, with loose drainer 3 35

Casserole.

Casseroles or Covered Vegetable Dishes—Round shape.
8-in. (actual size 8½-in.) 4 98

Cream.

Creams—Low fancy shape.
24's 1 10

Covered Soup or Oyster Tureen.

Covered Soup or Oyster Tureen—Round Shape.
Diam. 8¾ in. 5 65

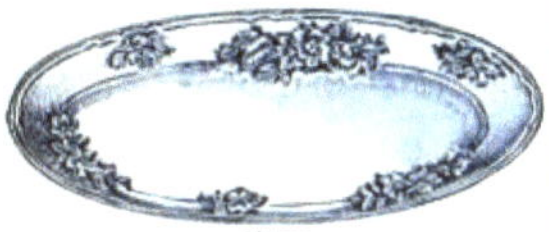

Platter.

Dishes or Platters—Footed, fancy oval shape.
4-in. (actual size 8-in.) 56
5 " " " 9 " 60
6 " " " 10 " 65
7 " " " 11 " 75
8 " " " 12 " 89
9 " " " 12¾" 1 12
10 " " " 13¾" 1 64
12 " " " 15¾" 2 80
14 " " " 17¾" 3 95
16 " " " 19 " 6 25

Sauce Boat.

Sauce Boats — Handled, footed, large fancy shape .... Doz. $1 50

Soup Tureen—Extra large oval shape, (actual size 11-in.). 16 50

Cup and Saucer.

Mug.

Cups and Saucers—Each doz. comprises 12 cups and 12 saucers
Teas—St. Denis, handled 75
" " " unhandled 63
" Baltimore, handled 63
" " unhandled 48
" Handled, low echo shape 75
Coffees—Handled, low echo shape 87
" St. Denis, handled 87
" " unhandled 75
After Dinner Coffees—Handled 63

Mugs — Handled and footed.
36's (Actual size ⅓ pt.) 59
30's " ½ " 72
24's " ¾ " 89

Comports—
8-in 3 95

Fruit Saucers—Round shape.
4-in. (actual size 5-in.) 28
4½-in. " 5¾-in.) 32

Ice Creams—
3½-in. (actual size 4½-in.) 24
4 " " 5 ") 26

Jug.

Jugs—
42's (Actual size ½ pt.) 78
36's " 1 " 89
30's " 2 " 1 10
24's " 3 " 1 30
12's " 4 " 2 20
6's " 6 " 3 35
4's " 7 " 5 00

Sugar Bowl.

Covered Sugar Bowls — Low fancy shape, double handles 2 20

Tea Pot.

Tea Pot—Large fancy swell shape 2 95

Covered Sauce Tureen — Footed, with double handle, (actual size 7-in.) 3 10

Covered Vegetable Dish.

Covered Vegetable Dishes—Oval shape.
7-in. (actual size 8½-in) 3 95
8-in. " " 9½ " 4 45

Nappy.

Nappies—Footed round shape. Doz.
3-in. (actual size 4½-in.) $0 65
4 " " 5¾ " 65
5 " " 6½ " 75
6 " " 7¼ " 89
7 " " 8 " 1 10
8 " " 9 " 1 69
9 " " 10¾ " 2 20
10 " " 11¾ " 2 75

Pickle Dishes—Deep oval shape.
Length 8½-in 1 10

Plate.

Plates—Flat Doz.
4-in. (actual size 6¼-in.) $0 33
5 " " 7¼ " 39
6 " " 8 " 45
7 " " 9¼ " 60
8 " " 10 " 72

Plates—Deep or soup.
7-in. (actual size 9¼-in.) 60

Coupe Soups—Round deep shape.
7-in. (actual size 7¾-in.) 60

"GREEN PRINT" DECORATED PLATE AND BOWL ASSORTMENT.

Slop Bowl.

Plate.

C58. White semi-porcelain body, all firsts, decorated in attractive leaf design in delicate green print. These job regularly at 78c per doz. The assortment comprises:
5 doz. 7-in. (actual size 9¼-in.) plates.
5 doz. 36's, round extra deep bowls, diameter 5-in.
Total 10 doz. in pkg. (pkg. 40c.) Per dozen, **45c**

Shipped direct from pottery near Bellaire, Ohio.

HOW TO PAY LEAST FREIGHT ON CROCKERY.

Our purpose in shipping crockery from the pottery instead of from our houses is two-fold. First, to save the double cost of shipping goods to our city and reshipping to you. Second, to save the extra breakage which is inevitable when goods are handled twice.

Railroad companies make an extremely wide difference between the rate on crockery in cases, and when packed in hogsheads, casks or crates. For instance, a $5 lot of cups, saucers and plates shipped from pottery to New England or Missouri river points, costs nearly as much freight as a $12 lot, because the latter is large enough to take a cask or a hogshead and therefore enjoys the low rate.

We quote below rates from our pottery to leading points over the country. We believe any buyer who studies these will agree with us that he cannot afford to make his crockery orders to small—that they should be made of the amount of $12 or more so he may get the benefit of the lower rate.

	Cases.	Hogsheads, Casks and Crates.
Alabama.		
Decatur	....	$0 68
Birmingham	....	68
Mobile	....	44
Arkansas.		
Little Rock	$1 15	95
Texarkana	1 29	1 17
Ft. Smith	1 20	1 05
Colorado.		
Denver	1 75	1 45
Pueblo	1 75	1 45
Leadville	2 70	2 25
Connecticut.		
Hartford	43	26
New Hartford	39	24
Illinois.		
Chicago	39	24
Peoria	44½	27
Quincy	56½	34
Indiana.		
Evansville	44½	27
Ft. Wayne	35	21
Indianapolis	37½	23
Indian Ter.		
So. McAlester	1 34	1 19
Wagoner	1 13	99½
Kansas.		
Topeka	99	84
Wichita	1 28	1 11
Ft. Scott	91	75
Kentucky.		
Owensboro	....	40
Lexington	....	24
Louisiana.		
Shreveport	1 24	1 10
New Orleans	....	44
Maine.		
Portland	43	26
No. Berwick	42	26
Maryland.		
Baltimore	31	22
Frederick	31	22
Massachusetts.		
Boston	43	26
Springfield	43	26
Michigan.		
Detroit	35	21
Saginaw	39	24
Mississippi.		
Holly Springs	....	81
Meridian	....	75
Natchez	....	44
Missouri.		
Chillicothe	$0 75	$0 65
Springfield	82	70
Kansas City	75	65
New Hampshire.		
Nashua	43	26
Portsmouth	43	26
New Jersey.		
Camden	33	23
Trenton	39	24
New Mexico.		
Santa Fe	2 20	2 00
Albuquerque	2 20	2 00
New York.		
Albany	39	24
Buffalo	31	18
New York City	39	24
Ohio.		
Cincinnati	35	21
Columbus	36	23
Toledo	31	18
Oklahoma.		
Oklahoma City	1 39	1 27
Oregon.		
Astoria, Commodity rate.		1 30
Portland, " "		1 30
Pennsylvania.		
Erie	28½	17½
Harrisburg	31	22
Philadelphia	33	23
Rhode Island.		
Providence	43	26
Tennessee.		
Knoxville	....	64
Nashville	....	44
Memphis	....	36
Texas.		
Ft. Worth	1 43	1 27
Austin	1 43	1 27
Houston	1 43	1 27
El Paso	1 56	1 45
Virginia.		
Alexandria	31	18
Richmond	47	24
Winchester	31	18
West Virginia.		
Charleston	31	18
Parkersburg	22	12½
Washington.		
Olympia, Commodity rate,	....	1 30
Seattle " "	....	1 30
Tacoma " "	....	1 30
Wisconsin.		
La Crosse	81½	50½
Milwaukee	41	26

NOTE—In western classification crockery in barrels and boxes same rate as in cases.

Investigate—Compare. We Seek Your Business Only on the Basis of Mutual Interest.

Our "IMPERIAL" Open=Stock Line of DECORATED SEMI-PORCELAIN WARE.
SHIPPED DIRECT FROM THE POTTERY.

Best quality, light weight, fancy shapes. Every piece elaborately embossed in beautiful scroll and lace edge design, decorated in dainty rose-bud and vine effect pattern. Edges, handles etc., all traced in gold. Decorations are not scant, but are on both sides and profuse. *Every piece warranted not to craze.* Positively the most beautiful line of dinner ware we have ever offered. We urge you to order a sample barrel, knowing that you will be pleased with the pattern and the value. Prices subject to our regular terms—1 per cent 20 days, net 40 days. Regular charge for packages.

Baker.
Bakers—Fancy oval shape. Doz.
3-in. (actual size 6 -in.) $0 92
7 "   "   9¼ " 1 60
8 "   "   10 " 2 40

Slop Bowl. **Bowl.**
Slop Bowls—Footed, fancy flared shape.
30's (diam. 5¼-in.) 1 08
Bowls—St. Denis, extra deep.
30's (diam. 5¼-in.) 1 08

Berry Saucer. **Bone Dish.**
Berry Saucers—Fancy shape.
Diam. 6½-in. 67
Bone Dishes—Fluted edge 82
Berry Dishes—Extra large, fancy shape,
length 10¼ in. 3 50

Covered Butter Dish.
Covered Butter Dishes—Loose drainer, flanged and footed 4 87
Casseroles—(Same shape as Oyster Tureen). Fancy shape, footed. 8-in. 7 20
Covered Dishes—(Same shape as Soup Tureen). Fancy shape, footed.
8-in. (actual 9-in.) 6 50

Cream.
Creams—Good size, fancy shape 1 50

Cake Plate.
Cake Plates—10-in. 1 35

Spoon Tray.
Spoon Trays—
8½-in. 1 20

Jug.
Jugs—Fancy shape, fancy handle.
36's (1-pint) 1 30
30's 2 " 1 60
24's 3 " 1 90
12's 4 " 3 05
6's 5 " 4 87

St. Denis.
Cups and Saucers—1 doz. comprises 12 Doz. cups and 12 saucers. Fancy ovide shape, handled $0 98
St. Denis, teas, good coffee size 98

After Dinner.
After Dinner, fancy shape 94

Celery Tray.
Celery Trays—Extra deep, 13¾-in. 3 05

Platter.
Dishes or Platters—Fancy shape.
4-in. (actual 7 -in.) 79
8 "   "   11¼ " 1 30
10 "   "   13 " 2 40
12 "   "   14½ " 4 10
14 "   "   17 " 5 75
16 "   "   19 " 8 90

Double Handled Cracker Jar.
Double Handled Cracker Jars—Extra large, low shape 4 50

Egg Cup. **Fruit.**
Egg Cups—Large size 92
Fruits—4-in. (actual 5-in.) 30

Ice Cream. **Relish Dish.**
Ice Creams—Plain.
4-in. (actual 4½-in.) 36
Relish Dishes—3½-in. (actual 4-in.) 36
Individual Butters—3¼-in. 28

Coupe Soup.
Coupe Soups—
Actual 7¾-in. 85

Cracker Jar.
Cracker Jar—Covered, large size, fancy shape 4 10

Nappy.
Nappy—Fluted. Doz.
5-in. (actual 6½-in.) $1 00
6 "   "   7¼ " 1 30
7 "   "   8½ " 1 60
8 "   "   9¼ " 2 40

Oyster Tureen.
Oyster Tureen—Covered, extra large round shape, footed.
Diam. 9¾-in. 10 80

Pickle.
Pickles—Fancy shape.
Actual 8-in. 1 60

Oblong Cake and Bureau Tray.
Oblong Cake and Bureau Trays—
10¾ x 7½ 1 50

Plate.
Plates—Flat.
4-in. (actual 6 -in.) 48
5 "   "   7¼ " 60
6 "   "   8 " 75
7 "   "   9 " 85
8 "   "   10 " 96

Deep Plate.
Plates—Deep.
7-in. (actual 9¼-in.) 85

Roll Tray.
Roll Trays—Deep boat shape.
12½-in. 2 75

Sugar Bowl.
Sugar Bowls—Covered, double handles .. 3 05

Sauce Tureen.
Sauce Tureen—Attached stand, large size, fancy shape 4 50

Jelly Dish. **Oatmeal Saucer.**
Jelly Dish—Fancy shape.
6½-in. .... Doz. $0 92
Oatmeal Saucers—
Actual 6½-in. 69

Sauce Boat.
Sauce Boat—Handled and footed, fancy shape 2 20

Salad Dish.
Salad Dishes—Low shape.
5-in. (actual 6½-in.) 1 00
6 "   "   7½ " 1 30
7 "   "   8½ " 1 60
8 "   "   9¼ " 2 40
9 "   "   10¾ " 3 05

Tea Pot.
Tea Pots—Large, fancy shape 4 25

3-Piece Mush and Milk or Oatmeal Set.
3-Piece Mush and Milk or Oatmeal Sets .... Doz. sets 3 20

Soup Tureen.
Soup Tureen—Covered, extra large oval shape, footed, length 10¾ in. .. 14 95

NO cartage charge

There is Satisfaction in Buying from a Catalogue That is Always Up-to-Date and Guarantees Prices.

A Well Advertised Bargain Paves the Way to Increased Business in Regular Lines.

OUR "PRINCESS" OPEN STOCK LINE
WHITE AND GOLD DECORATED SEMI-PORCELAIN WARE.

Shipped Direct From Pottery.

An entirely new line and one of the most beautiful ever offered.

All best quality thin, light weight, pure white semi-porcelain ware in new and beautiful shapes, fancy embossed desigu. Each and every piece with elaborate decorations in numerous beautiful and artistic floral displays in pure gold, decorations in the popular border design, nearly all the pieces having decorated centers. The knobs, handles, etc., on all large pieces are also richly decorated in gold, altogether making one of the richest and most elaborate lines we have shown. At the exceptionally low prices here named, nearly all the pieces can be retailed at popular prices. We positively guarantee the "Princess" line not to craze. Prices subject to our regular terms—1 per cent 20 days, net 40 days, regular charge for packages.

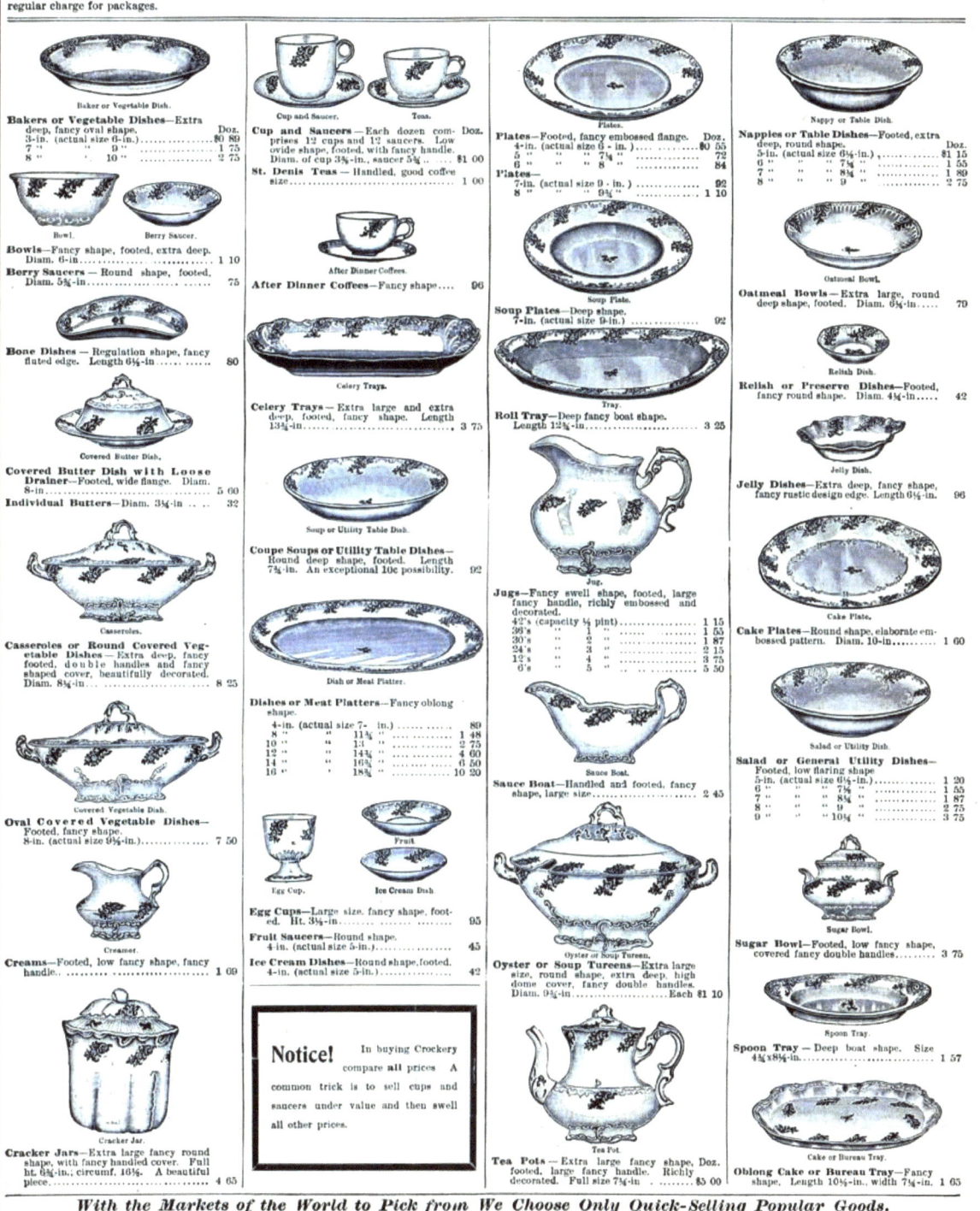

Baker or Vegetable Dish.

Bakers or Vegetable Dishes—Extra deep, fancy oval shape.

		Doz.
6-in. (actual size 6-in.)		$0 89
7 "	" 9 "	1 75
8 "	" 10 "	2 75

Bowl.

Berry Saucer.

Bowls—Fancy shape, footed, extra deep. Diam. 6-in. 1 10

Berry Saucers — Round shape, footed. Diam. 5⅜-in. 75

Bone Dishes — Regulation shape, fancy fluted edge. Length 6¼-in 80

Covered Butter Dish.

Covered Butter Dish with Loose Drainer—Footed, wide flange. Diam. 8-in 5 60

Individual Butters—Diam. 3¼-in 32

Casseroles.

Casseroles or Round Covered Vegetable Dishes—Extra deep, fancy footed, double handles and fancy shaped cover, beautifully decorated. Diam. 8¼-in 8 25

Covered Vegetable Dish.

Oval Covered Vegetable Dishes—Footed, fancy shape. 8-in. (actual size 9½-in.) 7 50

Creamer.

Creams—Footed, low fancy shape, fancy handle 1 09

Cracker Jar.

Cracker Jars—Extra large fancy round shape, with fancy handled cover. Full ht. 6¾-in.; circumf. 16½. A beautiful piece 4 65

Cup and Saucer.

Teas.

Cup and Saucers—Each dozen comprises 12 cups and 12 saucers. Low ovide shape, footed, with fancy handle. Diam. of cup 3⅜-in., saucer 5¾ .... Doz. $1 00

St. Denis Teas — Handled, good coffee size 1 00

After Dinner Coffees.

After Dinner Coffees—Fancy shape 96

Celery Trays.

Celery Trays — Extra large and extra deep, footed, fancy shape. Length 13¾-in 3 75

Soup or Utility Table Dish.

Coupe Soups or Utility Table Dishes—Round deep shape, footed. Length 7⅝-in. An exceptional 10c possibility. 92

Dish or Meat Platter.

Dishes or Meat Platters—Fancy oblong shape.

4-in. (actual size 7- in.)		89
8 "	" 11¾ "	1 48
10 "	" 13 "	2 75
12 "	" 14¾ "	4 60
14 "	" 16¾ "	6 50
16 "	" 18¾ "	10 20

Egg Cup.

Fruit.

Ice Cream Dish.

Egg Cups—Large size, fancy shape, footed. Ht. 3½-in 95

Fruit Saucers—Round shape. 4-in. (actual size 5-in.) 45

Ice Cream Dishes—Round shape, footed. 4-in. (actual size 5-in.) 42

Notice! In buying Crockery compare **all** prices. A common trick is to sell cups and saucers under value and then swell all other prices.

Plates.

Plates—Footed, fancy embossed flange.

		Doz.
4-in. (actual size 6 - in.)		$0 55
5 "	" 7¼ "	72
6 "	" 8 "	84

Plates—

7-in. (actual size 9 - in.)		92
8 "	" 9¾ "	1 10

Soup Plate.

Soup Plates—Deep shape. 7-in. (actual size 9-in.) 92

Tray.

Roll Tray—Deep fancy boat shape. Length 12⅝-in 3 25

Jug.

Jugs—Fancy swell shape, footed, large fancy handle, richly embossed and decorated.

42's (capacity ⅛ pint)			1 15
36's	"	1 "	1 55
30's	"	2 "	1 87
24's	"	3 "	2 15
12's	"	4 "	3 75
6's	"	5 "	5 50

Sauce Boat.

Sauce Boat—Handled and footed, fancy shape, large size 2 45

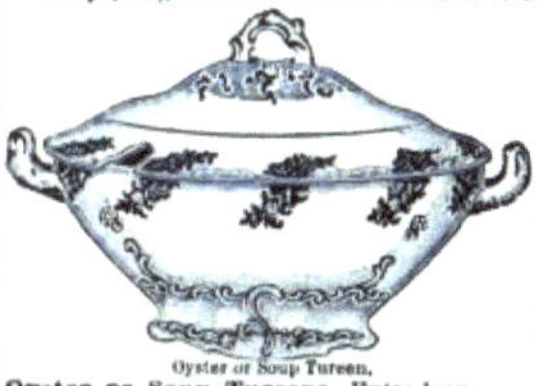

Oyster or Soup Tureen.

Oyster or Soup Tureens—Extra large size, round shape, extra deep, high dome cover, fancy double handles. Diam. 9⅛-in .... Each $1 10

Tea Pot.

Tea Pots — Extra large fancy shape, footed, large fancy handle. Richly decorated. Full size 7¼-in .... Doz. $5 00

Nappy or Table Dish.

Nappies or Table Dishes—Footed, extra deep, round shape.

		Doz.
5-in. (actual size 6½-in.)		$1 15
6 "	" 7¼ "	1 55
7 "	" 8¼ "	1 89
8 "	" 9 "	2 75

Oatmeal Bowl.

Oatmeal Bowls — Extra large, round deep shape, footed. Diam. 6⅜-in 79

Relish Dish.

Relish or Preserve Dishes—Footed, fancy round shape. Diam. 4¼-in 42

Jelly Dish.

Jelly Dishes—Extra deep, fancy shape, fancy rustic design edge. Length 6¼-in. 96

Cake Plate.

Cake Plates—Round shape, elaborate embossed pattern. Diam. 10-in 1 60

Salad or Utility Dish.

Salad or General Utility Dishes—Footed, low flaring shape

5-in. (actual size 6½-in.)		1 20
6 "	" 7¼ "	1 55
7 "	" 8¼ "	1 87
8 "	" 9 "	2 75
9 "	" 10¼ "	3 75

Sugar Bowl.

Sugar Bowl—Footed, low fancy shape, covered fancy double handles 3 75

Spoon Tray.

Spoon Tray — Deep boat shape. Size 4⅜x8½-in 1 57

Cake or Bureau Tray.

Oblong Cake or Bureau Tray—Fancy shape. Length 10½-in., width 7¼-in. 1 65

With the Markets of the World to Pick from We Choose Only Quick-Selling Popular Goods.

Decorated CHAMBER or TOILET SETS from Pottery.

From the best pottery in the United States. Absolutely the best values we have ever offered. Not merely are the prices low but goods are of SUPERIOR GRADE. Better ware and better decorations than most (even at higher prices), and **sizes honest.** Shipped from pottery, near Bellaire, Ohio.

Our New "LARGE STAPLE" 6-Piece Toilet Set.

C20—Large size, print decorations on every piece in a combination of floral designs in three colors—green, blue and brown. Set comprises:
1 extra size large body ewer or pitcher, ht. 11¼-in.
1 extra deep 14¼-in. basin, decorated in and out.
1 large covered chamber.
1 handled mug.
1 soap slab.
Packed 3 sets—one of each color—in barrel.
(Shipped from pottery. 3 sets in bbl. Bbl. 35c.) Per set, **$1.25**

Our New "GOOD MORNING" 10-Piece Toilet Set.

C21—Print decoration in floral designs in four colors. All large size pieces as follows:
1 large ewer, 11¼-in. high.
1 extra deep 14¼-in. basin, decorated in and out.
1 large covered chamber (2 pieces).
1 handled mug.
1 1-qt. jug, height 7-in.
1 upright 5¼-in. toothbrush holder.
1 medium size soap dish with cover and drainer. (3 pieces).
4 sets in cask, one each of the following colors—green, brown, blue and terra cotta.
(Shipped from pottery. 4 sets in cask. Cask 75c.) Per set, **$1.50**

Our "GOLD SHOWERED" 10-Piece Toilet Set.

C23—All fancy shapes, semi-porcelain. One set decorated in blue, the other in green. Decorations in large sprays of cornelius. Profuse gold stippling on all pieces. 10 pieces as above.
(Shipped from pottery. 2 sets in bbl. Bbl. 40c.) Per set, **$2.10**

Our "FLORAL WREATH EMBOSSED" 12-Piece Toilet Set.

C26—Quietly elegant pure white set of embossed floral design. Semi-porcelain ware. Tall and graceful pattern with daisies and japonicas in relief. Same pieces as "Complete" set.
(Shipped from pottery. 1 set in bbl. Bbl. 40c.) Per set, **$2.75**

OUR NEW "COMPLETE" 12-Piece Toilet Set.

C22—Each and every piece profusely decorated in handsome floral band vine effects. colors brown and blue. One set of each color in barrel.
1 extra size double handled slop jar and cover (2 pieces).
1 medium sized handled mug.
1 large lipped handled water jug.
1 tooth brush holder.
1 good size soap dish with drainer and cover (3 pieces).
1 extra deep basin.
1 extra size large body handled ewer or pitcher.
1 large chamber and cover (2 pieces).
(Shipped from pottery. 2 sets in cask, sold only by cask. Cask 60c.) Per set, **$2.65**

Our "NEW MASSIVE" Gold Clouded 12-Piece Toilet Set.

C61—An exceptionally rich set being in pure white semi-porcelain, richly embossed in beautiful floral and scroll design with elaborate decorations of rich gold clouds on all edges, handles and knobs, giving an extremely beautiful effect. Set comprises:

1 extra large fancy shape footed ewer or pitcher, ht. 12 in.
1 large footed and roll rimmed basin, diam. 15½ in.
1 extra large footed covered slop jar with double handles, ht. 15 in.
1 large covered chamber.
1 large oval soapdish and cover with loose drainer.
1 medium size footed hot water pitcher, fancy handle, ht. 7¼ in.
1 large fancy shape footed tooth brush holder.
1 large handled and footed mug.
(Shipped from pottery. Each set in pkg. Pkg. 40c.) Per set, **$3.85**

Our "MAGNIFICENT" Toilet Set.
An exceptionally rich set in an entirely new combination.

C69—Bodies of best pure white semi-porcelain, all the pieces are extra large and fancy swell shape, elaborately embossed and tinted in delicate pink, extra large fancy handles, decorations in rich hand painted filled-in roses in pink with green leaves. Each set consists of:
1 extra large rolled rim basin.
1 extra large ewer or pitcher.
1 large covered combinet with bail handle.
1 small ewer or hot water pitcher.
1 tall brush vase.
1 large covered soap dish with loose drainer.
1 fancy handled mug.
Total, 10 pieces in set. Do not confuse this with the regular 10-piece set. Note especially that it contains the combinet or combination chamber and slop jar, making it an especially desirable set. Per set, **$3.89**
(Shipped direct from pottery. Each set in pkg., pkg. 40c.)

We Never Sacrifice Quality for Price-- We Frequently Do Sacrifice PRICE for QUALITY.

"RICHLY TINTED" 12-PIECE TOILET SET.
Shipped direct from pottery. An extremely rich set.

C68—Best semi-porcelain body, an unusually artistic shape all embossed work and edges richly tinted in a new and beautiful effect. Comprises the same pieces as our No. 22 complete set. (2 sets in cask, 1 in pink and 1 in green. Cask 60c.) Per set, **$3.60**

Our "SPARE ROOM" Decorated 12-Piece Toilet Set.

C62—Body of best pure white semi-porcelain, all pieces extra large and of fancy shape, all elaborately decorated almost all over in beautiful band painted floral designs in delicate green, every piece having extra heavy gold clouded edges, handles and knobs. All pieces footed with gold clouded decorations on feet. Same composition as C61, "Massive Gold Clouded" Set.
(Shipped direct from pottery. Each set in Pkg. Pkg. 40c.) Per set, **$4.20**

Our "BRIDAL CHAMBER" Decorated 12-Piece Toilet Set.

C66—An extra large set of rare beauty, best semi-porcelain, extra large fancy shapes with elaborate hand painted decorations in large roses in pink with delicate green leaves. Not the usual scant decorations, but decorated on both sides, basin inside as well as out. Every piece heavily gold clouded on all edges and handles, making one of the most beautiful sets ever produced. Same composition and sizes as C67, "Palatial."
(Shipped direct from pottery. Each set in pkg. 40c.) Per set, **$4.75**

IMPORTANT NOTICE TO CUSTOMERS.

In order to facilitate the handling of direct shipments from pottery, crockery customers will please observe the following:

Order factory goods on separate order blanks as these orders are handled in a special department and when written on the same sheet with other goods are subject to delay. Always mention number, price and style of ware desired.

Customers dealing with us on a C. O. D. basis, when ordering crockery shipped from factory in the same order with goods shipped from our house, should send two separate deposits. That for crockery should equal 10 per cent of amount of order—in no case less than $5.00. Orders for less than $10.00 must be accompanied by full amount.

The above applies to all factory orders.

Our "PINK TINTED" 12-Piece Toilet Set.

C63—An entirely new and beautiful set, made of best semi-porcelain, richly embossed and tinted almost all over in beautiful pink shading into white, all pieces have extra wide heavily gold clouded edges and handles, altogether making an exceedingly handsome set and one that will sell wherever shown. Same number of pieces as C61, "Massive Gold Clouded" Set.
(Shipped direct from pottery. Each set in pkg. Pkg. 40c.) Per set, **$4.25**

Our "GREEN TINTED" 12-Piece Toilet Set.

C64—Same size and style as C63, only tinted in beautiful delicate green.
(Shipped direct from pottery. Each set in pkg. Pkg. 40c.) Per set, **$4.25**

Our "PALATIAL" Decorated 12-Piece Set.

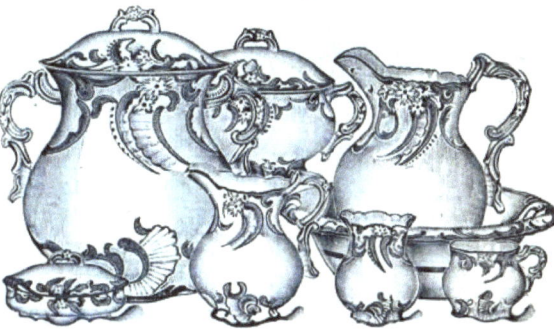

C67—Pure white semi-porcelain, extra large fancy shapes, elaborate embossed work in beautiful floral and scroll design, embossed work decorated in rich green with pure gold tracings producing a very artistic and elaborate effect, all pieces footed. Feet, handles, edges and knobs elaborately decorated in gold. Note especially the extra large sizes. Set comprises:

1 mammoth swell shape ewer or pitcher, ht. 12-in., fancy handle, large lip.
1 extra large and extra deep roll rimmed basin, diam. 15½-in.
1 mammoth footed slop jar with cover, ht. 14½-in., girth, 35½ long double handles.
1 large handled and covered chamber.
1 handled and footed hot water pitcher, ht. 7½-in.
1 large oval covered soap dish with loose drainer. Length 5¾-in.
1 large fancy shape brush holder. Ht. 5¼-in.
1 large fancy handled mug.
(Shipped direct from pottery. Each set in pkg. Pkg. 40c.) Per set, **$5.25**

Our "BIG AND BEAUTIFUL" TOILET SET Assortment.
Shipped direct from pottery. Four sets of different compositions that are rare values.

C70—Best La Belle china body, all pieces being extra large and well made, all of the same shape which is a new and exceptionally good one. Assortment comprises:

2 regular 6-piece sets. Elaborate wild flower decorations in plain print—1 set in blue and 1 in brown..Each, $1 25 $2 50
1 regular 10-piece set. Green decorations, gold edges and handles............... 1 95
1 regular 12-piece set. Extra large double handle slop jar, decorations hand painted and filled-in pink wild flowers and green leaves............... 3 75

(Cask 90c) Total for 4 sets in cask. Total, **$8.20**

We Drum Up Trade by Clear Statements, Low Prices and Goods of Honest Quality.

AMERICAN DECORATED TEA and DINNER SETS== SHIPPED FROM POTTERY NEAR BELLAIRE, OHIO.

We claim that the pottery whose output in Tea and Dinner Sets we practically control, produces the **very best goods** in America. That is a strong claim, but it is **easily** tested. **New shapes and new decorations.** Goods **honest** in every way—full sizes, all regular composition, covers where covers should be, all pieces **well covered** with decoration.

Our "PURITY" 56-Piece Embossed Tea Sets.

C75—Light-weight plain white semi-porcelain in neat embossed pattern, all pieces being in large new fancy shape. A set that is always a staple seller and at this price a rare bargain. (Shipped direct from pottery. 2 sets in pkg. Pkg. 40c.) Per set, **$1.89**

Our "COTTAGE HOME" 56-Piece Decorated Tea Set.

C76—Best light-weight semi-porcelain body in new and fancy shape, neat embossed patterns, decorations in plain print in floral and vine designs. Cups being decorated on the inside as well as outside. (Shipped direct from pottery. 2 sets in pkg., one in blue and one in brown.) (Bbl. 40c.) Per set, **$2.75**

Our "FAVORITE" 56-Piece Decorated Tea Set.

C1—Decorations in plain print, of the two sets in barrel, one is in lettuce green, the other in Sevres brown. Heliotrope design in from two to three sprays on every piece. Edges and handles traced in gold. Ware is light weight semi-porcelain, with artistic embossing in relief. Regular 56-piece composition. (Shipped from pottery. 2 sets in bbl. Bbl. 40c.) Per set, **$3.25**

Our "ELABORATE" 56-Piece Highly Decorated Tea Set.

C2—All hand-painted on light weight embossed and festooned edge porcelain. Handles and knobs traced in gold. Large sprays of morning glories in natural colors, pink and blue. Regular 56-piece composition. (Shipped from pottery. 2 sets in bbl. Bbl. 40c.) Per set, **$3.75**

COMPOSITION OF ALL OUR 56-PIECE TEA SETS.

Each 56-piece set comprises the following: 12 handled cups, 12 saucers, 12 plates, 12 sauce dishes, 1 extra deep bowl, 2 large bread or cake plates, 1 handled milk pitcher, 1 double handled sugar bowl with cover, 1 covered tea pot.

Our "RICH AND SHAPELY" 56-Piece Decorated Tea Set.

C77—Made of best grade light-weight pure white semi-porcelain, new and beautiful shape, all pieces in fancy embossed lace edge design, decorations very elaborate, being in hand-painted filled in sprays of small roses. All pieces have gold decorated edges and handles. One set in pink and one in combination of green and blue. (Shipped direct from pottery. 2 sets in pkg. Pkg. 40c.) Per set, **$3.50**

Our "OLD COLONIAL" 56-Piece Tea Set.

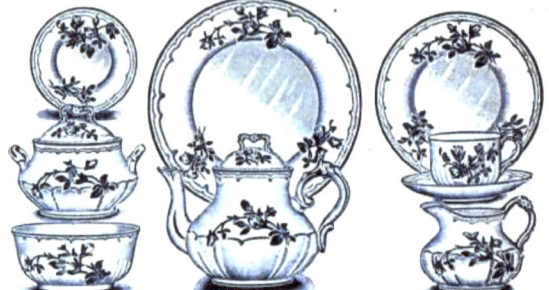

C78—Light weight semi-porcelain body, fancy new shape, each piece embossed in an artistic pattern, all decorations are hand painted moss roses in pink and delicate green leaves, all pieces have gold edges, handles of large pieces elaborately traced in gold. This is sure to be a popular seller. (2 sets in pkg., pkg. 40c.) Per set, **$3.60**

Our "RICHLY PLAIN" 106-Piece Complete Dinner Set.

C10—Plain white light weight semi-porcelain, all fancy shapes, raised festoon pattern with elaborate embossing on edges. Comprising 106 pieces. Please note the absence of small pieces useful for *counting* purposes only. *Sizes given are actual.*

12 7¾-in. plates.
12 8-in. plates.
12 9-in. plates.
12 individual butter plates.
12 5-in. sauce plates.
1 9¼-in. oval dish (covered and handled).
2 10-in. vegetable dishes.
1 handled sauce boat.
1 sugar bowl and cover.
1 large bowl.
1 10-in. bread plate.
12 handled cups and saucers.
1 13-in. "
1 11½-in. platter.
1 17-in. "
1 8-in. round vegetable dish and cover (handled).
1 9-in. pickle dish.
1 handled butter dish, covered, with drainer.
1 teapot and cover
1 milk pitcher.
1 10-in. cake plate.

(Shipped from pottery. 1 set in bbl. Bbl. 40c.) Per set **$5.75**

It Is the Number of ITEMS You Offer that Controls Your Sales, Not the Dollars Value of Your Stock.

Our "LACE EMBOSSED" 65-Piece Dinner Set.

C85—Light weight plain white semi-porcelain body in new and rich fancy embossed pattern in beautiful lace border design, all large fancy shape pieces. Sizes given are actual. Set comprises 65 pieces, as follows:

6 only 9¼-in. breakfast or dinner plates.	1 only large fancy shape footed and handled sauce or gravy boat.
6 " 8 " tea plates.	1 only 8½-in. footed pickle dish.
6 " 8¼ " soup plates.	1 " 9 " extra large round deep footed comport or salad bowl.
12 " 5 " fruit or sauce dishes.	1 only 7½-in. flanged butter dish with cover and loose drainer.
6 " 3¼ " individual butter plates.	1 only large fancy bell shape tea pot with cover.
6 " low fancy handled tea cups.	1 " double handled covered sugar bowl.
6 " saucers to match.	1 " fancy handled and footed cream pitcher.
1 " 9- in. deep oval baker or vegetable dish.	1 " round deep footed slop bowl.
1 " 11¼ " dish or platter.	
1 " 13¼ " oval dish or platter.	
1 " 9¼ " footed oval covered vegetable dish.	

(Shipped direct from pottery. Total 65 pieces in set. Each set in bbl. Bbl 35c.) Per set, **$3.25**

Our "EVERY-DAY" 65-Piece Decorated Dinner Set.

C86—Medium light weight semi-porcelain in new shape, fancy embossed pattern, profuse decorations in lilacs in delicate green print, making a very attractive and beautiful set, nearly all the pieces are footed. Same composition of pieces and same sizes as No. 85 "Lace Embossed" set. (Shipped direct from pottery. Each set in bbl. Bbl. 35c.) Per set, **$4.60**

OUR "GOLDEN ANNIVERSARY" 65-PIECE DINNER SET.

Shipped direct from pottery.

C84—A beautiful set made up specially for newly married couples or small families. The best thin, light weight, pure white semi-porcelain in beautiful and attractive shapes, each piece heavily embossed and artistically decorated in numerous sprays of pure gold in a neat floral design, handles, knobs, etc., also richly traced in gold. The set comprises 65 pieces as follows, sizes given being actual:

1 large oval covered Vegetable Dish, length 9 in.	1 extra deep round footed Bowl, diam. 5¼ in.
1 extra large oval footed Salad Bowl, 8½x11¼ in.	6 only 3½-in. individual Butter Plates.
6 9¼-in. Soup Plates.	1 large fancy shape Tea Pot and cover.
6 9¼-in. Dinner Plates.	1 fancy double handled Sugar Bowl and cover.
6 8¼-in. Breakfast or Tea Plates.	1 only 8-in. flanged Butter Dish and cover, with loose drainer.
1 handled footed Gravy Boat, fancy shape.	1 fancy handled Milk or Cream Pitcher.
1 11¼-in. Dish or Platter.	12 5-in. Fruit or Sauce Dishes.
1 13-in. Dish or Platter.	6 low shaped handled Tea Cups.
1 fancy shape Table or Utility Dish, size 5x8¼ in.	6 Saucers to match.
1 oval Baker or Vegetable Dish, length 9 in.	(One set in bbl., bbl 35c.) Per set, **$5.95**

Our "NEW POPULAR" Decorated 100-Piece Dinner Set.

C87—A large set at exceptionally low price. Medium light weight semi-porcelain of neat fancy embossed pattern, decorations being in green print and very elaborate. Sizes given are actual. Set comprises the following:

12 only 7½-inch tea plates.	1 only 9½-inch footed oval covered vegetable dish.
12 " 8 " breakfast plates.	1 only large fancy shaped footed and handled gravy boat.
12 " 9¼ " dinner plates.	1 only 8½-inch oval footed pickle dish.
12 " 5 " fruit or sauce dishes.	1 " 7½ " flanged covered butter dish with loose drainer.
10 " 3½ " individual butters.	1 only fancy low shaped handled milk or cream pitcher.
12 " low fancy handled tea cups.	1 only low shape double handled sugar, sugar bowl and cover.
12 " saucers to match.	1 only 5⅞-inch round deep slop bowl.
2 " 9¼ " footed oval deep baker's or vegetable dishes.	1 " 8 " handled cheese or cake plate.
1 only 11¼-inch oval footed dish or meat platter.	
1 only 15¼-inch oval footed dish or meat platter.	

Total 100 pieces in set. Each set in pkg. Pkg. 40c.
(Shipped direct from the pottery.) Per set, **$5.40**

Our "MANSION" 100-Piece Richly Decorated Dinner Set.

C7—Artistically embossed, hand-painted, filled in floral decoration, in a combination of delicate blue and green, rich gold traced handles and knobs. Fancy shape, light, weight, semi-porcelain. Sizes given are actual.
Set comprises 100 pieces, as follows:

12 tea plates, 7½ in.	1 bowl.
12 breakfast plates, 8½-in.	1 meat platter, 11¼-in.
12 dinner plates, 9½-in.	1 meat platter, 15¼-in.
12 round fruit saucers, 5¼-in.	1 sauce boat.
12 individual butters.	1 pickle dish.
12 teacups and saucers (24 pieces.)	1 butter dish, with cover and drainer.
2 9¼-inch oblong vegetable dishes.	1 milk pitcher.
1 9½-inch oblong vegetable dish, covered.	1 sugar bowl and cover.
1 cake plate.	

(Shipped from pottery. 1 set in bbl. Bbl. 35c.) Per set, **$7.20**

Your Profit Comes from Quick Returns--Don't Tie Your Capital Up in Slow Sellers.

OUR "BARGAIN SPECIAL" DECORATED 127-PIECE DINNER SET.

C91:.Best thin light weight La Belle china attractive and popular shapes, neat embossed border pattern and all richly decorated in numerous artistic filled-in hand decorated floral sprays in combination of heliotrope and delicate green. Handles and knobs of all pieces heavily decorated in gold. A set which jobs regularly at $12.00. Sizes given are actual.

Each Set Comprises the Following:

12 only 6¼-inch Bread and Butter or Pie Plates.
12 " 7¼ " Tea Plates.
12 " 8¼ " Breakfast Plates.
12 " 9¼ " Dinner Plates.
12 " 9¼ " Soup Plates.
12 " 5 " Fruit or Sauce Dishes.
12 " 3½ " Individual Butter Plates.
12 " Low Fancy shape Handled Tea Cups.
12 " 5¾ " Saucers to match.
2 " 9¾ " Extra Deep Oval Baker or Vegetable Dishes.
12 " 9¾ " Oval Footed Covered Vegetable Dishes.
1 only 9-inch Round Covered Oyster or Soup Tureen.
1 " 11¾ " Oval Dish or Meat Platter.
1 " 13¾ " " " " " "
1 " 17 " " " " " "
1 " 8¾ " " Footed Pickle or Preserve Dish.
1 " Large Fancy shape Handled and Footed Sauce or Gravy Boat.
1 " 7¾ " Flanged Covered Butter Dish with loose drainer.
1 " Fancy shape Sugar Bowl and Cover, with double handles.
1 " Handled Milk or Cream Pitcher.

(*Total 127 pieces in set. Each set in pkg. Pkg. 40c.*)
Shipped direct from pottery. Per set, **$8.50**

Our "BANQUET GOLD ILLUMINATED" 101-Piece Dinner Set.

C88—Thin light weight semi-porcelain, embossed in neat border design with profuse decortions in green ivy leaves filled in in gold, giving an unusually rich and attractive effect. The edges and handles of all pieces are also traced in gold. Sizes given are actual. Set comprises the following:

12 only 8-in. breakfast plates.
12 " 9¼-in. dinner plates.
12 " 9¼-in. soup plates.
12 " 5-in. fruit or sauce dishes.
12 " 3½-in. individual butters.
12 " low ovide shape handled tea cups.
12 " 6¼-in. saucers to match.
2 " 9¾-in. deep oval footed bakers or vegetable dishes.
1 " 11¾-in. oval dish or platter.
1 " 13¾-in. " "
1 " 15½-in. " "
1 only 9¼-in. oval, footed, covered vegetable dish.
1 " 8¼-in round, footed, covered casserole.
1 " extra large, fancy footed and handled sauce boat.
2 " 8¼-in. deep oval footed pickle or preserve dishes.
1 " 7½-in. flanged and footed covered butter dish with loose drainer.
1 " 9-in. round, covered soup or oyster tureen with opening for ladle.

Total 101 pieces in set. Each set in pkg.
(*Shipped direct from pottery. Pkg. 40c.*) Per set, **$8.75**

Our "GOVERNOR'S TABLE" 101-Piece Complete Dinner Set.

C9—Hand-painted. Filled in decorations in a delicate pink and very profuse floral design, all the embossed work, knobs, handles, etc., being elaborately traced in gold. All on light weight semi-porcelain. Large platters. Regular 101-Piece Composition.

(*Shipped from pottery. 1 set in bbl. Bbl. 40c.,*) Per set, **$10.95**

Our "KING'S FAVORITE" 127-Piece Decorated Dinner Set.

C90—Best thin light weight pure white semi-porcelain in new and artistic shapes, all embossed in neat and rich pattern. Decorations in beautiful sprays of marguerites in combination of pink and delicate green with the pink predominating. Not the usual scant decorations, but are almost all-over and are very elaborate, all open pieces decorated on inside as well as outside. Edges, handles, knobs and feet of all pieces heavily gold clouded. Sizes given are actual.
Set comprises the following:

12 only 6-in. bread and butter or pie plates.
12 " 7¼ inch tea plates.
12 " 8 " breakfast plates.
12 " 9 " dinner plates.
12 " 9 " soup plates.
12 " 5 " fruit or sauce dishes.
12 " 3¼ " individual butters.
12 " fancy shape ovide handled tea cups.
12 only 6-in. saucers to match.
2 only 9-inch deep oval footed bakers or vegetable dishes.
1 only 11¾ inch oval footed dish or meat platter.
1 only 13¾ inch oval footed dish or meat platter.
1 only 17-in. extra large dish or meat platter.
2 only 9 inch deep oval footed covered vegetable dishes.
1 only fancy shape handled and footed sauce boat.
1 only 8-inch footed fancy shape pickle dish.
1 only 8 " flanged covered butter dish with loose drainer.
1 only low fancy shape footed covered sugar bowl with double handles.
1 only fancy footed and handled cream pitcher to match.
1 only extra round deep footed and covered soup or oyster tureen, diam. 10-in.

Total 127 pieces. Each set in pkg. Pkg. 40c. (Shipped direct from pottery.) Per set, **$14.50**

We make no charge for cartage. We do make the usual charge for packages, believing it more straightforward to do so than to smuggle same into the price of goods. Reduce all quotations made you down to the same net basis as ours and you will find that we are **always the lowest on Glassware and Crockery.**

We Want MORE Than Trial Orders--For That Reason Sell Only Dependable Quality Goods.

Original Packages of CROCKERY SHIPPED FROM OUR HOUSE.

Our "10-CENT WONDER" Assortment of GOLD DECORATED SEMI-PORCELAIN WARE.

No better 10-cent bargain in this book. Half of them retail regularly at 25-cents.

Our "BARGAIN LEADER" Assortment of Filled-in and Gold Decorated SEMI-PORCELAIN TABLE WARE.

Shipped from our house.

If retailed at 10c these will not only pay you a good profit but will give you some excellent advertising as well.

C54—All in pure white, best thin light weight semi-porcelain in beautiful shapes with fancy embossed edges, all with elaborate decorations in profuse sprays of pure gold in an artistic floral design, all pieces also having gold decorated centers, decorations being exactly the same as in our new "Princess" line, listed in the regular pages of this book. Assortment comprises:
1 doz. extra large round deep footed nappies or salad dishes, diam. 9¼-in., fancy embossed scalloped edge, elaborately decorated.
2 " low fancy shaped handled teacups and saucers, diam. of cup 3⅝-in., saucer 5¾.
1 " 8¼-in. extra deep round footed table dishes.
1 " 7½-in. extra deep round footed nappies or table dishes.
2 " 5-in. (actual 7¼) tea plates.
2 " 6-in. (actual 8) breakfast plates.
1 " large deep footed oatmeal bowl, diam. 6¼ in.
2 " 7-in. (actual 9¼) breakfast or dinner plates.
(Total 12 doz. in pkg., pkg. 40c.)   Average price per dozen, **82c**

No cartage charge on any goods.

C51—All in the best pure white semi-porcelain, each and every piece beautifully decorated in filled-in floral and leaf designs in rich delicate green and pink combination, all the edges elaborately decorated in gold showered dapple effect. Decorations are not scant but profuse. Most of the pieces would retail readily at from 15 to 25c. Sizes givenare actual.

The Assortment Comprises 1-2 Doz. Each of the Following:
11-Inch Large Deep Meat Dish or Platter—Fancy oval shape. *Worth 25c.*
7¼-Inch Round Deep Table Dish—Fancy embossed and scalloped edge.
Extra Large 10¼-Inch Dinner Plate—Embossed flange. *A bargain at 15c.*
5-Inch Extra Deep Footed Bowl—Fancy shape, richly decorated.
9¼-Inch Large Fancy Plate—Neatly embossed edge.
6¼-Inch Deep Footed Oatmeal Bowl.
8¼-Inch Medium Size Plate—Decorated as above.
6¼-Inch Extra Deep Footed Nappy or Table Dish—Scalloped edge.
8¼-Inch Deep Oval Baker or Vegetable Dish—Would be cheap at 20c.
7½-Inch Embossed Plate—A size that always sells.
Fancy Handled Ovide Shape Tea Cup and Saucer—Never too many to sell at a dime.
7½-Inch Extra Deep Round Nappy or Table Dish—Footed, scalloped edge. *Worth 25c.*
(Total 6 doz. in barrel. Bbl. 35c.)   Per dozen, Temporarily Out.

"HOLLAND" SEMI-PORCELAIN CUP, SAUCER AND PLATE SET.

You can retail with a good profit at 15c and still be giving rare value.

C810-14—Body of pure white imported Holland semi-porcelain, medium light weight, but extra strong and well made. Each set consists of 9-in. plate; extra large St. Denis shape tea or coffee cup, ht. 3¼-in. diam. 3⅜, strong handle and extra deep saucer, diam. 6¼-in. 1 doz. sets in pkg. (No pkg. charge.)
Per doz. sets, **$1.30**

"10-CENT" DECORATED LAVA CUSPIDORS.

6¼-inch, painted, assorted spray decorations. Sold only by case. No charge for cases.
Case No. 1: 3 doz. Total (3 doz. at 76c) **$2.28**
Case No. 5: 6 " " (6 " " 72c) **4.32**

GLAZED CUSPIDORS.

Superb value in this popular ware.

C536—Good size, ht. 4½-in. diam. 6¼, extra strong and well made, white body, heavily glazed inside and out with all over decorations in cobalt blue mottled effect. Do not confuse this with the common painted cuspidor usually sold at this price. 2 doz. in bbl. (No charge for bbl.) Per dozen, **96c.**

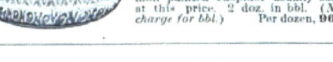

EMBOSSED GLAZED PITCHER ASSORTMENT.

Priced so you can retail with profit at 20 and 25 cents.

EMBOSSED GLAZED CUSPIDORS.

Usually a 50-center. We name a 25-cent price.

C535—Extra strong and well made, good shape, extra large size, being 7¼ in. in diam. at top, ht. 6 in. Elaborately embossed in rich scroll design heavily glazed inside and outside. Attractive dark colors having rich mottled effect. Assorted in crate of 2 doz. (No charge for crate.) Per dozen, **$2.10**

"BIG AND BEAUTIFUL" EMBOSSED GLAZED JARDINIERE ASST.

Richest of colorings, newest of shapes, extraordinary values to retail at 25, 50, 75c and $1.00.

Our NEW "TRADE WINNER"
Assortment of Decorated SEMI-PORCELAIN CUPS, SAUCERS AND PLATES.

Two popular sellers and two 10-cent bargains.

C55—Light weight, pure white body, fancy shape, fancy embossed edges. Decorations are in beautiful ivy leaf design and are very attractive.
6 doz. 7-in. (actual size 9¼) plates, 3 doz. green and 3 doz. brown decorations.
6 doz. large fancy ovide shape handled tea cups and saucers, 3 doz. green and 3 doz. brown decorations.
(Total 12 doz. in bbl., bbl. 35c.)   Average price per doz. **80c**

C830—Extra strong and well made, best fire-proof faience bodies in twist, fluted and floral embossed designs, elaborately decorated in all-over mottled effect in rich colors, such as blue, green and old gold. All having extra large handles and good pouring lips. Usually retailed at from 25 to 50 cents.

The Assortment Comprises the Following:
½ doz. medium size. Capacity 3-pint. *To retail at 20c*, at $1.69 doz. **$0.85**
½ doz. extra large low shape. Capacity 6-pint, at $2.25 doz. 1 13
1 doz. tall tankard shape. Capacity 4-pint 2 25
Total for 2 doz. in crate. (No charge for crate.) **$4.23**

C538—Made of the strongest and best faience ware in assorted solid, blended and mottled colors, such as maroon, green, onyx, etc. All elaborately embossed in various rich designs, and heavily glazed both inside and out. Note that this assortment contains the most popular selling sizes and a large variety of shapes and colors, no two being exactly alike.

Size		
	Girth.	
¼ doz. 7 25¾	..... $1 95	$0 49
¼ " 8 29¼	..... 3 95	99
¼ " 9 31	..... 5 75	1 44
¼ " 10 35¼	..... 7 50	1 88
Total for assortment of 1 doz.		**$4.80**
(Wt. 125 lbs. No charge for pkg.)		

Keep Your Windows Clean—Dirty Windows Not Only Keep Out Light, But Keep Out Customers.

CROCKERY SHIPPED FROM OUR HOUSE--Continued.

FLOWER POT AND SAUCER Assortment.

New Cream Color

The lowest prices on absolutely high grade goods.

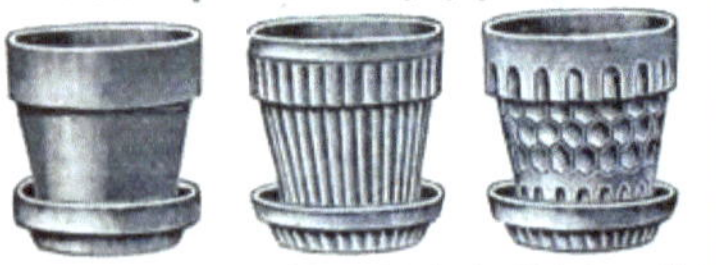

C1:.All mold made and finished by hand. Made from a high grade of potters' clay, very porous. Assortment contains equal quantities of 3 patterns in each size in cream colored ware.

2 doz. 4½-inch, at 18c.		$0 36
2 " 5½- " " 34c.		68
2 " 6½- " " 44c.		88
1 " 7½- " " 74c.		74
1 " 8½- " " 96c.		96
Total for assortment		**$3.62**

Total of 8 doz. in crate, sold only in crate. (*No charge for crate.*)

No Cartage Charge On Any Goods.

PAINTED FLOWER POT AND SAUCER Assortment.

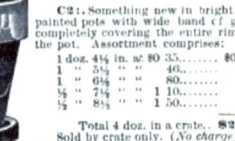

C2:.Something new in bright red painted pots with wide band of gold completely covering the entire rim of the pot. Assortment comprises:

1 doz. 4½ in. at $0 35		$0 35
1 " 5½ " " 46		46
1 " 6½ " " 80		80
½ " 7½ " " 1 10		55
½ " 8½ " " 1 50		75

Total 4 doz. in a crate.. **$2.91**

Sold by crate only. (*No charge for crate.*)

OUR "LEADER" GLAZED EMBOSSED JARDINIERE AND PEDESTAL.

One of the best dollar bargains ever offered.

C536½—Comprising large fancy shape jardiniere, ht. 7¼-in., diameter 8¼, standing on artistically shaped 8¾-in. pedestal. Full height of jardiniere and pedestal 16-in., both elaborately embossed in tropical design, heavily glazed inside and out. Assortment comprises the following: 1 light green, 1 dark green, 1 maroon and 1 dark yellow. (*Total 4 in bbl. No charge for bbl.*) Wt. 71 lbs. Each, **72c**

EXTRA LARGE GLAZED EMBOSSED JARDINIERE AND PEDESTAL.

Regular $5.00 combination which you can retail with good profit at $2.98.

C537 — This beautiful set comprises extra large fancy shape jardiniere, ht. 9-in., diam. 9¼, circumference 36. Extra tall fancy round shape pedestal, ht. 15 in., full ht. of jardiniere and pedestal 24½-in. Both pieces are heavily glazed and embossed in beautiful scroll and leaf design. Color being the popular dark green. Each in bbl. Price including jardiniere and pedestal. Each, **$1.95**

GLAZED JARDINIERE AND PEDESTAL.

Positively the richest ones ever produced.

C539, "Palace". Extra heavy, best faience body in new and exquisite design. Pedestal tall fancy column shape, ht. 15-in. with fancy wide foot. Extra large fancy footed jardiniere, diameter 10¼-in., fancy scalloped flaring top. Both jardiniere and pedestal in combination of rich green and brown, blending into pink, both heavily glazed inside and out. Full ht. of jardiniere and pedestal 24-in. Each in barrel, *no charge for bbl.* Price complete, **$2.95**

C540, "Mammoth":. As above, ht. of pedestal 17-in., jardiniere 11½, diam. 12½. Full ht. of jardiniere and pedestal 29-in. Each in bbl, *no charge for bbl.* Price complete, **$4.75**

ASSORTMENTS OF YELLOW AND ROCKINGHAM WARE.

A profitable staple line, needed in every stock. We have arranged five assortments of trade-drawing goods, which will answer our customers' needs nicely, as they include the right proportion of each article according to its usual sale. **All these assortments will be carried constantly in stock in our warehouse in this city. Orders can be filled promptly at all times. NO CARTAGE CHARGE.**

The following cuts are representative items of the line.

Rockingham Pie Plate

Yellow Bowl, Banded

Rockingham Nappy.

Pineapple Teapot.

Yellow Chamber, Open.

Rockingham Water Pitcher.

No. 1 "SENSIBLE" ASSORTMENT.

(Yellow Ware.)

:.Every article a staple every day seller. Assorted so all items will sell out clean. A profitable line of goods to put in your stock. Neatly banded.

1/12 doz.	4's.	Bowls	13-Pint.	13 inch	$2.50	$0 21
⅙ "	6's.	"	9 "	12 "	2.00	34
½ "	9's.	"	6½ "	10½ "	1.20	60
⅓ "	12's.	"	4¾ "	9½ "	90	30
⅓ "	18's.	"	3½ "	8¾ "	75	25
½ "	24's.	"	4 "	7 "	40	20
½ "	30's.	"	1½ "	6½ "	35	18
1 "	36's.	"	1⅛ "	6 "	27	27
1 "	42's.	"	¾ "	5¼ "	24	24
1/12 "	6's.	Open Chambers.		9½ "	2.00	17
1/12 "	6's.	Cov'd "		9½ "	3.00	25
¼ "	9's.	Open "		8½ "	1.25	31
¼ "	9's.	Cov'd "		8½ "	2.50	63
1/12 "	12's.	Open "		7½ "	85	07
1/12 "	12's.	Cov'd "		7½ "	1.50	13

(*5 1-6 doz. in bbl. Sold only by pkg. Bbl. 35c.*) Total, **$4.15**

No. 2 YELLOW CHAMBER ASSORTMENT.

:.Comprises the 3 everyday selling sizes in proper quantities of each size, both open and covered. Neatly banded. If you have not carried yellow chambers you have missed many sales.

⅙ doz.	6's.	Open.	9½-inch	$2 00	$0 34
1/12 "	6's.	Covered.	9½ "	3 00	25
½ "	9's.	Open.	8½ "	1 25	63
½ "	9's.	Covered.	8½ "	2 50	1 25
1/12 "	12's.	Open.	7½ "	85	07
1/12 "	12's.	Covered.	7½ "	1 50	13

(*15-12 doz. in bbl. Sold only by pkg. Bbl. 35c.*) Total, **$2.67**

No. 4 "COMBINATION" ASSORTMENT.

(Yellow and Rockingham.)

:. Just the thing for the dealer who finds he does not need No. C1 C2 and C5 assortments, or the customer who wants to try the line and is timid about ordering largely. We have combined the **pieces that sell** from out of the complete line of Yellow and Rockingham ware now made.

Yellow Ware, Banded.

⅓ doz.	No. 9	Bowls	6½-Pint.	10½-inch	$1.20	$0 40
⅓ "	" 12	"	4¾ "	9½ "	90	30
⅓ "	" 18	"	3½ "	8¾ "	75	25
½ "	" 24	"	2 "	7 "	40	20
½ "	" 30	"	1½ "	6½ "	35	18
½ "	" 36	"	1⅛ "	6 "	27	13
½ "	" 9	Open Chamber		8½ "	1.25	63
¼ "	" 9	Cov'd "		8½ "	2.50	63

Rockingham Ware.

⅙ doz.	42's. Teapots. Pineapple.	6¼ in.	2-Pints	$1.50	25
¼ "	36's. " "	7¼ "	2½ "	1.75	44
⅙ "	30's. " "	8 "	4 "	2.00	33
1/12 "	24's. " "	8½ "	4¾ "	2.40	20
¼ "	7-in. Rd. Pl. Nappy.	8 "	2 "	70	17
¼ "	9 " " "	9¾ "	4 "	1.10	28
¼ "	9 " Pie Plate	10½ "	1½ deep	60	15
1/12 "	6's Pl. Water Pitcher	9½-in. high.	6 pts.	2.70	23

(*4 3-4 doz. in bbl. Sold only by pkg. Bbl. 35c.*) Total, **$4.77**

"MONSTER" 10-Cent YELLOW BOWL ASSORTMENT.

Most Excellent Sellers--Most Unusual Values.

:.This is one of the biggest assortments ever offered for a dime. Order a sample assortment and see for yourself.

½ doz.	Milk Bowls,	banded, diameter.	8½ inches.
½ "	Cake "	" "	9⅝ "
½ "	Batter "	" "	10¼ "
½ "	Oval Baking Dish,	" "	10½ "
½ "	Round " "	plain, "	10½ "
½ "	" Vegetable Dish, fluted,	"	9½ "

(*3 doz. in pkg. Sold only by pkg. Bbl. 35c.*) **Per dozen 82c**

No. 3 "ROCKINGHAM" TEA POT Assortment.

:.You will find an extensive sale on these goods in all sizes, and the following assortment will sell out even and at a good profit. This perfectly plain shape is the favorite.

¼ doz.	48's.	5¾-inch.	1½-pint	$1 20	$0 30
½ "	42's.	6½ "	2 "	1 50	75
1 "	36's.	7¼ "	2½ "	1 75	1 75
½ "	30's.	8 "	4 "	2 00	1 00
¼ "	24's.	8½ "	4¾ "	2 40	60

(*2¼ doz. in bbl. Sold only by pkg. Bbl. 35c.*) Total, **$4.40**

"CLOVER LEAF" BOTTLE CAPS.

C1895:.All up-to-date dairy men now deliver in bottles. ... the common goods, but *of superior quality*, full wt., thoroughly waterproof. Fit full size milk bottles.

1000 in pasteboard box. Per M, **23c**

6000 in bushel basket, *no charge for basket.* Per M, **22c**

25,000 in a case. Per M, **19c**

"SANITARY" MILK BOTTLE CAPS.

These absolutely prevent leakage.

C1890:. Made of the very toughest stock paraffined. Turned edge which adapts itself to any irregularity in the neck of bottle, preventing leakage. Can be inserted without breaking. 1,000 in pasteboard box Per 1,000, **30c**

6,000 in strong, heavy bushel basket, no charge for basket.

GLASSWARE EXTRAORDINARY for March Buyers.

Bought specially for the yellow pages and priced to make them real bargains. We venture the bold assertion that you will not match a single ONE of these items in all America at the price. Try it and let us know if you succeed.

BEADED CRYSTAL NAPPY.

Special purchase for this bargain page.

LC145—Diameter 4½ in., extra deep, fancy footed, scalloped edge bright beaded crystal pattern. A regular 5-center as a "2 for 5" leader. 1 doz. in box. Per dozen, **20c**

"SATIN DIAMOND" SAUCE DISH.

A finished 5-cent gem.

LC154—4¼-in., the most popular size. Extra deep, round shape, cut design, fancy scalloped edge. Brilliant, full finished and fire polished. 1 doz. in box, *no pkg. charge.* Per doz. Out

"CRYSTAL AND GOLD" TABLE DISH.

You will be surprised at the size and beauty.

LC498—Fancy oblong shape, length 8-in., width 3¾, extra deep, rolled up ends, brilliant prism design, extra heavy, fire polished, gold decorated edge. Useful for many purposes. 1 doz. in box, *no pkg. charge.* Per dozen Out

EMBOSSED SHELL PATTERN SALTS AND PEPPERS.

Big and shapely 5-centers on which you can double your money.

LC259—Extra large size, tall shape, attractive embossed shell design in purest blown crystal, nickel plated dome top. Finished and brilliant. 6 salts and 6 peppers in box of 1 doz. *No pkg. charge.* Per dozen, **28c**

"HIGH SHAPE" SALTS AND PEPPERS.

A 5-cent advertiser; retails regularly for 10-cents.

LC255 — Extra large fancy twist twist and embossed, wide base, all-over decorations in bright blended colors and elaborate gold clouds. 6 salts and 6 peppers in box of 1 doz. *No pkg. charge.* Per doz. **43c**

OUR "HEAVY RICH" TABLE TUMBLER.

You would expect to pay more for one not so good.

LC440—A new and exceptionally good one. Medium heavy and very beautiful pattern. Heavy bottom, long fine flutes, 3 mould bands. Tall and shapely full size tumbler, brilliantly finished and fire polished. 1 doz. in box, no pkg. charge. Per dozen, **27c**

PLAIN BLOWN TABLE TUMBLER.

Exceptional value at this price.

LC399 — Purest of thin lead blown glass, medium table size, capacity about 7½-oz. A size that is always a seller. 1 doz. in box, no pkg. charge. Per dozen, **36c**

"GOLD BAND" OPTIC TABLE TUMBLER.

This is regularly a 10-center.

LC451 — Large size, good shape, purest crystal in brilliant reflecting optic pattern, pure burnt-in gold band, full finished and fire polished. One that will sell every day in the year. 1 doz. in box. No pkg. charge. Per dozen, **43c**

"GOLD BAND" MINERAL WATER TUMBLER.

Your loss if you do not sample this exceptional 5c possibility.

LC338—Pure lead blown, tall flaring shape, capacity 4 oz. 2 burnt-in bands of gold, 1 wide and one narrow. Retails regularly at 10c. 1 doz. in box. *No pkg. charge.* Per dozen, **45c**

OUR "BEAUTY" WINE GLASS.

A famous seller at a bargain price.

LC100—Brilliant twist cut diamond pattern, smooth finished edge. A staple 5-center—as a positive leader. 1 doz. in box. No pkg. charge. Price per dozen, **27c**

SPARKLING "CUT DIAMOND" SHERBET CUP.

A crystal gem. A dime bargain.

LC38—Large size, fancy shape, rich diamond and deep cut pattern, large handle, ground and polished bottom, brilliant finish. 1 doz. in box, *no pkg. charge.* Per dozen, **69c**

OUR "DIME" SYRUP PITCHER.

Unequaled at a 10-cent price.

LC380 — Tall shape, beaded and plain panel pattern, wide flaring base, large handle, strong top, capacity 8 oz. Brilliantly finished. 1 doz. in box, no pkg. charge. Per dozen, **87c**

"RICHEST" DECORATED OPAL VASE ASST.

New ones to retail at 10 cents or more.

LC584—Comprising 3 sizes in assorted shapes, all pure opal, embossed patterns, elaborate all-over decorations in rich bright blended colors and silver and gold clouds. 1 doz. each of 3 sizes, 5¼-inch, 6-inch and 6½-inch, total 3 doz. in case *(no charge for case).* Average per dozen, **79c**

TWO SPECIAL BARGAINS IN "GOLD DECORATED" WINE-RUBY GLASSWARE.

Values beyond compare.

"Gold Decorated" Wine-Ruby Salts and Peppers.

LC264 — Good size, fancy new shape, rich solid wine-ruby color in leaf embossed design, all the embossed work decorated in pure gold. Decorations burnt-in, will not wear off, extra heavy genuine silver plated tops. *Advertise yourself by retailing these at 10c.* 6 salts and 6 peppers in box of 1 doz., *no pkg. charge.* Per dozen, **75c**

"Gold Decorated" Wine-Ruby Toothpick Holder.

LC340 — Footed, fancy shape, good size, height 2¼-in., solid wine-ruby color with embossed decorations in pure burnt-in gold and fancy scalloped gold edge. *A 10-cent price ticket will sell these every day in the year.* 1 doz. in box, *no pkg. charge.* Per dozen, **75c**

Our "ARISTOCRACY" Water Set.

Only 28c for this big and brilliant set.

LC680—Beautiful new pattern in purest crystal, extra heavy massive panel design, richly fire polished. A high grade set. Each set comprises 1 extra large and extra heavy half gallon jug in fancy shape with wide flaring top and extra large handle and 6 heavy table tumblers to match. *(12 sets in bbl. Bbl. 35c).* Per set, **28c**

"RICH AND RARE" 5-PIECE CRUET SET.

A large and handsome set to retail at 50c.

LC57 — Extra heavy and beautiful scroll pattern, brilliantly fire polished. Set comprises — 6¼-inch round tray on 3 feet, large oil or vinegar bottle with glass stopper, large heavy salt shaker with silver top, pepper shaker to match salt, fancy toothpick holder. Comes in 4 colors —amethyst, green, blue and crystal. One of the handsomest sets ever produced, will be an exceptional seller. Each set in box (no pkg. charge.) Per set, **33c**

Note.—We suggest that customers order at least 4 sets and thereby get the full assortment of colors.

"COMMON SENSE" GLASS MILK BOTTLES.

A clean, economical and convenient way of handling milk and cream.

Crystal glass, *guaranteed extra quality,* very heavy and thick. Do not confuse with the green bottles which make milk look blue. Fruit preserves and pickles are safely put up in these bottles simply by pouring melted paraffine or common sealing wax on top of the cap.

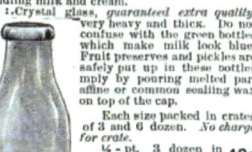

Each size packed in crates of 3 and 6 dozen. *No charge for crate.*

½-pt. 3 dozen in crate. Per dozen, **40c**
(6 doz. in crate, 38c doz.)

1-pt. 3 dozen in crate. Per dozen, **44c**
(6 doz. in crate, 41c doz.)

1-qt. 3 dozen in crate. Per dozen, **62c**
(6 doz. in crate, 60c doz.)

'JUPITER" GLOBE NIGHT LAMP.

Richest of 25c offerings.

LC726 — Large size, full height 9 in., square fancy shape fount and round fancy shape globe, both in embossed pattern and entirely new decoration, in blended orange and shaded green producing an old mosaic effect. Complete with best burner and wick. Each in carton, ½ doz. in pkg., *no pkg. charge.* Per dozen, **$2.10**

THE WELL KNOWN "VESUVIUS" GAS CHIMNEY.

Hard to match as a 10-center.

8-inch "Vesuvius". Etched base gas chimney. Each in carton. ½ doz. in pkg. Per dozen, **63c**

THE BIGGEST AND BEST 25c REFLECTOR LAMP EVER OFFERED.

Your competitors sell them for 50c.

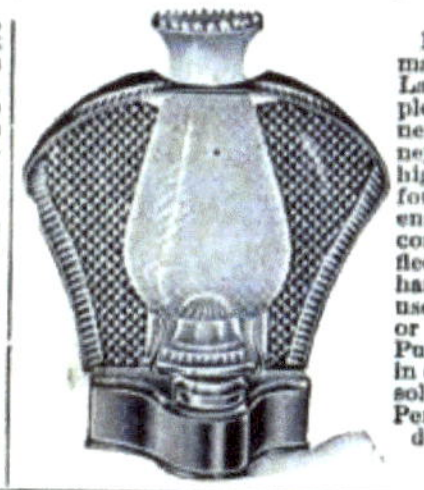

LC97. Climax Reflector Lamp. Complete with burner and chimney. 11-inch high. 1½ pint founts. Nicely enameled, large corrugated reflector, good handle. Can be used as a table or wall lamp. Put up 1 doz. in case, no less sold. Per doz., **$2.25**

Our "NEW COMPETITION" Tank Glass Tumbler Assortment.

Your opportunity to secure a rare leader.

LC551—Not equal in quality to our regular line, but exceptional value at this price. Medium size, height 3¾-inch, capacity about 7-oz., all with heavy bottoms and finished edges. Assortment comprises 5 dozen each of four patterns, all with fluted bases and neat mold bands. *(Total 20 doz. in bbl. Bbl. 35c).* Per dozen, **14½c**

OUR "DIME QUART" JUG ASSORTMENT.

You need these 10-cent leaders.

LC475—Assortment comprises 2 styles—1 tall almost plain tankard shape, height 8¼-in., footed, with handle and extra good lip; the other a rich reflecting panel design, graceful shape, with wide top, footed and large handle. Both brilliantly finished and fire polished, both so-called 1-quart. 1½ dozen each, total 3 doz. in bbl. *(Bbl. 35c.)* Per dozen, **89c**

"TWO BARGAINS" BERRY SET ASSORTMENT.

Exceptional value. *Regular 35-cent sets to retail at 25-cents.*

LC409—Comprises 2 patterns —1 a heavy cut diamond design; other a plain and frosted beaded panel pattern. Each set consists of 1 extra large and extra deep 8-in. berry bowl, and six 4¼-in deep nappies to match. 12 sets each of 2 patterns—total 24 sets in bbl. *(Bbl 35c.)* Per set, **14½c**

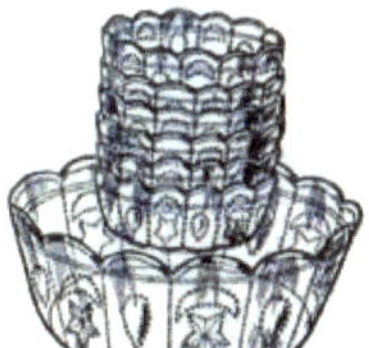

Our "ADVERTISER" 4-piece Table Set Assortment.

Big and bright sets at a bargain price.

LC513—Comprising 2 styles, one in new and brilliant plain and frosted panel design; the other a rich beaded drapery pattern. All pieces are extra large and all are footed, all the open pieces with fancy scalloped edges. 12 sets each of 2 patterns. *Total 24 pieces in bbl., bbl. 35c.* Per set, **15c**

BUTLER BROTHERS, 1221 TO 1237 WASHINGTON AVE., ST. LOUIS.

Always Sell a Leader to the GREATEST NUMBER OF PEOPLE POSSIBLE.

Our "BEST YET" 5-Cent Assortment.
All Extra Rich, Half of Them Being Regular 10-Centers.

LC114—While not quite equal in quality to most of our assortments, being made under the new tank glass process, they are *almost* equal to the best. All in bright new patterns. All exceptionally good sellers. More than half of them retail regularly at 10c.

The Assortment Comprises 1-2 Doz. Each of the Following:
7¼-in. Extra Large Flanged Butter Dish and Cover—Rich plain and frosted panel design.
Large Footed Spoon Holder with Scalloped Edge—Matches butter dish.
Large Handled and Footed Milk Pitcher—Also matches butter dish.
Large Fancy Footed Sugar Bowl and Cover—Of the same beautiful pattern.
4½-in. Extra Deep Berry or Sauce Dish—With attractive scalloped edge.
5¾-in. Extra Large and Extra Deep Utility Dish—With fancy open handle.
6½-in. Extra Deep Round Table Dish—Beautiful pattern and scalloped edge.
7½-in. Round Plate—For bread or cake.
6¼-in. Deep Round Table Dish—Extra heavy and brilliant cut pattern.
Fancy Footed Tankard Cream Pitcher—Ht. 5¼-in., large handle, beautiful embossed pattern.
5¼-in. Extra Deep Round Bowl—On fancy foot.
4¾-in. Deep Round Nappy—Fancy drapery pattern.
Shapely Wine Glass—Rich and brilliant.
4⅜-in. High Footed Jelly Dish—Beaded crystal pattern.
Fancy Handled and Footed Mug—Extra heavy and extra brilliant.
Full Finished Table Tumbler—Extra bright neat pattern.
4½-in. Extra Heavy and Round Sauce Dish—Brilliant pattern and scalloped edge.
High Footed Handled Sherbet Cup—Cut diamond pattern.
6¼-in. Tall Flower Vase—Brilliant pattern. *A regular 10-center.*
9½-in. Long Oval Table Dish—Extra brilliant. A 10-cent bargain.
(Total 10 dozen in bbl. Bbl. $5.) **Per dozen, 36c**

OUR "NEW FULL FINISHED" BOWL ASSORTMENT.
Magnificent 10-cent leader at a price which leaves you a profit.

LC391—The assortment comprises 2 patterns and 6 shapes, elaborate and brilliant cut glass patterns, all richly finished and fire polished. Footed, extra deep, average size about 8 in. These will sell themselves if shown. 1 doz. each of the 6 styles, total 6 doz. in bbl. (Bbl. 35c.) **Per dozen, 72c**

OUR "MAJESTIC" DINING SET ASSORTMENT.
Big and Beautiful Sets to Retail at Unusually Low Prices.

LC359—All pieces of the same pattern, which is an extra heavy and massive design, in beautiful all-over scrollwork. Exceptionally handsome in the rich solid colors. *These will sell themselves if marked 75 cents per set, and pay you a handsome profit.* Assortment comprises 3 sets each of the following, 1 each in blue, green and wine ruby:
7-piece Water Set, consisting of 1 extra large and extra heavy half-gallon jug and 6 tumblers to match.
4-piece Table Set, comprising massive flanged butter dish and cover, covered sugar bowl, milk pitcher and spoonholder.
7-piece Berry Set, consisting of mammoth 8-inch deep footed berry bowl and six 4½-inch footed nappies to match.
Total 9 sets in bbl. (Bbl. 35c.) **Average per set, 39c**

New Klondyke Gold Assortment.
A Magnificent Group of 10-cent Trade Stimulators.

LC278—Although you can retail these for 10 cents, most of them are *actually worth 25*. The pattern is one of the newest in crystal glass, prism panel design, all pieces in same pattern, and all extra heavy and brilliantly fire polished. Decorations in pure 18k gold and very elaborate, being all around the edges of each piece and extending almost the full length of panels.

The Assortment Comprises ½ Doz. Each of the Following:
Extra Large and Shapely Table Tumbler—Also used as a spoonholder.
Fancy Handled Cream Pitcher—Dainty and rich.
Large Size Open Sugar—To match cream pitcher.
8¼x4¼-in. Oblong Utility Tray—A big and beautiful piece.
6-in. Tall Fancy Flower Vase—With fancy scalloped edge.
4½-in. Extra Deep Sauce Dish—Fancy shape, useful and beautiful.
Fancy Footed Toothpick Holder—Large size, richest of decorations.
4½-in. Extra Deep Bonbon Dish—Fancy shape with large open handle.
Brilliant Wide Glass—Fancy stem and flaring top.
5¼-in. Bonbon or Card Tray—With fancy rolled-up sides.
Handled Sherbet or Lemonade Cup—With ground and polished bottom.
Extra Large and Shapely Goblet—Attractive and beautiful.
(Total 6 doz. in small bbl. Bbl. 25c.) **Per dozen, 75c**

Our "TREMENDOUS" 10-Cent Cask Assortment.
Twenty Big and Useful Pieces—All Exceptional 10-Centers.

LC276—A splendid collection of all staple and all bright pieces in attractive patterns—all of the purest crystal—which, if offered at 10 cents, would make sales lively on the dullest day. The assortment comprises ⅙ dozen each of the following:
8¼-inch extra large round berry bowl. Extra deep.
6½-inch extra deep round bowl with high dome cover.
11¼x8-inch large oval bread or cake plate with fancy scalloped edge.
Extra large footed sugar bowl and cover. Rich pattern. Always a staple seller.
7¼-inch flanged butter dish and cover. Extra large and extra brilliant.
6½x6½-inch square deep table dish. Bright pattern.
Tall, slender, flaring flower vase. Rich cut pattern, height 8¾ inches.
5½-inch high footed jelly dish, deep and fancy round shape.
8¼-inch extra large oval dish. Extra deep and useful.
7¼-inch fancy footed comport. Fancy flaring shape.
Extra large fancy footed cream or milk pitcher with wide and scalloped top.
Large fancy footed spoonholder. Matches sugar and cream.
7¼-inch extra deep scalloped flanged butter dish and cover of the same beautiful pattern.
7-inch fancy footed bent-up dish. Attractive 3-cornered shape.
8½-inch high footed cake salver. Worth 25 cents.
7⅛-inch extra deep round berry bowl. Always a big seller.
5⅜-inch high footed deep dish; for jellies, preserves, etc.
Tall syrup pitcher. Good top and handle.
Extra large fancy footed half-gallon jug with fancy handle and wide top.
Total 10 dozen in cask (cask 90c). **Price per dozen, 72c**

BUTLER BROTHERS, 1221 TO 1237 WASHINGTON AVE., ST. LOUIS.

If There Is Money in Another Line, GET INTO IT QUICK.

COMPOUNDING PROFIT.

It seems to us strange that so many good merchants should be blind to what is at once the plainest and most important lesson in modern merchandising, which is:

The best profit a merchant can possibly make is the COMPOUND profit which comes from frequent turns.

You have a certain fixed expense—say 15 per cent on sales. You make a more or less fixed average profit—say 25 per cent on sales. In other words, an article that costs you 75 cents you sell for a dollar. Out of that dollar 15 cents goes for expense, leaving you 10 cents net profit each time the stock is turned.

If you turn that item twice in a year you make 20 cents on the investment. If you turn it five times you make 50 cents, without a penny more investment.

Profit compounds in exact ratio with the number of times you turn your stock.

When you buy double the usual quantity of an item you double your investment but do not increase sales. You turn your stock but half as often. With twice as much money invested you make no more net profit.

This is all the "mystery" there is about the ease with which small stores, that buy their goods right hold their own against big neighbors. It tells why, of two stores side by side handling about the same lines, one may make twice as much "net" as the other.

Go to nine towns out of ten and you will find one or more old-line concerns that have made money in the past and are still well rated. They were bred in the old school where merchants were taught to buy a six months' supply at a time, and they seemingly can't forget their lesson. Their annual sales are perhaps twice their average investment.

To one of these towns comes a small concern with not more than a quarter as much capital as the present leader there. *Because* its capital is limited, it must buy in smaller quantities, buy oftener, watch stocks closer, keep every dollar on the turn all the time. It probably turns its stock eight or at least six times a year.

At the end of the first twelve-month the little store has probably made sales half as great and profits more than half as great as the big store.

At the end of five years the little store has become the big store and its one-time rival (pending the time when expense shall have eaten up its capital wholly) has little to do save to complain that trade is not what it used to be, unless—

Unless the old timer has the wit to see where the trouble lies and the grit to climb out of the rut.

In the latter case there will probably be two prosperous stores instead of one, for both the new firm and the old will fight aggressively for business and pull it from less enterprising towns around.

Every time you invest two dollars where one dollar would have served, you withdraw a dollar from the active part of your capital—you stop the growth of COMPOUND profit.

TO THE MAN WHO THINKS OF OPENING A NEW STORE.

The question "What line to choose" is an important one to the man who is about to launch his bark on the uncertain sea of business. Everywhere one sees exclusive stores doing a profitable business, and no doubt a fair share of the beginners in these lines hew their way to success. Yet we think any keen observer will confirm the statement that the stores that have made the *signal* success in the last decade have been those which handled a general line of merchandise—that started as "department stores in little" and grew to be "department stores in big."

If you contemplate opening a new store, let us ask your thoughtful consideration of the following points before you make your decision:

If you decide to handle simply dry goods or hardware, or boots and shoes or any single line, you automatically set a limit to your possibilities at the start. You can grow up to the consumption of your single line in your community and no further.

On the other hand, if you start with a diversified stock of goods, dipping into many lines of merchandise, the world is before you.

If in your town the dry goods business is not in strong hands, you will soon learn the fact and can develop the dry goods end of your business indefinitely.

If dry goods are overdone and experience shows that hardware competition is weak, then you can push in the direction of hardware and go slow in dry goods.

All progress is along the line of least resistance. When you begin with a general line you test possibilities in all directions, and can therefore avail yourself of any opening of any character in your locality. You have many chances to grow, not merely one.

You can settle your foot firmly after one step before you take another. You need not put in full fledged departments in the beginning. You can start small and grow.

If you run a dry goods store your people will expect you to sell domestics; if a grocery store, you must sell sugar; if a hardware store, you must sell nails; but if you conduct a variety store you need not sell anything on which you cannot make a fair profit.

It is our settled conviction that there is no other mercantile business on earth comparable in possibilities of growth and profit, in proportion to investment, with a retail variety store.

WHY NOT FIND OUT
WHICH CLASS THEY HAVE YOU IN?

As everyone knows, the big exclusive houses in each line have you retailers "classified." Roughly speaking, they divide you into three classes—"big," "medium" and "little." The head of the house makes these classes on the coldest sort of business grounds—on your real or supposed skill as a buyer and your ability to use quantities.

The salesman has nothing to say about the matter. Within certain bounds he can charge what he likes for *particular* items, but if he sells you on the average for less than your class he will hear from the house mighty quick.

The salesman has the hard task of making each man he calls on think *he* gets the inside price, and that it is always someone else who pays the long one. We pay cheerful tribute to the ability with which he does his work, for we have never met even one retailer who had the slightest idea that *he* was in the lowest class.

As a matter of fact the "little" class is much the largest. Outside of two or three leading stores in cities like Albany, Indianapolis and Memphis, the firms rated "big" are scarce, and to qualify for entry in the "medium" class a firm can't fall far short of fifty thousand dollars per year sales.

For example, take an ordinary 10-cent plain black hose. The exclusive house probably prices it to the "little" man at 93 cents, to the "medium" man at 89 cents, and to the "big" man (who is supposed to buy in case lots) at 86 cents.

If the "little" man puts the pressure on that particular number he can for an instant get out of his class and buy it for 89 cents or even less, but be very sure he will make it up on something else before the drummer gets through with him.

Why not find out on which of the three classes they have YOU?

Of course you believe you're high up. But have you any reason for your faith except the drummer's say-so? And, you know, he is hardly a disinterested witness.

It is not hard to find out all about it. Buy a bill from the salesman who gets most of your orders, then duplicate the goods from us as nearly as possible. As far as possible avoid leaders and staples, which everyone sells at about the same price. When the two shipments come in take them off in some corner and compare goods and prices.

Let the test be thorough and fair. Strip labels off goods until you have made up your mind so your judgment may not be unconsciously influenced.

If you find our tablet at $3.25 per hundred looks as good as his at $3.50, do not try to persuade yourself that his *must* be better than ours because the price is higher.

If not, why isn't that odd 25 cents as good in your pocket as in his?

If you find you have gotten more value for a dollar from the drummer than from us be very sure he has you on his highest class. If, after giving him the benefit of every doubt, values seem to be about even—some better here, some better there—it is reasonably sure you are on the "medium" class; and don't flinch if the result proves that you are on the list which requires you to pay the largest prices.

Not from idle curiosity, but for cash box reasons, if we were in your place, we'd want to know how the drummer had us classified.

CONCERNING FREIGHTS.

It seems to be a law of nature that one dollar spent in freight shall look as large to a buyer as two dollars spent in price, though when one stops to think he knows that the only thing that counts is *the cost of goods laid down at his store.*

We notice one very fruitful source of irritation on the freight question is in connection with very small shipments.

The rule among railroad companies is to make a minimum charge of the 100-lbs. rate. That is, freight will be as great on a shipment of 40 lbs. as on one of 100 lbs., though the value of the former may be $15.00 and of the latter $40.00. In other words the ratio of freight to the value of goods is nearly three times as great in the former case as in the latter.

Here is a case in point. One of our St. Louis house salesmen in Texas lately on personal business dropped in to visit one of the local merchants. The latter complained that on his last little bill of $12, freight had been $1.50. He picked up another invoice on his desk from a near-by jobber and showed that freight was only 80c on a purchase of $6. Though the ratio of freight we actually less from us than from the local merchant, yet 80c looked so much smaller to him than $1.50 that without figuring the matter through he decided against us. Comparison of prices on the two invoices showed a decided difference in our favor. If he had ordered just a few more "staples" from us to bring his shipment up to 100 lbs. the variation in our favor would have been still very marked.

We certainly do not wish to seem to urge our customers to buy larger bills than their business requires, yet we feel sure in many cases the sending of orders for less than 100 lbs. is a matter of sheer oversight.

Our line is so varied and includes so many goods of the ever-selling sort that we believe in nearly all cases buyers who bear this point will be able to buy at one time enough goods to make a shipment of 100 lbs. or more, which will entitle them to the minimum freight rates.

RETURN PRIVILEGE.

Any customer may at any time order goods he does not now handle, or which he has not heretofore bought from us, with the privilege of returning same, provided such return is made immediately upon receipt.

The above offer is made for the two-fold purpose of inducing customers to take hold of new lines and to enable them to easily test our values in lines which they now handle but have not heretofore bought of us. It is strictly opposed to our rules—and to our idea of commercial fairness—that merchants should order goods with which they are *familiar* and return them for other than valid cause.

Note that in order to be accepted goods must be returned immediately upon receipt. Be sure to enclose your name and address in the package, and to send us by mail (not in the parcel) notification, including itemized list of goods, date of invoice and reason for returning.

Any merchant NOT now a customer may send us one trial order with the privilege of returning any or all the goods if not satisfactory, provided such return is made within five days after receipt.

We recognize that a merchant to whom we are as yet strangers may properly wish to see what our goods are like before giving us his trade, and as an inducement to that end we make this special offer on entire first trial shipment.

We Extend a Cordial Invitation to You to Call and See Us—Either New York, Chicago or St. Louis.

4 Remember, This Book Quotes NET WHOLESALE PRICES—Keep It Out of Your Customers' Hands.

NEW YORK: Looking up Broadway (north) from the corner of Broome street, showing our giant building, extending through to Mercer street and with an "L" fronting on Broome street.

ST. LOUIS: Seven-story and basement building situated at the corner of Washington avenue and 12th street, embracing 1221, 1223, 1225, 1227, 1229, 1231, 1233, 1235 and 1237 Washington avenue, running through to Lucas avenue. Our new warehouse (nearly three hundred thousand square feet of floor area) is within a stone's throw.

Regular terms. 1 per cent 20 days—net 21 days. Net 40 days—no longer time.

No charge for cartage and none for cases except on glassware and crockery in original packages, for which we make the charge according to the schedule established by the Associated Manufacturers.

A deposit must accompany every C. O. D. order. If you desire goods sent C. O. D. you will please send us a deposit of at least 10 per cent of the presumable amount of the order, and on orders of any amount less than $50 you will please send at least $5. A guaranty of your acceptance of the goods. The amount of the deposit will be deducted from the draft. No C. O. D. shipments for less than $10 will be made. C. O. D. shipments from factory should be treated in same manner as above.

We send goods C. O. D. by freight, cases marked with your initials, not "Butler Brothers," same as all shipments made by us. The invoice is mailed direct to you, and the bill of lading (indorsed over to you), accompanied by a draft on you for the amount of invoice (less your deposit), is sent to your nearest bank for collection. Upon the payment of the same you can secure the bill of lading and thus get your goods from the railroad agent.

Please send bank draft or money order. By the recent action of the clearing houses in our three cities we are compelled to pay exchange on checks drawn on out-of-town banks. We therefore ask our customers to kindly send drafts or money orders.

We cannot break packages. All goods are put in as small packages as possible consistent with safe shipping. We will not furnish less quantities than indicated.

We do not sell to any one but merchants, neither do we sell to peddlers or agents.

We send catalogues only to storekeepers who handle our lines. Any merchant, customer or not, who sees our catalogue in the hands of any one not entitled to same, will do us a favor by reporting the fact to us.

Examine all cases, barrels, etc. and see that they are in good condition before accepting same from transportation company. All shipments made by us are in good order when taken by transportation lines and so receipted for. Our responsibility then ceases.

Goods cannot be returned except for cause. We guarantee every item as described, and are always ready to rectify errors. If goods received are not as ordered, notify us and await instructions. Never return them without notice.

Never send money by mail unregistered. Notwithstanding Uncle Sam's vigilance, money letters disappear in transit every day.

Please do not ask us to purchase goods outside our stock. We naturally wish to be accommodating, but so much difficulty has been experienced in endeavoring to even approximate such requests, often from very meager directions, we have been compelled to refuse them.

In ordering from us for the first time please send CASH IN FULL for first shipment in order to avoid the inevitable delay caused by the investigation of references which necessarily precedes the opening of a credit account. At the same time give us as references the names of a few wholesale houses with which you have an established credit and we will make investigation in readiness for next shipment.

Write your order on separate sheets from any other communication you have to make. This permits both being attended to at once.

Our order sheets are put up 20 in pad. If you have no pad, mention in your next order or drop us a card.

Use only one side of the paper in ordering as this sometimes prevents items being overlooked.

Shipping directions. Be sure to mention your nearest shipping point if you are not located on a railway or water route. If there are competing transportation companies name your preference. If express shipments, specify which company serves your town.

One item only on a line. Never write more than one item on a line, and carry out the price at which we catalogued it. This helps us to identify the exact article wanted.

In using our order blank write nothing upon it except the order. If you have other matters to communicate or a remittance to enclose, mention same on another paper.

Our principal banks of deposit are the following, to which we refer:

Chemical National Bank, New York.

Corn Exchange National Bank, Chicago.

State National Bank of St. Louis, St. Louis.

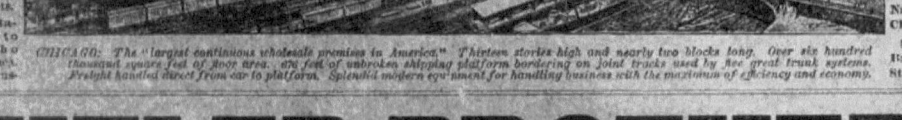

CHICAGO: The "largest continuous wholesale premises in America." Thirteen stories high and nearly two blocks long. Over six hundred thousand square feet of floor area. 476 feet of unbroken shipping platform bordering on joint tracks used by five great trunk systems. Freight handled direct from car to platform. Splendid modern equipment for handling business with the maximum of efficiency and economy.

BUTLER BROTHERS

IMPORTERS AND WHOLESALERS OF GENERAL MERCHANDISE.

NEW YORK:	CHICAGO:	ST. LOUIS:
491 TO 497 BROADWAY.	RANDOLPH BRIDGE.	1221 to 1237 Washington Ave.

MID-SUMMER 1906.   PRICES NAMED HEREIN SUPERSEDE ALL OTHERS

STILL MORE EXPANSION!

In Minneapolis — early in 1913 we shall have a new Distributing House. Construction work is well started and when complete the building will give us over 11 acres of floor space with a railroad track running through the property.

In Baltimore — we shall occupy every inch of floor space in the new factory-and-basement building at the corner of Howard and W. German Streets as a permanent Sample House. Here "the latch string will be out" to every Southern retailer soon after July 1.

In Dallas — we have leased the building at 338-340 Commerce St. and all of its 42,500 sq. ft. of floor area will be utilized for the permanent display of our complete lines. A hearty invitation is extended to every Southwestern retailer when in Dallas to look over our Texas Sample House.

In Chicago — we have added to our equipment another auxiliary warehouse containing 150,000 square feet of floor space, which should take care of our growth for at least a few months.

In St. Paul — we continue to occupy the entire building at 379-381 Sibley St. as our Twin City Sample House for the convenience of Northwestern retailers until the opening of our new Distributing House in Minneapolis.

Another Season of Special Effort in 5 & 10 Cent Goods

In every market of the world, months ago our buyers began their search for values with which a summer season of special effort in retail stores could be made most productive.

That season of special effort by us culminates in the offers—starting on the next leaf—of such window goods as crowd 5 and 10 cent stores in July not much less than in November.

You've got to get people **Inside** before you can sell them anything at all. Left to itself, trade slumps in summer. Dollar prices, however deeply cut, fail to draw when "it's too hot to go shopping."

Also you know that genuine 5 and 10 cent bargains **do** keep exclusive 5 and 10 cent stores busy—every day in the year.

Likewise a 5 and 10 cent store on the side—rightly run and no bigger than you yourself chose to make it—**would** draw trade into your own store this very summer.

Here as everywhere, though, the difference between being busy and being idle, between making a profit and taking a loss, is practically but the difference between pushing and loafing.

Provided, of course, that the ways and the means for the pushing are both available—as they are in this very catalogue which besides The Goods contains The Plans for using them resultfully.

On the green pages, ready to be turned to, are plain and simple directions easily followed for starting—little or big—your 5 and 10 cent store on the side.

It rests with you. Shall this be a busy and profitable summer, or the contrary—for **you?**

| MID SUMMER 1906 | Prices take effect June 29 and supersede all others. We guarantee them during July or until our August catalogue is out. Send all orders from this catalogue to our Chicago House. | Catalogue No. **580** |

BUTLER BROTHERS CHICAGO
EXCLUSIVE JOBBERS OF GENERAL MERCHANDISE—WHOLESALE ONLY

Comparison is the Only True Test of Value. We Court It On Every Line We Sell.

START IT NOW.

Every sticker on your shelves, every slow mover in your storeroom is a reason why you need a bargain department.

For a bargain department is a machine that makes Ready Money from remnants, fad things that fail to sell, stickers and slow movers of all sorts and descriptions.

To be that kind of a machine of course the bargain department must be kept in proper condition. But, merely by making the bargain department pay a profit as a department you may be sure that it is in proper condition.

Yes, that means buy new things regularly for your bargain department. But the best new goods for this use are big sellers that will pay profits while also moving your stickers.

Besides, with the people once drawn into your store by the bargain department, your sales in your other departments must increase—unless you fail to live up to your opportunities.

Facing a season sure to be dull, unless the right effort is made to avoid dullness—now surely is a time when it would seem a merchant could hardly keep from considering the addition of a bargain department.

Starting it as a 5 and 10 cent store on the side—as explained on another page—and running it in that form through the summer, you will have acquired the experience by September 1 on which to base your decision to continue it in that form, or with its scope enlarged to include goods at all sorts of prices.

You need never fear that you will lack fresh, new things for bargain department leaders for they are to be found in plenty in every catalogue of ours.

On the colored pages of this present catalogue are typical big values such as we make it a business to provide regularly every month.

You are perhaps familiar enough with advertising that involves an immediate outlay. Now consider well the bargain department—as a 5 and 10 cent store on the side or in any other form.

For the bargain department is the one kind of advertising which, while drawing more trade than any other kind of advertising, at the same time yields a direct profit.

Our New Distributing House
In Minneapolis

Rough sketch made from architect's plans.

Construction work is under way in Minneapolis. Early in 1907 we shall be located in a new building on Sixth St., N, extending from First Av., N, to Second Av., N.

The area of the site is 173x330, or 56,000 square feet. There will be eight stories and a basement and also a sub-basement under half the building making a net total of 541,000 square feet of floor area.

Thus we shall have more than 13 acres of floor space piled high with goods in our forty odd departments and equipped with every modern facility for doing a jobbing business right.

Understand that we have no "branches." Every Distributing House of ours is a distinct whole except when it comes to join in that tremendous buying which we do as ONE for all our houses.

The direct railroad tracks which will run through our property connecting with the Minneapolis & St. Louis railroad will enable us to handle most of our in and out shipments back and forth from car over our own platform.

That means the elimination of waste handling and the absence of cartage—savings to be reflected in the values afforded to our customers.

The greater the outlet, the greater the quantity of any one item it is safe to buy. And the greater the quantity we can buy, the more we can hammer down our costs and consequently our selling prices.

Hence every customer, present or prospective and wherever located, is vitally interested in the fact that we shall have a fourth great Distributing House—January 1, 1907, or thereabouts.

And until the opening of the new house, Northwestern retailers may continue to send their orders—which will be promptly filled at prices low enough to more than offset freight differences—to Chicago by mail or through

Our
Twin-City Sample House
379-381 Sibley Street
ST. PAUL

BEFORE YOU GO TO MARKET.

Before you go to market this summer, look around your store for all the hints you can get as to how to do better buying this season than you have ever done before.

Go thoroughly over your store—under the counter, up on the highest shelves and out where you have your reserve stocks stored. Miss nothing.

See all that you have. And take every hint without dodging.

That big lot of spring stuff you bought away back last January—that lot you know on which you got the last extra 5 per cent—how far short of being all sold is it?

Get out your pencil. Figure interest on the amount you have tied up in the lot. Add enough to cover its share of insurance and storage. Also add what you think you will have to lose in order to get rid of what's left.

Subtract that total from the profit you made on what you did sell. Are you satisfied?

Now estimate—for you never can tell exactly how big they might have been—the profits you have lost by not having for investment in other things the money tied up in the lot you had in storage. Then—are you satisfied with the result?

Follow this process throughout your stock and lose none of the other hints you can gain.

Then when you go to market act on the hints you have obtained from your own stock. Don't let some interested party over-persuade you again. Remember that the interests at stake are your own.

If you are in business for all the money you can make with the capital and capabilities you have, why help to play some other man's game to the extent of tying up an unnecessary proportion of your own means?

And when the salesman again whispers the "confidential inside" for taking an extra big lot, recall how large a quantity you have left of the last thing you bought big in order to save an extra "per cent off."

Get all the hints for better buying that your stock, in its present state, can give. Keep them fresh in mind so you will act on them when you get "within range" of the next temptation to repeat the buying mistakes now so evident—to yourself—in your own stock.

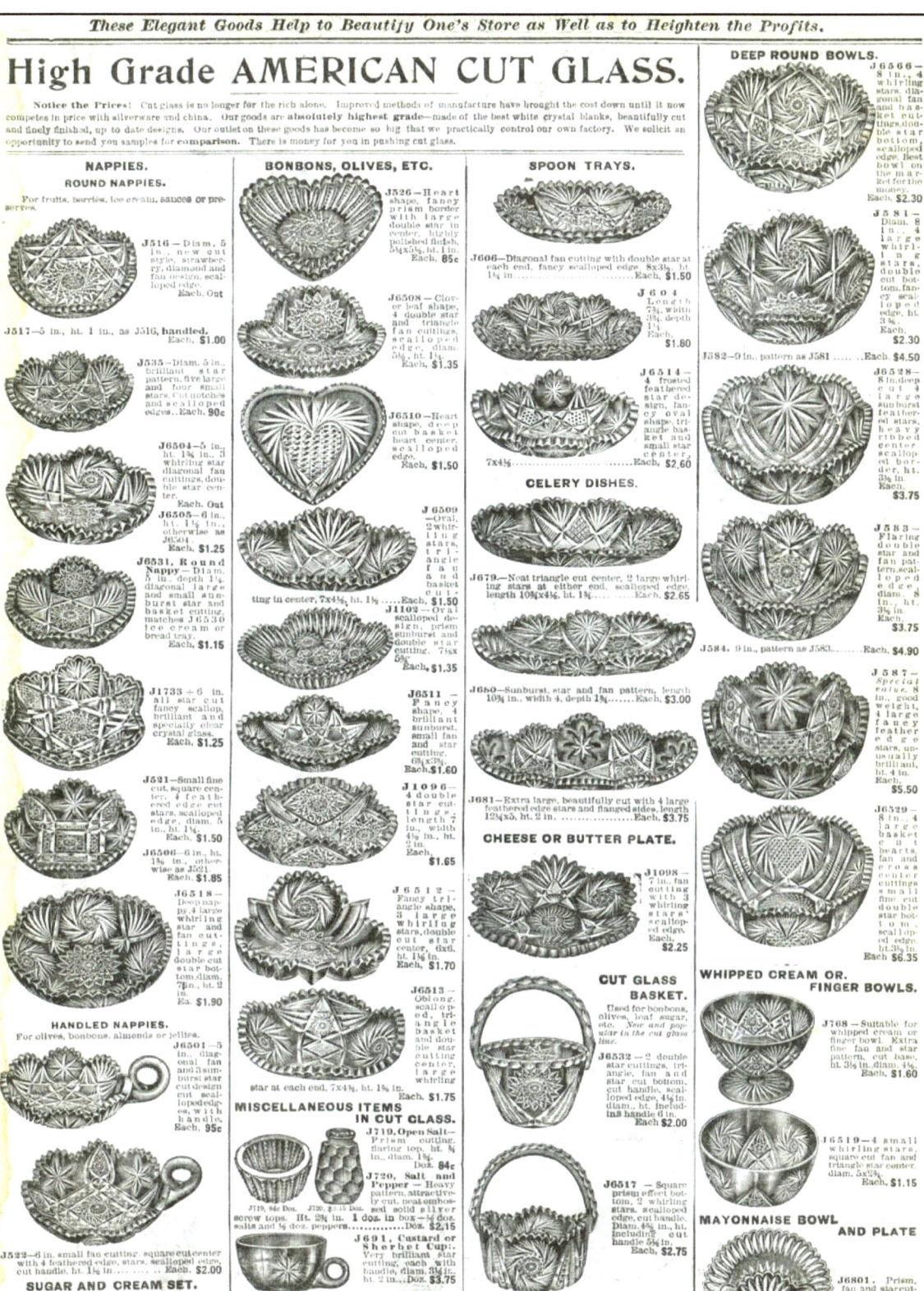

No Retailer Is So Large But He May Obtain Profitable Price Hints From This Catalogue.

TUMBLERS.

J6523, $4.40 Doz.   J1714, $8.10 Doz.    J6524, $9.75 Doz.

J6523—Triangle fan, 3 diamond star cutting, cut bottom, ht. 3¾ in. Matches J6653 water bottle. Extra heavy. .... Doz. **$8.10**

J1714—3¾ in. high, capacity ½ pt. Extra heavy, matches J1828 water bottle. .... Doz. **$4.00**

J6524—2 frosted feathered stars, star cut bottom, ht. 4 in. Matches J6525 water bottle. .... Doz. **$9.75**

OIL OR VINEGAR BOTTLES.

J653—Flaring star and fan design cutting, cut stopper. Ht. 6 in. Each. **$1.35**

J6522—Globe shape, 3 whirling star triangle fan cuttings, star bottom, notched neck, cut stopper. Ht. 7¾ in. Each. **$1.75**

J652—New square shape, triangle and prism cut, handle and stopper, ht. 6 in. Each. **$2.35**

FOOTED COMPORTS.

J6547—Sunbeams, star, triangle and basket cutting, star footed base with long stem, diam. 5 in. ht. 6¼ in. Each. **$1.75**

J6545—Triangle and basket fan cutting, scalloped edge, star cut foot. Ht. 5¼ in. diam. 4½ in. Each. **$1.85**

J573—The bronze in stem represents a long bubble made purposely when the blanks are molded. Scalloped and notched top, 5 in. diam. ht. 8 in. Best clear white glass, all hand cut. Each. **$3.10**

J6516—Diam. 6 in. ht. 9 in. 4 frosted feathered star cuttings, square fan and basket center, large star cut foot, notched stem. Each. **$4.95**

COLONIAL PATTERN CUT GLASS CANDLESTICKS.

J755—Colonial pattern, handsomely cut. Ht. 7¾ in. Each. Temp. out

J756—As J755 only larger. Ht. 9¼ in. Each. **$2.25**

VASES.

J6566, $1.50 Each   J734, $1.75 Each

J6568, Vase 1. Tall flaring shape, ht. 8 in., double whirling star, diagonal basket and fan cuttings, large star base, notched edge, scalloped edge. .... Each. **$1.50**

J734, Cut Glass Vase. Handsome design flaring top, scalloped edge, fancy small star and fan pattern cut stem, star cut base, ht. 8 in. .... Each. **$1.75**

J746, $2.25 Each   J6520 and J6521

J746—Large whirling star and fan cutting, 10½ in. diam at top 4⅜ in. Each. **$2.25**

J6520—8 in. 4 whirling star, triangle and round prism design, swell scalloped edge, star cut bottom. Each. **$3.75**

J6521—9 in., otherwise as J6520. Each. **$4.50**

WATER SETS AND BOTTLES.

J663½, Water Set—8 piece consisting of 1 qt. squat water bottle ht. 8½ and 6 tumblers to match capacity ⅓ pt. ht. 3⅜ in. complete with plain 14 in. plateau .... Set **$6.00**

J663, Water Bottle Only—Pattern as above. Squat shape 8½ in. 1 qt. .... Each. **$2.00**

J660, Water Set—8 pieces, consisting of 8½ in. globe water bottle capacity 1 qt. six tumblers, ht. 3¾ in. capacity ⅓ pt. complete with plain 14 in. plateau. .... Set **$8.45**

J672, Water Bottle Only—Pattern as above. Squat shape, 8¼ in., 1 qt. .... Each. **$2.75**

PLATEAUS.

For displaying cut glass. Double thick French plate glass. Beveled edge, metal back and rim.

Plain Pattern—
J775—8 in. .... Each. 54c
J776—10 in. .... Each. 72c
J777—12½ in. .... Each. $1.05
J778—14 in. .... Each. $1.30

Fancy Star Pattern—
J779—8 in. .... Each. 72c
J780—10 in. .... Each. $1.05
J781—12½ in. .... Each. $1.35
J782—14 in. .... Each. $1.75

AUSTRIAN GOLD INLAID CUT GLASS.

Fine white crystal, hand cut, with inlaid gold in floral and bead design, gold borders.

J541—Bonbon, ass't round and heart shapes, diam. 3¾ in., depth 1¼ in. .... Each. 65c

WATER BOTTLES.

J663, $2.00 Each   J672, $2.75 Each   J6525, $3.75 Each

J663—Squat shape, capacity 1 qt. fancy diamond star fancy cutting, star bottom, ht. 8¼ in. .... Each. **$2.00**

J672—Squat shape, 8¼ in. 1 qt. Our medium priced bottle and an excellent seller. Each. **$2.75**

J6525—Globe shape, 3 large frosted feathered stars, large diagonal fan and basket cutting, star bottom, notched neck, capacity 1 qt. ht. 8 in. .... Each. **$3.75**

JUGS.

J6526, $5.00 Each   J643, $6.50 Each   J6527, $8.25 Each

J6526—3 large handsome whirling stars, fan, diagonal and basket cuttings, notched lip, cut handle, capacity 3 pts., ht. 10½ in. .... Each. **$5.00**

J643—Beautifully cut, whirling star, prism and sunburst design, heavy cut handle, capacity 3 pts., ht. 11¼, diam. of base 5 in. .... Each. **$6.50**

J6527—2 large frosted feathered star, diagonal, small double star basket cuttings, notched lip, cut handle, 3 pts., ht. 8¼ in. .... Each. **$8.25**

SUGAR AND CREAM SETS.

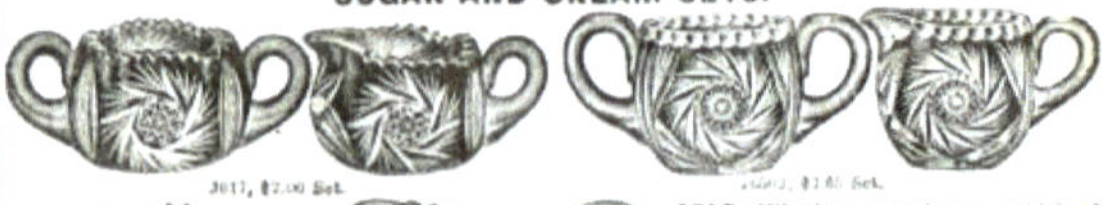

J617, $2.00 Set   J6502, $2.65 Set

J617—Whirling star design, width of sugar including handles 6 in. ht. 3¾ in., width of pitcher including handle and lip 6 in. ht. 3⅞ in. .... Set **$2.00**

J6502—Whirling star and triangle fan design cut handle, cut star bottom. Sugar ht. 3¼, 6¼ wide including handles, cream ht. 3 in. width including handle 4¾. .... Set **$2.65**

J620—Whirling star design, length of sugar including handles 7 in., length of pitcher including handle 6 in., ht. at lip 3¾ .... Set **$3.75**

J6503—New oval shape, 4 frosted feathered stars, fine diagonal and basket cutting, star bottom, cut handles. Sugar ht. 3¾, width including handle 7½ in. cream ht. 3¼ in., width including handle 5¾ in. .... Set **$4.50**

FANCY MANTEL VASES.

J1852, 6c Each   J1860, 78c Each   J1857, $1.10 Each   J1858, $1.65 Each   J1862, $2.25 Each

J1872—Opal glass pitcher, ground sides with hand painted rose decoration, embossed gold plated metal top and base, ht. 11¾ in. .... Each. **65c**

J1860—Pitcher design, embossed gold plated handle and base, opal glass center with tinted hand painted rose buds and leaves in colors, ht. 15½ in. .... Each. **78c**

J1857—Tinted opal glass center, decorated with 2 hand painted roses, gold scroll ornamentation, gold plated metal handle, top lip and 4 footed base, bright finish, neatly embossed, ht. 18 in. .... Each. **$1.10**

J1861—Embossed design, large base with 4 feet, gold plated top and handle, opal glass center with hand painted carnation decoration, ht. 17⅜ in. .... Each. **$1.60**

J1858—Guaranteed gold plated, heavy scroll openwork 4 footed base, neatly embossed openwork handle, top and lip, large tinted opal glass center, 2 hand painted roses in natural colors, ht. 19½ in. .... Each. **$1.65**

J1862—Large size pitcher design, heavy gold plated embossed and openwork top handle and base, ruby glass background with handsome hand painted picture, rose and gold scroll decoration. Ht. 22 in. .... Each. **$2.25**

J1859—Colonial design, heavy gold plated, embossed scroll square 4 footed base, openwork design top, lip and handle, ruby opal glass center with large hand painted rose cluster in natural colors, ht. 22½ in. .... Each. **$3.50**

To Test Our Prices, Glance at the Quotations Made on Goods You are Posted On.

PKG. CHARGE ABOLISHED On Glassware and Crockery

For years the package charge on glassware has been a matter of contention among makers, jobbers and retailers. We have never been satisfied with it, but have done as our neighbors did. We have now decided to cut the Gordian knot by abolishing the charge wholly. In the future our terms will be *"No package charge on any goods."*

Study the prices on the following pages, and we think you will agree that we not only *save you the package charge entire* as compared with other sellers, but give you larger and better pieces for any given price. We introduced the assortment plan in 1877, and have made a specialty of it ever since. We know how to put into our lots only the goods that will sell in a retail store. In comparing our assortment with those of the glassware factories and other jobbers, note the *uniform goodness* of our items and the *absence of small pieces.* We aim to make the smallest piece in each assortment worth the average price named. For over seventeen years we have been largest handlers of table glassware in America, and we are further ahead today than ever before. These are absolutely the same goods as offered you by other sellers at 10 to 30 per cent more.

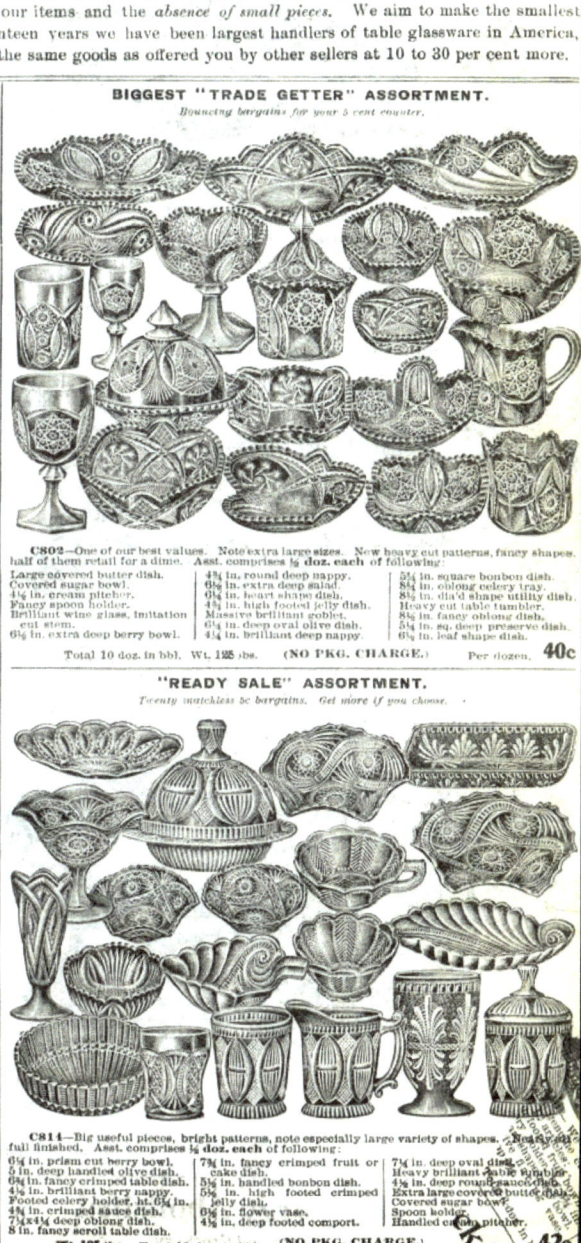

"BARGAIN DAY" ASSORTMENT.
5c possibilities comparable only with the 5c assortments offered by others.

C800—All large pieces usually retailed for 5c. Brilliant cut glass patterns, most of them full finished and fire polished. Asst. comprises 1 doz. each of following:

7¼ in. deep oval dish.
4½ in. scalloped sauce dish.
7¼ in. oval table dish.
Extra heavy deep cut tumbler.
5½ in. heavy cut flower vase.
4 in. optic berry nappy.
Heavy cut salt and pepper.
5 in. fan shape olive dish.
4 in. fancy cut flower vase.
Full finished wine glass.
4½ in. nappy or sauce dish.
6¼ in. fancy finished plate.

Total 12 doz. in bbl. Wt. 95 lbs. (NO PKG. CHARGE.) Per dozen. **25c**

"CONQUEST" 5 CENT ASSORTMENT.
In size and quality they look like 10 centers.

C817—Big useful pieces, bright new patterns, everyone a seller. Asst. comprises ½ doz. each of following:

6 in. round table dish.
5¾ in. footed comport, crimped.
5¼ in. tankard cream pitcher.
6¼x4¼ in. deep oblong dish.
Fancy handled sherbet cup.
5½ in. square bonbon.
Large brilliant goblet.
6¼ in. flaring berry bowl.
4½ in. deep round nappy.
6¼ in. fancy oval dish.
5½ in. square cake plate.
5¼ in. double handled dish.
5 in. extra deep round bowl.
5¼ in. fancy dish, bent-up sides.
10 in. deep oval celery tray.
5¾ in. high footed jelly dish.
Large covered sugar bowl.
Footed spoon holder.
Cream pitcher.
Large covered butter dish.

Wt. 125 lbs. Total 10 doz. in bbl. (NO PKG. CHARGE.) Per dozen. **38c**

CAUTION! When Opening Glassware Barrels **DO NOT DRIVE IN THE HEADS.**

Our assortments are all packed by professional packers at the factory before being shipped to us, and are not opened until they reach our customers' stores.

BIGGEST "TRADE GETTER" ASSORTMENT.
Bouncing bargains for your 5 cent counter.

C802—One of our best values. Note extra large sizes. New heavy cut patterns, fancy shapes, half of them retail for a dime. Asst. comprises ½ doz. each of following:

Large covered butter dish.
Covered sugar bowl.
4½ in. cream pitcher.
Fancy spoon holder.
Brilliant wine glass, imitation cut stem.
6¼ in. extra deep berry bowl.
4½ in. round deep nappy.
6½ in. extra deep salad.
6¼ in. heart shape dish.
4½ in. high footed jelly dish.
Massive brilliant goblet.
6¼ in. deep oval olive dish.
4¼ in. brilliant deep nappy.
5¼ in. square bonbon dish.
8¼ in. oblong celery tray.
8¼ in. dia'd shape utility dish.
Heavy cut table tumbler.
8½ in. fancy oblong dish.
5¼ in. sq. deep preserve dish.
5¼ in. leaf shape dish.

Total 10 doz. in bbl. Wt. 125 lbs. (NO PKG. CHARGE.) Per dozen. **40c**

"READY SALE" ASSORTMENT.
Twenty matchless 5c bargains. Get more if you choose.

C814—Big useful pieces, bright patterns, note especially large variety of shapes, full finished. Asst. comprises ½ doz. each of following:

6¼ in. prism cut berry bowl.
5 in. deep handled olive dish.
6¼ in. fancy crimped table dish.
4½ in. brilliant berry nappy.
Footed celery holder, ht. 6¼ in.
4¼ in. crimped sauce dish.
7¼x4¼ in. deep oblong dish.
8 in. fancy scroll table dish.
7¼ in. fancy crimped fruit or cake dish.
5¼ in. handled bonbon dish.
5¼ in. high footed crimped jelly dish.
6½ in. flower vase.
4½ in. deep footed comport.
7¼ in. deep oval dish.
Heavy brilliant table tumbler.
4½ in. deep round sauce dish.
Extra large covered butter dish.
Covered sugar bowl.
Spoon holder.
Handled cream pitcher.

Wt. 125 lbs. Total 10 doz. in bbl. (NO PKG. CHARGE.) Per dozen. **42c**

"PLAIN PATTERN" ASSORTMENT.

These regular 10 centers in size and quality offered on a 5 cent basis

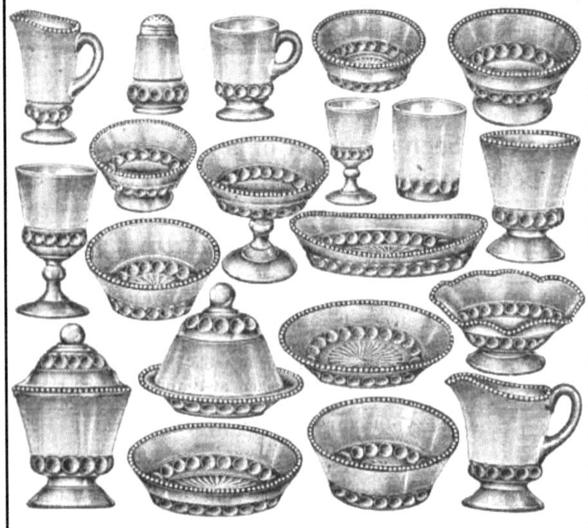

C808—All of same rich almost plain pattern, optic bullseye band, pearl beaded edges. All exceptional sellers. Comprises ½ **doz. each** of following:

Extra large covered butter dish.
Extra large covered sugar bowl.
Fancy footed spoonholder.
Large handled cream pitcher.
4½ in. round nappy.
Fancy flaring goblet.
5¼ in. deep round bowl.
7½ in. deep oval dish.
5¼ in. footed berry dish.
8¼ in. oval table dish.
Large family salt and pepper shakers.
4¼ in. footed comport.
Large handled mug.
5¼ in. footed, crimped comport.
7¼ in. round cake plate.
Tall tankard cream pitcher.
Brilliant table tumbler.
5¼ in. high footed berry dish.
Fancy wine glass.
6¼ in. deep berry bowl.

Total 10 doz. in bbl. Wt. 125 lbs. (NO PKG. CHARGE.) Per dozen, **40c**

"RICH CUT" 5 CENT ASSORTMENT.

Absolutely the finest quality assortment ever offered to retail at this price.

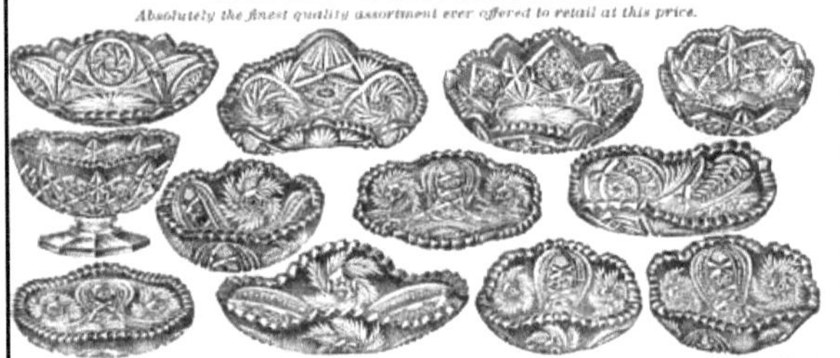

C816 — New and artistic shapes in the extra heavy well known "Prescut" glass. Each piece a regular 10 center. **1-2 doz. each** of 12 articles:

6¼ in. deep round nappy.
6½ in. clover leaf shape bonbon.
5½ in. star shape berry dish.
7½ in. fancy oval spoon or utility tray.
4⅝ in. deep round nappy.
4¾ in. high footed nut bowl.
6 in. fancy tray plate.
5 in. extra deep and heavy nappy.
5½ in. fancy round olive dish.
6½ in. deep oval bonbon dish
5 in. heavy deep triangle nappy.
6¼x4½ oblong utility dish.
6 doz. in case.

(NO PKG. CHARGE.) Per dozen, **42c**

MARVELOUS "SUNBURST CUT" ASSORTMENT.

A very special purchase. Will create a sensation if offered at 15 cents. **Every piece worth a quarter.**

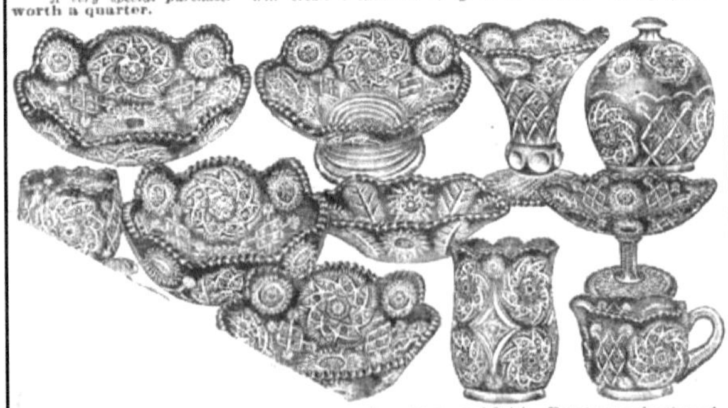

...ty, pattern and finish. Exact reproduction of ...s, pieces brilliantly fire polished. ½ **doz.**

...d berry
...nbon dish.
...ter dish.
Fancy shape spoonholder.
Fancy shape cream pitcher.
Large covered sugar bowl.
7¾ in. deep oval spoon or utility tray.
9¼ in. fancy salad dish.

...CHARGE.) Per dozen, **$1.10**

...arge Abolished

...sware and Crockery.

"LEADER" 10c CASK ASSORTMENT.

Big fancy pieces to sell at a good profit.

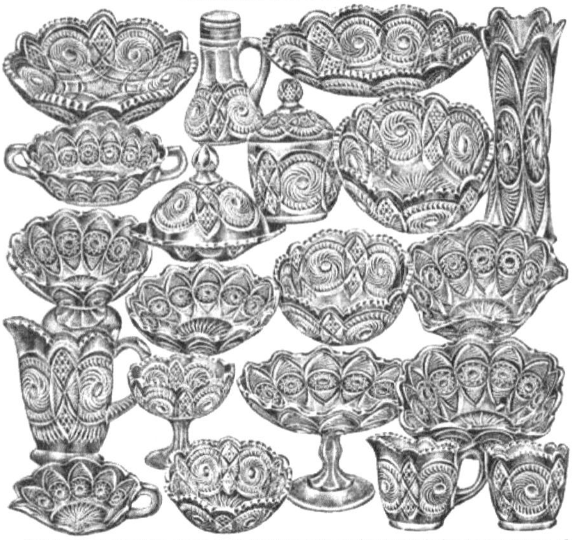

C818—20 big attractive pieces, new, brilliant patterns, heavy cut designs, note absence of undesirable pieces, every one a seller. **Asst.** comprises ½ **doz. each** of following:

9 in. round deep salad dish.
6¼ in. extra deep bowl.
Large syrup pitcher.
6¼ in. high footed bowl.
11 in. flower vase.
7¼ in. footed flared dish.
8½ in. crimped edge berry bowl.
8 in. double handled oval dish.
9 in. square berry bowl.
6¼ in. handled bonbon dish.
10¼ in. oval celery tray.
6½ in. deep fancy bowl.
7¾ in. round berry bowl.
4¾ in. high footed jelly dish.
Large milk pitcher.
Spoon holder
Covered butter dish.
Handled cream pitcher
Large covered sugar bowl.
8¾ in. high footed fruit bowl.

Total 10 doz. in cask. Wt. 185 lbs. (NO PKG. CHARGE.) Per dozen, **75c**

"RELIANCE" ASSORTMENT.

Big pieces and staple sellers to retail at 10 cents. The larger pieces will easily bring 15c or more.

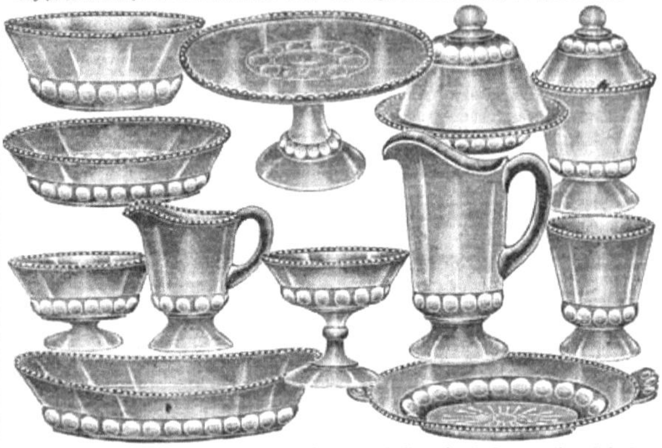

C873—Pure crystal, almost plain but rich pattern, bullseye band effect, pearl peaded edges well finished. Asst. comprises ½ **doz. each** of following:

11½ in. large oval bread tray.
7¼ in. deep round bowl.
5¾ in. high footed preserve dish.
8½ in. extra deep oval dish.
Large butter dish and cover.
Large footed sugar bowl and cover.
Footed cream pitcher.
Footed spoon holder.
11¼ in. heavy deep oval dish.
5½ in. deep footed comport.
8½ in. tankard pitcher.
9½ in. high footed cake salver.

Total. 6 doz. in bbl. Wt. 130 lbs. (NO PKG. CHARGE.) Per dozen, **79c**

"CRYSTAL GEM" ASSORTMENT.

You can retail at a dime though they will bring twice as much.

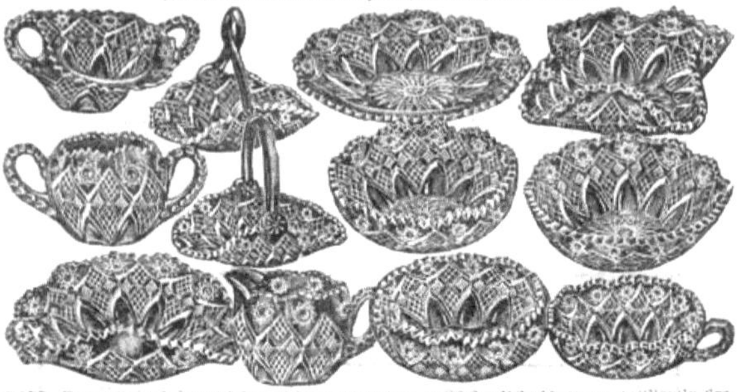

C875—Finest crystal, beautiful new deep cut pattern, ground polished bottoms, brilliantly fire polished. **Asst. comprises ¼ doz. each** of following:

8½ in. fancy cake dish, bent up sides.
6¼ in. bon bon dish, double open handles.
Large cream pitcher, diam. 4¼.
Fancy double handle open sugar.
8¼ in. fancy salad dish.
5½ in. heart shape handled olive dish.
6½ in. extra deep round bowl.
6 in. fancy basket, large ring handle. Wt. 111 lbs.
6¼ in. deep round nut bowl.
6 in. fancy basket, large stuck handle.
7½ in. deep round berry bowl.
8¼ in. round salad or cake dish.

Total 6 doz. in box. (NO PKG. CHARGE.) Per dozen, **85c**

We Notice the Merchant Who Is Always Working for Trade Seldom Complains of the Lack of It.

"NEW CHALLENGE" ASSORTMENT.
Nearly all of these are 19 centers in size and quality.

C804—All extra large, nearly all richly finished and fire polished. Asst. comprises ½ doz. each of following:
Heavy 7 in. covered butter dish.
Double handled sugar bowl.
Double handled spoonholder.
Heavy cream pitcher.
6½ in. flower vase.
6 in. deep round berry dish.
5½ in. extra deep footed bowl.
8¼ in. deep oval table dish.
6½ in. square footed nappy.
5⅜ in. footed dish, bent up sides.
4½ in. footed berry dish.
7½ in. fancy oval dish.
4¼ in. deep round sauce dish.
Rich deep cut table tumbler.
8½ in. fancy oblong dish.
7 in. round deep footed fancy dish.
5 in. deep olive dish, open handle.
High footed comport.
Fancy shape handled dish.
Large cake plate.

Total 10 doz. in tierce. Wt 130 lbs. (NO PKG. CHARGE.) Per dozen, **43c**

"NEW RECORD BREAKER" ASSORTMENT.
Business making bargains for your 10c counter.

C852—Very brilliant, full finished and fire polished. Very large, the smallest a bargain at 10c., several are 25 centers. Asst. comprises ½ doz. each of following:
7½ in. deep oval scalloped table dish.
7½ in. footed flaring square bowl or nappy.
10 in. extra large flared berry bowl.
12 in. fancy carnation vase.
Optic 3 pint jug.
Heavy cut oil or vinegar bottle.
Jewel cut wine glass.
9¼ in. oblong table dish.
8½ in. extra deep footed berry bowl.
7½ in. high footed comport or fruit bowl.
1 qt. water pitcher, footed tankard shape.
5¼ in. high footed jelly dish.

Total 6 doz. in bbl. Wt. 134 lbs. (NO PKG. CHARGE.) Per dozen, **79c**

"SUPREME GOLD" ASSORTMENT.
All new rich patterns. If offered at 10c it will surprise your customers.

C889—The best 10c asst. of gold decorated ware ever offered. Finest crystal, deep heavy cut patterns, brilliantly full finished, rich heavy gold decorations. Asst. comprises ½ doz. each of the following:
5¼ in. high footed jelly dish.
5½ in. deep round nappy.
Large handled mug.
6½ in. fancy pointed utility dish.
5 in. deep bonbon with open handle.
6½ in. deep oval dish.
Large brilliant goblet.
Jewel cut wine glass.
4½ in. square deep dish.
Rich table tumbler, ground bottom.
Fancy handled sherbet cup.
5½ in. extra deep pointed nappy.
Double handled open sugar.
Fancy shape cream pitcher.
7½x4¼ fancy oblong dish, turned up sides.

Total 7½ doz. in bbl. Wt. 77 lbs. (NO PKG. CHARGE.) Per dozen, **85c**

"ARTISTIC" ASSORTMENT OF ALL LEADERS.
12 possible "10 centers" whose usual retail price is double 10 cents.

C870—All one pattern, full finished fire polished, each with 3 jeweled feet and jewel beaded edge. This old colonial pattern appeals to people who appreciate beautiful plain crystal glassware. Asst. comprises ½ doz. each of the following:
6 in. deep round dish.
6½ in. 3 cornered dish, stuck handle.
6½ in. card tray.
7½ in. rolled up side dish.
7 in. useful dish fancy crimped sides.
6½ in. 3 cornered turned up dish.
7 in. high crimped dish.
1½ in. deep table bowl.
Rich milk pitcher, footed.
Sugar bowl and cover, extra size.
Spoonholder, or open sugar.
Butter dish and cover.

Total 6 doz. in tierce. wt. 120 lbs. Per dozen, **79c**

"NOX-EM-ALL" CASK ASSORTMENT.
Big trade winning bargains for a 10c sale.

C890—Mammoth size pieces, every day sellers, bright deep heavy cut patterns. Asst. comprises ½ doz. each of following:
6½ in. deep fancy berry dish.
10½ in. deep oblong celery tray.
Massive covered butter dish.
Large spoon holder.
Large cream pitcher.
Large covered sugar bowl.
8½ in. extra deep round berry bowl.
6½ in. high footed preserve dish.
Large 3 pt. jug, ht. 9 in.
Tall tankard oil or vinegar bottle.
7½ in. deep round berry bowl.
6½ in. high footed covered fruit bowl.
6½ in. massive high footed fruit bowl.
6½ in. wide top flower vase.
6½ in. high footed comport.
8½ in. diamond shape spoon or celery tray.
4¼ in. high footed jelly dish.
8½ in. deep round berry bowl.
Brilliant water pitcher, ht. 9in.
10 in. round salad dish.

Weight 235 lbs. Total 10 doz. in cask. Per dozen, **80c**

"FLORAL ENGRAVED" 10 CENT ASSORTMENT.
Splendid patterns. Excellent values. Entirely new at this unusually low price.

C893—Finest quality, brilliantly full finished, rich almost plain pattern, handsome lily of the valley engraving, nearly all with fluted bases. Many will retail at 15 or 20c. Asst. comprises ½ doz. each of following:
Fancy tankard syrup pitcher, stuck handle, ht. 5¼ in.
Medium covered sugar bowl, ht. 4½ in.
Fancy stuck handled cream pitcher. Matches sugar bowl.
4 in. high footed jelly dish.
Tankard milk pitcher, large stuck handle, ht. 5¼ in.
High footed sherbet cup, diam. 3¼ in.
Sugar shaker, nickel plated top, ht. 4¾ in.
Extra large celery holder, ht. 5½ in.
Fancy flaring goblet.
4½ in. low footed comport.
Large sherbet cup, stuck handle.
Heavy oil or vinegar bottle, fancy stopper.

Total 6 doz. in bbl. Wt. 75 lbs. Per dozen, **83c**

"RICH QUALITY" CASK ASSORTMENT

Brilliant new patterns. Every piece full finished.

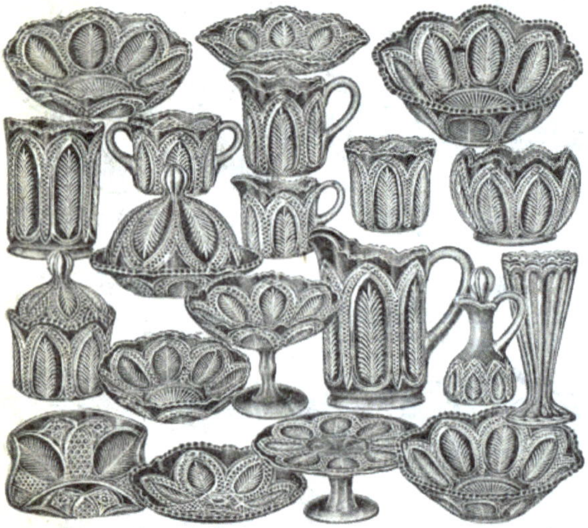

C864—An excellent asst., all self sellers, handsome feather panel and diamond band designs, finest crystal. Asst. comprises ½ **doz. each** of following:

- 8¼ in. round berry bowl.
- 8 in. flower vase.
- Fancy cream pitcher.
- Double handled open sugar.
- 5½ in. extra deep nut bowl.
- 7 in. high footed comport.
- 6¾ in. flared footed bowl.
- 8 in. fancy oval spoon tray.
- 9½ in. round berry bowl.
- Large covered butter dish.
- Fancy spoonholder.
- Cream pitcher.
- Covered sugar bowl.
- Large 3 pt. jug.
- Tall celery holder.
- 8½ in. salad dish.
- Fancy oil or vinegar bottle.
- 8½ in. high footed cake salver.
- 8½ in. crimped fancy dish.
- 8 in. salad or cake plate.

Total 10 doz. in cask. Wt. 174 lbs. (NO PKG. CHARGE.) Per dozen, **80c**

"MASSIVE BRILLIANT" 10 CENT CASK ASSORTMENT.

Hard to match at a 10 cent price. Looks like cut glass.

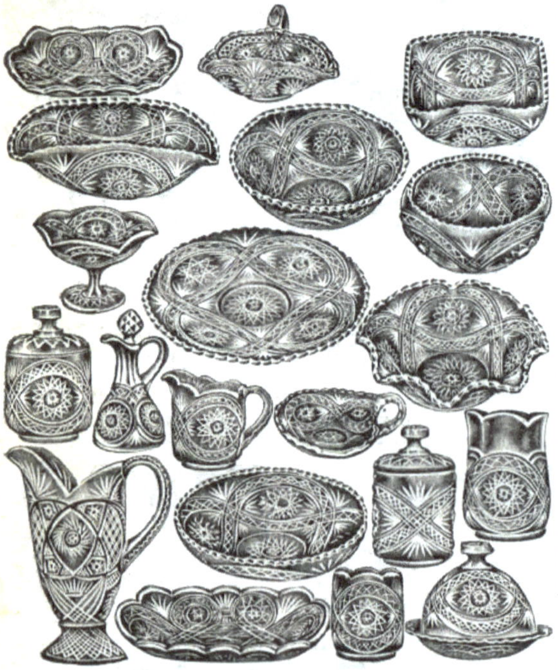

C886—20 big crystal beauties, all in rich deep cut star and jewel band design, extra heavy fire polished. Half of them retail for 25c. Asst. comprises ½ **doz. each** of following:

- 9 in. tall fancy footed jug.
- Large covered sugar bowl.
- 7¼ in. flanged covered butter dish.
- Footed spoon holder.
- Fancy handled cream pitcher.
- 7¼ in. deep berry bowl.
- 5¾ in. fancy handled olive dish.
- 10¾ in. footed cake or bread plate.
- Large brilliant oil or vinegar bottle.
- 8 in. deep fancy oblong dish.
- 6½x6½ in. extra deep square shape berry bowl.
- 5¾ in. tall fancy celery holder.
- 8¾ in. fancy crimped berry bowl.
- 5½ in. high footed jelly dish.
- 7 in. extra deep heavy nut bowl.
- 6¾ in. fancy handled spoon or bonbon tray.
- 8½ in. fancy pointed dish, turned up sides.
- 9¾ in. deep oblong celery tray.
- Large covered pickle jar.
- 8¾ in. fancy round berry bowl.

Total, 10 doz. in cask. Wt. 220 lbs. (NO PKG. CHARGE.) Per dozen, **81c**

OUR "HIGHEST AWARD" CASK ASSORTMENT.

All fire polished, full finished and all big sellers.

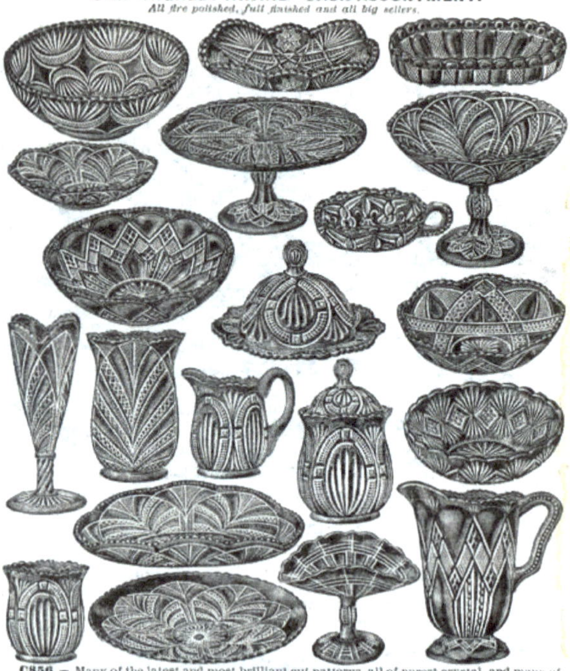

C856 — Many of the latest and most brilliant cut patterns, all of purest crystal, and many of them you would not expect to find in an assortment short of double the price. Asst. consists of ½ **doz. each** of the following:

- 8 in. extra heavy oblong dish.
- Rich cut pattern spoonholder.
- Large covered sugar bowl.
- Good size handled cream pitcher.
- 8 in. extra heavy butter dish and cover.
- 7 in. round deep berry bowl.
- 8¼ in. fancy deep oblong dish.
- 8 in. high footed fruit dish.
- Heavy footed 2 quart water pitcher.
- 6½ in. high footed card receiver or bonbon.
- 8¾ in. round brilliant berry bowl.
- 8½ in. round deep bowl.
- Large celery holder.
- 10¾ in. bread or cake tray.
- 7½ in. deep bowl.
- 11½ in. large celery tray.
- 8¼ in. high footed comport.
- 9¼ in. high footed cake salver.
- 5 in. handled bonbon dish.
- 9¾ in. flower vase.

Total 10 doz. in cask, wt. 230 lbs. (NO PACKAGE CHARGE.) Per dozen, **79c**

"BIG BRILLIANT" CASK ASSORTMENT.

Richest patterns, finely finished. Study sizes and compare with 25c offeringt of others.

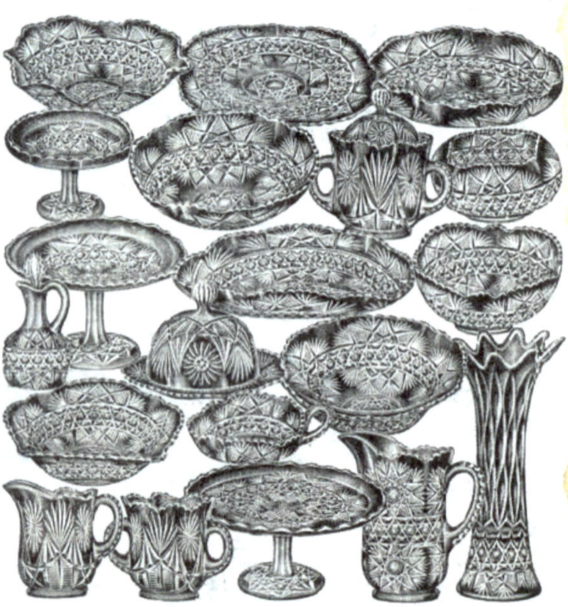

C859—An exceptional assortment. No small pieces put in to reduce the average, everyone a bargain. Asst. comprises ½ **doz. each** of following:

- 9¼ in. round deep salad dish.
- Extra large footed rose bowl. diam. 6 in.
- 8½ in. square footed berry bowl.
- 5½ in. high footed jelly dish.
- 11¼ in. deep oval celery tray.
- Large brilliant oil or vinegar bottle, ht. 6¼ in.
- 8¾ in. high footed fruit dish.
- Tall tankard jug, ht. 7½ in.
- 10¼ in. fancy footed cake plate.
- 5¼ in. deep handled olive dish.
- 7¾ in. extra deep footed bowl.
- 9¼ in. mammoth berry bowl.
- Large fancy flower vase, ht. 12 in.
- 9 in. deep berry bowl with crimped edge.
- Large double handled sugar bowl.
- Large double handled spoonholder.
- Large milk or cream pitcher.
- Large covered butter dish.
- 9¼ in. footed flaring berry bowl.
- 9½ in. high footed cake salver.

Total 10 doz. in cask. Wt. 235 lbs. (NO PKG. CHARGE.) Per dozen, **84c**

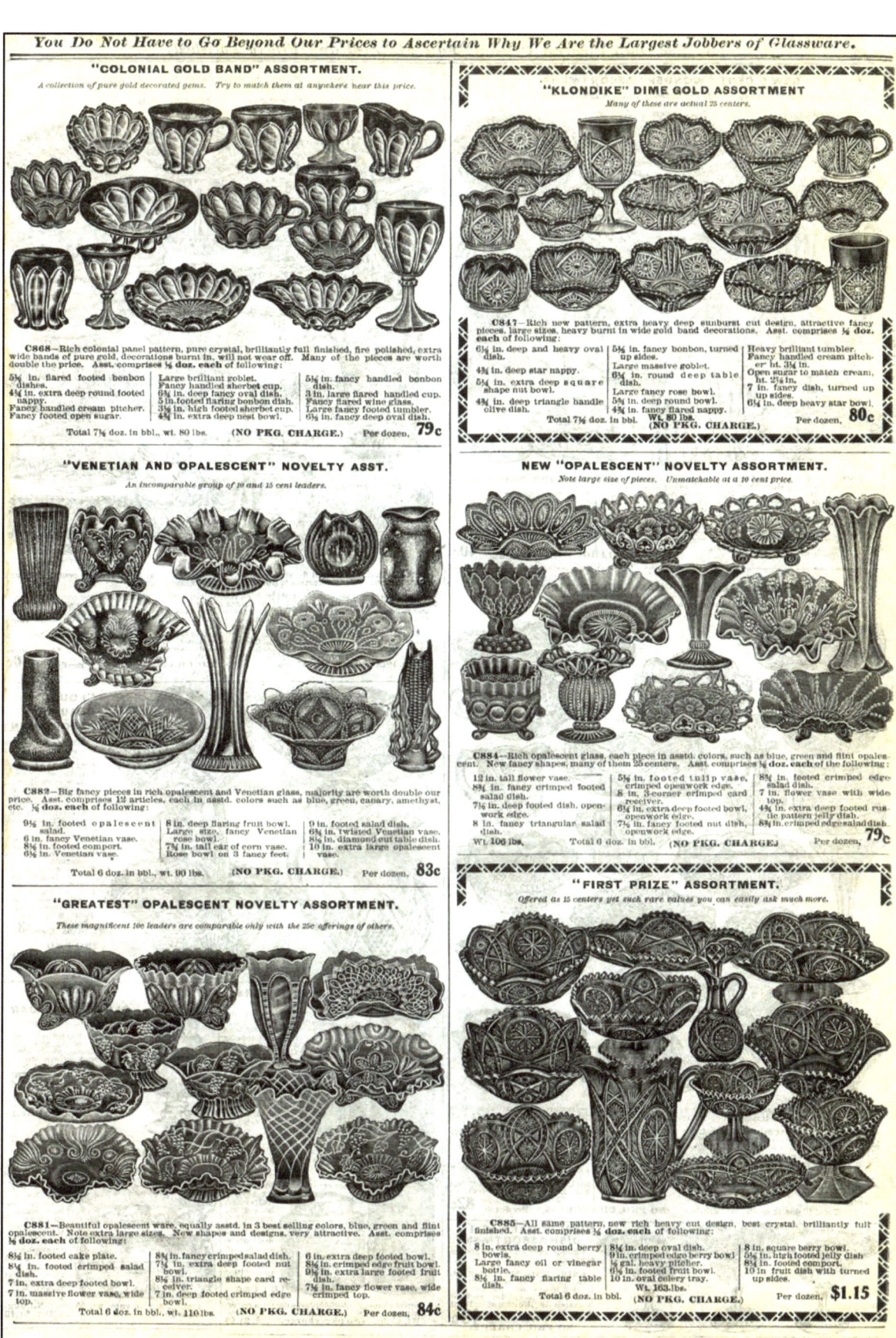

NEW 5 CENT "WONDER" ASSORTMENT.

A 5 cent assortment in name only. In size and quality more than half of them are 10 centers.

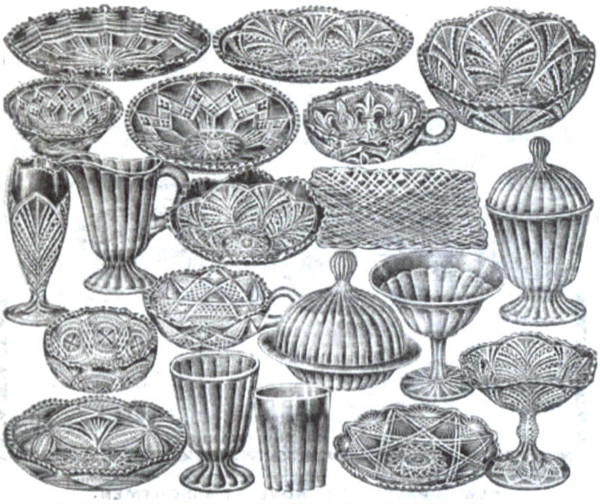

C803—Look at sizes and patterns. Excellent quality crystal, rich cut designs, nearly every piece full finished. ½ **doz. each** of the following 20 articles:

6¼ in. flower vase.
5¼ in. high footed jelly dish.
6¾ in. flaring berry bowl.
8¼ in. deep oval dish.
5 in. fancy footed berry nappy.
7 in. flaring table dish.
7¼x5¼ deep oval table dish.
7½ in. footed cake plate.
Rich optic table tumbler.
5 in. round deep nappy.
5 in. handle olive dish.
8¼ in. oval table dish.
4½ in. deep sauce dish.
Large optic covered butter dish.
Optic sugar bowl.
Optic cream pitcher.
Optic spoonholder.
5½ in. high footed jelly dish.
6 in. deep footed bowl.
5 in. deep bonbon dish with open handle.

Total 10 doz. in bbl. (NO. PKG. CHARGE.) Per dozen, **40c**

"FAMOUS CENTURY" CASK ASSORTMENT.

Positively the richest assortment ever offered for the money.

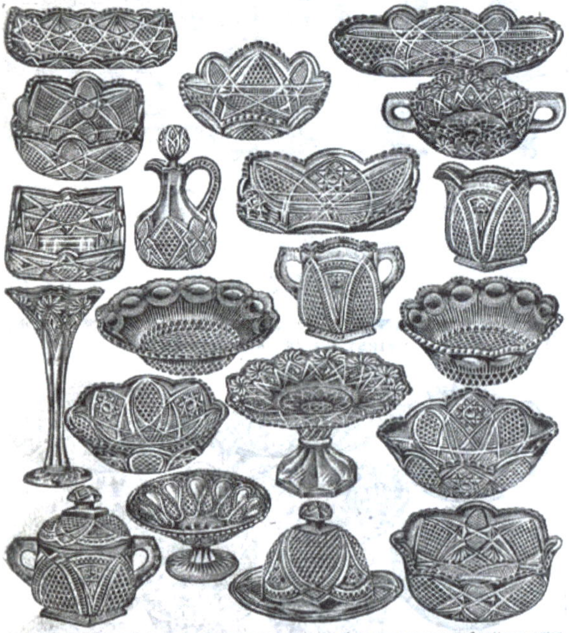

C861: This well known assortment is now better than ever, unsurpassed patterns, extra heavy, deep cut, exact imitations of costly cut glass. Asst. comprises ½ **doz. each** of following:

8¾ in. high footed fancy salver.
7¾ in. deep round berry bowl.
8¾ in. tall flaring flower vase.
5¼ in. heavy square deep dish.
7¾ in. extra deep round berry bowl.
7¼x4 in. heavy oblong dish.
8¼ in. extra deep fancy bowl.
Large heavy vinegar or oil bottle.
7¼ in. fancy round shape table dish.
5½ in. deep fancy olive dish, open handle.
5¼x5½ in. extra deep square bowl.
8½x6½ in. oblong table dish.
8¼ in. massive covered butter dish.
Large double handled covered sugar bowl.
Double handled spoonholder.
Large handled cream pitcher.
8¾ in. fancy flaring salad dish.
11 in. extra long deep celery tray.
6¾ in. high footed compor t.
8 in. extra deep berry bowl.

Total 10 doz. in cask. Wt. 225 lbs. (NO PKG. CHARGE.) Per dozen, **82c**

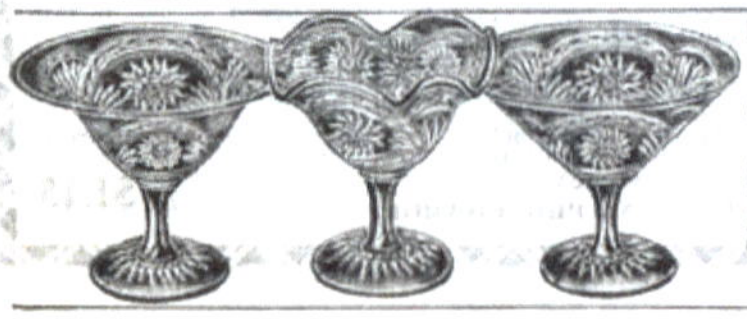

HIGH FOOTED JELLY DISH ASSORTMENT.

Popular selling 10 centers as be leaders.

C813. Diam. 5½ in., full ht. 5 in., fine full finished crystal in rich heavy deep cut pattern. Asstd. comprises 2 doz. each of 3 shapes as illustrated. Total 6 doz. in bbl. Per dozen, **48c**
(NO PKG. CHARGE.)

"TOP NOTCH" ASSORTMENT OF LEADERS.

A line of 10 centers which cannot be beat.

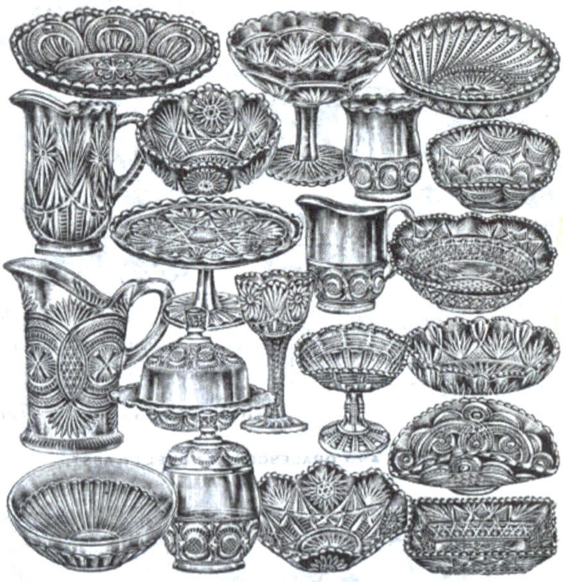

C855. Extra large full finished pieces, many will retail at from 15 to 25 cents. Brilliant crystal pattern. Asst. comprises ½ **doz. each** of following:

2 qt. jug, heavy cut pattern.
8 in. heavy flanged butter dish and cover.
Extra large covered sugar bowl.
Good size milk or cream pitcher.
Fancy scalloped edge spoonholder.
5½ in. high footed jelly dish.
10¼ in. oblong celery dish.
9 in. star shape berry bowl.
7 in. extra deep round bowl.
7¼ in. oblong dish.
8 in. deep round footed bowl.
8½ in. flaring berry bowl.
7¼ in. high footed pint bowl.
7½ in. new shape tulip vase.
Fancy tankard quart jug.
9½ in. high footed cake salver.
7¼ in. deep oval table dish.
8½ in. heavy brilliant salad dish.
8x5 in. footed tray, bent up edges.
10½x8 in. oval cake or bread tray.

Total 10 doz. in cask, wt. 217 lbs. (NO PKG. CHARGE.) Per dozen, **80c**

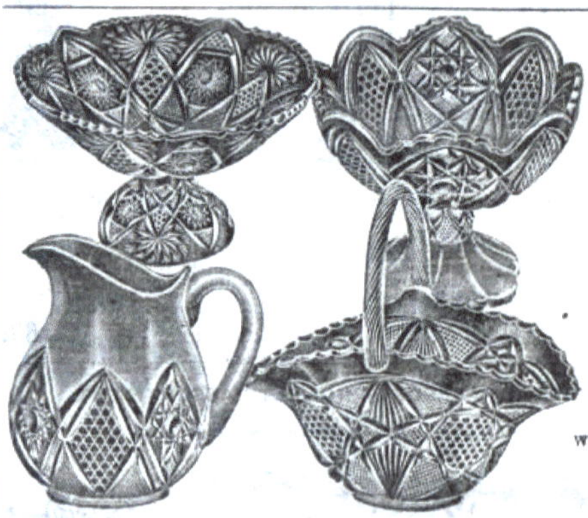

"FOUR BEAUTIES" ASSORTMENT

Offered as 50 centers, though really worth 75.

C921 — All mammoth size, finest pure crystal, richest new deep cut patterns, look like genuine cut glass. Assortment comprises 2 each of the following:

Mammoth ¾ gal stuck handle jug.
10¼ in. high footed compor t.
8½ in. extra deep high footed fruit dish.
11½ in. Extra deep basket with fancy twist stuck handle.
Total 8 pieces in bbl.

Wt. 76 lbs. Each, **32**

(NO PKG. CHARGE.)

"CROWN TOP" SHELF JARS.

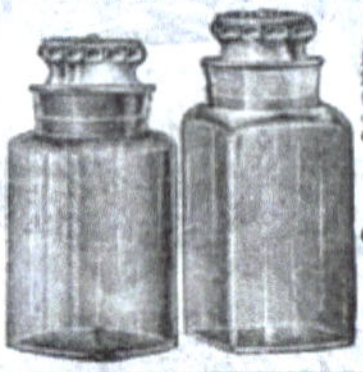

Best full finish, fire polished goods. Cut tops. Capacity 4½ lbs. Cut tops.

C1437, Round —½ doz. in case. 45 lbs. (**No pkg. charge.**) Doz. **$2.85**

C1438, Square —½ doz. in case. 45 lbs. (**No pkg. charge.**) Doz. **$2.85**

TIN TOP CANDY OR SHELF JARS.

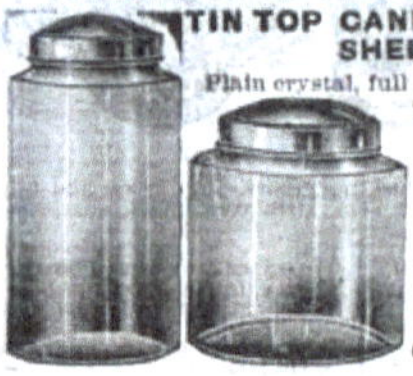

Plain crystal, full finish.

C1436—Tall round, ht. 9¼ in., capacity ½ gal., ground top, japanned tin cover. 1 doz. in case. Wt. 43 lbs. (**No pkg. chg.**) Doz. **$1.59**

C1435—Round squat shape, ground top, japanned tin cover, capacity ½ gal., ht. 6½ in. 1 doz. in case. Wt. 45 lbs. (**No pkg. charge.**) Doz. **$1.59**

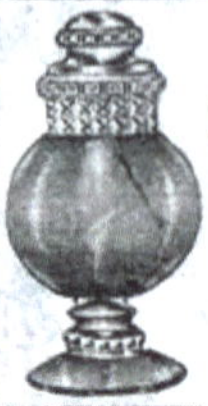

GLOBE SHOW JAR.

Best and most attractive made

C1440—Patented. Fine quality crystal, well made and finished, swell shape fancy neck, crown stopper, capacity 3 qts., full ht. 1 in. 4 in bbl.
Wt. 36 lbs. Each, **79**

(NO PKG. CHARGE.)

CANDY TRAYS.

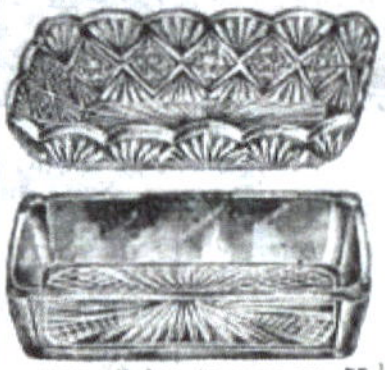

C1431—Oblong, 8x5½, extra deep. Heavy, bright, attractive pattern, scalloped edge. 2 doz. in case. Wt. 50 lbs. (**No pkg. charge.**) Doz. **$1.05**

C1432—Pure crystal goods, 5x8. Plain sides, smooth bottom. 2 doz. in case, wt. 55 lbs. (**No pkg. charge.**)............ Doz. **$1.10**

GENUINE "CUT STAR" ASSORTMENT.

High grade goods at prices which make them specially desirable.

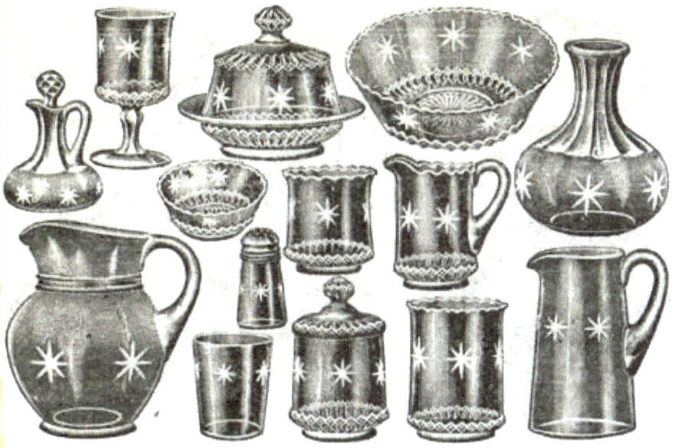

C911 — All rich almost plain pattern, nearly all pieces footed and brilliantly fire polished genuine deep cut stars. Entirely new and very rich design. Asst. comprises:

2 only 4 pieces table sets—large heavy covered butter dish, covered sugar bowl, fancy spoonholder and stuck handle cream pitcher	@$0 45	$0 90
2 only 7 piece berry sets—deep round footed berry bowl and six 4¼ in. deep footed nappies	@ 48	96
2 only 7 piece water sets—large fancy shape stuck handle, ½ gal. pitcher and 6 ground bottom tumblers	@ 57	1 14
2 only 7 piece water sets—large heavy low shape water bottle and 6 ground bottom tumblers	@ 55,	1 10
¼ doz. tall tankard blown jugs, stuck handle	@ 1 87	47
¼ doz. large celery holders, ht. 5¼ in.	@ 1 35	34
¼ doz. large fancy shape oil or vinegar bottles	@ 1 30	32
1 doz. fancy goblets at		87
1 doz. salt and pepper shakers, asstd., with nickel plated dome tops		84

(NO PKG. CHARGE.) Total for asst. of 83 pieces. **$6.94**

RICHLY COLORED AND DECORATED DINING SET ASSORTMENT.

Surprise your customers by retailing these at $1.00 per set.

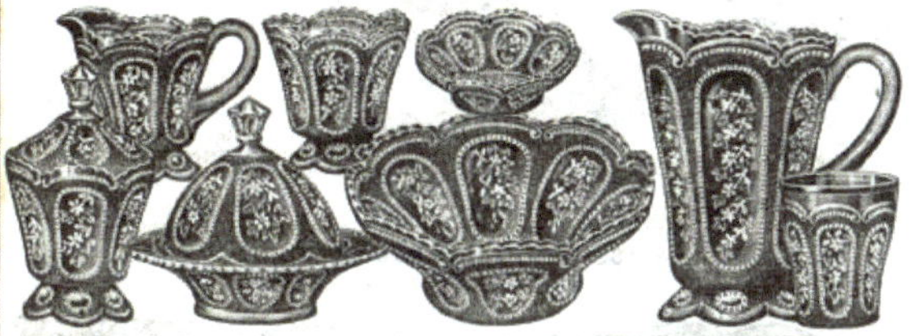

C961 — New fancy beaded panel pattern, solid colors, panels on all pieces decorated in enameled floral designs with gold illuminated leaves, edges, knobs, etc., with wide gold band decorations. **2 only each** of the following:
4 pc. table sets, butter dish, sugar bowl, cream pitcher and spoon holder.
7 pc. water sets, ½ gal. jug and 6 tumblers.
7 pc. berry sets, 8¼ in. deep bowl and six 4½ in. nappies.
One set each blue and green. Total 6 sets in bbl.
(NO PKG. CHARGE.) Per set, **72c**

"GOLD BAND" DINING SET ASSORTMENT.

Among the richest and most attractive patterns. You can make an extra profit on every one of these items

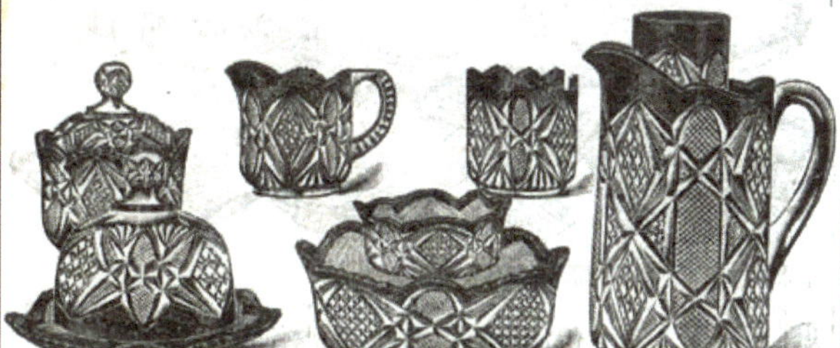

C950. Cut glass pattern, extra heavy, gold band around top, in some places 2 in. wide. Large size, fire polished. Asst. comprises **2 sets each of** the following:
7 piece berry sets: 8 in. deep bowl, six 4¾ in. nappies.
7 piece water sets: 9 in. jug, stuck handle and 6 full size tumblers.
4 piece table sets; creamer, sugar bowl, spoonholder and butter dish. Per set, **87c**
6 sets complete in bbl., wt. 74 lbs. (NO PKG. CHARGE.)

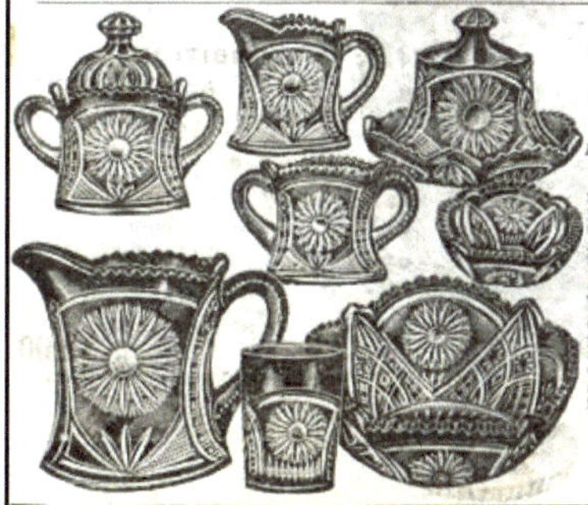

"BEAUTY" GOLD BAND DINING SET ASST.

Popular sellers in a magnificent pattern.

C955:. Rich sunburst pattern, massive and very brilliant. Wide pure burnt in gold band edges, solid gold decorated knobs, etc. Asst. comprises **2 only each** of the following:
7 piece water sets; large ½ gal. jug, 6 ground bottom tumblers.
7 piece berry sets; 8 in. round deep berry bowl, six 4¾ in. nappies.
4 piece table sets; covered butter dish, sugar bowl, spoonholder and cream pitcher. Total 6 sets in bbl., wt. 65 lbs.
Per set, **78c**
(NO PKG. CHARGE.)

NEW "GOLD AND WINE RUBY" DECORATED ASSORTMENT.

10c leaders comparable only with the 25c offerings of others.

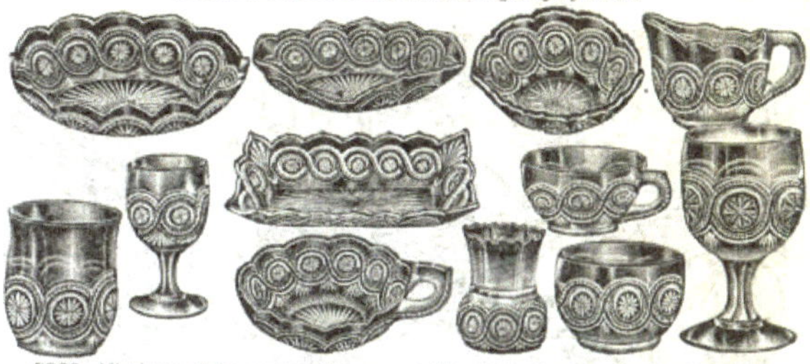

C866—All pieces of the same pattern, very brilliant new deep cut rosette, all pieces extra heavy and brilliantly full finished, rich wide ruby bands and gold decorated edges, both the ruby and gold decorations burnt in and will not wash off. Asst. comprises ½ **doz. each** of following:

6½ in. deep olive dish.
Tall fancy match or toothpick holder, ht. 3¼ in.
5 in. deep round nappy.
Fancy handled lemonade or sherbet cup.
Brilliant wine glass, imitation cut stem.
Large fancy table tumbler, 1½ in. wide ruby band.
Total 6 doz. in bbl.
6½ in. fancy diamond shape shape dish.
Fancy handled cream pitcher.
Fancy open sugar.
7¼x4½ deep oblong dish.
Large brilliant goblet.
5 in. deep handled olive dish.
Per dozen, **78c**

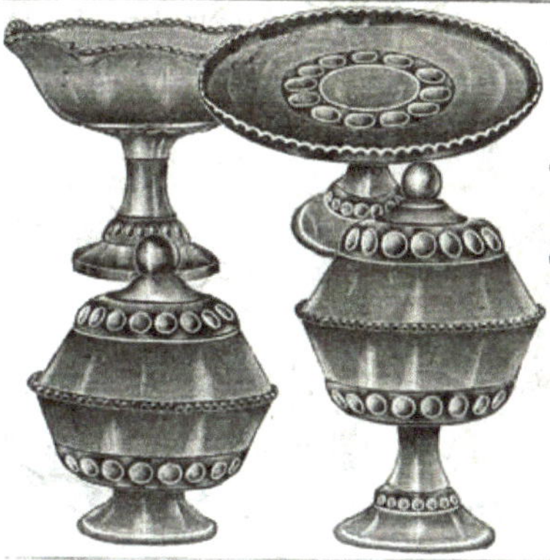

"CROWN" ASSORTMENT OF ALL LEADERS.

Four big pieces that will sell everywhere at 25c or more.

C914 — Rich almost plain pattern with optic bullseye and pearl beaded edges. 3 of them are actual 50 centers. Asst. comprises ½ **doz. each** of the following:
10¾ in. High footed cake salver.
7½ in. extra deep footed bowl with high cover.
8¾ in. high footed fruit bowl.
7½ in. high footed bowl and cover.
Total 2 doz. in bbl., wt. 106 lbs. Per dozen, **$1.75**
(NO PKG. CHARGE.)

FANCY OPALESCENT BASKET AND SALAD DISH ASST.

You can retail these at 25 cents although they will easily bring more.

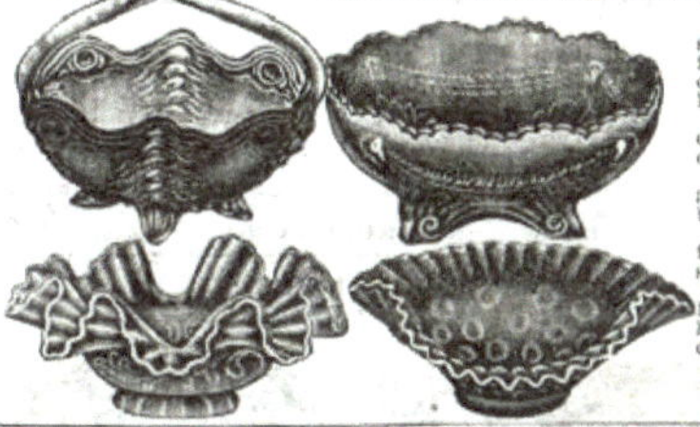

C910 — Extra large fancy shaped pieces in beautiful full finished opalescent ware. Asst. comprises ½ **doz. each** of 4 extra large pieces as follows:
9½ in. extra large salad or fruit dish, genuine ruby color, crimped edge.
9 in. extra large and deep berry and fruit bowl on 4 feet, asstd. blue and green opalescent.
11 in. extra deep footed salad or fruit dish, fancy crimped and scalloped edge.
7¾ in. extra large and deep footed basket with fancy rustic handle, asstd. blue and green opalescent.
Total 2 doz. in bbl. Per dozen, **$1.79**
(NO PKG. CHARGE.)

DRUGGISTS' SODA FOUNTAIN CLASSWARE SPECIALS.

Precisely same quality glassware that the "exclusive" jobber sells at 25 per cent more.

CRUSHED FRUIT BOWLS.

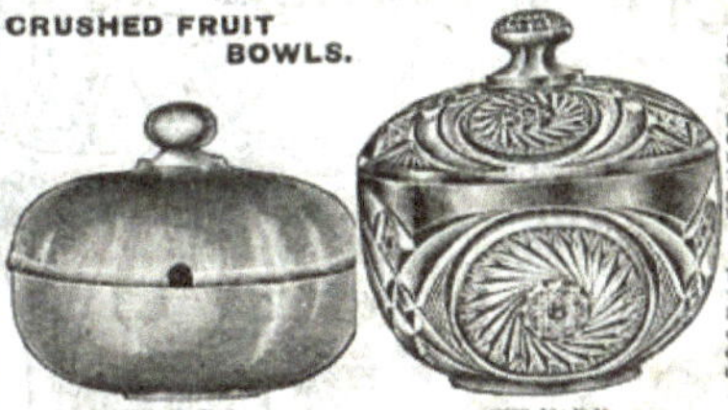

C681, 35c Each. C682, 50c Each.

In great demand, used at all the soda fountains.

C681 — Large, rich plain pattern, deep shape, diam. 8 in., high notched cover, fine full finished crystal, fancy ground star bottom. Each, **35c**

C682 — "Rich Sunburst" pattern. Massive round deep shape, diam. 8½ in., footed, fancy cover, ht. 8 in., finest crystal, beautiful deep cut design. Each, **50c**

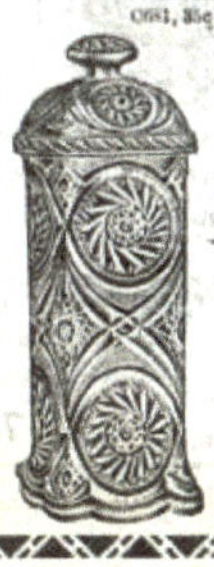

"SUNBURST" STRAW JAR.

A ready seller in a magnificent pattern.

C683—Square shape with flaring foot, fancy cover, ht. 12½ in., extra heavy deep cut crystal, brilliantly fire polished. Each, **50c**

PACKAGE CHARGE ABOLISHED
On all Crockery and Glassware

"MONUMENTAL" CASK ASSORTMENT.

Big dime leaders. Half of them actually worth 25 cents.

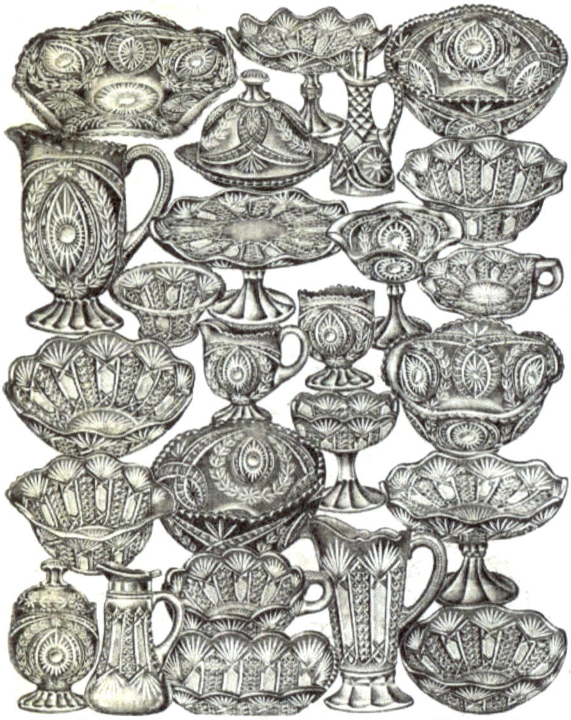

C848—Excellent quality and finish, brilliant new deep cut designs. Note especially extra large sizes. Assortment comprises:

- 6 only $8\frac{1}{2}$ in. bell shape berry bowls.
- 6 only $7\frac{3}{4}$ in. extra deep nut bowls.
- 6 only $5\frac{1}{2}$ in. footed comports.
- 6 only $8\frac{1}{2}$ in. extra deep oblong dishes.
- 6 only $6\frac{1}{2}$ in. double handled oval dishes.
- 6 only 8 in. deep round berry bowls.
- 6 only 5 in. high footed comports.
- 6 only $6\frac{1}{2}$ in. extra deep handled table pitcher.
- 6 only large brilliant syrup pitchers.
- 6 only 9 in. deep pointed salad dishes.
- 6 only fancy shape vinegar bottles.
- 6 only 6 in. high footed crimped jelly dishes.
- 3 only covered sugar bowls.
- 3 only footed spoonholders.
- 3 only cream pitchers.
- 3 only covered butter dishes.
- 3 only 7 in. extra deep berry bowls.
- 3 only 7 in. high footed fruit bowls.
- 3 only fancy tankard jugs, ht. $8\frac{1}{2}$ in.
- 1 only 8 in. extra deep berry bowl.
- 1 only $8\frac{1}{2}$ in. high footed comport.
- 1 only $9\frac{1}{2}$ in. high footed cake salver.
- 2 only extra large half gallon pitchers.
- 1 only $10\frac{1}{2}$ in. fancy cake dish.
- 1 only 8 in. deep berry bowl.

Total 100 pieces in cask. Wt. 158 lbs. **(NO PKG. CHARGE.)** Each, **$6\frac{3}{4}$c**

"MARVELOUS" GOLD ASSORTMENT.

The smallest piece easily worth a dime and some of them will retail from 25 to 50 cents.

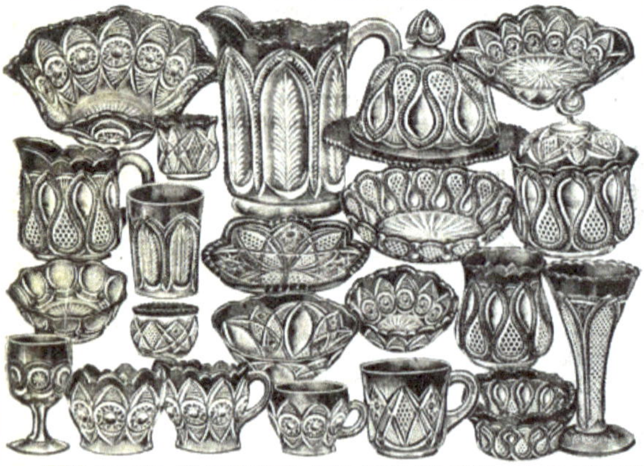

C869—Comprises 100 miscellaneous pieces, bright new crystal patterns, heavy and richly full finished, wide gold band decorations. Asst. comprises following:

- 1 only 3 pt. water pitcher, ht. $7\frac{3}{4}$ in.
- 6 only tumblers to match.
- 1 only $8\frac{1}{4}$ in. deep crimped berry bowl.
- 6 only $4\frac{1}{4}$ in. nappies to match.
- 6 only $7\text{x}5\frac{1}{2}$ fancy shape dishes.
- 6 only brilliant wine glasses.
- 6 only $4\frac{3}{4}$ in. extra deep footed nappies.
- 6 only $4\frac{1}{2}$ in. deep flaring berry dishes.
- 6 only footed open sugars, ht. $3\frac{1}{8}$ in., diam. $3\frac{1}{2}$.
- 6 only cream pitchers, ht. $3\frac{1}{4}$
- 6 only handled and footed sherbet cups.
- 6 only $6\frac{3}{4}$ in. fancy oblong dishes.
- 6 only fancy jewel or toilet boxes, solid gold covers.
- 6 only gold nugget toothpick holders.
- 6 only extra large and heavy handled mugs.
- 4 only tall flaring flower vases
- 1 only extra large covered butter dish
- 1 only spoonholder, matches butter dish.
- 1 only handled cream pitcher.
- 1 only large and heavy covered sugar bowl.
- 6 only $5\frac{1}{4}$ in. fancy bonbon dishes.
- 6 only 5 in. heavy brilliant nappies.

Total 100 pieces in bbl., wt. 85 lbs. **(NO PKG. CHARGE.)** Each, **$7\frac{1}{4}$c**

"SOVEREIGN" ASSORTMENT.

Big and beautiful pieces to retail at 25 cents.

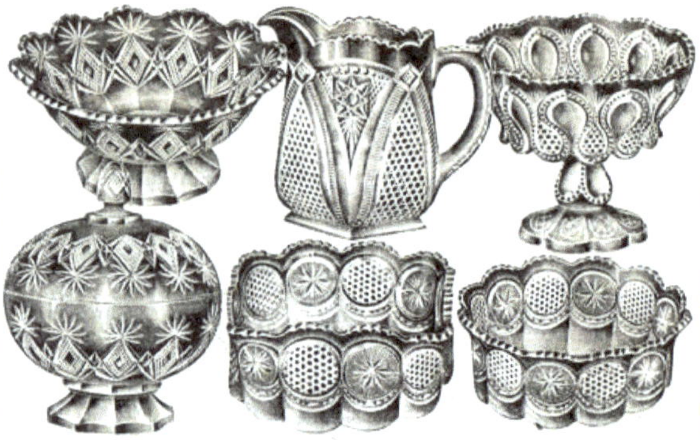

C902—Extra large fancy pieces, finest crystal, new rich deep cut patterns, full finished, Asst. comprises $\frac{1}{2}$ **doz. each** of following:

- $9\frac{1}{2}$ in. high footed fruit bowl,
- $8\frac{1}{2}$ in. extra deep round berry bowl.
- $7\frac{1}{4}$ in. deep footed bowl with cover.
- $9\frac{3}{4}$ in. fancy deep comport on high foot.
- $7\frac{3}{4}$ in. massive square deep berry bowl.
- $\frac{1}{2}$ gal. massive and brilliant pitcher.

Total 2 doz. in bbl., wt. 105 lbs. **(NO PKG. CHARGE.)** Per dozen, **$1.85**

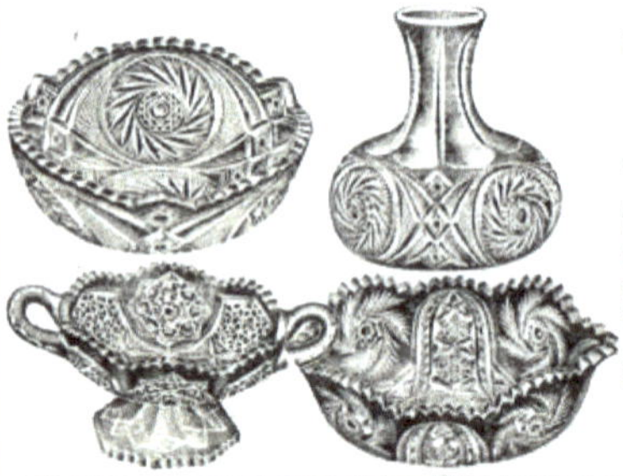

NEW "PRIZE WINNER" ASSORTMENT.

"PRESCUT" WARE.

Big crystal beauties to retail at 15 cents.

C904—Massive heavy rich patterns, all fine full finished crystal, new shapes that will sell on sight. Assortment comprises $\frac{3}{4}$ doz. each of the following:

- $8\frac{1}{2}$ in. mammoth deep dish.
- 7 in. large and heavy water bottle.
- 7 in. high footed double handled fruit dish.
- 10 in. extra deep oval salad dish.

Total 3 doz. in bbl. Wt. 120 lbs. Per dozen, **$1.87**

(NO PKG. CHARGE.)

"MASSIVE GOLD" ASSORTMENT.

Biggest and richest ones ever offered to retail at 25 cents.

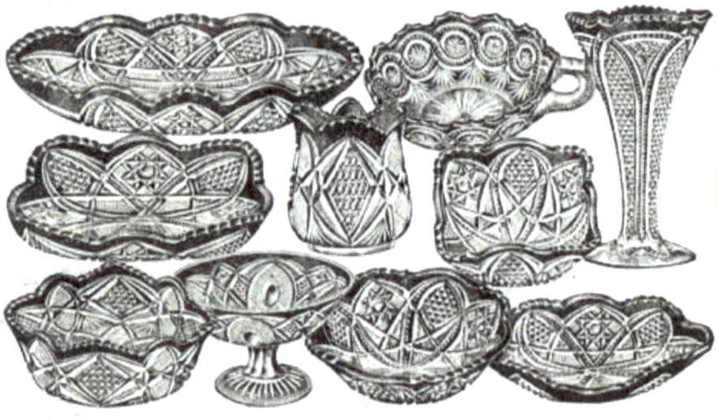

C916—Extra quality, heavy deep rich cut patterns brilliantly fire polished, extra wide gold band decorations. **Asst. comprises $\frac{1}{4}$ doz. each** of the following:

- $6\frac{3}{4}$ in. square deep bowl.
- $8\frac{3}{4}$ in. fancy table dish.
- 9 in. mammoth flaring flower vase.
- $7\frac{3}{4}$ in. extra deep pointed dish.
- $9\frac{3}{4}\text{x}6\frac{1}{2}$ in. fancy oblong table dish.
- $7\frac{3}{4}$ in. round deep berry bowl.
- Extra heavy tall celery holder.
- 6 in. deep handled dish.
- $6\frac{3}{4}$ in. deep high footed fruit bowl.
- Mammoth rich cut celery tray, length 13 in.

Wt. 73 lbs. Total $2\frac{1}{2}$ doz. in bbl. **(NO PKG. CHARGE.)** Per dozen, **$1.92**

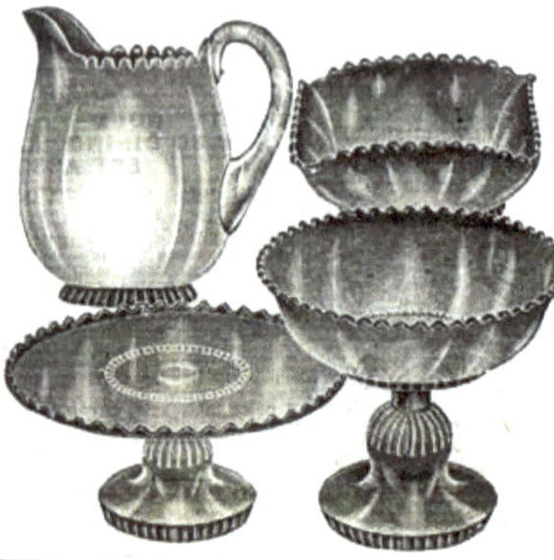

"EXHIBITION" ASSORTMENT.

Mammoth pieces richly finished.

C905—Rich, almost plain pattern, purest crystal. Full finished, fire polished. *Note extra large pieces.* $\frac{1}{2}$ **doz. each** of following:

- $\frac{1}{2}$ gal. pitcher, stuck handle.
- 7x7 4 corner bowl, extra deep, footed.
- 11 in. extra high cake salver.
- $8\frac{1}{2}$ in. high footed deep bowl.

Total 2 doz. in bbl., wt. 105 lbs.

Per dozen, **$2.00**

(NO PKG. CHARGE.)

Our Illustrations Are as Faithful as Possible, Yet They Do Not Do These Goods Full Justice.

"MAMMOTH" 4 PIECE ASST.

Extra large pieces; all full finished and fire polished.

C906—Much larger than usual 25 cent goods. Finest quality pure crystal, extra heavy, bright patterns. Asst. comprises ½ doz. each of following:
¼ gal. heavy water pitcher.
10 in. high footed cake salver.
6¼ in. extra deep high footed bowl and cover.
10 in. high footed flaring fruit bowl.
Total 2 doz. in bbl., wt. 116 lbs. Per dozen, **$1.85**
(NO PKG. CHARGE.)

"FLORAL ENGRAVED" SET ASSORTMENT.

You can retail at 75c per set—cheap at $1.00.

C945—Rich almost plain crystal, all pieces footed and with fancy ribbed base scalloped edges, full finish, fire polished, engraved floral decorations in banded design completely circle each piece. Asst. comprises 2 sets each of the following:
7 piece water sets; ½ gal. jug, genuine stuck handle, 6 optic ground bottom tumblers.
7 piece berry sets, extra deep berry bowl, six 4¼ in. nappies.
4 piece table sets.
Total 6 sets in bbl. Wt. 60 lbs. Per set, **54c**
(NO PKG. CHARGE.)

"WEDDING GIFT" DINING SET ASSORTMENT.

Unequaled values. Richest of the rich. Must be seen to be appreciated.

C960—Entirely new, massive deep cut pattern, exact reproduction of genuine cut, nearly all pieces footed, all full size and new artistic shapes, brilliantly fire polished. Asst. comprises 2 sets each of the following:
7 piece water sets; Mammoth ½ gal. pitcher, 6 ground bottom tumblers.
7 piece berry sets, 9¼ in. crimped ground bottom berry bowl, 6 5¼ in. ground bottom nappies.
Two 4 piece table sets. Total 6 sets in bbl., wt. 76 lbs. (NO PKG. CHARGE.) Per set, **59c**

"GOLD NUGGET" DINING SET ASSORTMENT.

None richer made. You can make a good profit on every one of these sets.

C959—Extra heavy massive deep cut patterns, finest quality and finish, all pieces with heavy pure burnt-in gold decorations. Asst. comprises 2 sets each of the following: 7 piece water sets, ½ gal. pitcher, 6 ground bottom tumblers; 7 piece berry sets, 9¼ in. mammoth berry bowl, six 4¼ in. nappies; 4 piece table sets.
Total 6 sets in bbl., wt. 67 lbs. Per set, **85c**
(NO PKG. CHARGE.)

PACKAGE CHARGE ABOLISHED
On All Glassware and Crockery.

"RICHEST OF ALL" SET ASSORTMENT—"Prescut" Ware.

Positively the richest crystal sets ever produced.

C954—Heavy deep cut pattern copied from the latest genuine cut design, brilliantly fire polished. Asst. comprises 2 sets each of the following:
7 piece water sets, low shape stuck handle jug, 6 ground bottom tumblers; 4 piece table sets.
7 piece berry sets, 8¼ in. berry bowl, 6 4¼ in. nappies.
Total 6 sets in bbl., wt. 70 lbs. (NO PKG. CHARGE.) Per set, **48c**

"MASSIVE CUT" DINING SET ASSORTMENT.

The biggest and richest sets ever offered at this price.

C940—Extra heavy deep cut pattern, finest quality crystal, every piece brilliantly finished. Note especially the extra large sizes. Asst. comprises 3 sets only each of the following:
7 piece water sets; mammoth ½ gal. jug, 6 ground bottom tumblers.
7 piece berry sets; 9 in. massive berry bowl, 6 4¼ in. nappies.
4 piece table sets; covered butter dish, sugar bowl, spoon holder and cream pitcher. Total 9 sets in bbl. Wt. 94 lbs. Per set, **42c**

"PURE GOLD" DINING SET ASSORTMENT.

The gem of the collections. One of the best you ever have seen.

C951—Handsomest of crystal patterns, heavily decorated with alternate crystal and genuine gold decorated panels. Asst. comprises 2 sets each of the following:
7 piece berry set, one 7½ in. deep bowl and 7 piece water set, wide top pitcher, 6 tumblers, six 4¼ in. nappies; 4 piece table set.
Total 6 sets complete in bbl., wt. 75 lbs. (NO PKG. CHARGE.) Per set, **80c**

"RICH GOLDEN" DINING SET ASSORTMENT.

Finest quality, richest pattern. You can retail these sets with a good profit.

C958—New jewel cut colonial design, extra heavy, very brilliant, all pieces with heavy pure burnt-in gold decorations, some of them nearly 2 in. wide. Asst. comprises 2 sets each of the following: 7 piece water sets, ¾ in. jug, 6 ground bottom tumblers; 7 piece berry set, 9¼ in. extra deep bowl, six 5 in. nappies; 4 piece table set, covered butter, sugar bowl, cream pitcher and spoon holder.
Wt. 70 lbs. 6 sets in bbl. (NO PKG. CHARGE.) Per set, **89c**

"FRENCH CRYSTAL" DINING SET ASSORTMENT.

Beautiful full finished sets to retail at 50c, although worth regularly much more.

C941—Beautiful Colonial panel pattern with fancy cut diamond band effect, finest quality full finished crystal, all pieces extra large and heavy, fancy shape. Asst. comprises 3 sets each of the following:
7 piece water sets, ½ gal. tankard pitcher, 6 ground bottom tumblers; 4 piece table sets; 7 piece berry sets, 8½ in. deep footed berry bowl and 6 4¼ in. nappies. Total 9 sets in bbl. Per set, **35c**
Wt. 85 lbs.
(NO PKG. CHARGE.)

Force Stickers Into Cash at a Loss and Put the Money Back Into Goods THAT SELL.

"DIADEM" BERRY BOWL ASSORTMENT.

Rare bargains if offered at 15 cents. You will be surprised at the quality and finish.

C983—Massive extra heavy deep cut patterns, finest quality full finished crystal with genuine ground and polished bottoms. Asst. comprises ⅔ doz. each of three fancy round shapes, 8 to 8½ (inches). Total 2 doz. in bbl. Per dozen, **$1.79**

"OPALESCENT" SALAD DISH ASSORTMENT.

No better 10 or 15 cent leaders than these.

C880—All in the beautiful opalescent ware, artistic patterns, equally asstd. in 3 colors, flint, blue, green. Asst. comprises 1¼ doz. each of 4 styles, sizes from 8¼ to 10¾, crimped and scalloped edges, brilliantly well made and finished, brilliantly fire polished. 6 doz. in bbl. wt. 128 lbs. Per dozen, **78c** (NO PKG. CHARGE.)

"BARGAIN BOWL" ASSORTMENT.

Four extra large and heavy 10 center leaders.

C77—You can easily get 15 cents each for two of the four. Assortment comprises 1¼ doz. each, average size about 8 in., all deep and heavy. Total 5 doz. in bbl. Per dozen, **82c** wt 140 lbs (NO PKG. CHARGE.)

"MATCHLESS" BOWL ASSORTMENT.

Excellent value at 15 cents. Rare advertisers if offered at a dime.

C982—Extra large sizes, diam. about 9¼ in., all footed, new brilliant cut patterns, first quality full finished crystal. 1 doz. each of 5 styles. Total 5 doz. in bbl., wt. 130 lbs. (NO PKG. CHARGE.) Per dozen, **89c**

"BIG" BERRY BOWL ASSORTMENT.

Extra heavy, new patterns.

C976. Note especially variety and size of pieces. They will prove rare leaders if offered "Your choice for 10 cents." Asst. comprises ⅜ doz. each of 8 patterns, all large deep round shapes, average size about 8 in. Total 3 doz. in bbl. Wt. 109 lbs. Per dozen, **75c** (NO PKG. CHARGE.)

DIME HANDLED BASKET ASSORTMENT.

Exceptionally good souvenir sellers.

C900. Asstd. new fancy basket shapes, large stuck handles, length 6½ in., rich heavy cut crystal jewel pattern, fine quality, ground polished bottoms. 4 doz. in case. Per dozen, **84c** (NO PKG. CHG.)

"ROYAL" BERRY BOWL ASSORTMENT.

Four big and beautiful pieces as 25c profit payers.

C988—Extra large and heavy, beautiful patterns, being among the richest ever produced in pressed glass. Asst. comprises ½ doz. each of 4 styles as illustrated, average size about 9½ in. Total 2 doz. in bbl. wt. 85 lbs. Per dozen, **$1.72** (NO PKG. CHARGE.)

"MAMMOTH" HEAVY CUT BERRY BOWL ASST.

Actually 50 centers to retail at 25 cents.

C990—Finest quality full finished crystal, extra heavy, footed, all the same pattern, a massive deep cut star and jewel band design. All pieces with fancy scalloped edges. Asst. comprises ½ doz. each of 5 fancy round shapes, all extra deep. Average size about 10½ in. Total 2½ doz. in bbl., wt. 128 lbs. (NO PKG. CHARGE.) Per dozen, **$1.95**

"MAGNIFICENT" BERRY BOWL ASSORTMENT.

Beautiful beyond description. As 25 centers these will startle your competitors.

C971—Beautiful new pattern, exceptionally rich, looks like genuine cut, finest quality crystal, brilliantly fire polished, fancy star bottoms ground and polished. Asst. comprises ⅔ doz. each of 3 deep round shapes, average diam. about 9 in. Total 2 doz. in bbl. Wt. 105 lbs. (NO PKG. CHARGE.) Per dozen, **$2.10**

HANGING FISH GLOBE ASSORTMENT.

You can retail with a good profit at about one-half usual price.

C1416. Round globe shape, best quality crystal glass. Asst. comprises:

1 only	½ gal		at $0 18
1 "	1 "		27
1 "	1½ "		36
1 "	2 "		43
1 "	2½ "		52
1 "	3 "		65

Wt. 50 lbs. Total for asst. of 6, **$2.40** (NO PKG. CHARGE.)

FOOTED FISH GLOBE ASSORTMENT.

The 3 best selling sizes in one package.

C1417—Large globe shape on fancy high foot, made of the best quality crystal, well finished. Asst. comprises:

1 only 1 gal		at $0 87
1 " 2 "		92
1 " 3 "		1 30

Wt. 50 lbs. Total for asst. of 3, **$2.98** (NO PKG. CHARGE.)

"EXTRA OFFERING" BOWL AND SALVER ASST.

Heretofore unknown as 10 cent sellers. If you show them, you will sell them.

C993: Heavy cut patterns, all high footed, full finished and fire polished. Asst. consists of 1 doz. each of the following:
9 in. high footed flared bowl.
8 in. deep bowl, high footed.
9½ in. high footed cake salver.
Total 2½ doz. in bbl. (NO PKG. CHARGE.) Per dozen, **$1.08**

"CRACKERJACK" BERRY BOWL ASSORTMENT.

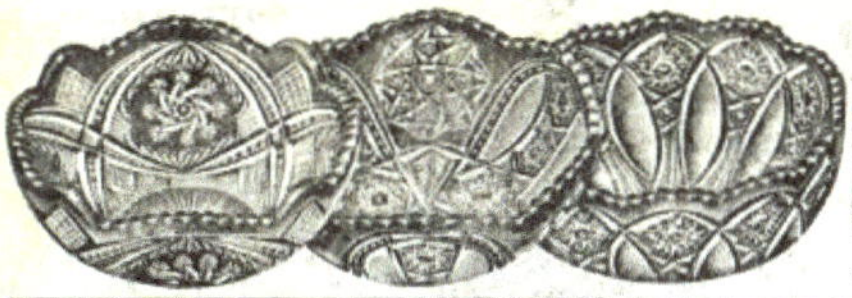

Trade winner of the sensational sort.

C972 — All extra large and heavy, diam. about 8½ in. 1 doz. each of 3 extra deep rich heavy cut patterns with fancy scalloped edges. Total 3 doz. in bbl. Wt. 105 lbs. Per dozen, **96c**

(NO PACKAGE CHARGE.)

MASSIVE COVERED BOWL ASST.

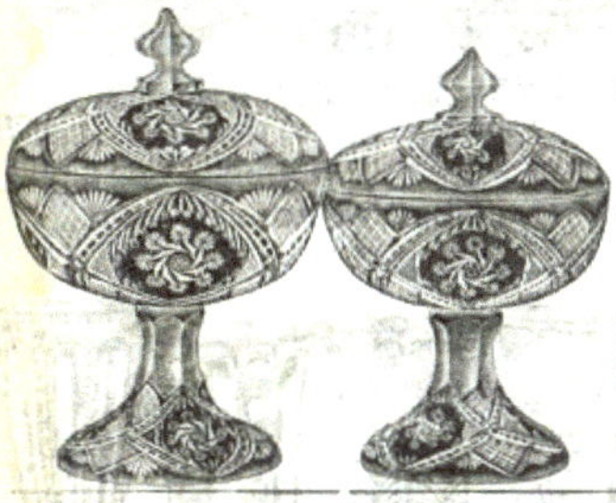

Regular 50 center. Your opportunity to acquire some big values.

C968—Comprising ¾ doz. 7¼ in., ½ doz. 8½ in. Both extra large, on high foot, rich and heavy deep cut pattern, fancy high dome covers. Total 1¼ doz. in bbl.

Per dozen, **$3.25**

(NO PKG. CHARGE.)

"RICHEST" FOOTED BOWL ASSORTMENT.

Four large profit paying 25 centers. Easily worth more.

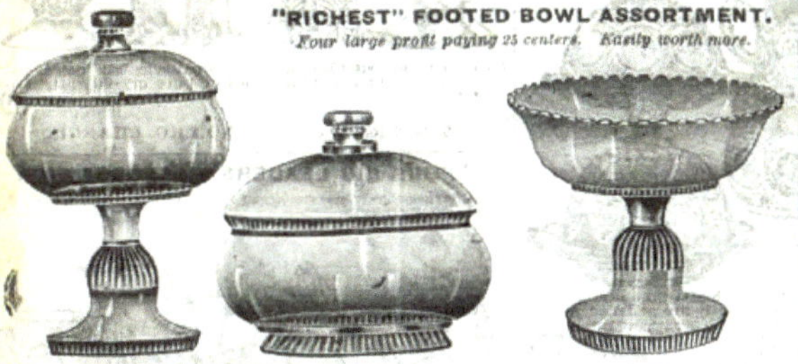

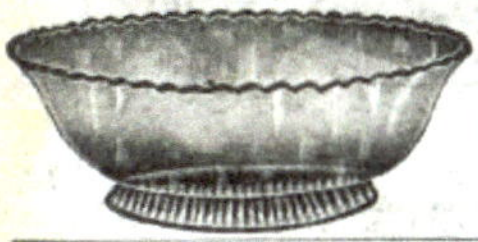

C984—In almost plain but beautifully rich pattern, half with covers and half without, all footed, richly finished and fire polished. Asst. comprises ½ doz. each of the following:

7 in. extra heavy bowl, footed, dome cover.
8½ " footed comport, scalloped edge.
6 " high footed bowl and cover.
7¼ " footed fruit bowl.

Total 2 doz. in bbl. Wt. 98 lbs. Per dozen, **$1.80**

(NO PKG. CHARGE.)

POPULAR SIZE COVERED BOWL ASSORTMENT.

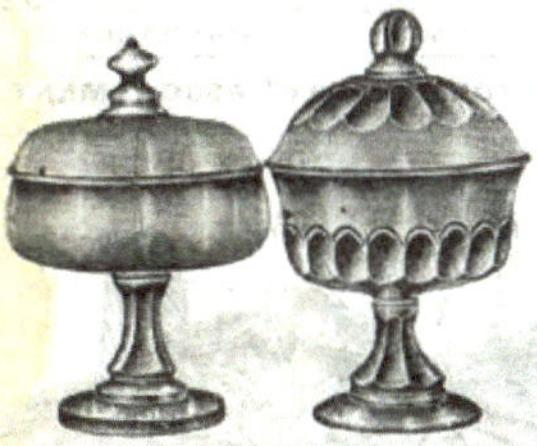

Big rich pieces to retail at unusually low prices.

C981—2 styles, one plain, the other almost plain with deep mirror flutes, both bowls and covers brilliantly fire polished, all on high feet. Asst. comprises ⅓ doz. each of 4 styles from 6 to 7¼ in. in diam.

Total 1⅓ doz. in bbl. Wt. 85 lbs. Per dozen, **$2.15**

(NO PKG. CHARGE.)

"PRINCELY" SALVER ASST.

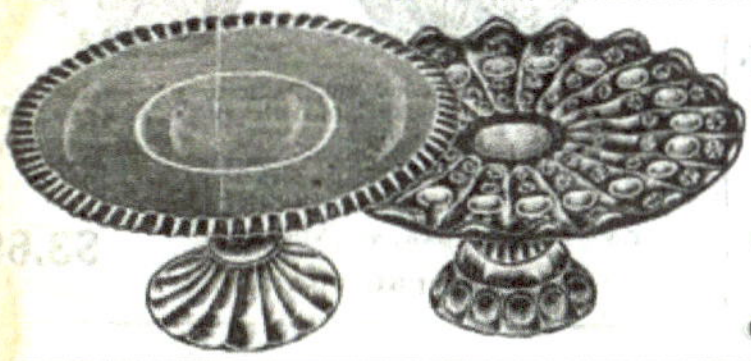

Excellent quality, cake salvers to sell at a quarter.

C927—Best crystal, brilliantly fire polished, richest of patterns. Asst. comprises: ⅔ doz. **Crimped Edge 10 in. Salvers.** ⅔ doz. **Scalloped Edge 10¼ in. Salvers.** Total of 1⅓ doz. to bbl., wt. 70 lbs.

Per dozen, **$1.95**

(NO PKG. CHARGE.)

"THREE SIZES" SALVER ASSORTMENT.

Possible 20 and 25 centers that usually retail for more.

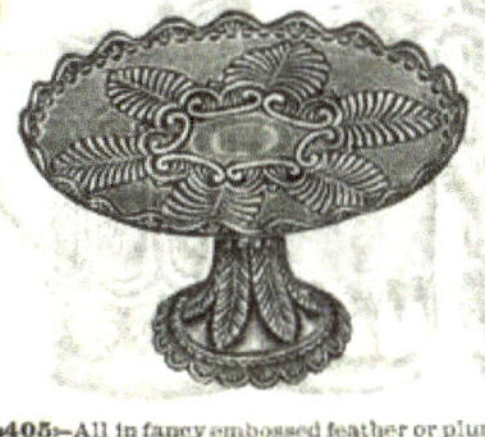

C1405—All in fancy embossed feather or plume design, rich full finished crystal. ½ doz. 9 in., ½ doz. 10 in., ¼ doz. 11 in. Total 1¼ doz. in bbl. Wt. 61 lbs.

Average price per dozen, **$1.85**

(NO PKG. CHARGE.)

"PLAIN SALVER" ASST.

Superior quality—the most staple seller in the salver line.

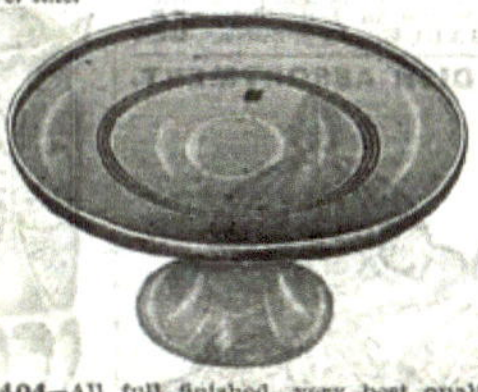

C1404—All full finished, very best quality ware, superior finish. Asst. comprises:

⅓ doz.	8 in.	@ 87c	$0 29
⅓ "	9 "	@ $1.67	56
⅓ "	10 "	@ $2.25	75
⅙ "	11 "	@ $3.00	50

1⅙ doz. in bbl., wt. 60 lbs.

Total for the 1⅙ dozen, **$2.10**

(NO PKG. CHARGE.)

10c COVERED BOWL.

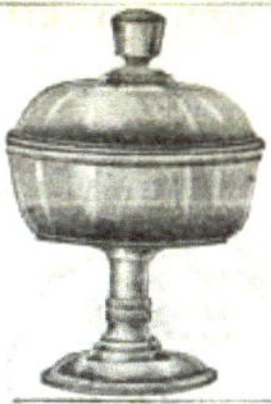

A sensational offering. Try and match it at anywhere near this price.

C969 — The staple plain crystal pattern, on high foot, extra deep, diam. 5¼ in., dome cover. 4 doz. in bbl.

Per dozen, ***85**

(NO PKG. CHARGE.)

"PRACTICAL" COVERED BOWL ASSORTMENT.

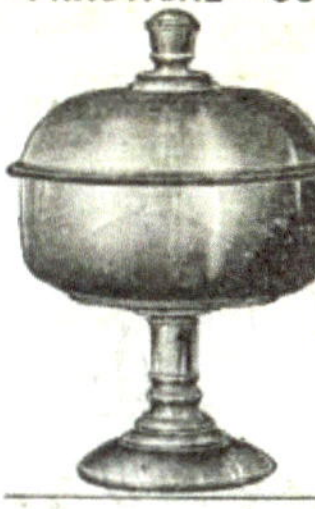

As 25 centers these are unequaled.

C970—Strong, well made, heavy plain crystal on high foot. Assortment comprises **1 doz. each 6¼ and 7¼ in. sizes.** Total 2 doz. in bbl. Wt. 110 lbs.

Per dozen, **$1.89**

(NO PKG. CHARGE.)

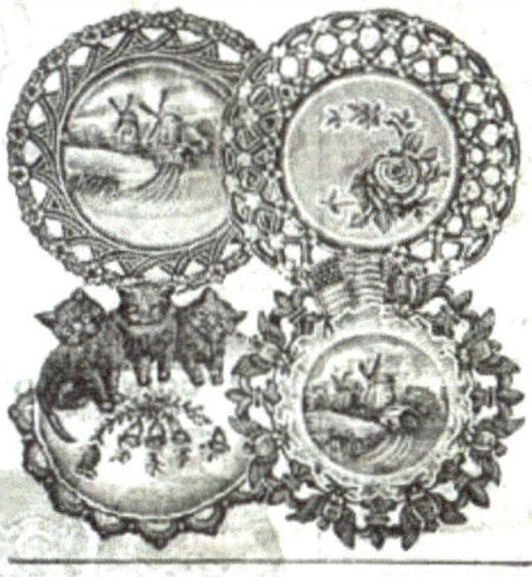

FANCY DECORATED PLAQUE ASSORTMENT.

Nothing better ever shown for a 10 cent sale.

C1448—4 styles, all opal, fancy embossed patterns with openwork edges, average size about 7¼ in., rich decorations: such as Holland scene, kittens in embossed effect, fancy floral designs. **1 doz. each** pattern. Total 4 doz. in case. Wt. 50 lbs.

Per dozen, **86c**

(NO PKG. CHARGE.)

"NOVELTY" PLAQUE ASST.

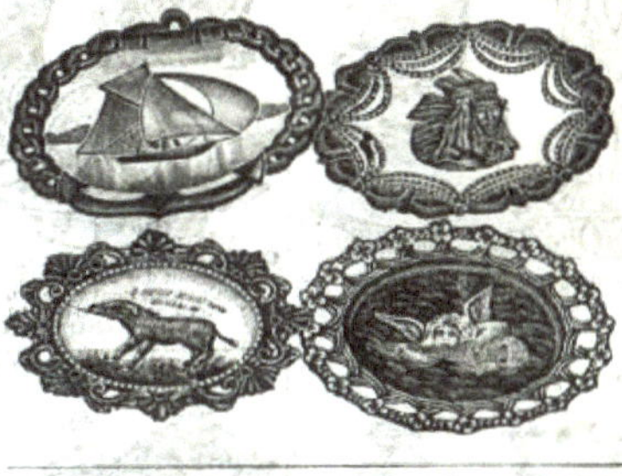

Up to date novelties in this line.

C1446—Exceptionally attractive decorations on opal, **1 doz. each of 4 styles.**

7¼ in. with embossed Indian head center and bow and arrow edge, Indian in natural colors, gold bronze.
7½ in., with anchor and chain openwork edge, embossed yacht and water scene center.
7¼ in., openwork edge, white angel in relief center with solid color mat back ground, fancy wreath embossed edge.
7¼ in., openwork edge, mat colors, donkey, "I'm from Missouri, Show Me" in gold bronze letters.

Total 4 doz. in case. Wt. 55 lbs. Per dozen, **87c**

(NO PKG. CHARGE.)

NOVELTY TURQUOISE BLUE HAND DECORATED ASST.

Priced as possible 10 centers, but more than half of them would be cheap if offered at 25 cents.

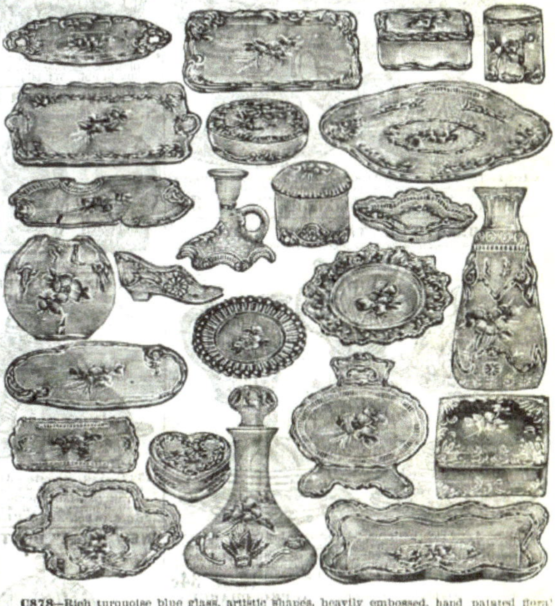

C878—Rich turquoise blue glass, artistic shapes, heavily embossed, hand painted floral decorations, embossed work decorated in gold bronze. Note large variety and extra large sizes. Asst. comprises:

8 only 9 in. flower vases, asstd. fancy shapes.
6 only 4¾ in. oval covered jewel boxes.
2 onlo 4¾ in. extra large rose bowls.
9 only 5 in. fancy slippers.
2 only 5x5 square covered handkerchief boxes.
6 only 3 in. fancy footed cigar holders.
2 only 8¼ in. fancy dishes with open handle.
3 only 4 in. oblong covered hairpin boxes.
6 only 8¾ in. fancy bureau trays
6 only fancy plaques, attached easel, ht. 6¾ in.
2 only 10¾ in. deep oblong celery trays.
6 only 5¾ in. fancy plates, openwork flange.
2 only 9¾x6 oblong comb and brush trays.
6 only fancy heart jewel boxes, cover.
6 only 5¾ in. pin trays, asstd. fancy shapes.
6 only 4¼ in. handled candle sticks.
4 only 8¾ in. fancy utility trays.
3 only 7¼ in. pin trays, double open handles.
3 only covered puff boxes.
6 only 7¾ in. openwork plaques
3 only 6x3¾ oblong trays.
2 only 8¾x6 oblong bureau trays.
2 only large toilet bottles with stopper.
2 only 11¼x8¾ comb and brush trays.

Total 100 pieces in asst. Wt. 105 lbs. (NO PKG. CHARGE.) Each **7½c**

The Country's Shrewdest Buyers Come Here for Their Glassware Needs. We Save Them Money.

4 PIECE TABLE SETS.

Each comprising covered butter dish, covered sugar bowl, cream pitcher and spoonholder.

"RARE VALUE" 4 PIECE TABLE SET ASST.
Note the patterns and large sizes. You can retail these at 25c a set.

C1026—3 inch patterns, all heavy cut design and all pieces full size. 8 sets each pattern. Per set, **17½c**

Total 24 sets in bbl., wt. 125 lbs. (NO PKG. CHARGE.)

NEW "PLAIN AND FANCY" TABLE SET ASST.
Bouncing big sets and bright bargains.

C1028—Comprises 8 sets each of 3 styles, plain with pearl edge, mirror panel and deep cut, all pcs. extra large. Per set, **19c**

Total 24 sets in bbl., wt. 150 lbs. (NO PKG. CHARGE.)

NEW "MAGNIFICENT" TABLE SET ASST.
Positively the most beautiful set ever offered at a low price.

C1034—Three elaborate and brilliant genuine cut glass patterns, all extra large, heavy and massive, richly finished and fire polished. 4 sets of 3 patterns. Total 12 sets in bbl. Wt. 110 lbs. Per set, **33c**

"BEAUTIFUL" TABLE SET ASST.
Magnificent crystal gems. The popular massive heavy pieces

C1033—3 new rich patterns, 2 being deep heavy cut designs, one with large double handles; one optic and cut diamond panel with wide plain edge. Each set consists of massive heavy covered butter dish, covered sugar bowl, spoonholder, cream pitcher. All pieces footed. 4 sets each pattern. Per set, **34c**

Total 12 sets in bbl., wt. 104 lbs. (NO PKG. CHARGE.)

"SURE THING" NEST EGG.
C750—Best opal nest eggs, large size, packed 1 gro. in partition case. Per gross, **$1.75**

C750½—As above, put up 1 doz. in pasteboard box. Per dozen, **17c**

"RICH COLONIAL" TABLE SET ASST.
Finest quality, beautiful patterns.

C1035—3 rich colonial patterns, one almost plain with deep flutes, the other two with wide panel designs. All are of purest crystal and brilliantly fire polished. 4 sets each of 3 patterns. Per set, **38c**

Total 12 sets in bbl., wt. 100 lbs. (NO PKG. CHARGE.)

"COIN GOLD" TABLE SET ASST.
The richest 4 piece table sets ever made.

C1045—3 rich patterns, one a fancy colonial flute and 2 heavy deep cut designs. All pieces brilliantly fire polished, all with extra heavy wide burnt in gold decorations, 2 sets of each pattern. Total 6 sets in bbl. Wt. 55 lbs. Per set, **77c**

"CRYSTAL" SUGAR BOWL.

C1320—One doz. each of 5 attractive patterns—2 low and 3 high shapes, one with large double handles. Total 5 doz. in bbl. Wt. 96 lbs. Per dozen, **73c**

"NEW" SUGAR BOWL ASSORTMENT.
A barrel will indeed convince you that we are indeed bargain givers.

C1321—One doz. each of 4 patterns, all bright and finished. A good variety of shapes and sizes. Regular 15 centers. Per dozen, **75c**

Total 4 doz. to bbl. Wt. 90 lbs. (NO PKG. CHARGE.)

"BIG SIX" BUTTER DISH AND SUGAR BOWL ASSORTMENT.

C1322.—Asst. comprises 3 doz. covered sugar bowls and 3 doz. covered butter dishes, all large full size and equally assrtd. in 3 patterns—fancy plume design, rich plain and pressed star—all of heavy crystal, well made and finished. Total 6 doz. in bbl. (NO PKG. CHARGE.) Per doz., **65c**

"NEW DIME" BUTTER DISH ASSORTMENT.

C1316—Assortment comprises 5 patterns, all large sizes, diam. 7¼ in., 4 heavy deep cut designs and one beaded panel, all pure crystal, well made and finished. 1 doz. of each. Total 5 doz. in bbl., wt. 130 lbs. (NO PKG. CHARGE.) Per dozen, **75c**

"BIG FOUR" BUTTER DISH ASSORTMENT
Every day sellers. All large and all bright.

C1317—Pure crystal, extra heavy and well finished. 4 styles as illustrated, extra deep and with high cover. 1 doz. each of 4 patterns. Per dozen, **79c**

Total 4 doz. in bbl., wt. 110 lbs. (NO PKG. CHARGE.)

TALL CELERY HOLDER ASST.
These large attractive holders are always in demand. Good value at 15c—possible dime leaders.

C1444—Comprising ½ doz. each of 4 patterns, all footed, extra large sizes, ht. about 6½ in., all of pure crystal, bright patterns. Per dozen, **89c**

Total 2 doz. in case. (NO PKG. CHARGE.)

"FOUR BIG LEADERS" ASSORTMENT.
A fortunate purchase enables us to offer these big high grade pieces as possible 10 centers.

C849—Beautiful colonial pattern, all pieces footed, brilliant full finished crystal. Can be retailed either in sets or separately. Asst. comprises 1½ doz. each of the following: Mammoth flanged covered butter dish, 8 in. Large milk or cream pitcher, ht. 4¼ in. Frosted spoonholder, ht. 4½ in. Extra large covered sugar bowl, ht. 7 in. Per dozen, **92c**

Wt. 123 lbs. Total 5½ doz. in bbl. (NO PKG. CHARGE.)

FANCY HANDLED BASKET ASSORTMENT.
To retail at 10, 15 and 25c or more if you choose. Will sell themselves if shown.

C901 — New, rich diamond cut pattern, purest brilliant crystal, extra deep shapes, large twist stuck handles. Asst. comprises:

1 doz. 4½ in.	$0.82	$0.82
½ doz. 6 "	1.32	.66
½ doz. 7½ "	1.84	.92
½ doz. 10 "	2.40	1.20

Total 2½ doz. in asst., wt. 75 lbs. Complete. **$3.60**

(NO PKG. CHARGE.)

"QUARTER BARGAIN" TANKARD JUG ASST.
Big values, large sizes, rich new bright patterns

C1287—⅔ doz. each of 3 styles, all extra large ½ gal. tall tankard shapes, ht. about 10 in., all footed and with large fancy handles. 2 being deep cut designs and the other rich plain. Total 2 doz. in bbl. Per dozen, **$1.90**

(NO PKG. CHARGE.)

We Ask the Same Courtesy for "Our Drummer" You Give the Drummer Who Calls in Person.

July "Specials" in GLASSWARE and CROCKERY

We have always been signally successful in securing the best values in the trade and July has been no exception. On the following four pages you will find listed *the very best bargains to be had in America*. Every item will yield a good profit at the bargain price you will ask for it.

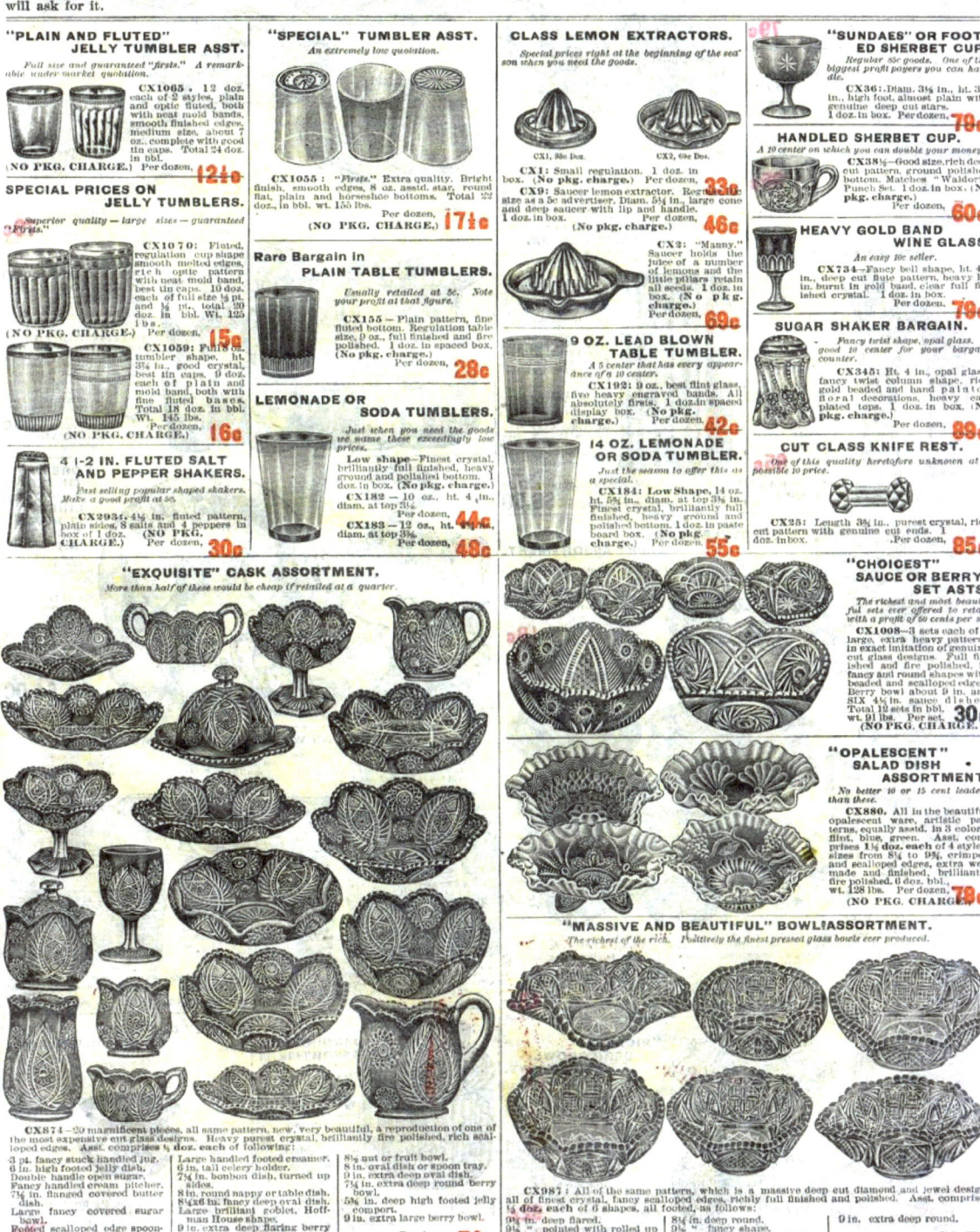

"PLAIN AND FLUTED" JELLY TUMBLER ASST.
Full size and guaranteed "firsts." A remarkable under market quotation.
CX1065 : 12 doz. each of 2 styles, plain and optic fluted, both with neat mold bands, smooth finished edges, medium size, about 7 oz., complete with good tin caps. Total 24 doz. in bbl. (NO PKG. CHARGE.) Per dozen, **12½c**

SPECIAL PRICES ON JELLY TUMBLERS.
Superior quality — large sizes — guaranteed "Firsts."
CX1070 : Fluted, regulation cup shape, smooth melted edges, rich optic pattern with neat mold band, best tin caps. 10 doz. each of full size ½ pt. and ⅓ pt., total 20 doz. in bbl. Wt. 125 lbs. (NO PKG. CHARGE.) Per dozen, **15c**

CX1059 : Fancy tumbler shape, ht. 3¾ in., good crystal, best tin caps, 9 doz. each of plain and mold band, both with fine fluted bases. Total 18 doz. in bbl. Wt. 145 lbs. (NO PKG. CHARGE.) Per dozen, **16c**

4 1-2 IN. FLUTED SALT AND PEPPER SHAKERS.
Fast selling popular shaped shakers. Make a good profit at 5c.
CX2931, 4½ in. fluted pattern, plain sides, 8 salts and 4 peppers in box of 1 doz. (NO PKG. CHARGE.) Per dozen, **30c**

"SPECIAL" TUMBLER ASST.
An extremely low quotation.
CX1055 : "Firsts." Extra quality. Bright finish, smooth edges, 8 oz. asstd. star, round flat, plain and horseshoe bottoms. Total 12 doz., in bbl. Wt. 155 lbs. (NO PKG. CHARGE.) Per dozen, **17½c**

Rare Bargain in PLAIN TABLE TUMBLERS.
Usually retailed at 5c. Note your profit at that figure.
CX155 — Plain pattern, fine fluted bottom. Regulation table size, 9 oz., full finished and fire polished. 1 doz. in spaced box. (No pkg. charge.) Per dozen, **28c**

LEMONADE OR SODA TUMBLERS.
Just when you need the goods we name these exceedingly low prices.
Low shape — Finest crystal, brilliantly full finished, heavy ground and polished bottom. 1 doz. in box. (No pkg. charge.)
CX182 — 10 oz., ht. 4 in., diam. at top 3⅛. Per dozen, **44c**
CX183 — 12 oz., ht. 3¾, diam. at top 3¾. Per dozen, **48c**

GLASS LEMON EXTRACTORS.
Special prices right at the beginning of the season when you need the goods.
CX1, 83c doz.   CX2, 69c doz.
CX1 : Small regulation. 1 doz. in box. (No pkg. charge.) Per dozen, **33c**
CX9 : Saucer lemon extractor. Regular size as a 5c advertiser. Diam. 5¼ in., large cone and deep saucer with lip and handle. 1 doz. in box. (No pkg. charge.) Per dozen, **46c**
CX2 : "Manny." Saucer holds the juice of a number of lemons and the little pillars retain all seeds. 1 doz. in box. (No pkg. charge.) Per dozen, **69c**

9 OZ. LEAD BLOWN TABLE TUMBLER.
A 5 center that has every appearance of a 10 center.
CX192 : 9 oz., best flint glass, five heavy engraved bands. All absolutely firsts. 1 doz. in spaced display box. Per dozen, **42c**

14 OZ. LEMONADE OR SODA TUMBLER.
Just the season to offer this as a special.
CX184 : Low Shape, 14 oz., ht. 5⅜ in., diam. at top 3¾ in. Finest crystal, brilliantly full finished, heavy ground and polished bottom. 1 doz. in pasteboard box. (No pkg. charge.) Per dozen, **55c**

"SUNDAES" OR FOOTED SHERBET CUP.
Regular 5c goods. One of the biggest profit payers you can handle.
CX36 : Diam. 3¼ in., ht. 3¾ in., high foot, almost plain with genuine deep cut stars. 1 doz. in box. Per dozen, **79c**

HANDLED SHERBET CUP.
A 10 center on which you can double your money.
CX38½ — Good size, rich deep cut pattern, ground polished bottom. Matches "Waldorf" Punch Set. 1 doz. in box. (No pkg. charge.) Per dozen, **60c**

HEAVY GOLD BAND WINE GLASS.
An easy 10c seller.
CX734 — Fancy bell shape, ht. 4½ in., deep cut flute pattern, heavy 1¼ in., burnt in gold band, clear full finished crystal. 1 doz. in box. Per dozen, **79c**

SUGAR SHAKER BARGAIN.
Fancy twist column shape, opal glass. A good 10 center for your bargain counter.
CX345 : Ht. 4 in., opal glass, fancy twist column shape, rich gold beaded and hand painted floral decorations, heavy cast plated tops. (No pkg. charge.) Per dozen, **89c**

CUT CLASS KNIFE REST.
One of the quality heretofore unknown at a possible 10 price.
CX25 : Length 3¾ in., purest crystal, rich cut pattern with genuine cut ends. 1 doz. in box. Per dozen, **85c**

"EXQUISITE" CASK ASSORTMENT.
More than half of these would be cheap if retailed at a quarter.
CX874 — 20 magnificent pieces, all same pattern, new, very beautiful, a reproduction of one of the most expensive cut glass designs. Heavy purest crystal, brilliantly fire polished, rich scalloped edges. Asst. comprises ⅓ doz. each of following:

3 pt. fancy stuck handled jug.
6 in. high footed jelly dish.
Double handle open sugar.
Fancy handled cream pitcher.
7½ in. flanged covered butter dish.
Large fancy covered sugar bowl.
Footed scalloped edge spoonholder.
Large handled footed creamer.
6 in. tall celery holder.
6 in. oval dish.
7¼ in. bonbon dish, turned up sides.
8 in. round nappy or table dish.
8¼ & 8 in. fancy deep oval dish.
Large brilliant goblet, Hoffman House shape.
9 in. extra deep flaring berry bowl.
8¼ in. nut or fruit basket.
6 in. oval dish or spoon tray.
9 in. extra deep oval dish.
7¾ in. extra deep round berry bowl.
5⅜ in. deep high footed jelly comport.
9 in. extra large berry bowl.

Total 10 doz. in cask. Wt. 195 lbs. (NO PKG. CHARGE.) Per dozen, **74c**

"CHOICEST" SAUCE OR BERRY SET ASTS.
The richest and most beautiful sets ever offered to retail with a profit of 50 cents per set.
CX1008 — 3 sets each of 4 large, extra heavy patterns in exact imitation of genuine cut glass designs. Full finished and fire polished, in fancy and round shapes with beaded and scalloped edges. Berry bowl about 9 in. and six 4½ in. same dishes. Total 12 sets in bbl. wt. 91 lbs. Per set, **30c** (NO PKG. CHARGE.)

"OPALESCENT" SALAD DISH ASSORTMENT.
No better 10 or 15 cent leaders than these.
CX880. All in the beautiful opalescent ware, artistic patterns, equally assted. in 3 colors, flint, blue, green. Asst. comprises 1¼ doz. each of 4 styles, sizes from 8½ to 9½, crimped and scalloped edges, extra well made and finished, brilliantly fire polished. 6 doz. in bbl. wt. 128 lbs. Per dozen, **79c** (NO PKG. CHARGE.)

"MASSIVE AND BEAUTIFUL" BOWL ASSORTMENT.
The richest of the rich. Positively the finest pressed glass bowls ever produced.
CX987 : All of the same pattern, which is a massive deep cut diamond and jewel design, all of finest crystal, fancy scalloped edges, richly full finished and polished. Asst. comprises ½ doz. each of 6 shapes, all footed, as follows:

9½ in. deep flared.   9 in. deep round.   9 in. extra deep round.
9½ in. pointed with rolled up sides.   9½ in. fancy shape.   7 in. extra deep, bent in sides.

Total 2 dozen in bbl., wt. 100 lbs. (NO PKG. CHARGE.) Per dozen, **$1.70**

BUTLER BROTHERS, RANDOLPH BRIDGE, CHICAGO.

You Cannot Afford to Pay Market Prices For These—WE SAVE YOU MONEY ON EVERY ITEM.

"SPECIALS" for JULY—Continued

"SPECIAL OFFERING" BOWL ASSORTMENT.
Your loss if you miss this opportunity. Possible 10 centers that will easily bring 15c.

GOLD DECORATED FANCY CUT TUMBLER.
A big bargain at the price offered.

CX738—Full size tapering shape, heavy brilliantly full finished crystal, deep diamond cut design, 1½ in. heavy gold band top, ground and polished star bottom. 1 doz. in box. Per dozen, **79c**

"DIME LEADER" JUG ASSORTMENT.
Matchless value at 15 cents.

10c COVERED BOWL.
A sensational offering. Try and match it anywhere near this price.

CX969—The staple plain crystal pattern, on high foot, extra deep, diam. 5¼ in. dome cover, 1 doz. in bbl. Per dozen, **85c** (NO PKG. CHARGE.)

CX1477: Large size, so called half gallon, footed with wide top and large handle, 1½ doz. each of 2 deep heavy cut designs. Total 2⅔ doz. in pkg., wt. 97 lbs. (NO PKG. CHARGE.) Per dozen, **$1.05**

EXTRAORDINARY MANTLE CABINET OFFERING.
For 30 days we offer the biggest bargain in high grade mantles ever put before a retail merchant.

CX1950—Our well known brands at prices that will enable you to make a special 10 cent mantle drive with goods that regularly wholesale at this price. We also give you FREE a Glass Front Oak Cabinet. Each cabinet contains:

25 Sensation Loop Mantles reg price .06½ **$1.63**
50 White City Cap Mantles reg price .06½ **3.25**
25 Defiance Cap Mantles reg price .09½ **2.38**

100 Mantles regular price, **$7.26**
Special price complete, **$6.50**

CX993: Artistic deep cut design, 5 new patterns, all extra brilliant full finished, best quality crystal, average about 9 in. asstd. shapes. Total 5 doz. in bbl. wt. 135 lbs. (NO PKG. CHARGE.) Per dozen, **79c**

"IMMENSE VASE" ASST.
Regular 25 cent values at a possible 10 cent price. Actually the biggest values we have ever offered in vases.

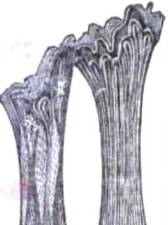

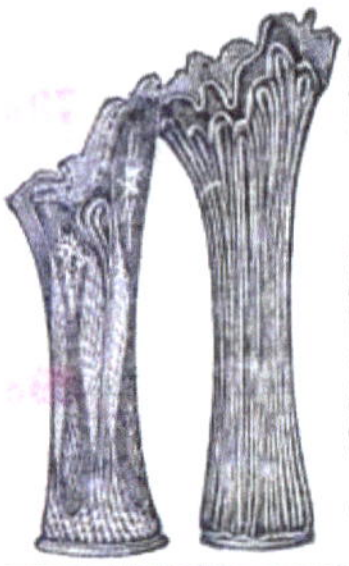

CX1202: Two beautiful patterns, one heavy cut effect, the other diamond, bead and panel. Average ht. from 12 to 14 in. Full finished pot glass. Total 3½ doz. in case. Per dozen, **95c** (NO PACKAGE CHARGE.)

"ENAMELED AND GOLD" DECORATED LEMONADE SET ASST.
No richer ones possible to retail at $1.00.

CX1244—3 large fancy shapes, ht. jugs about 10½ in., full ½ gal. size, stuck handles, large hand painted enameled floral decorations, wide gold edges. Each set comprises 1 jug and 6 tumblers. 5 sets each green, blue and crystal, total 9 sets in bbl. Wt. 78 lbs. Per set, **63c** (NO PKG. CHARGE.)

"SIX STYLE" BERRY NAPPY ASSORTMENT.
You can retail at a good profit at 2 for 5.

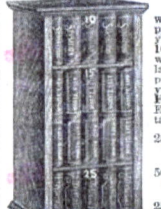

CX996: Average size about 4½ in., 6 bright new deep cut crystal patterns, all fancy shape, with scalloped edges. 2 doz. each. Total 12 doz. in case. Wt. 75 lbs. Per dozen, **18c** (NO PKG. CHARGE.)

"GREEN TINTED AND GOLD LINED" 12 PIECE TOILET SET.
At a special price for our month. Big value.

EX514: Regular composition, embossed white granite body in special green tinted and gold lined combination. Full size pieces. Each set in bbl. wt 60 lbs. Per set, **$4.00** (NO PKG. CHARGE.)

"OPALESCENT" 5 CENT NOVELTY ASSORTMENT.
All large bright attractive pieces. Many of them 10 cent values.

CX807—All bright full finished pieces in blue, green and flint opalescent. Not a piece in the lot that is not a useful article. Assortment consists of 1¼ doz. each of the following:

7½ in. fancy footed plate.   6½ in. fancy fluted card tray.
4½ in. flower vase.   4½ in. fancy handled dish.
5¼ in. deep round footed bowl.   4½ in. swan vase.
4½ in. colonial rustic vase.   5¼ in. fancy star nappy.   6½ in. beaded edge plate.
                      6½ in. triangle shape dish.   3¾ in. colonial vase.

Total 15 doz. in pkg. (NO PKG. CHARGE.) Per dozen, **42c**

BOHEMIAN WATER SET ASSORTMENT.

The entire stock of one of the largest makers and importers of this line is here represented. For purely financial reasons, we have taken the entire stock—not a part, but every set. This assortment consists of sets ranging in price from 75c to $2.00 per set, regular wholesale. This is a bargain not to be overlooked.

CX1243½: Assorted crystal, green, ruby and etched glass, assorted decorations in colored enameled flowers and design effect, most of them full gold treated. Each set consists of one pitcher and six tumblers. Total 11 sets in a bbl. (NO PACKAGE CHARGE.) Per set, **73c**

"RICHEST" BERRY BOWL ASSORTMENT.

Big massive brilliant pieces which were never before offered at such a price.

CX979—Beautiful beyond description, exact imitation of genuine cut glass, rich diamond cut star pattern, extra heavy and brilliantly fire polished. 1¼ doz. each of 4 deep fancy shapes, all footed average size about 8 in. Total 5 doz. in bbl. wt. 140 lbs. Per dozen, **92c** (NO PKG. CHARGE.)

JARDINIERE ASSORTMENT.
Big sellers this month.

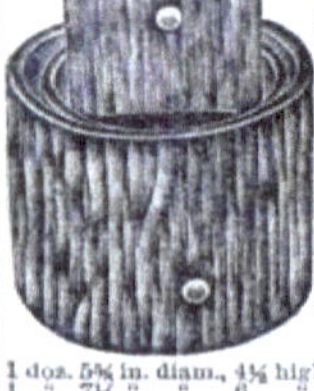

EX855. Hard burned body, embossed wood design, deep cut bark and knot pattern. Assorted colors, maroon and gilt; black, red and gilt; and green and gilt.

1 doz. 5⅜ in. diam., 4½ high ea. $0.75
1 " 7½ " 6 " 1.10
1 " 9 " 7½ " 1.68

Total 3 doz. in asst. **$3.53**
Special price, **$3.25**

"DIME" CUSPIDOR
In Original Package.
A big seller.

EX845: Diam 7 in. ht. 4½. Rustic design in red, green and olive colorings, half dull and half bright baked finish, artistic bronze decorations. Asstd. 6 doz. in crate. Per dozen, **78c** (NO PKG. CHARGE.)

BUTLER BROTHERS, RANDOLPH BRIDGE, CHICAGO.

"Is it Satisfactory?" This Question Decides the Selection of Every Number Here.

OUR ANNUAL "HARVEST SALE" of W. G. WARE (OPEN STOCK)

Net prices figured at 60 & 10 per cent off the White Granite list.

Our well known "Perfection" High Grade White Granite Ware. For 30 days only, we offer our well known "Perfection" line of White Granite Ware at the exceptionally low price of 60 & 10 per cent off the White Granite list. No package charge. F. O. B. Chicago. All orders shipped the same day received.

Best W. G. Ware in the United States. We guarantee it as to quality, color, selection, sizes and **against crazing**. Body the best that can possibly be made—baked extra hard—blue white color—clean, bright glaze. Very carefully selected R. K. grade. A ware that will stand the test.

NOTE—The following net prices are figured at 60 and 10 per cent off the White Granite list.

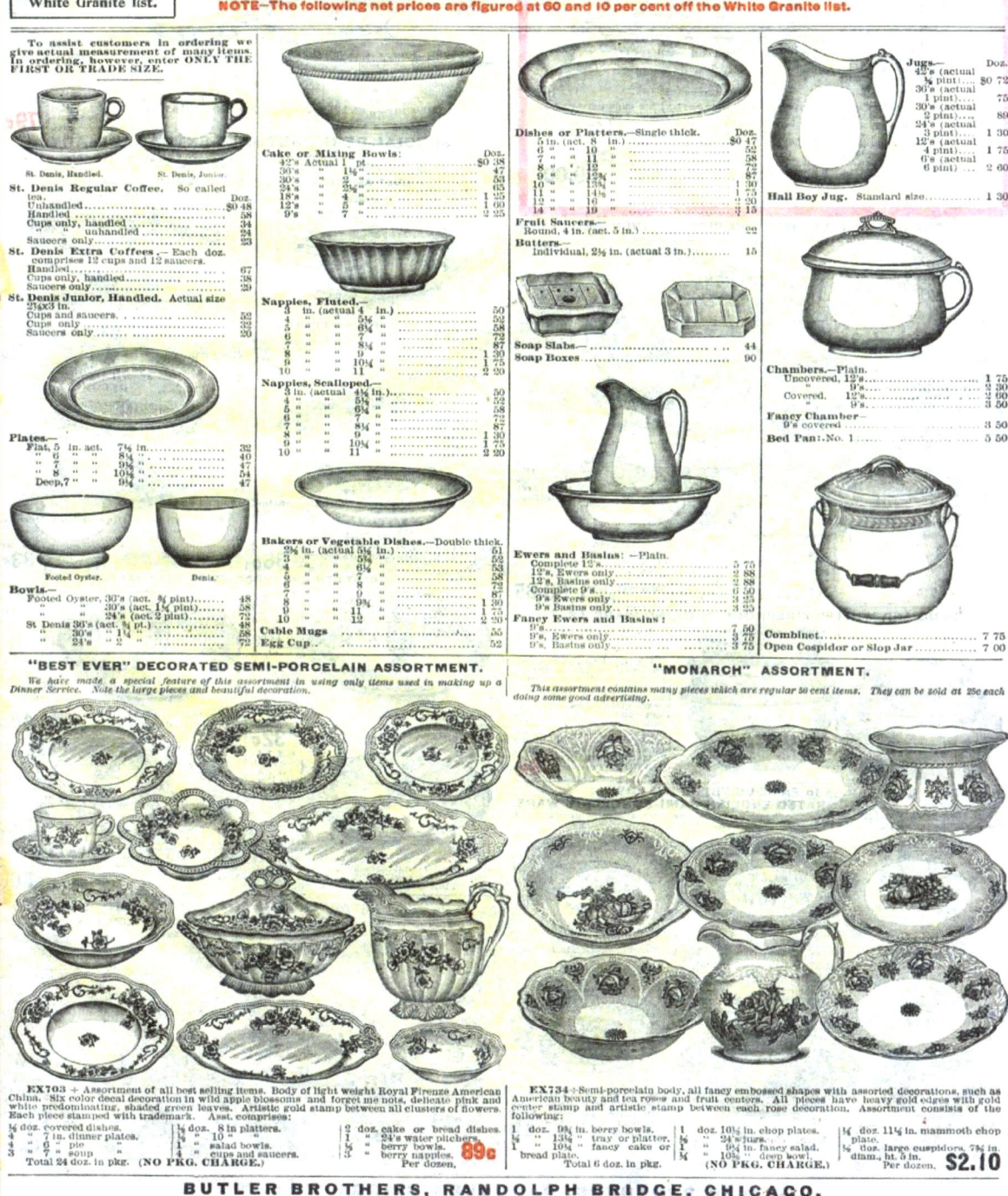

To assist customers in ordering we give actual measurement of many items. In ordering, however, enter ONLY the FIRST or TRADE SIZE.

St. Denis, Handled.   **St. Denis, Junior.**

St. Denis Regular Coffee. So called. Doz.
Unhandled, tea $0 48
Handled 58
Cups only, handled 34
    " " unhandled 24
Saucers only 23

St. Denis Extra Coffees.—Each doz. comprises 12 cups and 12 saucers.
Handled 67
Cups only, handled 38
Saucers only 29

St. Denis Junior, Handled. Actual size 2¼x3⅛ in.
Cups and saucers 52
Cups only 32
Saucers only 20

Plates.—
Flat, 5 in. act. 7⅞ in. 32
 " 6 " " 8¼ " 40
 " 7 " " 9⅜ " 47
 " 8 " " 10¾ " 54
Deep, 7" " 9¼ " 47

Bowls.—
Footed Oyster, 30's (act. ⅞ pint) ... 48
  "   " 30's (act. 1⅛ pint) ... 58
  "   " 24's (act. 2 pint) 72
St. Denis 36's (act. ⅝ pt.) 48
  "   " 30's " 1¼ " 58
  "   " 24's " 72

Cake or Mixing Bowls: Doz.
42's Actual 1 pt $0 38
36's " 1¼ " 47
30's " 1¾ " 58
24's " 2⅝ " 65
18's " 4 " 1 22
12's " 6 " 1 60
9's " 7 " 2 25

Nappies, Fluted.—
3 in. (actual 4 in.) 50
4 " " 5¼ " 52
5 " " 6¼ " 58
6 " " 7 " 72
7 " " 8¼ " 87
8 " " 9 " 1 30
9 " " 10¼ " 1 75
10 " " 11 " 2 20

Nappies, Scalloped.—
3 in. (actual 5¼ in.) 50
4 " " 5¼ " 52
5 " " 6¼ " 58
6 " " 7 " 72
7 " " 8¼ " 87
8 " " 9 " 1 30
9 " " 10¼ " 1 75
10 " " 11 " 2 20

Bakers or Vegetable Dishes.—Double thick.
2¾ in. (actual 5¼ in.) 51
3 " " 5¾ " 52
4 " " 6¼ " 58
5 " " 7 " 72
6 " " 8 " 87
7 " " 9¼ " 1 30
8 " " 11 " 1 75
10 " " 12 " 2 20

Cable Mugs 55
Egg Cup 52

Dishes or Platters.—Single thick. Doz.
5 in. (act. 8 in.) $0 47
6 " " 10 " 51
7 " " 11 " 58
8 " " 12 " 72
9 " " 12¾ " 87
10 " " 13¾ " 1 30
11 " " 14¼ " 1 75
12 " " 16 " 2 60
14 " " 19 " 3 15

Fruit Saucers.—
Round, 4 in. (act. 5 in.) .. 22

Butters.—
Individual, 2½ in. (actual 3 in.) .. 15

Soap Slabs 44
Soap Boxes 90

Ewers and Basins:—Plain.
Complete 12's 5 75
12's, Ewers only 2 88
12's, Basins only 2 88
Complete 9's 6 50
9's, Ewers only 3 50
9's, Basins only 3 25

Fancy Ewers and Basins:
9's 7 50
9's, Ewers only 3 75
9's, Basins only 3 75

Jugs.— Doz.
42's (actual ½ pint) ...
36's (actual 1 pint) ... $0 72
30's (actual 2 pint) ... 75
24's (actual 3 pint) ... 89
12's (actual 4 pint) ... 1 30
6's (actual 6 pint) 1 75
    .... 2 60

Hall Boy Jug. Standard size ... 1 30

Chambers.—Plain.
Uncovered, 12's 1 75
          9's 2 30
Covered, 12's 2 60
       9's 3 50
Fancy Chamber—
9's covered 3 50
Bed Pan: No. 1 .... 5 50

Combinet 7 75
Open Cuspidor or Slop Jar . 7 00

"BEST EVER" DECORATED SEMI-PORCELAIN ASSORTMENT.

We have made a special feature of this assortment in using only items used in making up a Dinner Service. Note the large pieces and beautiful decoration.

"MONARCH" ASSORTMENT.

This assortment contains many pieces which are regular 50 cent items. They can be sold at 25c each doing some good advertising.

EX703—Assortment of all best selling items. Body of light weight Royal Firenze American China. Six color decal decoration in wild apple blossoms and forget me nots, delicate pink and white predominating, shaded green leaves. Artistic gold stamp between all clusters of flowers. Each piece stamped with trademark. Asst. comprises:
¼ doz. covered dishes.   ¼ doz. 8 in. platters.   2 doz. cake or bread dishes.
4 " 7 in. dinner plates.   4 " 10 " "   ¼ " 24's water pitchers.
4 " 6 " pie   4 " salad bowls.   ⅙ " fancy cake plate.
3 " 7 " soup   4 " cups and saucers.   3 " berry nappies.
Total 24 doz. in pkg. (NO PKG. CHARGE.)   Per dozen. **89c**

EX734—Semi-porcelain body, all fancy embossed shapes with assorted decorations, such as American beauty and tea roses and fruit centers. All pieces have heavy gold edges with gold center stamp and artistic stamp between each rose decoration. Assortment consists of the following:
⅙ doz. 9⅜ in. berry bowls.   1 doz. 10¼ in. chop plates.   ⅙ doz. 11¼ in. mammoth chop plate.
⅙ " 13¼ " tray or platter.   ⅙ " 24's sugars.   ⅙ " large cuspidors, 7¾ in. diam., ht. 5 in.
⅙ " 10¼ " fancy salad.   ⅙ " 9¼ " fancy cake or bread plate.   ⅙ " 10¼ " deep bowl.
Total 6 doz. in pkg. (NO PKG. CHARGE.) Per dozen. **$2.10**

BUTLER BROTHERS, RANDOLPH BRIDGE, CHICAGO.

"ROSE AND GOLD BORDER" 100 PIECE DINNER SET.

A most excellent offering. Jobbed ordinarily at $10.00.

EX635. 100 Piece "A" Composition Dinner Set: 12 tea cups and saucers (24 pieces), 12 bread and butter plates, 12 breakfast plates, 12 dinner plates, 12 soup plates, 12 fruit or sauce dishes, 2 covered dishes, (4 pieces), 1 covered butter, (3 pieces), 1 covered sugar, (2 pieces), 1 open vegetable dish, 1 medium platter, 1 large platter, 1 sauce boat, 1 pickle dish, 1 cream pitcher, 1 slop bowl.

Fancy semi-porcelain body, light weight, decorations of beautiful rose border wreath pattern with heavy gold line and lace border decorations. All handles and knobs gold traced. An especially striking and attractive set. Each in pkg. Wt. 100 lbs. (**NO PKG. CHARGE.**) Per set, **$9.00**

"DEPARTMENT LEADER" 100 PIECE DINNER SET.

Extraordinary value in a high grade fancy semi-porcelain set.

EX626. Whitesemi-porcelain body, neatly embossed large full shape, decorations being in a combination cluster of natural colored flowers, pink predominating, beautifully shaded pink background, making a very artistic decoration. Asst. comprises:

12 dinner plates.	1 open vegetable dish.	1 large platter.
12 bread & butter plates.	1 covered vegetable dish.	1 small platter.
12 soup plates.	1 pickle.	1 covered sugar.
12 fruits.	1 covered butter, 3 pieces.	1 creamer.
12 cups.	1 cake plate.	1 24's jug.
12 saucers.	1 sauce boat.	
12 4 inch plates.	1 bowl.	

(**NO PKG. CHARGE.**) Each set in pkg. Per set, **$5.65**

"BLUE AND WHITE" FIREPROOF COOKING WARE ASST.

Popular goods at a very low price during July.

EX768: Heavy fireproof earthen body baking dishes, blue tinted inside and out, mixing bowl blue outside and white inside, all pieces with heavy smooth glaze. Asst. comprises 1 doz. each of 7, 8¾ and 10¼ in. round deep baking dishes, and 1 doz. each 7¼, 8 and 9¼ in. extra deep round footed mixing bowls. Total 6 doz. in crate. Wt. 236 lbs. (**NO PKG. CHARGE.**) Per dozen, **79c**

Some Extra Good Things in FAMOUS "BLUE WILLOW" DECORATED ENGLISH SEMI-PORCELAIN WARE.

Here are some specials that are specials. Everybody knows this ware as it is in great demand. Decorated in the ever staple allover blue willow pattern.

EX21, Special Tea—Fancy long low shape, 3¼ x 2¼, saucer 5½ ....Doz. **89c**

EX22, London Tea—Large size, medium low shape, 3½ x 2⅝, saucer 5½ ....Doz. **92c**

EX29, Fruit or Sauce Dish—4½ in.......Doz. **38c**

EX30, Oatmeal Bowl—Round deep shape, diam. 5¾ in..................Doz. **46c**

Plates—

EX23, Bread and Butter—4 in., actual 6 in....Doz. **43c**

EX24, Tea—5 in., actual 7 in...................Doz. **59c**

EX25, Breakfast—6 in., actual 8 in...........Doz. **72c**

EX26, Dinner—7 in., actual 9 in..................Doz. **86c**

EX27, Soup—7 in. actual 9 in.................. Doz. **85c**

EX28, Coupe Soup or General Utility Table Dish—7 in., actual 8 in. Doz. **86c**

Napples or Table Dishes—Extra deep shape. Doz.

EX31—6 in., act. 8¼ in. **$1.28**

EX32—7 " " 9⅝ " **1.86**

EX33—8 " " 10½ " **2.36**

"MAMMOTH" ASST. ROSE DECORATED SEMI-PORCELAIN WARE.

All nice large pieces worth from 10 to 25 cents.

EX705½: Fancy shapes, full sizes, light semi-porcelain body. Large rose decoration, green leaf background, gold lined edges. 1 doz. each of following:

Fancy tea cups and saucers.	7¼ in. extra deep salads.	7 in. nappies, actual 8¼.
36's fancy jugs.	7¾ " salad or table dish.	Bread plates, " 8½.
6 in. plates, actual 8¼.	Large oatmeal bowl.	Cake plates, " 7¼.
7 " " " 9½.	5 in. nappies, actual 6½.	8 in. platters, " 11¾.

Total 12 doz. in bbl., wt. 140 lbs. (**NO PKG. CHARGE.**) Per dozen, **79c**

SPECIAL BERRY SET SALE EXTRAORDINARY.

Sets made up from well known **Domestic** and **Imported English** lines **at very special prices.** The berry season is just beginning and at these prices you can do a handsome business.

BEST AMERICAN OR DOMESTIC SEMI-PORCELAIN.

EX10: French Rose Decoration. 1 only actual 8¾ in. bowl, 6 actual 5¼ in. fruit dishes. Deep bowl, fancy shape. Delicate pink roses with profuse shaded green sprays and back ground of wild flowers in seven color work. Light weight neatly embossed new china effect semi porcelain. Per set. **35c**

EX12: Princess Near China Decorations. 1 only actual 8¾ in. bowl, 6 actual 5¼ in fruit dishes. Delicate shaded pink and yellow roses in full bloom and bud effect with sprays of green leaves in two shades. Body of very light and thin domestic near china ware. Per set. **38c**

EX11: Royal Firenze Rose Decoration. 1 only actual 8½ in bowl, 6 actual 5½ in. fruit dishes. Shaded pink roses, wreath design with background of shaded green leaves and pink forget-me-nots. Gold stamp between each spray of flowers, also gold center stamp. Full gold traced. Extra light Royal Firenze ware. Per set. **36c**

ENGLISH "BLUE WILLOW" DECORATED WARE.

EX15: Famous Blue Willow Decorated. 1 actual 9¾ in. bowl, 6 actual 4¾ in. fruit dishes. Blue willow shape with the popular allover blue decorations. Good quality English semi-porcelain body. Each trade-marked. Per set. **33c**

BEST GENUINE IMPORTED ENGLISH WARE.

EX13: English Floral Green Decorated. 1 only actual 9¼ in. bowl, 6 actual 5 in. fruit dishes. Wideborder design in rich green floral underscroll effect. Good quality semi-porcelain, light weight, embossed, heavily glazed and guaranteed against crazing. Per set, **32c**

EX14: English Floral Blue Decorated. 1 only actual 9½ in. bowl, 6 actual 5 in. fruit dishes. Wide border design in rich blue floral and scroll effect. Good quality semi-porcelain light weight, embossed, heavily glazed and guaranteed against crazing. Per set, **32c**

EX16: Flow Blue Decoration. 1 actual 9½ in. bowl, 6 actual 5¼ in. fruit dishes. Finest quality ware, medium light weight, embossed, elaborate floral and scroll decorations in underglazed flow blue. Per set, **48c**

EX17: Victoria 6 color Decal Decoration. 1 actual 9 in. bowl, 6 actual 5⅜ in. fruit saucers. Profuse sprays of arbutus in combination of pink, green and white, pink predominating, producing an exquisite vine effect. Light weight royal vitreous semi-porcelain body. Per set. **50c**

"STARTLING" 12 PIECE TOILET SET.

Exceptionally good value at the regular price. At this figure a RARE BARGAIN.

EX510—Best semi-porcelain body—large fancy shape with neat embossing. Full gold lined beautiful six color American beauty rose decoration in full blown, pink and bud effect with shaded green leaf background. Regular composition. Each set in pkg., wt. 55 lbs. Per set. **$3.90** (**NO PKG. CHARGE.**)

BUTLER BROTHERS, RANDOLPH BRIDGE, CHICAGO.

"BRIGHT TANKARD" JUG ASST.

Extra good ones to retail at a dime or more.

C1275—So called qt. size, tall tankard shape. ht. 7¾ in. Asst. compromises 1 doz. each of 4 rich deep cut patterns, all brilliantly full finished and fire polished. Total 4 doz. in bbl., wt. 87 lbs. Per dozen, **89c**

(NO PKG. CHARGE.)

"DIME" QUART JUG ASSORTMENT.

Possible 10 cent leaders—you need these.

C1276—So called qt.—2 styles—1 tall almost plain tankard shape, ht. 8¾ in., footed, with handle and extra good lip; other rich reflecting panel design, with wide top, footed and large handle. Both brilliantly finished and fire polished 1½ doz. each. Total 3 doz. in bbl., wt. 100 lbs. Per dozen, **84c**

(NO PKG. CHARGE.)

"STAPLE" JUG ASSORTMENT.

C1278: All large (so called ½ gal.) and all full finished crystal. Asst. comprises ¾ doz. each of 3 patterns. Total 2¼ doz. in bbl., wt. 96 lbs. (NO PKG. CHARGE.) Per dozen. **$1.20**

CRYSTAL JUG ASSORTMENT.

Exceptional beauties at this price.

C1294—So called ½ gal. size, footed, wide tops, large handles, good quality crystal, full finished, **1 doz. each** of 3 patterns, two being heavy cut and 1 optic flute. 3 doz. in bbl. (NO PKG. CHARGE.) Per dozen, **96c**

"FANCY TANKARD" JUG ASSORTMENT.

Worth 25 cents yet can retail for less if you choose.

C1281—(So called ½ gal.) sizes, extra tall tankard shapes, best full finished crystal ⅔ **doz. each** of 3 rich patterns as illustrated, total 2 doz. in bbl., wt.127lbs. (NO PKG. CHARGE.) Per dozen. **$1.57**

"BIG PLAIN" CRYSTAL JUG ASST.

Two big fellows to retail with a profit at 25c or more.

C1284—2 styles, both footed, extra large and heavy, ½ gal. size, pure crystal, strong and well made, brilliant full finished and fire polished. 1 doz. each of 2 styles, total 2 doz. in bbl., wt. 80 lbs. Per dozen **$1.90**

(NO PKG. CHARGE.)

"HIGH GRADE" PITCHER ASSORTMENT.

Unequaled in quality, size and finish.

C1283—3 magnificent specimens of the glass worker's art, all half gallon size. ⅔ doz. each of 3 styles. Total 2 doz. in bbl., wt. 115 lbs. Per dozen, **$1.90**

(NO PKG. CHARGE.)

"MASSIVE" PITCHER ASSORTMENT.

None better ever offered to retail at 25 cents.

C1286.—Large full ½ gal., extra heavy brilliant full finished crystal. **1 doz. each** of 2 rich patterns. Per doz. **$2.00**

Total 2 dozen in bbl. Wt. 130 lbs.

"RICH CUT" JUG ASSORTMENT.

The heaviest and richest jugs that can be bought under a 50 cent price.

C1289—Extra massive, superbly finished. Exact imitation of choicest cut ware. 1 doz. each of the two styles one round, one square. Both highly polished. Made for high priced, high class trade. Total 2 doz. in bbl., wt. 125 lbs. Per dozen. **$2.20**

(NO PKG. CHARGE.)

"BEAUTY" BLOWN JUG ASSORTMENT.

Big rich profit paying 50 centers.

C1285—All large full ½ gal. size, pure lead blown crystal, genuine stuck handles, asstd. tankard and fancy swell shapes. ¼ doz. each of plain and optic, ¼ doz. asstd. engraved band tankard, ¼ doz. low shape floral engraved. Total 1½ doz. in bbl., wt. 68 lbs. Per dozen, **$3.35**

(NO PKG. CHARGE.)

"GIANT" GLASS PITCHER.

Extra large size, brilliant pattern.

C1288—Mammoth size, capacity almost 4 quarts, ht. 10 in., wide top and large handle, brilliant optic panel pattern, richly fire polished. 1 doz. in bbl., wt. 97 lbs. Per dozen. **$3.65**

(NO PKG. CHARGE.)

"FANCY OPALESCENT" BLOWN JUG ASST.

Four styles, all in beautiful opalescent.

C1290—Asst. comprises 4 each of 3 patterns asstd. flint, blue and green opalescent. 1 doz. in bbl., wt. 70 lbs. (NO PKG. CHARGE.) Per dozen. **$3.25**

"BARGAIN COUNTER" WATER SET.

A big attractive set at a small price.

C1250 — Large so called ½ gal. jug, rich optic fluted pattern, wide top, neat mold band, 6 tumblers to match. Total 15 sets in bbl., wt. 100 lbs. Per set, **21c**

(NO PKG. CHARGE.)

SENSIBLE PLAIN WATER SET.

Popular pattern at a popular price.

C1251 — Large so called ½ gal. jug, footed almost plain with bull's eyes in band effect. 6 full size tumblers to match. Total 12 sets in bbl. Wt. 100 lbs Per set, **25c**

(NO PKG. CHARGE.)

FANCY ENGRAVED WATER SET ASST.

Usually retail at one dollar but you can offer as leaders at 75 cents.

C1260 — All pure crystal, large fancy ½ gal. blown jugs with genuine stuck handles, full finished tumblers. Asst. comprises 3 beautiful shapes, 2 sets with engraved band decorations; 2 with wide engraved Grecian band; 2 with lily of the valley floral engraving; 2 optic with large floral and leaf engraving. Each set comprising large jug and six tumblers. Total 8 sets in bbl., wt. 72 lbs. Per set, **52c**

(NO PKG. CHARGE.)

"SUNBURST" WATER SET ASST.

("Prescut" Ware.)

One of the most beautiful patterns ever produced.

C1257—Very heavy "Prescut" ware and brilliantly fire polished. Asst. comprises three 7 piece sets, each consisting of a tall ½ gal. stuck handle jug and 6 ground bottom tumblers, and 3 sets with large water bottle instead of jug. Total 6 sets in bbl., wt. 70 lbs. Per set, **62c**

(NO PKG. CHARGE.)

"WIDE GOLD BAND" WATER ASST.

Magnificent patterns and decorations.

C1248—3 patterns, all extra heavy and very brilliant, good quality crystal, all with extra wide gold decorations. Set comprises large tankard half gallon jug, 6 tumblers. 2 sets each pattern. Total 6 sets in bbl. Per set, Wt 70 lbs. **87c**

(NO PKG. CHARGE.)

Goods That Force Immediate Appreciation Are the Proper Sort for Ourselves and Our Customers.

COLORED BLOWN LEMONADE SETS.

C1247—3 shapes, large ½ gal. blown jugs, ht. about 10 in., genuine stuck handle, optic and fancy embossed designs. Each set comprises 1 jug and 6 tumblers. 3 sets each crystal, blue and green, total 9 sets, in bbl. Per set, **47c**

"OPALESCENT" LEMONADE SET ASST.

C1261—3 patterns—serpentine, polka dot and scroll. Each set consists of large fancy ½ gal. blown jug, fancy crimped top and genuine stuck handle and 6 thin tapering tumblers to match. 3 sets each green, blue and flint opalescent. Total 9 sets in bbl., wt. 90 lbs. Per set, **53c**

"ALL OVER DECORATED" SET ASST.

C1271—Comprising 2 styles—tall tankard and large swell shape—full ½ gal. size blown jugs, genuine stuck handles, each with 6 tumblers to match. Decorations comprise rich enameled floral effects with colored bands, etc. Asstd. colors, crystal, blue and green, 8 sets in bbl., wt. 75 lbs.
(NO PKG. CHARGE.) Per set, **60c**

"ENGRAVED BLOWN" WATER SET ASST.

LC1273, Set comprises tall tankard shape ½ gal. jug, 10¾ in., thin blown crystal, large genuine stuck handle and six 10 oz. thin lead blown tumblers. Both jug and tumblers with rich engravings, 2 sets each of new choice patterns. Total 8 sets in bbl. Wt. 65 lbs. (NO PKG. CHARGE.) Per set, **55c**

DECORATED LEMONADE SET ASST.

C1243—New fancy shapes, genuine stuck handles and burnt in gold edges, rich floral enameled decorations. 1 style embossed, average ht. 10½ in. Each set comprises large ½ gal. blown jug and six decorated tumblers. 3 sets each crystal, blue and green. Total 9 sets in bbl. Per set, **75c**
(NO PKG. CHARGE.)

"HAND DECORATED" LEMONADE SET ASST.
Regular $1.50 sets as possible dollar leaders.

C1263—3 large fancy shapes, ½ gal. size, large stuck handles, rich hand painted and enameled floral decorations, wide gold band edges. Each set comprises 1 jug and 6 tumblers, 2 sets each shape, asstd. crystal, blue and green, total 6 sets in bbl. Wt. 84 lbs. Per set, **72c**
(NO PKG. CHARGE.)

ENAMELED AND GOLD DECORATED TANKARD SHAPE LEMONADE SETS.
Exceptionally rich sets at this low price.

C1264—2 shapes, both tall tankard, average ht. of jugs 12½ in., large stuck handles, hand painted enameled decorations in 3 elaborate designs, ¼ in. gold band edges. Each set comprises 1 jug and 6 tumblers. 2 sets each crystal, blue and green. Total 6 sets in bbl. Wt. 77 lbs. Per set, **78c**
(NO PKG. CHARGE.)

RICHEST HAND DECORATED LEMONADE SET ASST.
Elegant shapes, magnificent decorations. Note that no two are alike.

C1246—6 shapes, all large half gallon blown jugs, profuse rich gold leaf effect, richest enamel, satin etched and floral decorations, wide gold bands and edges. 3 crystal, 2 green, 1 blue set (6 sets in bbl.) wt. 80 lbs. Per set, **89c**
(NO PKG. CHARGE.)

"FLORAL ENGRAVED" WATER SET.
Surprise your customers by offering this rich set for 50 cents.

C1249—Large footed jug, ht. 9 in., 6 tumblers, plain crystal, fancy engraving, floral and wreath design. 12 sets in bbl.
(NO PKG. CHARGE.) Per set, **36c**

"MAMMOTH" 15 CENT WATER BOTTLE.
Will easily bring 25c.

C1448: Full size, fancy bowl, long heavy octagon shape neck, 48 oz. capacity. 3 doz. in bbl. Per dozen **92c**
(NO PKG. CHARGE.)

FLORAL AND GOLD DECORATED WINE SET ASSORTMENT.
$1.50 value as possible dollar leaders.

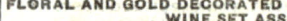

C1428—3 fancy shape extra large stuck handle decanters, average ht. 12 in., 2 with rich floral enamel and gold decorations, one with wide gold bands, all have gold edges. Each set comprises 1 decanter, 6 fancy stem glasses. 2 crystal, 2 blue and 2 green sets. 6 sets in case. Wt. 30 lbs.
(NO PKG. CHARGE.) Per set, **75c**

"FANCY DECORATED" WINE SET.
Surprisingly rich. Extraordinary value to retail at $1.00.

C1424—12½ in., decanter, fluted base, cut stem and stopper, 6 fancy glasses. 11½ in. round tray. Rich enamel floral and cupid decorations burnt in and will not wash off. Six sets in case. Wt. 45 lbs. Per set, **67c**
(NO PKG. CHARGE.)

"RICH GOLD" DECORATED WINE SET.
A regular $1.50 set as a possible $1.00 leader.

C1426—12½ in. fancy shaped decanter with glass stopper, round deep tray, diam. 10½ in., 6 fancy wine glasses. Heavy burnt in gold decorated panels and wide gold bands, 8 pieces in set, 3 sets in case. Wt. 27 lbs. Per set, **78c**
(NO PKG. CHARGE.)

RICH TINTED AND HAND DECORATED LEMONADE SET ASST.
Big, attractive $1.00 sets at a profit paying price.

C1245—Comprising 3 styles, large, tall tankard shapes, genuine stuck handles, crimped tops, allover enameled floral decorations, upper part in asstd. ruby, green and blue tints. Set comprises 1 jug and 6 tumblers. 3 sets each crystal, blue and green, total 9 sets in bbl. Per set, **67c**

"HIGH FOOTED" BERRY SET.
An extra good 25 cent leader.

C1001—Rich, almost plain pattern, with optic bullseye band and pearl beaded edge. Set comprises 7¼ in. extra deep high footed comport, and SIX 4¼ in. deep nappies. Total 24 sets in bbl. (Bbl. 35c.) Per set, **15c**

PACKAGE CHARGE ABOLISHED

On All Glassware and Crockery.

"VENETIAN" VASE ASST.

Marvelous value; these are good enough for 25 centers.

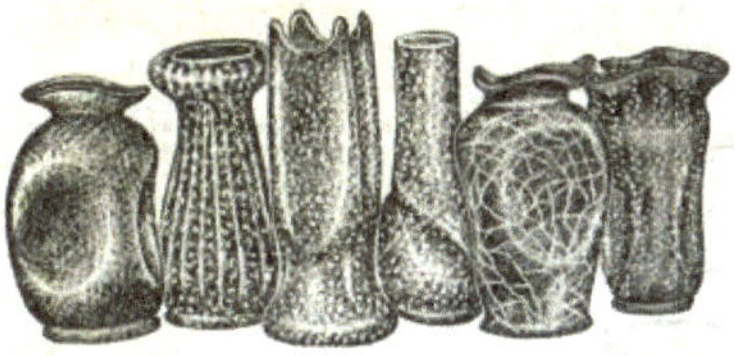

C1211—Domestic glass, exact reproductions of the expensive imported vases. Asst. comprises 1 doz. each of 6 fancy shapes, average ht. about 6¾ in. Beautiful iridescent silver effects, assorted colors—blue, green and amethyst. Total 6 doz. in bbl., wt. 80 lbs. Per dozen, **84c**

"SLENDER" FLOWER VASE ASSORTMENT.

Brilliant crystal beauties to retail at 10c or more.

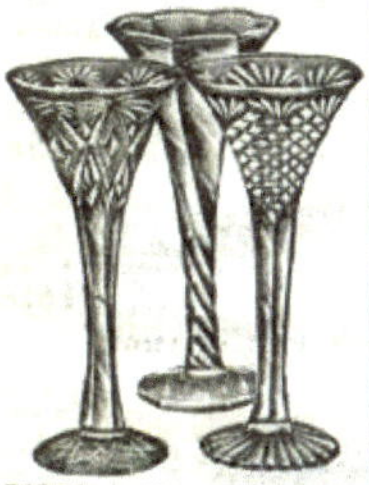

C1206—4 patterns; plain colonial flute, flute twisted, rich cut diamond, strawberry and fan designs. Tall and slender with wide flaring tops, ht. about 9 in. ½ doz. each of 4 styles. Total 2 doz. in case, wt. 40 lbs. Per dozen, **84c**

"COLORED AND CRYSTAL" VASE ASSORTMENT.

Matchless 10c leaders. Will sell on the dullest days.

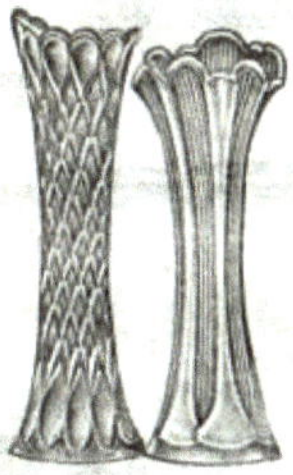

C1209—Extra large sizes, ht. from 12 to 15 in. 2 styles—optic diamond and fancy ribbed, wide floral shape tops. Asstd. colors, 2 doz. crystal, 1¼ doz. blue, 1¼ doz. green. Total 4½ doz. in bbl., wt. 90 lbs. Per dozen, **87c**

"RICH VARIETY" VASE ASST.

Possible 10 centers though you will readily get more.

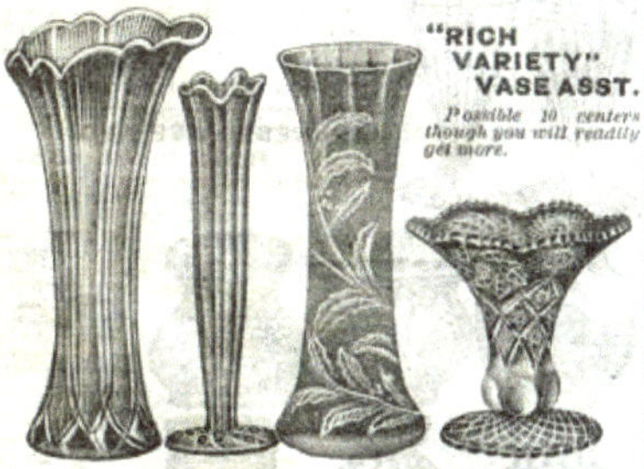

C1201—Comprises 4 patterns—leaf, embossed colonial and fancy ribbed. All extra large sizes, new shapes, ht. from 10 to 12 in., rich crystal, brilliantly finished. 1¼ doz. each, of 4 styles. Total 5 doz. in bbl. Wt. 80 lbs. Per dozen, **87c**

"OPALESCENT" AND COLORED VASE ASST.

The first time ever offered as 10 centers.

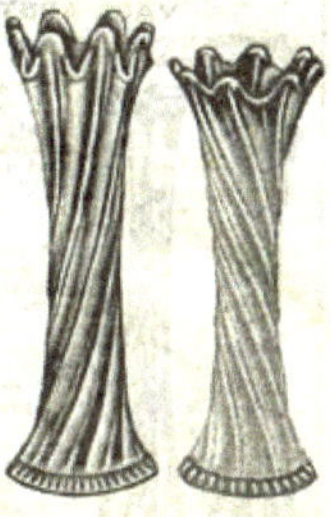

C1219—Twist panel pattern, wide base, fancy shape tops, average ht. from 12 to 15 in. Asst. comprises: 1¼ doz. crystal, 1 doz. nile green, 2 doz. opalescent. Total 4¼ doz. in bbl. Wt. 85 lbs. Per dozen, **84c**

"MAMMOTH" VASE ASST

Big and beautiful 25 cent leaders which are easily worth 50c.

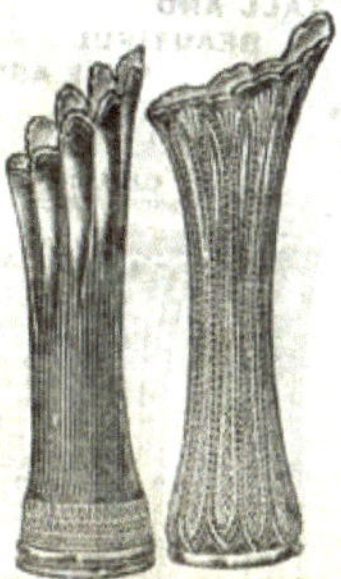

C1213—Extra large, ht. about 12 in., girth 11, fancy cut diamond and ribbed pattern, scalloped floral shape tops. 1 doz. each 2 styles asstd. colors crystal, blue, green and amber. Total 2 doz. in bbl., wt. 87 lbs. Per dozen, **$1.63**

"BIG COLORED" VASE ASSORTMENT.

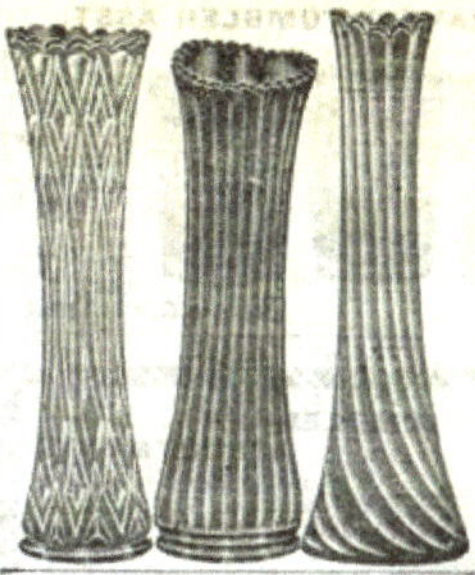

Possible 10 centers though worth much more.

C1223—3 patterns—optic, spiral and diamond panel. Heavy and brilliant, wide bases, floral shape tops, ht. about 12 in. Asst. patterns and colors, 1⅓ doz. each pattern—⅓ crystal, ⅓ blue, ⅓ green, ⅓ amber. Total 4 doz. in bbl. Per dozen, **84c** Wt. 110 lbs.

"GIANT" VASE ASST.

Biggest of 25 cent possibilities. Wonderfully attractive sellers.

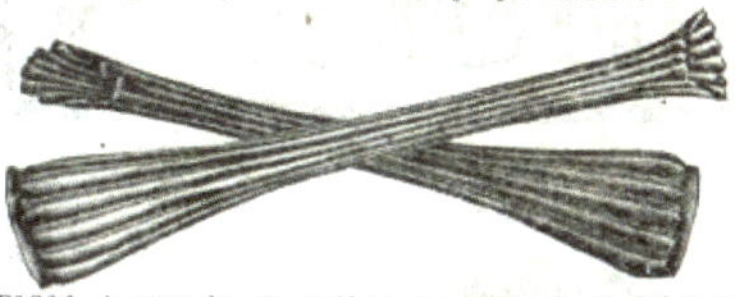

C1214—Average ht. about 21 in., beautiful tall panel design, heavy wide base, fancy tops. Asstd. 1½ doz. crystal, ¼ doz. amber and ¼ doz. blue. Wt. 85 lbs. Total 2 doz. in bbl. Per dozen, **$1.87**

EXTRA LARGE CRYSTAL VASE ASST.

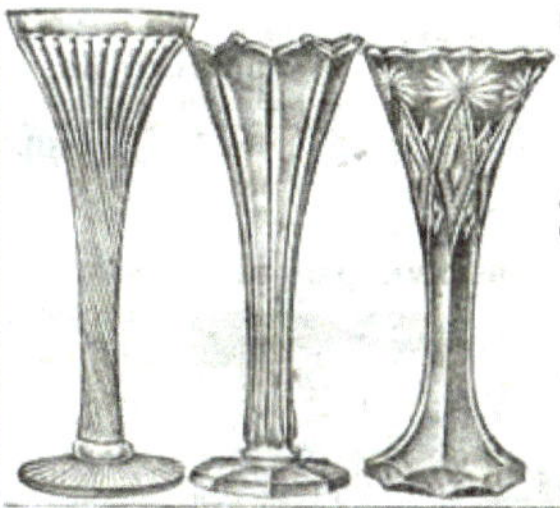

Big and beautiful 25 centers.

C1215—Tall flaring shape, ht. about 12 in., purest full finished crystal, ⅓ doz. each cut diamond, colonial flute and serpentine patterns. Total 1 doz. in case., wt. 40 lbs. Per Dozen, **$1.85**

RICH "PRESCUT" VASE ASST.

Offer them at 50c and see them go.

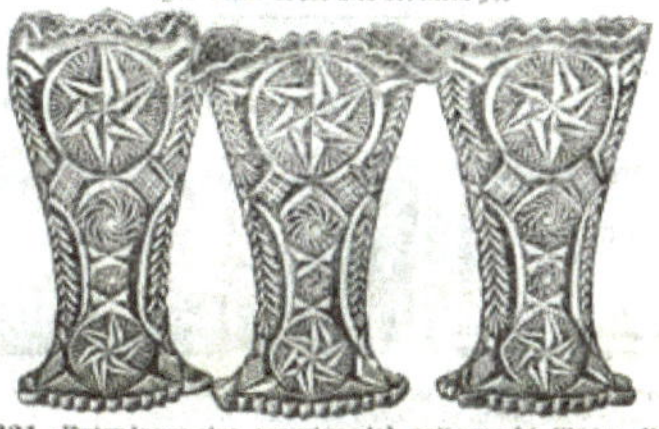

C1221—Extra large size, massive rich patterns, ht. 8¼ in., diam. top about 5¼, asstd. flaring, triangular and tulip shapes, all with fancy cut bases., wt. 23 lbs. Total 6 in case. Each, **30c**

"OLD MILL SCENE" DECORATED VASE ASSORTMENT.

Big fancy shapes with popular landscape decorations to retail at popular prices.

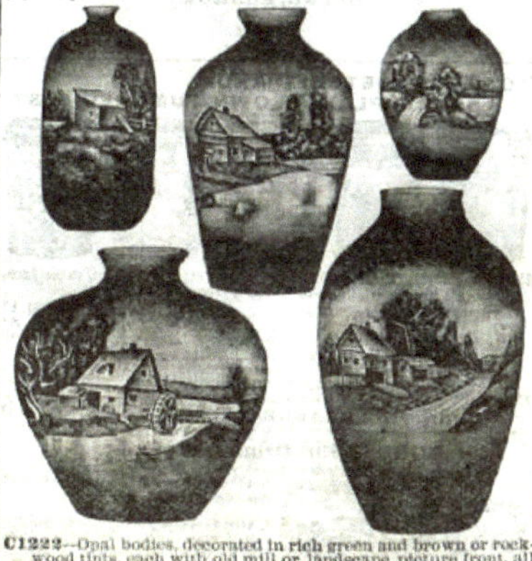

C1222—Opal bodies, decorated in rich green and brown or rockwood tints, each with old mill or landscape picture front, all decorations are burnt in and will not wash off. Note especially the extra large sizes. Asst. comprises:

2 only,	low shape,	Ht. 6¾ in.,	girth 14 in.	...@	$0 19	$0 38
2 "	"	" 8 "	" 13¾ "	...@	35	70
2 "	"	" 10¾ "	" 19¾ "	...@	57	1 14
2 "	"	" 9½ "	" 28 "	...@	72	1 44
2 "	tall "	" 12¾ "	" 22¾ "	...@	75	1 50

Wt. 50 lbs. Total for assortment of 10 vases, **$5.16**

GLASS VASES

—1 doz. in pasteboard box.

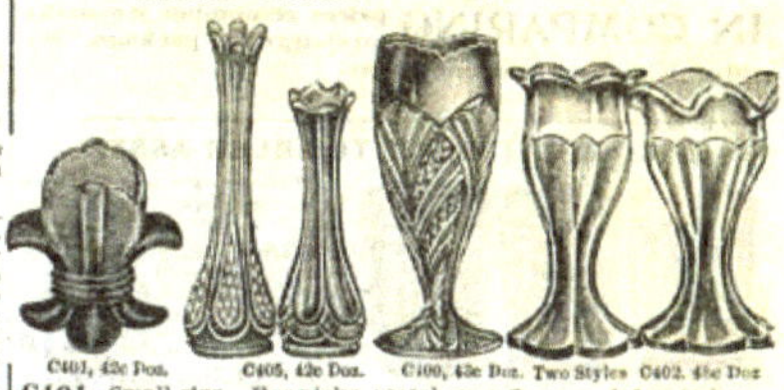

C401, 42c Doz. C405, 42c Doz. C400, 43c Doz. Two Styles C402, 48c Doz

C401—Small size. For picks, matches or flowers. 1 doz. in box. Doz. **42c**

C405—New shape, ht. from 5½ to 7 in., asstd. colonial and cut diamond panel patterns with fancy floral shape tops. Asstd. shapes in pkg. of 1 doz... Doz. **42c**

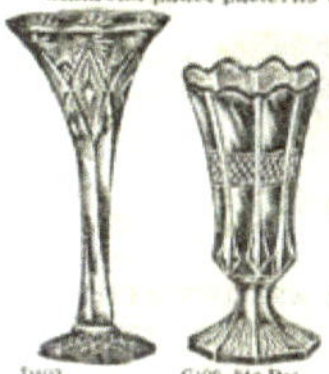

D403, C406, 84c Doz.

C400—Fancy tulip shape, ht. 6½ in 1 doz. in box.............. Doz. **43c**

C402—"Tiffany" Asst. 3 shapes, one tulip design, other two with wide flaring tops, rich Colonial design, ht. about 6 in. 1 doz. in pkg., asstd. Doz. **48c**

C403—Ht. about 8 in., slender wide flaring top and fancy base, strawberry and fan pattern. ½ doz. in box.............. Doz. **79c**

C406:.Ht, 6¼ in., bright reflecting panel design, scalloped top. Panels and edges decorated in pure gold.............. Doz. **84c**

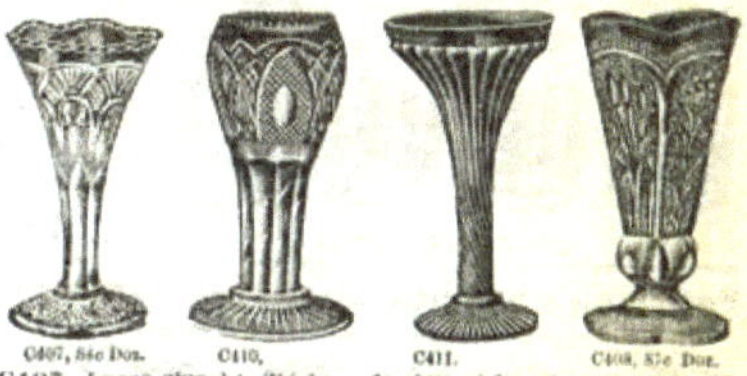

C407, 84c Doz. C410, C411, C408, 87c Doz.

C407—Large size, ht. 6¼ in., slender, rich cut pattern, extra heavy 1¼ in. gold band around top. 1 doz. in box... Doz. **84c**

C410—Heavy and brilliant, ht. 6¼ in., wide base, tulip shape top, deep cut crystal, ruby and gold decorations. 1 doz. in box.............. Doz. **84c**

C411—Ht. 7 in., fancy serpentine twist pattern with wide flaring top, pure full finished crystal with ½ in. wide gold band around top. *A regular 15 center, but you can retail at a dime.* Per dozen, **85c**

C408—Ht. 6¼, embossed floral relief pattern, extra wide gold decorated edge. 1 doz. in box.............. Doz. **87c**

"IMPERIAL" FLOWER VASES.

Ideal leaders that will pay their share of expenses.

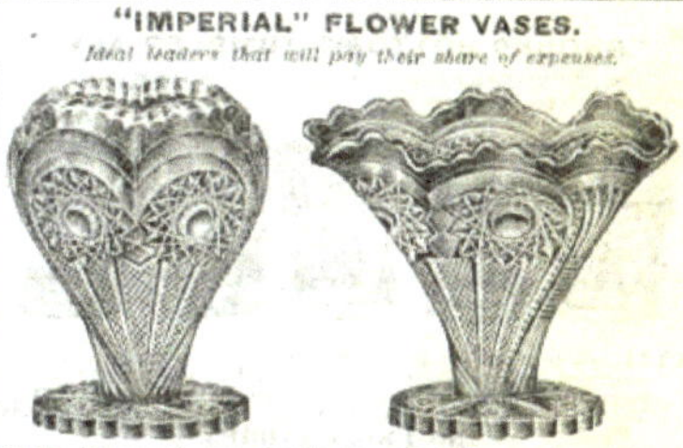

C687—Mammoth size, ht. 8½ in., cir. 20¼ massive, rich cut pattern on fancy foot, finest quality brilliant crystal. Each in pkg. Each, **39c**

C688—"Imperial" Crimped Vase. Wide flaring crimped top, diam. at top 9¾ in. Each, **39c**

"BRILLIANT CUT" VASE ASSORTMENT.

You can retail at 30 cents, yet would regularly bring 50 cents.

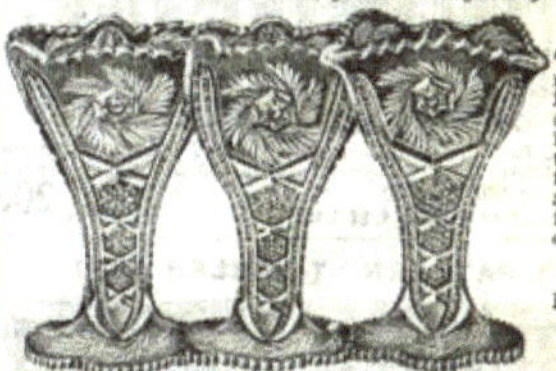

C1224—Rich "Prescut" glass, massive whirling star cut designs, ht. 8¼ in. asstd., round, triangular and flaring shapes, all brilliantly fire polished. 1 doz. in case. (NO PKG. CHARGE). Per dozen, **$2.25**

BIG CRYSTAL VASE ASSORTMENT.

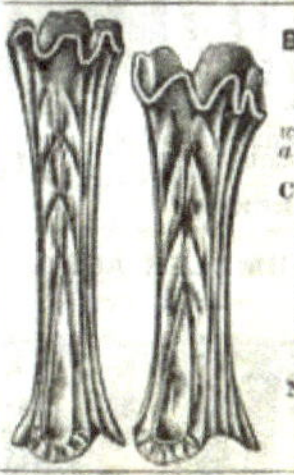

Nothing to equal them was ever offered to retail at a dime.

C1208—Entirely new fancy floral shape on 3 fancy feet, with large shape tops, all in pure crystal, full finished and richly fire polished, average ht. 12 to 14 in. 4½ doz. in bbl. (*Bbl. 35c.*) Per dozen, **87c** NO PKG. CHARGE.

BIG "BEAUTY" VASE ASST.

Nothing to equal them was ever offered to retail at a dime.

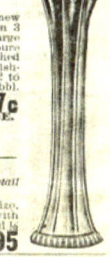

C1218—Colonial fluted pattern, extra large size, ht. about 18 in., diam. at base 4¾ in. with fancy floral shape tops. 1 doz. crystal and ½ nile green, total 1½ doz. in bbl. Per dozen, **$1.95**

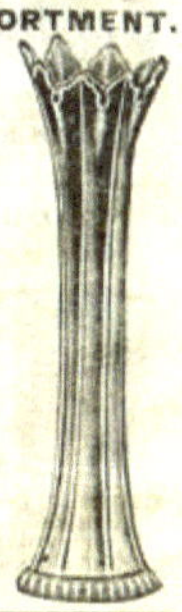

Our Customers Have the Satisfaction of Selecting From a Stock Which is Always Up-to-Date.

IN COMPARING prices remember we make no charge for package. We ship all goods from our house.

"COMPETITION" TUMBLER ASST.

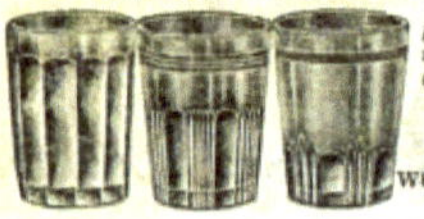

They are the best ones we have ever offered at anywhere near this price.

C1048—7 oz. good quality crystal, smooth finish bottom and edges, 8 doz. each of 3 attractive patterns. Total 24 doz. in bbl. Wt. 140 lbs. Per dozen, **12½c**

(NO PKG. CHARGE.)

"DEPARTMENT ADVERTISER" TUMBLER ASST.

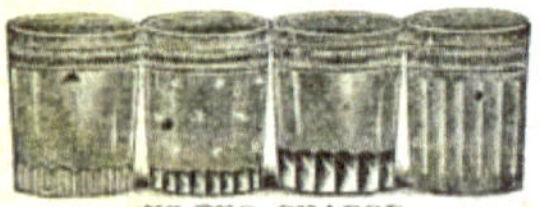

Shipped from our house at less than a Pittsburg price.

C1050—About 7 oz. smooth finished edges. 5 doz. each of 5 patterns. 25 doz. in bbl. Wt. 182 lbs. Per dozen, **15c**

(NO PKG. CHARGE.)

"STAPLE" TUMBLER ASSORTMENT.

Don't judge them by price alone. You will be surprised at the quality and finish.

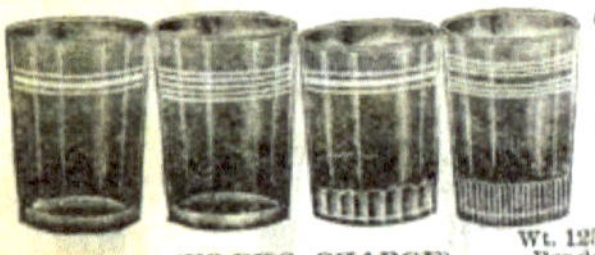

C1053—8 oz., tall shape, smooth finished bottoms and edges. 5 doz. each of 4 patterns. Total 20 doz. in bbl. Wt. 125 lbs. Per dozen, **16½**

(NO PKG. CHARGE)

"STYLISH & SERVICEABLE" TUMBLER ASST.

One of the best tumbler values we have offered.

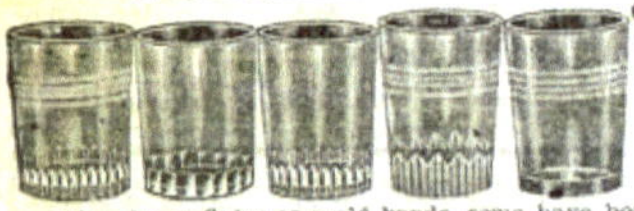

C1049—8 oz. table size, smooth finish bottoms and edges. All have either fancy flutes or mold bands, some have both, 4 doz. each of 5 patterns. Total 20 doz. in bbl., wt. 150 lbs Per dozen, **18c**

(NO PKG. CHARGE)

"GROUND BOTTOM" TUMBLER ASST.

Advertise yourself by retailing these regular 5 centers at 3c. Exceptional values.

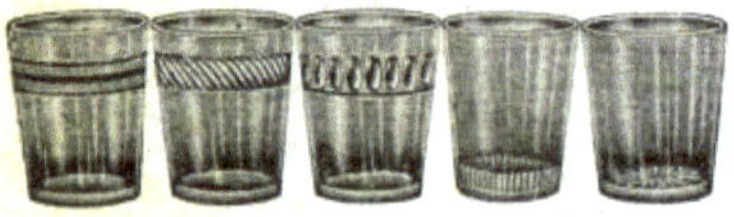

C1047—½ pint size in best pot glass. All with ground and polished bottoms. Asst. consists of 4 doz. each of 6 patterns, comprising plain and fancy designs. Total 24 doz. in bbl. Wt. 140 lbs. Per dozen, **25c**

(NO PKG. CHARGE.)

"BIG VALUE" NICKEL TUMBLER ASST.

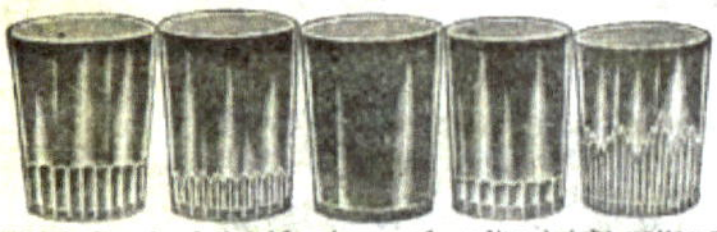

C1056—Regular full table size, good quality, bright patterns, allover brilliantly full finished. 4 doz. each of six styles. Total 24 doz. in bbl. Wt. 160 lbs. Per dozen, **20c**

(NO PKG. CHARGE.)

"FANCY PATTERN" TUMBLER ASST.

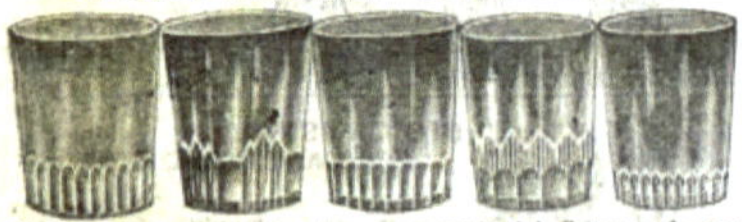

C1057—Large full table size, some with rich flutes and some with neat mold bands. 4 doz., each 6 styles. Total 24 doz. in bbl. Wt. 145 lbs. Per dozen, **21c**

(NO PKG. CHARGE.)

"GROUND BOTTOM" TUMBLER ASST.

Advertise yourself by retailing these regular 5 centers at 3c.

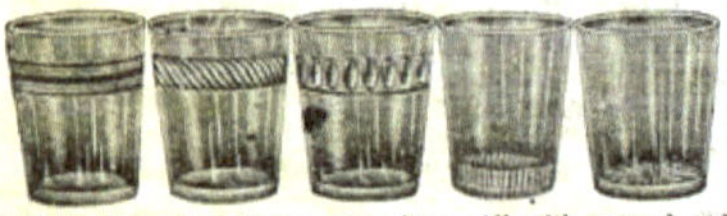

C1047—½ pint size in best pot glass. All with ground and polished bottoms. Asst. consists of 4 doz. each of 6 patterns, comprising plain and fancy designs. Total 24 doz. in bbl. Wt. 140 lbs. Per dozen, **25c**

(NO PKG. CHARGE.)

"RICH ENGRAVED" TUMBLER ASST.

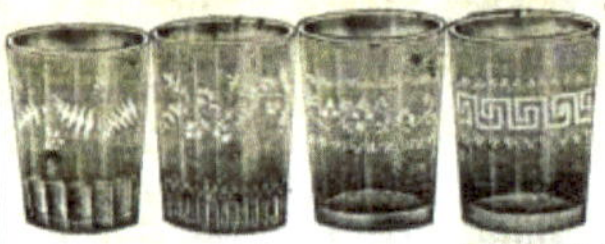

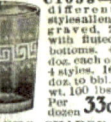

C1058—4 different styles all engraved, 2 with fluted bottoms. 4 doz. each of 4 styles. 16 doz. to bbl., wt. 100 lbs. Per dozen **33c**

(NO PKG. CHARGE.)

"HEAVY CUT" TUMBLER ASSORTMENT.

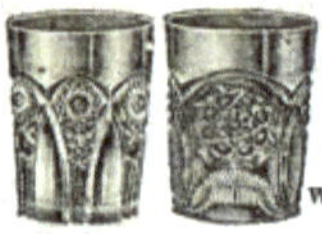

Looks like 10 centers, but you can retail with a profit for 5c.

C1061¼—Regulation size, straight shape, good full finished crystal, brilliant deep genuine cut patterns, fancy star bottoms. 6 doz. each of 2 styles as illustrated. Total 12 doz. in bbl. Wt. 108 lbs. Per dozen, **39c**

(NO PKG. CHARGE.)

EXTRA FINE BLOWN GLASS TABLE TUMBLER.

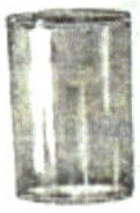

C1071—10 oz., plain lead blown glass, finished melted edges. 18 doz. in patent case. Wt. 70 lbs. Per dozen, **37c**

(NO PKG. CHARGE.)

"BANDED" BLOWN TUMBLER ASST.

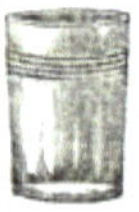

C1072—10 oz. size, thin lead blown glass, finished melted edges. 4 doz. each of 3 neat band engraved patterns. Wt. 70 lbs. 12 doz. in patent case. Per dozen, **40c**

(NO PKG. CHARGE.)

"ETCHED BLOWN" TUMBLER ASST.

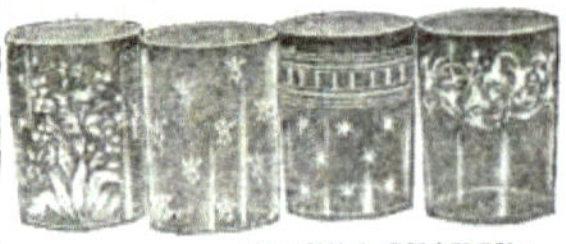

C1075—Thin lead blown glass, full 10 oz. table size, smooth melted edges. 4 doz. each of 4 beautiful engraved patterns. 16 doz. in bbl. Wt. 72 lbs. Per dozen, **45c**

(NO PKG. CHARGE.)

"ENGRAVED AND PLAIN" BLOWN TUMBLER ASST

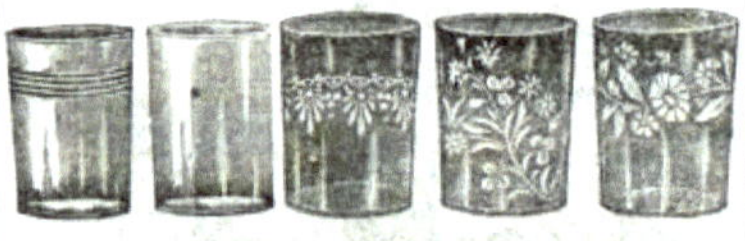

C1073—Lead blown glass, strictly firsts, all regulation 10 oz. table size, plain, engraved band and engraved floral designs. Assortment comprises:

6 doz.	plain	$0 37½	$2 25
2 "	engraved four band	42	84
1 "	" 1 wide and 2 narrow bands	43	43
1 "	" floral band pattern	46	46
1 "	leaf and floral engraved	46	46
1 "	allover floral engraved	46	46
12 "	in patent case. Wt. 70 lbs.		

Total for asst. **$4.90**

(NO PKG. CHARGE.)

"6 STYLES" ETCHED AND PLAIN BLOWN TUMBLER ASST.

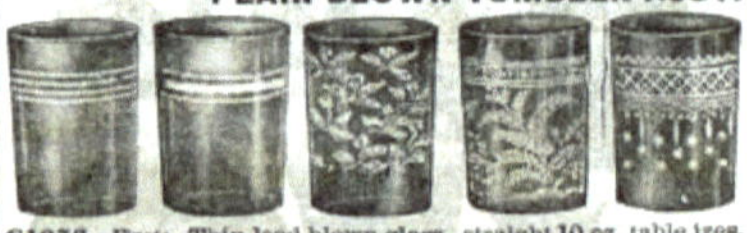

C1076—*Firsts.* Thin lead blown glass, straight 10 oz. table sizes, smooth melted edges. Asst. comprises:

3 doz.	plain	$0 37½	$1 13
2 "	engraved	42	84
1 "	one wide and 2 narrow bands	43	43
2 "	allover floral engraved	46	92
2 "	fancy band and fern engraved	46	92
2 "	wide fancy band and star engraved	46	92

12 doz. in patent case, wt. 70 lbs.

(NO. PKG. CHARGE.) Total for asst. **$5.16**

GOBLETS in Original Package.

Finest quality and very best finish for the prices named. Only the best selling styles are offered. *Sold only by bbl.*

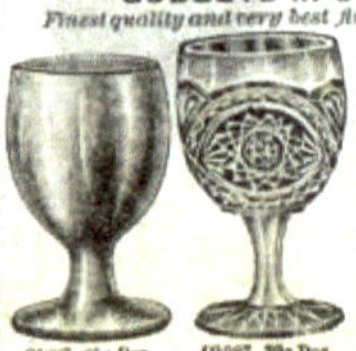

C1087, 35c Doz. C1087, 39c Doz.

C1084—Low shape hotel goblet, full size, heavy crystal glass, smooth mouth edge 9 doz. in bbl., wt. 117 lbs. Per dozen, **35c**

(NO PKG. CHARGE.)

C1087—Large size, ht. 5⅛ in., extra heavy and deep cut pattern, imitation cut stem. 9 doz. in bbl. Wt. 117 lbs. Per dozen, **39c**

(NO PKG. CHARGE.)

HOTEL TUMBLERS.

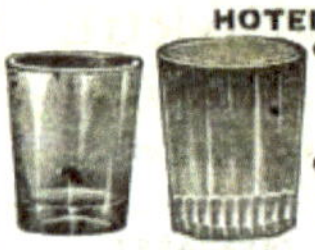

C1062—Best crystal glass, extra heavy and with double thick bottom extra large size. 6 doz. case, wt. 60 lbs. Per dozen, **33c**

(NO PKG. CHARGE.)

C1060—Large size, almost straight shape, rich flutes, ground and polished bottom. 6 doz. in case., wt. 55 lbs. Per dozen, **36c**

(NO PKG. CHARGE.)

JELLY TUMBLERS—"Firsts."

Superior quality—large sizes—guaranteed "Firsts." There are cheaper tumblers in the market than the following, but they are cheaper in quality as well as in price. Note that our ½ pint jelly tumblers are full 8 oz. size—not the 6 oz. commonly sold as ½ pint and worth fully 2 cents per doz. less. *Sold only by package.*

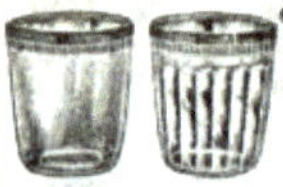

C1065. Plain and Fluted Jelly Tumbler Asst: 12 doz. each of 2 styles, plain and optic fluted, both with neat mold bands, smooth finished edges, medium size, about 7 oz., complete with good tin caps. Total 24 doz. in bbl., wt. 12? lbs. Per dozen, ***12½**

(NO PKG. CHARGE.)

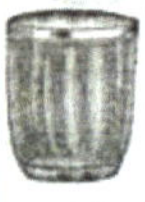

C1066—Plain ⅓ pt., regular, medium size. Complete with best tin tops. 24 doz. to pkg., wt. 160 lbs. Per dozen, **15c**

(NO PKG. CHARGE.)

C1067—Plain large ½ pts., really holding full 9 ounces. Complete with best tin tops. 18 doz. in bbl., wt. 143 lbs. Per dozen **16½**

(NO PKG. CHARGE.)

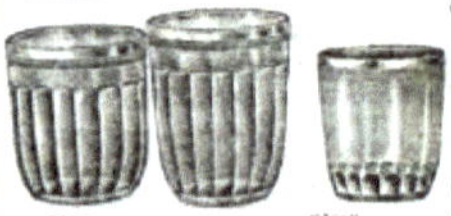

C1070. C1069.

C1070—Fluted regulation cup shape, smooth melted edges, rich optic pattern with neat mold band, best tin caps. 10 doz. each of full size ½ pt. and ⅓ pt. Total 20 doz. in bbl., wt. 125 lbs. Per dozen, ***15**

(NO PKG. CHARGE.)

C1069—Cup shape, plain with fluted base, flutes on the inside. Complete with best tin top. 12 doz. medium size, capacity 6 oz. 12 doz. large size, capacity 8 oz. 24 doz. in bbl., wt. 150 lbs. Per dozen, **15c**

(NO PKG. CHARGE.)

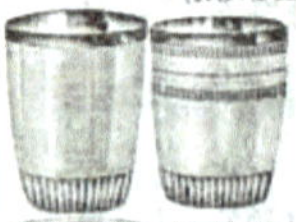

C1059—Full 8 oz., tumbler shape, ht. 3¾ in., good crystal, best tin caps. 9 doz. each of plain and mold band, both with fine fluted bases. Total 18 doz. in bbl., wt., 145 lbs. Per dozen, ***16½c**

(NO PKG. CHARGE.)

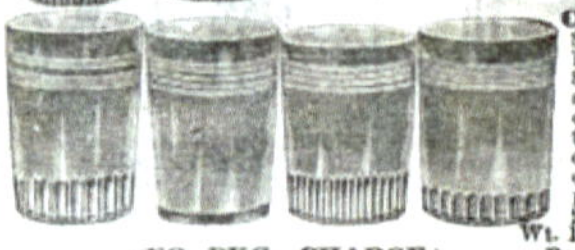

C1068½. Straight tumbler shape. Full 8 oz., ½ pt., tall smooth edges, complete with tin tops. Asst. comprises 5 doz. each of 4 patterns. Total 20 doz. in bbl. Wt. 130 lbs. Per dozen, Out

(NO PKG. CHARGE.)

"SPECIAL LEADER" VASE ASSORTMENT.

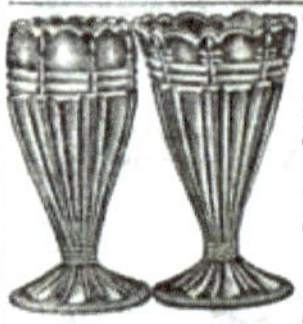

C404—Ht. 6¾ in., extra heavy prism panel pattern, asstd. tulip and flaring shapes, scalloped tops. 1 doz. in pkg. Per dozen, **45c**

(NO PKG. CHARGE.)

JAPANESE VASE AND ROSE BOWL ASST.

Entirely new, exceptionally rich. Art store 50 centers as dime leaders. Note especially the artistic shape.

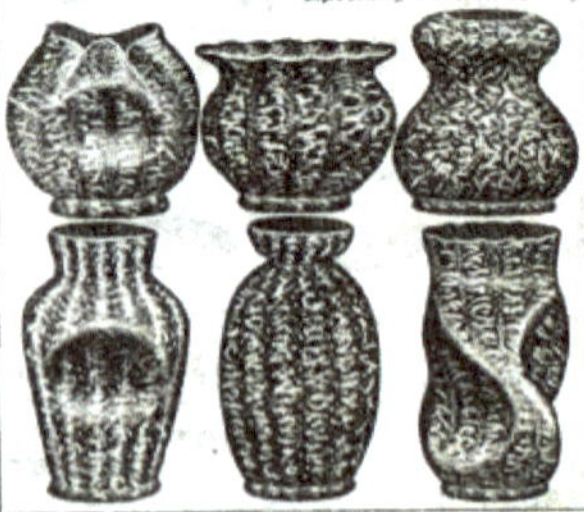

C1225—New oriental or Venetian mottled effect, in rich blue, green and opalescent colors, allover gold and silver illuminations. Asst. comprises 6 styles 3 rose bowl shape, ht. about 4½ in., 3 vases, ht. 6 in. Asstd. shapes, decorations and colors, 6 doz. in bbl. Per dozen, **82c**

(NO PKG. CHARGE.)

"TALL AND BEAUTIFUL VASE ASST.

Very attractive and on a good profit paying basis.

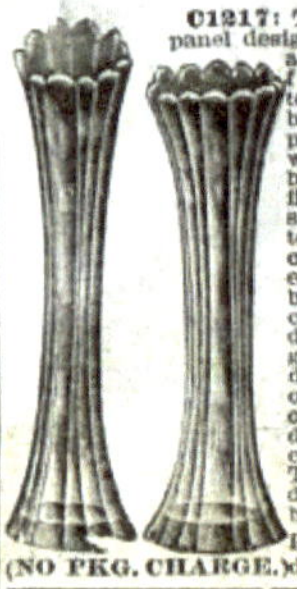

C1217: Tall rich panel design, average ht. from 12 to 15 in., beautiful pattern with wide base and flower shape tops. Asst comprises 2 doz. brilliant crystal, 1 doz. nile green, 1 doz. rich opalescent, ½ doz. delicate blue. Total 4½ doz. in bbl. Per doz. Out

(NO PKG. CHARGE.)

"PARISIAN" DECORATED VASE ASST.

Possible 10 centers which are actually worth 25c.

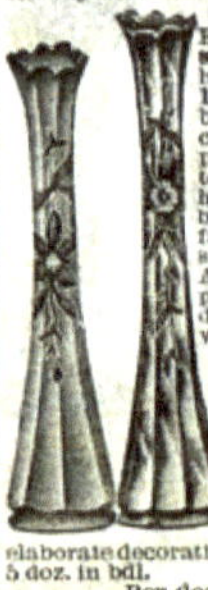

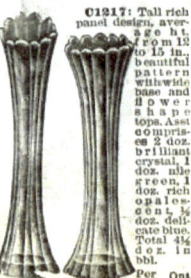

C1204: Extra large tall shape, ht. about 15½ in., beautiful colonial panel pattern with heavy wide base and fancy floral shape top. Asst. comprises: 2½ doz. crystal with large hand painted floral and gold bronze decorations; 2½ doz. opal, also with elaborate decorations. Total 5 doz. in bbl. Per dozen, **89c**

(NO. PKG. CHARGE.)

PUNCH SETS OF STANDARD GRADE.

We challenge any jobber or wholesaler to name regular net prices on similar quality punch sets that will average as low as these.

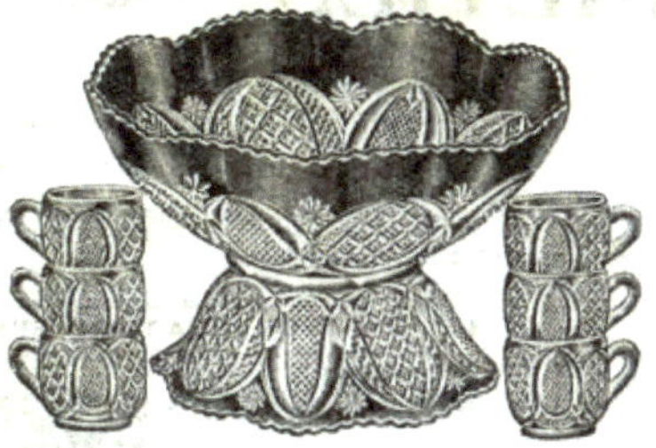

C1399—Our "Duchess" set. Large 12 in. deep bowl, rich cut pattern, scalloped edge, with separate stand, 6 handled sherbet cups to match, brilliantly finished and fire polished, full ht. of stand and bowl 8¾ in. 3 complete sets in bbl., wt. 55 lbs. Per set, **85c**

(NO PKG. CHARGE.)

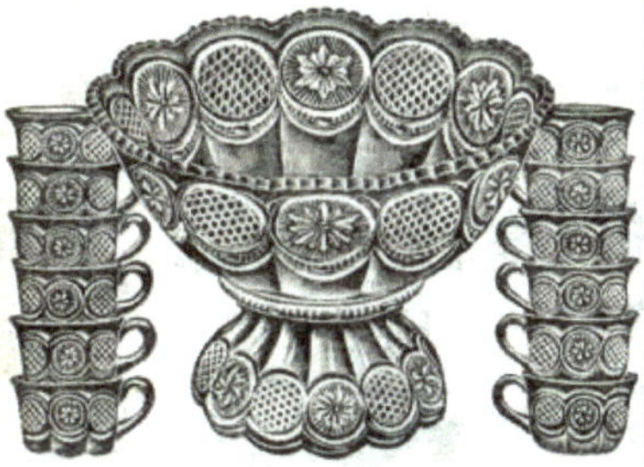

C1397—"Diamond Jewel." 12¾ in. extra deep bowl on separate stand, and 12 fancy handled cups, all in alternating star and deep jewel cut design, finest quality brilliant full finished crystal. Each set in case, wt. 33 lbs. Per set, **$1.39**

(NO PKG. CHARGE.)

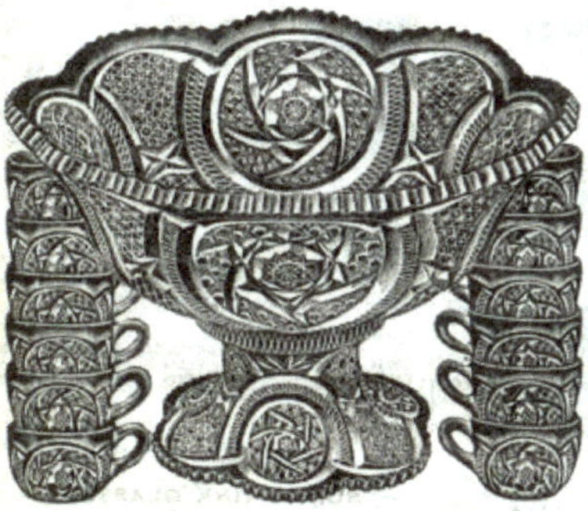

C1395—"Waldorf Cut." Massive deep heavy cut pattern, finest quality brilliant full finished crystal, looks exactly like real cut glass. Mammoth 15 in. bowl on fancy stand, 1 doz., ground bottom handled cups. Each set in bbl., wt. 56 lbs. Per set, **$3.00**

(NO PKG. CHARGE.)

C1396—As C1395, only 2 sets in bbl., wt. 77 lbs. Per set, **$2.87**

(NO PKG. CHARGE.)

"MASSIVE" PUNCH OR ORANGE BOWL.

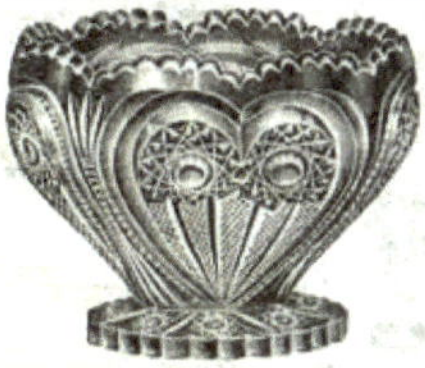

A rich one to retail at $1.00.

C685 — Diam. 9½ in., massive deep shape, footed, ht. 7¼ in., finest quality full finished crystal, extra heavy deep cut pattern. Each in pkg. Each, **57c**

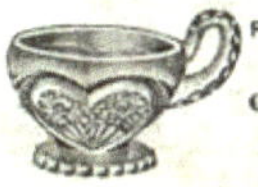

FOOTED PUNCH OR SHERBET CUP.

C686 — Diam. 3¾ in., extra deep shape with large fancy handle. 1 doz. in pkg. Per dozen, **78c**

(NO PKG. CHARGE.)

"DIAMOND JEWEL" BERRY SET ASST.

Well named. None more beautiful ever made and the price is exceptionally low.

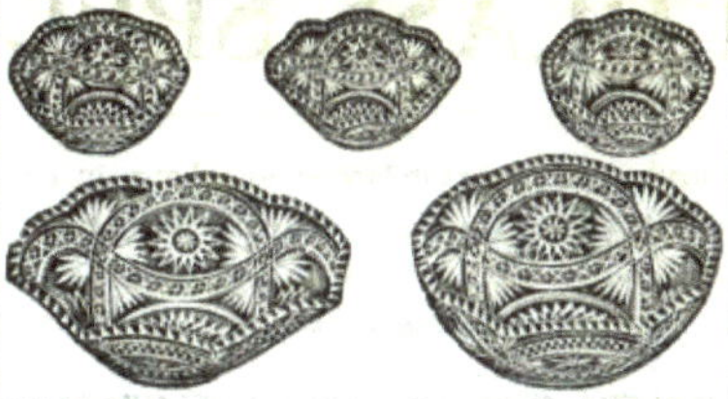

C1006—Extra heavy crystal, deep diamond cut band and star pattern, looks like genuine cut glass, brilliantly fire polished. Asst. comprises 6 sets each of 3 shapes, deep round, flared and fancy crimped, all pieces footed. Each set consists of 8¾ in. large deep berry bowl and SIX 4¾ in. nappies to match. Total 18 sets in bbl., wt. 100 lbs. Per set, **29c**

(NO PKG. CHARGE.)

"BIG VALUE" BERRY SET ASSORTMENT.

Rich 25 cent sets. Will sell on sight.

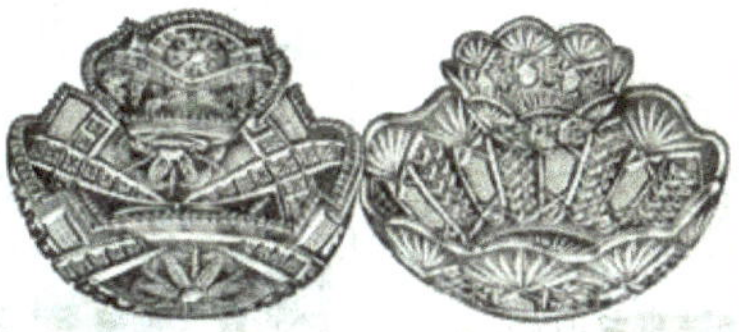

C1011—2 patterns, both rich deep cut designs in pure crystal. Set comprising one 8½ in. deep bowl, six 4½ in. nappies. 12 sets each pattern. Total 24 sets in bbl. Per set, **16½c**

(NO PKG. CHARGE.)

"BRILLIANT CUT" BERRY SET ASST.

Richest ones ever offered at a 50 cent price.

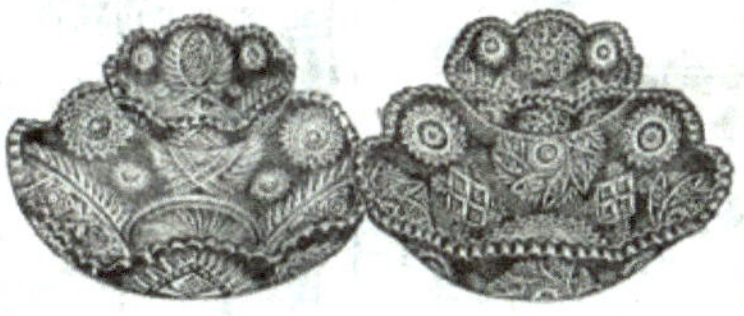

C1007—2 patterns, both exact imitation of genuine cut glass in full finished crystal. Each set consists of 9 in. large fancy shape berry bowl and SIX 4¼ in. deep nappies. 6 sets each pattern. Total 21 sets in bbl., wt. 115 lbs. Per set, **28c**

(NO PKG. CHARGE.)

"ROCK CRYSTAL" BERRY SET.

Magnificent set to retail at $1.00. Will easily bring more. Fine enough for any table.

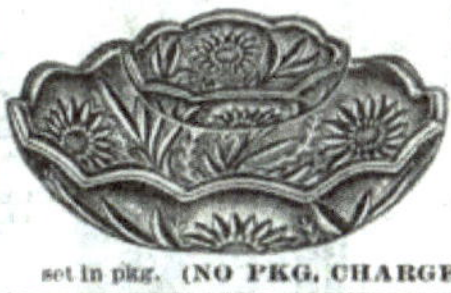

C390—Entirely new and most beautiful pressed glass ever made, extra heavy and brilliant, heavy cut floral and leaf design in exact reproduction of the famous and expensive Rock crystal. Each piece trademarked. Set comprises 10 in. deep round berry bowl and six 5¼ in. nappies. Each set in pkg. (NO PKG. CHARGE.) Per set, **67c**

"SIX STYLE" BERRY NAPPY ASSORTMENT.

You can retail at a good profit at "2 for 5."

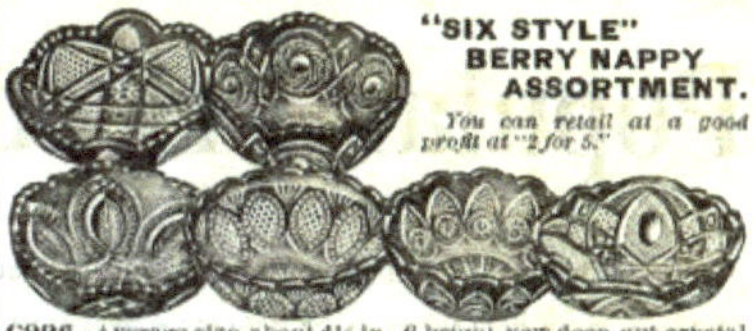

C996—Average size about 4½ in., 6 bright new deep cut crystal patterns, all fancy deep shape, with scalloped edges. 2 doz. each. Total 12 doz. in case, wt. 75 lbs. Per dozen, **19c**

(NO PKG. CHARGE.)

"BIG WINNER" BERRY SET ASST.

Popular and quick selling berry sets at a price which makes them unusually attractive.

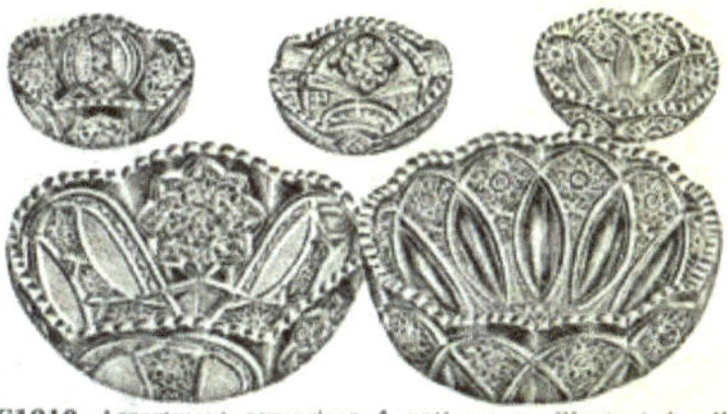

C1010—Assortment comprises 4 patterns as illustrated, all heavy deep cut. Each set consists of 8¼ in. deep round berry bowl and SIX 4¼ in. nappies to match. 6 sets each pattern. Total 24 sets in bbl., wt. 126 lbs. Per set, **14½c**

(NO PKG. CHARGE.)

"CHOICEST" SAUCE OR BERRY SET ASST.

The richest and most beautiful sets ever offered to retail with a profit of 50 cents per set.

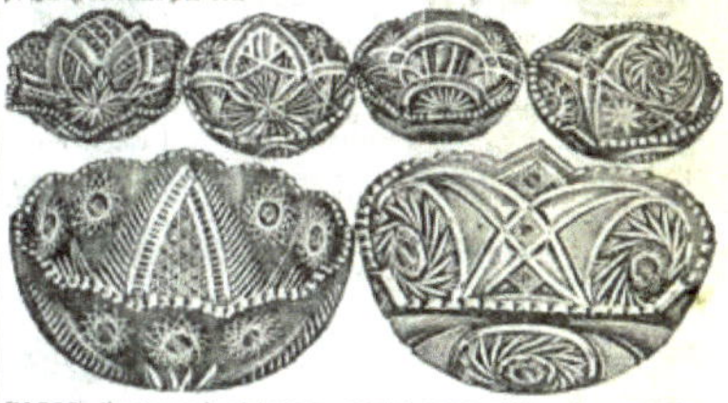

C1008—3 sets each of 4 large, extra heavy patterns in exact imitation of genuine cut glass designs. Full finished and fire polished, in fancy and round shapes with beaded and scalloped edges. Berry bowl about 9 in. and SIX 4½ in. sauce dishes. Total 12 sets in bbl., wt. 91 lbs. Per set, **32c**

(NO PKG. CHARGE.)

"EXCELLENT" BERRY SET ASST.

Two extra large and brilliant 25 cent possibilities, although actually worth much more.

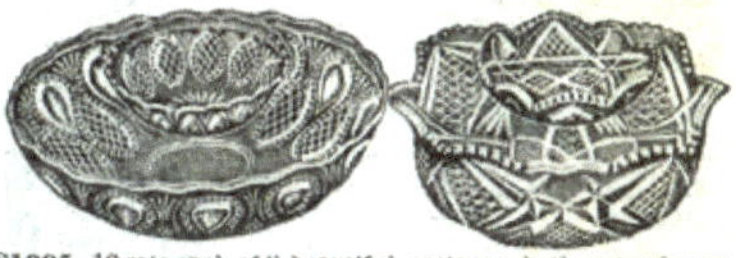

C1005—12 sets each of 2 beautiful patterns, both extra heavy and fire polished. 9¼ in. footed flaring bowl, brilliant cut diamond design and SIX 4½ in. nappies; 8¾ in. deep berry bowl, heavy cut pattern, and SIX 4½ in. nappies. Total 24 sets in bbl., wt. 130 lbs. Per set, **18½c**

(NO PKG. CHARGE.)

IMPORTED LEAD BLOWN GLASSWARE.

Only the most rapid selling items. While known to the trade as "Bar" Glassware, are sold and used largely for table, etc. Best imported thin lead blown glass, well finished, smooth melted edges. *1 doz. of a number in pkg.*

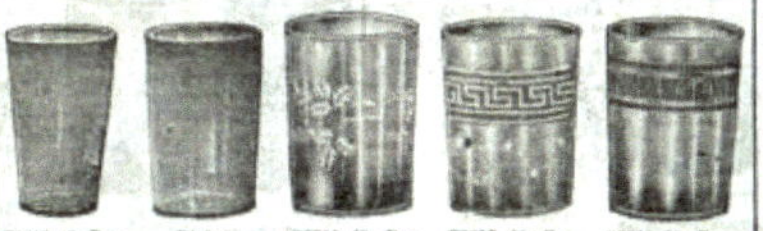

C2312, 40c Doz. Plain. C2316, 48c Doz. C2317, 48c Doz. C2318, 72c Doz.

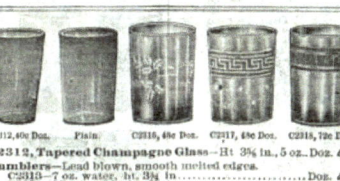

C2312, Tapered Champagne Glass—Ht 3⅝ in., 5 oz.. Doz. **40c**

Tumblers—Lead blown, smooth melted edges.

C2313—7 oz. water, ht. 3¾ in.	Doz.	42c
C2314—10 oz. table, ht. 3⅞ in.	"	42c
C2316—9 oz. table, floral and leaf engraved	"	48c
C2317—9 oz. table, Grecian band and star engraved	"	48c
C2318—9 oz. table, 1 wide and 2 narrow needle etched bands.	Doz.	72c

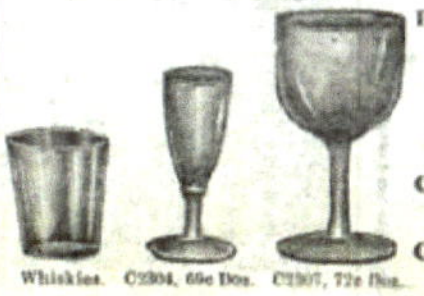

Whiskies. C2304, 69c Doz. C2307, 72c Doz.

Lead Blown Whiskey Glasses — All thin lead blown glass, slightly tapering shape. 1 doz. of a number in pkg.

C2299—1½ oz.	Doz.	32c
C2300—2 "	"	33c
C2301—2½ "	"	34c

C2304, Pousse Cafe—Regulation size, fancy stem. 1 oz. Doz. **69c**

C2307, Claret Glass—4 oz. Doz. **72c**

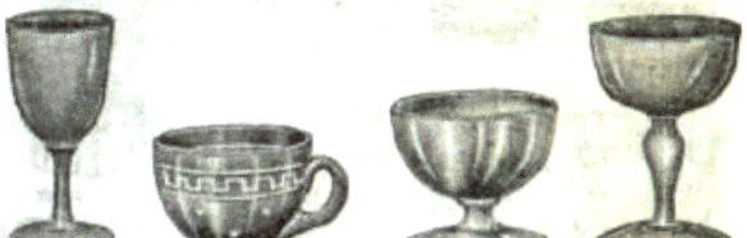

C2305 & C2306. C2303, 89c Doz. B2319, 92c Doz. C2308, 82c Doz.

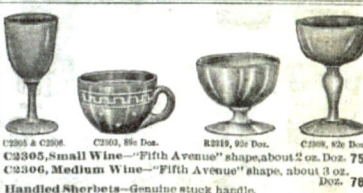

C2305, Small Wine—"Fifth Avenue" shape, about 2 oz. Doz. **75c**

C2306, Medium Wine—"Fifth Avenue" shape, about 3 oz. Doz. **78c**

Handled Sherbets—Genuine stuck handle.

C2303—Engraved, diam. 3⅛, ht. 2¼, Grecian band and star engraved. Doz. **89c**

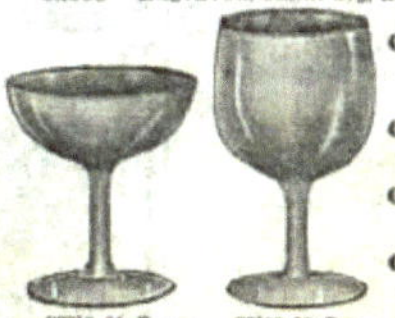

C2310, 96c Doz. C2309, 96c Doz.

C2319, Footed Sherbet or Sundae.—Good size, deep shape. Diam. 3¾ in., ht. 2¾, with fancy foot. Doz. **92c**

C2308, Cocktail Glass—Regulation size, 3½ oz., diam. top 2¾ in. Doz. **82c**

C2310, Saucer Champagne Glass—Diam. top 3½ in., 5 oz., long thin stem. Doz. **96c**

C2309, Goblet—"Hoffman House" shape, 10 oz. universally used for table, etc. Doz. **96c**

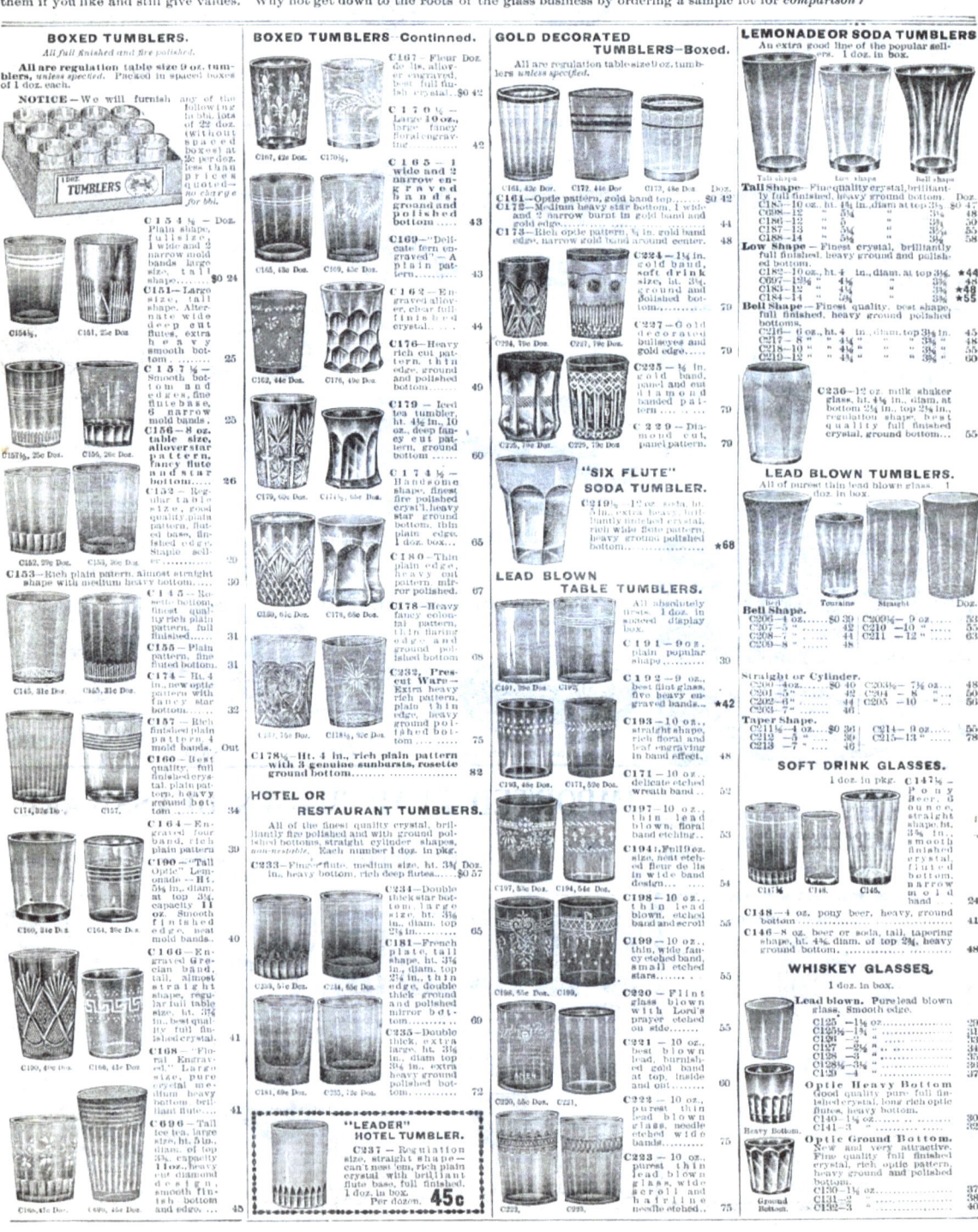

Competition Lessens in the Same Ratio That Energy and Push Ar' Increased.

LEAD BLOWN STEM WARE.

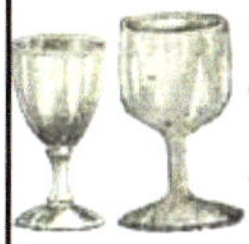

C79—2 oz. wine. "5th Ave." shape, dainty stem and foot. Doz. $0 89

C80: 3oz. claret "Hoffman House" shape. Out

WINE GLASSES—*1 doz. in box.*

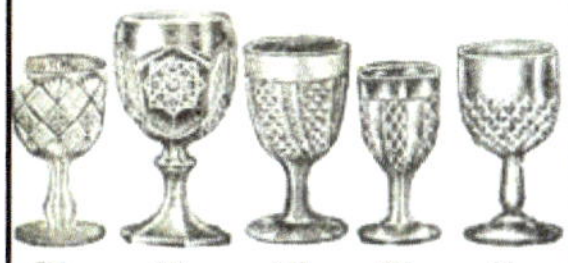

C56, 25c Doz. C50, 29c Doz. C68, 29c Doz. C53, 30c Doz. 52, 31c Doz.

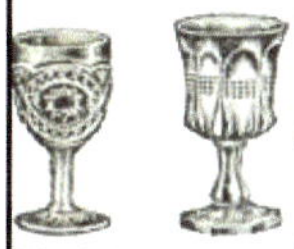

C54½, 32c Doz, C55, 34c Doz.

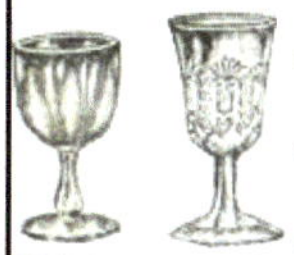

C60, 34c Doz. C58, 36c Doz.

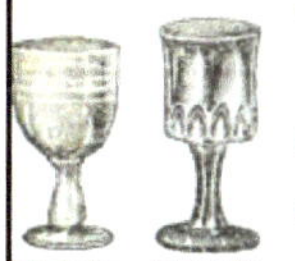

C59, 37c Doz. C66, 40c Doz.

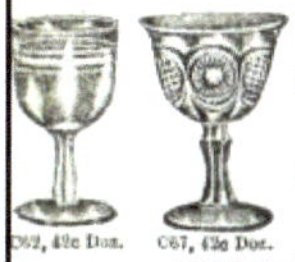

C62, 42c Doz. C67, 42c Doz.

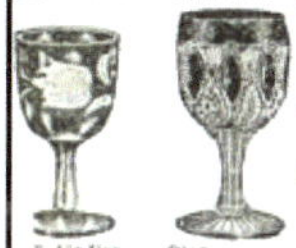

C63, 43c Doz. C103,

C56—Medium size, ht. 3½ in., bright cut diamond pattern, fancy stem. Doz. $0 25

C50—2 oz., ht. 4 in., imit. cut pattern and stem, smooth plain edge. 29

C68—Brilliant twist, cut diamond pattern, smooth finish edge. 29

C53—1½ oz. cordial, pointed edge cut panel pattern. 30

C52—Imitation cut diamond pattern, smooth plain edge. 31

C54½—Medium size, heavy rich cut pattern. 32

C55—Good size colonial flute pattern, fancy diamond cut band, imit. cut stem. 34

C60—Medium size, plain cut stem. 34

C58—Rich cut diamond pattern, brilliant finish. 36

C59—Medium size, 3 oz. 3 mold bands. 37

C66—About 2 oz. bell shape, deep cut flutes, fancy imit. cut stem. 40

C62—Medium size, 1 wide and 2 narrow engraved bands. 42

C67—Flaring shape, deep cut jewel pattern, fancy imit. cut stem. 42

C63—Regular size, delicate floral engraving 43

C103—Brilliant jewel cut pattern, heavy gold band, gold decorated panels. 79

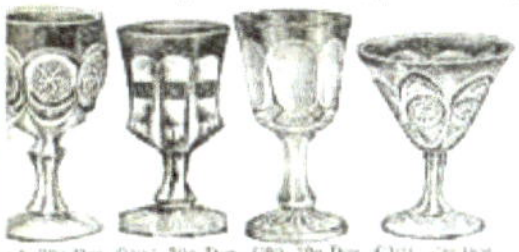

C101, 79c Doz. C102, 79c Doz. C99, 79c Doz. C104, 79c Doz.

C101—Rich deep cut jewel pattern, ¾ in. wide burnt in gold band. 79

C102—Brilliant cut panel pattern, ½ in. gold band. 79

C99—Medium size, ht. 4½ in., deep cut Colonial pattern, wide gold band edge. 79

C104—Large, fancy flaring shape, rich rosette and panel pattern, wide burnt in gold band decorations. 79

CUP FOOT WINE GLASSES.

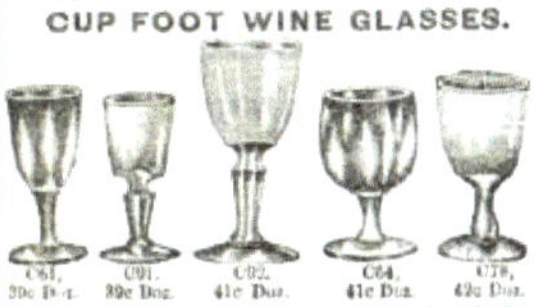

C61, 39c Doz. C91, 39c Doz. C92, 41c Doz. C64, 41c Doz. C78, 42c Doz.

C61—Regulation size, 1 oz. cordial tall fancy shape. Doz. $0 39

C91—Cut stem cordial, plain finished pattern, fancy imitation cut stem. 39

C92—Medium size, plain pattern, fancy cut stem. 41

C64—"Hoffman House" regulation low shape, slender stem. 41

C78, "Sherry" Wine—Finest of crystal. 42

WINE GLASS ASSTS.

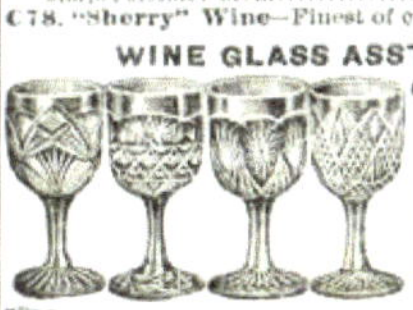

C1407—Richest cut patterns, 1 dozen each of 4 patterns, 4 doz. in wood case, sold by case only. Doz. 33c

GENUINE DEEP "CUT STAR STEM WARE.

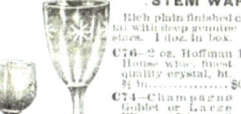

Rich plain finished crystal with deep genuine cut stars. 1 doz. in box.

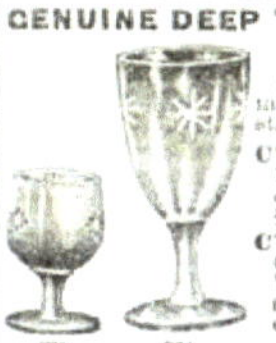

C76, 72c Doz. C74, 72c Doz.

C76—2 oz. Hoffman House wine, finest quality crystal, ht. 3¾ in. Doz. $0 72

C74—Champagne Goblet or Large Wine. "5th ave." shape, capacity 6 oz., ht. 5⅝ in. 72

GOBLETS.

1 doz. in box.

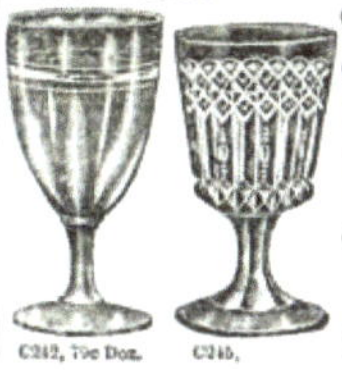

C242, 79c Doz. C245,

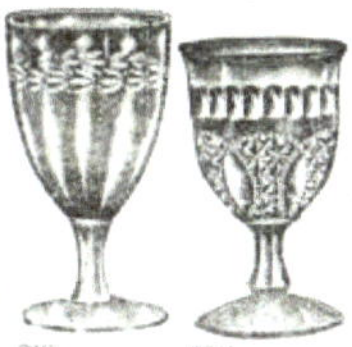

C243, C244,

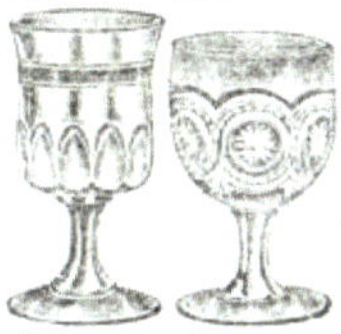

C246, C247,

C242—"5th ave." shape, 1 wide and 2 narrow engraved bands. (Bbl. lots, 10 doz. 67c.) 79

C245—Fancy flaring shape, rich cut diamond panel pattern, fancy stem, ⅛ in wide burnt in gold band. 80

C243—"5th ave." shape, fancy engraved wreath band. (In bbl. lots 10 doz., 72c) 80

C244: Large fancy shape, ht. 6 in., rich finished crystal, brilliant pattern with ¼ in. burnt in gold band decoration, gold decorated edge. 80

C246—Ht. 6 in. Deep opetic cut flutes and imit. cut stem, 1 wide and 2 burnt in gold bands, gold edge. 80

C247: Rich deep cut rosette pattern, 1 in. burnt in ruby band, gold decorated edge. 82

"HOFFMAN HOUSE" GOBLETS.

Regular "Hoffman House" shape, finest quality of full finished crystal. 1 doz. in box.

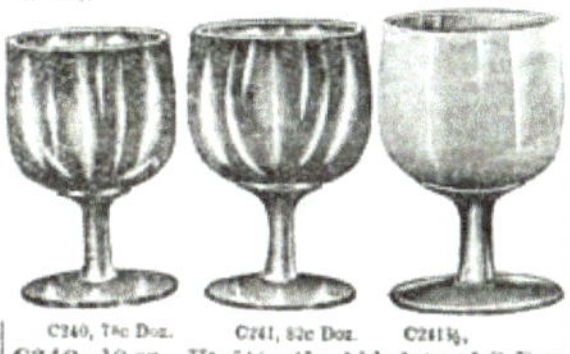

C240, 78c Doz. C241, 82c Doz. C241½,

C240—10 oz. Ht. 5⅛. (In bbl. lots of 9 doz., 70c doz.) Doz. $0 78

C241—12 oz. Ht. 5⅜. (In bbl. lots of 8 doz., 80c doz.) 82

C241½—14 oz. Ht. 5⅝ in. (In bbl. lots of 7 doz. 77c doz.) Out

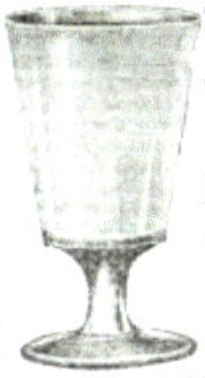

WEISS BEER GOBLETS.

You can sell these well known goods at a good profit.

Regulation shape, finest quality heavy full finished crystal, brilliantly full finished.

C694—14 oz. size. (In bbl lots of 6 doz. 89c doz.) 96

HANDLED ST. LOUIS BEER MUGS.

Big staple sellers at saving prices.

Large handles, ground polished bottoms, finest quality crystal, full finished and fire polished. 1 doz. in pkg. No pkg. charge.

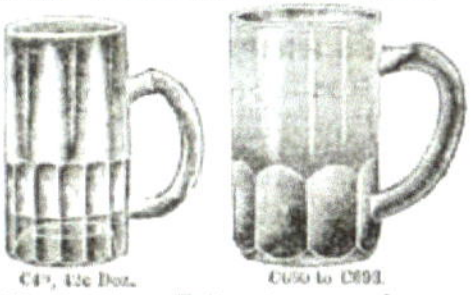

C49, 42c Doz. C690 to C693.

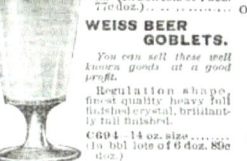

Picnic Mug—Tall and narrow shape C49—7 oz., ht. 4½ in. 42

Regulation Beer Mug.

C690—8 oz.,	ht. 4½ in.		57
C691—10 "	" 4¾ "		69
C692—12 "	" 5 "		81
C693—14 "	" 5⅝ "		1 25

BEER MUGS.

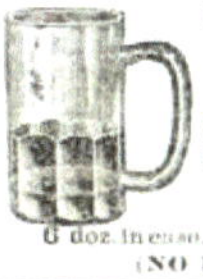

C1465—Standard 8 oz. "Picnic," lower part fluted, smooth finished bottom, 8 doz. in case. Wt. 79 lbs. 43

(NO PKG. CHARGE.)

C1466—Standard 8 oz. "St. Louis." Smooth finish bottom, will not scratch the table or bar. 6 doz. in case. Wt. 84 lbs. 48

(NO PKG. CHARGE.)

HIGH GRADE GLASS FLASKS.

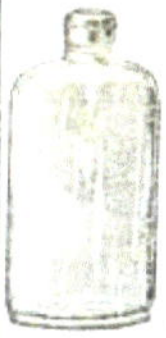

Good shape bottle, ground top with heavy cork-lined nickel plated cap. This makes the only absolutely unbreakable flask on the market.

C1413: 12 oz. (½ gro. in case). Doz. 39c

C1414: 16 oz. (½ gro. in case). Doz. 59c

HANDLED SHERBETS—*1 doz. in box.*

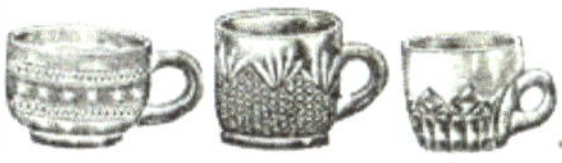

C30, 33c Doz. C33, C34, 42c Doz.

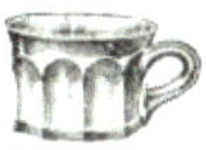

C32½, 67c Doz.

C30—Low shape, footed, large handle, fancy cut star and mold bands. Doz. 33c

C33—Brilliant cut design, smooth edge. Doz 37c

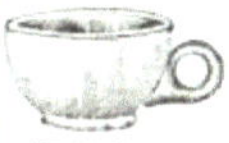

C39, 69c Doz.

C34—Custard, punch or sherbet, fancy fluted bottom. Doz. 42c

C32½—Regulation sized fancy bell shape, colonial cut flutes, thin edge, ground bottom. Doz. 67c

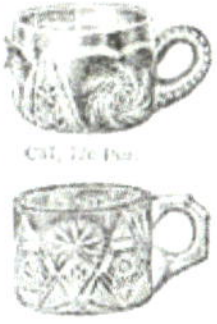

C37, 72c Doz. C46½, 80c Doz.

C39—Regulation size plain star ground bottom. Doz. 69c

C37, Prescut ware—Brilliant "Sunburst" pattern, ground and polished bottom. Doz. 72c

C46½—Straight shape, diam. 2¾ in., ht. 2½ in. heavy genuine cut pattern, rich red rose shading on upper part with wide gold decorated edge. Doz. 80c

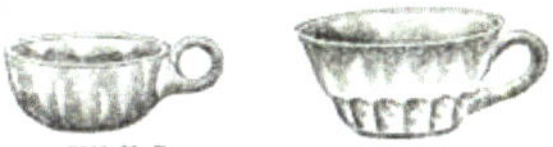

C662, 77c Doz. C679, 75c Doz.

C662—High class. Diam. 3⅜ in., thin plain pressed glass, stuck handle, ground genuine cut bottom. Doz. 77c

C679: Large size, diam. 4 in., fancy bell shape almost plain with fluted base, ground and polished star bottom, thin pressed glass. Doz. 75c

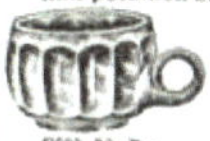

C663, 78c Doz.

C663—Deep cut shape, diam. 2¾ in., thin pressed glass, optic paneled sides, star ground bottom, large stuck handle. Doz. 78c

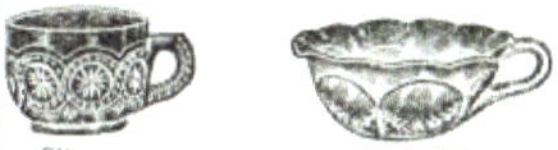

C44, C680, 84c Doz.

C44—Cup shape, rich deep cut pattern, wide burnt in gold decorated edge. Doz. 79c

C680—Large size, fancy shape, diam. 4⅛ in., rich colonial pattern, large handle, fancy crimped edge, ground polished bottom. Doz. 84c

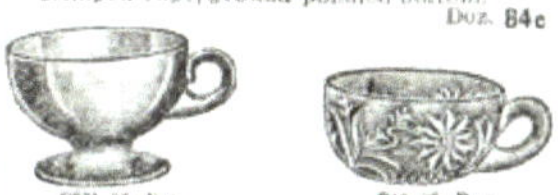

C671, 85c Doz. C48, 87c Doz.

C671—Diam. 3⅝x2⅝, large size, extra deep shape, fine thin pressed crystal with large genuine stuck handle. Doz. 85c

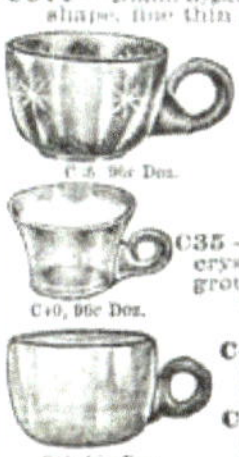

C35, 96c Doz. C40, 96c Doz. C41, 96c Doz.

C48—Rock Crystal. Diam. 3½ in., popular low shape, rich floral and leaf rock crystal cut pattern, heavy genuine cut polished bottom. Each piece trade marked. Doz. 87c

C35—Low shape, thin pressed crystal, genuine cut stars, ground and polished bottom, large stuck handle. Doz. 96c

C40—Bell shape, French lead blown ground top, stuck handle. Doz. 96c

C41—French blown ground tops, purest lead glass, stuck handle. Doz 96c

FINGER BOWLS.

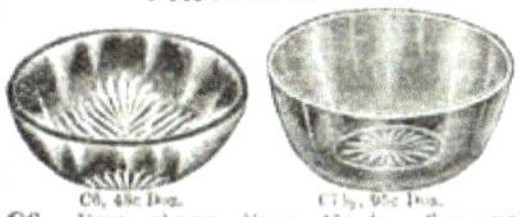

C6, 48c Doz. C7½, 95c Doz.

C6—Deep shape, diam. 4⅝ in., fine quality crystal, cut diamond pattern, ground bottom. Doz. 48c

C7½—Large size, extra deep round shape, diam. 4½ in., rich thin pressed crystal, star ground bottom, finest quality, brilliantly finished. 1 doz. in pkg. Per dozen. **95c**

"SUNDAES" OR FOOTED SHERBETS.

Used for ice cream, sherbets, etc. All 1 doz. box.

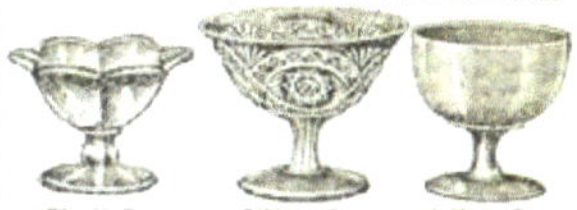

C38, 43c Doz. C672, 46c Doz. C673, 67c Doz.

C38—High footed, colonial pattern. Doz. 43c

C672—Diam. 4¼ in., fancy flaring shape, high footed, rich heavy cut pattern. Doz. 46c

C673—Diam. 3½ in., extra deep, high foot, plain pattern. Doz. 67c

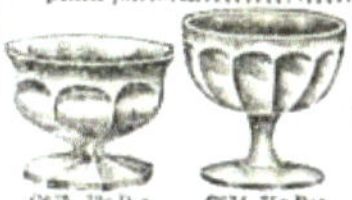

C675, 72c Doz. C674, 75c Doz.

C675—Diam. 3⅜ in., high foot, colonial flute pattern. Doz. 72c

C674—Diam. 3⅜ in., deep shape, high foot, rich optic pattern. Doz. 75c

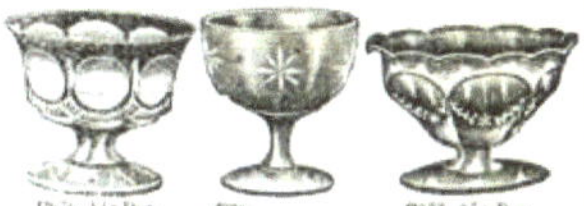

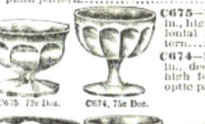

C676, 84c Doz. C36, C677, 87c Doz.

C676—Diam. 3⅝ in., extra deep flaring shape on high foot, colonial and diamond cut pattern, ⅛ in. gold decorated edge. Doz. 84c

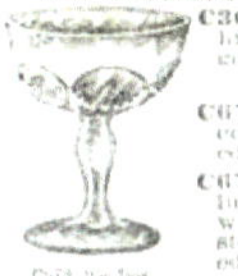

C678, 96c Doz.

C36—Diam. 3¼ in., ht. 3¼ in., high foot, almost plain with genuine deep cut stars. Doz. ★79

C677—Diam. 4¼ in. beautiful colonial design, fancy crimped edge. Doz. 87c

C678—Diam. 3⅝ in., ht. 4⅜ in., rich colonial pattern with fancy imitation cut stem, brilliantly full finished. 1 doz. in box. Doz. 96c

SUGARS AND CREAMERS.

No pkg. charge.

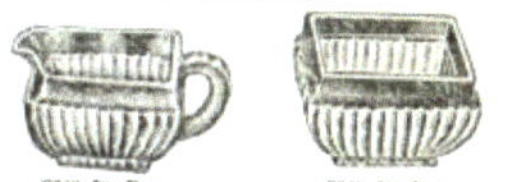

C762, 79c Doz. C763, 79c Doz.

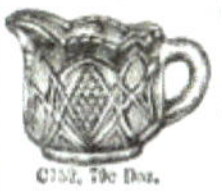

C752, 79c Doz.

C762—Square shape, 3x3⅛, footed, fancy handle, rich prism pattern, ⅛ in. gold decorated edge. 1 doz. in pkg. Doz. 79c

C763—Square shape, 3⅛x3⅛, rich prism pattern, ¼ in. gold band edge. 1 doz. in pkg. Doz. 79c

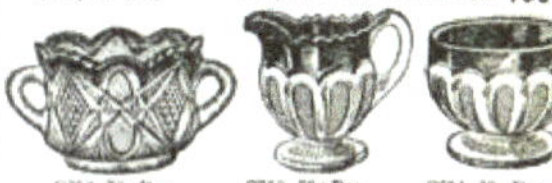

C754, 79c Doz. C750, 79c Doz. C751, 79c Doz.

C752—Ht. 3 in., diam. of top 3⅛, heavy deep cut pattern, large handle, wide burnt in gold band decorations. 1 doz. in pkg. Doz. 79c

C753—Ht. 2¾ in., diam. at top 3⅜ in., double handles, heavy goldband scalloped edge. 1 doz. in pkg. Doz. 79c

C750—3½ in. high, 1 in. gold band around top, neat foot. Doz. 79c

C751—3 in. across top, ⅜ in. gold band around top, neat foot. Doz. 79c

ASSORTED IN PKG.

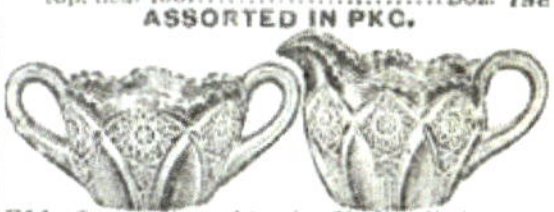

C11: Sugar, diam. 4 in., ht. 2¾, handled, cream entirely new deep heavy imitation cut pattern. 6 creams and 6 sugars in pkg. Doz. pieces. 48c

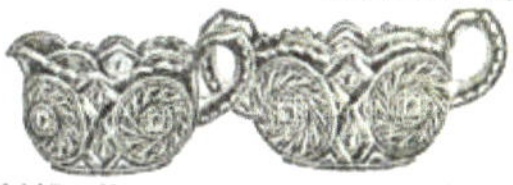

C1449: Heavy cut pattern, sugar, 4⅜x2⅝, creamer to match. 1 doz. each sugar and creamer, total 2 doz. Doz. pieces. 82c

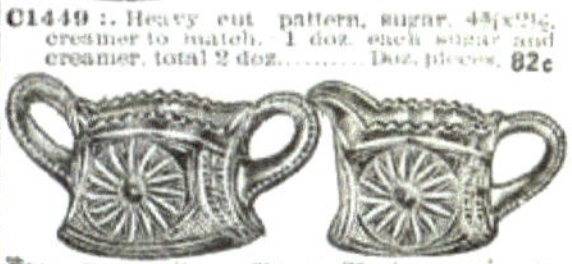

C9½: Sugar, diam. 3¾ ht. 2⅜ in., cream to match. Rich cut design, extra heavy with scalloped edges and fancy beaded handles. Assd. 6 sugars and 6 creams, total 1 doz. pieces in pkg. Doz. pieces, 84c

GLASS SOAP DISHES.

1 doz. in box.

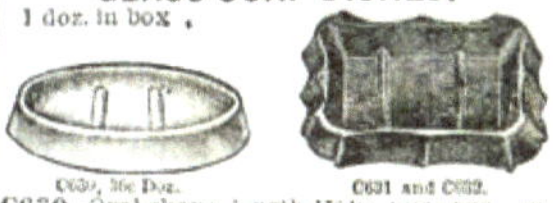

C630, 36c Doz. C631 and C632.

C630—Oval shape, length 4⅛ in., pure opal, extra heavy, well made and finished. Doz 36c

C631—Pure opal, fancy oblong shape, 3¼x3⅜. Doz 3[illegible]c

C632: Handsome turquoise colored soa[illegible] Do[illegible]

SAUCE DISHES AND NAPPIES.

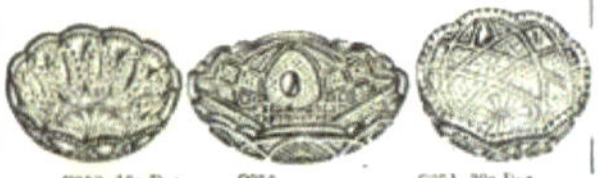
C350, 16c Doz. C356, C351, 20c Doz.

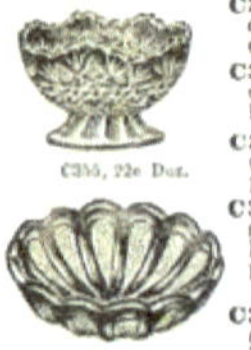
C355, 22c Doz.

C357, 23c Doz.

C350 — Diam. 3½ in., extra deep, fancy embossed beaded pattern.........Doz. **16c**

C356, Sauce — Diam. 4⅜ in., deep cut diamond pattern, heavy fancy edge. Doz. **Out**

C351 — Diam. 3½ in., deep shape, brilliant cut jewel pattern............Doz. **20c**

C355 — Diam. 3½ in., deep shape on fancy foot, brilliant deep cut diamond pattern, fancy edge. Doz. **22c**

C357 — Diam. 4⅜ in., deep shape, scalloped edge, brilliant panel pattern. Doz. **23c**

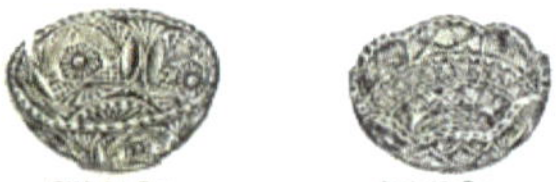
C352, 24c Doz. C353, 26c Doz.

C352 — Diam. 4¼ in., extra deep, brilliant deep cut diamond and rosette pattern, scalloped edge.... ....Doz. **24c**

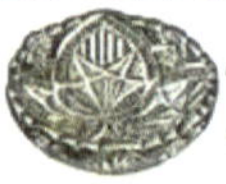
C373, 27c Doz.

C383 — Diam. 4½ in., deep shape, rich new pattern. Doz. **26c**

C373, Sauce — Diam. 4¼ in., brilliant genuine cut glass pattern, scalloped edge Doz. **Out**

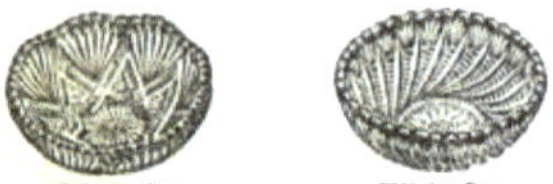
C374, 28c Doz. C368, 30c Doz.

C374 — Diam. 4¼ in., extra deep, scalloped edge. Doz. **28c**

C368 — Deep, diam. 4¼ in., extra heavy scroll twist pattern.......................Doz. **30c**

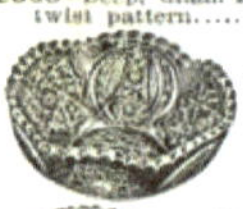

C382 — Diam. 4⅜ in., extra deep round shape, heavy new deep cut pattern, scalloped edge, fancy rosette bottom. Doz. **31c**

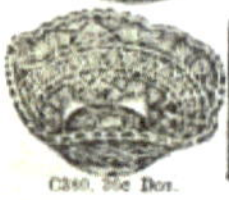
C380, 36c Doz.

C380 — 4½ in., square deep shape, footed, brilliant new cut pattern, full finished. *None prettier at a 5c price.* Per dozen, **36c**

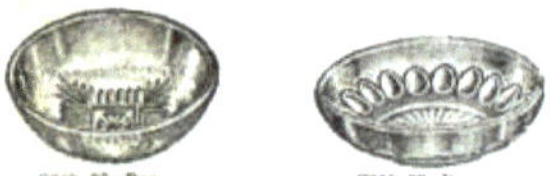
C360, 37c Doz. C369, 39c Doz.

C360 — Deep shape, diam. 4½ in., plain sides, diamond cut ground bottom ....Doz. **37c**

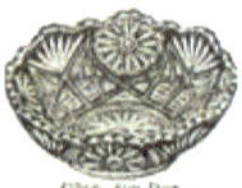
C366, 40c Doz.

C369 :. Round shape, diam., 5⅝ in., footed, fancy optic flutes. Doz. **Out**

C366 :. Diam., 4⅝ in., fancy deep shape, brilliant deep cut design, fancy scalloped edge. Doz. **Out**

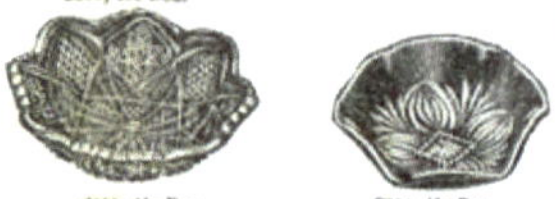
C388, 41c Doz. C384, 41c Doz.

C388 — Diam. 5 in., fancy star shape, brilliant deep cut pattern.....................Doz. **41c**

C384—"Beauty" Diam. 4⅝ in., pure French crystal, fancy cut ground bottom, wide plain crimped edge, brilliantly finished. *A rich 5 center.* 1 doz. in pkg. Per dozen. **41c**

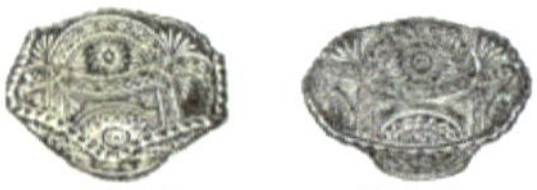
C362, 42c Doz. C363, 42c Doz.

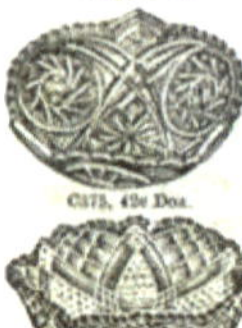
C375, 42c Doz.

C376, 42c Doz.

C362 :. Diam. 4⅜ in., fancy shaped footed brilliant deep genuine cut pattern...Doz. **42c**

C363 — Diam. 4½ in., fancy shape, brilliant deep genuine cut pattern. Matches C979 Bowl asst.....Doz. **42c**

C375 — Diam. 4⅜ in., heavy jewel cut glass "Sunburst" Prescut pattern. 1 doz. in pkg. Doz. **Out**

C376 :. Diam. 5½ in., rich cut glass pattern, scalloped edge. Doz. **42c**

SAUCE DISHES AND NAPPIES—Continued.

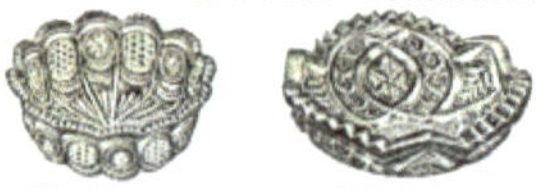
C370, 42c Doz. C377, 43c Doz.

C370 :. Diam. 4¼ in., extra deep, heavy crystal deep cut jewel pattern, scalloped edge. Doz. **42c**

C377 — Diam. 3⅞ in., extra heavy rich Prescut pattern, fancy scalloped edge......Doz. **43c**

MISCELLANEOUS DISHES—BON BON, UTILITY, ETC.

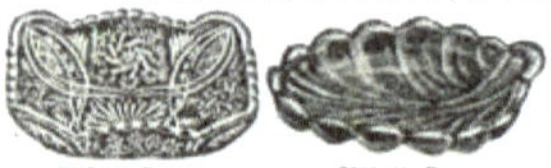
C365, 34c Doz. C389, 41c Doz.

C365, Bonbon :. Square shape, 5⅛x 5⅛, extra heavy and brilliant deep cut pattern, heavy fancy edge ....Doz. **34c**

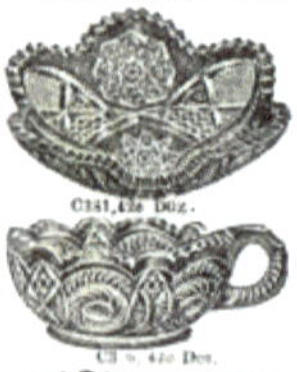
C381, 42c Doz.

C386, 42c Doz.

C389—Olive or Bon Bon. Length 5⅜ in., fancy deep leaf shape, heavy brilliant crysal. Doz. **41c**

C381, Olive— 6⅛ in. fancy leaf shape, rich heavy cut design, scalloped edge. 1 doz. in pkg. Per doz., **42c**

C386 — Diam. 4⅜ in., extra deep round shape, large open handle, heavy deep cut pattern. Doz. **42c**

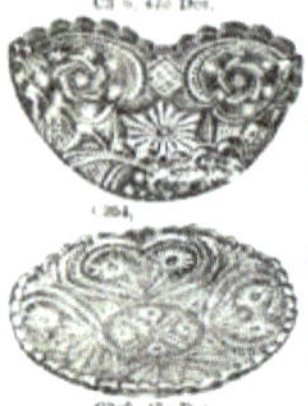
C364,

C385, 47c Doz.

C364, Utility — 6 x 5⅜, heavy deep cut pattern, fancy scalloped edge. Doz. **41c**

C385 — Diam. 5¼ in., fancy round shape, extra heavy brilliant jewel cut pattern, scalloped edge and ground polished bottom.. Doz. **47c**

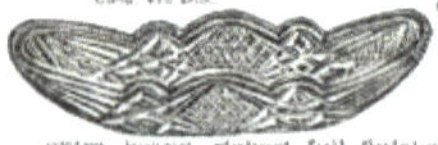

C372, Spoon Tray— Length 9 in., fancy deep shape, extra heavy, richest full finished crystal, diamond and jewel cut pattern.... Doz. **78c**

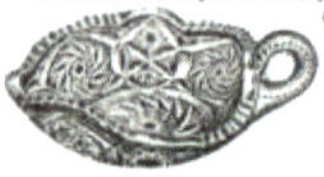

C379, Handled Olive Dish— Prescut pattern, large size, length 5⅜ in. fancy deep triangular shape, large open handle. Doz. **82c**

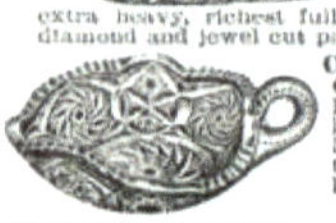

MISCELLANEOUS GOLD DECORATED DISHES.

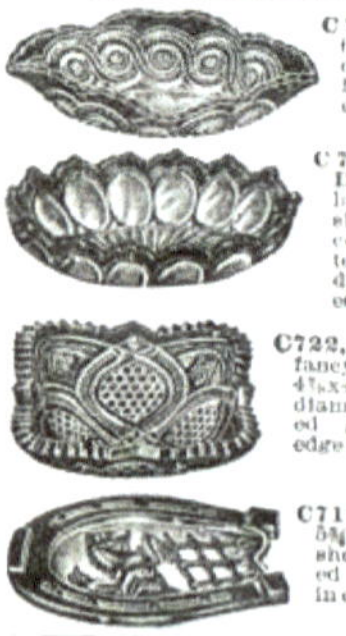

C711, Utility :. 6⅛ x 5⅛, brilliant cut glass pattern, heavy gold decorated fancy edge. Doz. **Out**

C709, Scalloped Dish — 5⅜x5 in. large deep oval shape, brilliant colonial fluted pattern, heavy gold decorated scalloped edge... Doz. **82c**

C722, Bonbon :. Deep fancy square shape, 4⅞x4⅞, heavy rich diamond cut, scalloped gold decorated edge ....Doz. **82c**

C717, Tray—Length 5⅜ in., fancy horseshoe shape, embossed horse and rider in center, gold edges. Doz. **82c**

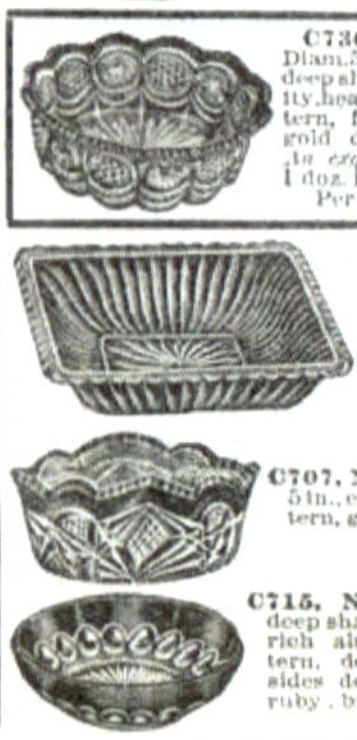

C730, Utility— Diam. 5 in., round extra deep shape, finest quality, heavy deep cut pattern, fancy scalloped gold decorated edge. *An exquisite 10 center.* 1 doz. in pkg. Per dozen, **82c**

C718, Table Dish :. Square extra deep shape, 6⅜x6⅜, rich prism pattern, heavy gold band edge. Doz. **82c**

C707, Nappy — Length 5 in., elaborate cut pattern, gold band edge. Doz. **82c**

C715, Nappy — Round deep shape, diam. 4⅜ in. rich almost plain pattern, deep optic flute, sides decorated in rich ruby, burnt in gold edge. Doz. **82c**

GOLD DECORATED—Continued.

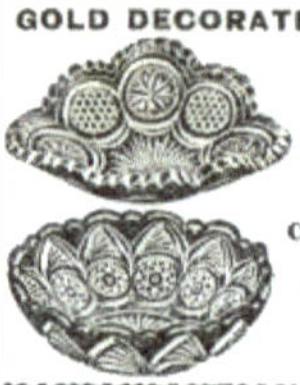

C731, Olive Dish — Length 6 in., turned up sides, brilliant jewel cut pattern, heavy scalloped gold decorated edge. Doz. **79c**

C713, Utility — Diam. 5¼ in., extra deep, brilliant rosette and feather panel pattern, heavy gold decorated sides and edges. Doz. **82c**

"GOLDEN ROSE" NAPPY.

Entirely new and very rich.

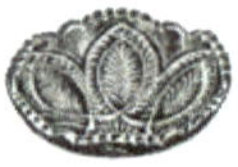

C729 — Round deep shape, diam. 4⅜ in., deep cut feather panel design, panels decoroted in rose red, heavy gold decorated edge. Per dozen, **82c**

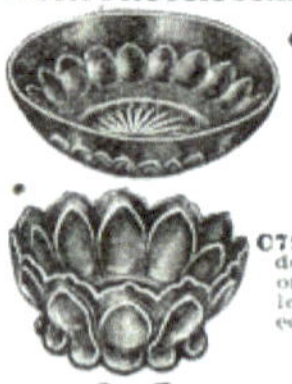

C727, Jelly Dish — Round extra deep. 5⅛ in., footed, deep cut flutes and star bottom, 1 in. wide gold band edge...Doz. **83c**

C725, Nut Dish—Extra deep, 4⅜ in., wide Colonial flute pattern scalloped gold decorated edges..........Doz. **84c**

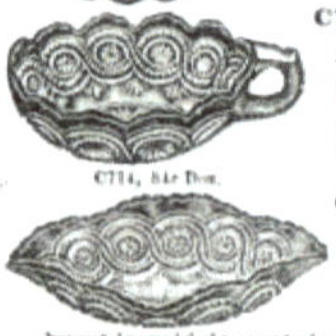
C714, 84c Doz.

C714, Handled Olive — Large, diam. 5 in., deep shape, fancy open handle, brilliant deep cut rosette pattern, gold decorated scalloped edge. Doz. **84c**

C716, Fancy Dish —4⅝ x 5⅜, diamond shape brilliant deep cut rosette pattern, wide ruby decorated border and burnt in gold decorated edge..........Doz. **84c**

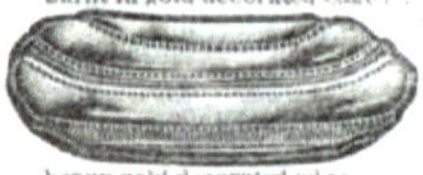

C703, Table Dish Oblong 8x5⅜, rolled up ends, brilliant prism design, extra heavy gold decorated edge..........Doz. **84c**

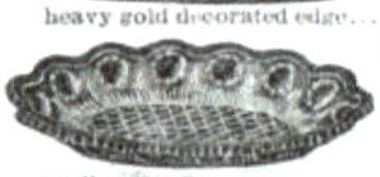

C700, Bureau Tray— 7⅝x6 in., rich jeweled pattern, heavy burnt in gold decorations, scalloped gold edge.................Doz. **84c**

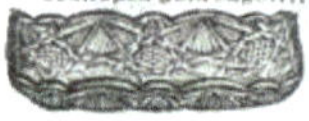

C704, Tray—7⅛x4, extra heavy and deep, brilliant cut glass pattern, scalloped and decorated gold edge. Doz. **84c**

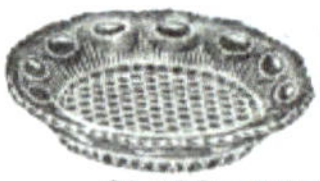

C706, Utility — Diam. 6 in., in. extra heavy and deep cut diamond pattern, gold decorations. Doz. **84c**

GLASS CANDY TRAY.

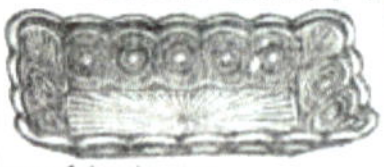

C616 — Candy Tray. Deep oblong shape, size, 7⅛x4⅛, rich brilliant crystal, fancy rosette pattern. 1 doz. in pkg.............................Doz. **43c**

GOLD DECORATED TRAY.

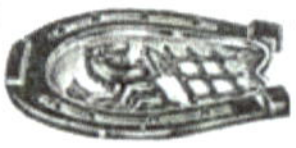

C717. Length 5⅜ in., fancy horseshoe shape, embossed horse and rider in center, gold edges. Doz. **82c**

CUT GLASS KNIFE RESTS.

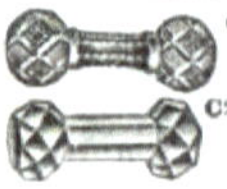

C27—4½ in. long, deep cut diamond pattern, genuine cut ends. 1 doz. in box..............Doz. **84c**

C25—Length 3⅞ in., purest crystal, rich cut pattern with genuine cut ends. 1 doz. in box...... Doz. **87c**

GLASS LEMON EXTRACTORS.

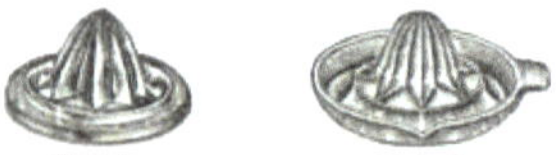
C1, 38c Doz. C9, 48c Doz.

C1—Small size regulation ....Doz. **38c**

C9—Diam. 5¼ in., large cone and deep saucer with lip and handle. 1 doz. in box. Doz. **48c**

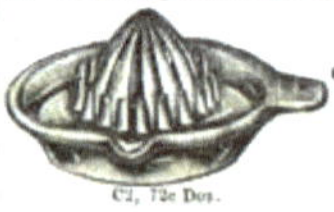
C2, 72c Doz.

C2—"Manny" saucer holds the juice of a number of lemons and the little pillars retain all seeds. Doz. **72c**

HOLDERS FOR TOOTHPICKS, MATCHES, ETC.

1 doz. in box.

C475—Pure crystal glass, barrel shape. Doz. **29c**

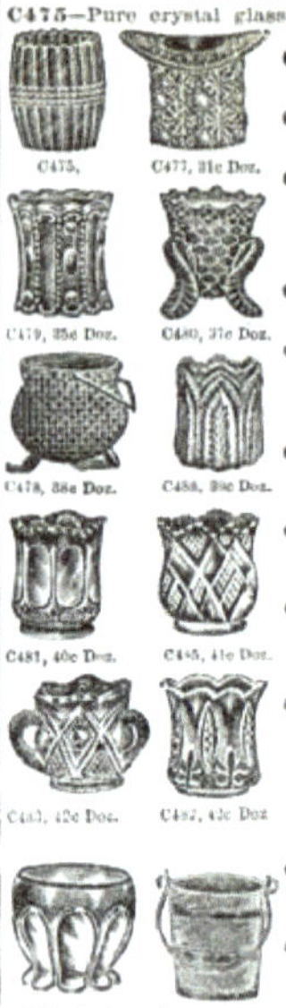
C475, C477, 31c Doz. C479, 35c Doz. C480, 37c Doz. C478, 38c Doz. C488, 39c Doz. C481, 40c Doz. C485, 41c Doz. C483, 42c Doz. C482, 42c Doz. C484, 42c Doz. C490, 85c Doz.

C477—*"Fineallstik"* Best flint glass, hat shape.....Doz. **31c**

C479—Rich reflecting panel design. Doz. **35c**

C480—Good size, ht. 2⅞ in., fancy feet, embossed optic design, asstd. green and blue colors. Doz. **37c**

C478—Minature glass gypsy kettle, handle....Doz. **38c**

C488—Good shape ht. 2⅝ in., rich new deep cut diamond, feather panel design.... ..Doz. **39c**

C481 :. Full finished crystal, colonial panel pattern. Doz. **40c**

C485— *Reproduction of cut glass.* Large size, scalloped and flared top. Doz. **41c**

C483—Imitation cut glass pattern, 3 handles, scalloped top, loving cup shape.....Doz. **42c**

C482 — Ht. 2⅝ in., extra heavy fancy embossed fleur de lis pattern. Asstd. blue, canary and flint opalescent. Doz. **42c**

C484 :. Large size, fancy footed, rich colonial flute pattern.......Doz. **Out**

C490—2⅛ in., asstd. ruby and emerald pails, heavy nickeled frame, nickel ball handle.....Doz. **85c**

DECORATED OPAL TOOTHPICK OR MATCH HOLDER.

A bargain at 5c., will easily bring 10c.

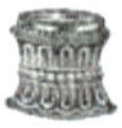

C487—Ht. 2⅛ in., fancy urn shape, decorated all over in tints and embossed gilt tracing, embossed nickel plated metal rim. Asstd. colors, 1 doz. in box. Per dozen, **42c**

GOLD DECORATED HOLDERS.

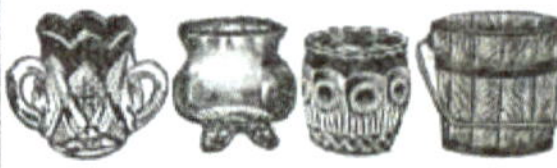
C496, 79c Doz. C493, 80c Doz. C494, 80c Doz. C492, 82c Doz.

C496—3 handles and heavy gold band around top, loving cup style................Doz. **79c**

C493—Ht. 2⅓ in., diam. 2⅛, gold decorated feet and edge.............................Doz. **80c**

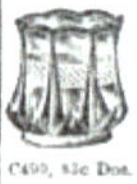
C499, 83c Doz.

C494—Ht. 2⅓ in., optic bullseye effect, bullseyes and ⅛ in. band decorated in pure gold. Doz. **80c**

C492—2⅜ x 2⅜, embossed, burnt in gold bands, metal bail handle. Doz. **82c**

C499—Cut panel design, imit. of cut glass, solid burnt in rose red color, gold edge.....Doz. **83c**

BURNT MATCH RECEPTACLE.

Exceedingly rich 10 center.

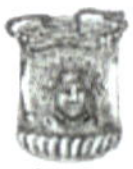

C503—Opal, length 2⅞ in., fancy embossed pattern, Indian's head, matches and pipe in relief, decorated in natural colors, "For Burnt Matches" in gold letters. Each with fancy satin ribbon for hanging. Asstd. colors, such as pink, blue and green in box of 1 doz. Per dozen, **78c**

HANDLED MUGS.

1 doz. in box unless specified.

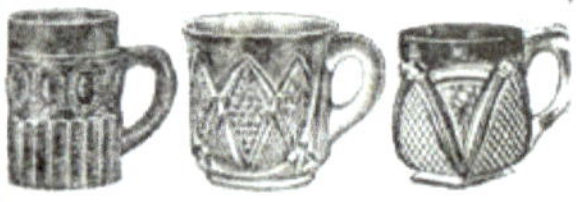
C574, 25c Doz. C580, 42c Doz. C579, 79c Doz.

C574—Children's colored, ht. 3⅛ in., solid amber, blue and crystal. Asstd in box. Doz. $0 25

C580—Extra large size, ht. 3¼ in., diam. of top 3¼, rich heavy cut diamond pattern, large handle........................ 42

C579—3⅛ in. high, jewel effect ⅜ in. gold band around top, ½ doz. in box.......................... 79

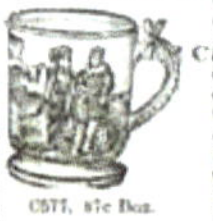
C577, 87c Doz.

C577 — Opal, ht. 3⅛ in., diam. of top 2⅛ in., footed. Red Riding Hood, Children at Play, etc., gold band foot gold edge and gold decorated handles, all decorations burnt in, pink or blue ribbons on handle....... 87

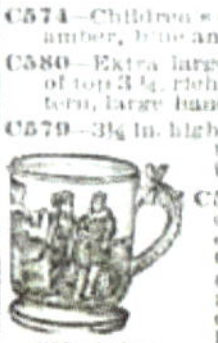

Test, Examine, Compare—The Keener the Investigation the Surer We Feel of Your Order.

CRYSTAL SALTS AND PEPPERS.

salts and 6 peppers in box of 1 doz.

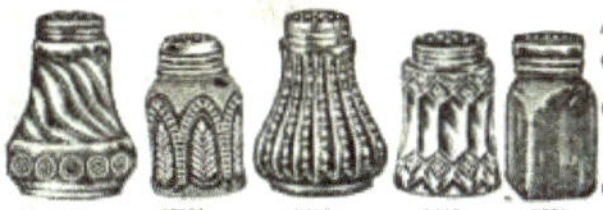

C251, C250½, C252, C257, 27c Doz. C254, 27c Doz.

C251—Large size, serpentine and rosette pattern.......Doz. **24c**

C250½—New tall shape, ht. 3¼ in., brilliant feather and beaded panel design, good tops. Doz. **25c**

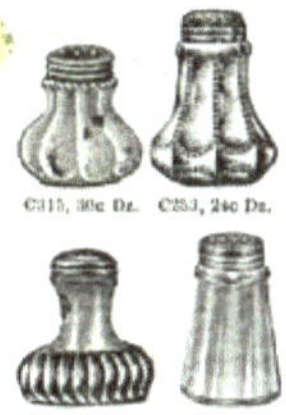

C315, 30c Dz. C253, 24c Dz. C258, 28c Dz. C255, 29c Dz.

C252—Large size, brilliant, blown crystal, fancy prism pattern with good tops. Doz. **25c**

C257—Low shape, nickeled tops Doz. **27c**

C254—Square, nickel plated tops.. Doz. **27c**

C315—Low optic melon shape, fancy beaded neck, embossed nickel caps...Doz. **27c**

C253—Swell pattern, beaded finish. Doz. **24c**

C258—Wide fluted bottom, nickeled top. 7 salts and 5 peppers in box of 1 doz. Doz. **28c**

C255—Tall shape nick-tops.......Doz. **29c**

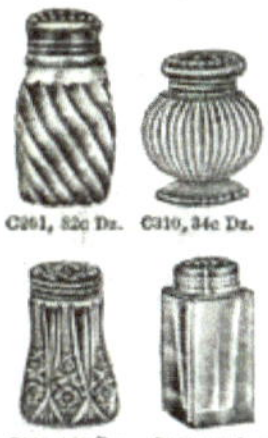

C261, 32c Dz. C310, 34c Dz. C298, 39c Doz. C262, 39c Doz.

C261—Ht. 4 in., extra heavy twist pattern best nickeled dome tops.......Doz. **32c**

C310—Fancy melon shape, brilliant ribbed pattern, heavy embossed nickel plated tops. Doz. **34c**

C298—Tall shape, heavy new deep cut pattern, very brilliant, embossed nickel plated caps.......Doz. **39c**

C262—Plain and rich extra heavy. Fancy embossed, nickeled top..........Doz. **39c**

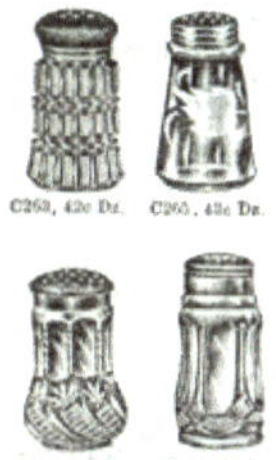

C263, 42c Dz. C265, 43c Dz. C266, 46c Dz. C292, 75c Dz.

C263—Tall shape, ht. 3½ in., extra heavy deep cut prism pattern, heavy nickeled dome tops... Doz. **42c**

C265—Large size, tall shape, fancy floral engraving, nickeled tops Doz. **43c**

C266—Ht. 3½ in., extra heavy, heavy cast plated tops..Doz. **46c**

C292 :. Heavy crystal, panel pattern, heavy cast plated tops, patent metal breaker inside of salt.......Doz. **75c**

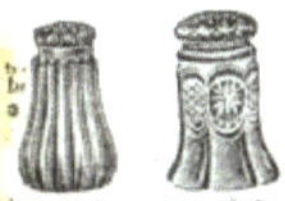

C279, 78c Dz. C294, 79c Dz.

C279—Fancy beaded cut prism pattern, fancy embossed silver plated tops..Doz. **78c**

C294—Large fancy shape, wide flaring base, rich optic panel patterns, deep jewel cutting, fancy embossed sterling tops. Doz. **79c**

C296—Extra heavy, Prescut ware pattern, heavy plated top. 6 salts and 6 peppers in box of 1 doz. Doz. **80c**

C295—Large size, tall square shape, heavy style fancy embossed tops..........Doz. **84c**

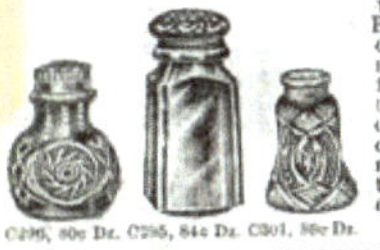

C296, 80c Dz. C295, 84c Dz. C301, 89c Dz.

C301 :. 3½ in., rich deep cut Prescut pattern, combination nickel and perforated pearl top. Contents do not come in contact with metal and will therefore not corrode or clog. Doz. **89c**

FANCY EMBOSSED DECORATED S. & P.

A regular 10 center as 5c leader.

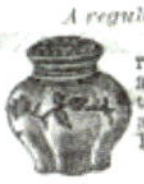

C306—New melon shape, relief embossed floral decorations, heavy nickel plated tops. Asstd. pink, canary and green tints in box of 1 doz. Per dozen, **42c**

PATENT CELLULOID TOP S. & P.

Never clogs, corrodes or gathers verdigris. 6 salts and 6 peppers in box of 1 dozen.

C300—Good size, ht. 3¼ in., fancy shape, wide base, attractive embossed pattern..Doz. **42c**

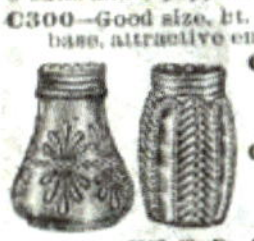

C300, 42c Dz. C302, 43c Dz.

C302—Ht. 3 in., alternating prism and plain panel pattern, brilliant crystal. Doz. **43c**

C303—Good shape, ht. 3 in., extra heavy deep cut pattern. ½ salts and ½ peppers.......Doz. **48c**

C289—Large size, ht. 4¼ in., heavy brilliant crystal, rich panel pattern. Specially desirable for restaurant or hotel use. Doz. **65c**

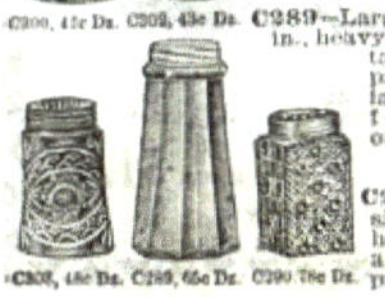

C303, 48c Dz. C289, 65c Dz. C290 78c Dz.

C290 :. Medium size, ht. 2¾ in., heavy square and diamond pattern. Doz. **78c**

TINTED AND DECORATED OPAL SALTS AND PEPPERS.

6 salts and 6 peppers in box of 1 dozen unless specified.

C281—Low round shape, allover floral decorations, nickeled tops.................Doz. **41c**

C313—Ht. 3 in., new fancy shape, heavily embossed rich tints, hand painted floral designs, gold bronze, asstd. pink, green and blue. Doz. **41c**

C314—Ht. 3 in., attractive shape, wide base, floral and bow-knot embossed effect, bright colors and rich gold bronze, asstd. tints such as pink, blue & green...............Doz. **42c**

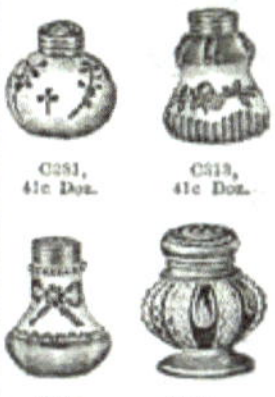

C281, 41c Doz. C313, 41c Doz. C314, 42c Doz. C309, 42c Doz.

C309—Footed, rich cut diamond crystal pattern, panels decorated in rich stained colors, asstd. ruby and emerald embossed nickel plated caps. Asstd. colors.......Doz. **42c**

C305—Large swell shape, embossed colored floral decorations, gilt beaded foot, asstd. pink, green and blue tints embossed nickeled tops. Doz. **42c**

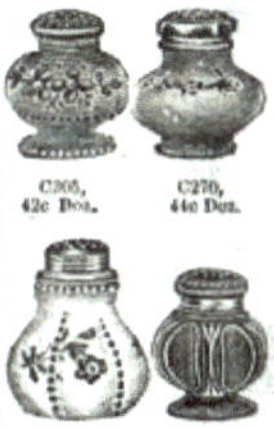

C305, 42c Doz. C270, 44c Doz. C283, 44c Doz. C308, 45c Doz.

C270—Richly tinted allover, floral embossed work, patent embossed nickeled tops. Asstd. pink, green and yellow. Doz. **44c**

C283—Extra large melon shape, wide shape, wide base, hand painted, decorations, gilt beaded panels.......Doz. **44c**

C308—Large size, fancy fluted pattern, allover variagated sunset tints, rich gold tracing, heavy embossed nickeled caps. Doz. **45c**

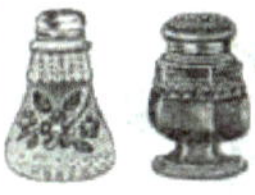

C312, 46c Doz. C307, 47c Doz.

C312—Fancy shape, ht. 3½ in., pure opal, embossed rich colored floral decorations, nickeled caps. Doz. **46c**

C307—Tall Colonial shape, ht. 3½ in., solid pink, blue and green, wide gilt band decoration, heavy embossed nickeled caps. Doz. **47c**

C277—Large fancy twist shape, rich solid tints, floral embossed work in bright colors, nickeled tops. Matches C534 Syrup Pitcher. Doz. **47c**

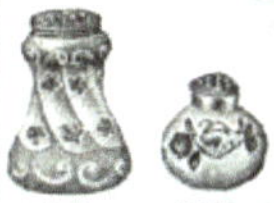

C277, 47c Doz. C286, 80c Doz.

C286—Solid colors, hand painted rose decorations burnt in, heavy silver plated tops. Asstd. red, blue and green.... Doz. **80c**

C272—Tinted and enameled hand painted decorations burnt in. Asstd. pink, blue and green tints.. Doz.. **82c**

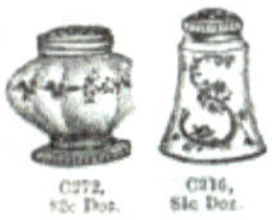

C272, 82c Doz. C316, 84c Doz.

C316—Tall shape with wide base, fancy floral fired decorations forming letters "S" and "P," heavy cast plated tops. Per dozen, **84c**

C317—Tall column shape, asstd. pink, green and light brown tints, hand painted "Old Mill" and scene decorations, cast plated tops......Doz. **85c**

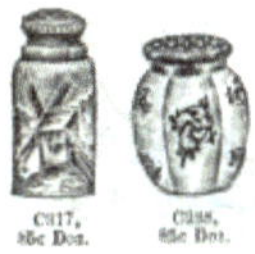

C317, 85c Doz. C288, 85c Doz.

C288—Tinted hand painted decorations burnt in, heavy silver plated tops. Asstd. tints and decorations. Doz. **85c**

GOLD DECORATED S. & P.

Remember -- Our gold decorated is burnt in and will not wear off. *6 salts and 6 peppers in box of 1 doz.*

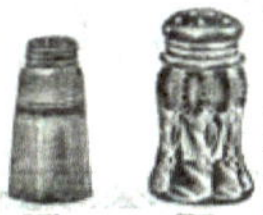

C291, 43c Doz. C330, 79c Doz.

C291—Medium size 1 wide and 2 burnt in gold bands, good nickel caps........ Doz. **43c**

C330—Heavy crystal, fancy tall shape, rich gold decorations, heavy cast plated top. Doz. **79c**

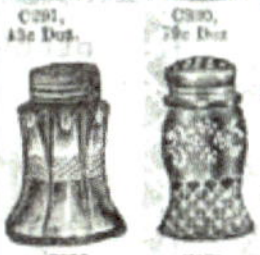

C332, 79c Doz. C333, 79c Doz.

C332—Ht. 3¼ in., panel pattern, rich rose red color, elaborate gold decorations,..Doz. **79c**

C333—Fancy shape, ht. 3¼ in., heavy rich ruby glass, hand painted enamel and gold decorations, gold bands round top, heavy nickeled dome tops. Doz. **79c**

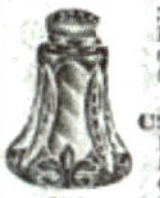

C285, 80c Doz.

C285—Large size, fancy shape, heavily embossed, rich panel and fleur de lis pattern, heavy gold decorations, asstd. green, blue and amethyst, heavy cast plated tops. Doz. **80c**

EXTRA SIZE SALT SHAKER.

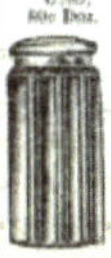

C280—Ht. 4 in., deep cut beaded panel pattern, heavy nickeled restaurant or hotel size.. Doz. **72c**

INDIVIDUAL SALTS.

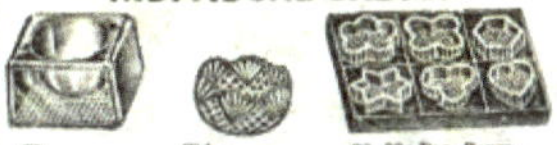

C5, C5½, C3, 80c Doz. Boxes.

C5—Extra heavy, square shape, 1¼x1¼, brilliant crystal, diamond cut bottom, 2 doz. in box..........Doz. **16c**

C5½—Cut diamond, large size, diam. 2 in., deep shape, rich strawberry and fan cut diamond pattern. 1 doz. in box..............Doz. **16c**

C3—Fancy shapes, average size 1¼ in., brilliant cut diamond pattern. Asstd. shapes in box of 6. 1 doz. boxes in pkg. Doz. boxes, **80c**

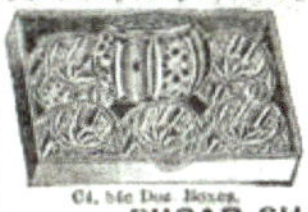

C4, 84c Doz. Boxes.

C4—6 salts of choice pattern in a box to run at 10c per box. 1 doz. boxes in pkg. Doz. boxes, **84c**

SUGAR SHAKERS.

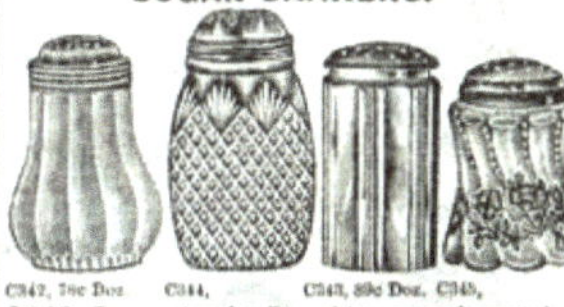

C342, 78c Doz. C344, C343, 89c Doz. C345,

C342—Large size, ht. 5 in, thin pressed crystal, optic pattern, nickeled dome top. 1 doz. in box..........Doz. **78c**

C344—Extra large size, ht. 5¼ in., extra heavy deep cut pattern, nickled dome top..Doz. **84c**

C343—Large size, ht. 4¾ in., extra heavy brilliant prism pattern, heavy cast plated top. 1 doz. in box..........Doz. **89c**

C345—Ht. 4 in., opal glass, fancy twist column shape, rich gold beaded and hand painted floral decorations, heavy cast plated tops. Per dozen, ***89c**

CASTER SETS.

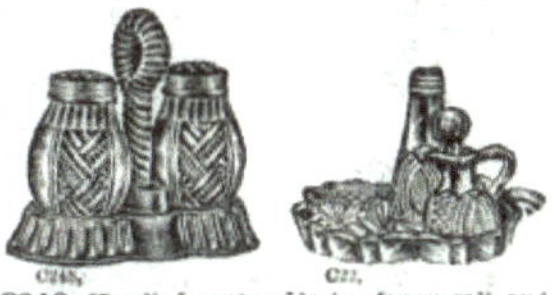

C248, C22,

C248—Handled caster, 5¾ in. fancy salt and pepper shakers, nickel plated caps, fancy cut pattern. Each set in carton, 1 doz. sets in pkg..........Doz. sets, **79c**

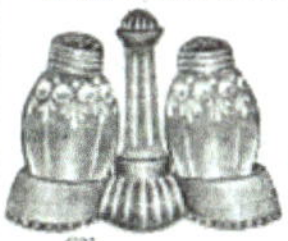

C21,

C22—Open salt, tall pepper with nickel top, small oil or vinegar with glass stopper, 4 in. handled tray. Each set in box. Doz. sets, **85c**

C21—1 salt and 1 pepper shaker, stand with heavy glass handle. Each in pasteboard box. Doz. sets, **84c**

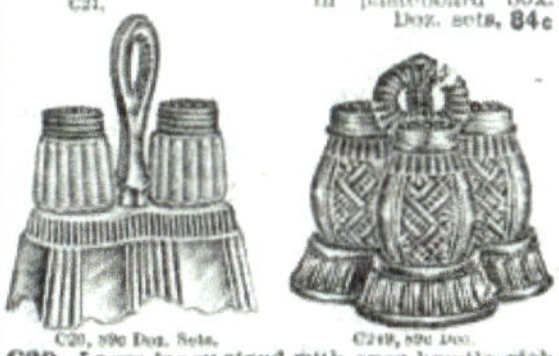

C20, 89c Doz. Sets. C249, 89c Doz.

C20—Large fancy stand with open handle, rich optic salt and pepper with nickeled caps. Each set in carton. 1 doz. pkg..Doz. sets, **89c**

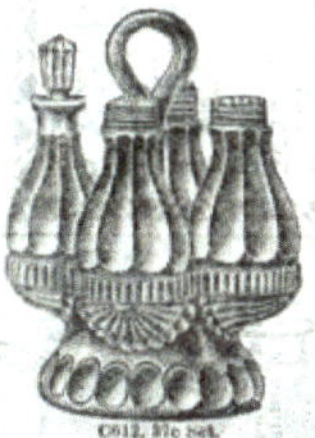

C612, 37c Set.

C249 :. Triangular shape handled caster, diam. of base 5½ in., fancy salt and pepper shakers and mustard pot, nickeled tops, rich new cut patterns. Each set in carton, ½ doz. sets in pkg. Doz. sets, **$1.89**

C612—Large size high foot, heavy glass handle, large salt and pepper shaker, mustard, with nickel plated tops, vinegar or oil bottle with glass stopper. Each set in carton. Set, **37c**

DECORATED PLAQUES.

1 doz. in box.

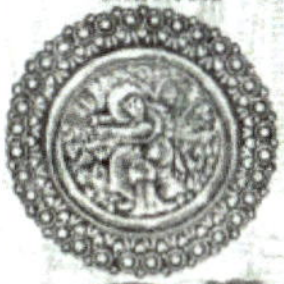

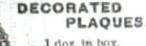

C615—5½ in., scalloped openwork edge, etched centers in asstd. subjects, such as Mary and her little Lamb, Children at Play, etc....Doz. **42c**

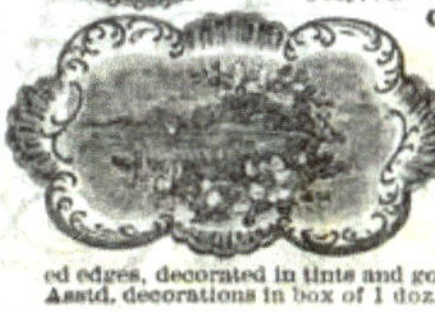

C622—Oblong shape, 9x6 centers decorated in rich hand painted floral designs, fancy embossed edges, decorated in tints and gold bronze. Asstd. decorations in box of 1 doz..Doz. **89c**

5 PIECE CRUET SETS.

Each set in package.

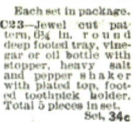

C23—Jewel cut pattern, 6¾ in. round deep footed tray, vinegar or oil bottle with stopper, heavy salt and pepper shaker with plated top, footed toothpick holder. Total 5 pieces in set. Set, **34c**

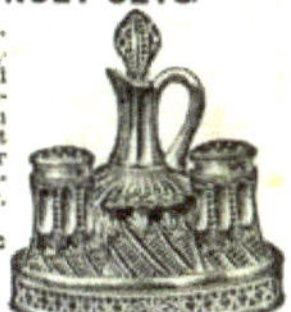

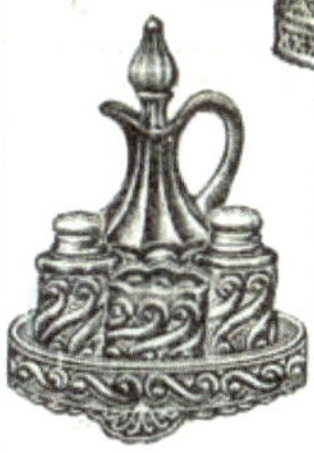

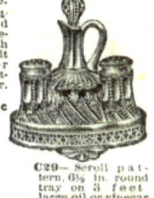

C29—Scroll pattern, 6½ in. round tray on 3 feet large oil or vinegar bottle with glass stopper, large salt shaker with nickel top, pepper shaker to match salt, toothpick. 3 colors, green, blue and crystal. Set, **35c**

Note—Order at least 3 sets and thereby get the full assortment of colors.

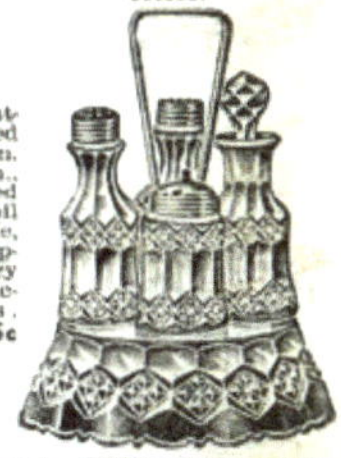

C24—Deep cut pattern, large spaced glass base, diam. at bottom 7 in., heavy nickeled handle; fancy oil or vinegar bottle, large salt and pepper shaker, fancy mustard pot, nickel plated tops. Set, **35c**

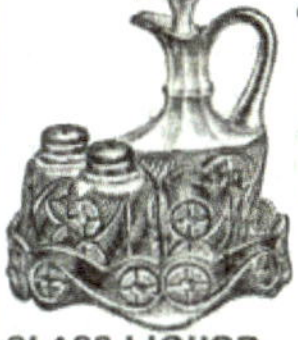

C29½—Rich pattern, extra heavy and brilliant pieces. 6½ in. deep footed tray; large oil or vinegar bottle, ht. 7½ in.; salt and pepper shaker, cast plated top; fancy toothpick holder. Each set in pkg., asstd. colors — crystal, blue and green. Set, **35c**

GLASS LIQUOR SETS.

Each set in box. (**No pkg. charge.**)

C16—Large handled decanter, ht. 8 in. with fancy glass stopper, six 2 oz. ground bottom tumblers, deep cut diamond pattern. Set, **33c**

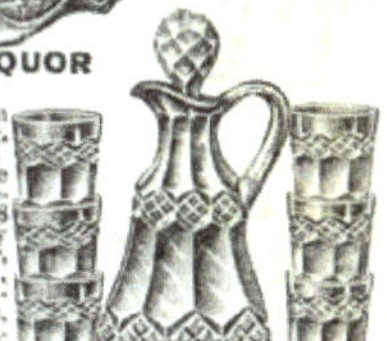

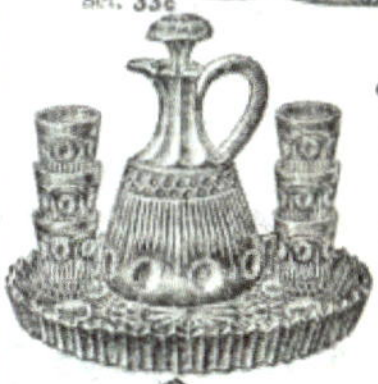

C17—8½ in. deep round tray, large handled decanter with stopper, 6 glasses, rich jewel cut pattern. Total, 8 pieces in set. Set, **35c**

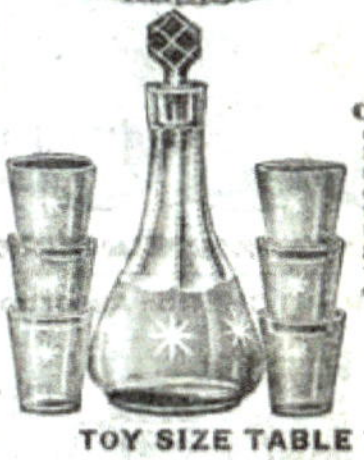

C19—8 in. decanter with imitation cut stopper, six 1½ oz. ground bottom tumblers, both decanter and tumblers with genuine deep cut stars. Set, **48c**

TOY SIZE TABLE WARE.

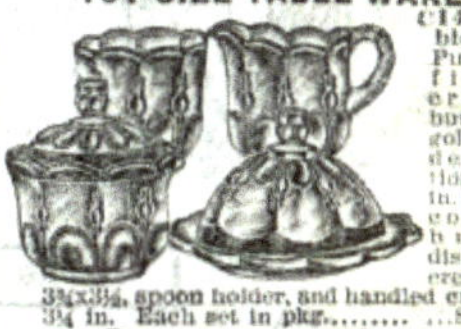

C14½, Table Set—Pure full finish crystal, burnt in gold band decorations. 5½ in. flanged covered butter dish, covered sugar 3¾x3¾, spoon holder, and handled creamer, 3¾ in. Each set in pkg.........Set, **35c**

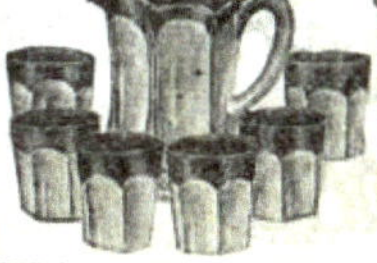

C18, Water Set—Heavy wide burnt in gold band decorations, tall tankard jug, ht. 4¾ in., rich colonial crystal pattern, 6 small tumblers. Each set in pkg. Set, **35c**

We Bid for Your Business on the Merits of Our Merchandise and the Lowness of Our Prices.

"DIAMOND CUT" SPOONHOLDER.

A ready seller at 10 cents.

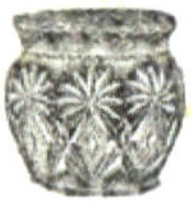

C547—Ht. 4¼ in., fancy swell shape, heavy cut diamond pattern, full finished crystal. 1 doz. in pkg. Per dozen, **78c**

CREAM PITCHERS.

1 doz. in box—*no pkg. charge.*

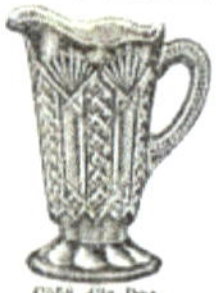

C558, 42c Doz.

C550, 42c Doz.

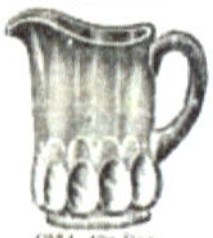

C554, 43c Doz.

C558—Ht. 5¾ in., brilliant pattern, well made and finished.............Doz. **42c**

C550—Tiffany pattern, fancy bottom, fluted tops, heavy handle.....Doz. **42c**

C554—Ht. 4½ in., tankard shape, large handle, plain with deep optic flutes around base......Doz. **43c**

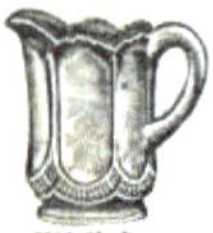

C556, 80c Doz.

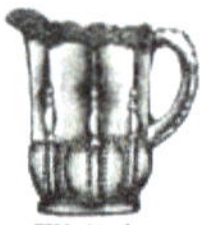

C555, 80c Doz.

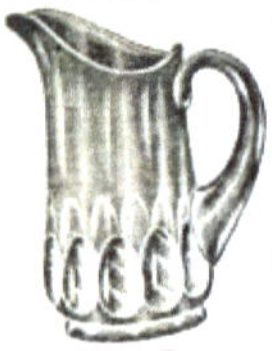

C557, 96c Doz.

C556—Tall tankard shape, ht. 4¼ in., mirror panel pattern, rich wide burnt in gold band edge. Doz. **80c**

C555—Fancy tankard, ht. 4 in., optic panel design, fancy handle, wide gold band edge. Doz. **80c**

C557—Tall tankard shape, 6¾ in., large *stuck* handle, plain with heavy deep cut flutes around wide base........Doz. **96c**

"SANITARY" COVERED PITCHER.

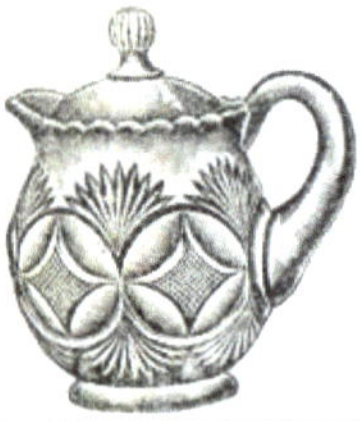

Entirely new. The housewife will appreciate its many uses.

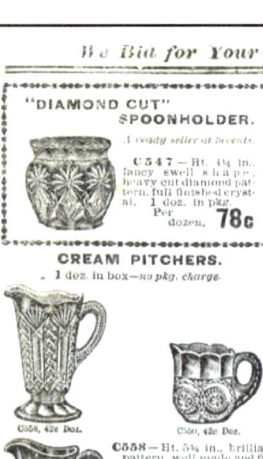

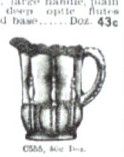

C689 — Extra large, full ½ gal. ht. 9 in., heavy rich cut pattern, large stuck handle and fancy cover. Each in pkg. Each, **37c**

GLASS SYRUP PITCHERS.

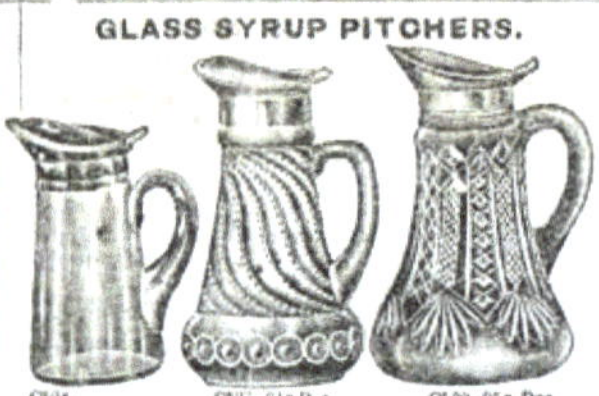

C524, C527, 81c Doz. C530, 95c Doz

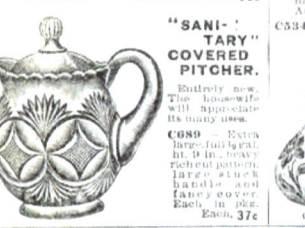

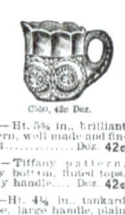

C524—8 oz. tankard shape, genuine stuck handle, spring top, 5¼ in. 1 doz. in box.........Doz. **75c**

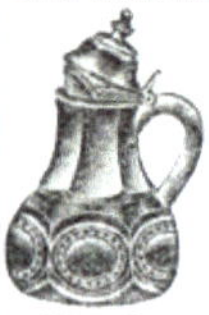

C529, 95c Doz.

C527—About 9 oz. fancy tall serpentine pattern, wide base, large handle, ht. 6¾ in. 1 doz. box. Doz. **81c**

C530—14 oz. tall fancy shape, wide base, rich brilliant cut pattern, spring top. ht. 6¾ in.... Doz. **95c**

C528—Ht. 6 in., glass lip, crystal jewel band around bulb base, cut flute effect neck, heavy nickel plated Britannia top 1 doz. box...Doz. **$1.20**

C539 — 10 oz., ht. 6¾ in. heavy rich colonial flute pattern, nickel plated dome top. ½ doz. in box. Doz. **$1.69**

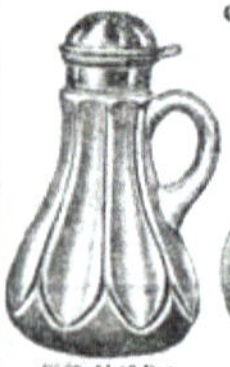

C539, $1.69 Doz.

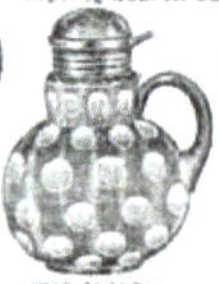

C537, $1.72 Doz.

C537—16 oz. **opalescent blown glass**, polka dot pattern, nickeled dome top. Asstd. flint, blue and green. 1 doz. box...Doz. **$1.72**

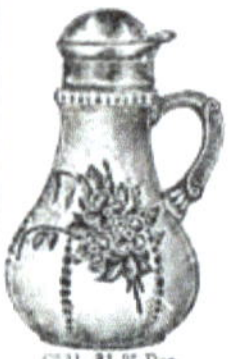

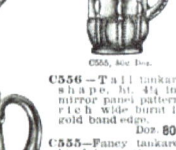

C531, $1.95 Doz.

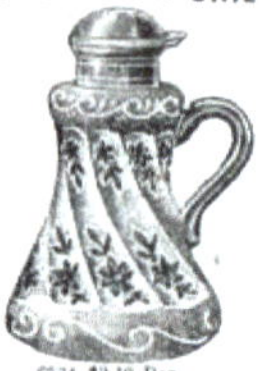

C534, $2.10 Doz.

C531—13 oz., nickeled dome top, gilt beaded, hand painted floral decorations, **opal body.** Asstd. decorations in box of ½ doz. Doz. **$1.95**

C534—16 oz., tall fancy shape, embossed twist pattern, ht. 7 in. nickeled dome top. **Tinted opal body,** hand painted floral designs. Each in carton ½ doz. pkg., asstd. pink, red, yellow.......Doz. **$2.10**

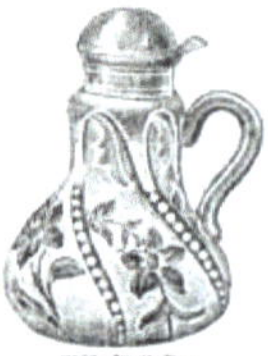

C535, $2.25 Doz.

C535—16 oz. low fancy shape, ht. 6½ in. **fancy opal**, heavily embossed and richly decorated in asstd. tints and bright colored floral design, best nickeled dome top. Each in carton, ½ doz. in pkg., asstd. green, red and pink. Doz. **$2.25**

HOTEL "SPECIAL" ASSORTMENT.

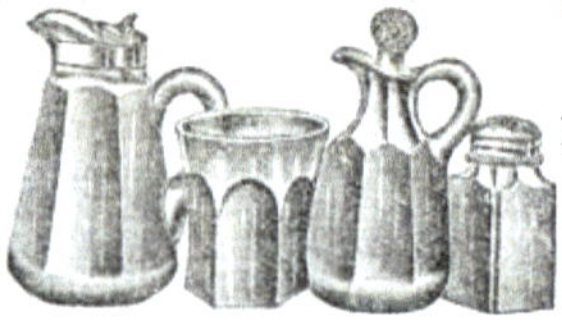

Four staple sellers at an attractive price.

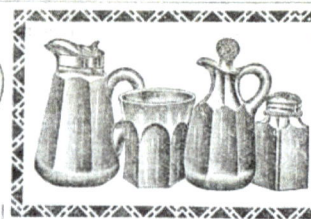

C898—Finest quality crystal, extra heavy rich colonial pattern. Asst. comprises:

- 1 doz. 8 oz. syrup pitchers, cast nickel plated tops,
- 1 doz. 8 oz. oil or vinegar bottles.
- 1 " large salt and pepper shakers, heavy cast nickel plated tops.
- 3 doz. ground bottom tumblers.

Total 6 doz. in wood case, sold by case only. Wt. 70 lbs. Per dozen, **78c**

VINEGAR OR OIL BOTTLES.

1 doz. in box.

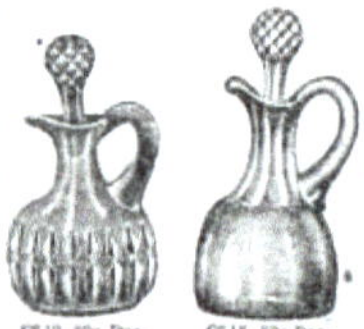

C512, 80c Doz. C518, 82c Doz.

C512—Extra heavy rich pattern about 5 oz. Doz. **80c**

C518, Plain—Ht. 4¾ in., about 5 oz., rich plain body with fluted neck and stopper. Doz. **82c**

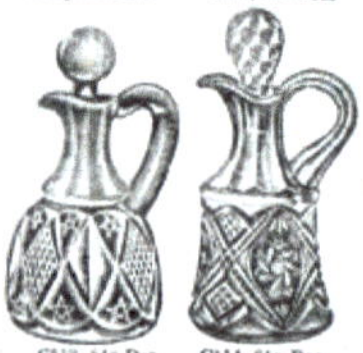

C513, 84c Doz. C514, 84c Doz.

C513—Diamond imit. cut glass, heavy and brilliant. Glass stopper, 5 oz...Doz. **84c**

C514—Tall tankard shape, 4½ oz., rich and heavy deep cut pattern. Doz. **84c**

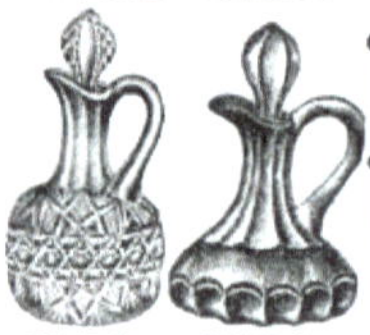

C515, 85c Doz. C511, 87c Doz.

C515 — Large size, full ht. 5¾ in., rich pattern, fancy stopper....Doz. **85c**

C511 — Large size, fancy low shape, ht. 6¾ in., almost plain with deep optic flutes, fancy stopper. Doz. **87c**

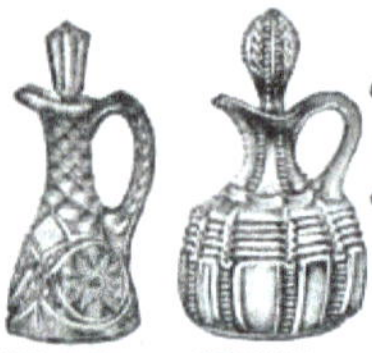

C510, 88c Doz. C516, $1.15 Doz.

C510 — New heavy all over cut pattern, large size. Doz. **88c**

C516—9 oz., rich cut pattern, fancy cut stopper. Doz. **$1.15**

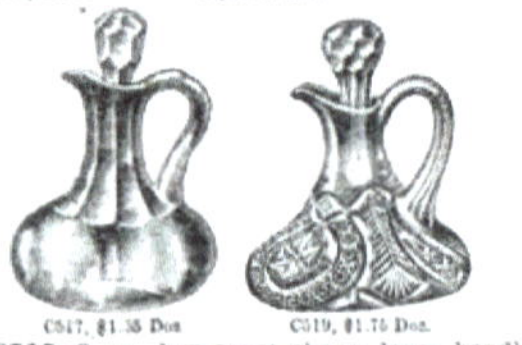

C517, $1.35 Doz C519, $1.75 Doz.

C517—9 oz., low squat shape, large handle, fancy imit. cut stopper, heavy crystal. Hotel or restaurant size. ½ doz. in box. Doz. **$1.35**

C519—Vinegar bottle Present ware, large size, low fancy shape, diam. at base, 4¾ large handle and fancy ground stopper. ½ doz. in pkg.......................Doz. **$1.75**

VINEGAR OR OIL BOTTLE ASST.

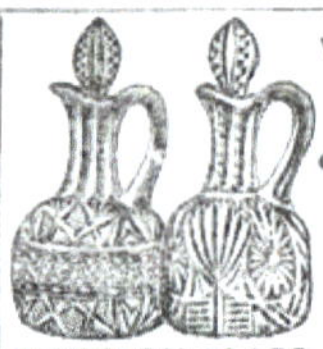

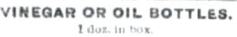

C1412, "Delmonico"—Medium size, purest crystal, genuine cut pattern. 1 doz. each of 2 patterns. 2 doz. in case, sold by case only Doz. **81c**

SANITARY GLASS KITCHEN UTENSILS.

Have proven their popularity over same articles of wood or tin by enormous increase of sales during last few years. 1 doz. in pkg.

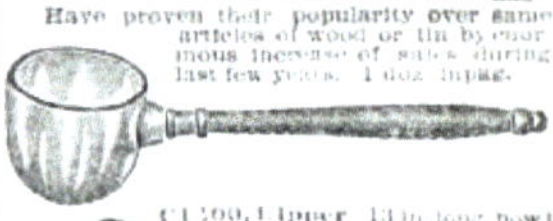

C1300, Dipper 13 in. long bowl about the size of a tea cup, black enamel handle, extra heavy, wt. 10 lbs.........Doz. **72c**

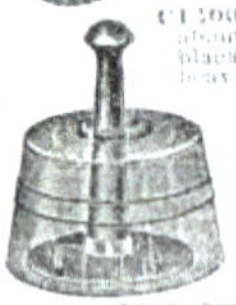

C1443, Homer Butter Mold—Crystal bowl shape mold, diam. at top 3¾ in., bottom 4¾, ht. 3, with 5 in. hardwood handle and 3⅛ in. glass stamp, imprints cow or clover design. 2 stamps with each, wt. 35 lbs. Doz. **$1.45**

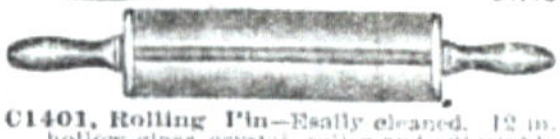

C1401, Rolling Pin—Easily cleaned. 12 in. hollow glass crystal roller and adjustable hardwood handles, full lgth. 21 in. Dz. **$2.25**

5c Glass Kitchen Utensil Asst.

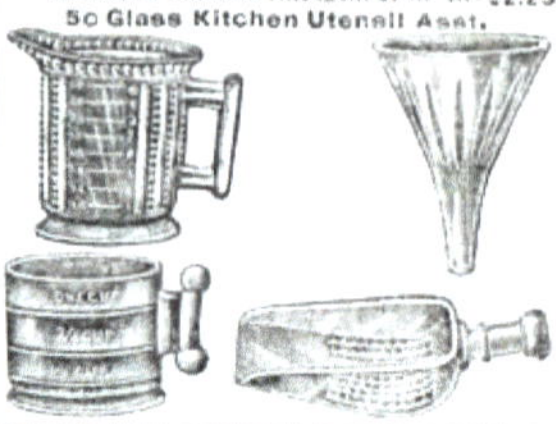

C1410: 1 doz. graduated measuring pitchers, 4x4¼. 1 doz. handle glass scoops 3x6¾. 1 doz. glass funnels, 3¾ in. diam. 1 doz. measuring cups. 4 doz. in wood case, sold by case only.............................Doz. **39c**

GRADUATED COOKING CUPS.

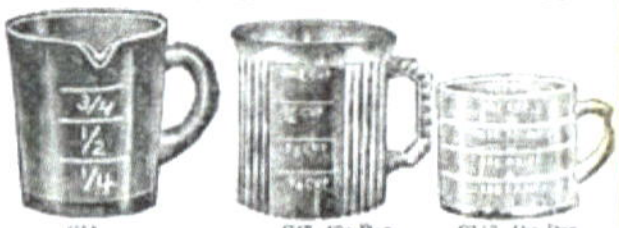

C14, C47, 43c Doz. C143, 48c Doz.

C14—Large size, capacity 1 cup, graduated for measuring ¼, ½, ¾ and 1 cup. Ht. 3⅝ in. Large handle and **good pouring lip.** Doz. **42c**

C47—Large size, capacity 8 oz., graduated for measuring ozs., cups, etc......... Doz. **43c**

C143—Heavy and well finished, capacity 1 cup, graduated spaces measuring ¼, ⅓, ½ and ¾ cups...............................Doz. **48**

"DIME" CREAM PITCHER ASSORTMENT.

Pattern, quality and price combined make this an exceptionally desirable assortment.

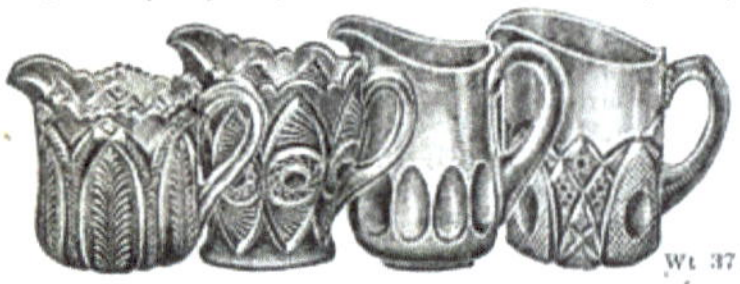

C1451 — ½ doz. each of 4 rich patterns, deep cut, French plate, feather, panel and rosette design. All large sizes, average ht. about 5 in., finest quality full finished crystal. Total 2 doz. in case. Sold by case only. Wt. 37 lbs. Per dozen, **80c**

SYRUP PITCHERS—Assortments.

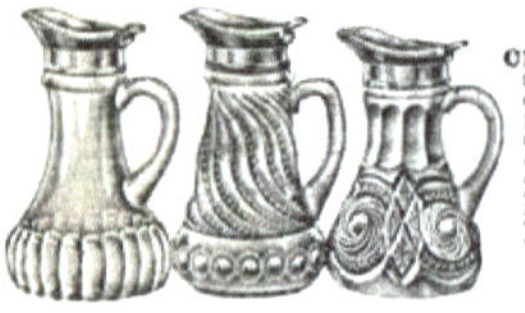

C1301 — Ht. 6¼ in., rich plain and fluted patterns in purest crystal, wide spread base, good spring top. ⅔ doz. of each style. Total 2 doz. in case. Wt. 32 lbs. (**No pkg. charge.**). Doz. **87c**

NO PKG. CHARGE.

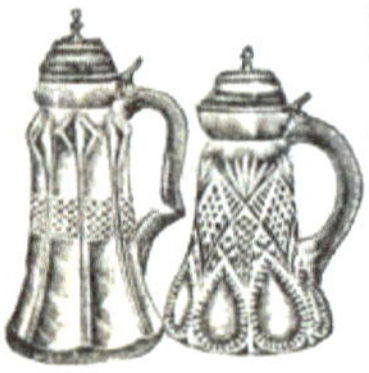

C1302—Ht. about 7 in., glass lip and patent britannia top. Wide spread base, one style in panel design; 1 cut diamond pattern. Both richly finished. 1 doz. each of 2 sizes. 2 doz. in case. Wt. 35 lbs. (**No pkg. charge.**)............Doz. **$1.15**

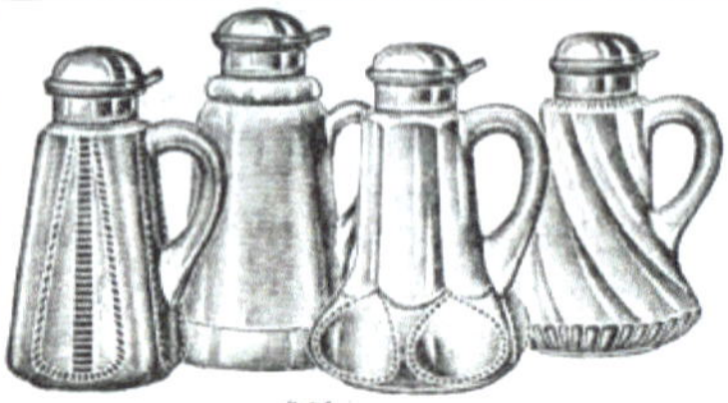

C1305

C1305 — ½ doz. each of 4 styles, all large fancy shapes, **capacity 16 to 18 ounces,** nickel plated dome tops with patent clinch collars (no plaster.) Total 2 doz. in case. Wt. 47 lbs........Doz. **$1.55**

(**NO PKG. CHARGE.**)

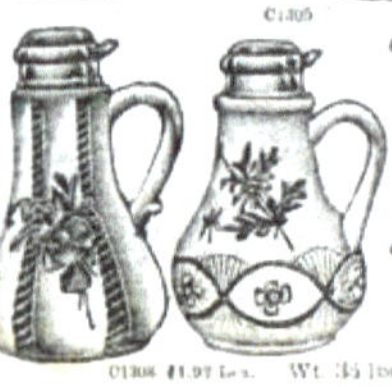

C1308 $1.92 Doz.

C1308: Large size, 13 oz., **opal** embossed and hand painted, floral and gold bronze decorations, heavy nickel plated dome tops. 1 doz. each of 2 styles. 2 Wt. 35 lbs. doz. in case.....Doz. **$1.92**

DECORATED OPAL SYRUP PITCHER ASST.

Striking values to retail at 25c.

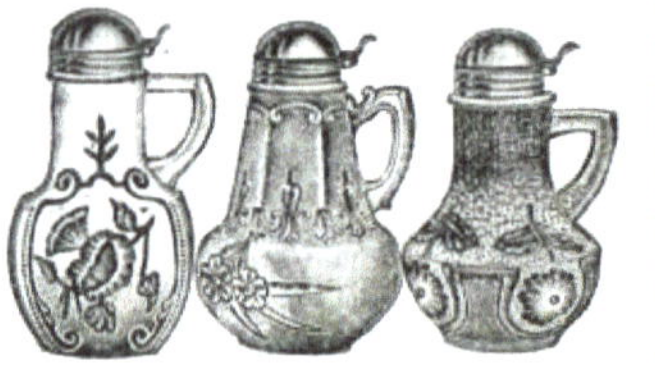

C1309—Large sizes, average ht. 6½ in., heavy embossed floral and gold decorations, asstd. rich tints. nickel plated dome tops. ⅔ doz. each of 3 patterns. Total 2 doz. in case, sold by case only. Wt. 40 lbs. Per dozen, **$1.67**

(**NO PKG. CHARGE.**)

"CUT JEWEL" TUMBLER AND PITCHER.

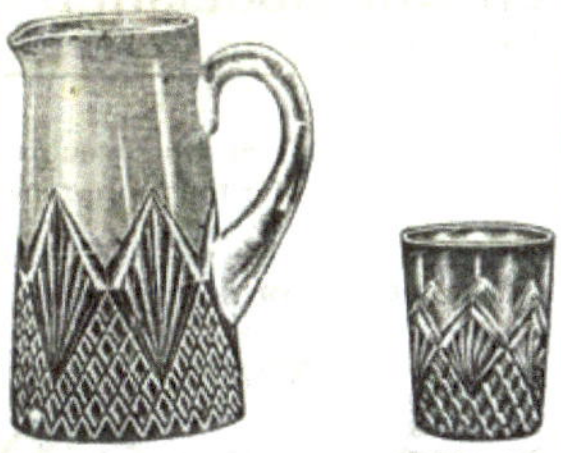

C12—Large ½ gal. tankard pitcher, ht. 8¾ in., large genuine stuck handle, extra heavy and brilliant genuine deep cut pattern, ground and polished mirror bottom. Each in pkg. Each, **39c**

C180 — Large size, thin plain edge. 1 doz. in box....Doz. **67c**

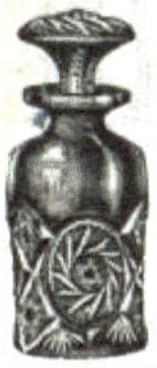

"PRESCUT" COLOGNE BOTTLE.

C545 — Tall fancy cylindrical shape, ht. 6¾ in., with fancy cut ground stopper, extra heavy rich deep cut design, brilliantly fire polished. ½ doz. in pkg.......... Doz. **$1.15**

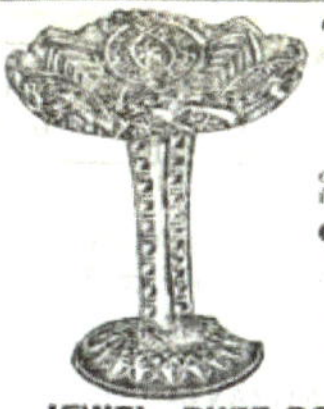

"PRESCUT" HIGH FOOTED COMPORT.

A popular seller at a price which makes it doubly interesting.

C974 — Large size, diam. 6¾, ht. 7 in., slightly turned up sides, heavy imitation cut stem, brilliant star pattern foot. 6 in case. Each **29c**

JEWEL, PUFF BOXES, ETC.

1 doz. in pkg., *no package charge.*

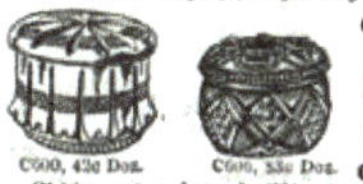

C600, 42c Doz. C606, 83c Doz.

C600. Diam. 2⅜ in. pure crystal, panel and cut diamond design, deep cut glass cover. Doz. **42c**

C606—Diam. 2¾ in. extra deep, brilliant crystal with solid burnt in gold decorated cover in green jeweled effect. .... Doz. **83c**

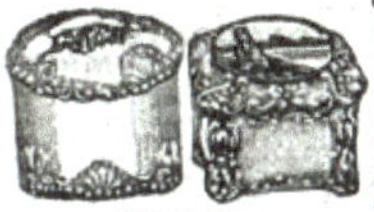

C603, 89c Doz.

C603: Round and square, both extra large, fancy embossed, rich tints, hand painted floral and water scenes and gold bronze, 6 of each shape. Doz. **89c**

BIRD CAGE FITTINGS—*1 doz. in box.*

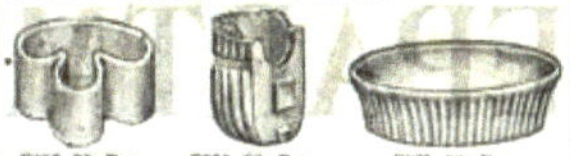

C637, 28c Doz. C638, 32c Doz. C635, 36c Doz.

C637, Opal Seed or Water Cup — Pure opal, the largest patent shape, fits all cages. Doz. **28c**

C638, Opal Seed Cup— Pure white, fancy ribbed design, ht. 2¾ in., patent knob for fastening to cage.......................... Doz. **32c**

C635, Opal Bird Baths—Fancy ribbed sides, 4½x2⅝, footed and fancy pressed bottom. Doz. **36c**

C636—As C635, 5⅛x3⅜................. Doz. **39c**

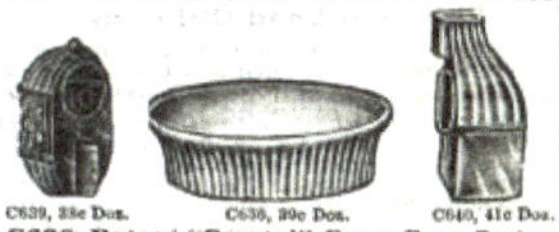

C639, 38c Doz. C636, 39c Doz. C640, 41c Doz.

C639, Patent "Crystal" Cage Cup—Projection by which it is held between the wires of any cage. .... Doz. **38c**

C640, Patent Cage Cup—Large size, 3 corner shape, crystal glass patent knob at top, fits any cage............ .. .. Doz. **41c**

C325½, Opal Seed or Water Cup—Regulation shape, 2 openings, 2¾x2, pure opal, rich tints, hand painted floral decorations, asstd. to the doz., tints and decorations burnt in .... Doz. **48c**

PACKAGE CHARGE ABOLISHED

On All Glassware and Crockery.

MILK BOTTLE CAPS.

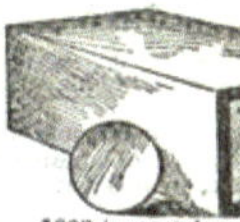

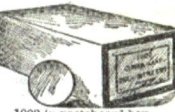

C1895, "Clover Leaf": Not the common goods, but *of superior quality*, full wt., thoroughly waterproof. Ft. full size milk bottles.

1000 in pasteboard box.......... Per M, **19c**

8000 in bushel basket, *no charge for basket.* Per M, **17c**

25000 in barrel..................... Per M, **16c**

C1890, "Sanitary": Toughest stock, paraffined. Turned, preventing leakage. Can be inserted without breaking.

1000 in pasteboard box. Per M, **25c**

8000 in strong, heavy bushel basket, *basket free*.... Per M, **24c**

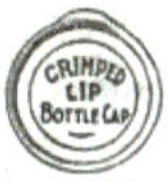

C1898, Crimped Lip: Extra tough stock, crimped edges, which prevent leaking. This cap is so made that to remove same from battle, the lip is used in place of some sharp instrument, thus making it very handy. 1000 in box. Per M, **33c**

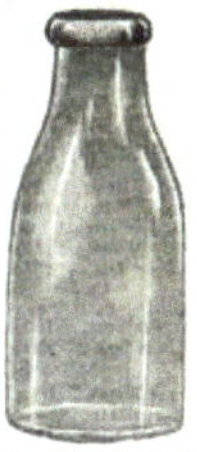

"COMMON SENSE" GLASS MILK BOTTLES.

—Crystal glass, *guaranteed extra quality*, very heavy and thick. Do not confuse with the green bottles which make milk look blue. Fruit, preserves and pickles are safely put up in these bottles simply by pouring melted paraffine or common sealing wax on top of the cap.

Each size packed in crates of 6 doz., *no charge for crate.*

½ pt.	6 doz.	in crate	...	**33c**
1 "	6 "	"	....	**39c**
1 qt.	6 "	"	....	**55c**

DECORATED OPAL BOX ASSORTMENT.

Newest and best ones on the market.

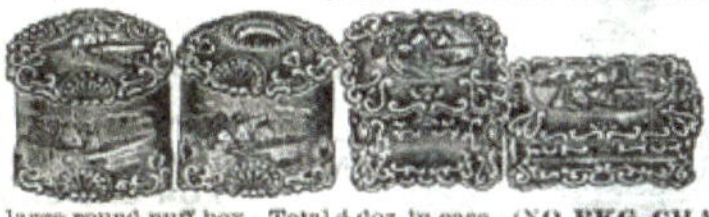

C1452 — All opal, new shapes, fancy embossed, each style in new hand painted Holland scene and floral decorations with gold bronze tracings. Assortment comprises 1 doz. each of following: large square puff box; fancy hair receiver; oblong jewel box; large round puff box. Total 4 doz. in case. Wt. 47 lbs. (**NO PKG. CHARGE.**) Per dozen, **88c**

MISCELLANEOUS SPECIALTIES.

1 doz. in box.

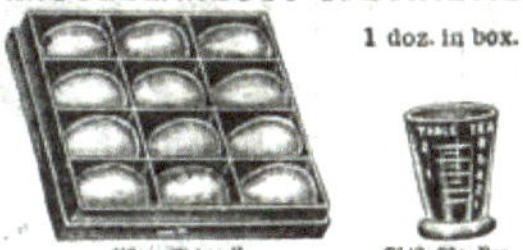

"Sure Thing." C142, 37c Doz.

"Sure Thing" Nest Egg—Heavy opal glass. "Firsts." (Case of 1 gro. $1.75 gro.) Doz. **17c**

C142, Lipped Medicine Glass—Has measuring scale for tea spoon, table spoon, etc. Doz. **37c**

TUBULAR LANTERNS.

Standard crank tubular. Positively best ever made.

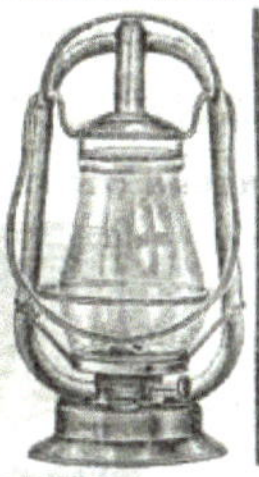

NO PACKAGE CHARGE.

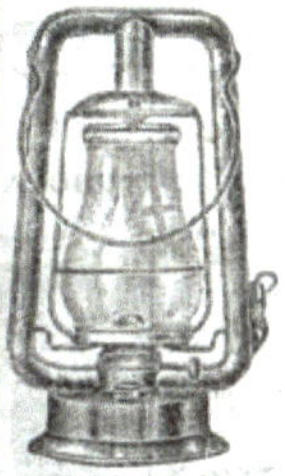

C50. C55, $4.20 Doz.

C50—Large fount, outside filler, concaved top, heavy round tubes, strong wire guard and bail handle. No. 0 rimmed steel burner, automatic steel lift, globe being raised or lowered by moving wire at top. Complete with globes. 1 doz. in case. Wt. 36 lbs. (**NO PACKAGE CHARGE.**) Doz. **$3.95**

C55—Side lift. Solid stamped base, extra large oil fount, outside filler, No. 0 brass burner, strong tubes made from one piece heavy tin, bail handle and guard. Globe is raised by improved side lift crank which throws globe upwards and outward, easy access to burner. Complete with globe. 1 doz. in case (**NO PACKAGE CHARGE.**) Doz. **$4.20** Wt. 37 lbs.

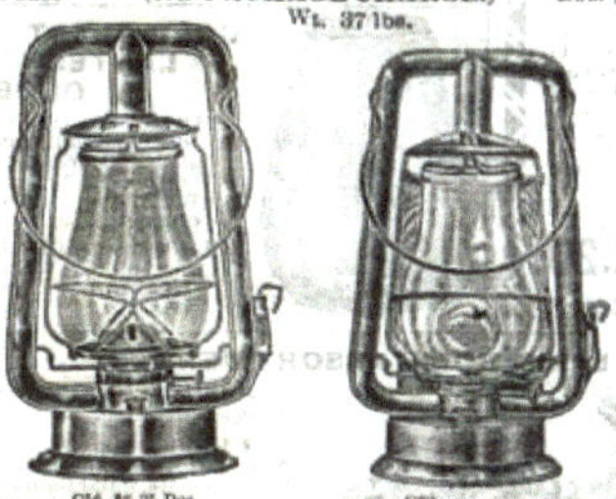

C56, $6.25 Doz. C60.

C56—Side lift, most convenient and substantial lantern offered at price. Solid stamped base, solid extra oil fount with outside filler, best No. 2 brass burner, strong tubes, made from one piece heavy tin, bail handle and guard. Globe raised by improved side lift crank which throws globe upward and outward, giving easy access to burner. Complete with globe. 1 doz. in case.................................. Doz. **$6.25**

(**NO PACKAGE CHARGE.**)

C60. Stable or Dashboard Lantern—Size and style as C56. Best blued japanned tin with reflector and firmly attached wire spring hook. Made to fit dashboard of wagon or carriage, or to hang up in stable. Fitted with bullseye globe. ½ doz. in case. Wt. 28 lbs.... .... Doz. **$6.40**

(**NO PACKAGE CHARGE**)

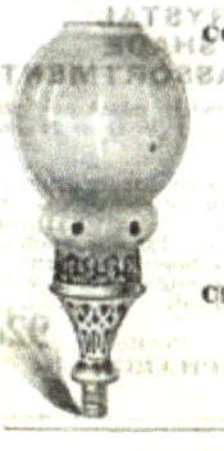

A SPECIAL GAS LAMP.

C9: Especially made for natural gas. Can also be adjusted to artificial gas. Has leather packed regulator that absolutely prevents gas leaking. A high class burner built on correct principle. Lindsay air hole globe. Each in box. .... Doz. **$5.25**

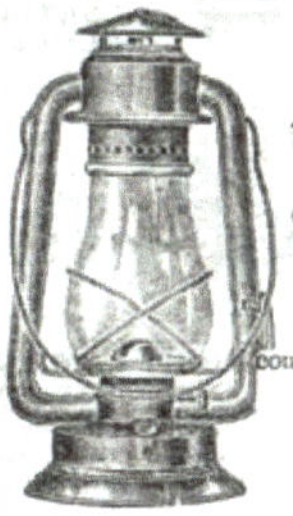

TUBULAR LANTERNS —Continued

C65, Celebrated "Cold Blast"—Perfect combustion, flame being wind proof. Ht. without handle 15 in., heavy block tin, oil tank, outside filler, No. 2 brass burner, crank lift for raising and lowering globe, bail handle and guard. ½ doz. in case. Complete with globes. Wt. 24 lbs. Doz. **$7.75**

(NO PACKAGE CHARGE.)

STORE OR HALL LAMPS.

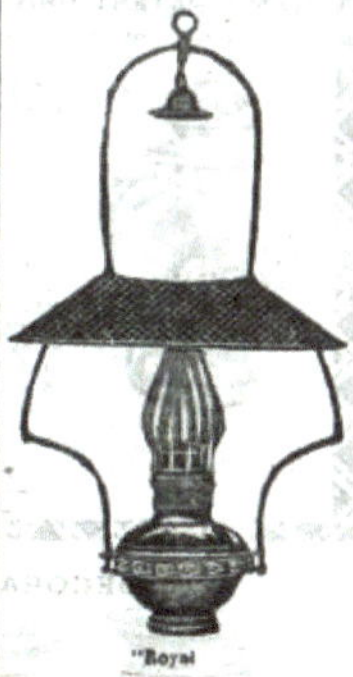

"Royal"

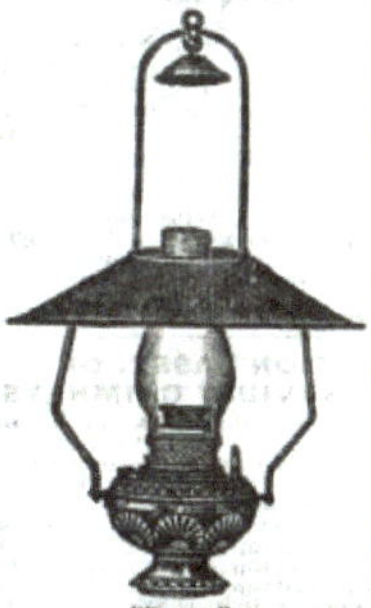

"Banner."

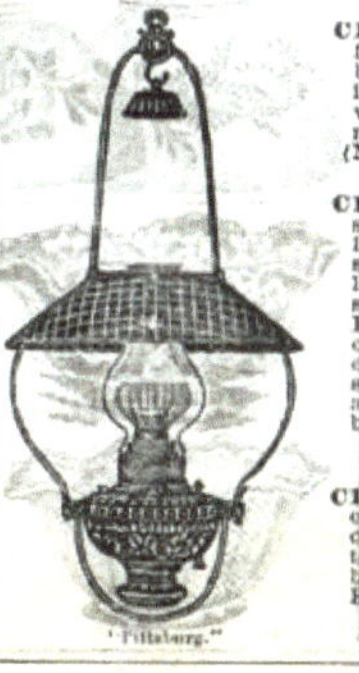

"Pittsburg."

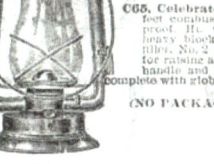

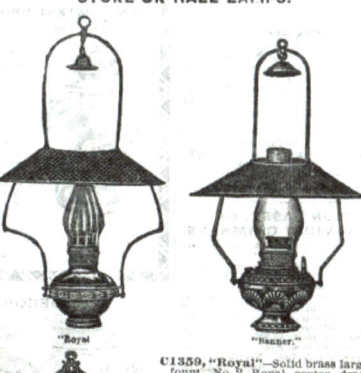

C1359, "Royal"—Solid brass large fount. No. 2 Royal center draft burner, oil drip cup, large harp, 15 in. embossed tin shade, complete with smoke bell, wick and chimney. Each in box. Wt. 19 lbs. (**NO PKG. CHARGE**). Each, **$1.69**

C1358, "Pittsburg"—Non-explosive, burns 10 hours without refilling. Perfect draft, no dirt, no odor, smallest wick exposure of any lamp made. Patent dial indicator showing quantity of oil in lamp. Extra feeder wick and oil drip cup on handle of tube to carry any overflow back to wick. 20 in. tin shade. No. 3 burner, fount, wick and chimney. Each complete in box, wt. 24 lbs. Each, **$2.35** (**NO PKG. CHARGE.**)

C1357, "Banner"—Has extra feeder wick and oil drip cup on inside of tube to carry any overflow back to wick. 20 in. tin shade. No. 3 burner, fount, wick and chimney. Each in box complete. Wt. 25 lbs. Each, **$2.60**

(**NO PKG. CHARGE.**)

COMPLETE GAS PORTABLES.

All except C1530 fitted with the celebrated "Lindsay" burner and air hole glassware. Each in pkg., *no charge for pkg.*

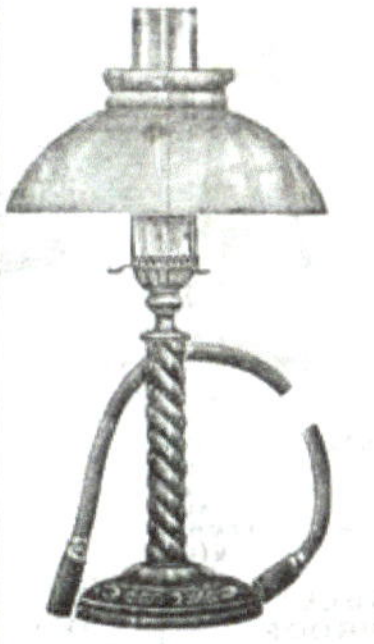

C1530, 95c Each.

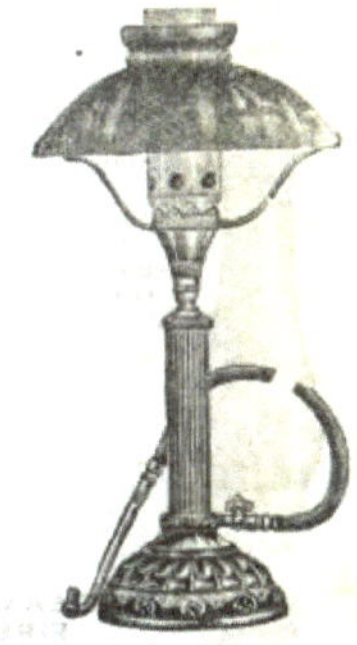

C1532, $2.30 Each.

C1530: Heavy twist column design, maroon enameled black metal trimmings, fancy black metal base. Complete with 6 ft. patent end tubing, post burner, special loop mantles, 8 in. flint glass chimneys, and 10 in. opal shade. Full ht. 19 in. Each, **95c**

C1532: Polished brass, fancy base, ribbed column. 10 in. green shade, Lindsay adjustable burner, mantle, air hole chimney and 6 ft. mohair tubing with gooseneck. Full ht. 20 in. Each, **$2.30**

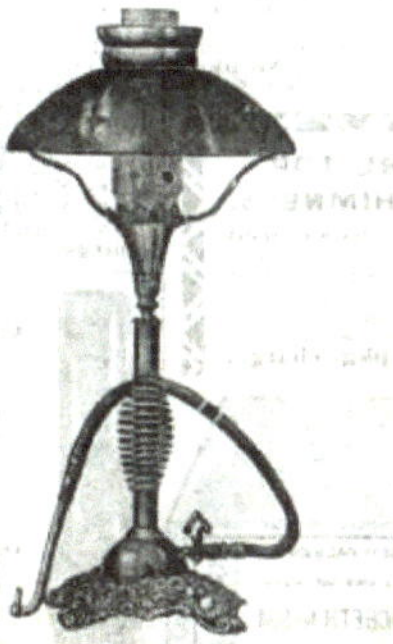

C1533, $3.00 Each.

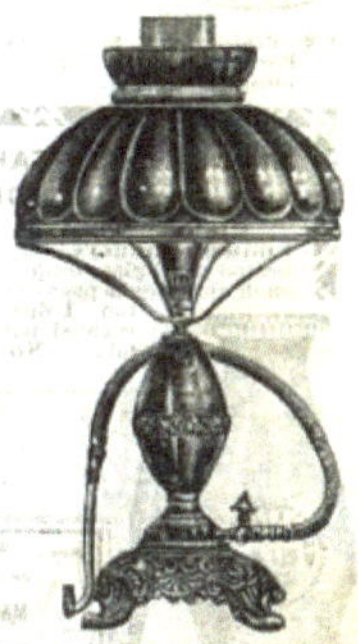

C1534, $3.35 Each.

C1533: Black metal base with green and black combination column. Complete with 10 in. plain green shade, Lindsay adjustable burner, mantle, air hole chimney and 6 ft. mohair tubing with gooseneck. Full ht. 20½ in....... ..... Each, **$3.00**

C1534: Vase shape body of dark coach green metal wreath trimmings, footed black enameled base, 6 ft. mohair tubing with brass connection and gooseneck, Lindsay burner, mantle, air hole chimney, green ribbed shade. Ht. 20 in.. Each, **$3.35**

Add a New Department Every Few Months. The Bigger Your Line the More You Will Sell.

LAMP DEPARTMENT

PACKAGE CHARGE ABOLISHED
On All Glassware and Crockery.

A complete line of the goods that *sell.* When you buy lamps here you have a chance to make more profit for yourself than when you pay market prices. If you will order sample packages you will find that when there are two or more grades of an article ours is never the poorest and USUALLY THE BEST. We have the goods you want and our prices thrive on comparison.

Note that our quotations on Chimneys are now named WITHOUT PACKAGE CHARGE.

LIME CHIMNEYS.

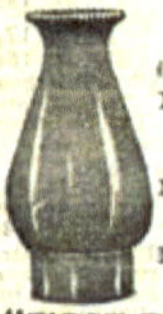

First class quality. Each packed in corrugated tube.

No. C0—Best crystal sun burner, crimped top. 6 doz. in case, wt. 37 lbs. **(No pkg. charge.)** Doz. **24c**

No. C1—As C0, larger. 6 doz. in case, wt. 41 lbs. **(No pkg. charge.)**............Doz. **27c**

No. C2—As C1, but larger. 6 doz. in case, wt. 50 lbs. **(No pkg. charge.)**...........Doz. **37c**

"FIRST TEST" LEAD CHIMNEYS.

(Trademarked.)

"FIRE TEST"

Sold only in pkg. lots.

Strictly "firsts." While not equal in quality and quantity of lead to "Vesuvius," yet will compare in fire or melting test with any lead chimneys at 10 per cent higher prices.

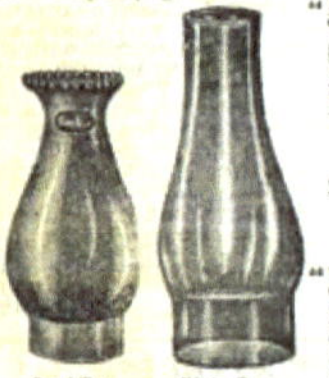

Bead Top. Plain Top.

"Fire Test" Bead Top—German glass. Will not break in hottest fire. *Each wrapped.* No. 1—6 doz. in case, wt. 41 lbs. **(No pkg. chg.)** Doz. **39c**

No. 2—6 doz. in case, wt. 51 lbs. **(No pkg. chg.)** Doz. **50.**

"Fire Test" Plain Top Slim Chimney—Diam. at base 3 in., fits medium and low priced decorated globe lamps.

C2—3 doz. in case. Wt. 24 lbs. Doz. **65c**

"Fire Test" Rochester Lead—Satisfactory in every particular.

No. 2—Diam. at bottom 2⅝ in. 6 doz. in case, wt. 62 lbs. **(No pkg. charge)**......Doz **65c**

No. 3—Diam. at bottom 4 in. 2 doz. in case, wt. 46 lbs. **(No pkg. charge.)** Doz. **$1.25**

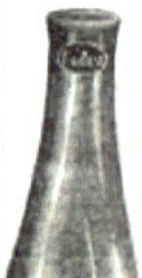

Rochester Lead.

Note—No. 3, fits Rochester, Banner, Yale and Aurora mammoth lamps.

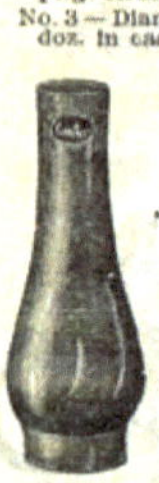

Electric.

"Fire Test" Electric—For use on Climax and other No. 3 wick burners.

No. 2—Diam. at bottom 3 in. 3 doz. in box, wt. 36 lbs. **(No pkg. chge.)** Doz. **67c**

No. 2 Slim Shape—Diam. at bottom 3 in. For globes with 4 in. openings. 3 doz. in box, wt. 37 lbs. **(No pkg. charge.** Doz. **67c**

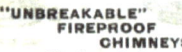

"UNBREAKABLE" FIREPROOF CHIMNEYS.

(Trademarked)

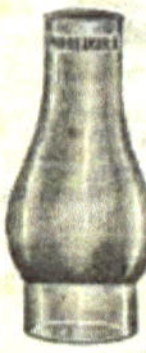

Best and most durable made, extra heavy, finest tempered, pure lead glass, absolutely fire proof, clear as crystal. Each branded "Unbreakable," none genuine without trademark.

C1—Plain top, ht. 7¾ in., diam. at bottom 2¼. Each in attractive carton. 3 doz. in a case. Wt. 31 lbs. **(No pkg. charge)** Doz. **92c**

C2—Plain top, ht. 8¼ in., diam. at bottom 3 in. Each in carton. 3 doz. in case. **(No pkg. charge.)**........................Doz. **$1.10**

MACBETH'S PEARL TOP CHIMNEYS.

Right prices on these well known chimneys. Each bear the celebrated pearl glass trade mark. Note that each chimney is packed in separate carton. 1 doz. in heavy corrugated paper sealed container. **No pkg. charge.**

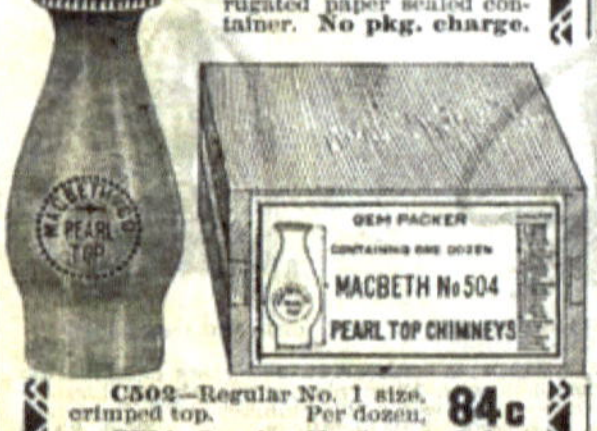

C502—Regular No. 1 size, crimped top. Per dozen, **84c**

C504—Regular, No. 2 size. Per dozen, **96c**

GENUINE "VESUVIUS"

(Trademarked.)

Fireproof Lead Chimneys.

Each chimney packed in attractive pasteboard carton. Reduces breakage to a minimum—clean and convenient to handle.

Have won highest award against all other chimneys in severe fire test competitions. Absolutely the best pure lead chimneys. None genuine without "Vesuvius" etched on chimney. Sold only by case.

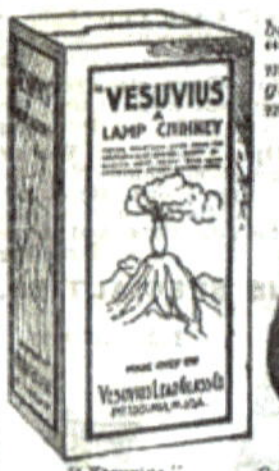

"Vesuvius." Trademark registered May 1, 1900.

Impossible to make a better chimney than our **"VESUVIUS,"** *which is made from purest lead glass under a secret formula.*

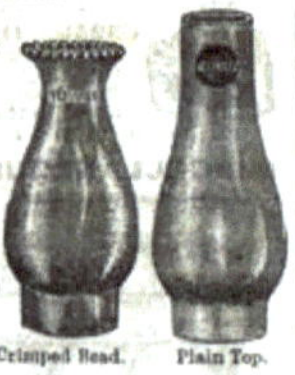

Crimped Bead. Plain Top.

"Vesuvius" Crimped Bead Top—

No. 1 Each in carton, 6 doz. in case, wt. 41 lbs. **(No package charge.)** Doz. **60c**

No. 2—Each in carton, 6 doz. in case, wt. 57 lbs. **(No package charge.)** Doz. **72c**

"Vesuvius" Plain Top—

No. 1—Each in carton, 6 doz. in case, wt. 41 lbs. **(No package charge.)** Doz. **60c**

No. 2—Each in carton, 6 doz. in case, wt. 57 lbs. **(No package charge.)** Doz. **72c**

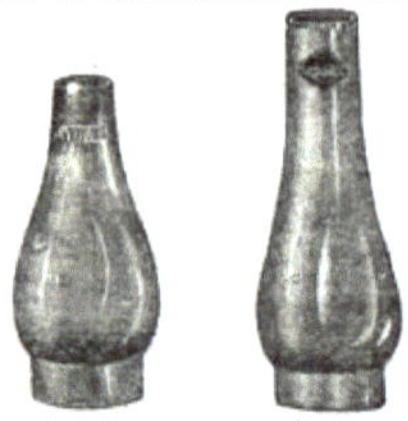

Rochester. Electric.

"Vesuvius" Rochester—

No. 2—Diam. at bottom 2⅝ in. Each in carton, 6 doz. in case, wt. 42 lbs. **(No package charge.)**....................Doz. **84c**

No. 2—12 in., extra long, for large globes. Diam. at bottom 2⅝ in. Each in carton. **(No package charge)**...Doz. **$1.45**

No. 2—12 in., as above, each in carton, 3 doz. in case, wt. 42 lbs. **(No package charge.)**........................Doz. **$1.30**

No. 3—Diam. at bottom, 4 in. Each in carton, 2 doz. in case, wt. 46 lbs. **(No pkg. charge.)**........................Doz. **$1.52**

"Vesuvius" Electric—For Climax and other burners where globes are used.

No. 2—Diam. at bottom 3 in. Each in carton, 3 doz. in box, wt. 36 lbs. Sold only by box. **(No pkg. charge.)**......Doz. **87c**

No. 2—Diam. at bottom 3 in. Each in carton. Slim shape, for globes with 4 in. openings. 3 doz. in box, wt. 37 lbs. **(No pkg. charge.)**....................Doz. **87c**

"INTRODUCTION" ASST. OF "VESUVIUS" CHIMNEYS.

We want **all** our customers to know the "Vesuvius"—*the very best* lead chimney. Accordingly we make up an asst. comprising a small lot of each style. Good variety. Will sell out evenly (each chimney in carton):

1 doz.	No. 1 Sun, plain top....................	$0 56
1 "	No. 1 Sun, bead top....................	56
1 "	No. 2 Sun, plain top....................	69
1 "	No. 2 Sun, bead top....................	69
½ "	No. 2 Rochester, 10 in. @ 82c........	41
½ "	No. 2 Electric, slim, @ 87c............	44

Total 5 doz. in case. Wt. 50 lbs. **(No pkg. charge.)** Complete, **$3.35**

"BELGIAN" CHIMNEY.

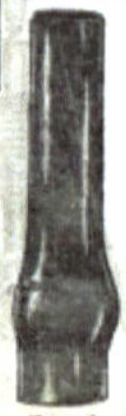

C1—Lead glass, fits Belgian and Success burners. Ht. 10¼ in., diam., at bottom 2¼. 3 doz. in case. Wt. 25 lbs. **(No pkg. charge.)**...............Doz. **85c**

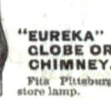

"EUREKA" GLOBE OR CHIMNEY.

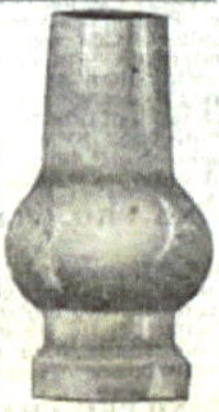

Fits Pittsburg store lamp.

—Pure lead glass, mammoth size, ht. 11 in., diam. at base 4¼ in. 1½ doz. in bbl. Wt. 50 lbs. **(No pkg. charge.)**.......Doz. **$1.80**

(Less than bbl. lots, $1.95 doz.)

ENGRAVED GLOBE CHIMNEYS.

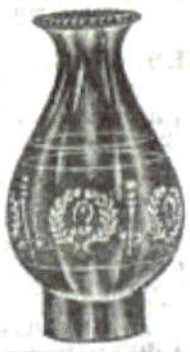

No. 2—Equal quantities, each of 3 designs of engraved and banded chimneys, large No. 2 size swelled center globe shape. Regularly sold at 20c. 6 doz. in case. Wt. 73 lbs. Doz. **84c**

No. 1 Size—As No. 2. 3 doz. in case. Wt. 25 lbs. **(No pkg. charge.)**...Doz **75c**

DECORATED GLOBE CHIMNEY.

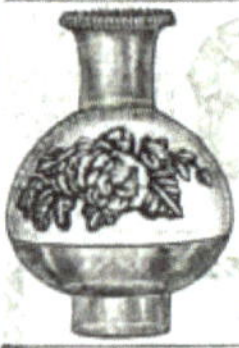

C1903, Regular B or No. 2 size—Large bulb shape circum. 17¾ in., bead top, globe decorated in white enamel and colored floral design. 3 doz. in bbl., asstd. decorations. Wt. 50 lbs. **No package charge.)** Doz. **$1.00**

MAMMOTH ENGRAVED GLOBE CHIMNEY.

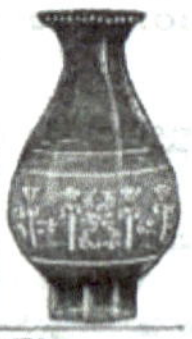

C2—Diam. at base 3 in., fits all No. 2 Sun burners, ht. 10½ in., extra large bulb, girth 18 in., pearl beaded top, engraved in 3 patterns. Asstd. in case of 2 doz. Wt. 35 lbs. **(No pkg. charge.)**..........Doz. **$1.25**

MAMMOTH "SATIN ETCHED" GLOBE CHIMNEY.

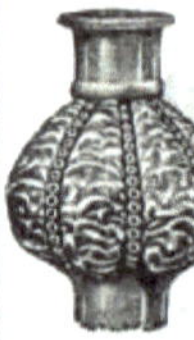

Fits our C 1352 and C 1353 Satin Etched Lamps.

C2—Pure lead glass, ht. 9 in., crimped top, extra large swell bulb, circum. 21 in., alternating panels of satin etching and beaded crystal, giving rich frosted effect. Fits regular No. 2 Sun burner, 1½ doz. in bbl. wt. 46 lbs. **(No pkg. charge.)** Doz. **$2.20**

NIGHT LAMP CHIMNEYS.

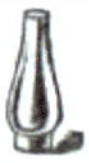

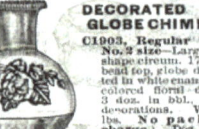

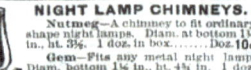

Nutmeg—A chimney to fit ordinary shape night lamps. Diam. at bottom 1¼ in., ht. 3½. 1 doz. in box........Doz. **10c**

Gem—Fits any metal night lamp. Diam. bottom 1½ in., ht. 4¾ in. 1 doz. in box.................................Doz. **14c**

HAM'S PATENT DRIVING LAMP.

Entirely new, best one made. Big value.

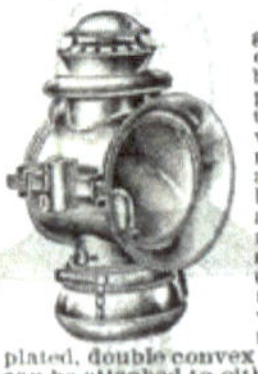

C439—A high grade lamp, built on celebrated cold blast principle, perfect combustion, absolutely windproof, will not jar out, gives an excellent light, handsome, suitable for finest carriage, made of steel, black enameled outside, interior finished with nickel, back reflector silver plated, double convex magnifying lense, can be attached to either side or center of dashboard. Each in pkg. Each, **$2.20**

CHIMNEYS FOR GAS LAMPS.

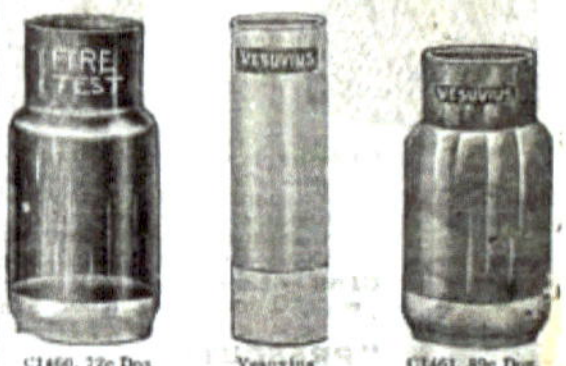

C1460, 72c Doz. Vesuvius. C1461, 89c Doz.

8 inch "Fire Test" Gas—Lead glass, best quality. 3 doz. in case, wt. 50 lbs..Doz. **54c**

C1460, Cylinder Shape Welsbach Gas—Same grade as our "Fire Test" brand. Etched base, pure lead glass, strictly firsts. 3 doz. in case. Wt. 25 lbs. **(No package charge.)**..............................Doz. **72c**

8 inch "Vesuvius"—Etched base gas chimney. Each in corrugated carton. 3 doz. in case. Wt. 32 lbs. **(No pkg. charge.)**....Doz. **75c**

C1461, "Vesuvius" Etched Base Combination Gas Chimney Asbestos Ringed—Suitable for all incandescent gas lamps and our "Suns-Ray" lamp. Goes over outside of burner upright and rests on springs at bottom of burner. Purest lead glass, and being large poes not break easily. Each in carton. 3 doz. in case. **(No Pkg. Charge.)**..........Doz. **89c**

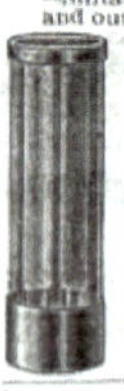

MICA CHIMNEY FOR GAS LAMP.

C124, 7 in. Mica Chimney—6 piece. Fits incandescent gas burners, made of most transparent mica, does not break, saves mantle bill. Clean with vinegar and hot water. Packed in pasteboard carton............Doz. **52c**

MICA CANOPY.

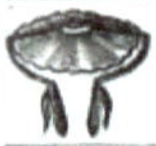

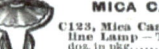

C123, Mica Canopy for Gasoline Lamp—Two supports. 1 doz. in pkg...............Doz. **35c**

TUBULAR LANTERN GLOBES.

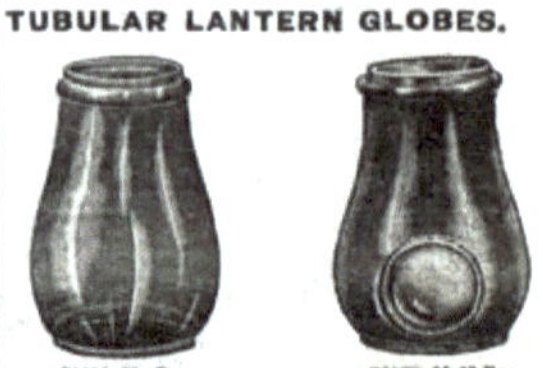

C1420, 33c Doz. C1423, $1.25 Doz.

C1420—Regular No. 0 size. Best goods, *ground top and bottom,* fits any tubular lantern 5 doz. in pkg. Wt. 66 lbs. **(No package charge.)**...............................Doz. **33c**

C1423, "Bulls Eye"—Regulation size, fits all tubular lanterns, best crystal glass, large optic bulls eye. 1 doz. in case. Wt. 20 lbs. **(No pkg. charge.)**... ....Doz. **$1.20**

COLD BLAST LANTERN GLOBES.

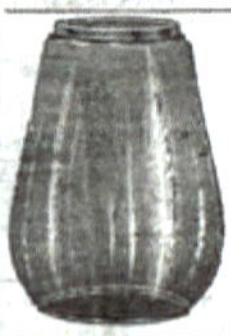

C1421—Large size for cold blast lanterns, best glass ground tops and bottoms. 2 doz. in case. Wt. 37 lbs. **(No pkg. charge.)**......Doz. **55c**

C1422—As C1421. 4½ doz. in bbl. Wt. 74 lbs. **(No Pkg. Charge.)** Doz. **47c**

DECORATED LAMP DOME ASSORTMENT.

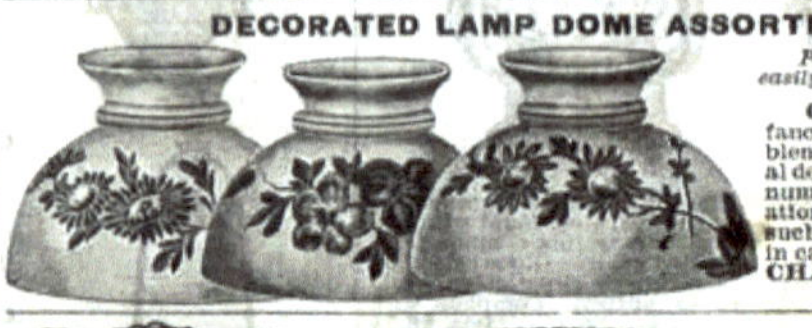

Possible 50 centers, though easily worth 75c.

C1369—Opal body, 10 in., fancy bell top, decorated in rich blended tints, hand painted floral designs; pansies, chrysanthemums, etc., all pieces and decorations burnt in asstd. colors; such as pink, blue and green in case of ¼ doz. **(NO PKG CHARGE.)** Wt. 36 lbs. Each, **37½c**

FANCY CRYSTAL GAS SHADE ASSORTMENT.

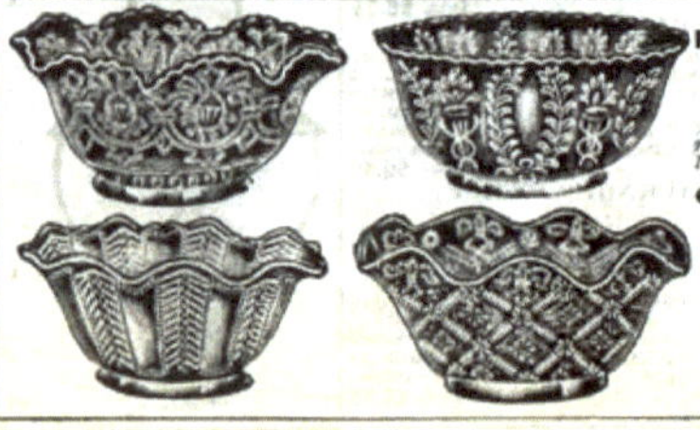

Usual 25 centers which you can retail with a good profit as 10 cent leaders.

C1200—Full size, all brilliantly finished, diam. of bottom 4 in. Fit all regular gas fixtures. Asst. comprises 1¼ doz. each of 4 fancy embossed patterns, 3 with crimped edges and 1 with pearl beaded edge. Total 5 doz. in bbl. Per dozen, **92c**

(NO PKG. CHARGE)

MANTLES—*For gas fixtures, etc.*

Standard goods. *Why pay more?*

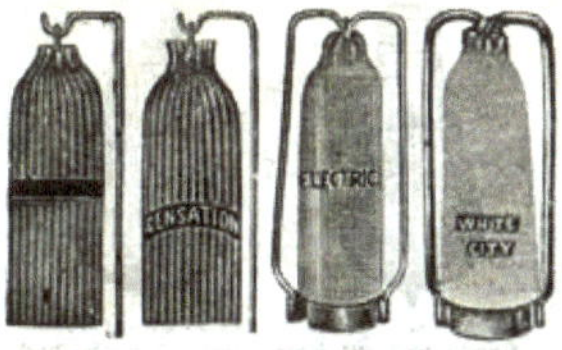

C1924, "White City" Best for the money. For gas or gasoline. Gives a bright, white, high candle power light. Very durable. 25 in box.................................Each, **5c**

C1925, "Sensation":. Perfect in shape and construction, gives an intense incandescent light for either gasoline or gas. 25 in box. Each, **6½c**

C1932, Cap Mantles:. Electric Cap, made of 6 cord thread. Each in box. 1 doz. in carton.................................Each, **7c**

C1933, "White City" Cap: Guaranteed non-shrinkable, made of special fibre thread which gives it strength and increases light. Full 100 candle power, looks and burns like a 25c mantle. Close fine weave, correct length, only best chemicals used. For gas only. 1 doz. in box............. Each, **6½c**

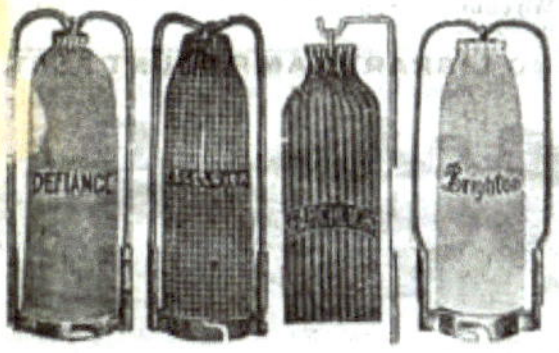

C1929, Defiance":.Cap mantle, 100 candle power, close fine weave, only the best chemicals used. Gives a strong white light. 12 in box. no less sold..................... Each, **9½c**

C1930 "Excelsior Cap:.Triple weave, extra strong, only the best chemicals used. Guaranteed as good as any mantle made, bar none. Has stood a 90 day test and will give satisfaction. 1 doz. in display box.Each **12c**

C1931, "Searchlight":.A perfect double thread mantle made from finest chemicals. Special double woven net permits double the absorption of chemicals, producing a heavier and stronger mantle. 12 in showy case............................ ....Each, **10c**

C1934, Brighton. Cap, full 100 candle power, close fine weave, extra well made, best brass cap, nickel steel wire support. 1 doz. in box. Each, **15c**

ANTLES FOR GRAVITY, HOLLOW WIRE SYSTEM AND PRESSURE LAMPS.

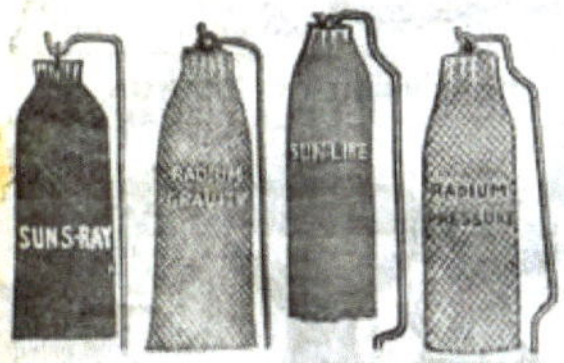

C1926, "Suns - Rays":.Treated by special process which greatly increases incandescence and strength, extra coated at top. For gasoline or gas. Our own copyrighted brand. 12 in box ... .Each, **9½c**

C1935, "Radium Gravity": Made especially for Gravity Lamp—extra strong close fine weave. Will stand any test. 3½ inch. 1 doz. in box..... ....Each **11c**

C1927, "New Sun Like": For pressure lamps only. 5 in. red color. We guarantee this to be the best pressure mantle made. Double weave, extra strong, best chemicals, gives a clear, brilliant light. 1 doz in box. Each, **15c**

C1936, "Radium Pressure": For Hollow Wire System. Special heavy weave—strong and durable. Made to stand great pressure. Best chemicals and material. Thoroughly tested. 5 in bh. 1 doz. in box.....Each, **15c**

SHADES FOR GAS LAMPS.

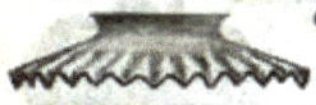

C74, 8 in.—Fits incandescent, common, or gasoline burners. 2 doz in box........Doz. **72c** Wt. 40 lbs.

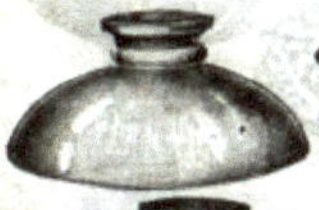

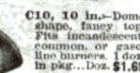

C10, 10 in.—Dome shape, fancy top. Fits incandescent, common, or gasoline burners. 1 doz. in pkg...Doz. **$1.69**

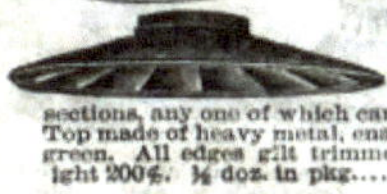

C1800: 10in. flat mirror reflector shade. Made of 3½ in. mirror sections, any one of which can be replaced. Top made of heavy metal, enameled in dark green. All edges gilt trimmed. Increases light 200%. ½ doz. in pkg........Doz. **$3.25**

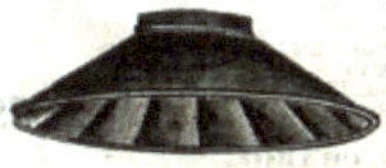

C1801: 10in. deep cone mirror reflector shade. 4 in. mirror sections. Otherwise as above. Doz. **$3.50**

GLOBES FOR GAS LAMPS.

Fits all incandescent gas burners.

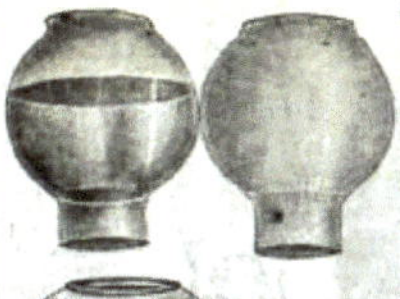

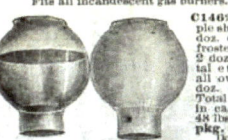

C1462—Apple shape. 2 doz. crystal frosted top; 2 doz. crystal etched all over; 2 doz. opal. Total 6 doz. in case, wt. 48 lbs. (**No pkg. chg.**) Doz. **54c**

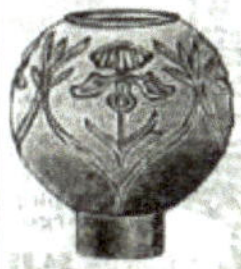

C1464—Ht. 5½ in., diam. bottom 2in., fits all incandescent burners, fancy floral and leaf embossed design. Asstd. 2 doz. each opal, sea green and turquoise blue, total 6 doz. in bbl. (**No pkg. charge.**) Doz. **87c**

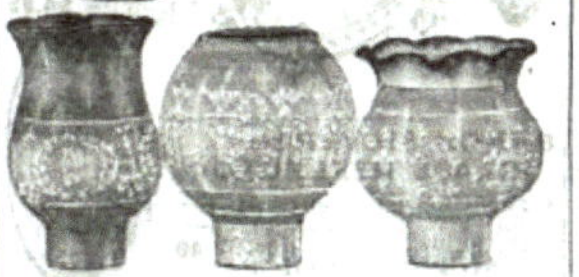

C1463—1 doz. apple shape band and medallion etching; 1 doz. with crimped top and medallion etching, etched top and bottom; 1 doz. bell shape, band and fleur de lis etching. Fits all incandescent gas burners. 3 doz. in case. (**No pkg. charge.**)...... Doz. **92c**

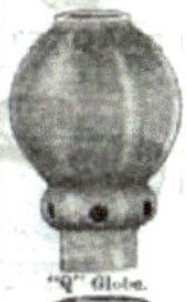

"Q" Globe.

C1459, "Q" Globe: High grade opal glass, fire temperature, strictly "firsts." 5 doz. in bbl. (**No pkg. charge**).. .... Doz. **86c**

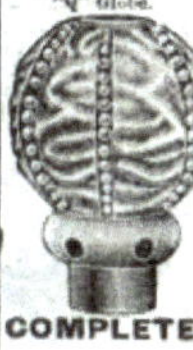

C1457—Regular "Q" size, ht. 6½ in., diam. bottom 2 in., fits all incandescent burners, fine quality crystal, embossed and allover satin etched finish. 5 doz. in bbl. (**No pkg. charge.**) Doz. **$1.20**

C1458—As C1457 only in rich asstd. colors. 2 doz. cardinal red. ½ doz. azure blue. ½ doz. light green, total 3 doz. in bdl. (**No pkg charge.**) Doz. **$2.20**

COMPLETE GAS OR CASOLINE LIGHTS.

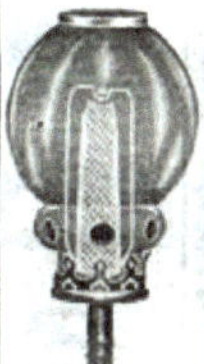

C7, $3.00 Doz.

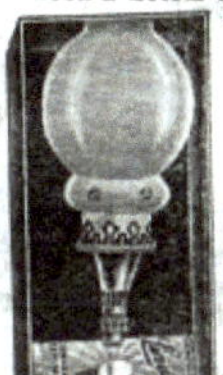

C8, $5 25 Doz.

C7, Ury Block: New combination brass burner for natural, manufactured or gasoline gas. Regulation size Q air hole globe, good cap mantle. ½ doz. in pkg. Doz. **$3.00**

C8, Simplex Block: Combination brass burner with wheel regulator, burns natural, manufactured or gasoline gas. Q air hole opal globe, burner and high grade mantle. Each in box complete ready to hand to customer........Doz. **$5.25**

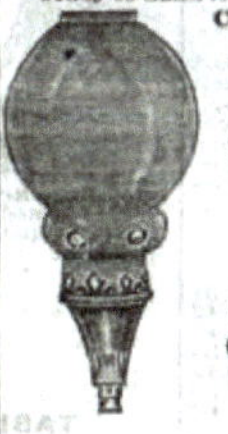

C5—Lindsay. Complete with adjustable burner, special loop mantle with a magnesia center rod and Q. Jena globe. 300 candle power. Guaranteed to give satisfaction. Each in box complete, ready to hand to hand to your customer. Doz. **$6.60**

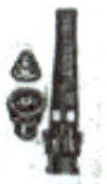

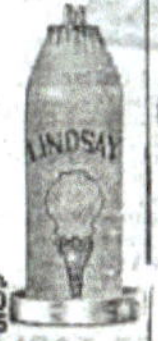

Fittings for Lindsay Light.

Lindsay Mantle with magnesia support.................Doz. **$1.80**
Q. Lindsay Opal Globe..... " **1.45**

"ANTI-VIBRATOR" LIGHT.

"The new money-saver light." Burns 10% gas and 90% air, saves 50% of your mantle bill—almost impossible for mantle to break on this light. *A practical light for factories, shops, stores and all places where vibration causes mantles to break. You save money by saving your mantles.*

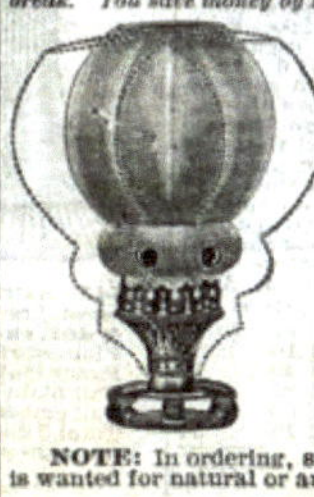

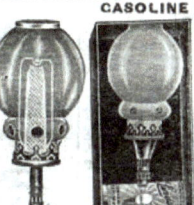

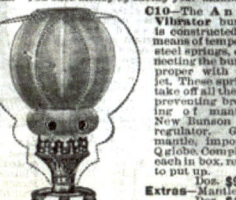

C10—The Anti-Vibrator burner is constructed by means of tempered steel springs, connecting the burner proper with gas jet. These springs take off all the jar, preventing breaking of mantles. New Bunson gas regulator. Good mantle, imported Q globe. Complete, each in box, ready to put up. Doz. **$9.00**

Extras—Mantle. Doz. **$1.80**
—Q Globe. Doz. **$1.45**

NOTE: In ordering, state whether burner is wanted for natural or artificial gas.

GLASS NIGHT LAMPS.

Each complete with base burner, wick, and chimney.

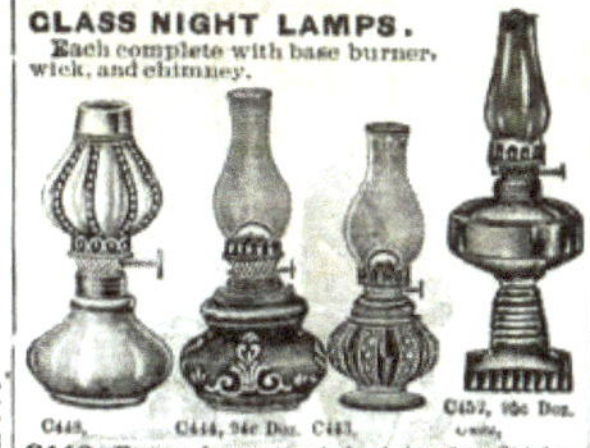

C448, C444, 94c Doz. C443, C457, 90c Doz.

C448—Fancy fount, beaded globe, ht. 6½ in., asstd. crystal, blue and green. 1 doz. in box. Doz. **88c**

C444—Large size, fancy shape embossed fount, asstd. ruby and emerald colors, embossed work gold traced, full ht. 7 in., Asstd. colors in box of 1 doz.................Doz. **94c**

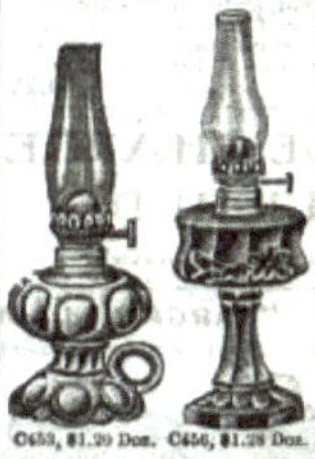

C453, $1.20 Doz. C456, $1.28 Doz.

C443—Fancy footed shape, cut diamond crystal pattern, asstd. green and ruby stained panels. Full ht. 6½ in. 1 doz. in box. Doz. **89c**

C452—Plain fount on high foot. Handsome pattern, purest crystal. ½ doz. box. Doz. **95c**

C453—Footed, fancy open handle, full ht. 7 in. 1 doz. box. Doz. **$1.20**

C456—Fancy floral embossed body, rich emerald green color, full ht. 9 in. ½ doz. in box....Doz. **$1.28**

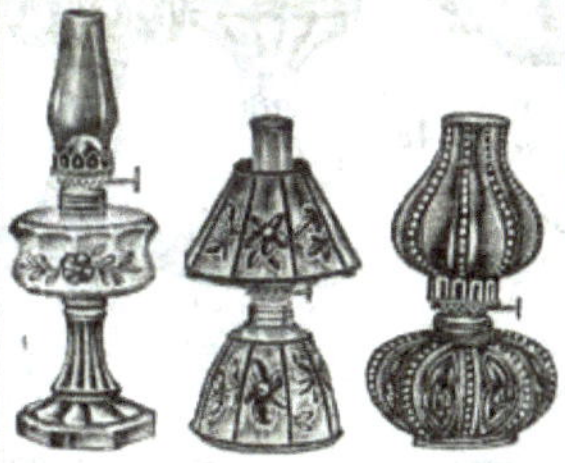

C454, $1.67 Doz. C455, $1 87 Doz. C459, $2.10 Doz.

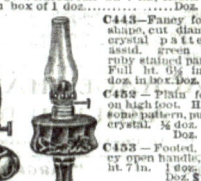

C454—Full ht. 9 in., rich red stand, satin edge fount, embossed and decorated in colored floral designs. With burner, chimney and wick. ½ doz. in box............ Doz. **$1.67**

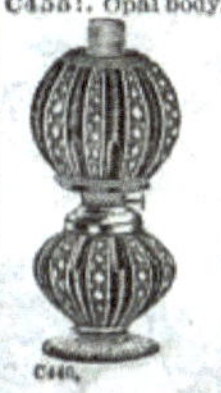

C440.

C455:. Opal body, fancy oriental shape, decorated all over in rich tints, such as pink, green and yellow, hand painted floral designs dividing panels decorated in black in bamboo effect. Complete with fancy shade decorated to match, crystal chimney. "Nutmeg" burner, wick and tripod, full ht. 7½ in. Each in carton. ½ doz. in pkg. ....Doz. **$1.87**

C459—Good size, fancy shape, wide low shape fount, fancy globe, both embossed in solid burnt in colors. Full ht. 7½ in. Complete with brass "Gem" burner and wick. Asstd. colors, pink, blue, opal and yellow. Each complete in carton. ½ doz. in pkg. Doz. **$2.10**

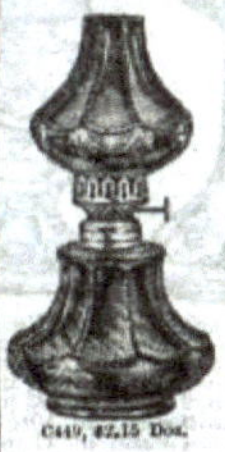

C449, $2.15 Doz.

C446—Fancy diamond cut crystal pattern, footed, nutmeg burner, globe ring and chimney, body and globe with decorated panels, asstd. ruby and emerald colors, full ht. 7½ in. Each in carton, ½ doz. in pkg. Doz. **$1.95**

C449—Ht. 9 in., large fancy shape fount and combination globe chimney, both heavily embossed and decorated in rich ruby color, brass "gem" burner and wick. 2 shapes, each in carton, ½ doz. asstd. in pkg...............Doz. **$2.15**

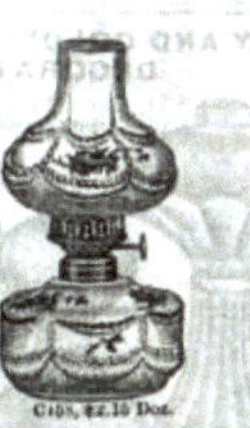

C458, $2.15 Doz.

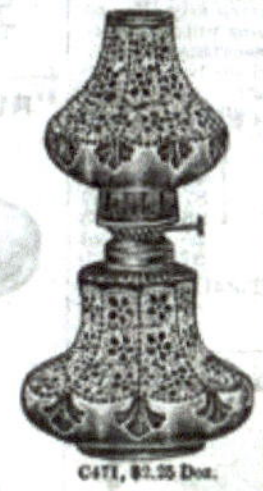

C471, $2.25 Doz.

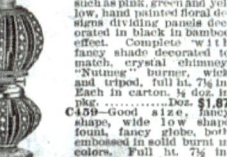

C458—Large fancy opal body, diam. of base 4½ in., fancy globe shade, full ht. 8½ in., body and globe with embossed hand painted rose and pansy decorations in colors with green leaves, embossed work gilt traced. Brass burner and wick. Each in carton, ½ doz. in pkg....... ... .Doz. **$2.15**

C471—Japanese. Large fount and globe, colonial panel pattern, asstd. green, blue and amethyst, enameled and gold bronze decorations. Brass burner and wick. Full ht. 8½ in. Each in carton. ½ doz.in pkg. Doz. **$2.25**

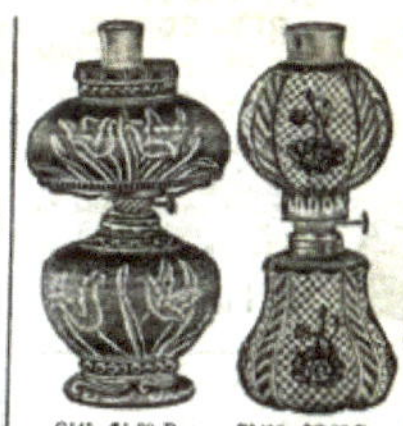

C445, $1.90 Doz. C1450, $2.20 Doz.

C445—Fancy floral embossed, footed fount, 4½ in. dome shade, solid ruby stained color, nutmeg burner, wick, tripod and chimney, full ht. 8½ in. Each in carton, ½ doz. in pkg. Doz. **$1.90**

C1450-Large, ht. 9½ in., fancy embossed fount and globe, decorated in rich colors, hand painted floral designs, gold bronze tracing, etc. 2 shapes, asstd. colors in crystal, blue and green, complete with best "Gem" burners and wicks. 1 doz. in case. wt. 33 lbs.....................Doz. **$2.20**

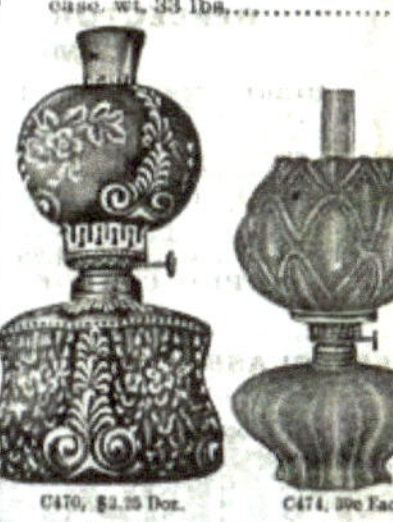

C470, $2.25 Doz. C474, 39c Each.

C470:.Full ht. 9 in., extra large fount, brass collar, 'Gem' burner and wick, large globe chimney in 3 colors, blue green and amethyst, both lamp and globe embossed and decorated in gold and colored floral designs. Each in carton. ½ doz. in pkg. asstd. colors. Doz. **$2.25**

C474—Fancy fount and globe, heavily embossed and satin etched, finished in Kopps' rich solid colors, asstd. cardinal, pink and light green. Nutmeg gallery burner, globe ring, chimney and wick. Full ht. 9½ in. Each in carton.............................Each, **39c**

METAL NIGHT LAMPS.

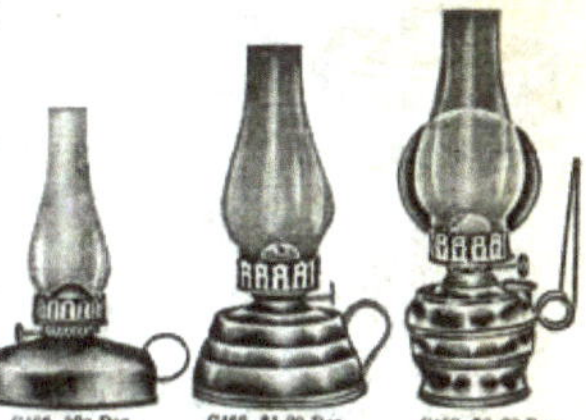

C466, 89c Doz. C468, $1.20 Doz. C469, $2.20 Doz.

C466—Full ht. 7 in., extra wide fount, never upsets, brass gem burner, wick and large chimney. 1 doz. in box..............Doz. **89c**

C468—*Brilliant lacquered brass.* 7 in. high, body 4 in. Burner, wick and large chimney. ½ doz. in box........................ Doz. **$1.20**

C469, "Bridgeport."—Full nickeled, fount has screw cap, adjustable reflector, burner, chimney, finger holder and hanger. Full ht. 8 in., no odor. 1 doz. in pkg.....Doz. **$2.20**

"DIME LEADER" NIGHT LAMP ASST.

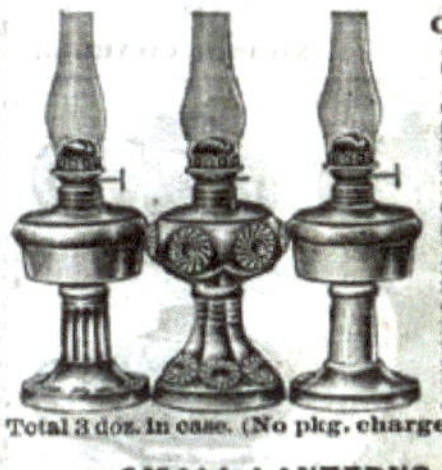

C1348—Large sizes on high foot, extra strong, best nutmeg burners, chimneys and wicks, full ht. 9½ in. 1 doz. each of 3 rich patterns, all in full finished crystal. Total 3 doz. in case. (No pkg. charge.) Doz. **96c**

SMALL LANTERNS.

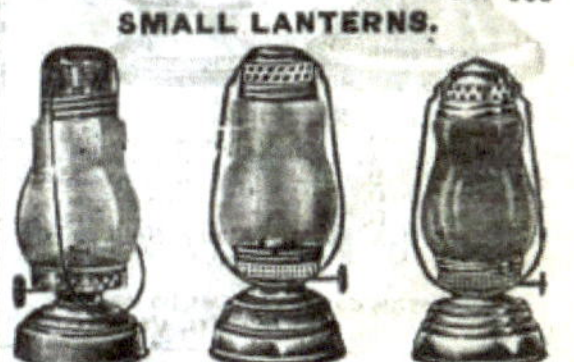

C462, C463, $1.62 Doz. C464, $1.95 Doz.

C462, "The Jewel"—Same size and style as the brass lantern which costs twice as much, heavy tin. ht. not including handle, 7 in. 1 doz. in box, complete with wicks. **82c**

C463, "Klondike"—Ht., not including handle, 7½ in. Brass ventilated top. Complete with wick. ½ doz. in box.................Doz. **$1.62**

C464, "Red, White and Blue"—Ht., including handle, 11½ in. With burner, wick and asstd. red, white and blue globes. Colors equally asstd. in box of ½ doz.........Doz. **$1.95**

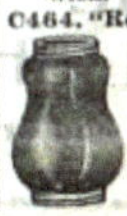

"Klondike" Lantern Globes.—To fit "Klondike" lanterns. 1 doz. in pkg.......................Doz. **40c**

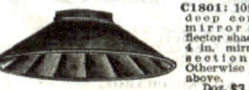

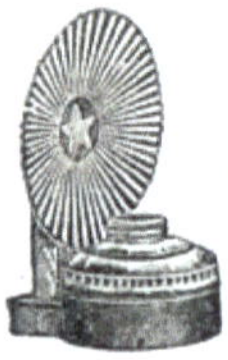

"BRILLIANT" REFLECTOR LAMP.

Extraordinary value at 19 cents.

C1360 :. Frame of heavy block tin, handsomely painted, tin reflector, 4½ in. glass front made for No. 2 burner. Packed 3 doz. in case. Wt. 75 lbs. Doz. **77c**
(Less than case, 79c doz.)
(NO PKG. CHARGE.)

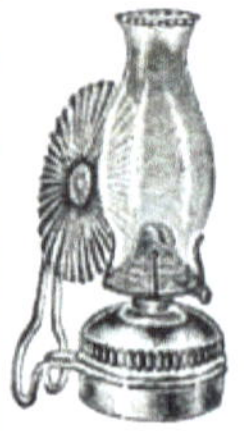

"READY TO LIGHT" COMPLETE REFLECTOR LAMP.

C1361 :. Made from 1 piece of 7 gauge steel wire very strong and springy, complete with 7 in. bright tin reflector and 4½ in. fount, fitted with No. 2 burner and chimney. 1 doz. in case, wt. 26 lbs.....Doz. **$1.95**
(NO PKG. CHARGE.)

COMPLETE BRACKET LAMPS.

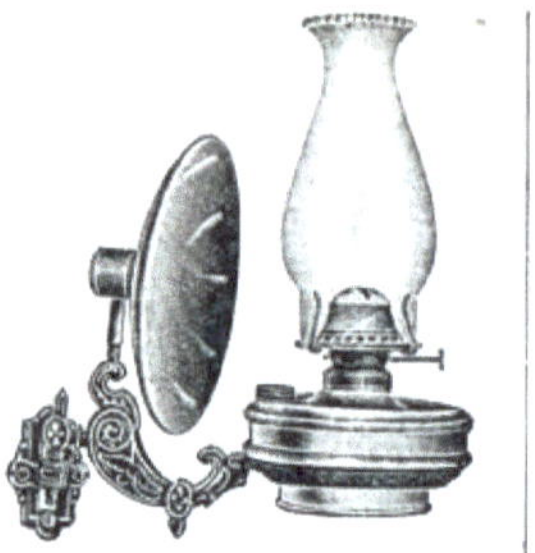

C1362:.Bronze bracket, swinging socket, complete with No. 2 filler fount, No. 2 sun burner, No. 2 sun crimped chimney and 8 in. silvered glass reflector. 1 doz. complete in case ....Doz. **$4.25**

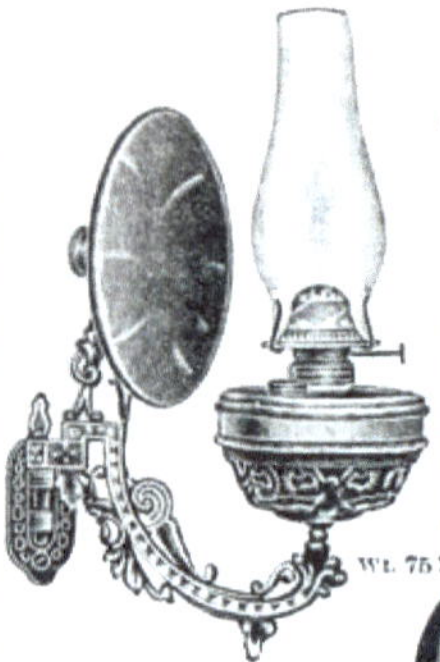

C1363.—French bronze bracket, No. 2 filler founts 8 in. silvered glass reflector, 2 Sun burner. Complete with crimped top chimney. Sold in lots of 1 doz. (No pkg. charge.) Doz. Wt. 75 lbs. **$4.95**

PACKAGE CHARGE ABOLISHED

On All Crockery and Glassware.

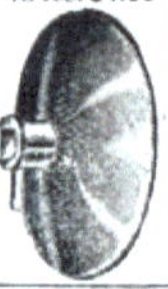

8 INCH SILVERED GLASS REFLECTOR.

C2—No. 2 brightly silvered, non dull goods. 1 doz. in case, wt. 20 lbs ....Doz. **$1.48**
(NO PKG. CHARGE.)

"CHICAGO" HIGH GRADE ELECTRIC LAMPS.

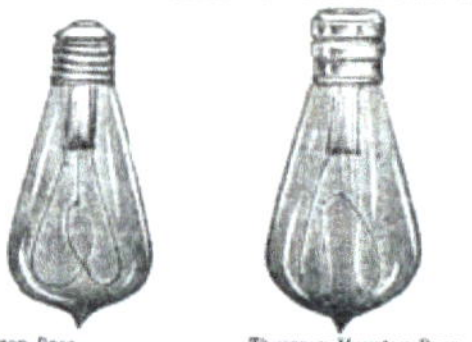

Edison Base. Thomson Houston Base

Guaranteed 900 hour lamp. Strictly high grade. Made and guaranteed by one of the best makers in the country. Cellulose anchored filament, closely selected as to voltage.

"Chicago" Edison Base:

				Doz.
C400.	8 candle power,	110 vlt.	1 doz. box	$1 80
C401.	16 " "	110 "	1 " "	1 80
C402.	25 " "	110 "	1 " "	1 80
C403.	8 " "	104 "	1 " "	1 80
C404.	16 " "	104 "	1 " "	1 80

"Chicago" Thomson-Houston Base:

C405.	8 candle power,	110 vlt.	1 doz. box	$2 10
C406.	16 " "	110 "	1 " "	2 10
C407.	25 " "	110 "	1 " "	2 10
C408.	8 " "	104 "	1 " "	2 10
C409.	16 " "	104 "	1 " "	2 10

Caution—The above lamps come in two styles of base, Edison and Thomson-Houston, which are not interchangeable. When ordering specify base, candle power and voltage wanted. We cannot accept return of lamp when filled as ordered.

"PIONEER" GLASS HAND LAMP ASST.

First class quality, bright patterns, large sizes.

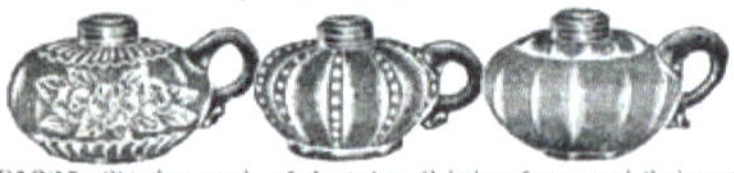

C1325—2¼ doz. each of 4 styles, 2 being fancy and 2 almost plain, all pure crystal, well made and finished, large stuck handles. No. 1 brass collars. Total 9 doz. in bbl. Wt. 100 lbs. Per dozen, **61c**
(NO PKG. CHARGE.)

GROOVED FLAT FILLER FOUNT.

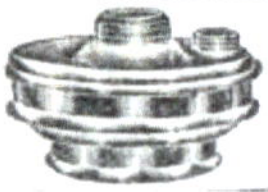

Fit with bracket reflector, chimney and burner then sell for what you would pay for complete lamp from lamp jobbers.

C1350 No. 2, superior goods, 1 doz. incase, wt. 25 lbs. Per dozen, **86c**
(NO PKG. CHARGE.)

"ALL LEADERS" LAMP ASST.

The best bargain of the year in fine glass lamps.

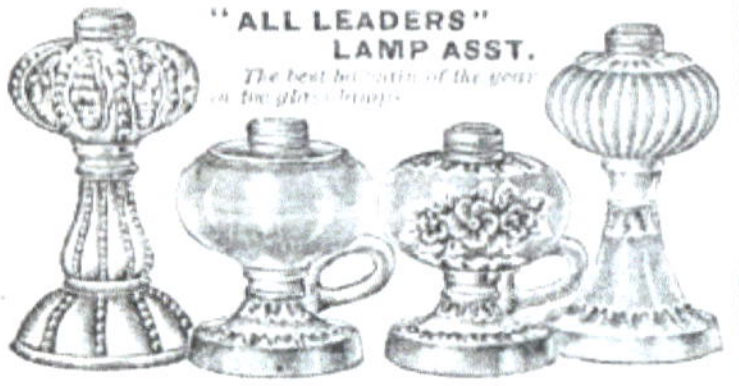

C1327—Best full finished crystal, bright attractive patterns, No. 1 brass collars. Asst. comprises **1 doz. each** of following:
1 doz. plain footed handled, ht. 5¼ in.
1 " fancy handled footed stand, ht. 5¾ in.
1 " optic stand, ht. 7⅝ in.
1 " fancy beaded stand, ht. 7¾ in.
1 " plain ribbed base stand, ht. 8¼ in.
1 " fancy embossed stand, ht. 8½ in.
Total 6 doz. in bbl. Wt. 114 lbs. Per dozen, **80c**
(NO PKG. CHARGE.)

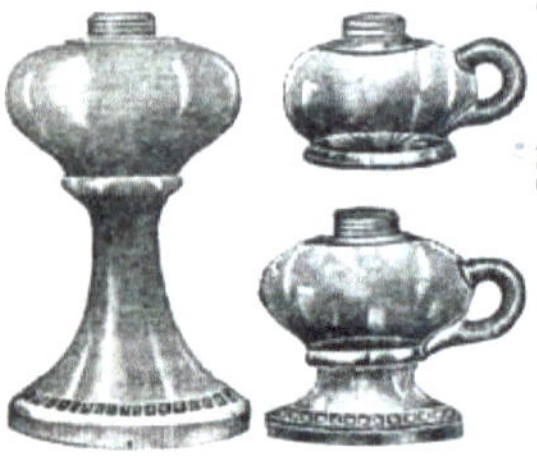

"ALL SIZES" LAMP ASSORTMENT.

Extra lamp value. New patterns and large sizes.

C1332:.Best selling patterns shown in years. An assortment of all best sizes at prices 10 per cent below market. Remember—these sizes are "*extra large*," and none marked up. Assortment comprises the following:

1 doz.	OOA. No. 1 collar	at $0 84	$0 84
½ "	OA. " 1 "	" 89	45
⅓ "	A. " 1 "	" 1 15	38
¼ "	B. " 2 "	" 1 48	37
¼ "	C. " 2 "	" 1 87	47
⅙ "	D. " 2 "	" 1 98	33
⅔ "	½A. Flat hand lamp, No. 1 collar..	" 65	44
⅓ "	½A. Footed lamp, " 1 "	" 87	29
		Total,	**$3.57**

Total of 3⅛ doz. in pkg., wt. 95 lbs.
(NO PKG. CHARGE.)

PACKAGE CHARGE ABOLISHED

On All Glassware and Crockery.

"BARGAIN" LAMP ASSORTMENT.

Choice brilliant patterns, well made and finished. Very special values.

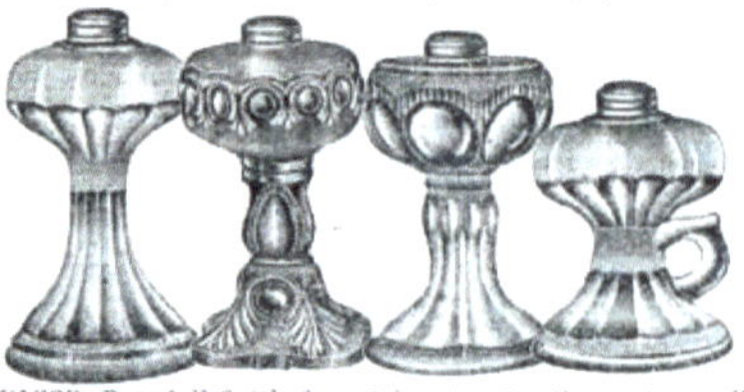

C1329—Pure full finished crystal, new, attractive patterns, all fitted with best No. 1 brass collars.
Asst. comprises 1 doz. high footed handled stand, and 1 doz. each of 4 tall stand. Average ht. 7¾ in.
Total 5 doz. in bbl. Per dozen, Out
(NO PKG. CHARGE.)

"DEFIANCE" LAMP ASST.

Up to date patterns. Always popular sellers.

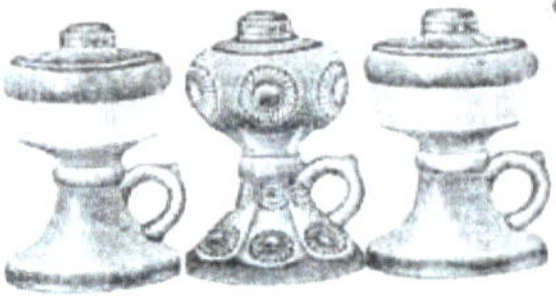

C1328 Pure crystal new patterns, ht. 5¾ in. Footed well made and finished. Large handles. No. 1 brass collars. 1 doz. each of 5 styles. Total 5 doz. in bbl. Wt. 100 lbs. Per dozen, **85c**
(NO PKG. CHARGE.)

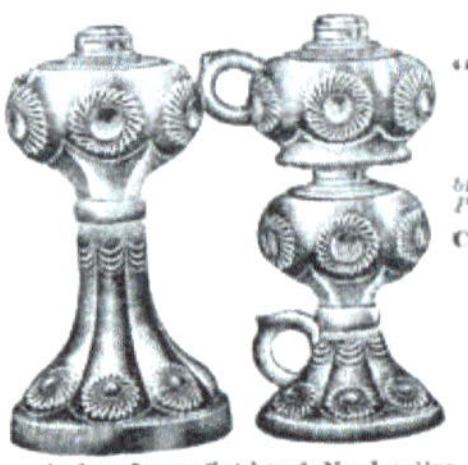

"BIG BRILLIANT" ALL SIZES LAMP ASST.

Strong and durable. New bright crystal patterns. Prices speak for themselves.

C1330—Best full finished crystal extra strong, well made. One half of each size plain with star foot and optic column; one half fancy embossed rosette design. Best brass collars. Asst comprises:

½ doz.	Large flat hand, No. 1 collar................	$0 67	$0 34
½ "	Footed hand, No. 1 collar....................	84	42
½ "	No. 0 stand, ht. 8⅛ in., No. 1 collar........	80	45
⅓ "	No. 1 stand, ht. 8¾ in., No. 1 collar........	1 15	38
⅓ "	No. 2 stand, ht. 9⅝ in., No. 1 collar........	1 35	45
⅓ "	No. 3 stand, ht. 10½ in., No. 2 collar......	1 59	53
⅓ "	No. 4 stand, ht. 11 in., No. 2 collar.......	1 80	60
⅓ "	Large sewing, ht. 8½ in., No. 2 collar......	1 95	65
		Total,	**$3.82**

Total 3⅓ doz. in bbl. Wt. 100 lbs.
(NO PKG. CHARGE.)

"RUBY AND GOLD" DECORATED TABLE LAMP ASST.

Very attractive. Will sell readily and pay you a good profit.

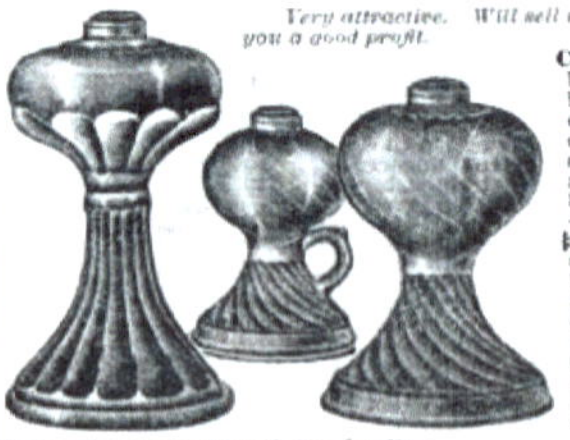

C1349:.All large and extra heavy. Made of one piece of glass. Each size equally assorted. In 2 bright patterns—one with ruby and gold bronze stand, the other in emerald and ruby tints. All decorations are on inside of stands and will therefore not wash off. Asst. comprises:

½ doz.	No. 1 footed hand, No. 1 collar..............	$0 89	$0 45
½ "	No. 1 stand, ht. 7⅞ in., No. 1 collar........	1 10	55
½ "	No. 2 stand, ht. 9¼ in., No. 1 collar........	1 40	70
½ "	No. 3 stand, ht. 9¼ in., No. 2 collar........	1 85	93
½ "	No. 4 stand, ht. 10½ in., No. 2 collar......	2 00	1 00
¼ "	No 4, sewing, ht. 8¾ in., No. 2 collar......	2 15	54
		Total,	Out

Total 2¾ doz. in bbl. Wt. 105 lbs.
(NO PKG. CHARGE.)

BRACKET AND LIBRARY LAMP FOUNT ASST.

Clinch collar founts at price of common goods.

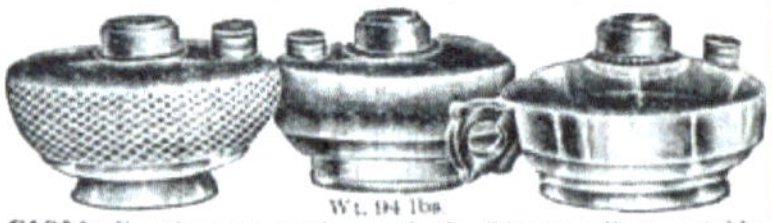

Wt. 94 lbs.

C1351:—Regular size good crystal, No. 3 brass collars, outside fillers. Asst. comprises:
2 doz. plain bracket founts. | 1 doz. fancy library founts.
1 " handled " " | Total 4 doz. in bbl.
No. chg. for bbl. | Average price dozen **95c**

"RELIABLE" LAMP ASSORTMENT.

Four huge sizes in popular, almost plain patterns.

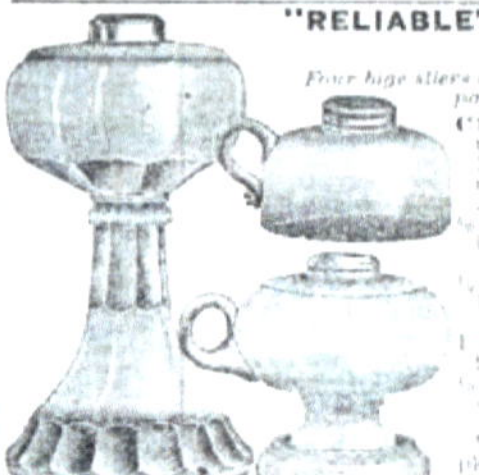

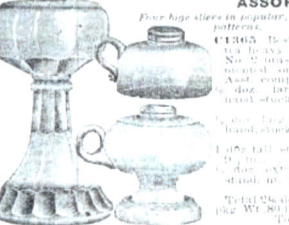

C1365 Best crystal, extra heavy, well made No. 2 brass collars cemented on, noplaster. Asst. comprises:
½ doz. large flat hand, stuck handle ... $0 62 $0 [illegible]
½ doz. large footed hand, stuck handle ... 1 35 [illegible]
1 doz. tall stand, ht. 9½ in. ... 1 72 1 7[illegible]
½ doz. extra large stand, ht. 10⅛ in. ... 1 9[illegible]
Total 2½ doz. in pkg. Wt. 80 lbs. Total, **$3.[illegible]**
(NO PKG. CHARGE.)

"BIG VARIETY" CLINCH COLLAR LAMP ASST.

No better glass lamps made—no plaster, no cement.

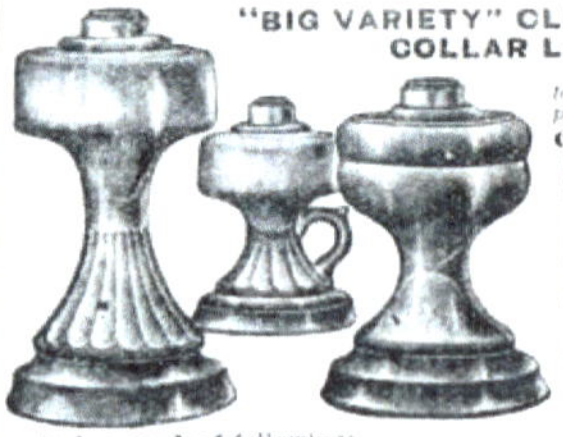

C1346—Extra quality, full finished crystal, extra heavy. **Made of one piece of glass,** almost unbreakable. Best patent clinch brass collars. Equal quantities in each size of plain and optic fluted design. Asst. comprises ½ **doz. each** of following:

No 1 footed hand, No. 1 collar.........................	$0 95	$0 48
No. 1 stand, ht. 8¾ in., No. 1 collar..................	1 20	60
No. 2 " " 9⅝ in., No. 1 "	1 44	72
No. 3 " " 10 in., No. 2 "	1 89	95
No. 4 " " 11 in., No. 2 "	2 15	1 08
No. 4 sewing, ht. 8⅝ in., No. 2 collar................	2 25	1 13
	Total,	**$4.96**

Total for 3 doz. in bbl. Wt. 120 lbs.
(NO PKG. CHARGE.)

TABLE AND SEWING LAMP ASST.

Four big ones at an exceptionally low price.

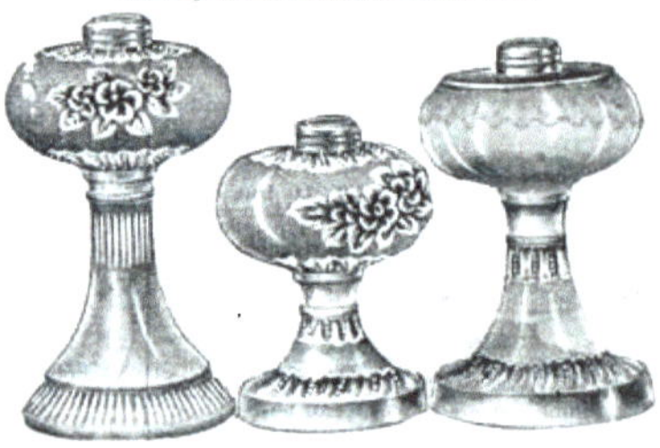

C1345—Extra large new bright patterns, pure crystal, well finished, fire polished, best No. 2 brass collars. Asst. comprises ¾ **doz. each of 4 styles.**
Plain sewing lamp, ht. 8½ in.
Fancy embossed sewing lamp, ht. 8¼ in.
Tall plain table lamp, ht. 10 in.
Tall embossed table lamp, ht. 10⅝ in.
Total 3 doz. in bbl. Wt. 110 lbs.
Average price Per dozen, **$1.75**
(NO PKG. CHARGE.

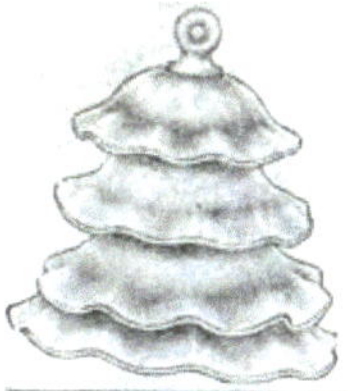

OPAL SMOKE SHADE ASSORTMENT.

All the popular selling sizes asstd. in one package.

C1368—Regulation shape, pure opal, crimped edge, ring for hanging. Asst. comprises:

½ doz. 5 in.
1 " 6 "
1 " 7 "
½ " 8 "

Total 3 doz. in case, wt. 56 lbs. Average price per dozen, **87c**

"ELABORATE" ASST. OF DECORATED GLASS TABLE LAMPS.

These will sell rapidly, paying you a good profit.

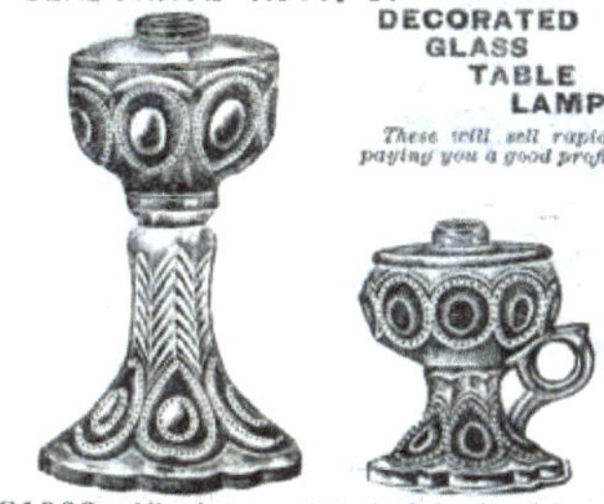

C1333—All of same pattern, both bowl and base in attractive beaded heart design, elaborate decorations, alternating in red green and yellow with gold bronze. Not burnt in, but will wear a long time. Asst. comprises:

½ doz. medium size stand, ht. 7½ in. No. 1 collar at	$1 25	$0 62
½ doz. footed hand, ht. 6 in., No. 1 collar at	1 35	68
½ " stand, ht. 8¼ in., No. 1 collar at	1 45	73
½ " stand, ht. 8¾ in., No. 1 collar at	2 10	1 05
⅓ " large stand, ht. 9½ in., No. 2 collar at	2 40	80
⅙ " extra large stand, ht. 10½ in., No. 2 collar at	3 00	50

Total 2⅓ doz. in bbl. Wt. 85 lbs. Total, **$4.38**

(NO PKG. CHARGE.)

"TABLE LAMP" ASST.

Popular in pattern, unsurpassed in quality, unequaled in price

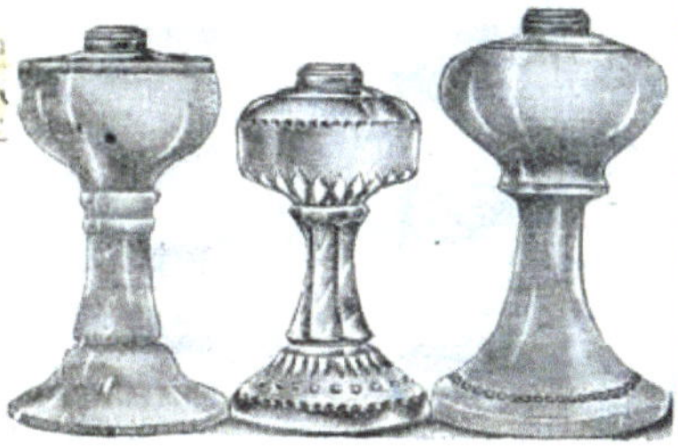

C1331—Best crystal glass, attractive patterns, extra heavy, well finished. *No "tank glass" in our lamps.* No. 2 collars.

Large,	½ doz.,	$1.48	$0 74
Large,	½ "	1.65	83
Extra large,	½ "	2.10	1 05
Extra large,	½ "	2.20	1 10

Total 2 doz. in pkg., wt. 95 lbs. (NO PKG. CHARGE.) Total, **$3.72**

"SEWING LAMP" ASST.

A much used pattern that carries a good profit.

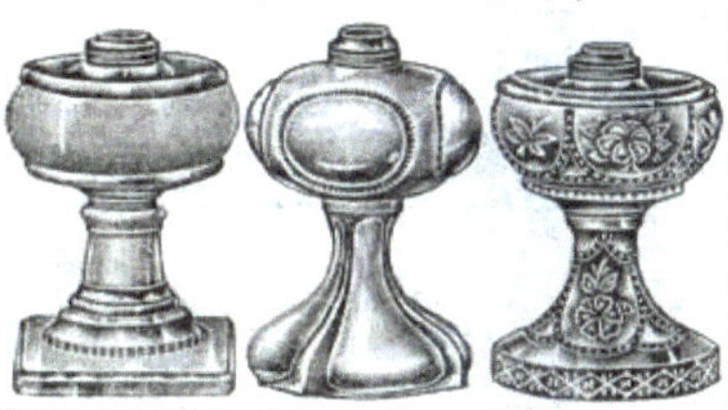

C1347—4 styles, No. 2 brass collars, extra large low shape, large founts. Pure crystal brilliantly finished, up to date patterns. ½ doz. of each style. 2 doz. in bbl. Wt. 80 lbs. (NO PKG. CHARGE.) Per dozen, **$1.89**

"MAMMOTH" CLINCH COLLAR ASST.

Strongest and best glass table lamps made.

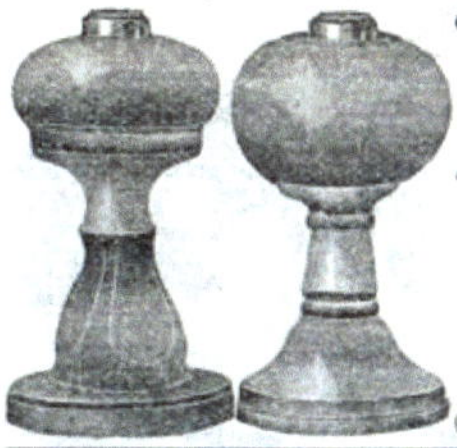

C1334—Made of one piece heavy crystal glass, thereby rendering them almost unbreakable, brilliantly finished, best brass clinch collars, all take No. 2 burners.

Asst comprises—
½ doz. 9¾ in. plain.
½ " 10 " fluted stem.
¼ doz. 10¼ " extra large plain.
¼ doz. 10¾ in. extra large fluted stem.

Total 1½ doz. in bbl. Wt. 80 lbs. Average price per dozen, **$2.35**

(NO PKG. CHARGE.)

PATENT "CLINCH COLLAR" LAMP ASST.

Best glass lamps made—no plaster, no cement.

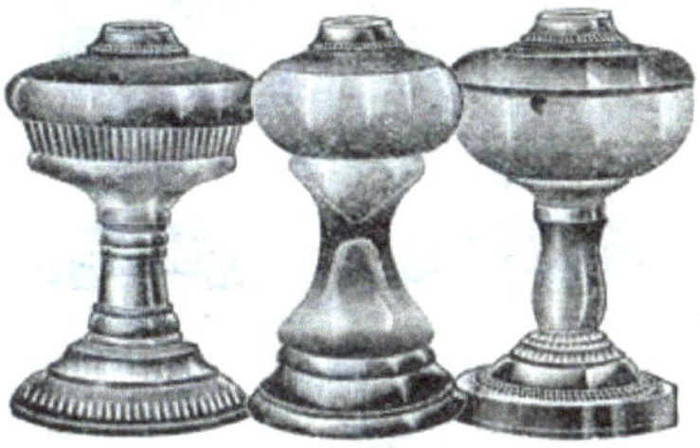

C1335—Large sizes, extra heavy, well made, best No. 2 clinch collar. Asst. comprises:

½ doz. stand, ht. 8½ at	$1 95	$0 98
½ " sewing, ht. 8¾ at	2 25	1 13
½ " stand, ht. 9½ at	2 50	1 25
¼ " large stand, ht. 10 at	2 75	69
¼ " extra large stand, ht. 9¾ at	2 95	74

Total for asst. of 2 doz. Wt. 90 lbs. (NO PKG. CHARGE.) **$4.79**

"GIANT" AND SEWING LAMP ASST.

Note especially the extra large sizes.

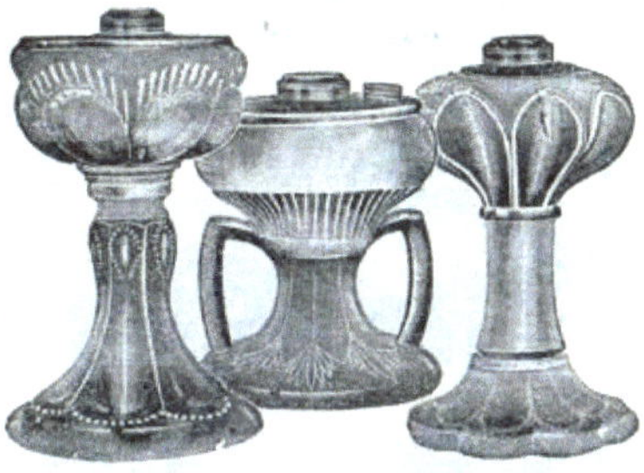

C1344:.4 styles. Extra heavy, best crystal glass, extra large founts, capacity about 1 quart. No. 2 brass collars. Asst. comprises ¼ **doz. each** of the following: Extra large and heavy low shape sewing lamp, ht. 8½ in. Large double handles. Mammoth sized table lamp. The popular almost plain pattern. Ht. 10¾ in. Large double handled sewing lamp, ht. 8½ in., with outside screw top filler. Giant table lamp, ht. 11 in., fancy pattern. Total 1 doz. in bbl. Wt. 65 lbs. Av. price, per dozen, **$2.95**

(NO PKG. CHARGE.)

"DECORATED" COMPLETE LAMP ASST.

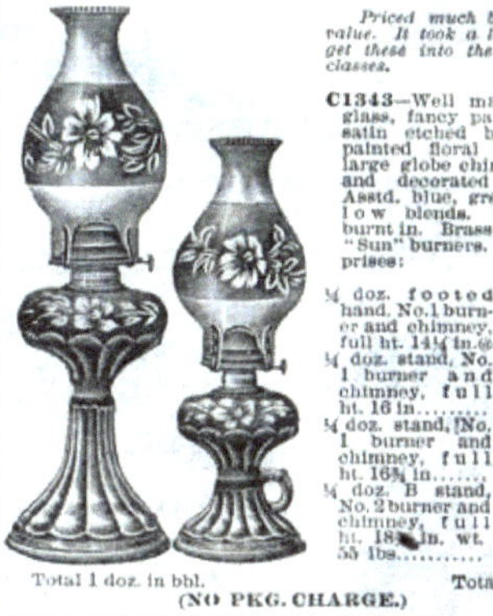

Priced much below regular value. It took a lot of work to get these into the 25 and 50c classes.

C1343—Well made, crystal glass, fancy pattern, tinted satin etched bodies, hand painted floral decorations, large globe chimneys tinted and decorated to match. Asstd. blue, green and yellow blends. Decorations burnt in. Brass collars and "Sun" burners. Asst. comprises:

¼ doz. footed hand, No. 1 burner and chimney, full ht. 14¼ in. @	$2 25	$0 56
¼ doz. stand, No. 1 burner and chimney, full ht. 16 in.	3 25	84
¼ doz. stand, No. 1 burner and chimney, full ht. 16¾ in.	3 95	99
¼ doz. B stand, No. 2 burner and chimney, full ht. 18¾ in. wt. 55 lbs.	4 25	1 06

Total 1 doz. in bbl. (NO PKG. CHARGE.) Total, **$3.45**

PACKAGE CHARGE ABOLISHED

On All Glassware and Crockery.

"ALL READY" LAMP ASST.

Full rigged ready to pass over the counter for 25c or 35c.

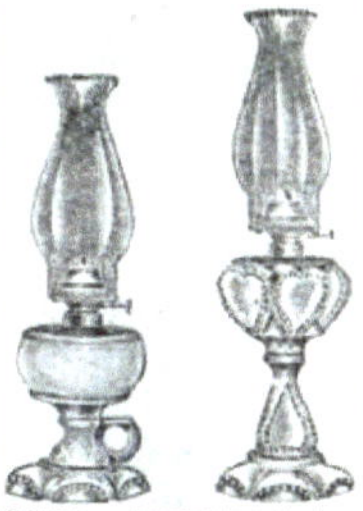

C1337 — Comprising 1 doz. **each** of hand and high stand lamps. Clinch collar — no plaster. With chimney, burner and wick. Total 2 doz. in bbl. wt. 80 lbs. Per dozen, **$2.20**

(NO PKG. CHARGE.)

MAMMOTH COMPLETE READING LAMP.

Will sell readily if offered a 75 cents.

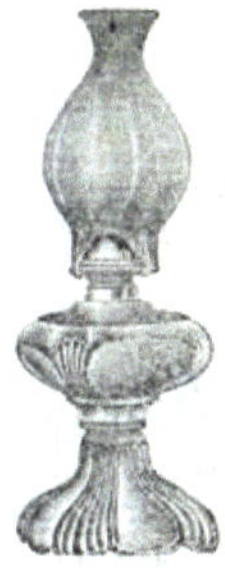

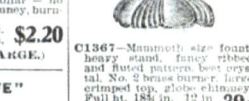

C1367—Mammoth size fount, heavy stand, fancy ribbed and fluted pattern, best crystal, No. 2 brass burner, large crimped top, globe chimney. Full ht. 18¾ in. 12 in bbl. Wt. 76lbs. Each, **39c**

(NO PKG. CHARGE.)

"BIG AND SAFE" COMPLETE LAMP ASST.

The best 50c complete lamps ever offered. All with patent clinch collars. No plaster, no cement, no dirt, no working loose.

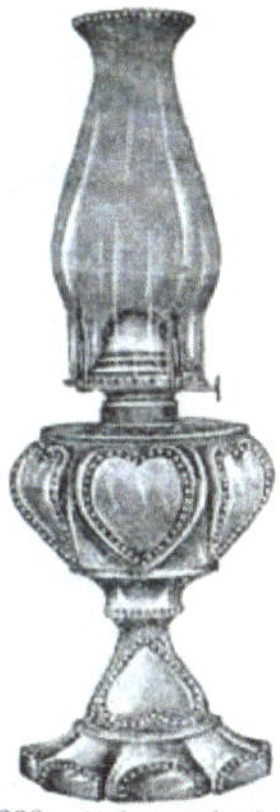

C1338 — ½ doz. each of two patterns of high stand lamps, 19½ in. to top of chimneys and ½ doz. of large sewing lamps, ht. 18 in., No. 2 burner, chimney and wick. Total of 1 doz. in pkg., wt. 70 lbs. Per dozen, **$4.10**

(NO PKG. CHARGE.)

COMPLETE LAMPS

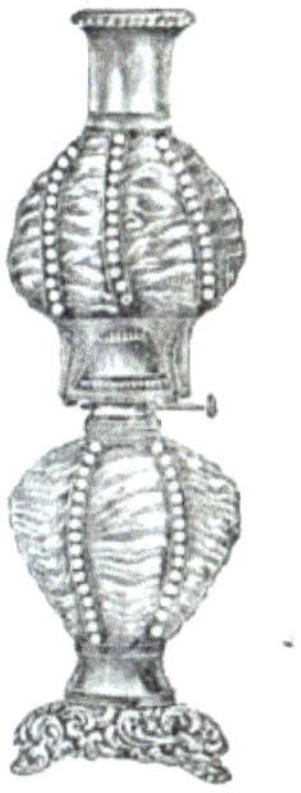

C1353—Large fancy body in all over embossed satin etched glass, beautiful frosted effect. Swell globe chimney to match, fancy gilt metal base. No. 2 Sun burner. Ht. 17¼ in.. 12 complete in bbl., wt. 60 lbs. Each, **42c**

(NO PAKCAGE CHARGE.)

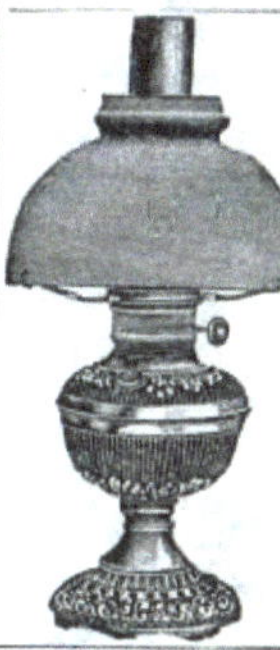

NICKEL PLATED CENTER DRAFT READING LAMP.

C1355 — Solid brass, openwork metal foot, No. 2 Royal center draft burner, nickeled tripod, wick, chimney and 10 in. opal dome shade. No better center draft lamp made. 6 in bbl. Wt. 58 lbs. Each, **$1.10**

(NO PACKAGE CHARGE.)

PACKAGE CHARGE ABOLISHED

ON GLASSWARE AND CROCKERY

NICKEL TABLE OR SEWING LAMP.

C460 — Full nickeled, No. 2 nickeled burner, 10 in. high, without chimney. Outside filling device, extension wick raiser, broad safety base. Each in pasteboard box...Each, **45c**

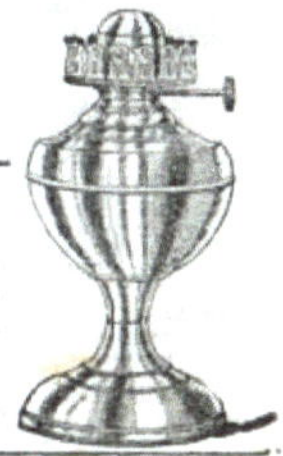

DECORATED LAMPS.

One might expect to pay a premium for these masterly decorations, but *we never overlook the selling price* and are able, therefore, to offer these truly artistic lamps *at prices below* the market on common goods. **(NO PACKAGE CHARGE)**

NOTICE—All our Decorated Lamps are complete, INCLUDING CHIMNEYS. All our founts are of solid brass, not the cheap tin affairs used by some makers.

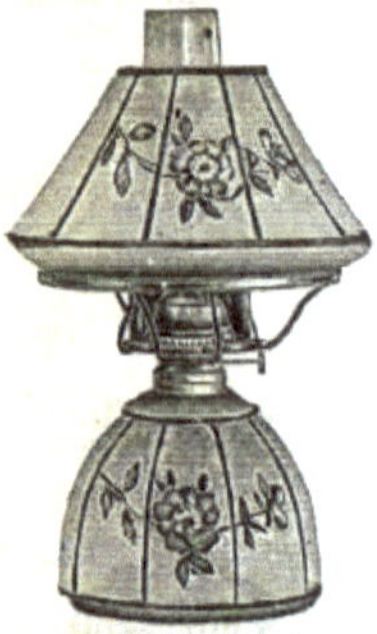

One Style C1476, 65c Each.

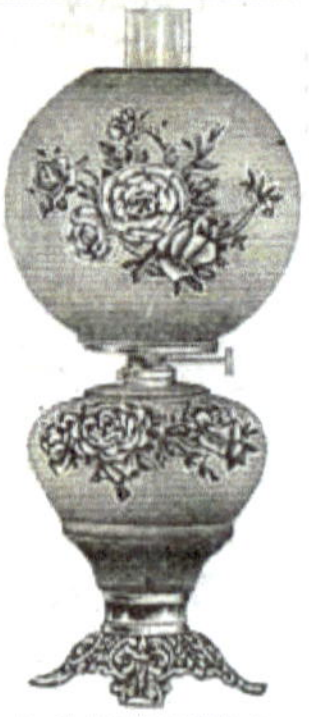

One Style C1484, $1.25 Each.

C1476 Asst—8 lamps, 4 with 7½ in. globes, 4 with 7 in. dome shades, Japanese panel effect design, extra large founts, No. 2 brass burners, shade rings and chimneys, full ht. 15½ in., rich asstd. colors, attrative floral decorations, raised panel work in black. 3 pink, 3 green, 1 yellow and 1 blue. 8 in bbl., wt. 65 lbs.......................................Each. **65c**

C1484 Asst—All same size and shape, 9½ in. globes, heavy floral embossed pattern in rich blended tints with large medallion effect decorations, heavy gilt metal bases, No. 3 climax burners, globe rings and chimneys, full ht. 20½ in. 2 red and brown blend and 2 red and green blend, 4 in bbl. wt. 55 lbs.......................................Each. **$1.25**

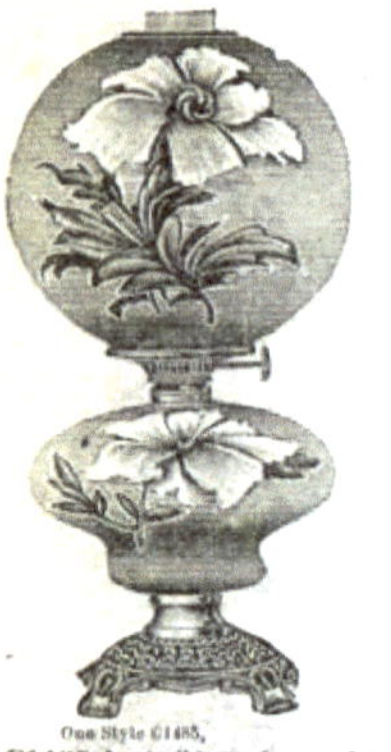

One Style C1485,

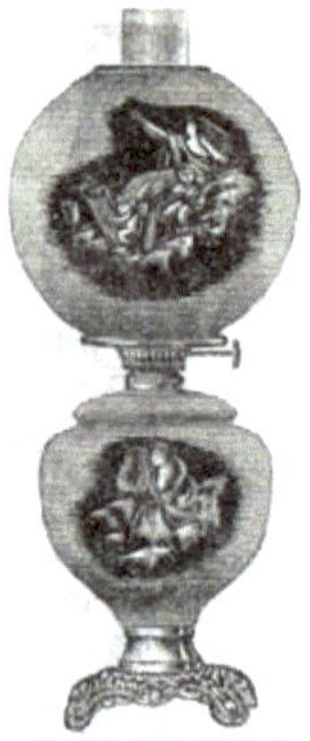

One Style C1486, $1.39 Each.

C1485 Asst—3 large lamps, fancy squat bodies, 10 in. globes, elaborate decorations of large peonies in natural colors on tinted grounds, gilt finished metal bases, No. 3 Climax burners, globe ring and chimneys, full ht. 21 in. 1 red, 1 green and 1 purple. 3 in bbl., wt. 50 lbs........................Each. **Out**

C1486 Asst—New fancy body, 9 in. globe, allover satin etched effect, gilt finished metal base, No. 3 Climax burner, globe ring and chimney, full ht. 22 in. 2 with stag and 2 with water nymph decoration. 4 in bbl., wt. 52 lbs.............Each. **$1.39**

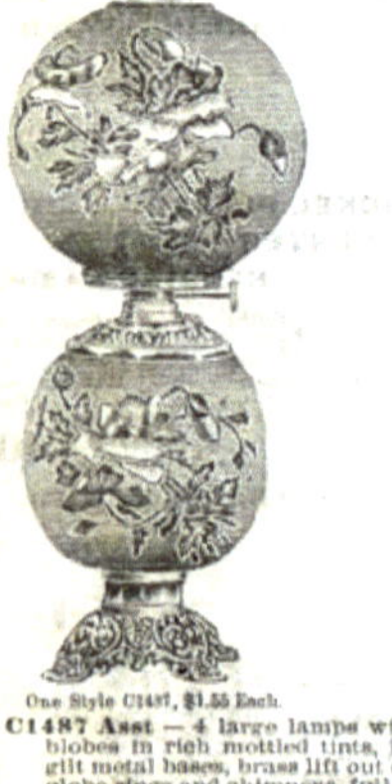

One Style C1487, $1.55 Each.

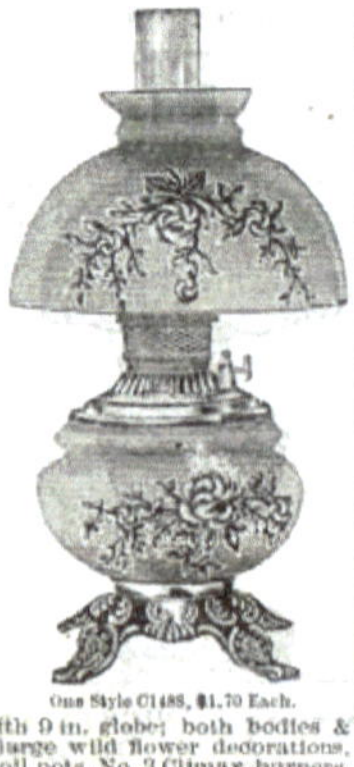

One Style C1488, $1.70 Each.

C1487 Asst — 4 large lamps with 9 in. globe; both bodies & blobes in rich mottled tints, large wild flower decorations, gilt metal bases, brass lift out oil pots, No. 3 Climax burners, globe rings and chimneys, full ht. 22 in. 2 pink and 2 green. 4 in bbl., wt 55 lbs.......................................Each, **$1.55**

C1488 Asst. Center draft, 2 with 8in. globes and 2 with 10 in. dome shades, all have large fancy shape bodies, decorated in rich tints and large floral design complete with heavy gilt finished metal bases, removable brass founts, No. 2 Royal center draft burners, globe rings, chimneys and wicks, full ht. 19 in. 2 pink and 2 green. 4 in bbl., wt. 54 lbs.Each, **$1.70**

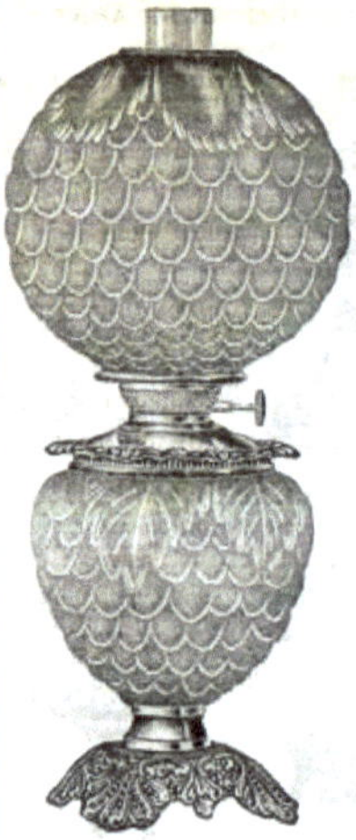

One Style C920, $2 69 Each.

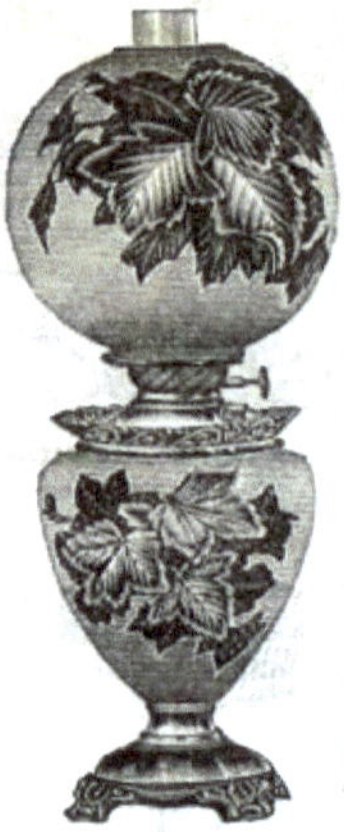

One Style C1494, $2.75 Each.

C920 Asst: 3 shapes—1 semi-tall with 9 in. globe, full ht. 22 in.; 1 low squat with 10 in. globe, full ht. 20¼ in.; 1 tall vase shape with 10 in. globe, embossed grape design, full ht. 24¼ in. Both bodies and globes in Kopd's genuine **solid cardinal red**, elaborately embossed and etched all over. All have extra heavy gilt finished metal bases, ornamental crown, removable brass founts, "Success" **center draft burners**, globe rings, No. 1 Belgian chimneys. 3 in bbl.wt. 52 lbs. Each, **$2.69**

(NO PACKAGE CHARGE.)

C1494 Asst—3 rich lamps, all different, large swell bodies, 10 in. globes, one new satin etched effect with art nouveau floral decorations in bright colors with rich gold tracings, old English brass trimmings, one red and delicate blue blend with rich Autumn leaf decoratons and oxidized metal trimmings, one delicate blue with large hand painted fruit decorations, gilt finished metal trimmings, heavy metal bases, ornamental crowns, removable founts, No. 2 Success center draft burners, globe rings, chimneys and wicks, average ht. 24½ in. 3 in bbl., wt. 55 lbs.......................................Each, **$2.75**

(NO PACKAGE CHARGE.)

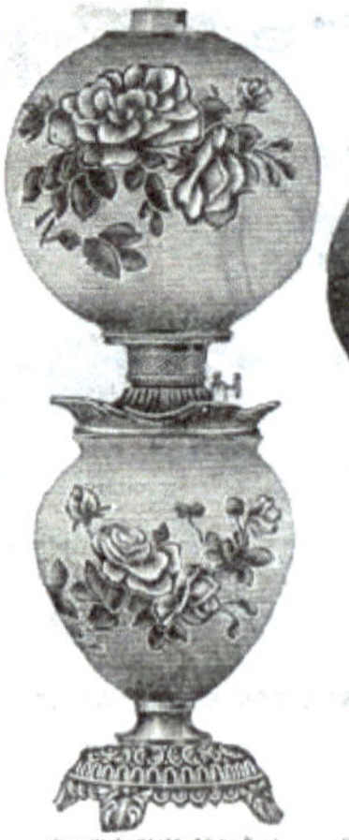

One Style C1496, $2.90 Each.

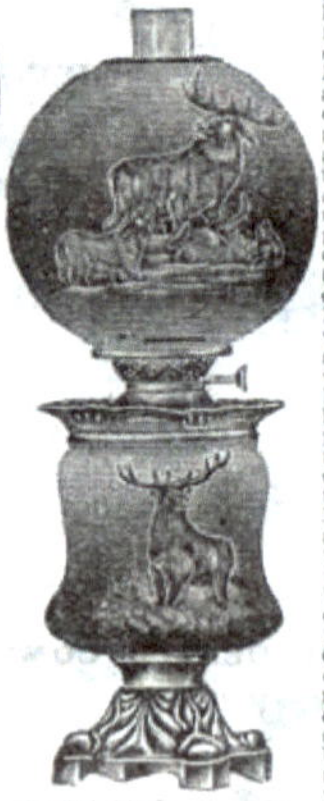

One Style C1497,

C1496 Asst — 2styles, large fancy shapes, 10 inch globes, one in rich green blended ground, monk picture decorations in colors, 1 rookwood ground with large hand painted rose decorations. Heavy gilt finished metal bases, double handled ornamental crowns, solid brass removable founts, No. 2 Royal center draft burners, globe rings, chimneys and wicks, full ht. about 25½ in., 2 in bbl., wt. 49 lbs., wt. 49 lbs. Each, **$2.90**

(NO PACKAGE CHARGE.)

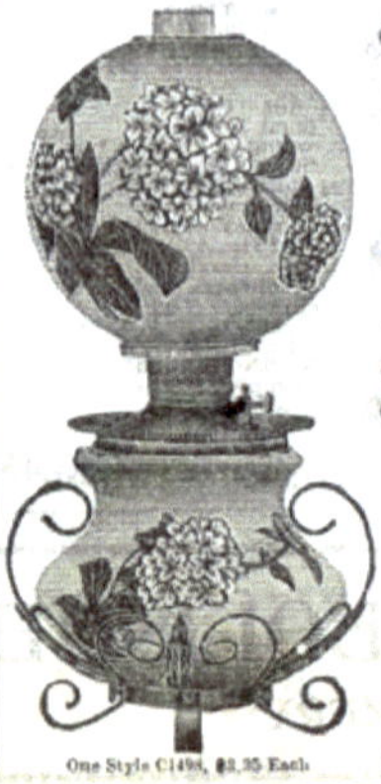

One Style C1498, $3.35 Each

C1497 — Asst, 2 large lamps, 10 in. globes, one in rich rookwood colors wth large shepherd picture decorations, oxidized metal trimmings, the other in rookwood and green blended ground, stag decoration. Old English brass finished metal trimmings, neavy metal bases, ornamental crowns, best removable brass founts, No. 2. Success draft burners, globe rings, chimneys and wicks, full ht. 4 in. Total 2 lamps in bbl., wt. 52 lbs.....................Each, **Out**

(NO PACKAGE CHARGE.)

C1498 Asst.—2 lamps, popular low shapes, one with 10 in. globe, both body and globe in rich green blended ground, large pink hydrangeas and green leaves, black Florentine design metal trimmings, spun crown, the other with large 11 in. globe, rich pink blended ground, large wild flower decoration, heavy gilt finished metal base and crown. Removable founts, No. 2 Royal center draft burners, globe rings, chimneys and wicks, full ht. 22¾ in. 2 in bbl., wt. 52 lbs.....................Each, **$3.35**

(NO PACKAGE CHARGE.)

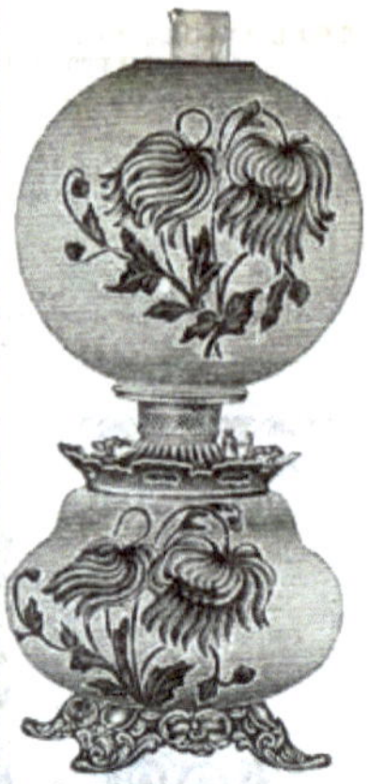

One Style C1499,

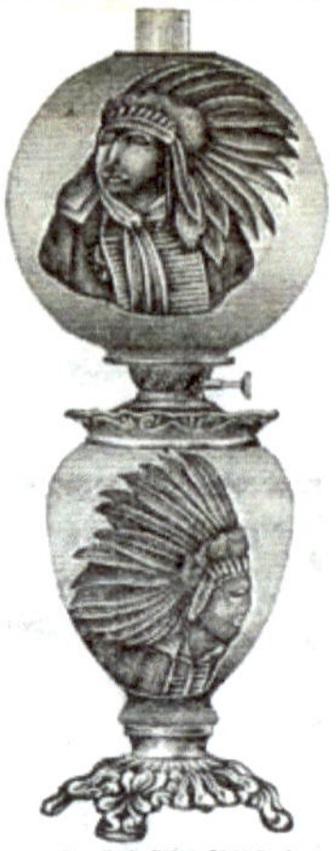

One Style C1500, $3 65 Each.

C1499—Large low swell shape body 11 in. globe, allover pink and green blended ground, large hand painted chrysanthemums, heavy ornamental gilt metal base and crown, solid brass removable fount, No. 2 Royal center draft burner, globe ring, chimney and wick, full ht. 24 in. Each in bbl., wt. 45 lbs.......................................Each, **Out**

(NO PACKAGE CHARGE.)

C1500—Tall vase shaped body, 11 in. globe, rich red and ivory ground, large Indian Chief decorations, heavy oxidized metal base and crown, removable fount, No. 2 Success center draft burner, globe ring, chimney and wick, full ht. 28¼ in. Each in bbl., wt. 41 lbs.......................................Each. **$3.65**

(NO PACKAGE CHARGE)

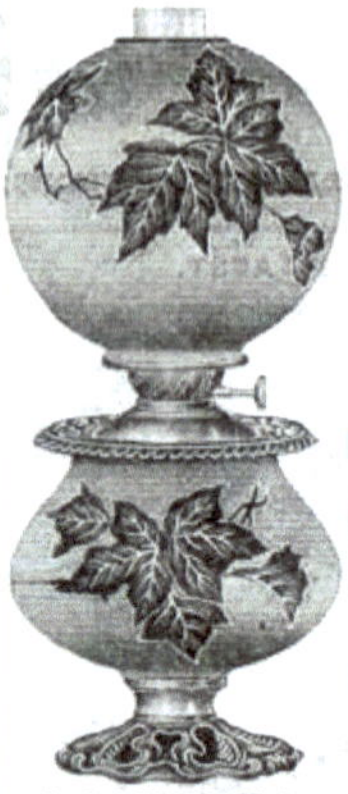

One Style C1501, $3.87 Each.

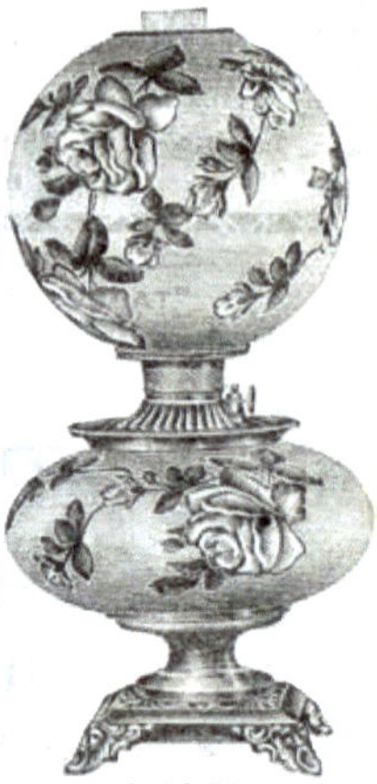

C1507, $5 50 Each.

C1501—Medium size, very beautiful. Swell shape body, 10 in. globe, rich satin etched finish, large oak leaf decorations in Autumnal colors with gold tracings, stems, etc., decorations profuse and on both sides, ornamental base and crown, removale fount, No. 2 Success center draft burner, globes, ring, chimney and metal trimmings in the popular old English brass and verd finish, full ht. 23¾ in. Each in bbl., wt. 28 lbs.......................................Each. **$3.87**

(NO PACKAGE CHARGE.)

C1507. Large fancy shape body with 11 in. globe, both in pure white ground with allover hand painted rose decorations in red and green, decorations richly enameled and very elaborate covering almost the entire lamp, extra heavy gilt finished metal base and crown, removable brass fount, No. 2 Royal center draft burner, globe ring, chimney and wick, full ht. 26½ in. Each in bbl.......................................Each. **$5.50**

(NO PACKAGE CHARGE.)

CARDINAL RED LAMP ASST.

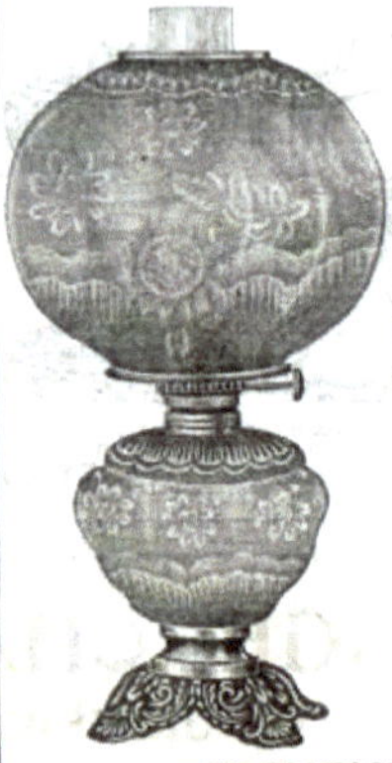

Both dome and globe shapes in the most popular colors and biggest profit paying lamps which could go on your counters. Our sales on these have been enormous; yours should be likewise.

C910 Asst. — 4 lamps, all in rich embossed satin etched solid cardinal red. Gilt finished metal bases. Complete with burners, globe and shade rings and chimneys. Asstd. as follops:

1 only, No. 1, 7 in. globe, full ht, 19 in., No. 2 burner.....................@ $1 20

1 only, No. 2, 3¾ in. dome, ht. 19 in., No. 2 "Sun" burber.....................@ 1 20

1 only, No. 3, 9 in. globe, ht. 19¾ in., No. 3 "Climax" burner.......@ 1 50

1 only, No. 4, large 10 in. dome, ht. 19¾ in., No. 3 "Climax" burner.@ 1 50

Total of 4 in asst., **$5.40**

(NO PACKAGE CHARGE.)

We Do Not Depend on One Line of Goods for Our Profit, Hence Can Sell Cheaper.

VASE SHAPE MELON DESIGN LAMP ASSORTMENT.

Popular sellers. At $5.00 each you will advertise yourself.

C1503 — 2 styles, both fancy vase shapes in the new melon design with 10½ in. globes, one in the rich allover Pompeian or onyx effect with old English brass finished metal trimmings, the other in solid lavender color, allover satin etched effect with gun metal trimmings, both have ornamental crowns, removable founts, No. 2 Success center draft burners, globe rings, chimneys and wicks, ht. 25¼. 2 in bbl. Wt. 50 lbs. Each. **$3.60**

NICKEL PLATED ROYAL CENTER DRAFT LAMP ASST.

The best center draft lamps made.

C1354 — Well made, heavy, full nickeled brass, with tripod, chimney, wick and 10 in. opal dome shade. Full ht. 19¼ in. Royal center draft burners. Asst. comprises:
1 only No. 5, plain, with embossed foot $1.32
1 only No. 10, fancy openwork metal foot 1.37
1 only No. 15, fancy openwork metal foot and large double handles 1.62

3 complete in bbl. Total, **$4.31**
(NO PKG. CHARGE.)

NICKEL PLATED STUDENT LAMP.

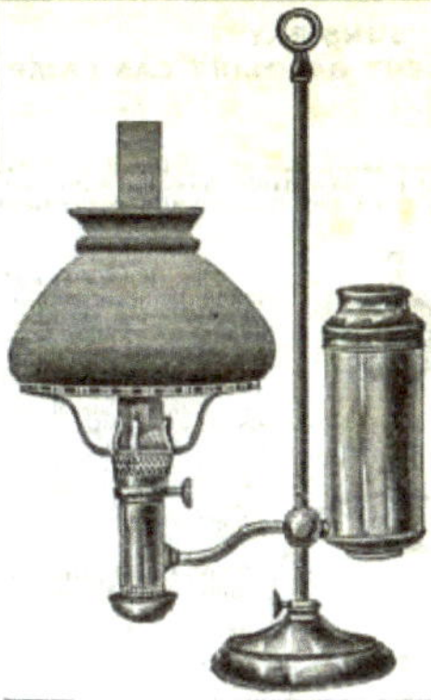

C1356 — Solid brass, full nickeled heavy base, thumb screw adjustment for raising and lowering. No. 0 center burner, chimney, wick and 7 in. opal dome shade. Each in case. Wt. 20 lbs. Each, **$3.00**

Student Lamp or "Junior Rochester" Chimney.

C0 — Fits C1356 Student lamp. 1 doz. in pkg. Doz. **30c**
(NO PKG. CHARGE.)

PACKAGE CHARGE ABOLISHED
ON GLASSWARE AND CROCKERY.

C1506, $4.60 Each.   C1510, $9.50 Each.

C1506 — Extra tall fancy vase shape body with 10 in. globe, both in rich dark rookwood ground with large enameled hand painted floral decorations, gilt finish metal base, ornamental double handled crown, removable fount, No. 2 Royal center draft burner, globe ring, chimney and wick, full ht. 15 in. Each in bbl., wt. 45 lbs. Each, **$4.60**
(NO PACKAGE CHARGE.)

C1510 — Solid royal ruby, fancy vase shape body, known to the trade as royal copper. Extra large fancy shape body with 11 in. globe both in the expensive solid ruby, decorated on both sides with large needle etched dragon in pure gold, large gun metal finished base and crown, gun metal finished removable fount, No. 2 success center draft burner, globe ring, chimney and wick, full ht. 29 in. Each in bbl., wt. 45 lbs. Each, **$9.50**
(NO PACKAGE CHARGE.)

DECORATED LAMP GLOBE ASST.

Big globes at unusually low prices.

C935 — All elaborately tinted and profusely decorated with hand painted floral and leaf designs. Asst. comprises three best selling sizes as follows:
3 only 8 in. 1 blue, one green and 1 pink .... at 25c $0.75
3 only 9 in. 1 blue, 1 purple and 1 pink .... at 35c 1.05
2 only 10 in. 1 pink and 1 green .... at 50c 1.00

Total for asst. of 8 globes **$2.80**
(NO PKG. CHARGE.)

RICH GOLD EXTENSION LIBRARY LAMPS.

Big values in these popular lamps. Although known to trade as library lamps, are universally used for dining room, parlor, etc.

C1515 — Rich gold metal, fancy embossed harp, ball extension, length closed 30 in., extended 55 in., large bell shape opal dome shade, crystal fount, No. 2 "Sun" burner, crimped top chimney, 4 complete in bbl., wt. 45 lbs. (No pkg. charge.) Each **$1.30**

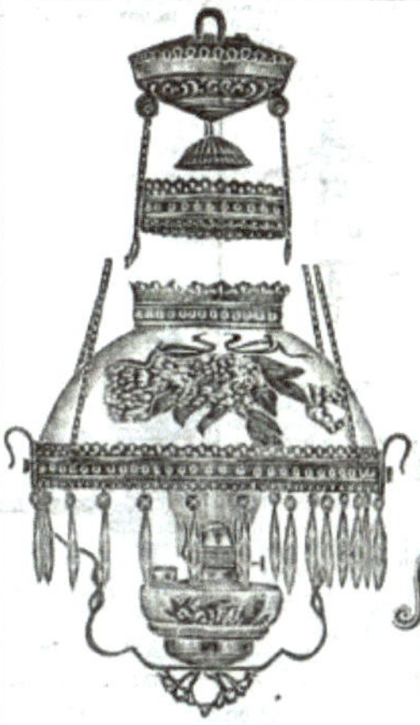

C1518 — Large rich gold harp and frame, ball extension, large opal fount, 14 in. dome shade, hand painted lilac decorations in lavender and green, 28 cut glass prisms length closed 44 in., extended 63 in. No. 2 "Sun" burner, crimped top chimney. Each in bbl. Wt. 45 lbs. (No pkg. charge.) .... Each, **$3.60**

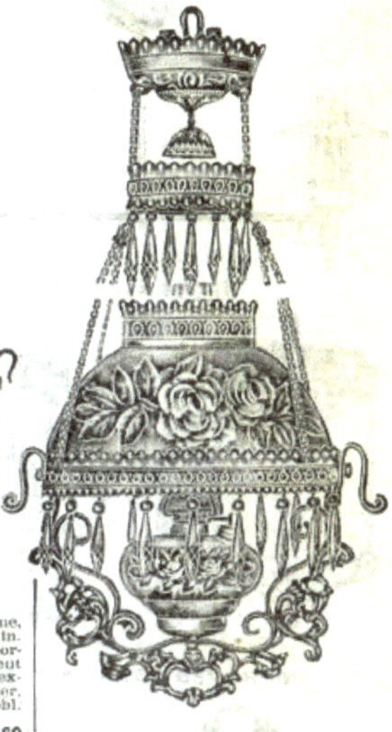

C1524 — Extra large frame and wide bands, all in rich gold, heavily chased, best spring extension, large opal body, 14 in. dome shade both in brown and green blended tints, large hand painted cherry and leaf decorations. Complete with 28 cut glass prisms, best gold finish solid brass removable fount, center draft burner, wick and chimney. Length closed 36 in., extended 78 in. Each in bbl., wt. 50 lbs. (No pkg. charge.) .... Each, **$4.95**

CARDINAL RED HALL LAMP.

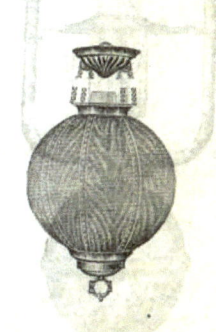

C1517 — Fancy shape harp, handsomely chased, all in rich gold, will not tarnish, patent spring extension, large opal fount, 14 in. dome shade, fount and shade in pink and green blended tints with large hand painted peonies, length closed 27 in., extended 64 in. No. 2 "Sun" burner and crimped top chimney. Each in bbl. Wt. 45 lbs. (No packing charge.) Each, **$3.25**

C1521 — Extra large size, rich gold fancy frame, patent spring extension, length closed 30 in., extended 72, large tinted and floral decorated body, 14 in. tinted and floral decorated dome shade, removable fount, "Success" center draft burner, wick and chimney. Each in bbl., wt. 45 lbs. (No pkg. chg.) Each, **$3.95**

C1527 — Rich gold finish metal trimmings, pulley extension, 10½ in. embossed cardinal red satin etched globe, glass fount. No. 1 burner and chimney. Each in case. Wt. 50 lbs. (NO PKG. CHARGE.) Each, **$2.29**

We Reserve Our Orders and Money for Goods We Can BUY RIGHT and SELL RIGHT.

THE IMPROVED "SUNS-RAY" INCANDESCENT GASOLINE GAS LAMP.

(Approved by the National Board of Fire Insurance Underwriters.)

Not merely the best lamp for the price, but **THE BEST AT ANY PRICE.** Positively has no superior. We invite comparison with any lamp made regardless of name or price.

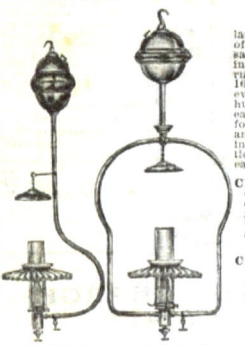

The "Suns-Ray" lamps are made entirely of solid brass, one-quart safety reservoirs, holding sufficient gasoline to run one burner for about 16 hours. Steady and even light of about one hundred candle power for each burner—more light for less money than by any other mode of illumination. Full instructions as to operating with each lamp.

C1605, One-light Pendent; All brass, oxidized finish, stationary reservoir. Complete with chimney, mantle and shade.
Each, **$2.50**

C1606, Plain Harp Lamp: All brass, polished brass finish. For home, church or hall. Complete with chimney, mantle and shade.
Each, **$3.50**

C1607, Two-light Pendant; All brass oxidized finish, stationary reservoir. Complete with chimneys, mantles and shades. Each, **$4.50**

Spring Extension.

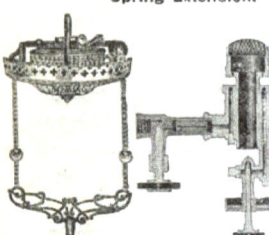

For Suns-Ray or other lamps. Automatic, extends 3 foot.
C 2, Suns-Ray extension, brass. Each, **$1.10**
C 1, Suns-Ray extension, nickel plate. Each, **$1.20**

Improved Suns-Ray Burner. Fits any gravity lamp with 3/4 in. Standard Tubing. Burner complete $1.00
Burner with Gallery..$1.10

IMPROVED "SUNLIKE" LAMP.

New and improved style, splendid illuminators, reasonable in cost.

C1601: For indoor use. About 800 candle illuminating power — more than 5 times that of the ordinary gravity gasoline lamps. The best substitute for electric arc light yet devised and perfectly safe, being Approved by the National Board of Fire Insurance Underwriters. When the gasoline in the reservoir is renewed it is put under an arc pressure by means of a pump. Handsomely finished in oxidized copper, ht. 30 in., wt. 10½ lbs., 5½ qt. reservoir, fitted with nickeled reflector, mantle chimney and extra quality 16 in. pump, complete. Each in case, no charge for case.
Each, **$8.00**

C1602: Fitted with pressure gauge as shown on cut.
Each, **$9.25**

C1603: For outdoor use. Same as C1601, but fitted with a heavy hood and globe, thus protecting the generator and mantle. Each in case, no charge for case.
Each, **$9.00**

NOTE. We can furnish a pressure gauge with which you can tell the exact pressure on your lamp. Each...**$1.25**

We can furnish all repairs for "Sunlike" lamp. Order by number.

No.			No.		
4	Air Mixer Cup	$0 20	19	Generator Rod complete	$0 10
6	Gas Tip	12	25	Gauge screw Set	07
7	Cleaning Needle and Nut	1"	31	Filler Plug	60
9	Generator Tube	40			

THE "RADIUM" INCANDESCENT GASOLINE GAS LAMP.

The up-to-date gasoline store lamps, more light for less cost than any gravity gasoline lamp made. Made of brass, oxidized finish, fitted with special burners, made of air-hole glassware which increases your light 100 per cent, giving you a 200 candle power light for each burner. Approved by the National Board of Fire Insurance Underwriters. Each lamp complete with mantle, air-hole globe, torch, etc. Each in box.

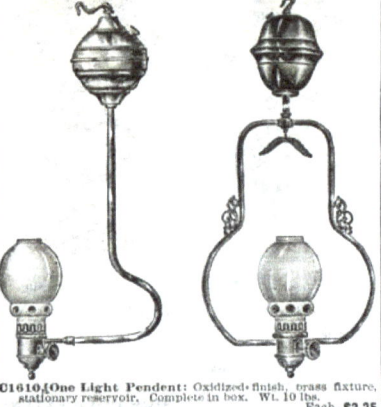

C1610, One Light Pendent: Oxidized finish, brass fixture, stationary reservoir. Each in box. Wt. 10 lbs.
Each, **$2.25**

C1612, Fancy Harp Lamp: Oxidized finish, brass. Complete in box. Wt. 11 lbs. Each, **$3.00**

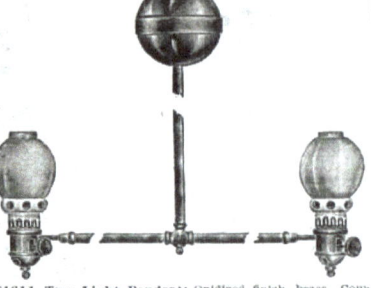

C1611, Two Light Pendent: Oxidized finish, brass. Complete. Wt. 15 lbs. Each, **$3.85**

"DAYLIGHT" ARC PRESSURE GASOLINE LAMP.

"NEW RADIUM" ARC PRESSURE GASOLINE LAMP.

The maximum of light with the minimum of gasoline.

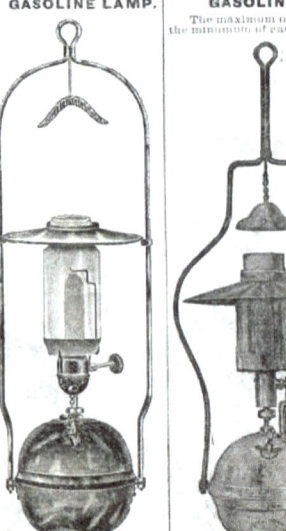

C1600: Constructed of best material, tank of heavy spun brass. Each tested to full 200 lb. pressure while lamp requires but 6 to 10 lbs. to operate. Burner is high class. Absolutely safe, clean and durable. Approved by the National Board of Fire Underwriters. Each in case. (No package charge.)
Each, **$5.00**

C1604: 750 candle power, under generator type. Nickel finish, all brass lamp. Special burner of simple construction, making lamp very easy to operate. Burns 12 hours with one filling. Complete with pump, wrench, mantle shade and glassware. Instructions with each. Each in box.
Each, **$5.00**

"PRINCESS" ARC GASOLINE PRESSURE LAMP.

One of the best, cheapest, simplest and most economical lamps on the market, cost of lighting not to exceed 2c per day and gives a light of about 750 candle power. Not only one of the handsomest but one of the safest gasoline lamps on the market, for home as well as store lighting. Burner produces soft white light of about 750 candle power. With 2 qts. of gasoline it will burn upwards of 20 hours. We cannot speak too highly of our "Princess" Arc Lamp. Each tested before leaving factory and a year's guarantee goes with each lamp. No needle and valve to get out of order. The gasoline is forced through a gauze wire. NOTE: Four strokes of the pump is all that is required, making about four lbs. pressure. Do not give more.

C1620—New artistic design, solid copper, oxidized finish. Equipped with new, patent non-clogging burner, best pressure burner. Jena Air Hole globe, extra large. Pump wrench, etc., complete in box. Wt. 20 lbs. Each, **8.00**

C1621—Nickel Plated, otherwise, same as above....Each, **8.25**

THE "RADIUM" PRESSURE SYSTEM LIGHT.

Cheapest artificial light known. Computed on a basis of 1200 C. P. The comparative costs per hour are:
Gasoline 1c. Gas with burner 6c.
Electricity 5c. Kerosene 18c.
These figures are from an actual test.

This system is so constructed that the supply tank may be placed outside the building and the gasoline forced through a hollow copper wire to lamp by air pressure. Approved by the Fire Underwriters. Each lamp guaranteed against defects for two years. Very simple to operate and absolutely safe. A four lamp system can be lighted in five minutes in the coldest temperature. Each system complete with tank, mantles, pump wrench, torch, etc., and includes one extra burner.

A Two Light System will light a store 24x50 ft. as light as day. For effective lighting use one lamp for a square of 25x25 ft.

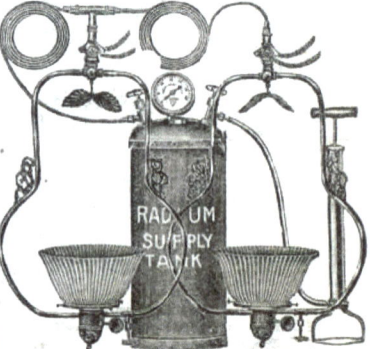

C1613, One Light System: One 600 C. P. lamp. Complete with 2 gal. tank. Wt. 28 lbs. Brass oxidized lamp with 25 ft. hollow wire connection. Imitation cut glass shade.
Each, **$11 50**

C1614, Two Light System: Complete with two 600 C. P. lamps, 4 gal. tank, 50 ft. hollow wire and 12 in. auto pump. Wt. 36 lbs. Each, **$15.95**

C1615, Three Light System: Complete with three 600 C. P. lamps, 4 gal. tank, 75 ft. hollow wire and 22 in. auto pump. Wt. 41 lbs. Each, **$19.75**

C1616, Four Light System: Complete with four 600 C. P. lamps, 8 gal. tank, 100 ft. hollow wire and 22 in. auto pump. Wt. 55 lbs. Each, **$23.50**

C1617, Five Light System: Complete with five 600 C. P. lamps, 8 gal. tank, 125 ft. hollow wire and 22 in. auto pump. Wt. 65 lbs. Each, **$27.50**

NOTE.—To customers who desire to increase the size of their systems, we can furnish the following supplies at any time.
Single lamps with 25 ft. wire..............Complete, **$3.75**
Hollow wire in 15 and 25 ft. coils................Pr. ft., .05
Four gal. tanks...Each, 7.00
Ten gal. tanks.. 8.20
T connections.. .20
Straight connections..................................Doz. 1.75
Globe.. Each
Burners complete...

CROCKERY OR QUEENS WARE DEPT.

Look Over Every Line of Crockery in the Trade and Then Come Here and Save Money.

Package Charge Abolished

All Goods Shipped from Our House

In the last eighteen months we have revolutionized the crockery business by carrying all goods in stock, making it possible to make shipment the same day orders reach us. We now take the final step by abolishing the last vestige of package charge.

We are today very much the largest distributers in America of these important goods. By reason of our ability to use the entire output of several potteries, we were able to make a number of long-time contracts at prices ruling before the last big advance. While those contracts last, we propose to give our customers the benefit. Our line is complete, the goods we supply are all of standard grade, and our prices set the pattern for America.

"PERFECTION" HIGH GRADE WHITE GRANITE WARE (OPEN STOCK)

Best W. G. Ware in the United States. We guarantee it as to quality, color, selection, sizes and against crazing. Body the best that can possibly be made—baked extra hard—blue white color—clean, bright glaze. Very carefully selected R. K. grade. A ware that will stand the test. Do not judge "Perfection" ware by the very low prices named—order a sample lot and COMPARE. Shipped from our house—no package charge.

NO PACKAGE CHARGE On any Goods.

The New "ROYAL FIRENZE" ROSE DECORATED DINNER WARE (OPEN STOCK)

Unheard of introductory prices. When this ware is once known and the grade and decoration seen we have reason to believe that this will be the best selling ware on the market. Fine quality, extremely handsome, up to date decoration. Body, new Royal Firenze Ware, neatly embossed design, extra light and artistic. All full sizepieces, decorations in shaded pink roses, wreath design, with background of shaded green leaves and pink forget me nots. Gold stamp between each spray of flowers, also gold center stamp. All pieces full gold traced.

SHIPPED FROM OUR HOUSE—**NO PACKAGE CHARGE.**

Plates.
4 in., actual 6½ in..Doz. $0 55
5 " " 7½ " .. " 68
6 " " 8¾ " .. " 84
7 " " 9⅛ " .. " 98
7 " deep, actual 9¾ in.... " 99
7 in., coupe, actual 8⅞ in. .... Doz. 99

Cake Plates—
11 in. ....Doz. 2 40

Bone Dish ....Doz. 92

Fancy Handled Cup and Saucer..Doz. **1 15**

Sauce Boat........Doz. 2 40

Fancy Creamer: Doz. 1 65

Dishes or Platters:
8 in., act. 11⅜ in..Doz. 1 50
10 " " 13¾ " .. " 2 70
12 " " 15¾ " .. " 4 50
14 " " 17⅜ " .. " 6 30

30's Bowls—
Capacity 1½ pt.... Doz. $1 20

4 in. Fruit—
Actual 5¼ in........Doz. 48

Covered Butter...Doz. 5 40

Individual Butters. Doz. 32

Covered Dishes:
7 in. oblong, actual 9 in..............Doz. 6 30
8 in. oblong, actual 10 in.............. " 7 20

Covered Casserole:
8 in. round.......... " 8 10

Fancy Tea Pot: ... " 4 80

Nappies:
5 in., actual 6½ in..Doz. 1 20
6 " " 7½ " . " 1 50
7 " " 8¾ " . " 1 80
8 " " 9⅝ " . " 2 70

Jugs:
42's actual ½ pt....Doz. $1 45
36's " 1 " .... " 1 50
30's " 2 " .... " 1 80
24's " 3 " .... " 2 55
12's " 4 " .... " 3 60

Bakers.
6 in., actual 8¾ in. Doz. 1 50
7 " " 9¾ " " 1 80
8 " " 10 " " 2 70

Fancy Sugar: ....Doz. 3 60

Pickles........ Doz. 1 80

"ROYAL" FIRENZE WARE-- TEA AND DINNER SETS.

For composition of tea and dinner sets see page 269

56 Piece—Tea Set. ...$3 80
65 Piece—Dinner Set... 5 45
100A Piece—Dinner Set. 8 00
100B Piece—Dinner Set. 7 75
112 Piece—Dinner Set... 8 50

PACKAGE CHARGE ABOLISHED

On All Glassware and Crockery

"PRINCESS" Delicate Rose Decorated Near China (OPEN STOCK)

Very fine high-class ware at extremely low prices. Positively the best American ware made. Built on very graceful lines. Body of domestic near china ware—very light and thin. Pieces all full size and of beau-t'ful shapes and design. Artistically embossed, full gold traced and lined. Decorations in delicate shaded pink and yellow roses in full bloom and bud effect with sprays of green leaves in two shades. Better than a great many of the high priced lines of imported china. SHIPPED FROM OUR HOUSE, **NO PACKAGE CHARGE.**

Cups and Saucers: Doz.
Martha regular coffees, so called teas..........$1 20
Iris regular coffees, so called teas............ 1 20
5 o'clock teas............ 1 00

Plates:
4 in., actual 6½ in....... 56
5 " " 7¼ "....... 75
6 " " 8¼ "....... 90
7 " " 9⅛ "....... 1 00
8 " " 10¼ "...... 1 18
7 in. coupe soup, actual 9 in.................... 1 00
7 in. deep soup, actual 9¼ in.................... 1 00

Fancy Pickle: 1 92

Dishes or Platters:
7 in., actual 10⅝ in..... 1 30
8 " " 11¾ "..... 1 60
10 " " 13⅜ "..... 2 90
12 " " 15⅜ "..... 4 80
14 " " 17¾ " 6 70

Nappies: Doz.
6 in., actual 7½ in.......$1 60
7 " " 8⅝ "....... 1 95
8 " " 9¾ "....... 2 90

Fruits:
4 in., actual 5¼ in........ 49
5 " " 6¼ "........ 56

Oatmeals: 36's 1 00

Bakers:
3 in., actual 5¾ in....... 1 15
6 " " 8¼ "....... 1 60
7 " " 9¼ "....... 1 95
8 " " 10¼ "....... 2 90

Covered Butters: 5 75

Individual Butters: .. 32

Bowls:
36's, Oyster Bowl, 1 pt.. 1 10
30's, " " 1¼ " 1 30
36's, Fancy " 1 " 1 10
30's, " " 1¼ " 1 25

Sugar and Cover: 30's.. 3 85

Tea Pot: 5 10

Covered Dishes:
7 in., actual 9¼ in....... 6 72
8 " " 10⅜ " 7 65

7 in. Casserole: Actual 8⅛ in.................... 7 65

Doz.
Bone Dish: $0 96
Sauce Boat: 2 55
Spoon Holder: 3 20
Creamer: 1 95

Jugs:
42's, capacity ¾ pt...... 1 60
36's, " 1 "...... 1 65
30's, " 2 "...... 1 92
24's, " 3 "...... 2 90
12's, " 4 "...... 3 85
6's, " 5 "...... 5 75

"PRINCESS" TEA AND DINNER SETS.

For composition tea and dinner sets see page 269

56 Piece Tea Set $3 95
65 Piece Dinner Set.... 5 00
100 Piece A Dinner Set.. 8 20
100 Piece B Dinner Set.. 8 00
112 Piece Dinner Set... 8 95

PACKAGE CHARGE ABOLISHED

On All Glassware and Crockery

"FRENCH ROSE" DECORATED SEMI-PORCELAIN (OPEN STOCK)

Owing to the extraordinary demand we have decided to reinstate this beautiful ware. Grade is much finer than our old pattern, though decoration is the same but much more profuse, both in the decal and gold tracing. "French Rose" ware is noted for its beautiful colorings which are in delicate pink roses with abundant shaded green sprays and background of wild flowers in seven color work. Body of new china effect semi-porcelain ware, light weight, neatly embossed. SHIPPED FROM OUR HOUSE—**NO PACKAGE CHARGE.**

Cups and Saucers—Handled
Fancy shape, regular Doz. coffee, so called tea...$1 10
Cups only.................. 65
Saucers only............... 45
Fancy extra large coffe. 1 25
Cups only.................. 73
Saucers only............... 52

Plates—Fancy scalloped edge.
4 in., actual 6¾ in....... 52
5 " " 7¾ " 45
6 " " 8¾ " *72c
7 " " 9⅝ " 95
8 " " 10¼ " 1 15
7 " deep, actual 9¼ in. 95

Coupe Soup—Actual 8⅛ in........................ 95

Fancy Cake Plate...... 2 30

Dishes or Platters—
Fancy shape.
7 in., actual 11 in....... 1 20
8 " " 12 " 1 45
9 " " 13 "....... 1 75
10 " " 14 "....... 2 65
12 " " 16 "....... 4 50
14 " " 18 "....... 6 25

Fruit or Sauce Dishes—
4 in., actual 5¼ in...... 45
5 " " 6¾ in...... 48

Bakers or Vegetable Dishes—Fancy deep oval shape. Doz.
6 in., actual 8¼ in.......$1 45
7 " " 9½ " 1 72
8 " " 10 " 2 65

Nappies—Round deep fancy shape
6 in., actual 7¼ in....... 1 45
7 " " 8⅝ " 1 72
8 " " 9¾ " 2 65

Covered Butter—
(3 pieces)................ 5 40

Individual Butter—
3 in........................ 30

Oval Covered Vegetable Dishes—Fancy shape footed.
7 in., actual 9 in........ 6 25
8 " " 10 " 7 00

Cassarole or Round Covered Vegetable Dish—
8 in., actual 8⅛ in....... 8 00

Sauce Boat—
Fancy shape............ 2 85

Covered Tea Pot........ 4 50

Covered Sugar Bowl—
Fancy 30's, large size... 3 60

Bone Dish— Doz.
Fancy shape..............$0 90

Pickle Dish—
Fancy shape.............. 1 70

Spoon Holder—
Fancy shape............. 2 35

Bowls—
30's, footed oyster, 1⅛ pt. 1 10
30's, " deep 1⅛ " 1 20

Jugs—
42's, capacity ½ pt...... 1 40
36's, " 1 "...... 1 50
30's, " 2 "...... 1 75
24's, " 3 "...... 2 20
12's, " 4 "...... 3 50

Cream Pitcher— Doz.
Fancy 30's, large size...$1 75

"FRENCH ROSE" TEA AND DINNER SETS.

For composition of Tea and Dinner Sets see page 269

56 Piece Tea Set.........$3 50
65 Piece Dinner Set...... 5 20
100 Piece A Dinner Set.. 7 90
100 Piece B Dinner Set.. 7 65
112 Piece Dinner Set.... 8 30

PACKAGE CHARGE ABOLISHED

On All Glassware and Crockery

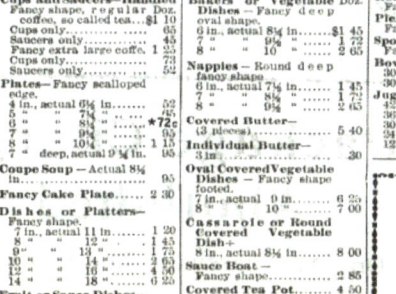

Dept. of ENGLISH CROCKERY

Standard brands, whose well known trademarks are a guarantee of quality. Long established English makers like John Maddock & Sons need no introduction to American dealers or users. Note how our prices on this staple English earthenware compare with those of exclusive crockery jobbers, who have heretofore almost monopolized the business. Note that we quote *net prices* in United States currency—not in pounds, shillings and pence as is usual. We think you will find our quotations from 15 to 20 per cent under those usually charged.

We carry all English crockery in open stock, hence can make shipment same day order is received. No charge for package. We shall carry the open patterns indefinitely. You can make up sets to suit your trade, in any composition you like, and know that you will be able to re-order pieces as wanted.

MADDOCK'S "Royal Vitreous" White Semi-Porcelain (OPEN STOCK)

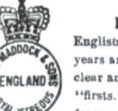

Famous John Maddock & Sons' make. Each piece trademarked. Positively the best English semi-porcelain made. Each piece guaranteed against crazing. Has been on the market 40 years and hasn't crazed yet. Made of finest materials, medium light weight, strong and durable, fine clear and brilliant white glaze, all pieces full size, fancy shape and attractively embossed and absolutely "firsts." Among the most staple merchandise that can go on your shelves. Always in season. Shipped from our house—**no package charge.**

Cups and Saucers—Handied. Doz.
- E103, After dinner coffees. Fancy shape, 2¾x2¼, saucer 4¾.. Out
- E100, London tea, fancy low shape, 3¾x2¼, saucer 6 95
- E101, Grecian tea, large size, fancy bell shape, 3¾x2⅝, saucer 6 96

Plates—Flat.
- E104, 4 in. actual 5⅝.. Out
- E106, 6 " " 7¾.. 72
- E107, 7 " " 9 .. 84
- E109, Deep soup, 7 in. flat, actual 9.......... 84

E114, Individual Butters—Diam. 3⅛ in..... 20

E116, Egg Cup—Regulation double deck, ht. 4⅛ in.................. Out

Dishes or Platters—Fancy oval shape. Doz.
- E124, 5 in., actual 8¾ $0 85
- E125, 7 " " 9¾ 1 05
- E126, 8 " " 10¾ 1 33
- E127, 9 " " 11⅜ 1 60
- E128, 10 " " 12⅜ 2 40
- E129, 12 " " 14¾ 2 95
- E130, 14 " " 16¾ Out

Nappies or Scollops—Fancy round deep shape.
- E123, 8 in., actual 10.. Out

Jugs—Fancy swell shape, footed.
- E133, 42's, ½ pt....... 1 25
- E134, 36's, 1 " 1 33
- E135, 30's, 2 " 1 57
- E136, 24's, 3 " .... 1 [illegible]
- E137, 12's, 4 " 3 15

E143, Covered Tea Pot—Large size, 24's, fancy shape, full ht. 7⅛ in.................. Out

Bakers or Vegetable Dishes—Fancy oblong, deep shape— Doz.
- E117, 3 in., actual 5⅜ $0 92
- E118, 6 " 7⅜ 1 30
- E119, 7 " 8⅝ 1 57

Oval Covered Vegetable Dishes—Fancy shape, footed.
- E131, 7 in., actual 9.. Out

E140, Covered Butter Dish—Large size, fancy shape, diam. 7⅛ in., loose drainer 4 75

E142, Covered Sugar Bowl—30's, fancy low shape, double handles 3 10

E141, Cream Pitcher— Doz. 30's fancy low shape .. 1 57

E139, Handled Sauce Boat—Large size, fancy shape.............. 2 10

"ROYAL VITREOUS" TEA AND DINNER SETS.

For composition of Tea and Dinner Sets see 209

Set.
- E64—56 piece Tea Set ...
- E65—45 piece Dinner Set.
- E66—100 piece Dinner Set
- E68—112 piece Dinner Set

Out

PACKAGE CHARGE ABOLISHED On All Crockery and Glassware.

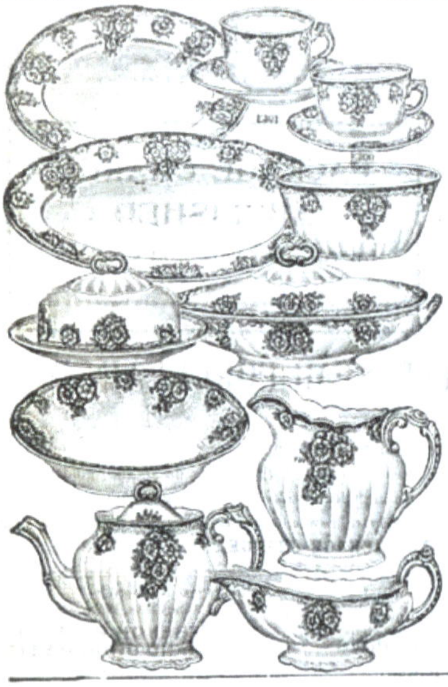

"EVERY DAY" Green Print Decorated ENGLISH SEMI-PORCELAIN (OPEN STOCK)

Attractively decorated line at prices usually charged for plain white. Good quality English white semi-porcelain body, light weight, run of the kiln "firsts," absolutely guaranteed against crazing. All pieces full size, fancy shape, attractive floral green print decoration in wide border effect, all handles, knobs, etc., also decorated in green. Send for a sample line and you will like this ware. Shipped from our house—**no package charge.**

Cups and Saucers Handled—
- E300, "Elite," tea, 3¼x 2¼, saucer 6.......... Doz. $0 95
- E301, "Crown" tea. Large size, low shape, 3½x 2½, saucer 6.......... 96
- E302, Coffees. Large size, fancy low shape 1 25

Plates—Flat.
- E304, 4 in., actual 6..... 45
- E305, 5 " " 7..... 62
- E306, 6 " " 8..... 75
- E307, 7 " " 9..... 89
- E308, 8 " " 10.... 96
- E309, Deep soup, 7 in. actual 9.............. 89
- E310, Coupe shape soup 7 in., actual 7¾....... 89

Fruit or Sauce Dishes—
- E311, 4 in., actual 4¾... 41
- E312, 4½ in., actual 5¾. 43

E313, Oatmeal Bowl— Deep shape, diam. 5¾ in. 47

Dishes or Platters— Fancy oval shape. Doz.
- E323, 7 in., actual 9... $0 [illegible]
- E324, 8 " " 10½. 1 35
- E325, 9 " " 11... 1 65
- E326, 10 " " 12... 2 40
- E327, 12 " " 14... 4 10
- E328, 14 " " 16... 5 75

Nappies— Round deep shape.
- E320, 6 in., actual 8..... 1 35
- E321, 7 " " 9¾... 1 65
- E322, 8 " " 10... 2 45

E338, Pickle Dish— Long oval shape, length 8¾ in., double handles.............. 1 70

E314, Individual Butters— Diam. 3¼ in.............. 28

E315, Utility or Slop Bowl—Round deep shape, diam. 6⅛ in. ht 3. 1 05

E316, Egg Cup— Double deck, regulation 95

Bakers or Vegetable Dishes—Fancy oval shape.
- E317, 6 in., actual 8..... 1 35
- E318, 7 in., actual 9..... 1 65
- E319, 8 in., actual 10.... 2 45

Oval Covered Vegetable Dishes— Doz.
- E329, 7 in., actual 9..... 5 80
- E330, 8 " " 10..... 6 75

E337, Handled Sauce Boat— Footed, large size, fancy shape.................. 2 25

E339, Covered Butter Dish— Flanged, diam. 7¾ in., loose drainer............ 4 80

E340, Cream Pitcher— 30's fancy low shape.... 1 85

Jugs—Tall fancy shape, fancy handles.
- E332, 42's, capacity ½ pt.. 1 35
- E333, 36's " 1 " . 1 55
- E334, 30's " 2 " . 1 85
- E335, 24's " 3 " . 2 10
- E336, 12's " 4 " . 3 25

E342, Covered Tea Pot—Large size, ht. 7⅛ in... 4 25

E341, Covered Sugar Bowl— Doz. Fancy low shape, double handles.................. $3 45

E331, Round Covered Soup Tureen— Large size, diam. 10 in... 10 50

"EVERY DAY" TEA AND DINNER SETS.

For composition of Tea and Dinner sets see page 209

Set.
- E70—56 piece tea set.. $3 13
- E71—65 " dinner set . 4 00
- E72—100 " " " . 6 05
- E73—102 " " " . 8 28
- E74—112 " " " . 7 09
- E75—130 " " " ..10 70

PACKAGE CHARGE ABOLISHED On All Crockery and Glassware.

All Goods Now Shipped From Our House

Package Charge Abolished

On All Glassware and Crockery.

A REQUEST

Please write Crockery orders on separate sheets from all other goods. Orders made in this way need not be copied, but can go at once to the crockery department for filling. This means a saving of time for YOU.

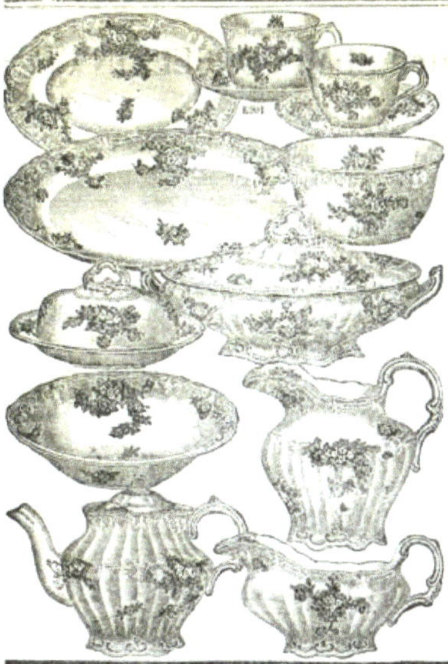

MADDOCK'S "VICTORIA" NATURAL 6 COLOR DECAL Semi=Porcelain (OPEN STOCK)

JOHN MADDOCK & SONS ENGLAND ROYAL VITREOUS

Victoria

Splendid value—will stand a profit. Light weight royal vitreous semi-porcelain body, absolutely guaranteed against crazing. Beautiful emb ssed fancy shape, profuse floral decorations, comprising large sprays of trailing arbutus in combination of pink, green and white, pink predominating, producing an exquisite vine effect. Decorations are not stingy, but very profuse, being on both sides of all the high pieces and inside as well as outside of open pieces. All handles, knobs and feet on all high pieces are elaborately traced in gold. Shipped from our house—**no package charge.**

Cups and Saucers, Handled— Doz.
E200, London teas, low fancy shape, 3¾x2¼, saucer 6 .... $1 67
E201, Grecian teas, large low bell shape, 3¼x2¼, saucer 6 .... 1 69
E202, Coffees, large size, fancy low shape, 4¼x2¼, saucer 6¾ 1 95
E203, After-dinner coffee, fancy shape, 2½x2¼, saucer 2¾ 1 25

Plates—Flat.
E204, 4 in., actual 5⅝ ... 72
E205, 5 " " 7 ... 89
E206, 6 " " 8 ... 1 15
E207, 7 " " 9 ... 1 35
E208, 8 " " 9¾ ... 1 55
E209, Deep soup, 7 in., actual 9 .... 1 35
E210, Coupe shape soup, 7 in., actual 8 .... 1 35

E214, Individual Butter Plates—Round, diam. 3¼ in 40

E241, Pickle Dish—Long fancy oval, 8¾ in .. 3 00

Dishes or Platters—Fancy deep oval shape. Doz.
E224, 7 in., actual 9¾ . $1 80
E225, 8 " " 10¾ . 2 25
E226, 9 " " 11¾ . 2 75
E227, 10 " " 12¾ . 4 00
E228, 12 " " 14¾ . 6 50
E229, 14 " " 16¾ . 9 00

Napples—Deep round shape.
E221, 6 in., actual 8 ... 2 25
E222, 7 " " 9 ... 2 75
E223, 8 " " 9⅞ ... 4 05

Fruit or Sauce Dishes—Fancy shape.
E211, 4 in., actual 5¾ . 64
E212, 4½ " " 5¾ . 67

E213, Oatmeal Bowl—Good size, deep shape, diam. 6⅜ in 75

E217, Egg Cup—Ht. 4¼ in., regulation double deck 1 38

E243, Handled Cream Pitcher—30's, low fancy shape 3 00

E244, Covered Sugar Bowl—Low fancy shape, footed, double handles .. 5 25

Bakers or Vegetable Dishes—Fancy deep oval shape. Doz.
E218, 6 in., actual 7¾ ... $2 25
E219, 7 " " 8¾ ... 2 75
E220, 8 " " 9¾ ... 4 05

Oval Covered Vegetable Dishes—Large, fancyshape, footed.
E230, 7 in., actual 9 .... 9 00
E231, 8 " " 9⅞ 10 50

Casseroles or Round Covered Vegetable Dishes—
E232, 6 in., actual 8 .... 10 50
E233, 8 " " 8⅞ .. 11 50

E234, Covered Soup Tureen—Large size, fancy round shape, diam. 9⅜ in., notched cover 16 90

E240, Handled Sauce Boat—Large, fancy shape, footed 3 45

E242, Covered Butter Dish—Large size, fancy shape, diam. 7¼ in., with loose drainer 7 75

E215, Bone Dish. Regulation size and shape, length 5¾ in .... Out

Jugs—Fancy shape, footed, large fancy handles. Doz.
E235, 42's, capacity ½ pt. $2 10
E236, 36's, " 1 " 2 35
E237, 30's, " 2 " 2 75
E238, 24's, " 3 " 3 10
E239, 12's " 4 " 5 15

E245, Large Covered Teapot—Fancy shape, large fancy handle, ht. 7⅛ in 6 95

E216, Utility or Slop Bowl—Large size, deep shape, diam. 5 in., ht. 3 .. 1 75

"VICTORIA" TEA AND DINNER SETS.

For composition of Tea and Dinner Sets see page 269. Set

E88—56 pc. tea set 4 75
E89—65 " dinner 7 55
E90—100 " " 10 00
E91—102 " " 12 10
E92—112 " " 11 9)
E93—130 " " 15 75

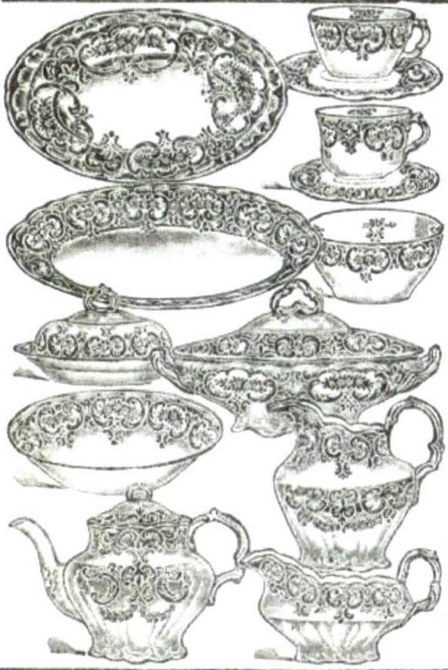

MADDOCK'S "FLOW BLUE" English Semi=Porcelain

JOHN MADDOCK & SONS ENGLAND ROYAL VITREOUS

Flow Blue

Each piece trademarked with John Maddock & Son's well known symbol. Entirely new. The most beautiful flow blue decoration ever produced. Ware is of the finest quality, medium light weight, fancy shape, attractively embossed, each piece with elaborate floral and scroll decorations in the popular underglazed flow blue which will never wear off. Illustrations cannot do justice to this line. *Every piece absolutely guaranteed against crazing.* Shipped from our house—**no package charge.**

Cups and Saucers—Handled—
E150, London teas. Fancy low shape, 3¾x2⅝, saucer 5¾ .... Doz. 1 50
E151, Grecian teas. Large size, fancy bell shape, 3¾x2¾, saucer 5¾ 1 52
E152, Coffees. Large size, fancy shape, 4⅛x2¼, saucer 6¾ 1 78
E153, After-dinner coffees. Fancy shape, 2¾x2¼, saucer 4¾ 1 10

Plates—Flat—
E154, 4 in., actual 5⅝ . 68
E155, 5 " " 6¾ 84
E156, 6 " " 8 . 1 04
E157, 7 " " 9 1 25
E158, 8 " " 10¾ . 1 45
E159, Deep soup, 7 in., actual 9 .... 1 25
E160, Coupe soups, 7 in., actual 8 in., deep shape 1 25

E164, Individual Butters—
Diam. 3¼ in 38

E165, Bone Dish—
Regulation fancy shape, 5¾ in 1 15

E166, Utility or Slop Bowl—
Large size, fancy shape, diam. 6 in., ht. 3 in ... 1 50

Dishes or Platters— Doz.
Fancy oval shape.
E174, 7 in., actual 9¾ . 1 50
E175, 8 " " 10¾ . 1 95
E176, 9 " " 11¾ . 2 28
E177, 10 " " 12¾ . 3 42
E178, 12 " " 14¾ . 5 70
E179, 14 " " 16¾ . 7 85

Nappies—Fancy, round, deep shape.
E171, 6 in., actual 8 ... 1 90
E172, 7 " " 9 ... 2 28
E173, 8 " " 10 ... 3 45

Fruit or Sauce Dishes—
E161, 4 in., actual 5⅛ .. 55
E162, 4½ " " 5¾ .. 62

E163, Oatmeal Bowl.
Fancy Shape—
Good size, diam. 6¼ in .. 68

E167, Egg Cup—
Ht. 4¼, regulation double deck 1 35

E191, Pickle Dish—
Fancy oval shape, length 8¾ in 2 20

E193, Cream Pitcher—
30s, fancy shape, footed, 2 25

E192, Covered Butter Dish—
Large size, fancy shape, flanged, diam. 7¾ in., loose drainer 6 85

Bakers or Vegetable Dishes—Fancy deep oval shape. Doz.
E168, 6 in., actual 7¾ .. 1 90
E169, 7 " " 8⅝ .. 2 25
E170, 8 " " 9¾ .. 3 45

Oval Covered Vegetable Dishes—
Fancy shape, footed.
E180, 7 in., actual 9 .... 8 60
E181, 8 " " 10 ... 9 10

Casseroles or Round Covered Vegetable Dishes—
E182, 6 in., actual 8 .... 9 10
E183, 8 " " 8¾ .. 10 25

E184, Covered Soup Tureen—
Large round fancy shape, diam. 9 in., with notched cover 15 45

E190, Handled Sauce Boat—
Large size, fancy shape, footed 3 45

Jugs—Fancy shape, footed Doz.
E185, 42's, capacity ⅜ pt. 1 85
E186, 36's, " 1 " 1 90
E187, 30's, " 2 " 2 28
E188, 24's, " 3 " 2 85
E189, 12's, " 4 " 4 42

E194, Covered Sugar Bowl—
Fancy shape, footed, with double handles. 4 45

E195, Covered Tea Pot—
Large size, fancy shape, ht. 7⅜ in 6 35

"FLOW BLUE" TEA AND DINNER SETS.

For composition of Tea and Dinner Sets see page 269. Set

E82—56 piece tea set .. 4 50
E83—65 " dinner set 7 20
E84—100 " " " 9 80
E85—102 " " " 11 75
E86—112 " " " 11 25
E87—130 " " " 15 10

PACKAGE CHARGE ABOLISHED On All Crockery and Glassware.

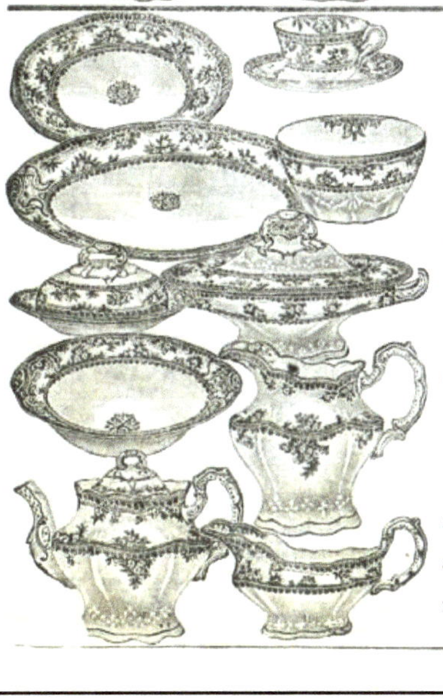

MADDOCK'S "BUCKINGHAM" Green & Gold Illuminated. Semi=Porcelain (OPEN STOCK)

JOHN MADDOCK & SONS ENGLAND ROYAL VITREOUS

"Buckingham"

Fine quality, beautiful shape, rich decoration. Each piece trademarked. All pieces full size, fancy shape, medium light weight, but strong and durable. Absolutely first selection, every piece guaranteed against crazing. Rich green print decoration in a combination of many sprays of delicate flowers and leaves, with outer and inner Grecian band, producing a wide border pattern effect. All pieces have gold edges, inner gold bands, gold decorated knobs and handles. All flat pieces with gold medallion centers. High pieces with gold bands around feet, and all large pieces otherwise gold illuminated. Shipped from our house—**no package charge.**

Cups and Saucers Handled—
E250, Fancy teas, low shape, 3⅝x2¼, saucer 6 .... Doz. $1 75
E251, Coffees. Large size, fancy shape, 4x2¼, saucer 6¼ 2 05
E252, After-dinner coffees, 2¾x2¼, saucer 4¾ 1 30

Plates—Fancy scalloped edge.
E253, 4 in. actual size 5¾ 75
E254, 5 " " " 7 96
E255, 6 " " " 8 1 20
E256, 7 " " " 9 1 40
E257, 8 " " " 9¾ 1 65
E258, Deep soup, 7 in. actual size 9 .... 1 40
E259, Coupe shape soup, 7 in., actual 7¾ 1 40

E263, Individual Butters—Round, diam. 3¼ 43

Fruit or Sauce Dishes—
E260, 4 in., actual 5¼ 65
E261, 4½ " " 5¾ 69

E262, Oatmeal Bowl—
Fancy deep shape, diam. 6 in 77

Dishes or Platters—
Fancy deep oval shape. Doz.
E273, 7 in., actual 9¼ $1 85
E274, 8 " " 10¼ 2 25
E275, 9 " " 11¼ 2 75
E276, 10 " " 12⅜ 4 10
E277, 12 " " 14¾ 6 75
E278, 14 " " 17 9 50

Nappies—Deep fancy shape.
E270, 6 in., actual 8 2 20
E271, 7 " " 9¼ 2 75
E272, 8 " " 10 4 10

E290 Pickle Dish—
Long oval shape, length 8¾ 2 75

E292, Cream Pitcher—
30's, fancy shape 2 75

Bakers or Vegetable Dishes—Fancy deep oval shape.
E267, 6 in., actual 8 2 25
E268, 7 " " 9 2 75
E269, 8 " " 9⅞ 4 10

E283, Covered Soup Tureen—Fancy round shape. Diam. 9 in., with notched cover 18 00

Casseroles or Round Covered Vegetable Dishes— Doz.
E281, 6 in. act'l size 8 $10 95
E282, 8 " " " 8¾ 12 00

Jugs—Tall fancy shape, footed, with large fancy handle.
E284, 42's capacity ¼ pt. 2 10
E285, 36's " 1 " 2 45
E286, 30's " 2 " 2 75
E287, 24's " 3 " 3 40
E288, 12's " 5 " 5 60

E264, Bone Dish—
Length 5¾ in., regulation fancy shape 1 30

E266, Egg Cup—
Regulation double deck, ht. 4⅜ in 1 55

E265, Utility or Slop Bowl—
Large size, deep shape, diam. 6 in., ht. 3⅝ ... 1 80

Oval Covered Vegetable Dishes—
Fancy shape footed. Doz.
E279, 7 in. act'l size 8¾ $9 00
E280, 8 " " " 9¾ 10 95

E289, Handled Sauce Boat—
Large size, fancy shape 3 60

E291, Covered Butter Dish—Round, diam. 7¾ in., with loose drainer 7 80

E294, Covered Teapot—
Large size, ht. 7¾ in ... 7 25

E293, Covered Sugar Bowl—
30's, fancy shape, with double handles 5 50

MADDOCK'S "BUCKINGHAM" TEA AND DINNER SETS.

For composition of Tea and Dinner Sets see page 269.

E94—56 piece tea set. Set $ 5 28
E95—65 " dinner set " 8 10
E96—100 " " " " 11 30
E97—102 " " " " 13 53
E98—112 " " " " 12 98
E99—130 " " " " 17 65

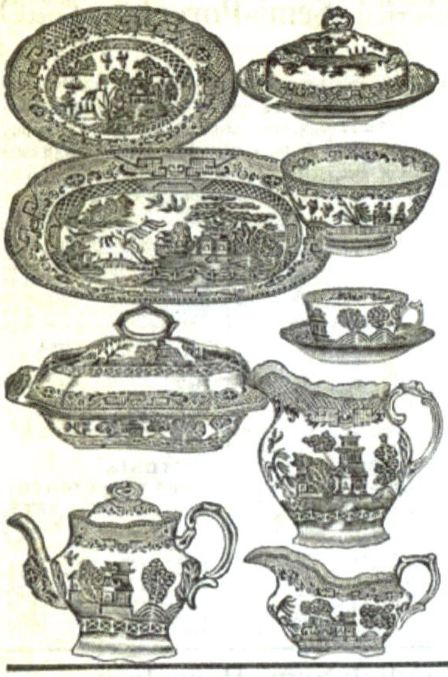

"PEKIN" Blue Willow Decorated SEMI-PORCELAIN (OPEN STOCK)

At special prices for March. This famous historical decoration is now more popular than ever. No crockery stock is complete without it. Prices named are exceptionally low. We invite comparison of quality and price with the offerings of other jobbers. Good quality English semi-porcelain body, all pieces full size, each one trademarked and absolutely guaranteed against crazing. Famous blue willow shape with the popular allover blue decoration. These goods sell twelve months in the year. Shipped from our house—**no package charge.**

E350, Handled Tea Cups and Saucers—Good size fancy shape.. Doz. $1 20

Plates—Flat.
- E351, 5 in., actual 7.... 69
- E352, 6 " " 7.... 84
- E353, 7 " " 8.... 96
- E354, 8 " " 10.... 1 20
- E355—Deep soup, 7 in., actual 9.... 96

E357, Individual Butters—Diam. 3¼ in....... 32

E356, Fruit or Sauce Dish—Deep shape, 4 in., actual 4¾.......... 48

E367, Pickle Dish—Fancy oblong shape, length 8¾ in.......... 1 85

E374, Covered Sugar Bowl—Fancy shape, footed, double handles.. 3 75

E373, Handled Cream Pitcher—Fancy shape, 30's.......... 1 95

E366, Utility or slop Bowl—Round deep shape, footed. Diam. 5¾ in., ht. 3½.......... Doz. $1 35

Dishes or Platters—Fancy oblong shape.
- E363, 10 in., actual 11½x9¼.......... 2 90
- E360, 7 in. act. 8x6½.... 1 25
- E361, 8 in. act. 9½x7¾.. 1 60
- E364, 12 in., actual 13¾x11¼.......... 4 70
- E365, 14 in., actual 15½x12¾.......... 6 70

E372, Covered Butter Dish—Large size, flanged, diam. 7¾ in., loose drainer.......... 5 70

Bakers or Vegetable Dishes—Deep oblong shape.
- E358, 7 in. act. 8⅜x6½.. 1 55
- E359, 8 in., act. 9½x7¼.. 2 90

E368, Handled Sauce Boat—Darge size fancy shape.......... Doz. $2 60

E375, Covered Teapot—Large size fancy shape.. 5 10

Covered Vegetable Dishes—Large fancy oblong shape.
- E369, 7 in., actual size, 10¾ in.......... 6 65
- E370, as E369, only larger.......... 7 50

E371, Covered Soup Tureen—Extra large size, deep oblong shape, length 12¾ in., notched cover.......... Doz. $11 80

"PEKIN" BLUE WILLOW TEA AND DINNER SETS.

For composition of Tea and Dinner Sets see page 269

E76—56 pc.	Tea	Set	$3 72
E77—65 "	Dinner	"	5 72
E78—100 "	"	"	7 91
E79—102 "	"	"	9 49
E80—112 "	"	"	9 13

PACKAGE CHARGE ABOLISHED On All Crockery and Glassware.

SPECIALTIES IN ENGLISH SEMI-PORCELAIN WARE.

Nearly all to retail at 5 and 10 cents. These are all "staples" and the prices are interesting. Good quality semi-porcelain, light weight, guaranteed against crazing. Shipped from our house—**no package charge.**

"BLUE FLORAL" AND GREEN FLORAL PRINT DECORATED LINE.

Embossed, heavily glazed, decorations in wide border design in rich blue and green floral and scroll effect.

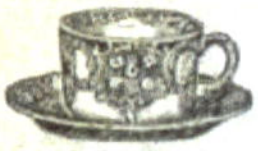

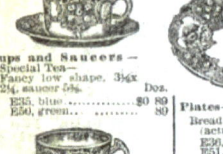

Cups and Saucers—
Special Tea—Fancy low shape, 3½x2¼, saucer 5¾. Doz.
- E35, blue.......... $0 89
- E50, green.......... 89

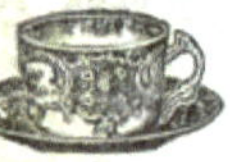

London Tea—Large size, cup 3½x2¾, saucer 6.
- E34, blue.......... 92
- E49, green.......... 92

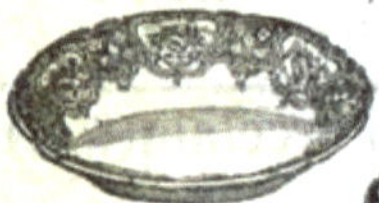

Coupe Soup or Utility Table Dish—7 in. (actual 8 in.)
- E41, blue.......... 87
- E56, green.......... 87

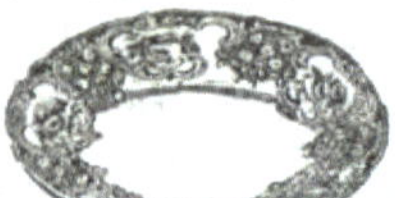

Plates—Flat.
Bread and Butter—4 in., (actual 6 in.) Doz.
- E36, blue.......... $0 43
- E51, green.......... 43

Tea or Fruit—5 in. (actual 7 in.)
- E37, blue.......... 60
- E52, green.......... 60

Breakfast—6 in. (actual 8 in.)
- E38, blue.......... 72
- E53, green.......... 72

Dinner—7 in. (act. 9 in.)
- E39, blue.......... 87
- E54, green.......... 87

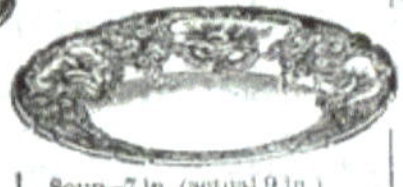

Soup—7 in. (actual 9 in.)
- E40, blue.......... 87
- E55, green.......... 87

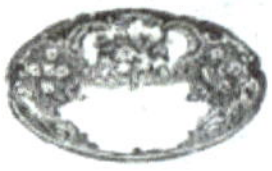

Fruit or Sauce Dish—Round shape, diam. 5 in. Doz.
- E43, blue.......... $0 41
- E58, green.......... 41

Oatmeal Bowl—Round deep shape, diam. 6 in.
- E42, blue.......... 48
- E57, green.......... 48

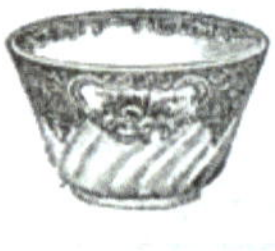

Footed Bowls—Round extra deep shape, spiral pattern.
- E48—36's, diam. 5¼ in., blue.......... 89
- E63—36's, diam. 5¾ in., green.......... 89
- E47—30's, diam. 6 in. (actual 4¼ in.) blue... 1 10
- E62—30's, diam. 6 in. (actual 4¼ in.) green.. 1 10

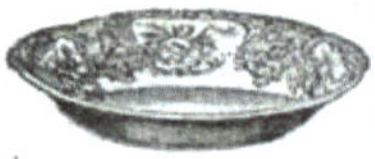

Nappies or Table Dishes—Fancy deep round shape.
- E44—6 in. (actual 8¼ in.) blue.......... Doz. $1 30
- E59—6 in. (actual 8¼ in.) green.......... 1 30
- E45—7 in. (actual 9⅛ in.) blue.......... 1 87
- E60—7 in. (actual 9⅛ in.) green.......... 1 87
- E46—8 in. (actual 10¼ in.) blue.......... 2 25
- E61—8 in. (actual 10¼ in.) green.......... 2 25

"SENSATION" DECORATED NAPPY ASST.

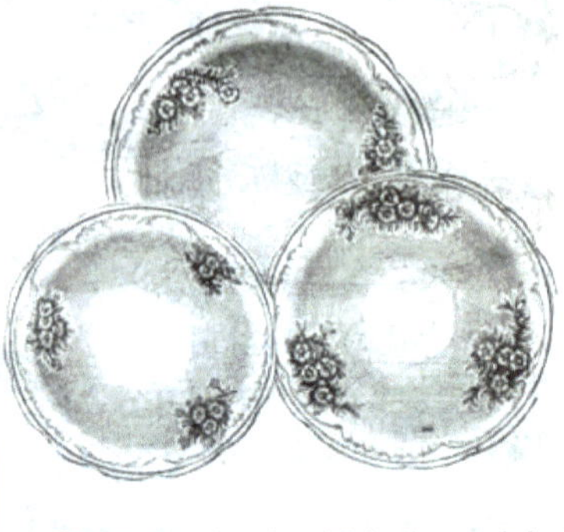

E171. White granite body, embossed design, deep round shape with slightly fluted edge. Asstd. decal decoration with gold line. Asst. consists of **2 doz. each** of the following:
Deep nappy—7¼ in. diam. Deep nappy—9¾ in. diam.
Deep nappy—8¾ in. diam.
Total 6 doz. Per dozen, **96c**

"BEST EVER" DECORATED SEMI-PORCELAIN ASSORTMENT.

We have made a special feature of this assortment in using only items used in making up a Dinner Service. Note the large pieces and beautiful decorations.

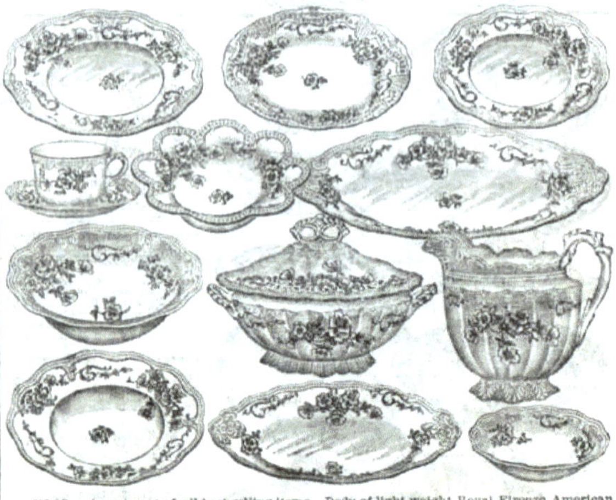

E703—Assortment of all best selling items. Body of light weight Royal Firenze American China. Six color decal decoration in wild apple blossoms and forget me nots, delicate pink and white predominating, shaded green leaves. Artistic gold stamp between all clusters of flowers. Each piece stamped with trademark. Asst. comprises:

½ doz. covered dishes.	½ doz. 8 in platters.	2 doz. cake or bread dishes.
4 " 7 in dinner plates,	½ " 10 " "	1 " 24's water pitchers.
4 " 6 " pie "	1 " salad bowls.	½ " berry bowls.
3 " 7 " soup "	4 " cups and saucers.	3 " berry nappies.

Total 24 doz. in pkg. (NO PKG. CHARGE.) Per dozen, **89**

FAMOUS "BLUE WILLOW" DECORATED ENGLISH SEMI-PORCELAIN WARE.

Decorated in the ever staple allover blue willow pattern.

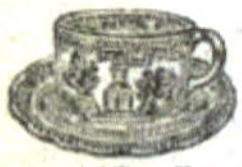

E21. Special Tea—Fancy long low shape, 3¼x2¼, saucer 5½.......... Doz. ★89

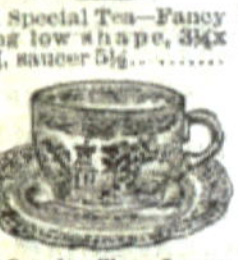

E22. London Tea—Large size, medium low shape, 3½x2⅝, saucer 5¾.......... ★92

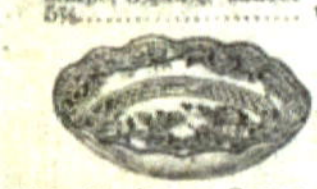

E29, Fruit or Sauce Dish—4¾ in.......... ★38

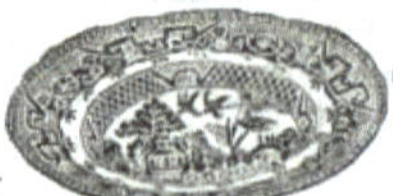

Plates—
- E23, Bread and Butter—4 in., actual 6 in.......... Doz. ★43
- E24, Tea—5 in., actual 7 in.......... ★59
- E25, Breakfast—6 in., actual 8 in.......... ★72
- E26, Dinner—7 in., actual 9 in.......... ★86

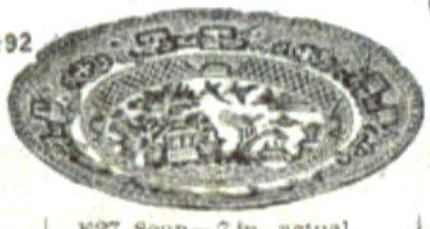

E27, Soup—7 in. actual 9 in.......... ★85

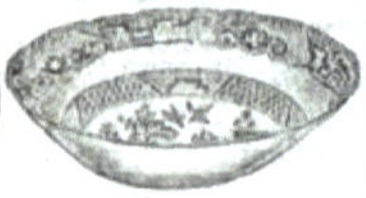

E28, Coupe Soup or General Utility Table Dish—7 in., actual 8 in. ... Doz. ★86

Nappies or Table Dishes—Extra deep shape.
- E31—6 in., act. 8¼ in.. ★1 28
- E32—7 " " 9¾ " ★1 86
- E33—8 " " 10½ " ★2 36

Here is Your Chance to Save in Buying—Black and White Figures Tell Their Own Story.

CARMINE ROSE DECORATED ASST. OF SEMI-PORCELAIN.

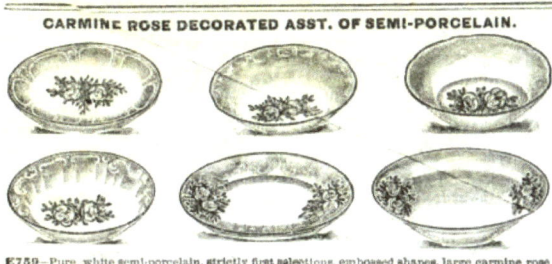

E759—Pure white semi-porcelain, strictly first selections, embossed shapes, large carmine rose decorations in bright colors, green leaves, gilt edges. Asst. comprises 2 doz. each of following:
6 in. deep oatmeal bowl.   7¼ in. tea plate.
6¼ in. bread and butter plate.   6¼ in. berry or sauce dish.
6 in. fancy shape oatmeal or fruit dish.   5½ in. deep table dish.
Total 12 doz. in bbl. Wt. 100 lbs. (NO PKG. CHARGE.) Per dozen, **43c**

"BIG SPECIAL" SEMI-PORCELAIN ASSORTMENT.

E706. Fancy shape semi-porcelain ware. New hand painted rose effect decal, all pieces gold traced. Asst. contains the following:
1 doz. 8 in. nappies, act. 9¼ in.   ½ doz. 10 in. platters, actual 14 in.   2½ doz. 7 in. dinner plates, actual 9¼ in.
1 " 7 "   "   8½ "   1½ doz. 30's fancy bowls 3½ x 5¼ in.   2¼ doz. fancy cups and saucers.
1 " 8 " bakers, " 10 "   1 doz. 8 in. platters, act. 12 in.
1 " 7 "   "   9¼ "
Total 12 doz. (NO PKG. CHARGE.) Per dozen, **89c**

"MONEY MAKER" ASSORTMENT.

E707—Cluster effect, rose and wild flower decoration in bright pink and shaded green; artistic decoration, all gold traced body of pure white semi-porcelain. Composition as follows:
1 doz. fancy cups and saucers.   ½ doz. 7¼ in. bread and butter plates.   ½ doz. 8¼ in. fancy cake plates
1 " 9¼ in. dinner plates.   ½ " 12½ in. meat platters.
½ " 8½ in. breakfast plates.   ½ " 7¼ in. coupe soups   ½ " jugs, 36's.
½ " 7½ in. round nappies.   ½ " fancy bowls, 30's.
Wt. 125 lbs. Total 6 doz. in pkg. (NO PKG. CHARGE.) Per dozen, **82c**

"DECAL AND TINT" ASSORTMENT OF SEMI-PORCELAIN WARE.

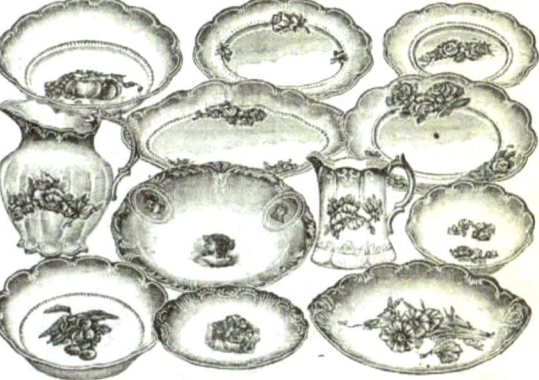

E714—Light wt. semi-porcelain body, fancy shapes, neat embossing, asstd. blue, green and pink tinted with asstd. decal decorations, such as large floral, fruit and head decorations. Every piece extra value. Asst. comprises:
1 doz. 11 in. chop plates.   ½ doz. 30's fancy jugs.   ½ doz. 36's tankard jugs.
2 " 9¼ " dinner plates.   ½ " 7¼ in. cake plates.   1 " 6 in. oatmeal bowls.
2 " 8½ " breakfast plates.   ½ " 8½ " deep nappies.   ½ " 9¼ " large berry dishes.
1 " 7½ " pie plates.   2 " 8¼ " low salads.   ½ " 11 " platters.
Total 12 doz. in pkg. wt. 135 lbs. (NO PKG. CHARGE.) Per dozen, **92**

"DRESDEN" ASST. OF DECORATED SEMI-PORCELAIN WARE.

E753—Pure white semi-porcelain body, clear, hard glaze guaranteed not to craze, 4 color decal decorations, pink roses and forget me nots, green leaves. All gold treated. Asst. comprises:
8½ in. deep bowl.   Fancy handled cup and saucer.   9½ in. jugs or pitcher.
6 in. oatmeal.   8½ in. table dish.   12 in. platter.
7¼ in. table plates.   8½ in. bread plate.   30's bowl.
9½ in. dinner plate.   8½ in. deep bowl.   1 doz. each of 12 items.
10 in. bread plate.
Total 12 doz. in bbl. Wt. 160 lbs. (NO PKG. CHARGE.) Per dozen, **82c**

"IMPERIAL" ASST. OF DECORATED SEMI-PORCELAIN.

E710: Fine light wt. semi-porcelain. New 7 color decalcomania decorations of autumn leaves and blackberries showing the 3 stages—the flowers, the green fruit and the ripe berry. The colorings are perfect, all pieces full gold traced. Asst. consists of 1 doz. each of the following:
10 in. high artistic vase.
10 in. fancy berry bowl.
9¼ in. fancy salad dish.
9¼ in. fancy high footed fruit bowl.
10¾ in. fancy handled cake plate.
8¼ in. fancy high tankard jug.
Total, 6 doz. in bbl. (NO PKG. CHARGE.) Per dozen, **Out**

"MAMMOTH" ASST. ROSE DECORATED SEMI-PORCELAIN WARE.

E705½—Fancy shapes, full sizes, light semi-porcelain body. Large rose decoration, green leaf background, gold lined edges. 1 doz. each of following:
Fancy tea cups and saucers.   7¼ in. extra deep salads.   7 in. nappies (actual 8¼).
30's fancy jugs.   7⅞ " salad or table dish.   Bread plates (" 8¼).
6 in. plates (actual 7¼).   Large oatmeal bowl.   Cake plates (" 7¼).
(" 5¾).   8¼ in. nappies (actual 6¼).   8 in. platters (" 11¾).
Total 12 doz. in bbl. Wt. 140 lbs. (NO PKG. CHARGE.) Per dozen, **79**

"BIG TWO" DECORATED SEMI-PORCELAIN WARE.

Extraordinary values as 25 cent leaders.

E667—Best semi-porcelain body, clear hard glaze, beautifully decorated, high color decal and gold, 10½ in. embossed rose and gold decorated chop dish. 24's large full shape jug—gold stippled with rose and leaf decoration. 1 doz. each of 2 items. 2 doz. in pkg. Per dozen, **$2.25**
(NO PKG. CHARGE.)

"DAISY" NAPPY AND SALAD ASSORTMENT.

E730—Pink daisies and green sprig with delicate background of blue, and vine effect of purple. Center sprays and gold lined edges. 4 doz. each of 3 items. 8¼ in. low salad, 7¼ in. deep round bowl, 8¼ in. deep fruit bowl. Total, 12 doz. Per dozen, **85c**

NEW "BEST YET" ASSORTMENT.

All items big value—some of them being retailed regularly for 50 cents.

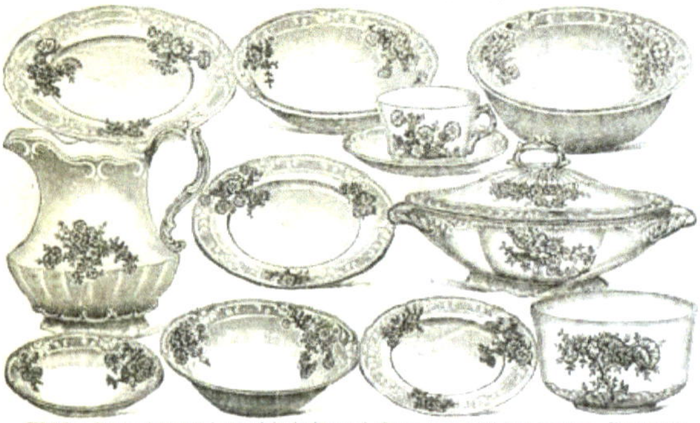

E708 + Pure white semi-porcelain body, good shape, neat border embossing. Pure white, good hard glaze, decorations in beautiful pink with background of shaded foliage, making a large cluster effect. First grade selection. Asst. comprises:

½ doz. large covered dishes, actual 9¼ in.	2 doz. fancy teas.
½ " 24's bowls, capacity 2 pts.	½ " 6 in. nappies, actual 7¼.
1 " oatmeals, actual 6 in.	½ " 7 in. nappies, actual 8¼.
2 " 6 in. pie plates, actual 7¼.	½ " 8 in. nappies, actual 10¼.
2 " breakfast plates, actual 8¼.	½ " 24's jugs, capacity 3 pts.
2 " dinner plates, actual 9¼.	

Total 12 dozen in package. **(NO PKG. CHARGE.)** Per dozen, **89c**

"NOVELTY" SEMI-PORCELAIN ASSORTMENT.

New, up to date decorations on quick selling items.

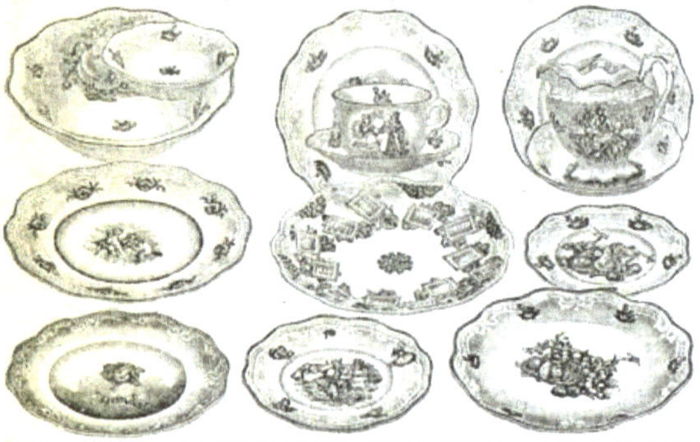

E704, Assortment: All good novelties, special decorations. Firenze porcelain body artistically embossed and decorated. Assortment consists of sets and plaques as follows:

2 doz. actual 7⅛ in. "Tiny Todkin" decorated plate.
3 doz. 9¼ in. cupid decal center plate.
1 doz. 8¼ in. decal center and tinted flange plate.
½ doz. 9¾ inch calendar plate with floral and calendar decorations.
1 doz. Japanese cereal sets, consisting of 1 each 7¼ in. plate, 6 in. oatmeals and 42's jug: all with beautiful Japanese decal.
Holland cup, saucer and plate assortment consisting of 3 doz. actual 8¼ in. plates and 2 doz. fancy cups and saucers with Holland decal decorations.
2 only fruit sets, consisting of ½ doz. 5⅛ in. fruit saucer and one 8¾ in. large fruit nappy with beautiful fruit decal decorations.
4 only cake sets, consisting of ½ doz. actual 6¼ in. plates and one 9¼ in. large cake plate. Gold stamp and line and decal decorated. Total of 18 dozen. **(NO PKG. CHARGE.)** Per dozen, **84c**

"BUSINESS GETTER" 5 CENT SEMI-PORCELAIN ASSORTMENT.

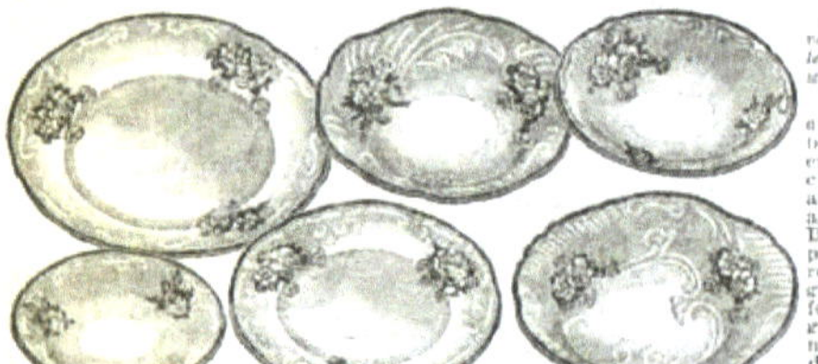

All extraordinary values as 5 cent leaders. Comparable with most 10 centers.

E719: Fancy semi-porcelain body, all with neat embossing, good clear glaze, guaranteed absolutely against crazing. Decorated in large pink full blown roses with background of green foliage. All pieces gold lined. Assortment consists of 1 doz. each of the following items:

Fancy plate actual 6⅛ in.	Fancy shape jelly dish actual 6⅜ in.
Fancy plate actual 7⅜ in.	Fancy nappy actual 6¾ in.
Berry dish actual 5 in.	Total 6 doz. in pkg.
Oatmeals actual 5⅛ in.	

Per dozen, **45c**

"TINY TODKIN" PLATE ASSORTMENT.

Something new in the way of domestic decorated semi-porcelain ware. Bound to sell. Be the first to offer them.

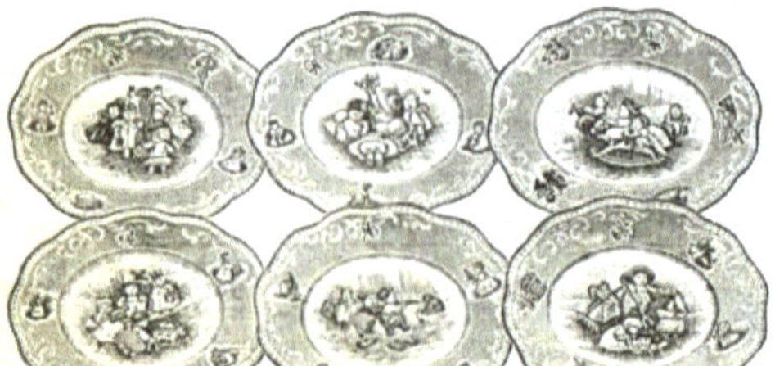

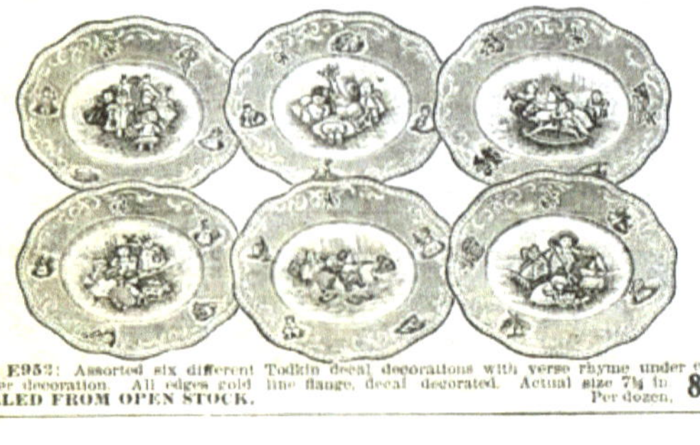

E952: Assorted six different Todkin decal decorations with verse rhyme under each center decoration. All edges gold line flange, decal decorated. Actual size 7⅛ in. Per dozen, **84c**
FILLED FROM OPEN STOCK.

ROYAL THREE-COLOR TINT AND DECAL ASSORTMENT.

An all leader assortment. Values that cannot be equaled at a similar price.

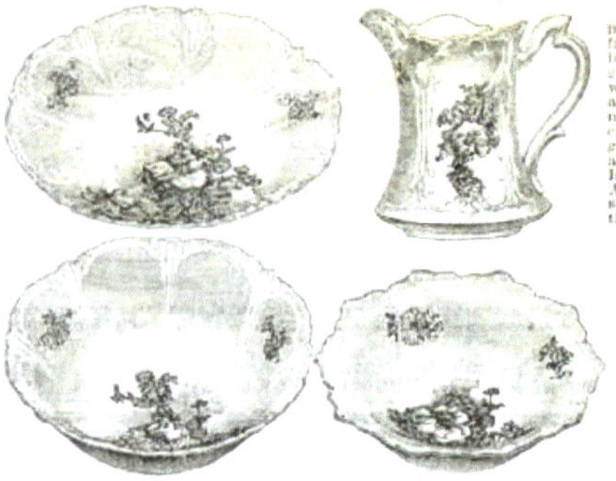

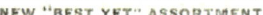

E1100—Light semi-porcelain body neat fancy shapes, new combination 3 color tint in green, pink and buff which harmonizes with a beautiful decalcomania of delicate natural colored poppies and green foliage, making a beautiful contrast. Heretofore unknown in American pottery. Assortment consists of the following:

½ doz. actual 10¼ in. deep salad bowls.
¼ doz. 24's 3 pint tankard jugs.
½ doz. actual 10¼ in. fruit bowls.
¼ doz. 10 in. fancy chop dish.

Total, 1 dozen.
(NO PKG. CHARGE)
Per dozen, **$2.25**

"HIGH ART" PLAQUE OR PLATE ASSORTMENT.

Something new—artistic and up to date. Will sell when shown. All popular and artistic decorations

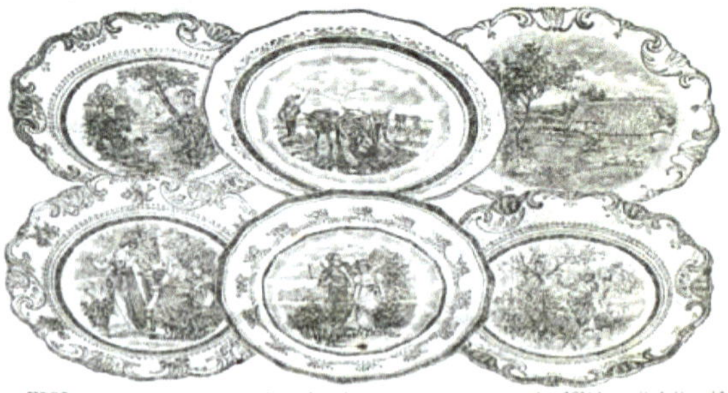

E737—Assortment consists of twelve large plaques, average size 10⅜ in.—all full gold treated with stamp, line and foil tracing; some with green, coral, rose and pure silver laid. All with center decalcomania decorations representing a variety of subjects in beautiful natural colorings bordered with artistic gold treatment. Best semi-porcelain body. Nothing like them ever offered before. *No two alike.* Complete set of 12 in pkg. **(NO PACKAGE CHARGE.)** Per dozen, **$5.00**

"ART" SALAD BOWL AND CHOP DISH ASSORTMENT.

Very handsome ware that will serve both as an advertisement and a profit maker.

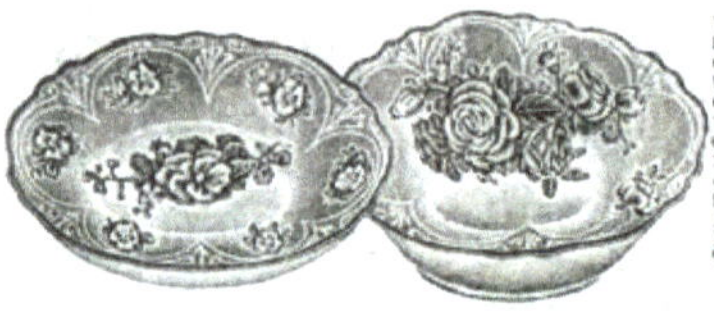

E732.—High grade light weight semi-porcelain body, fancy shapes, beautifully decorated in eight color assorted decal decorations, such as combination color effect in roses, poppies, chrysanthemums, etc. All edges decorated with a heavy gold line, making a very beautiful and artistic combination. 1½ doz. each of two items:

10⅜ in. chop or cake dish.
10¼ in. deep salad bowl.
Total 3 doz. in pkg. Per dozen, **$2.25**
(NO PKG. CHARGE.)

"SENSIBLE" YELLOW AND ROCKINGHAM ASSORTMENT.

All large and useful pieces. You never saw better values for the money.

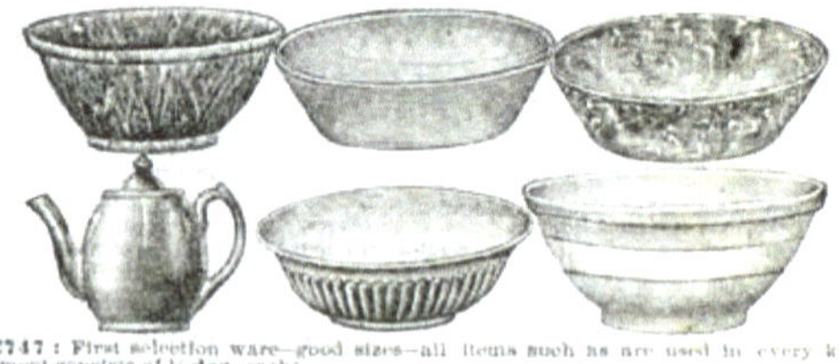

LE747: First selection ware—good sizes—all items such as are used in every kitchen. Assortment consists of ½ doz. each:

18's actual 9 in. deep Rockingham mixing bowl.	8 in., actual 9⅛ in. deep fluted nappy, actual 10⅛ in.
9 in. actual 9⅜ in. Rockingham nappy.	9 in. banded yellow mixing bowl.
42's teapot, capacity 2 pints.	Total 3 doz. in pkg.
9's yellow nappy, actual 9⅜ in.	

Per dozen, **92c**

EXTRAORDINARY COMBINET OFFERING.

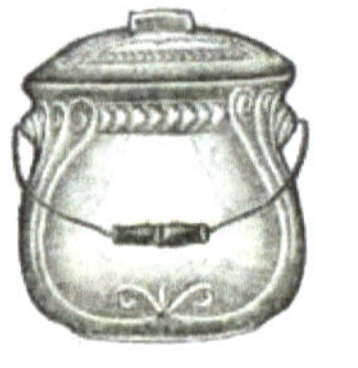

E775: White bristol body, large full shape, neatly embossed with fancy handle. Covered. Glazed inside and out with clear hard glaze. Complete with bail and handle. Full height 12 inches, diameter 10 inches. Per dozen, **$5.00**

GOLD STAMP & LINE SEMI-PORCELAIN CUP, SAUCER & PLATE ASSORTMENT.

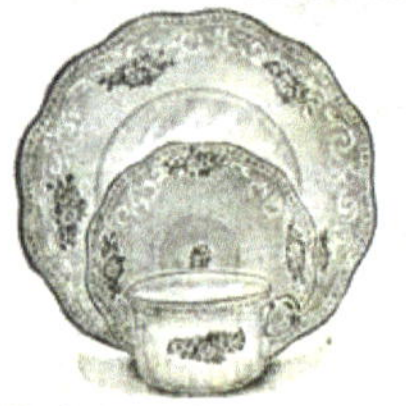

E725: Light weight semi-porcelain body, neat embossing, gold decorated large floral stamp and gold line. Assortment consists of 3 doz. 9¼ inch dinner plates and 3 doz. fancy cups and saucers. Total 6 doz. in package. Per dozen, **85c**

"ROSE AND GOLD STAMP" SEMI-PORCELAIN ASSORTMENT.

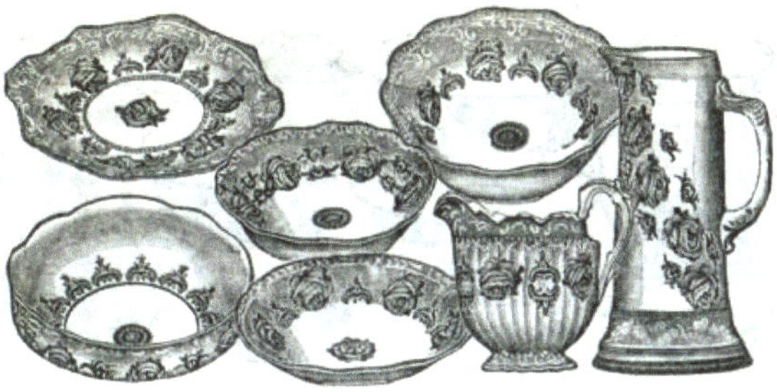

E712 :– Fancy light weight semi-porcelain body with beautiful large rose with filled in gold stamp. All pieces gold traced, all bowls have center decorations. As 25 cent offerings these are unequaled. Complete as follows:

1 doz. 9¼ in. round fruit bowls.
1 " 11 " fancy bread or cake plates.
½ " 9½ " orange bowls.
1 " 24's fancy jugs.
1 doz. 10½ in. deep fruit bowls.
1 " 8¾ " salad bowls.
½ " 12¼ " high tankards.

Total 6 doz. in bbl. (NO PKG. CHARGE.) Per dozen, **$2.25**

GLAZED PITCHER ASST.

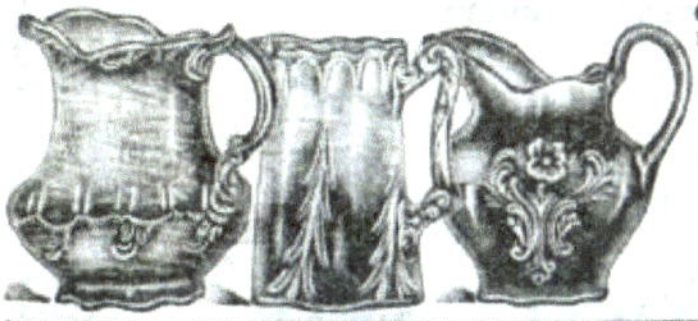

E816—Extra strong and well made, good faience body, large fancy shapes, embossed in rich, solid colors such as wine, brown, etc., all heavily glazed both outside and inside. Asst. comprises ⅓ doz. each of following:
24's, fancy shape, capacity 4 pts.
12's, tall tankard shape, capacity 5 pts.
12's, large fancy shape, capacity 5 pts.
Total 1 doz. in pkg., wt. 140 lbs. Per dozen, **$1.89**

GLAZED PITCHER ASST.

No better 10 centers ever offered.

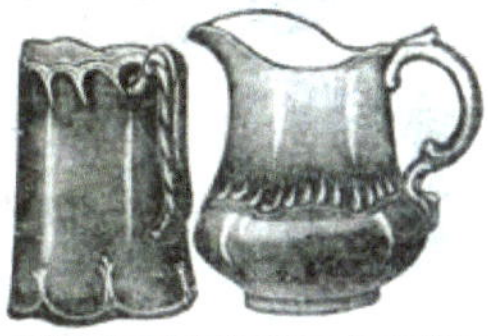

E815—Good faience strong fancy shapes, embossed in asstd. colors—brown, green, wine, etc., all heavily glazed inside and out. Asst. comprises:
½ doz. 42's tankard shape, ht. 5¾ in.
½ doz. 36's fancy shape, ht. 5¾ in.
½ doz. 30's tall tankard shape, ht. 6½ in.
½ doz. 30's large fancy shape, ht. 6¾ in.
Total 2 doz. in pkg., wt. 65 lbs. Per dozen, **89c**

"ART DECORATED" JUG ASSORTMENT.

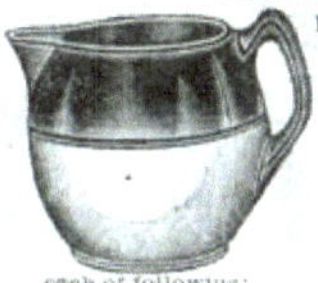

E819—Ivory color faience body, artistic barrel shape, wide band effect decorations, asstd. cobalt blue, pink and green, solid color handles, gold band top and foot, double gold band around center, gold traced handles. ½ doz. each of following:

Ht. 4¾ in., girth 14½	@	$2 10	$1 05
Ht. 5¼ in., girth 17¾	@	3 00	1 50
Ht. 6½ in., girth 21	@	3 89	1 95

Total 1½ doz. in crate, wt. 63 lbs. Per assortment, **$4.50**

MAMMOTH SIZE NESTED MIXING BOWLS.

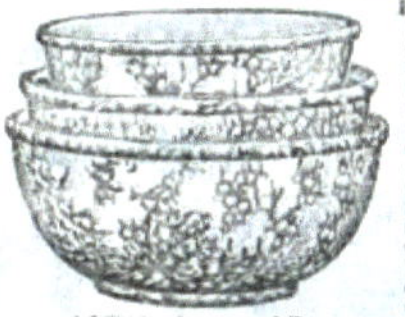

E766—Heavy faience body, ivory color inside, allover green stippled decorations outside, extra deep round shape, footed, glazed inside and out. 1 each of 10½, 11½ and 12½ in. in nest of 3. Nest, **57c**

EMBOSSED DECORATED JUG ASSORTMENT.

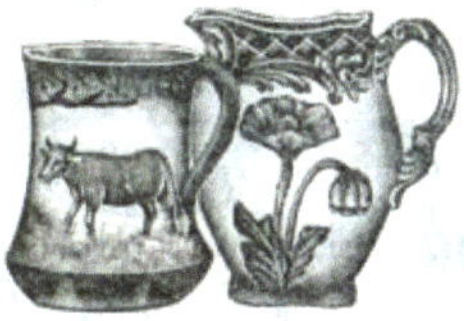

E793—2 styles—large tankard, fancy swell shape, both ivory color earthen body, extra large sizes, average ht. about 9 in., heavily embossed, asstd. green and brown tints, one with cow in relief, the other with large embossed floral decoration, ½ doz. each style. Total 1 doz. in crate, wt. 76 lbs. Per dozen, **$2.90**

"DEFIANCE" FIRE CLAY COOKING KETTLE ASSORTMENT.

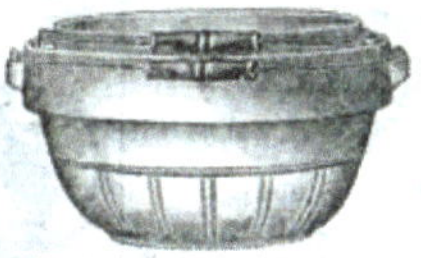

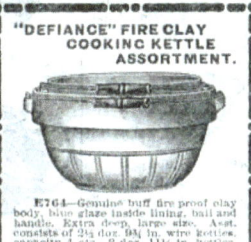

E764—Genuine buff fire proof clay body, blue glaze inside lining, bail and handle. Extra deep, large size. Asst. consists of 2½ doz. 9¾ in. wire kettles, capacity 4 qts., 2 doz. 11½ in. kettles, capacity 7 qts. Total 4½ doz. Wt. 313 lbs. Per dozen, **$1.20**
(NO PKG. CHARGE.)

ROYAL BLUE JUGS.

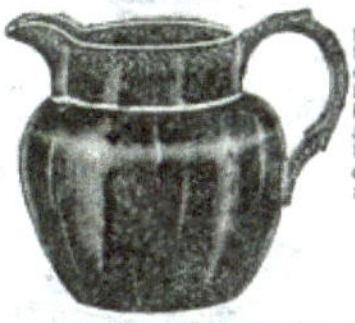

Good semi-porcelain body, fancy shape, all over decoration in rich royal blue, gold band around center, heavy gold clouded edges and handles.
E806—36's Doz. **$2.25**
E807—30's Doz. **$2.95**
E808—24's Doz. **$3.60**

LARGE ICE WATER PITCHER.

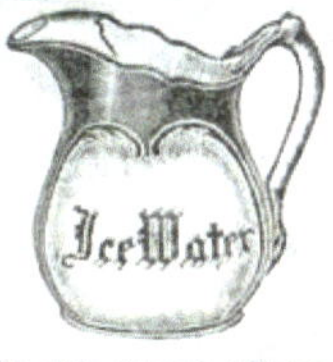

E824: 6's. Gold lettered and traced—decorated in three colors, blue, pink and red burned in color. Lip to hold back ice. Per dozen, **$9.50**

FIREPROOF PRESERVING KETTLES.

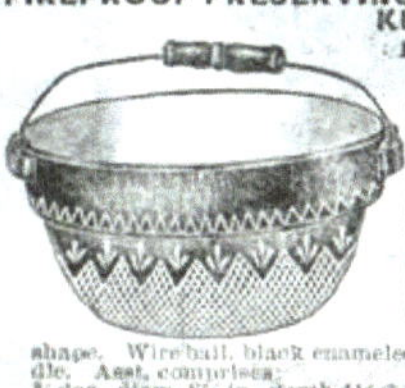

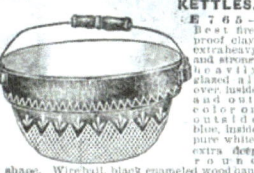

E765—Best fireproof clay, extra heavy and strong, heavily glazed all over, inside and out, color on outside blue, inside pure white, extra deep round shape. Wire bail, black enameled wood handle. Asst. comprises:
¾ doz., diam. 8⅝ in., depth 4½ @ $0 89 $0 67
¾ doz., diam. 10 in., depth 5...@ 1 87 1 41
Total 1½ doz. in pkg. Wt. 95 lbs. Total for asst., **$2.08**

"MONARCH" ASSORTMENT.

This assortment contains many pieces which are regular 50 cent items. They can be sold at 25c each doing some good advertising.

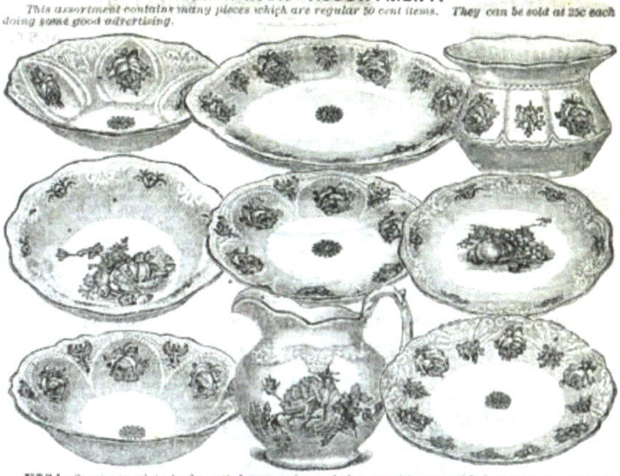

E734—Semi-porcelain body, all fancy embossed shapes with assorted decorations, such as American beauty and tea roses and fruit centers. All pieces have heavy gold edges with gold center stamp and artistic stamp between each rose decoration. Assortment consists of the following:

1 doz. 9¾ in. berry bowls.
½ " 13½ " tray or platter.
1 " 10¼ " fancy cake or bread plate.
1 doz. 10½ in. chop plates.
½ " 24's jugs.
1 " 9¾ in. fancy salad.
¼ " 10½ " deep bowl.
¼ doz. 11½ in. mammoth chop plate.
¼ doz. large cuspidors, 7⅝ in. diam., ht. 5 in.

Total 6 doz. in pkg. (NO PKG. CHARGE.) Per dozen, ***$2.10**

DECORATED STONE WARE NESTED BOWLS AND NAPPIES.

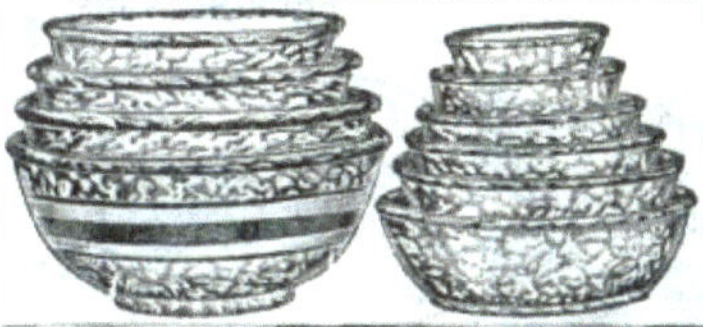

E767: Heavy well made gray stone; body with all over blue and green stippled decorations, bowls having alternate blue and white bands, well glazed inside and out.
4 nests Footed Mixing Bowls. Each nest consisting of 6 bowls—one each 7½, 8½, 9½, 10½, 11½ and 12½ in.
2 nests Nappies. Each nest consisting of 6 nappies—one each 5, 6¼, 7¼, 8¼, 9¼ and 10½ in.
Total 6 nests in bbl. Wt. 120 lbs. Per nest, **58c**

"ALL LEADERS" ASST. OF FIREPROOF COOKING WARE.

If you've handled this ware we merely call on you to NOTE THE PRICE. If you haven't as yet handled it you're missing the most satisfactory cooking ware on the market.

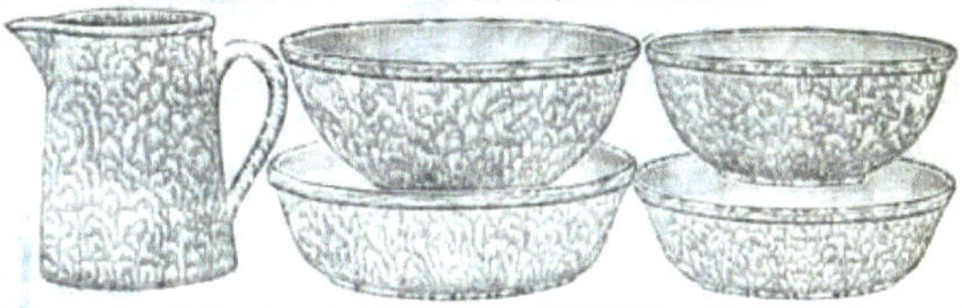

E741—Very attractive. Body of rich ivory color, strong and well made, allover decorations in mottled green, heavily glazed inside and out. Used in oven and on table. Asst. comprises **2 doz. each** of following:

Large 3 pt. deep pudding dish, diam. 8¼ in.
7½ in. extra deep round footed bowl.
9 in. deep round pudding or baking dish.
2 pt. tankard jug ht. 6 in.
8¼ in. round extra deep bowl.
Wt. 275 lbs.

Total 10 doz. in crate. Per dozen, **96c**

FIREPROOF PRESERVING KETTLE ASSORTMENT.

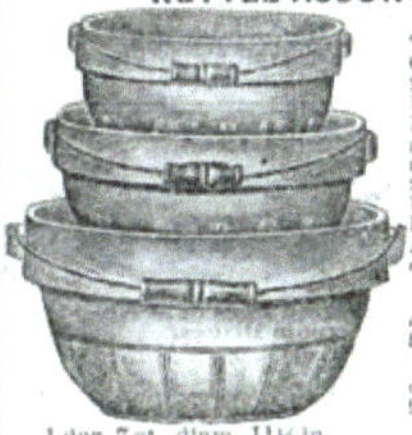

E769—Twentieth Century fireproof buff body, light blue glaze inside, each fitted with bail and handle. Assortment consists:
2 doz. 2 qt., diam. 8⅜ in.
2 doz. 4 qt., diam., 9⅞ in.
1 doz. 7 qt., diam. 11⅛ in.
Total 5 doz. in pkg. Per dozen, **89c**

BLUE AND WHITE FIREPROOF BAKING DISH.

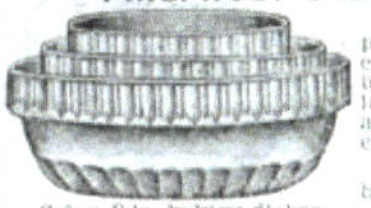

E763 — Fireproof clay, buff color outside, blue glaze lining. Will stand any heat. Asst. consists of:
2 dozen 7 in. baking dishes.
2 doz. 9 in. baking dishes.
2 " 10½ in " "
Total 6 doz. in pkg. Per dozen, **68c**

SPECIAL WHITE BRISTOL GLAZED CHAMBERS.

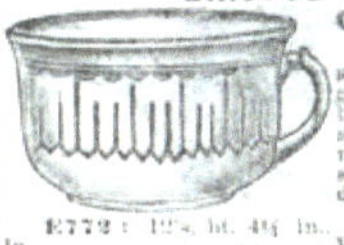

Regular C. C. shape, uncovered, good quality white bristol body, strong and well made, glazed inside and out. 1 doz. in pkg.
E772: 12's, ht. 4¾ in., diam 7⅜ in. Per dozen, **92c**
E773: 9's, ht. 5¼ in., diam. 9 in. Per dozen, **$1.20**
(NO PKG. CHARGE.)

"ROSE" DECORATED EWER AND BASIN.

High class decal and gold decorated ewer and basin at plain print price.

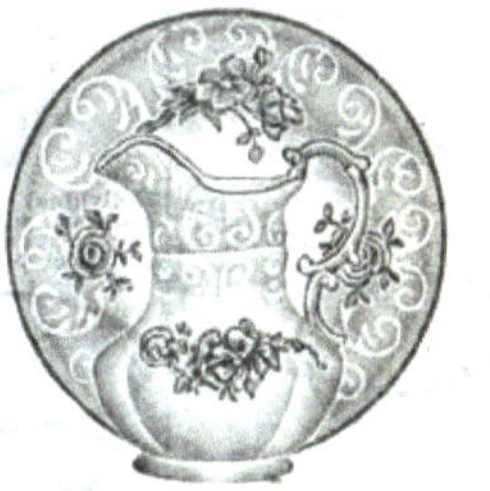

E951—Fancy shape, large pattern ewer, fancy handle, neatly embossed large roll edge basin. Gold edges illuminated handle. Decorations of large spray of pink roses and buds with background of delicately shaded green leaves, *no pkg. charge.* Per set, **92c**

BLUE TINTED COMBINET.

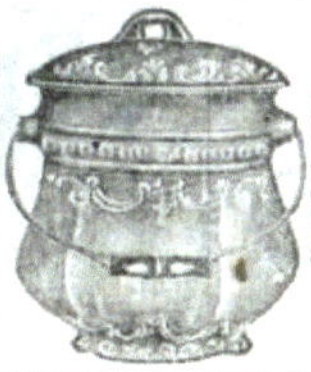

E774 — Large size, footed with cover and heavy wire bail with enameled wood handle, full ht. 12 in. heavy earthenware body, embossed in allover blue tint heavily glazed. Per dozen, **$5.20**

Every Dollar Invested Here Buys Full Value—No Inflated Prices Creep Into This Book.

Splendid Line of AMERICAN TEA AND DINNER SETS.

NO PKG. CHARGE.

New shapes and decorations. Goods **honest** in every way—full sizes, all regular composition, covers where covers should be, all pieces **well** covered with decoration. We invite comparison with sets in the market costing more money. Shipped from our house. No package charge.

"NEW PURITY" 56 PIECE TEA SET.

E601—Plain white, light weight semi-porcelain body, fancy shapes, neatly embossed. The style set always in demand. 2 sets in pkg. Wt. 75 lbs. Per set, **$1.95** (NO PKG. CHARGE.)

"NEW WINNER" 56 PIECE TEA SET.

E603—Plain print light weight white granite body, neat attractive decorations in blue and delicate green. New shapes, richly embossed. 2 sets in pkg. Wt. 75 lbs. Per set, **$2.70** (NO PKG. CHARGE.)

"CHOICEST" 56 PIECE TEA SET.

E608—Light weight, semi-porcelain body, neatly embossed, decorated in combination shaded green scroll and festoon of roses—very beautiful. All pieces gold lined edges, handles and knobs gold traced. 2 sets in pkg. Wt. 75 lbs. Per set, **$3.50** (NO PKG. CHARGE.)

"LEADER" 65 PIECE GOLD TRACED DINNER SET.

E621. Light wt. embossed semi-porcelain body with large rose decoration, interspersed with shaded pink and white forget me not flowers with a background of shaded green leaves. All edges gold lined with knobs and handles full gold traced. Special gold treatment on all covers with inside and outside decorations on hollow ware. Regular 65 piece composition. 2 sets in bbl. Wt. 95 lbs. NO PACKAGE CHARGE. Per set, **$5.50**

"EVERY DAY" 100 PIECE PLAIN PRINT DINNER SET. Composition "B."

E624: Fancy shape, light weight, semi-porcelain body. Green decorated, plain print in combination scroll and flower pattern. Not strictly first selection but splendid value for the money. Each set in bbl. Per set, **$5.35** (NO PKG. CHARGE.)

"FRENCH ROSE" 100 PIECE DINNER SET.

E643: Body of light weight, semi-porcelain, decalcomania decoration in the popular French Rose colorings. All pieces gold traced. Each set in bbl. Wt. 100 lbs. Per set, **$7.85** (NO PKG. CHARGE.)

"CHELSEA" 100 PIECE DINNER SET.

E620—Plain white body of pure semi-porcelain, beautifully embossed, new fancy shape, all large pieces. Each set in pkg., wt. 100 lbs. Per set, **$4.20** (NO PKG. CHARGE.)

"ORIENTAL BORDER" 100 PIECE SEMI-PORCELAIN DINNER SET. Composition "C."

E679—New up to date oriental border decoration in genuine oriental designs and colorings consisting of 10 distinct colors. All pieces gold lined with inner line of green, making very beautiful combination. All flat pieces with set centerpiece, all handles and knobs gold traced. This set is for your high toned trade. Each in pkg. Per set, **$10.75** (NO PKG. CHARGE.)

COMPOSITION OF ENGLISH AND AMERICAN TEA AND DINNER SETS.

56 Piece Dinner Sets—12 tea cups and saucers (24 pieces), 12 breakfast plates, 12 fruit or sauce dishes, 2 cake plates, 1 covered sugar, (2 pieces), 1 covered tea pot (2 pieces), 1 cream pitcher, 1 slop bowl.

65 Piece Dinner Sets—6 tea cups and saucers (12 pieces), 6 tea plates, 6 dinner plates, 6 soup plates, 12 fruit or sauce dishes, 6 individual butters, 1 covered butter (3 pieces), 1 covered dish (2 pieces), 2 cake plates, 1 open vegetable dish, 1 salad dish, 1 sauce boat, 1 medium platter, 1 large platter, 1 pickle dish, 1 cream pitcher, 1 slop bowl.

100 Piece "A" Composition Dinner Sets—12 tea cups and saucers (24 pieces), 12 bread and butter plates, 12 breakfast plates, 12 dinner plates, 12 soup plates, 12 fruit or sauce dishes, 2 covered dishes (4 pieces), 1 covered butter (3 pieces), 1 covered sugar (2 pieces), 1 open vegetable dish, 1 large platter, 1 medium platter, 1 pickle dish, 1 cream pitcher, 1 slop bowl.

100 Piece "B" Composition Sets—Same composition as 100 piece "A" except there are 12 individual butters instead of 12 bread and butter plates.

100 Piece "C" Composition Sets—12 handled cups and saucers (24 pieces), 12 6 in. flat plates, 12 7 in. flat plates, 12 coupe soups, 12 4 in. fruits, 12 individual butters, 1 covered butter (3 pieces), 1 covered dish (2 pieces), 1 8 in. covered dish (2 pieces), 1 covered sugar (2 pieces), 1 8 in. platter, 1 12 in. platter, 1 cake plate, 1 creamer, 1 30's bowl, 1 sauce boat, 1 pickle dish.

112 Piece Dinner Sets—12 tea cups and saucers (24 pieces), 12 tea plates, 12 breakfast plates, 12 dinner plates, 12 soup plates, 12 fruit or sauce dishes, 12 individual butters, 2 covered dishes (4 pieces), 1 covered butter (3 pieces), 1 covered sugar (2 pieces), 1 open vegetable dish, 1 large platter, 1 extra large platter, 1 pickle dish, 1 sauce boat, 1 cream pitcher, 1 slop bowl.

128 Piece Composition Sets—12 handled tea cups and saucers (24 pieces), 12 4 in. flat plates, 12 5 in. flat plates, 12 6 in. flat plates, 12 in. flat plates, 12 coupe soups, 12 4 in. fruits, 12 individual butters, 1 covered butter (3 pieces), 1 7 in. covered dish (2 pieces), 1 8 in. covered dish (2 pieces), 1 casserole (2 pieces), 1 covered sugar (2 pieces), 1 12's jug, 1 covered, 1 7 in. baker, 1 7 in. nappy, 1 sauce boat, 1 30's bowl, 1 8 in. platter, 1 10 in. dish, 1 12 in. platter.

130 Piece Composition Sets—12 handled tea cups and saucers (24 pieces), 6 handled coffee cups and saucers (12 pieces), 12 5 in. plates, 12 6 in. plates, 12 7 in. plates, 12 deep plates, 12 4 in. fruits, 12 individual butters, 2 8 in. covered dishes (4 pieces), 1 10 in. notched casserole (2 pieces), 2 7 in. bakers, 1 covered butter (3 pieces), 1 covered sugar (2 pieces), 1 7 in. dish, 1 8 in. dish, 1 10 in. dish, 1 12 in. dish, 1 30's bowl, 1 creamer, 1 sauce boat, 1 pickle dish, 1 12's jug.

We Constantly Watch The Market For NEW AND WORTHY GOODS.

"PRINCESS" 100 PIECE DINNER SET.
Composition "B."

E634: Near china, body decorations in delicate pink and yellow roses in full bloom and effect with sprays of green leaves in two shades. Total 100 pieces. Set, **$7.95** (NO PKG. CHARGE.)

NOTE: This set is made up from our High Grade Near China Open Stock pattern and you can order any of the pieces from open stock at any time.

"GOLD BORDER" 100 PIECE DINNER SET.
"A" Composition.

E636 — New fancy shape, light weight semi-porcelain body with solid gold decorations. All edges with one heavy and one fine gold line with an inner gold lace decoration. All handles with solid Roman gold finish with extra gold tracing on all hollow pieces. New and artistic treatment making a very striking set. Each in a pkg. Per set, **$8.50** Wt. 100 lbs. (NO PKG. CHARGE.)

Note: Composition "A" includes bread and butter plates in place of individual butters.

"EXQUISITE FLORAL AND GOLD" 100 PIECE DINNER SET.
Composition "C."

E630 — New artistic shape, light semi-porcelain body with new bead and scroll effect embossing. Profuse decorations in seven color decal. Large pink roses with cluster of pink chrysanthemums, background of shaded green and autumn colorings. All pieces gold lined with hand traced gold design between each decal spray. Handles and knobs full gold traced. Hollow pieces decal decorated on the inside—flat pieces with center spray. Each set in pkg. Wt. 110 lbs. Set, **$8.75** (NO PKG. CHARGE.)

IMPORTED "ORLEANS ROSE" 100 PIECE CHINA DINNER SET.

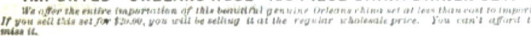

We offer the entire importation of this beautiful genuine Orleans china set at less than cost to import. If you sell this set for $20.00, you will be selling it at the regular wholesale price. You can't afford to miss it.

E650: Regular 100 piece genuine Orleans rose china dinner set. Beautiful pure white china body, large new shape with a neat embossed design on all pieces. Decorations being delicate pink Orleans roses, interspersed with shaded green foliage in wreath effect, making a complete border pattern. All flat pieces have center decoration, double gold lined, knobs and handles full gold traced. Each set in pkg. Set, **$13.50** (NO PKG. CHARGE.)

"COMPLETE" 112 PIECE DINNER SET.

E641: Seven color decal decoration in clusters of mammoth rose. Interspersed with delicate wild flowers and green leaves, making a beautiful effect. Covered dish and hollow pieces with inside decoration. All handles and knobs gold traced. A selection high grade semi-porcelain body. Each in bbl. (NO PKG. CHARGE.) Wt. 115 lbs. Set, **$8.75**

"ROSE AND GOLD BORDER" 100 PIECE DINNER SET.
Composition "A."

E635 — Fancy semi-porcelain body, light weight, decorations of beautiful rose border wreath patterns with heavy gold line and lace border decorations. All handles and knobs gold traced. An especially striking and attractive set. Each in a pkg. Wt 100 lbs. (NO PKG. CHARGE.) Per set, **$9.50**

Note: Composition "A" includes bread and butter plates in place of individual butters.

"PRESIDENT'S TABLE" 128 PIECE DINNER SET.

E642 — Heavy stippled edges and handles. Decoration in artistic cluster of beautiful pink roses and green leaves. Background of delicate vine and sprig of pink flowers. Hollow pieces and covered ware with inside decoration. Light semi-porcelain ware, very delicate embossing.

Wt. 114 lbs.   Each set in pkg.   (NO PKG. CHARGE.)   Set, **$11.25**

"FERN AND ROSE" 130 PIECE DINNER SET.

E640 — Body of light weight near China Ware with an entirely new and up-to-date decoration of delicate shaded green fern with rose and wild flower combination in natural colors. This class of decoration is totally used only on Higher grade of china. All pieces with gold lined edges. All knobs and handles full gold traced. Each in a pkg. Wt. 120 lbs. (NO PKG. CHARGE.) Set, **$12.50**

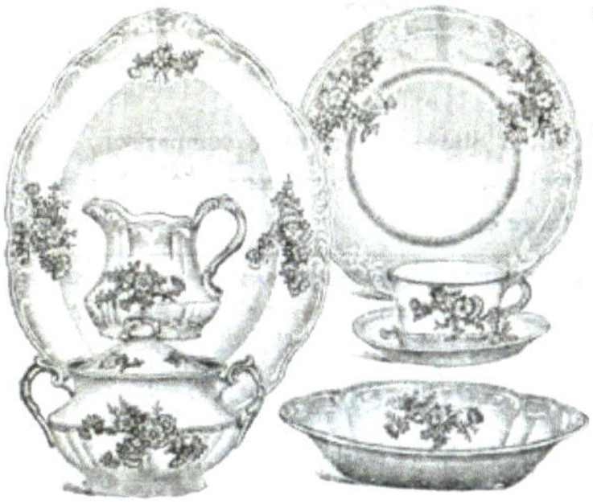

"GEM" 42 PIECE SEMI-PORCELAIN DINNER SET.

Excellent value.

E612—Light weight, semi-porcelain body, neat design, clear hard glaze. One set decorated in a combination of roses and daisies in pink, white and green coloring. The other decorated in beautiful spray of natural colored flowers with green foliage. Regular composition. Two sets in package.

6 tea cups and saucers. (12)
6 7 in. plates.
6 5 in. plates.
6 individual butters.
6 fruit dishes.
1 open vegetable dish.
1 large platter.
1 fancy bowl.
1 covered sugar (2).
1 creamer.
Per set, **$2.50**

(NO PKG. CHARGE.)

"SUPERB" 100 PIECE DINNER SET. COMPOSITION A.

Special value at a remarkably low price.

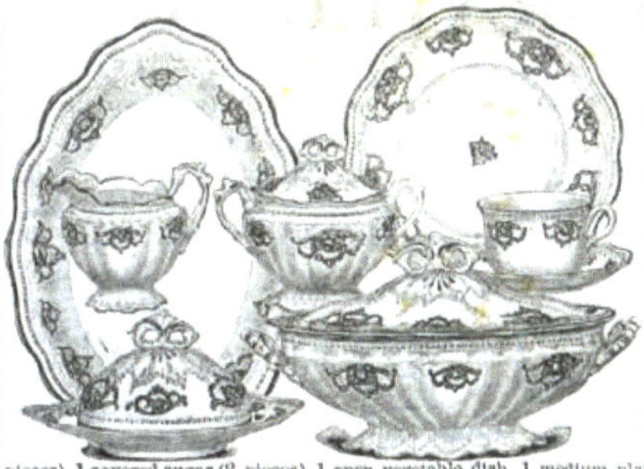

E681: Firenze body, light weight fancy embossed shape, good clear glaze decorations being in a combination of pink and white roses with a leaf and scroll effect of dark wild flowers, making a very beautiful contrast. All pieces are double lined with a gold outer and a delicate delft blue inner line. All flat pieces with center decorations. Knobs and handles of all hollow ware full gold traced. Set comprises 12 tea cups and saucers (24 pieces), 12 bread and butter plates, 12 breakfast plates, 12 dinner plates, 12 soup plates, 12 fruit or sauce dishes, 2 covered dishes (4 pieces), 1 covered butter (3 pieces), 1 covered sugar (2 pieces), 1 open vegetable dish, 1 medium platter, 1 large platter, 1 sauce boat, 1 pickle dish, 1 cream pitcher. Per set, **$9.00**

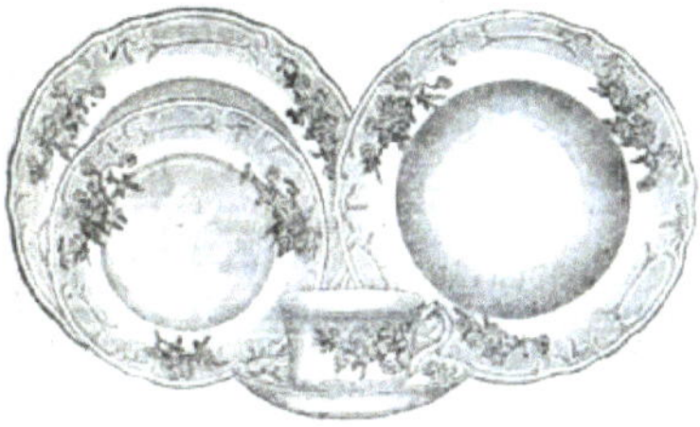

"ROSE DECORATED" TEA CUP AND PLATE ASSORTMENT.

Exceptional 10 cent values.

E722—Fancy embossed semi-porcelain body—first selection, good clear glaze, decorations in six-color rose and daisy in a combination of pink, green and blue with green leaf background. Assortment comprises:
6 doz. fancy teas.
3 " dinner plates, act. 9¼.
2 " bread & butter plates, actual 7½.
1 " soup plates, actual 10¼.
Total 12 doz. in pkg. Per dozen, **78c**

(NO PKG. CHARGE.)

DECAL & GOLD DECORATED SEMI-PORCELAIN JUG.

A matchless value for a quarter leader.

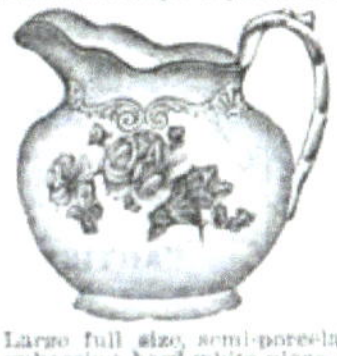

E922: Large full size, semi-porcelain body, neat embossing, hard white glaze, **guaranteed not to craze.** Floral rose decal decoration. Gold lined edges. Size 24's. Capacity 3 pints. Per dozen **$2.25**

WE do not say that you ought to buy all your goods from us. No one house can possibly undersell all others on each item in its line and make any money. But we do say, and say it earnestly, that unless you buy SOME of your goods from Butler Brothers you pay more than you ought.

"HIGH ART" AMERICAN CHINA.

Decorations very carefully executed in rich, lustrous colors and gold on a vitrous earthen body that is positively warranted not to craze. Decorations in the expensive mineral colors thoroughly amalgamated with the glaze, and cannot be effaced by continuous use, heat or moisture. Each piece wrapped.

PLATES—*¼ doz. in pkg.*

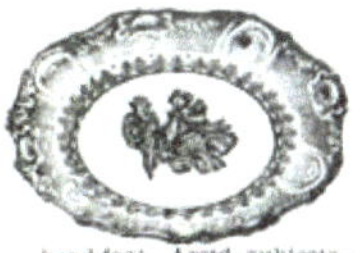

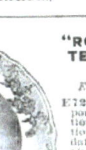

E1001—8¼in. coupe, panel embossing, white ground, asstd. fancy picture centers with rich gold framework, wide gold cloud scalloped edge, gold band foot. Asstd. subjects.. .... Doz. **$3.75**

E1004—8⅝ in. coupe, panel embossed flange, mother of pearl, cobalt blue and dark green flanges, asstd. bust centers inside gold framework, heavy gold outlining, colored inlay and gold scalloped edges, outer wide gold band at base, 3 colors and 3 subjects asstd.......................Doz. **$6.00**

CAKE PLATES.

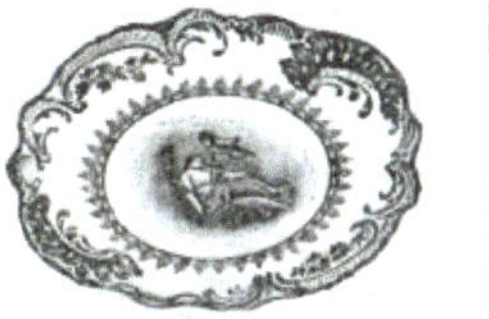

E1008—10¼ coupe, handled ivory, green and cobalt blue flanges with shell and floral embossing, heavily decorated and gold outlined, scalloped edges with asstd. gold band and gold showered decorations, asstd. 3 styles picture centers inside gold frame work, outer wide gold band at base. Each in pkg. Each, **75c**

PLAQUE OR CHOP PLATE.

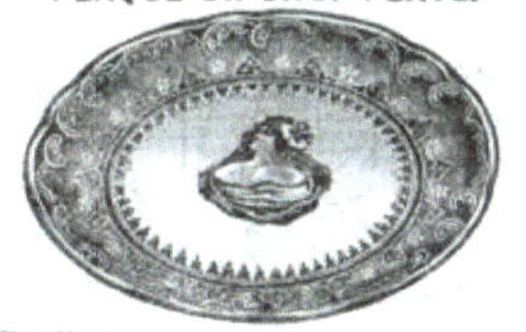

E1039—13 in., luster cobalt blue flange with shell embossing outlined with gold, wide gold band edge, bust picture center on flow blue tinted background surrounded by wide and narrow gold bands, gold lace wreath and outer ornamental wreath of gold and enameled flowers, flow blue shaded outside, flow blue band at base. Each in pkg. Each, **$1.20**

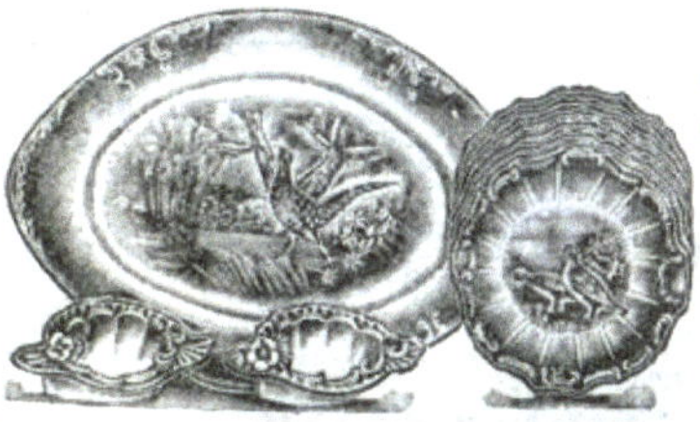

FISH AND GAME SETS.

E1033, Game Set—1 platter 18⅝x12⅜, 6 coupe plates, 8⅝ in. with embossed paneled flanges, 2 shell design jelly dishes 7x5¼. Each piece in shaded rookwood with gold edges and asstd. pictures of game with landscape backgrounds, pheasant, duck, snipe, etc. in groups, outer gold band on base. Each set in case.............. Set, **$3.75**

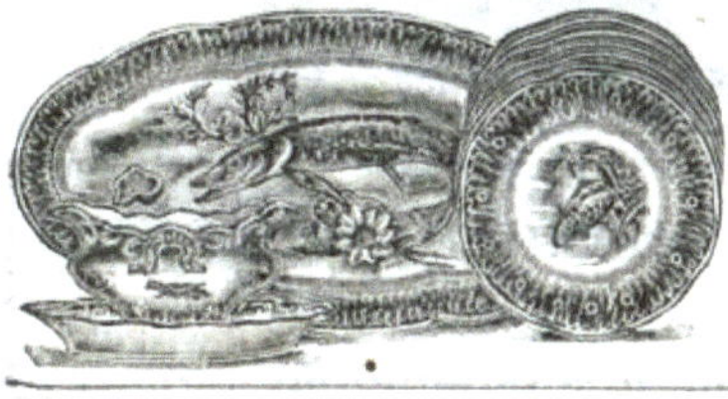

E1034, Fish Set—Six 9 in. plates, 1 large platter 22x11, 1 double handled sauce boat 8¼x5¾x4½ with detached tray size 10⅝x6⅜. Mottled embossed flanges in shaded green with asstd. fish picture centers combined with marine plants and water effect, gold edges. Each set in case. Set, **$4.25**

CUP AND SAUCER.

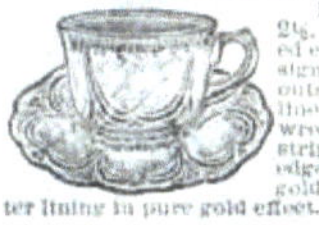

E1031—Cup 3¾x2⅝, saucer 6, scalloped embossed panel design, iridescent luster outside with gold outline and gold lace wreath around top, gold striped handle, gold edge and inner fillet gold band, yellow luster lining in pure gold effect. ½ doz. in pkg. Doz. **$2.95**

ENAMELED AND GOLD DECORATED ENGLISH ROCKINGHAM TEAPOTS.

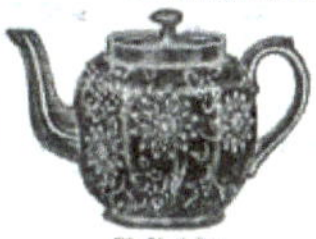

E5, $2.25 Doz.

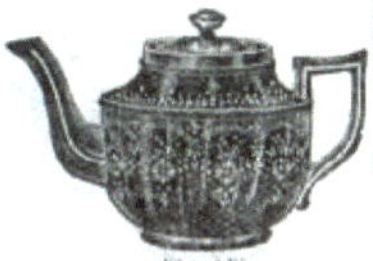

E6 and E7.

Best quality jet black color heavily glazed inside and outside, allover rich enamel decorations; gold decorations on edge handle, spout and cover, gold band around top. All decorations burnt in and will not wear off.

E5—Globe shape, size 42, ht. 5 in. Doz. **$2.25**

E6—As E5, only large fancy low shape, size 36, ht. 5¼ in. Doz. **$2.95**

E7—As E6, only much larger, size 30, ht. 5⅜ in. Doz. **$3.60**

PERFECTION GOLD BAND WHITE GRANITE WARE.

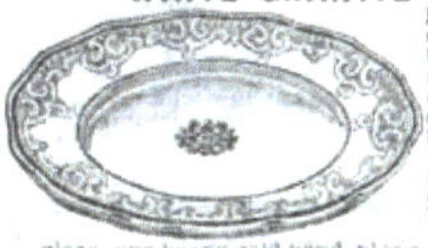

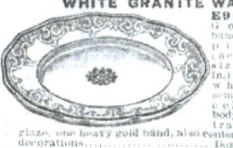

E963: Gold band 9 in. plate (actual size 8¼ in.) Fine white semi-porcelain body, extra fine glaze, one heavy gold band, also center gold decorations.............................Doz. **65c**

E962—7 in., actual 9¾ in ....Doz. **75c**

E965—7 in. flat plate, actual 9¾ in.....Doz. **75c**

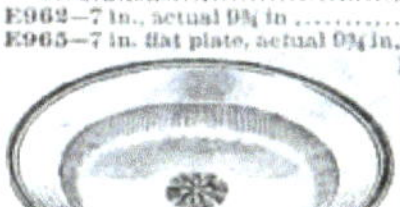

E964: Gold band, 7 in plate (actual size 9¾ in.) Fine white semi-porcelain body, extra fine glaze, heavy gold band. Doz. **75c**

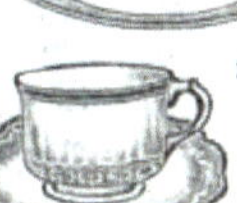

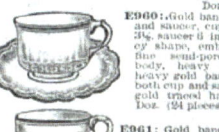

E960: Gold band cup and saucer, cup 2¼x3½, saucer 6 in., fancy shape, embossed fine semi-porcelain body, heavy body, heavy gold band on both cup and saucer, gold traced handle. Doz. (24 pieces) **85c**

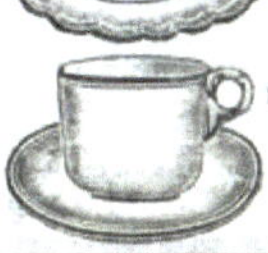

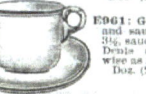

E961: Gold band cup and saucer, cup 3¼x3½, saucer 6¼ in. St. Denis shape, otherwise as above. Doz. (24 pieces) **85c**

"PERFECTION" NAPPY ASSORTMENT.

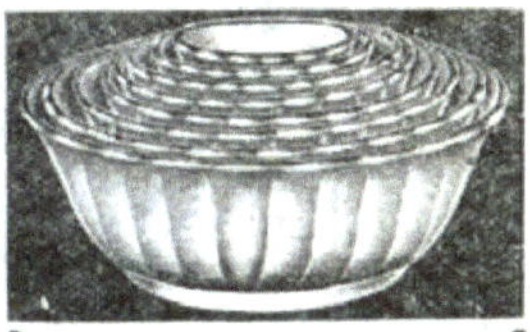

E711: The best selling numbers, all fluted regulation sizes, best quality ware, good clear glaze guaranteed not to craze. Each asst. comprises following:

¼ doz.	2½ in.	(act. 4 in.) @	$0 51	$0 13
¼ "	3 "	" 4½ " "	52	13
½ "	4 "	" 5½ " "	53	27
½ "	5 "	" 6⅜ " "	59	30
1 "	6 "	" 7 " "	76	76
1 "	7 "	" 8¼ " "	90	90
½ "	8 "	" 9 " "	1 55	78
¼ "	9 "	" 10¼ " "	1 76	44
¼ "	10 "	" 11 " "	2 20	55

Total for assortment, **$4.26**

UMBRELLA STANDS—*Each in pkg.*

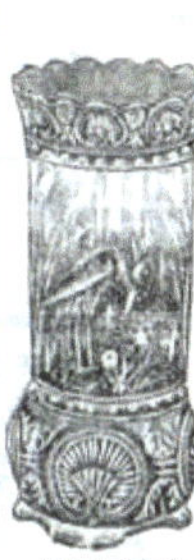

E938, $1.25 Each.

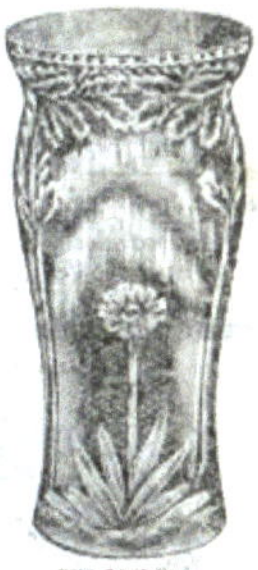

E939, $2.95 Each.

E938—Large size, ht. 19¾ in., girth 24 in., extra heavy, strong faience wares. Scalloped edge, richly embossed all over in tropical scenes. Beautiful blends of dark maroon or brown shading into green or blue, heavily glazed all over, wt. 35 lbs................Each, **$1.25**

E939—Extra large, ht. 23 in., diam. of top 11¼ in., fancy swell shape, very elaborate floral and wreath embossed work, beautiful relief effect, rich blended dark colors such as maroon, greens, etc., heavily glazed inside and out, wt. 48 lbs.........................Each, **$2.95**

NO PACKAGE CHARGE On any Goods

We Undercut Not By Cheapening Quality, But By Careful Buying and Economical Selling.

DECORATED DOMESTIC TOILET SETS.

NO PACKAGE CHARGE

Values that are positively unequaled. From the best pottery in United States. We invite comparison. Not merely are the prices low but the goods are of **SUPERIOR GRADE**. Better ware and better decorations than most (even at higher prices) and sizes honest. Shipped from our house—no package charge.

"LEADER" 6 PIECE TOILET SET

E550—Regular composition. Good white body, fancy embossed pattern, large floral print decoration. 1 olive green, 1 terra cotta and 1 myrtle green. Total 3 sets in bbl. Wt. 94 lbs. (NO PKG. CHARGE.) Set, **$1.30**

"NEW YEAR" 10 PIECE TOILET SET.

E552—Regular composition. All pieces full size, roll edge baxin, good white body, embossed and decorated in large carnation prints, 1 green and 1 blue. Total 2 sets in bbl. Wt. 75 lbs. (NO PKG. CHARGE.) Set, **$1.65**

"VIRGINIA" 10 PIECE TOILET SET

E506—Regular composition. Vastolta pearl decoration in beautiful pink and white coloring, interspersed with buds and green leaves. All pieces gold lined, handles and knobs gold traced. 2 sets in bbl. (NO PKG. CHARGE.) Wt. 70 lbs. Set, **$2.40**

"FULL VALUE" 6 PIECE TOILET SET.

E501—Asstd. floral designs in blue, brown and gray print decorations. Regular composition. 3 sets in barrel. Wt. 85 lbs. (NO PKG. CHARGE.) Set, **$1.35**

"ARTISTIC" 10 PIECE TOILET SET.

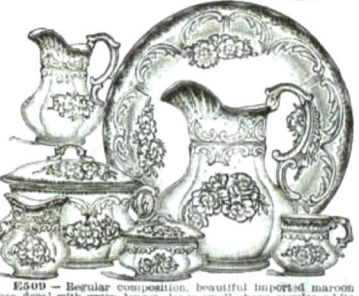

E509—Regular composition, beautiful imported maroon rose, decal with green leaves, large swell shape regular white granite body, all edges and handles full stippled, gold treated. 2 sets in bbl. Wt. 82 lbs. (NO PKG. CHARGE.) Set, **$2.80**

"REAL BARGAIN" 10 PIECE TOILET SET.

E539—New artistic design, wreath embossed pattern, best semi-porcelain body. Decorations in 7 color decal large pink American beauty and white roses in full blown and bud effect with a combination of green foliage in autumn colored tints. 2 sets in pkg. (NO PKG. CHARGE.) Per set, **$2.50**

"HOTEL" 7 PIECE TOILET SET.

E504—Body of best white granite, cable shape, large full size pieces. Comprises large ewer and basin, uncovered slop jar, covered chamber, soap dish and hall boy jug. Total 7 pieces. 3 sets in bbl. Wt. 100 lbs. (NO PKG. CHARGE.) Set, **$1.80**

WHITE AND GOLD 7 PIECE HOTEL TOILET SET.

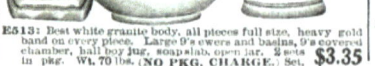

E513: Best white granite body, all pieces full size, heavy gold band on every piece. Large 9's ewers and basins, 9's covered chamber, hall boy jug, soap dish, open jar. 2 sets in pkg. Wt. 70 lbs. (NO PKG. CHARGE.) Set, **$3.35**

"DECORATED HOTEL" 7 PIECE TOILET SET.

E502—Hotel granite body, plain cable shapes, assd. print decorations in green and maroon. Large ewer, basin, open cuspidor, 9's chamber and cover, hall boy jug, drainer soap. 2 in bbl. (NO PKG. CHARGE.) Set, **$2.75**

"CHALLENGE" 6 PIECE TOILET SET ASST.

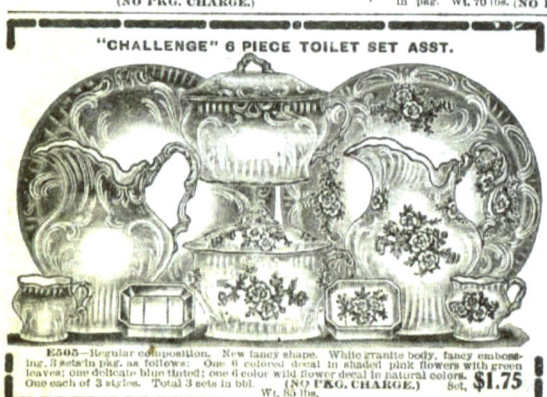

E505—Regular composition. New fancy shape. White granite body, fancy embossing, 3 sets in pkg. as follows: One 6 coloresl decal in shaded pink flowers with green leaves; one delicate blue tinted; one 6 color wild flower decal in natural colors. One each of 3 styles. Total 3 sets in bbl. Wt. 85 lbs. (NO PKG. CHARGE.) Set, **$1.75**

"EVERYDAY" 12 PIECE TOILET SET.

E573: Regular composition. Strong earthen body, all over solid color decoration—one blue and one light chocolate. Total 2 sets in crate. Wt. 145 lbs. Set, **$1.95** (NO PKG. CHARGE.)

PACKAGE CHARGE ABOLISHED
On All Crockery and Glassware

You Make One Good Profit In Close Buying Here—You Can't Beat These Prices.

"MAGNIFICENT" 10 PIECE TOILET SET.

E517: Fine white semi-porcelain body, embossed decorations of hand painted poppies with background of wild flowers in natural colors. Regular composition. Each set in pkg., wt. 50 lbs. (NO PKG. CHARGE.) Per set, **Out**

"BEAUTY" 12 PIECE TOILET SET.

E520: Decorations in beautiful natural color flowers in a combination of delicate pink and green. Large fancy shape semi-porcelain body. All full sizes pieces. Regular composition. Each set in pkg., wt. 55 lbs. (NO PKG. CHARGE.) Set, **Out**

"IMMENSE" 12 PIECE TOILET SET.

E511—Regular composition, large fancy shape in green and brown floral decorations, all edges gold lined, handles and knobs gold traced. 2 sets in cask, one of each color, wt. 95 lbs. Per set, **$3.40** (NO PKG. CHARGE.)

"AMERICAN BEAUTY" 10 AND 12 PIECE TOILET SETS.

Absolutely unmatchable at these prices. Two beautiful and ready sellers.

E559—10 piece. Semi-porcelain body, large full shape, embossed pattern, large American Beauty decal decorations, flowers beautiful pink, green spray back ground, shaded autumn coloring. All gold lined, gold traced handles and special gold tracing on body. Regular composition. 2 sets in cask. wt. 75 lbs. (NO PKG. CHARGE.) Per set, **$2.45**

E560—As E559, 12 piece including large fancy covered slop jar. Each in pkg., wt. 55 lbs. (NO PKG. CHARGE.) Per set, **$4.10**

"COMPLETE" 12 PIECE TOILET SET.

E512: Regular composition, 7 color imported decal decoration in natural color flower. Very artistic combination. Fancy embossed white granite body. All large sizes. 1 set in bbl., wt. 55 lbs. Per set, **$3.65** (NO PKG. CHARGE.)

"GOLD CLOUDED" 10 AND 12 PIECE TOILET SETS.

E525—10 piece regular composition, full size pieces basin with rolled rim, semi-porcelain body, fancy shape, heavily embossed, edges, handles, knobs, etc. gold clouded. 2 sets in bbl. wt. 75 lbs. Per set, **$2.25** (NO PKG. CHARGE.)

E526: 12 piece, regular composition, with large fancy covered slop jar. 1 set in bbl. wt. 55 lbs. (NO PKG. CHARGE.) Per set, **$3.90**

"GREEN TINTED AND GOLD LINED" 12 PIECE TOILET SET.

E514: Regular composition embossed white granite body in special green tinted and gold lined combination, Full size pieces. Each set in bbl., wt. 60 lbs. Per set, **$4.00** (NO PKG. CHARGE.)

DECAL AND GOLD 10 AND 12 PIECE DECORATED TOILET SETS.

E523, 10 Piece—New shape embossed semi-porcelain body. All pieces large full sizes. 10 color decal decorations in beautiful combination of wild flowers and green sprays—handle and edge stippled. 2 sets in bbl., wt. 75 lbs. Per set **$2.90** (NO PKG. CHARGE.)

E524, 12 Piece—With large fancy covered slop jar. Each set in bbl., wt. 55 lbs. (NO PKG. CHARGE.) Per set **$4.60**

"STARTLING" 12 PIECE TOILET SET.

E519—Best semi-porcelain body—large fancy shape with neat embossing. Full gold lined beautiful six-color American beauty rose decoration in full blown pink and bud effect with shaded green leaf background. Regular composition. Each set in pkg., wt. 55 lbs. (NO PKG. CHARGE.) Per set, **$3.90**

"GROUND LAID" 10 AND 12 PIECE TOILET SETS.

E527, 10 Piece—Regular composition. Tall stately shape, beautiful decal rose decoration, bright red and yellow colorings with green leaf and bud background, completely encircled with elaborate gold tracing, making a double panel effect. Ground laid, beautiful shade of green. All pieces gold lined and full gold traced. All pieces decorated on both sides with full gold tracing and gold lines. The newest and most artistic decoration of the day. 2 sets in a pkg., wt. 75 lbs. (NO PKG. CHARGE.) Per set, **$3.15**

E528, 12 Piece—As E527, including large fancy covered slop jar. Each set in a pkg., wt. 55 lbs. (NO PKG. CHARGE.) Per set, **$5.75**

In Our Sample Rooms Goods Are Marked in Plain Figures—You KNOW You Get Bottom Prices.

CUSPIDORS.
In Original Packages.

E845, 79c Doz. E844,

E845:. Diam. 7 in., ht. 4½ in. Rustic design in red, green and olive colorings, half dull and half bright baked finish, artistic bronze decorations. Asstd. 6 doz. in crate. Doz. ★**78**

E844: 6½ in., painted lava, asstd. spray decorations. 3 doz. in crate- Wt. 94 lbs Doz. **80c**

E846:. Asstd. designs. Colorings in dark green, red and light green, with gold bronze decorations in leaf and wreath designs. All decorations baked, glazed inside with white enamel flange. 6 doz. in crate.........Doz. **84c**

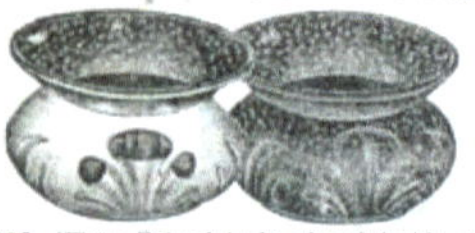

E837—White Bristol body, glazed inside and out. 2 patterns: blue mottled and bristol white with embossed decorated sides. Large size, diameter 7 inches, height 4½ inches. 2¼ doz. each. Total 4½ doz. in pkg. Doz. **92c**

E838—Large size, 4¾x6½. Faience body, embossed, heavily glazed outside and in. Asstd. light and dark green, maroon, brown, yellow, etc. 4 doz. in crate. Wt. 155 lbs. Doz. **92c**

E826: Glazed inside, with hard baked outside decoration. Asstd. colors, green, red and blended effects. 1 doz. 8 in. floral decorated, 1 doz. 7½ in. floral and embossed decorated, 1 doz. 7½ in. blended with embossed floral decoration. Total 3 doz. in crate..........Doz. **95c**

E832: Faience body, embossed, heavily glazed inside and out. ⅓ doz. large low shape, asstd. blended colors, ⅓ doz. large low shape, in solid cobalt blue, ⅓ doz. high shape in rich blended colors. Total 1 doz. in case..........Doz. **$1.89** Wt. 50 lbs.

E833—Extra large, heavily embossed, in rich floral and scroll designs, all in rich dark blended colors, combinations of red, green, maroon, etc. ½ doz. each of 2 styles; diam. 7¾ in., average ht. 5½. Total 1 doz. in case ..Wt. 63 lbs..........Doz. **$2.10**

IN OPEN STOCK.

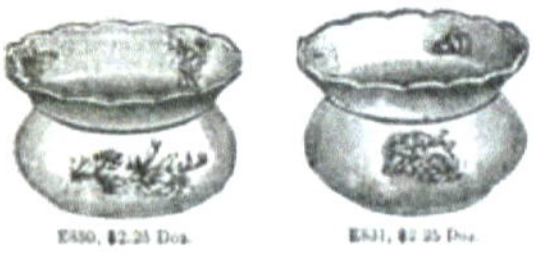

E830, $2.25 Doz. E831, $2.25 Doz.

E830. "Carnation and Gold"—Large size, ht. 4½ in., diam. of top, 7½ in., good shape, well made, semi-porcelain body, large sprays of pink carnations, gold band around center and gold edge..............Doz. **$2.25**

E831—Large size, ht. 4½ in., diam. at top 7½ in., white semi-porcelain, cupid decorations on both sides of body and on flange, gold band and gold decorated edge.....Doz. **$2.25**

E847, $2.25 Doz.

E847:. White granite body, 7½ in. diam. at top, 5 in. high, asstd. decal decorations in natural colors. Gold lined, large full shape. Doz. **$2.25**

E811—Large size, ht. 5½ in., diam. of top 7¾ in., semi-porcelain body, solid cobalt blue inside and out, heavily glazed and embossed in tulip design traced and outlined with gold, wide gold band base, heavy gold clouded flange. ½ doz. in case....Doz. **$2.25**

NEW RED CLAY FLOWER POT ASST.
Terra Cotta Color.

E930— All mold made and finished by hand. Made from a high grade of potter's clay, very porous. Asst. contains equal quantities of 3 patterns in each size in terra cotta brown ware, red burned.

2 doz. 4½ in.	@	$0 18	$0 36
2 " 5½ "	@	30	60
2 " 6½ "	@	42	84
1 " 7½ "	@	72	72
1 " 8½ "	@	92	92

Wt. 277 lbs. Total for assortment **$3.44**

Total of 8 doz. in crate, sold only in crate.

RED CLAY FLOWER POT ASSORTMENT.

E931—Assorted patterns in mold made pots, best pattern clay. Popular sizes.

2½ doz. 5½ in., at 30c......$0 75
2½ doz. 6½ in., at 42c...... 1 05
2½ doz. 7½ in., at 72c...... 1 80
Total 7½ doz.
Total for asst......**$3.60**
Wt 330 lbs.

PAINTED FLOWER POT AND SAUCER ASSORTMENT.

E933. Bright red painted pots with wide band of gold completely covering the entire rim. Assortment comprises:

1 doz. 4½ in. at $0.35..	$0 35
1 doz. 5½ in. at $0.46..	46
1 doz. 6½ in. at $0.80..	80
½ doz. 7½ in. at $1.10..	55
½ doz. 8½ in. at $1.57..	79

Sold in crate only. Total 4 doz. in crate, **$2.95**

FLOWER POT AND SAUCER ASST.
Terra Cotta Brown.

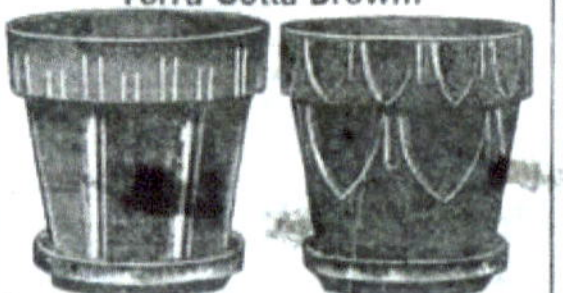

E932:. Mold made, hand finished. Made from best pottery clay, assorted patterns. Complete with saucers. Assortment contains the following:

1 doz.	8½ in.,	at $0.96	$0 96
½ "	9½ "	" 1.15	58
½ "	10½ "	" 1.30	65
½ "	12½ "	" 1.50	75

2½ doz. in crate. Total for asst. **$2.94**

Wt. 300 lbs. (**NO PKG. CHARGE.**)

JARDINIERES AND PEDESTALS.

Two Styles, E841, 62c Each.

E841, — Average size of jardiniere diam. 7¾ in., girth 23. Ht. of pedestal 8½ in., rich blended colors. Elaborately embossed and glazed all over. 1 each of 4 styles, in bbl. Each **62c**

E867, $1.20 Each. E865, $1.95 Each.

E867, "Blended"—9 in. jardiniere, 14 in. pedestal, full ht. 22¾ in., fancy embossed, pedestal with wide foot, jardiniere with flaring scalloped edge, both pieces in rich dark blended colors. 2 in pkg. Each, **$1.20**

E865, Extra Large Glazed Embossed—Jardiniere 9x9½, girth 36. Pedestal 15 in. high, full ht. of jardiniere and pedestal 24½ in. Both heavily glazed and embossed in scroll and leaf design in rich dark green. Each in bbl.............. Wt. 38 lbs. ..Each. **$1.95**

EMBOSSED GLAZED FERN DISHES.

E794—Diam. 7¾ in., deep shape, fancy embossed faience body in light and dark green blended colors, heavily glazed inside and out. Inside perforated clay fern pot. Doz. **2.15**

E795—Larger, diam. 8¾ in..........Doz. **$3.75**

JARDINIERES IN ASSORTMENTS.

E850:. Best faience body, heavily embossed in artistic scroll effect, glazed inside and out, asstd. colors—light and dark green, maroon, etc. 1 doz. each of 4½, 5½ and 6½ in. Total 3 doz. in crate. Wt. 115 lbs. Doz. **96c**

E312—Hard burned body, 3 up-to-date shapes, 7½x6, stork and floral decorations; 7½x6, rustic body with band of variegated floral decorations; 7x6, beautiful floral decorations. Assorted colors in terra cotta, olive and nile green with rustic and honeycomb background. 2 dozen each of 3 items. Total 6 doz. in pkg... Wt. 300 lbs. .....Doz **96c**

E852: Hard burned, painted body, baked red and green colorings with heavy embossed gold decorations. Five distinct patterns. Average diam. about 8 in., av. ht. about 6½, all full shapes, good patterns. ½ doz. each of 6 items. Total 3 doz. in pkg. Per dozen, **95c**

E849, $1.85 Doz. E851.

E849: Faience body, footed, large fancy shape, ht. 6½ in., diam. 8, girth 25, attractively embossed, scalloped edges, all in rich dark blended colors, ½ doz. each of 2 shapes, total 1 doz. in pkg.... Wt. 71 lbs. .Doz. **$1.85**

E851—1 dozen each of 8 and 9 in., all extra large fancy shapes, good faience bodies, heavily embossed with rich dark blended colors, heavily glazed both inside and out. Total 2 doz. in crate..........Doz., **$2.15**

E855—Hard burned body, embossed wood design, deep cut bark and knot pattern. Assorted colors, maroon and gilt; black, red and gilt; and green and gilt.

1 doz. 5½ in. diam., 4½ high at ★**66**
1 doz. 7½ in. diam., 6 high at.......... ★**97**
1 doz. 9 in. diam., 7½ high at ... ★**1.62**
Total 3 doz. in asst. ★**3.25**

E858. Embossed Glazed—Best strong faience ware, heavily glazed inside and out, elaborately embossed in rich blended light and dark green maroon, etc. Not the cheap plain colored but the expensive blended colors. Asst. comprises 12 jardinieres, no 2 exactly alike.

¼ doz.	7 in.	@	$1 75	$0 44
¼ "	8 "	"	2 10	53
¼ "	9 "	"	3 40	57
¼ "	10 "	"	4 75	79
¼ "	11 "	"	7 20	1 20

Wt. 100 lbs. Total for assortment, **$3.53**

E899: Dull finish, rustic pattern, large full shape, fluted tops, asstd. colors. Flower and leaf pattern in bronze colorings, very artistic.

1 doz. 6½ in. high, 7 in. diam. at top, at 98c. $0 98
½ doz. 8 in. high, 9 in. diam. at top, at $3.00 .... 1 50
¼ doz. 10 in. high, 11 in. diam. at top, at $4.48 .... 1.12
Wt. 150 lbs. Total for assortment. **Out**

E845: 4 jardinieres of the same pattern, a beautiful panel design. Elaborately embossed in scroll and fleur de lis design. Embossed work in ivory with elaborate gold tracings, panels in solid colors, such as reds, greens and blues. Insides of ivory color and edges are elaborately gold clouded.

1 medium size, 7½ in., girth 25 in., @.....
1 large size, 8¾ in., girth 31 in., @..........
1 extra large size, 9½ in., girth 33¾ in., @..
1 mammoth size, 10¾ in., girth 37½ in., @..
Total 4 in asst. Total for assortment. **Out Out**

E857: Best faience ware, elaborately embossed in artistic all over designs. Rich blended colors, underglazed decorations. Large variety of shapes and colors—no 2 exactly alike. All heavily glazed both inside and outside. Asst. comprises:

¼ doz.	6½ in.,	girth	21	in.,	at	$1 95	$0 49
¼ "	7½ "	"	24		"	2 10	55
⅙ "	8½ "	"	27		"	3 95	66
⅙ "	9½ "	"	30		"	6 00	1 00
⅙ "	11 "	"	34½		"	8 40	1 40

Total 1 doz. in pkg. Wt. 115 lbs. Total for asst.. **$4.10**

E859: Faience body, large fancy shapes, heavily embossed, white inside, outside with rich blended tinted groundwork such as light and dark greens blending into pinks, yellows, etc. Decorations very elaborate, comprising large hand painted floral designs in roses, pansies, lilies, etc., bright natural colors. All have scalloped gold decorated edges. Asst. comprises:

1 only	7 in.,	rose decoration	....	$0 33
1 "	8½ "	pansy "	....	42
1 "	9 "	lily "	....	62
1 "	9½ "	pansy "	....	75
1 "	10 "	lily "	....	88
1 "	10½ "	rose "	....	1 20

6 in., asst. Wt. 59 lbs. Total for assortment **$4.20**

E541: Best faience ware, all embossed almost all over in artistic design, richest blended colors in underglazed decorations. Large variety of shapes—*no two exactly alike*. All heavily glazed, both in and out. Asst. comprises:

¼ doz., 6½ in., girth 20½ in. at $2.20. $0 55
¼ doz., 7¾ in., girth 24 in. at $3.10.. 78
⅙ doz., 8½ in., girth 26 in. at $4.50..... 75
⅙ doz., 9½ in., girth 30 in. at $7.95.......... 1 33
⅙ doz., 10½ in., girth 32 in. at $10.50... 1 75
Total for assortment, **$5.16**
Total of 1 doz. in bbl. Wt. 85 lbs.

"NEW ART" JARDINIERE ASSORTMENT.

New, artistic and up to date assortment, *worth double the price we quote.*

E860: Beautiful combination colorings in shaded green, brown and rookwood effects. Embossed floral designs, all stems, leaves and flowers hand colored.

3 only 7 in. (actual about 7½) @ 51....$1 53
3 only 9 in. (actual about 9) @ 72....... 2 15
2 only 10 in. (actual about 10½) @ 99.. 1 98
Total, 8 in asst. complete, *no pkg. charge.*
Wt. 103 lbs. Total. **$5.66**

ADD A SIDE LINE.

There is no better time than now to think of making room and using a little capital for a Profitable Side Line or two.

That results of such a step are quick and satisfying is proved by the fact that almost without an exception the merchant who has made even the smallest of an experiment almost immediately extends his Side Line showing.

No other attempt to better business can be so safely made for in no other venture will so small an investment so soon or so certainly indicate what results will be.

A look through our catalogue would suggest many things that could be utilized as Profitable Side Lines in your store. For a compact and varied lot of hints on this subject see the index of this very book.

One good way to experiment would be to watch results of using an assortment of 5 and 10 cent goods during the coming summer.

The variety in 5 and 10 cent goods is so great that you could test many things to determine just what Profitable Side Lines would pay best in your locality.

Besides, 5 and 10 cent goods used as your summer leaders would help you in cleaning up your regular stocks while avoiding summer dullness.

Look into this matter of Profitable Side Lines at once—for the **extra** profit, all things considered, there is in them for you at this particular time.

SPECIAL SALES THAT FAIL.

There was never a better example of why some special sales fail than a recent occurrence in one of our houses.

A certain merchant had sold out at one place and found a new location where he proposed to start another store. After buying for his opening stock he cast about for something to be used for his "grand" opening sale.

His choice fell upon an assortment of articles of various kinds and sizes, the whole averaging to cost him 81c per dozen. His special bought, he counseled with our Expert Service Bureau as to the way of presenting it.

His idea was to indulge in a great deal of "circus" talk about the phenomenal "special" which he proposed to have on sale opening day as a remarkable "Choice 10 cents" article.

When it was pointed out to him that the successful 5 and 10 cent or department store owner would almost certainly make a 5 cent offering of the article for such an occasion, this merchant came back with the statement "Why every dozen I sold would then represent a loss of 24 cents on first cost!"

It took argument to convince this particular merchant that the loss of 24 cents per dozen should be charged as part of the cost of advertising his opening day. And it took much more argument to convince him that the practice would pay him if followed regularly one day of every week after his store was opened.

Incidentally he remarked that special sales had never paid him. One reason was obvious. The man who would think of selling a regular 10 cent article as a remarkable opening day "special at 10 cents" could hardly have had bargains that really deserved the name for his other special sales.

Also his talk disclosed that he had never made it a point to have a few new things for his special sales and that he had never tried a special sale on any other basis than a certain straight "per cent. off all through the store."

And it is almost needless to say that preparatory to granting the straight per cent off all over the store, this merchant marked up goods so that after the deduction had been made there still was left what he called a "fair" profit on his goods.

This man, remember, had sold out in one location because results had proved unsatisfactory and yet proposed to start anew with immediate repetition of practices that at least had not made good in the first business.

It is easy to say that one understands why —with him—special sales had not been successful. Yet a great many other merchants are dissatisfied perhaps for reasons the same in kind though perhaps not in degree.

Can you go on describing goods as "bargains" and "specials" and failing to make them that—can you go on thus for any length of time without finally having your advertising of special sales fail to be believed and therefore fail to be effective.

Can you go on advertising "new" things as reasons why people should come to your special sales and then spreading before them nothing but the same old stocks perhaps not even rearranged—can you go on thus and yet be surprised when your special sales fail to draw?

And in spite of the fact that results have never been fully satisfactory, will you go on taking a loss on too many things but not enough loss on a few things to be so convincing as to draw people into your store?

If you are one of those merchants whose special sales "have not been successful"— frankly, ask yourself why and just as frankly aim to make the right answer however much the process may hurt your self-esteem.

For special sales will be successful—if you put the right methods of conducting them back of the right goods for special sales.

THERE IS A DIFFERENCE.

When it comes to low priced goods—there is a difference. And it behooves every retailer, for his own sake, not to lose sight of that fact.

The very popularity of the prices is a source of danger for through the efforts of mistaken as well as of unscrupulous manufacturers and merchants, wholesale and retail, there is popular priced merchandise on the market whose only recommendation is the price.

While popular priced merchandise has always been our specialty, our specializing does not go below the point where quality ceases to exist.

In every department we begin our line with the very lowest priced thing to be found which possesses merit enough to make it good worth for the price retailers will ask for it.

Indeed, our low priced specializing, even more than to the lowering of prices is directed toward the making of bigger worth possible at any given popular price.

Take the 5 and 10 cent specials in the sale that's the big feature of this catalogue as examples of what our low priced specializing means.

Observe how many are the things you have been buying as good values at higher prices that we have crowded down to 45 and 95 cents the dozen.

Observe, too, that things have not been skimped nor weakened in the process of making them such phenomenal values.

Consider well where you shall buy your popular priced merchandise. Don't get too far away from value. For, without value, in the long run it will profit you nothing to have secured merely low prices.

The low priced goods you can sell *the second*

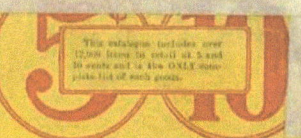

time to the same customer—that's the kind of popular priced merchandise it will pay you to handle. And that's the only kind of popular priced merchandise we sell.

OUR HOLIDAY GOODS.

In each of the six cities—New York, Chicago, St. Louis, Baltimore, Dallas and St. Paul— where we shall have our line displayed complete, the samples of our holiday goods will be ready for inspection on or about July 15.

And on or about August 20 we shall have ready for mailing the big fall catalogue in which the same immense line will be laid before buyers in their own homes.

As admittedly the largest handlers of holiday goods we could anticipate these dates were we so disposed. But—**we will not show an incomplete line.**

No one buys holiday goods farther in advance than we. But the risk of advance purchases we think belongs to the jobber alone.

As holiday goods are handled today, there is absolutely no reason why any retailer need buy his stocks earlier than we make it possible for him to buy.

At this writing holiday goods are pouring in on us from all over the world. The larger part of these goods of course was bought many months ago.

But—we are still picking up and shall be doing so until the latest possible moment those new goods which give spice and freshness to a line.

Do not be satisfied with leftovers from last season and the mere staples for the coming season, which together must constitute the holiday stocks that are offered early.

Do not be swept off your feet by the arguments of clever drummers, hurrying to capture all possible of the orders that may be lost to them when, later on, the complete big lines are available to retailers.

Whether you buy of us or not—for your own sake see our line either in one of our houses or in our catalogue before—not after— you buy your holiday goods this year.

For your own sake—remember.

All goods sold with privilege of returning within five days after receipt.

We want our customers to be satisfied in the fullest sense of the word.

We cannot afford to sell you even one article that does not please you after you have taken it out of the case. On any single sale the profit is small. It becomes great only when an army of satisfied customers are sending in their orders every few days.

It may seem unnecessary to say that this rule must be construed with reason. If any merchant abuses it, we shall of course withdraw the return privilege from him.

When returning goods always enclose your name and address and an itemized list of goods in THE PACKAGE. Also send us notification by mail.

Goods returned must positively be sent back within 5 days after receipt.

Remember, This Book Quotes NET WHOLESALE PRICES—Keep It Out of Your Customers' Hands.

TERMS:
1 per cent 20 days—Net 31 days. Net 40 days—no longer time. No further discount given under any circumstances.

No charge for package or cartage on any goods.

All goods sold with the privilege of returning within five days after receipt.

In sending us a first order, unless you remit cash in full, please state whether you wish the order shipped C. O. D., or on open account.

In asking us to open an account new customers should remember that their names may not as yet appear, with satisfactory information, in the commercial reports. Therefore to save delay, kindly send us as reference the names of other wholesale houses with which you deal on open account, or of your banker. (When goods are wanted immediately, it is well to send cash with first order, as the investigation of references necessarily consumes some time.)

We send goods C. O. D. by freight, cases marked with your initials (not "Butler Brothers"), same as all shipments made by us. The invoice is mailed direct to you, and the bill of lading (indorsed over to you), accompanied by a draft on you for the amount of invoice (less your deposit), is sent to your nearest bank for collection. Upon the payment of this draft you can secure the bill of lading and thus get your goods from the railroad agent.

Please remit by bank draft or money order. We are compelled to pay exchange on checks on out-of-town banks. *We therefore ask our customers to kindly send drafts or money orders.*

Never send money by mail unregistered. Notwithstanding Uncle Sam's vigilance, money letters disappear in transit every day.

Gross prices are for lots of ½ dozen or more, unless otherwise specified.

We cannot break packages. All goods are put in as small packages as possible consistent with safe shipping. We will not furnish less quantities than indicated.

When sending an additional order to be packed with one sent in an earlier mail, you will help us to give good service if you will instruct us what to do in case the second order is too late to connect with the first—that is, whether to ship goods separately or return same to stock.

WE SELL AT WHOLESALE ONLY.

Broadway Bldg. (495 & 497 Broadway).   *Jersey City Building (Washington, Morgan, Warren and Bay Streets).*

OUR NEW YORK HOUSE. In Broadway building (8 stories and 2 basements) are general offices and sales rooms. In Jersey City building are merchandise and operating departments. The latter is one of the largest two wholesale structures in the world, the other being our Chicago premises. Private railroad tracks on two sides. Total area of the two buildings about 600,000 square feet.

OUR CHICAGO HOUSE. One of the largest two wholesale structures in the world, the other being our New York plant. An eighth of a mile of thirteen-story buildings. More than 600,000 square feet (16 acres) of connected floor area. 670 feet of unbroken shipping platform, bordering on joint tracks used by five great trunk systems. Freight handled direct from car to platform.

Store "A," 1221 to 1237 Washington Avenue.   *Store "B," Corner St. Charles and Thirteenth Streets.*

OUR ST. LOUIS HOUSE. The two buildings above shown are a short half block apart. Store "A" (7 stories and basement) runs through from Washington Avenue to Lucas Avenue; in same are our sales rooms, offices and open stock goods. Store "B" (7 stories and basement) contains surplus stock and original packages, and from same all shipping is done. Magnificent modern equipment for handling business economically and efficiently.

We do not sell to any one but merchants, neither do we sell to peddlers or agents.

Write your order on separate sheets from any other communication you have to make. This permits both being attended to at once.

You can help to expedite the handling of your orders when you group all goods of a department together. The letter prefixed to number indicates the department to which an item belongs.

Please use our regular order sheets, which are put up 20 in pad. If you have not a pad, mention in your next order or drop us a card. You will help us to give you best and quickest service by observing the suggestions on the back of our order sheet.

Be sure to mention your nearest shipping point if you are not located on a railway or water route. If there are competing transportation companies, name your preference. If express shipment, specify which company serves your town.

We send catalogues only to storekeepers who handle our lines. Any merchant, customer or not, who uses our catalogue in the hands of anyone not entitled to same, will do us a favor by reporting the fact.

When returning goods always enclose your name and address and an itemized list of goods IN THE PACKAGE. Also send us notification by mail.

Examine all cases, barrels, etc., and see that they are in good condition before accepting same from transportation company. All shipments made by us are in good order when taken by transportation lines and so receipted for. Our responsibility then ceases.

Please do not ask us to purchase goods outside our stock. We naturally wish to be accommodating, but so much difficulty has been experienced in endeavoring to even approximate such requests, often from very meager directions, that we have been compelled to refuse them.

Our principal banks of deposit are the following, to which we refer:

Chemical National Bank, New York.

Corn Exchange National Bank, Chicago.

National Bank of Commerce, St. Louis.

BUTLER BROTHERS

Wholesalers of General Merchandise—By Catalogue Only

NEW YORK:	CHICAGO:	ST. LOUIS:	AND MINNEAPOLIS
495 and 497 BROADWAY	RANDOLPH BRIDGE	1221-1237 Washington Ave.	after Jan. 1, 1907